T0181418

Communications
in Computer and Information Science 1906

Rationale

The CCIS series is devoted to the publication of proceedings of computer science conferences. Its aim is to efficiently disseminate original research results in informatics in printed and electronic form. While the focus is on publication of peer-reviewed full papers presenting mature work, inclusion of reviewed short papers reporting on work in progress is welcome, too. Besides globally relevant meetings with internationally representative program committees guaranteeing a strict peer-reviewing and paper selection process, conferences run by societies or of high regional or national relevance are also considered for publication.

Topics

The topical scope of CCIS spans the entire spectrum of informatics ranging from foundational topics in the theory of computing to information and communications science and technology and a broad variety of interdisciplinary application fields.

Information for Volume Editors and Authors

Publication in CCIS is free of charge. No royalties are paid, however, we offer registered conference participants temporary free access to the online version of the conference proceedings on SpringerLink (http://link.springer.com) by means of an http referrer from the conference website and/or a number of complimentary printed copies, as specified in the official acceptance email of the event.

CCIS proceedings can be published in time for distribution at conferences or as post-proceedings, and delivered in the form of printed books and/or electronically as USBs and/or e-content licenses for accessing proceedings at SpringerLink. Furthermore, CCIS proceedings are included in the CCIS electronic book series hosted in the SpringerLink digital library at http://link.springer.com/bookseries/7899. Conferences publishing in CCIS are allowed to use Online Conference Service (OCS) for managing the whole proceedings lifecycle (from submission and reviewing to preparing for publication) free of charge.

Publication process

The language of publication is exclusively English. Authors publishing in CCIS have to sign the Springer CCIS copyright transfer form, however, they are free to use their material published in CCIS for substantially changed, more elaborate subsequent publications elsewhere. For the preparation of the camera-ready papers/files, authors have to strictly adhere to the Springer CCIS Authors' Instructions and are strongly encouraged to use the CCIS LaTeX style files or templates.

Abstracting/Indexing

CCIS is abstracted/indexed in DBLP, Google Scholar, EI-Compendex, Mathematical Reviews, SCImago, Scopus. CCIS volumes are also submitted for the inclusion in ISI Proceedings.

How to start

To start the evaluation of your proposal for inclusion in the CCIS series, please send an e-mail to ccis@springer.com.

Miguel Félix Mata-Rivera ·
Roberto Zagal-Flores · Cristian Barria-Huidobro
Editors

Telematics and Computing

12th International Congress, WITCOM 2023
Puerto Vallarta, Mexico, November 13–17, 2023
Proceedings

 Springer

Editors
Miguel Félix Mata-Rivera (iD)
UPIITA - Instituto Politécnico Nacional
México, Mexico

Roberto Zagal-Flores (iD)
ESCOM - Instituto Politécnico Nacional
México, Mexico

Cristian Barria-Huidobro (iD)
Universidad Mayor
Santiago, Chile

ISSN 1865-0929 ISSN 1865-0937 (electronic)
Communications in Computer and Information Science
ISBN 978-3-031-45315-1 ISBN 978-3-031-45316-8 (eBook)
https://doi.org/10.1007/978-3-031-45316-8

This Springer imprint is published by the registered company Springer Nature Switzerland AG
The registered company address is: Gewerbestrasse 11, 6330 Cham, Switzerland

Paper in this product is recyclable.

Preface

The 12th International Congress in Telematics and Computing (WITCOM 2023) was held in hybrid modality, with some participants attending in person in Puerto Vallarta, Mexico, and some participations attending online. This year authors came from the following countries: USA, Sri Lanka, Spain, Chile, Colombia, and Mexico. This volume shows some of the advances in various fields of knowledge, such as Artificial Intelligence techniques, Cybersecurity, Data Science, Environment Monitoring, Information Systems, IoT, Education, and Energy, with applications to different areas of study.

WITCOM 2023 attracted numerous students, researchers, and entrepreneurs to share experiences and knowledge and establish collaboration among universities and research centers. These proceedings contain selected research papers after a thorough peer-review process. We received 88 research papers; three members of the Program Committee reviewed each one of them, and 35 were accepted (an acceptance rate of 40%).

The conference program featured a broad set of session topics that extended beyond the documents contained in these proceedings. Materials for all sessions are available on the conference website at www.witcom.upiita.ipn.mx and www.witcom.org.mx.

All the tracks and workshops at WITCOM 2023 contributed to making a consistent program. We want to thank God and all those who contributed to this effort, especially ANTACOM A.C., IPN, and UPIITA-IPN, which supported the event. Of course, thanks go to UDI-UPIITA, the managers and administrators, the Geospatial Intelligence and Mobile Computing Laboratory, the article authors, session presenters, coordinators, members of the Program Committee, UPIITA Staff, and Sponsors. Without your help and collaboration, the event could not have been successful.

November 2023

Miguel Félix Mata-Rivera
Roberto Zagal-Flores
Cristian Barria-Huidobro

Organization

Organizing Committee

General Chair

Miguel Félix Mata-Rivera   UPIITA-IPN, Mexico

Co-chair

Roberto Zagal-Flores   ESCOM-IPN, Mexico

Cybersecurity Track Chair

Cristian Barria-Huidobro   Universidad Mayor, Chile

Local Manager

Jairo Zagal-Flores   UNADM, Mexico

Applied Maths Chair

Christian Carlos Delgado   UNAM FES Acatlán, Mexico
     Elizondo

Staff Chair

Sergio Quiroz Almaraz   UNAM FES Acatlán, Mexico

Program Committee (Research Papers)

Christophe Claramunt	Naval Academy Research Institute, France
Clara Burbano	Unicomfacauca, Colombia
Gerardo Rubino	Inria, France
Cesar Viho	IRISA, France
Jose E. Gomez	Université de Grenoble, France
Ken Arroyo Ohori	Delft University of Technology, The Netherlands

Mario Aldape Perez	CIDETEC-IPN, Mexico
Anzueto Rios Alvaro	UPIITA-IPN, Mexico
Ludovic Moncla	UFR S&T de Pau, France
Jose M. Lopez Becerra	Hochschule Furtwangen University, Germany
Walter Renteria-Agualimpia	University of Zaragoza, Spain
Shoko Wakamiya	Kyoto Sangyo University, Japan
Patrick Laube	ZAUW, Switzerland
Sergio Ilarri	University of Zaragoza, Spain
Sisi Zlatanova	TU Delft, The Netherlands
Stephan Winter	University of Melbourne, Australia
Stephen Hirtle	University of Pittsburg, USA
Steve Liang	University of Calgary, Canada
Tao Cheng	University College London, UK
Willington Siabato	Universidad Nacional, Bogotá, Colombia
Xiang Li	East China Normal University, China
Andrea Ballatore	King's College London, UK
Carlos Di Bella	INTA, Argentina
Haosheng Huang	University of Zurich, Switzerland
Hassan Karimi	University of Pittsburgh, USA
Luis Manuel Vilches	Universidad Politecnica de Madrid, Spain
Victor Barrera Figueroa	UPIITA-IPN, Mexico
Adrián Castañeda Galván	UPIITA-IPN, Mexico
Thomaz Eduardo Figueiredo Oliveira	CINVESTAV-IPN, Mexico
Hiram Galeana Zapién	CINVESTAV-Tamaulipas, Mexico
Laura Ivoone Garay Jiménez	SEPI-UPIITA, Mexico
Domingo Lara	CINVESTAV-IPN, Mexico
Aldo Gustavo Orozco Lugo	CINVESTAV-IPN, Mexico
Omar Juarez Gambino	ESCOM-IPN, Mexico
Itzama Lopez Yañez	CIDETEC-IPN, Mexico
Miguel Ángel León Chávez	BUAP, Mexico
Alberto Luviano Juarez	UPIITA-IPN, Mexico
Mario H. Ramírez Díaz	CICATA-IPN, Mexico
Mario Eduardo Rivero Angeles	CIC-IPN, Mexico
Francisco Rodríguez Henríquez	CINVESTAV-IPN, Mexico
Patricio Ordaz Oliver	Universidad Politécnica de Pachuca, Mexico
Izlian Orea	UPIITA-IPN, Mexico
Rolando Quintero Tellez	CIC-IPN, Mexico
Grigori Sidorov	CIC-IPN, Mexico
Rosa Mercado	ESIME UC, Mexico
Blanca Rico	UPIITA-IPN, Mexico
Blanca Tovar	UPIITA-IPN, Mexico

Noe Sierra Romero	UPIITA-IPN, México
Chadwick Carreto	ESCOM-IPN, Mexico
Ana Herrera	UAQ, Mexico
Hugo Jimenez	CIDESI, Mexico
Jose Antonio Leon Borges	UQROO, Cancún, Mexico
Rene Rodriguez Zamora	ITMAZ, Mexico
Homero Toral	UQROO, Chetumal, Mexico
Lorena Renata Galeazzi Ávalos	Universidad Mayor, Chile
Marcela Rosana Ulloa Zamora	Universidad Mayor, Chile
Rosa María de la Paz Fuentes Valdebenito	Universidad Mayor, Chile
Hernaldo Andrés Salazar Mendoza	Universidad Mayor, Chile
Daniel Eduardo Soto Carabantes	Universidad Mayor, Chile
Saul Ortega Alvarado	Universidad Mayor, Chile
Lorena Fabiola Soto Silva	Universidad Mayor, Chile
Sergio Rosales Guerrero	Universidad Mayor, Chile
Cristian Arcadio Contreras Gómez	Universidad Mayor, Chile
Yenny Alexandra Méndez Alegría	Universidad Mayor, Chile
Ismael Osuna Galán	UQROO, Mexico
Julio Cesar Ramírez Pacheco	UQROO, Mexico
Yolanda Pérez Pimentel	UQROO, Mexico
David Ernesto Troncoso Romero	UQROO, Mexico

Sponsors

ANTACOM A.C.
UPIITA-IPN

Collaborators

FES Acatlán
Alldatum Systems
CISCO Systems

Contents

A Decision Tree as an Explainable Artificial Intelligence Technique for Identifying Agricultural Production Predictor Variables in Mexico

Héctor M. Ruiz-Juárez[1,3], Juliana Castillo-Araujo[2,3],
Mauricio Gabriel Orozco-del-Castillo[1(✉)], Nora Leticia Cuevas-Cuevas[1],
Francisco Cárdenas-Pimentel[1], and Raúl Cáceres-Escalante[1]

[1] Tecnológico Nacional de México/IT de Mérida, Departamento de Sistemas
y Computación, Mérida, Yucatán, Mexico
{le19081442,mauricio.od,nora.cc,francisco.cp,raul.ca}@merida.tecnm.mx,
mauricio.orozco@itmerida.edu.mx
[2] Universidad de Cundinamarca, Seccional Ubaté, Cundinamarca, Colombia
jcastilloa@ucundinamarca.edu.co
[3] AAAI Chapter of Mexico (AAAIMX), Mérida, Mexico

Abstract. Agriculture has been an essential and foundational activity for human societies since the dawn of civilization and nowadays serves as the backbone of economies worldwide. Efforts to understand and to enhance agricultural productivity are crucial for addressing global challenges and achieving sustainable development goals. This research study focuses on analyzing the factors influencing production of the flagship crops of the 32 states in Mexico. A regression tree model was employed as an explainable artificial intelligence technique to gain insights into the production patterns. The study utilized a dataset containing various agricultural variables, including territorial extension, precipitation mean, and temperature measurements across different months. Quantitative and qualitative approaches were employed to understand the significance of predictors. Through permutation importance analysis, it was identified that territorial extension, precipitation mean, and specific temperature measures, such as minimum temperature in January and mean temperature in November, had a substantial impact on crop production. Additionally, a visual analysis of the pruned regression tree further confirmed the importance of these predictors. The findings led to the formulation of seven production rules, which provide valuable guidance for agricultural decision-making. The results highlight the potential of the regression tree model as an explainable tool for understanding and predicting crop production.

Keywords: Agriculture · Machine learning · Decision trees · Crop production

M. F. Mata-Rivera et al. (Eds.): WITCOM 2023, CCIS 1906, pp. 1–14, 2023.
https://doi.org/10.1007/978-3-031-45316-8_1

1   Introduction

Agriculture, the practice of cultivating crops and raising livestock for human consumption, has been an essential and foundational activity for human societies since the dawn of civilization. It serves as the backbone of economies worldwide and plays a pivotal role in ensuring food security, rural development, and sustainable livelihoods. The significance of agriculture extends beyond the production of food alone; it encompasses a wide range of interrelated sectors, including agribusiness, food processing, and agricultural technology [14]. In a world grappling with a growing population, climate change, and resource scarcity, the importance of agriculture becomes even more pronounced [35]. Efforts to understand, and consequently to enhance agricultural productivity, are crucial for addressing global challenges, eradicating hunger, and achieving sustainable development goals.

Mexico's agriculture plays a vital role in the nation's economy, culture, and food security [17]. Agriculture in Mexico encompasses a wide array of crops in basically all of its 32 states, which include maize, beans, tomatoes, avocados, citrus fruits, among others [38]. Due to its favorable geographic and climatological conditions, Mexico has become a major global producer and exporter of agricultural products. The sector not only contributes significantly to the country's gross domestic product (GDP) but also supports the livelihoods of several rural communities [5]. However, agriculture in Mexico faces various challenges, such as water scarcity, climate change impacts, and the need for sustainable land management practices.

Artificial intelligence (AI) has rapidly gained prominence as a powerful tool for solving complex problems and making informed decisions across various domains. In recent years, the application of AI in the agricultural sector has shown great potential in enhancing productivity, reducing costs, and ensuring sustainable practices [25]. Understanding and harnessing the power of AI techniques in agriculture can unlock transformative solutions, enabling farmers and policymakers to make informed decisions, optimize resource allocation, and propel agricultural systems towards greater resilience and efficiency. However, one critical challenge in deploying AI models in agriculture is their lack of transparency and interpretability, which hinders the understanding of the decision-making process and limits the trust that stakeholders can place in these systems [37].

Explainable AI (XAI) has emerged as a promising field within AI research, aiming to bridge the gap between the predictive power of complex AI models and the need for human interpretability. By providing insights into how AI systems arrive at their decisions, XAI techniques enable users to understand the underlying factors driving predictions and gain confidence in the results. However, applying and understanding various XAI techniques, such as SHAP (SHapley Additive exPlanations), LIME (Local Interpretable Model-agnostic Explanations), Feature Importance, ALE (Accumulated Local Effects), and others, can be a complex endeavor [22]. Each technique has its own underlying assumptions, computational requirements, and limitations, making it essential to carefully consider their applicability and interpretability in specific contexts. For instance, SHAP and LIME focus on generating local explanations for individual predictions, providing insights into how specific features contribute to the model's output. However, understanding and interpreting the complex interactions between multiple features can still be challenging. Feature Importance methods provide a global perspective by ranking features based on their contribution to the overall model performance, but they may oversimplify complex relationships. ALE, on the other hand, captures the non-linear effects of individual features on the predictions but may require substantial computational resources for large datasets. Furthermore, challenges arise in selecting the appropriate XAI technique for a given problem, ensuring its compatibility with the underlying ML model, and effectively communicating the explanations to end-users or stakeholders [2].

Despite these complexities, leveraging XAI techniques remains crucial in enhancing transparency, trust, and accountability in AI systems, enabling stakeholders to better understand the decision-making process and make informed decisions in domains like agriculture [6]. By considering the strengths, limitations, and interpretability aspects of each technique, practitioners can navigate the complexities of XAI and harness its potential for valuable insights in agricultural applications. Particularly, by exploring and identifying key predictor variables using XAI techniques we can gain invaluable insights into the factors driving agricultural production in Mexico, paving the way for evidence-based decision-making, sustainable farming practices, and the achievement of Mexico's agricultural goals. In the context of agricultural production, particularly in a country as diverse and agriculturally significant as Mexico, the need for accurate and interpretable AI models becomes even more crucial. Mexico boasts a rich agricultural sector, contributing significantly to the national economy and ensuring food security for its population. However, numerous factors, including climatic variations, land conditions, and socio-economic dynamics, influence agricultural productivity and success [19].

This article focuses on utilizing a very common machine learning (ML) technique, decision trees (DTs), but not as a classification or regression tool, but rather as an XAI tool which can easily help decision makers identify predictor variables that significantly impact agricultural production in Mexico, particularly the highest produced crop for a given state. By employing DTs, we aim to uncover the key factors driving agricultural production in Mexico, providing valuable insights for farmers, policymakers, and stakeholders in the agricultural sector. For this, we leverage comprehensive agricultural data from Mexico, encompassing various relevant variables from 2004 to 2021. By utilizing DTs, we aim to extract meaningful patterns and relationships from this data, ultimately providing actionable insights that can inform agricultural practices and policy-making.

The outline of this paper is as follows. In Sect. 2 we describe the agricultural and technical considerations of this work, along with a brief section about how ML has been applied in agriculture. In Sect. 3 we describe the process from the data acquisition, data processing, and the regression tree (RT) implementation which allowed us to identify key predictors for agricultural production. We include a discussion and the concluding remarks in Sect. 4, and finally state possible future lines of work in Sect. 5.

2   Background

2.1   Agricultural Considerations

Agriculture is a crucial component of the economy [23], serving as the primary environment for generating descriptive reports on the ascending or descending levels in the final stages of production. In the decision-making process to achieve success in the planting and harvesting process, temperature and precipitation factors are not directly related, as farmers often rely on years of experience to attain optimal yields [33]. Agriculture encompasses diverse processes and holds significant estimated values, which are closely linked to annual projections. By 2050, the world's population is projected to exceed 9 billion people [28]. As the population continues to grow, there will be a substantial increase in demand for food, including fruits, vegetables, and grains. This surge in demand poses a challenge for countries for the foreseeable future, with estimates exceeding 60% [36]. This growing demand has prompted a greater emphasis on understanding the primary factors that influence agricultural production, particularly temperature, precipitation, land area, among others.

Temperature, a perception captured by physical entities, allows measuring thermal intensity, whether hot or cold, and has a significant impact on crops. Various investigations have observed that an increase in temperature results in a reduction in the production of different crops [18]. Under production conditions, temperature plays a decisive role, since higher temperature levels can lead to greater evaporation and, consequently, a decrease in the amount of water captured [4]. Crops are highly dependent on the weather in their sowing and harvesting process [30]. In fact, farmers are often forced to modify the chronological order of sowing due to climatic threats that could affect final food production [30].

Precipitation, in the form of rain, snow, or hail, plays a vital role in agricultural ecosystems, serving as a primary source of water for crop growth and overall agricultural productivity [13]. It is a fundamental component of the hydrological cycle and contributes significantly to soil moisture replenishment, ensuring the availability of water for plant uptake and irrigation. Adequate and well-distributed precipitation is crucial for germination, plant development, and yield formation [8]. Insufficient precipitation can lead to drought conditions, negatively impacting crop growth, yield potential, and overall agricultural output [12]. On the other hand, excessive precipitation, such as heavy rainfall or prolonged periods of rain, can result in waterlogging, soil erosion, and increased vulnerability to diseases and pests [15]. Farmers rely on accurate precipitation forecasts and historical patterns to plan their planting and irrigation schedules, manage water resources effectively, and make informed decisions to optimize crop production.

In regions where water resources are limited or unreliable, the careful monitoring and management of precipitation become even more critical.

2.2 Machine Learning

AI is normally considered as broadly divided into two types, knowledge-based systems, which perform based on knowledge explicitly programmed in them, and ML, which focuses on acquiring knowledge directly from the data without the need for explicit programming [1]. In order to achieve this, large amounts of data to identify patterns, extract insights, and make accurate predictions are needed [11]. ML algorithms excel at analyzing complex patterns within large datasets, enabling us to gain a deeper understanding of various phenomena.

Decision Trees. DTs are a widely used ML model, particularly for classification and regression tasks [21]. As the name suggests, DTs resemble tree-like diagrams, structures composed of nodes and branches. Each node represents a decision based on a feature, while the branches correspond to the possible outcomes or values of that feature. The end points are called leaves, representing the final predictions (regression) or decisions (classification). While DTs are not considered within the most powerful techniques of ML, what makes them appealing is their interpretability and ease of understanding. Input features can be transparently mapped to target variables, especially in shallow trees, making them valuable in domains where interpretability is critical. DTs are capable of handling both numerical and categorical data, and as well as missing values and outliers effectively. As other ML techniques, DTs have the ability to capture non-linear relationships and interactions between variables. While DTs are not commonly recognized as explicit XAI techniques, they have proven valuable in delivering interpretability and transparency to classification and regression models. For instance, they have been successfully employed to enhance trust management in cybersecurity applications [24].

Machine Learning and Explainable Artificial Intelligence in Agriculture. In the context of agriculture, ML holds immense potential [31]. By leveraging ML techniques, we can process vast amounts of agricultural data, including climate data, soil characteristics, crop growth patterns, and pest and disease information. This enables us to develop predictive models that can forecast crop yields, optimize resource allocation, identify potential risks, and facilitate precision farming practices. ML in agriculture has the power to revolutionize decision-making processes, enhance productivity, and contribute to sustainable and efficient agricultural systems.

ML applications in agriculture have usually been classified into four categories: crop, livestock, water and soil management [23]. Crop management, correspondingly, has been classified into five separate areas 1) yield prediction, the mapping, estimation, matching of crop supply with demand, and crop management to increase productivity; 2) disease detection, including pest and disease control in open-air and greenhouse conditions; 3) weed detection, being weed the most important threat to crop production [23]; 4) crop quality, identification of features connected with crop quality to increase product price and reduce waste; and 5) species recognition, the automatic identification and classification of plant species.

Even though ML models have been extensively used in agriculture, the same cannot be said about XAI techniques [29], where most of them remain largely unintroduced [31]. For instance, in [20] a system (PBI-CBR) to predict grass growth is presented. This case-based reasoning system combines predictive accuracy and explanation capabilities do improve user adoption. Case-based reasoning has also been explored for the explanation of black-box time series and image models in smart agriculture [10]. A different approach in which a knowledge map model and an ontology design, OAK4XAI, to explain the knowledge mined in agriculture, is proposed in [27]. Other applications where only a few particular XAI techniques are used and do not emphasize the usage, include [31] crop yield estimate [34], crop type and trait classification [26], water flux and quality assessment [16], biomethane production [9] and agricultural land identification [39]. Very few studies have explored XAI techniques for agricultural production explanation and interpretation.

3   Development and Results

3.1   Data Acquisition

The data used in this work includes: monthly precipitation, monthly temperature (minimum, average, and maximum), territorial extension and annual production, all these for each one of the 32 states of Mexico. These data were downloaded directly from the website of the Mexican National Water Commission (Comisión Nacional del Agua, CONAGUA) [7] and the Agro-Food and Fisheries Information Service (Servicio de Información Agroalimentaria y Pesquera, SIAP) [32], covering from 2004 to 2021. The data was organized in such a way that they are represented as 56 variables: 1 a numerical value describing the federal entity, 12 describing the average precipitation per month, 1 describing the average precipitation, 36 describing the minimum, average and maximum temperatures, 3 describing their average temperatures (minimum, average, and maximum), 1 describing the territorial extension, 1 describing the current year, and finally 1 describing the production of the crop with the highest production for that state during that year, *i.e.*, the *flagship product* (from here on, for simplicity purposes we will refer to it simply as *production*). These values for the 32 states over 18 years result in 576 different instances.

3.2   Decision Tree Implementation

With their ability to handle complex datasets and generate understandable rules, DTs, including RTs, offer a powerful tool for identifying important predictor variables in agricultural production. Even though the aim of this work is to identify these predictors, we explored the potential of the data to be estimated through the design of several ML regression models: RT, boosted trees, support vector machines (SVM) and Gaussian process regression (GPR), using 5-fold cross-validation. The R-squared values indicate the proportion of variance explained by each model, reflecting their goodness-of-fit. The R^2 values reported in Table 1 suggest that the models are able to explain from a moderate (0.58) to a strong (0.80) level of fit, achieved by the GPR. This means data up to 80% of the variance in the data can be explained and there are underlying patterns which could be used to provide accurate predictions.

Table 1. Comparison of Regression Models and R^2 Values

Model	R^2	Parameters
Regression tree	0.58	Minimum leaf size: 12
		Surrogate decision splits: Off
Boosted trees	0.76	Minimum leaf size: 8
		Number of learners: 30
		Learning rate: 0.1
Support Vector Machine	0.58	Kernel: Gaussian
		Kernel scale: 7.5
Gaussian Process Regression	0.80	Basis function: Constant
		Kernel function: Exponential

After it was shown that there are underlying patterns in the data which could be used to yield predictions, we used the complete dataset to fit a RT: 55 variables and 576 observations. This was done because this model was not aimed to estimate or predict production, but to explain it. This yielded a RT with a depth of 98, as shown in Fig. 1. The predicted versus actual plot (Fig. 2a) and the residual plot (Fig. 2b) obtained from the RT analysis reveal valuable insights into the performance of the model. With an R-squared value of 0.90, the model shows a stronger fit than the one obtained by the GPR (which was to be expected due to the use of the complete dataset). The root mean squared error (RMSE) of 1.9976e+05 quantifies the average deviation between the predicted and actual values, providing an estimate of the model's accuracy. The mean squared error (MSE) of 3.9905e+10 reflects the average squared difference between the predicted and actual values, highlighting the magnitude of the errors. Additionally, the mean absolute error (MAE) of 8.4022e+04 provides an absolute measure of the average prediction error.

Since the focus of the work relies on the explainability issue, two different approaches were followed: quantitative and qualitative. For the quantitative approach we calculated the importance of the predictors in the RT using permutation importance [3]. This algorithm measures the impact of each predictor on the model's performance by permuting the values of a single predictor while

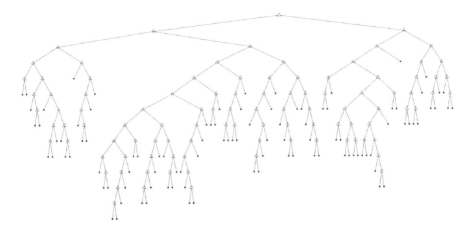

Fig. 1. A diagram of the complete decision tree structure, displaying the complexity of the model.

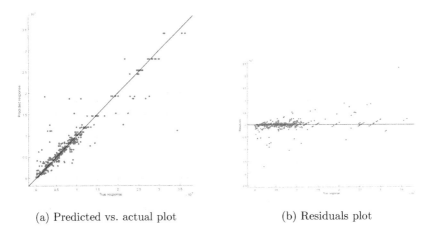

(a) Predicted vs. actual plot   (b) Residuals plot

Fig. 2. Comparison of (a) predicted versus actual values and (b) residual plot of the regression tree using the complete dataset. The predicted versus actual plot illustrates the relationship between the predicted values and the corresponding actual values, showing a strong model performance. The residual plot showcases the distribution of the residuals, with a high percentage located around low values, as expected due to the 0.9 R-squared value.

keeping the other variables unchanged and observing the resulting change in the model's performance metric. According to the analysis of predictor importance, the following variables emerged as the most influential predictors in the RT model, highlighting their significant contribution to the model's predictive power:

1. Territorial extension
2. Precipitation mean
3. November's mean temperature
4. July's mean precipitation
5. January's minimum temperature
6. December's maximum temperature
7. May's mean temperature

For the qualitative approach, which meant a visual analysis after pruning the RT to identify and highlight the main predictors at the root of it (Fig. 3), results are consistent with the quantitative analysis. Following this approach, the following variables were identified as the most relevant:

1. Territorial extension
2. Precipitation mean
3. January's minimum temperature
4. July's mean precipitation
5. November's mean temperature

All of these also included in the quantitative analysis, confirming their importance. This also allowed us to establish several rules, which are shown in Table 2.

From analysis of Table 2, it can be observed that the maximum production tends to occur when the territorial extension is higher than 71,636 km^2, the mean precipitation is higher than 67.05 mm/m^2, and the mean temperature during november is lower than 22.35 °C (~24.9 MM). On the other hand, the minimum production occurs when the territorial extension is higher than 71,636 km^2, the mean precipitation is lower than 67.05 mm/m^2, and the mean precipitation during July is higher than 200.6 mm/m^2 (~1.8MM).

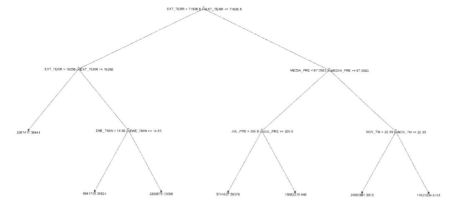

Fig. 3. A diagram of the pruned tree up to 4 levels. This display allows us to identify the most significant predictors and rules for production.

Table 2. Most significant rules for production.

Rule	Territorial extension (km²)	Mean Prec. (mm/m²)	Min. Temp. Jan. (°C)	Mean Prec. July (mm/m²)	Mean Temp. Nov. (°C)	Production (MM Tons.)
1	< 16256					2.3
2	16256 − 71636		< 14.65			6.8
3			> 14.65			3.3
4	> 71636	< 67.05		< 200.6		5.7
5				> 200.6		1.8
6		> 67.05			< 22.35	24.9
7					> 22.35	11.8

4   Discussion and Conclusions

This article presents a novel approach to tackle the challenge of explainability in AI models applied to agricultural production in Mexico. By employing DTs, particularly RTs, we aim to unravel the relationships between predictor variables and agricultural productivity, offering a transparent and interpretable framework for stakeholders. This study aims to improve the decision-making processes in the agricultural sector, empowering farmers and policymakers with reliable and actionable information to drive sustainable agricultural practices and ensure food security in Mexico.

The findings of our study highlight several significant predictors that strongly influence agricultural production. The quantitative analysis using permutation importance revealed that territorial extension, precipitation mean, and various temperature measures, such as November's mean temperature and January's minimum temperature, emerged as the most influential variables in the RT model. These findings underscore the importance of environmental factors and climatic conditions in determining crop yield.

Our qualitative analysis, which involved a visual examination of the pruned RT, further confirmed the importance of these predictors. The qualitative approach allowed us to identify and highlight the main predictors at the root of the tree, providing additional clarity and insight. Consistent with the quantitative analysis, the qualitative findings emphasized the critical role of territorial extension, precipitation mean, January's minimum temperature, July's precipitation, and November's mean temperature as the most relevant variables in predicting agricultural production.

Based on these findings, we established a set of rules Table 2 that link specific combinations of predictor variables to production outcomes. These rules provide practical guidance for understanding and predicting production levels under different conditions. Further analysis of the seven established rules for predicting agricultural production reveals interesting patterns and aligns with existing knowledge in the field. Rule 1 indicates that smaller territorial extensions correspond to lower production levels, which is consistent with the relatively evident understanding that limited land area imposes constraints on agricultural output. Rule 2 highlights the interaction between territorial extension and minimum temperature in January, suggesting that certain temperature thresholds can significantly impact crop yield. Rules 4 and 5 emphasize the combined effect of territorial extension, mean precipitation, and July's mean precipitation, reflecting the influence of water availability on agricultural productivity. Rules 6 and 7 demonstrate the interaction between territorial extension, mean precipitation, and November's mean temperature, corroborating the known sensitivity of crops to temperature fluctuations during critical growth stages. Particularly Rules 2 and 3, and 6 and 7, appear to confirm previous studies where, under the same conditions, an increase in temperature yields a decrease in production [4,18]. Overall, these rules provide meaningful insights that align with reported knowledge, further confirming the relevance of the identified predictors and their impact on production outcomes.

These rules, but moreso the methodology here described, could serve as valuable decision support tools for farmers, policymakers, and stakeholders in the agriculture sector. They provide actionable insights into the specific conditions that lead to different production levels, enabling stakeholders to make informed decisions and implement targeted strategies. By considering the identified predictors and the associated rules, stakeholders can optimize resource allocation, improve crop management practices, and enhance overall agricultural productivity.

The combination of quantitative and qualitative approaches in our study strengthens the validity and reliability of the findings. The consistency between the two analyses reinforces the significance of the identified predictors and the established rules, further validating their practical applicability.

5   Future Work

The findings presented in this study provide a solid foundation for future research in the field of agricultural production prediction. Several avenues for further exploration and improvement can be pursued based on the outcomes and limitations of this study.

Firstly, expanding the dataset to include additional variables such as soil composition and sunlight exposure could enhance the accuracy and comprehensiveness of the predictive models. This would enable a more comprehensive understanding of the intricate relationships between these factors and agricultural production.

Furthermore, incorporating more advanced ML models, such as ensemble methods or DL models, could potentially yield higher predictive performance. These models have the ability to capture more complex nonlinear relationships and interactions within the data, providing a more nuanced understanding of the predictors' influences on production outcomes. Additionally, conducting a comparative analysis of different XAI techniques, beyond RTs, would be valuable to determine the most effective and interpretable approach for explaining agricultural production. Exploring methods such as SHAP or LIME could provide deeper insights into the relative importance and impact of predictors in the context of production prediction.

Finally, incorporating temporal and spatial analysis could enhance the predictive capabilities by accounting for seasonal variations and regional disparities. Understanding how the identified predictors and rules evolve over time and across different geographic regions could provide valuable information for decision-makers in the agricultural sector.

By addressing these avenues for future work, we can further refine and improve the accuracy, interpretability, and practical applicability of predictive models in agricultural production. This would contribute to more informed decision-making, better resource allocation, and ultimately, sustainable and efficient agricultural practices.

Acknowledgements. This work was supported by projects 13933.22-P and 14601.22-P from Tecnológico Nacional de México/IT de Mérida.

References

1. Alsharef, A., Aggarwal, K., Sonia, Kumar, M., Mishra, A.: Review of ML and AutoML solutions to forecast time-series data. Arch. Comput. Methods Eng. **29**(7), 5297–5311 (2022). https://doi.org/10.1007/s11831-022-09765-0
2. Ávila, D.D., Ramírez-Arrieta, V.M.: If an image is worth than thousand words: how much a box plot can say? Revista del Jardin Botanico Nacional **41**(November), 57–69 (2020)
3. Breiman, L.: Random forests. Mach. Learn. **45**, 5–32 (2001)
4. Caira Mamani, C.M., Lopez Loayza, C., Carhuarupay Molleda, Y.F.: Efecto de la temperatura y precipitacion sobre la agricultura en la cuenca Coata-Puno, Perú. Revista Alfa **5**(14), 285–296 (2021). https://doi.org/10.33996/revistaalfa.v5i14.118
5. Canales, E., Andrango, G., Williams, A.: Mexico's agricultural sector: production potential and implications for trade. Choices **34**(3), 1–12 (2019)
6. Cartolano, A., Cuzzocrea, A., Pilato, G., Grasso, G.M.: Explainable AI at work! what can it do for smart agriculture? In: 2022 IEEE Eighth International Conference on Multimedia Big Data (BigMM), pp. 87–93. IEEE (2022)
7. Conagua: Climatología, resúmenes mensuales de temperatura y lluvia (2022). https://smn.conagua.gob.mx/es/climatologia/temperaturas-y-lluvias/resumenes-mensuales-de-temperaturas-y-lluvias
8. Dannehl, D., Huber, C., Rocksch, T., Huyskens-Keil, S., Schmidt, U.: Interactions between changing climate conditions in a semi-closed greenhouse and plant development, fruit yield, and health-promoting plant compounds of tomatoes. Sci. Hortic. **138**, 235–243 (2012). https://doi.org/10.1016/j.scienta.2012.02.022
9. De Clercq, D., Wen, Z., Fei, F., Caicedo, L., Yuan, K., Shang, R.: Interpretable machine learning for predicting biomethane production in industrial-scale anaerobic co-digestion. Sci. Total Environ. **712**, 134574 (2020)
10. Delaney, E.: Case-based explanation for black-box time series and image models with applications in smart agriculture. ICCBR Doctoral Consortium **1613**, 0073 (2022)
11. Dogan, A., Birant, D.: Machine learning and data mining in manufacturing. Expert Syst. Appl. **166**, 114060 (2021)

12. Donatelli, M., Magarey, R.D., Bregaglio, S., Willocquet, L., Whish, J.P., Savary, S.: Modelling the impacts of pests and diseases on agricultural systems. Agric. Syst. **155**, 213–224 (2017). https://doi.org/10.1016/j.agsy.2017.01.019
13. Dwamena, H.A., Tawiah, K., Akuoko Kodua, A.S.: The effect of rainfall, temperature, and relative humidity on the yield of cassava, yam, and maize in the Ashanti region of Ghana. Int. J. Agron. **2022**, 1–12 (2022). https://doi.org/10.1155/2022/9077383
14. Friha, O., Ferrag, M.A., Shu, L., Maglaras, L., Wang, X.: Internet of things for the future of smart agriculture: a comprehensive survey of emerging technologies. IEEE/CAA J. Automatica Sinica **8**(4), 718–752 (2021). https://doi.org/10.1109/JAS.2021.1003925
15. Galindo, V., Giraldo, C., Lavelle, P., Armbrecht, I., Fonte, S.J.: Land use conversion to agriculture impacts biodiversity, erosion control, and key soil properties in an Andean watershed. Ecosphere **13**(3), 1–19 (2022). https://doi.org/10.1002/ecs2.3979
16. Garrido, M.C., Cadenas, J.M., Bueno-Crespo, A., Martínez-España, R., Giménez, J.G., Cecilia, J.M.: Evaporation forecasting through interpretable data analysis techniques. Electronics **11**(4), 536 (2022)
17. Hendrickson, J.R., Hanson, J.D., Tanaka, D.L., Sassenrath, G.: Principles of integrated agricultural systems: introduction to processes and definition. Renewable Agric. Food Syst. **23**(4), 265–271 (2008). https://doi.org/10.1017/S1742170507001718
18. Jacobs, L., Quack, L.: The end of the diesel subsidy: distributional effects of a CO2-based energy tax reform. Wirtschaftsdienst **98**(8), 578–586 (2018). https://doi.org/10.1007/s10273-018-2334-3
19. Kawakura, S., Hirafuji, M., Ninomiya, S., Shibasaki, R.: Analyses of diverse agricultural worker data with explainable artificial intelligence: XAI based on SHAP, LIME, and LightGBM. Eur. J. Agric. Food Sci. **4**(6), 11–19 (2022). https://doi.org/10.24018/ejfood.2022.4.6.348
20. Kenny, E.M., et al.: Predicting grass growth for sustainable dairy farming: a CBR system using Bayesian case-exclusion and *Post-Hoc*, personalized explanation-by-example (XAI). In: Bach, K., Marling, C. (eds.) ICCBR 2019. LNCS (LNAI), vol. 11680, pp. 172–187. Springer, Cham (2019). https://doi.org/10.1007/978-3-030-29249-2_12
21. Kingsford, C., Salzberg, S.L.: What are decision trees? Nat. Biotechnol. **26**(9), 1011–1013 (2008)
22. Langer, M., et al.: What do we want from explainable artificial intelligence (XAI)? - a stakeholder perspective on XAI and a conceptual model guiding interdisciplinary XAI research. Artif. Intell. **296**, 103473 (2021). https://doi.org/10.1016/j.artint.2021.103473
23. Liakos, K.G., Busato, P., Moshou, D., Pearson, S., Bochtis, D.: Machine learning in agriculture: a review. Sensors (Switzerland) **18**(8), 1–29 (2018). https://doi.org/10.3390/s18082674
24. Mahbooba, B., Timilsina, M., Sahal, R., Serrano, M.: Explainable artificial intelligence (xai) to enhance trust management in intrusion detection systems using decision tree model. Complexity **2021**, 1–11 (2021)
25. Megeto, G.A.S., da Silva, A.G., Bulgarelli, R.F., Bublitz, C.F., Valente, A.C., da Costa, D.A.G.: Artificial intelligence applications in the agriculture 4.0. Revista Ciência Agronômica **51**(5), 1–8 (2020). https://doi.org/10.5935/1806-6690.20200084

26. Newman, S.J., Furbank, R.T.: Explainable machine learning models of major crop traits from satellite-monitored continent-wide field trial data. Nat. Plants **7**(10), 1354–1363 (2021)
27. Ngo, Q.H., Kechadi, T., Le-Khac, N.A.: OAK4XAI: model towards out-of-box explainable artificial intelligence for digital agriculture. In: Bramer, M., Stahl, F. (eds.) SGAI-AI 2022. LNCS, vol. 13652, pp. 238–251. Springer, Cham (2022). https://doi.org/10.1007/978-3-031-21441-7_17
28. Organización de las Naciones Unidas para la Alimentación y la Agricultura: La agricultura mundial en la perspectiva del año 2050. Fao, pp. 1–4 (2009). http://www.fao.org/fileadmin/templates/wsfs/docs/I
29. Posadas, B.B., Ogunyiola, A., Niewolny, K.: Socially responsible AI assurance in precision agriculture for farmers and policymakers. In: AI Assurance, pp. 473–499. Elsevier (2023)
30. Ramirez-Villegas, J., Jarvis, A., Läderach, P.: Empirical approaches for assessing impacts of climate change on agriculture: the EcoCrop model and a case study with grain sorghum. Agric. Forest Meteorol. **170**, 67–78 (2013). https://doi.org/10.1016/j.agrformet.2011.09.005
31. Ryo, M.: Explainable artificial intelligence and interpretable machine learning for agricultural data analysis. Artif. Intell. Agric. **6**, 257–265 (2022). https://doi.org/10.1016/j.aiia.2022.11.003. https://www.sciencedirect.com/science/article/pii/S2589721722000216
32. SAGARPA: SIAP - Servicio de Información Agroalimentaria y Pesquera Datos Abiertos (2014). http://infosiap.siap.gob.mx/gobmx/datosAbiertos.php. http://www.siap.gob.mx/datos-abiertos/
33. Shakoor, M.T., Rahman, K., Rayta, S.N., Chakrabarty, A.: Agricultural production output prediction using supervised machine learning techniques. In: 2017 1st International Conference on Next Generation Computing Applications, NextComp, pp. 182–187 (2017). https://doi.org/10.1109/NEXTCOMP.2017.8016196
34. Sihi, D., Dari, B., Kuruvila, A.P., Jha, G., Basu, K.: Explainable machine learning approach quantified the long-term (1981–2015) impact of climate and soil properties on yields of major agricultural crops across conus. Front. Sustainable Food Syst. 145 (2022)
35. Sohail, M.T., Mustafa, S., Ali, M.M., Riaz, S.: Agricultural communities' risk assessment and the effects of climate change: a pathway toward green productivity and sustainable development. Frontiers Environ. Sci. 10 (2022). https://doi.org/10.3389/fenvs.2022.948016
36. Sosa Baldivia, A., Ruíz Ibarra, G., Sosa Baldivia, A., Ruíz Ibarra, G.: La disponibilidad de alimentos en México: un análisis de la producción agrícola de 35 años y su proyección para 2050. Papeles de Población 23(93), 207–230 (2017). 10(22185/24487147), pp. 93, 2017.027. https://rppoblacion.uaemex.mx/article/view/9111
37. Spanaki, K., Sivarajah, U., Fakhimi, M., Despoudi, S., Irani, Z.: Disruptive technologies in agricultural operations: a systematic review of AI-driven AgriTech research, **308** (2022). https://doi.org/10.1007/s10479-020-03922-z
38. Torres, R.: Linkages between tourism and agriculture in Mexico. Ann. Tour. Res. **30**(3), 546–566 (2003). https://doi.org/10.1016/S0160-7383(02)00103-2
39. Viana, C.M., Santos, M., Freire, D., Abrantes, P., Rocha, J.: Evaluation of the factors explaining the use of agricultural land: a machine learning and model-agnostic approach. Ecol. Ind. **131**, 108200 (2021)

APOS is Not Enough: Towards a More Appropriate Way to Estimate Computational Complexity in CIC Decimation Architectures

David Ernesto Troncoso Romero[1]([⊠]) [iD], Julio César Ramírez Pacheco[1],
José Antonio León Borges[1], and Homero Toral Cruz[2]

[1] Departamento de Informática y Redes, División de Ciencias, Ingeniería y Tecnología,
Universidad Autónoma del Estado de Quintana Roo, Campus Cancún, Av. Chetumal SM 260
MZ 21 y 16 LT 1-01, Fracc. Prado Norte, 77519 Cancún, Quintana Roo, México
`david.troncoso@uqroo.edu.mx`
[2] Departamento de Informática y Redes, División de Ciencias, Ingeniería y Tecnología,
Universidad Autónoma del Estado de Quintana Roo, Campus Chetumal Bahía, Blvd. Bahía S/N,
esq. I. Comonfort, Col. Del Bosque, 77019 Chetumal, Quintana Roo, México

Abstract. The number of Additions Per Output Sample (APOS) is, currently, a standard way to estimate the computational complexity of Cascaded Integrator-Comb (CIC) decimators. This metric originates from a perspective with a high level of abstraction, where the amount of additions performed by the CIC hardware architecture accounts in general for the switching activity of the system, and therefore represents the power consumption in a direct proportion. In this paper we introduce an approach that leads towards a more appropriate way to estimate the computational complexity of CIC decimators, which considers the width of the internal buses of the architecture. We employ the pruning scheme by Hogenauer, and we provide explicit formulas to find, through a simple procedure, the number of Atomic Additions Per Output Sample (AAPOS), which accounts for the computational complexity on a bit-by-bit (i.e., atomic) basis. Three detailed examples are included to show how the AAPOS provides different results for systems with apparently equal computational complexity when estimated with APOS, leading to a more precise and trustable estimation.

Keywords: Computational complexity · Decimation · CIC filter

1 Introduction

Decimation is the process of decreasing the sampling rate of a digital signal. Being a sampling rate reduction, decimation requires a digital filter prior to the downsampling operation in order to prevent aliasing [1].

The design of anti-aliasing filters is a challenging task when the decimation processes are implemented for high-end applications, such as in modern communication systems [2–9]. The reason is that there are difficult constraints to meet in terms of magnitude-response characteristics, power consumption, utilization of hardware resources, and

M. F. Mata-Rivera et al. (Eds.): WITCOM 2023, CCIS 1906, pp. 15–25, 2023.
https://doi.org/10.1007/978-3-031-45316-8_2

maximum achievable frequency of operation. These constraints are, besides, conflicting among each other.

One of the most popular filters for decimation by an integer R is the Cascaded Integrator-Comb (CIC) filter, which consists of a cascade of N integrator-comb pairs. Its transfer function is

$$H(z) = \left(\frac{1 - z^{-R}}{1 - z^{-1}} \right)^N. \tag{1}$$

The CIC decimation architecture, proposed in [3], is obtained by moving the comb part to the low-rate section via multirate identities. The CIC decimator is very popular because of its simple and regular structure. Therefore, this system is ubiquitous in modern battery-operated mobile digital communication systems, either in programmable Digital Down-Conversion (DDC) algorithms for multi-standard receivers [4–6], or in Radio Frequency (RF)-to-baseband Analog to Digital Converters (ADCs) [7–9]. Recent refinements to the CIC architecture have been introduced in [10–14].

In general, but especially for battery-operated systems, it is important to have design metrics that help to estimate the power consumption. Particularly, in early design phases of decimation filters, this estimation is performed by means of the computational complexity, which is accounted with the number of arithmetic operations performed to compute an output sample. Since the CIC decimator is a multiplierless system, currently, the standard metric for computational complexity is the number of Additions Per Output Sample (APOS), as we see in the recent works [12, 13]. The APOS metric originates from a perspective with a high level of abstraction, where the amount of additions performed by the CIC hardware architecture accounts in general for the switching activity of the system, and therefore represents the power consumption in a direct proportion.

In this paper we introduce a model that leads towards a more appropriate way to estimate the computational complexity of CIC decimators, which takes into account the width of the internal buses of the architecture. To this end, we employ the pruning scheme devised by Hogenauer in [3], and we provide explicit formulas to find, through a simple procedure, the number of Atomic Additions Per Output Sample (AAPOS), which accounts for the computational complexity on a bit-by-bit (i.e., atomic) basis.

Following this introduction, Sect. 2 presents the frequency response characteristics of the CIC filter, and describes the CIC decimation structure. Section 3 introduces the proposed AAPOS metric, where the size of every bus in the structure is taken into account. Section 4 details three examples to show how the AAPOS provides different results for systems with apparently equal computational complexity when estimated with APOS, leading to a more precise and trustable estimation. Finally, Sect. 5 draws our conclusion.

2 The CIC System

The frequency response characteristics of the CIC filter can be obtained from its transfer function by first replacing $z = e^{j\omega}$ in (1). This results in the expression

$$H(e^{j\omega}) = \left\{ \frac{e^{-j\omega R/2}}{e^{-j\omega/2}} \left(\frac{e^{j\omega R/2} - e^{-j\omega R/2}}{e^{j\omega/2} - e^{-j\omega/2}} \right) \right\}^N, \tag{2}$$

which is obtained after factorization of the terms $e^{-j\omega R/2}$ and $e^{-j\omega/2}$ in the numerator and in the denominator, respectively. Using Euler's equivalence

$$2j \sin(\theta) = e^{j\theta} - e^{-j\theta} \tag{3}$$

inside the parenthesis in (2), and the equivalence

$$\frac{e^{-j\omega R/2}}{e^{-j\omega/2}} = e^{-j\omega(R-1)/2} \tag{4}$$

outside the parenthesis but inside the curly braces in (2), we get

$$H(e^{j\omega}) = \left(\frac{\sin(\omega R/2)}{\sin(\omega/2)} \right)^N e^{-j\omega N(R-1)/2}. \tag{5}$$

We can observe from (5) that the filter has a linear phase response and an amplitude response based on the Dirichlet kernel. Figure 1 shows an example of the magnitude response for $N = 4$ and $R = 16$. The nulls make the filter useful for a multi-stage decimation chain. The CIC filter rejects aliasing components around its nulls, whereas other parts of the aliasing power spectrum gets cancelled by the remaining decimators in the chain (details of this technique are covered in [1]). In Fig. 1, the amplitude response has been normalized by R^N, the gain of the filter, in order to represent a unitary gain (0 dB) at $\omega = 0$.

Figure 2 shows the CIC decimation structure, introduced by the first time in [3]. There are N integrators working at the high-rate section, and N comb blocks working at the low-rate section, separated by the downsampling operation. Integrators work concurrently to each other, and so do the combs. Notice that, in order to produce an output sample, the integrators must operate R times faster than the combs. Therefore, the computational complexity of the CIC decimator, measured in APOS, is (see [12, 13])

$$APOS = N \times R + N. \tag{6}$$

It is worth highlighting that the term "additions" in APOS refers in general to either additions o subtractions because these operations have the same complexity [15].

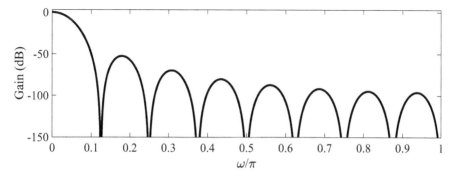

Fig. 1. Magnitude response of a CIC filter with parameters $R = 16$ and $N = 4$.

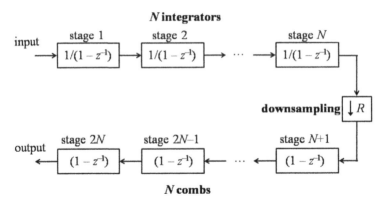

N integrators

Fig. 2. CIC decimation structure.

3 Introducing the Atomic Additions Per Output Sample (AAPOS) Metric

Is a "small" addition the same as a "big" one in terms of computational complexity, considering that "small" and "big" refer to the size of the physical adder implemented in hardware? The answer is no. A small adder consumes less power than a big one because it has less internal switching activity. Therefore, the "size" of the addition must be taken into account in order to reflect this fact in the estimation of computational complexity.

In the CIC structure, integrators and combs operate concurrently to their peers because they are all physically implemented in hardware. This is a necessary requirement in high-speed modern communication systems where there is little room for time-multiplexed processing units. Therefore, we can take into account an "atomic" perspective, i.e., a bit-by-bit basis where the size of every integrator and comb is included.

To this end, let us consider the CIC structure of Fig. 3. Every slash mark represents the bus width of the individual stage that appears after it (i.e., the k-th stage), and W_k is the number of bits in that stage. With this, we write the AAPOS metric as

$$AAPOS = R\left(\sum_{k=1}^{N} W_k\right) + \left(\sum_{k=N+1}^{2N} W_k\right). \tag{7}$$

The first N terms, W_1 to W_N, have a weight R because they represent the width of the integration blocks that run R times faster than the comb blocks. The last N terms, W_{N+1} to W_{2N}, represent the width of the comb blocks.

Every stage in the CIC structure, from the first integrator to the last comb, should have in its internal buses enough room to express the gain of the filter, R^N, in 2's complement, which is the standard representation employed in CIC systems (see [3] for details). In other words, every stage must have a bus width of

$$G = D + \left\lceil \log_2(R^N) \right\rceil + 1, \tag{8}$$

where D is the number of bits of the input data. However, we can prune some Least Significant Bits (LSB) in every stage, at the cost of increasing the variance of the output.

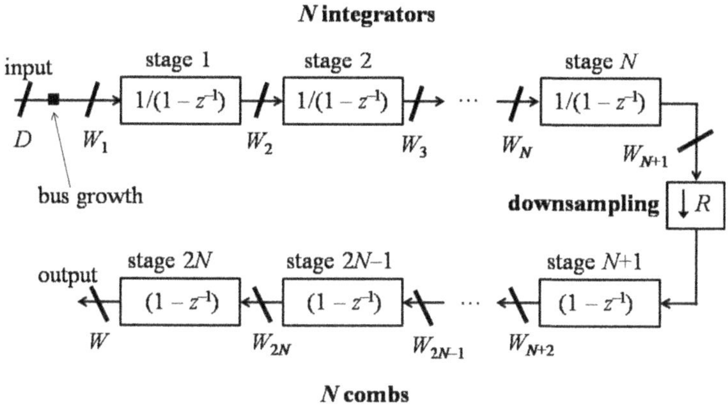

_N_ integrators

Fig. 3. CIC decimation structure with sizes of internal buses.

If the number of LSBs pruned in the k-th stage is called B_k, we can define W_k as

$$W_k = G - B_k. \tag{9}$$

From the classic quantization analysis, we can consider that the error at the k-th stage has a uniform probability density function of width 2^{Bk}, and a variance $2^{2Bk}/12$. The total variance contributed to the output by every stage is the sum of the variances over all k, each one scaled by F_k^2, which is the squared gain of the filter seen from the k-th pruning position to the output (moving the downsampler to the output and using multirate identities when necessary). Hogenauer suggested making such a total variance equal to the variance σ_o^2 which is obtained by pruning B bits from the output, and distributing it equally among all the stages. With this, we can express B_k as follows (see details in [3, 10, 11, 14]):

$$B_k = \left\lfloor -\log_2\left(\sqrt{F_k^2}\right) + \log_2(\sigma_o) + \frac{1}{2}\log_2\left(\frac{6}{N}\right)\right\rfloor. \tag{10}$$

Since we consider a uniform probability density function for the error after pruning B bits from the output, we have

$$\sigma_o = \frac{2^B}{\sqrt{12}}. \tag{11}$$

Besides, we stick to the standard scenario where the output word-length W of the CIC decimator, the input word-length D, and the parameters R and N are known a priory. Hence, the value for B can be obtained simply as

$$B = G - W. \tag{12}$$

From the analysis above, the procedure to estimate the AAPOS for a given CIC structure is given as follows:

Step 1: Given R (the downsampling factor), N (the number of integrator-comb pairs), D (the word-length for the input of the CIC decimator) and W (the word-length for the output of the CIC decimator), use (8) to compute G.

Step 2: Given G, compute B using (12).

Step 3: Given B, compute σ_o using (11).

Step 4: Given σ_o, compute B_k using (10) for $k = 1, 2, ..., 2N$, taking into account that F_k^2 is the squared gain of the filter seen from the k-th pruning position to the output.

Step 5: Given B_k, compute W_k using (9) for $k = 1, 2, ..., 2N$.

Step 6: Given W_k, compute AAPOS using (7).

4   Examples and Discussion

In this section we explore the computation of APOS and AAPOS metrics. For the latter case, we follow, step by step, the procedure given in Sect. 3. To this end, let us consider the case of a CIC decimator with the following characteristics:

- Downsampling factor is $R = 16$.
- Number of integrator-comb pairs is $N = 4$.
- Bus-width of the input port is $D = 16$ bits.
- Bus-width of the output port is $W = 16$ bits.

We consider two cases:

- Case A allows internal pruning in the buses of the architecture.
- Case B does not allow internal pruning in the buses of the architecture.

The APOS metric only uses R and N as input parameters and it does not take into account the details about pruning. From (6) we have

$$\text{Case A}: APOS = N \times R + N = 4 \times 16 + 4 = 68.$$

$$\text{Case B}: APOS = N \times R + N = 4 \times 16 + 4 = 68.$$

The AAPOS metric uses R and N as input parameters, but also takes into account the details about pruning, starting with the values D and W according to the steps introduced in Sect. 3. For Case A, we have

Step 1: From (8), we get $G = 33$.

Step 2: From (12), we get $B = 17$.

Step 3: From (11), we get $\sigma_0 = 37837.23$.

Step 4: From (10), for $k = 1, 2, ..., 8$, we get $B_1 = 2$, $B_2 = 5$, $B_3 = 8$, $B_4 = 11$, $B_5 = 12$, $B_6 = 13$, $B_7 = 14$, $B_8 = 15$.

Step 5: From (9), for $k = 1, 2, ..., 8$, we get $W_1 = 31$, $W_2 = 28$, $W_3 = 25$, $W_4 = 22$, $W_5 = 21$, $W_6 = 20$, $W_7 = 19$, $W_8 = 18$.

Step 6: From (7), we get

$$\text{Case A}: AAPOS = 1774.$$

For Case B, we have

Step 1: From (8), we get $G = 33$.
Step 2: From (12), we get $B = 17$.
Step 3: From (11), we get $\sigma_0 = 37837.23$.
Step 4: Since pruning is not allowed, we do not use (10). Instead, we have $B_k = 0$ for $k = 1, 2, \ldots, 8$.
Step 5: From (9), we have $W_k = G = 33$ for $k = 1, 2, \ldots, 8$.
Step 6: From (7), we get

$$\text{Case B}: AAPOS = 2244.$$

Table 1 summarizes the results from this experiment. Notice that the CIC structure for Case A has an estimate of 21% less computational complexity than the CIC structure for Case B, owing to the fact of using integrators and combs with reduced sizes. This aspect can not be seen with the standard APOS metric.

Table 1. APOS and AAPOS metrics for the two cases of the CIC decimator structure under test ($R = 16, N = 4, D = 16$ and $W = 16$): Case A allows pruning; Case B does not allow pruning.

	APOS	AAPOS
Case A	68	1774
Case B	68	2244
Information upon comparing Case A and Case B	None (they are equal)	Case A is 21% more efficient than Case B

Since the ultimate goal of the AAPOS metric is representing the power consumption of the CIC system, let us detail a second example, taken from [11]. In that reference, dynamic power consumption has been directly reported in milliwatts (mW). Thus, we will validate the approximation of the AAPOS computation with the data of power consumption presented in [11]. For this example, we have a CIC decimator with the following characteristics:

- Downsampling factor is $R = 8$.
- Number of integrator-comb pairs is $N = 5$.
- Bus-width of the input port is $D = 16$ bits.
- Bus-width of the output port is $W = 16$ bits.

Again, we consider two cases:

- Case A allows internal pruning in the buses of the architecture.
- Case B does not allow internal pruning in the buses of the architecture.

The APOS metric from (6) results as follows,

$$\text{Case A}: APOS = N \times R + N = 5 \times 8 + 5 = 45.$$

$$\text{Case B}: APOS = N \times R + N = 5 \times 8 + 5 = 45.$$

Steps to compute the AAPOS metric for Case A are given as follows:

Step 1: From (8), we get $G = 32$.

Step 2: From (12), we get $B = 16$.

Step 3: From (11), we get $\sigma_0 = 18918.61$.

Step 4: From (10), for $k = 1, 2, \ldots, 10$, we get $B_1 = 1$, $B_2 = 4$, $B_3 = 6$, $B_4 = 8$, $B_5 = 9$, $B_6 = 10$, $B_7 = 11$, $B_8 = 12$, $B_9 = 13$, $B_{10} = 13$.

Step 5: From (9), for $k = 1, 2, \ldots, 10$, we get $W_1 = 31$, $W_2 = 28$, $W_3 = 26$, $W_4 = 24$, $W_5 = 23$, $W_6 = 22$, $W_7 = 21$, $W_8 = 20$, $W_9 = 19$, $W_{10} = 19$.

Step 6: From (7), we get

$$\text{Case A}: AAPOS = 1157.$$

For Case B, we have

Step 1: From (8), we get $G = 32$.

Step 2: From (12), we get $B = 16$.

Step 3: From (11), we get $\sigma_0 = 18918.61$.

Step 4: Since pruning is not allowed, we do not use (10). Instead, we have $B_k = 0$ for $k = 1, 2, \ldots, 10$.

Step 5: From (9), we have $W_k = G = 32$ for $k = 1, 2, \ldots, 10$.

Step 6: From (7), we get

$$\text{Case B}: AAPOS = 1440.$$

Table 2 presents the results from this experiment. The AAPOS metric estimates 19.65% less power consumption for the CIC structure with pruned buses (Case A) with respect to the CIC structure with complete buses (Case B). According to the dynamic power consumption reported in [11] for the CIC decimator under test, Case A consumes 4.73 mW, whereas Case B consumes 5.62 mW. Therefore, there is a real saving of 15.85% in power consumption. The error in the estimation is only 3.8%.

Table 2. APOS and AAPOS metrics along with real dynamic power consumption (in mW) for two cases of the CIC decimator structure under test ($R = 8$, $N = 5$, $D = 16$ and $W = 16$): Case A allows pruning; Case B does not allow pruning.

	APOS	AAPOS	Power consumption (see reference [11])
Case A	45	1157	4.73 mW
Case B	45	1440	5.62 mW
Information upon comparing Case A and Case B	None (they are estimated as equal)	Case A is estimated to be 19.65% more efficient than Case B	Case A is indeed 15.85% more efficient than Case B

Finally, it is worth highlighting that the APOS and AAPOS metrics are suitable for any decimation filter that has the main characteristic of being multiplierless, i.e., they are not limited only to CIC systems. The APOS approximation only needs the number of adders and the rate reduction in the decimation process (the downsampling factor). The AAPOS model, on the other hand, needs also the number of bits of every adder. Therefore, let us present a concluding example where we contrast the full-bitwidth vs pruned versions of a decimation core called Approximated Dirichlet kernel with Concurrent Integrator-Combs (or ACIC for short), introduced in [11].

In this case, the ACIC decimator has the following characteristics:

- Downsampling factor is $R = 128$.
- Number of integrator units working concurrently at the high-rate section is 5.
- Sizes of the integrators are, respectively, $W_1 = 49$, $W_2 = 42$, $W_3 = 36$, $W_4 = 30$, $W_5 = 25$.
- Number of comb units working concurrently at the low-rate section is 4.
- Sizes of the combs are, respectively, $W_6 = 21$, $W_7 = 20$, $W_8 = 19$, $W_9 = 19$.
- Bus-width of the input port is $D = 16$ bits.
- Bus-width of the output port is $W = 16$ bits.
- Internal bus-width without pruning is $G = 50$ bits.

Again, we consider two cases:

- Case A allows internal pruning in the buses of the architecture.
- Case B does not allow internal pruning in the buses of the architecture.

The algorithm to compute the bus widths W_k is detailed in [11], and power consumption for both cases of the ACIC system is also reported in [11]. Therefore, we will validate the approximation of the AAPOS computation with the data of power consumption presented in that reference.

The APOS metric from (6) results as follows,

$$\text{Case } A : APOS = 5 \times 128 + 4 = 644.$$

$$\text{Case } B : APOS = 5 \times 128 + 4 = 644.$$

The AAPOS metric from (7) is,

$$\text{Case } A : AAPOS = (49 + 42 + 36 + 30 + 25) \times 128 + (21 + 20 + 19 + 19) = 23375.$$

$$\text{Case } B : AAPOS = 50 \times 5 \times 128 + 50 \times 4 = 32200.$$

Table 3 summarizes the results. The AAPOS metric estimates 27.41% less power consumption for the structure with pruned buses (Case A) with respect to the one with complete buses (Case B). On the other hand, the dynamic power consumption reported in [11] for the decimation system under test is, for Case A, 4.52 mW, whereas for Case B is 6.88 mW. As a consequence, there is a real saving of 34.3% in power consumption. The error in the estimation is 6.89% which is, again, very acceptable.

In general, we can notice that the proposed AAPOS metric is not blind to the advantages of pruning, and reveals good estimations of power consumption. However that metric is not exact because the real power consumption is not only dependent on the computational complexity, but also involves a number of implementation variables, such as target technology, size of the chip die, temperature, time of operation, type of signals being processed, and so on.

Table 3. APOS and AAPOS metrics along with real dynamic power consumption (in mW) for two cases of an Approximated Dirichlet kernel with Concurrent Integrator-Combs (ACIC) decimator: Case A allows pruning; Case B does not allow pruning.

	APOS	AAPOS	Power consumption (see reference [11])
Case A	644	23375	4.73 mW
Case B	644	32200	5.62 mW
Information upon comparing Case A and Case B	None (they are estimated as equal)	Case A is estimated to be 27.41% more efficient than Case B	Case A is indeed 34.3% more efficient than Case B

5 Concluding Remarks

The Atomic Additions Per Output Sample (AAPOS) metric has been introduced to quantify the computational complexity of Cascaded Integrator-Comb (CIC) decimation structures. This metric has arisen from two observations. On the one hand, from the hardware perspective, a small adder consumes less power than a big one because it has less internal switching activity. Therefore, the "size" of the addition must be taken into account in order to reflect this fact in the estimation of computational complexity. On the other hand, in the CIC structure, integrators and combs operate concurrently to their peers because they are all physically implemented in hardware. Therefore, we can take into account an "atomic" perspective, i.e., a bit-by-bit basis where the bus width of every integrator and comb is included. Through detailed examples, we have observed that counting Additions Per Output Sample (APOS) is not enough to discover computational efficiency of CIC decimators that are implemented under the pruning scheme. AAPOS, on the other hand, can give value to this scheme and reveal appropriately an estimation of its advantages with respect to computational cost.

References

1. Harris, F.: Multirate Signal Processing for Communication Systems, 2nd edn. River Publishers, Gistrup (2021)
2. Luo, F.-L.: Digital Front-End in Wireless Communications and Broadcasting: Circuits and Signal Processing. Cambridge University Press, Cambridge (2011)
3. Hogenauer, E.: An economical class of digital filters for decimation and interpolation. IEEE Trans. Acoust. Speech Sig. Process. 29(2), 155–162 (1981)
4. Abinaya, A., Maheswari, M., Alqahtani, A.S.: Heuristic analysis of CIC filter design for next-generation wireless applications. Arab. J. Sci. Eng. 46, 1257–1268 (2021)
5. Datta, D., Mitra, P., Dutta, H.S.: FPGA implementation of high performance digital down converter for software defined radio. Microsyst. Technol. (2019)
6. Gautam, D., Khare, K., Shrivastava, B.P.: A novel approach for optimal design of sample rate conversion filter using linear optimization technique. IEEE Access (2021)

7. Aggarwal, S.: Efficient design of decimation filters using linear programming and its FPGA implementation. Integr. VLSI J. **79**, 94–106 (2021)

8. Martens, E., et al.: RF-to-baseband digitization in 40 nm CMOS with RF bandpass Σ-Δ modulator and polyphase decimation filter. IEEE J. Solid State Circuit **47**(4), 990–1002 (2012)

9. Pavan, S., Shcreier, R., Temes, G.C.: Understanding Delta-Sigma Data Converters. Wiley, Hoboken (2017)

10. Troncoso-Romero, D.E., Jimenez, M.G.C., Meyer-Baese, U.: Alternative data paths for the Cascaded Integrator-Comb decimator. IEEE Sig. Process. Mag. **38**(3), 194–200 (2021)

11. Troncoso-Romero, D.E., Jimenez, M.G.C., Meyer-Baese, U.: Hardware-efficient decimation with spectral shape approximating the Nth power of a Dirichlet kernel. Circuits Syst. Sig. Process. **41**, 4886–4905 (2022)

12. Dudarin, A., Vucic, M., Molnar, G.: Decimation filters with minimum number of additions per output sample. Electron. Lett. **58**(6), 246–248 (2022)

13. Jovanovic, G.: Update on the CIC multistage decimation filter with a minimum number of additions per output sample (APOS): can we still decrease the number of APOS? IEEE Sig. Process. Mag. **40**(2), 151–172 (2023)

14. Troncoso-Romero, D.E.: Simplifying zero rotations in Cascaded Integrator-Comb decimators. IEEE Sig. Process. Mag. **40**(3), 50–58 (2023)

15. Meyer-Baese, U.: Digital Signal Processing with Field Programmable Gate Arrays, 4th edn. Springer, Heidelberg (2014). https://doi.org/10.1007/978-3-642-45309-0

Shape-Based Object Detection
for Industrial Process Improvement

Manuel Matuz-Cruz[1]📷, Enrique Quezada-Próspero[1]📷,
Andrea Ramos-Córdova[1]📷, Dante Mújica-Vargas[2]📷,
and Christian García-Aquino[1(✉)]📷

[1] Tecnológico Nacional de México, Campus Tapachula, Tapachula, Mexico
cj.garciat51@gmail.com
[2] Tecnológico Nacional de México, Campus CENIDET, Cuernavaca, Mexico

Abstract. In this work, the objective is to implement a convolutional neural network (CNN) to automate some processes in companies and with this, avoid human participation and not spend more resources than necessary, in addition to recovering in less time the investments that companies made. The CNN was implemented through the YOLOv5x algorithm, and this classifies 10 different object classes. The corresponding images for the training of the CNN were obtained with the AllImage extension which allowed downloading all the images that were on the screen. In addition to this, multiple dates bank were accessed and large number of images were downloaded having to filter a total of 700,000 images approximately, additionally photos were taken manually to complement the dataset, after the image filter, a dataset with a volume of 10673 images was obtained. Once the image filter was carried out, the network was trained with a single class, applying a k-fold cross-validation to calibrate the model and obtain an optimal percentage of images for training and validation. After having obtained these values, different versions of YOLO (YOLOv3-SPP, YOLOv5x and YOLOv7x) were trained to determine which of them was more accurate, YOLOv5x being the best with an AUC of .8811. Subsequently, the network was trained with the 10 classes. To measure the efficiency and quality of the proposed method, the following metrics were used with their respective values: 95.1% Accuracy, 92.8% Recall, 97.4% Specificity, 97.8% Precision, 95.1% F1 Score. The results obtained show a better classification performance in the neural network with a detection greater than 95% of the evaluation metrics for each class.

Keywords: Digital images · Artificial Vision · Convolutional neural network · YOLO · Industrial tools

1 Introduction

The automation of processes has been of great importance in companies, it allows to avoid errors in addition to optimizing and improving production, this

M. F. Mata-Rivera et al. (Eds.): WITCOM 2023, CCIS 1906, pp. 26–43, 2023.
https://doi.org/10.1007/978-3-031-45316-8_3

translates into more profits. However, the problem with implementing this in companies is that sometimes it can consume more resources. Thought due to the fact that some systems can be very complex and for this reason are very expensive causing the company's return on investment time to be prolonged [1].

Another problem is the low efficiency of the models, some have a high margin of error causing the company to lose production and therefore, profits, making the implementation of the system is counterproductive. This is due to the number of classes or objects that the model is capable of detecting, the more classes are configured, the more difficult is for the model to have an efficiency desired, which is why the models must be correctly tuned. To achieve a desired efficiency, it is necessary to have a sufficiently large dataset that includes images with characteristics of angle, color and shape of the objects to be detected, in addition to correctly configure the hyperparameters of the network [3].

Artificial Vision is a technology that allow to obtain significative information of images and videos, based on this, computers make recommendations based on the obtained information, computer equipment that implements this technology use cameras, data and algorithms that simulate human vision system. From this arise convolutional neural networks (CNN), they are in charge of make detections and classification duties, these networks are deep learning algorithms that are designed to work with images, assigning weights to the elements on them with the objective of discriminating [2].

The CNN's consist of multiple layers of filters of 1 or more dimensions through which the characteristics and/or values of the input images are analyzed. At the end of these layers, an activation function is applied, this function is in charge of performing a non-linear mapping [4].

The feature extraction phase resembles to the stimulating process of the visual cortex cells, this phase is composed of alternating layers of downsampling convolutional neurons, ad the data progresses through this phase, their dimension decreases, being the neurons of the posterior layers less sensitive to disturbances in the input data [5].

Automation process is important as it optimize production and allows manage resources in the best way. Object classification is a time-consuming task, and to conteract this problem, computer vision techniques can be used.

Works supported in the estate of the art demonstrate a versatility in detection and classification techniques of objects.

An example of this is [6], where the YOLO algorithm was used for the detection of shoots in oil palms, having a 92% accuracy.

In [7], artificial vision techniques are used for the measurement of the opening and coverage of the light environment under the forest canopy, reducing by 73.49% the time of carrying out this task, in addition to eliminating the risk that may present wildlife.

In [8] the AlexNet model is used to detect pests in plant images, reaching an accuracy of 83%.

In [9], convolutional neural networks are used to detect abnormalities in mammograms, obtaining an efficiency of 94% using a model based on AlexNet.

In [10] the use of CNNs applied to thermal imaging for stress detection, the model proposed is the inception architecture, the result of the experiments show a precision of 96%.

In [11] a convolutional neural network is used for the digit recognition, the ConvNet model was implemented and this achieved a detection rate of 93%.

In [12] the YOLO neural network was trained with the aim of detect that workers wear the equipment correctly necessary protection, the model achieved a higher precision 80%.

In short, CNNs can deliver promising results, these are varied depending on the algorithm and tuning used, however, are acceptable and reliable. The CNN's models are in constant development offering architectures that generate more accurate and reliable results. In this work, the YOLO algorithm was used, which is currently in its version 7, however, a comparison was made between versions 3, 5 and 7 to verify if there is any improvement between these versions.

The methodology used in this work is the following: Internet images were obtained which were filtered, eliminating "junk" images; after the filter, the model was trained with a single class in search of obtaining an optimal percentage for the validation and training images, for this a k-fold cross validation was used, after this calibration, 3 different versions of the algorithm YOLO were trained to verify which of them was the most efficient to achieve the objective of this work, after having determined the best option, the model was trained with the images of the 10 classes of industrial tools.

The rest of the work is organized as follows; In Sect. 2 details the proposed methodology; in the Sect. 3 presents the experimentation and the results obtained; and finally, in Sect. 4 the conclusions are presented, discussion of the results and future work.

2   Methods

For the development of this work, the followings topics were used:

The composition of digital images is based on the RGB spectrum which is the combination of the colors red, green and blue. The maximum value for each color that can be allocate is 255, depending on the combination of these values, new colors will be obtained, which are the ones that the user displayed on the screen. The possible color combination is represented by $255 \times 255 \times 255$, which is equal to 16,777,216 different colors [14].

Convolutional Neural Networks (CNN): They are part of the deep learning which has led to rapid development of the object detection field. CNNs constitute currently the state of the art of various computational vision problems due to its good performance in solving problems recognition and interpretation of images. Within the CNNs there are convolution layers, which are those in charge of extracting the characteristics of the images depending on the filter applied to them, the value of the new pixels will be determined by the scalar sum of the filter (Fig. 1).

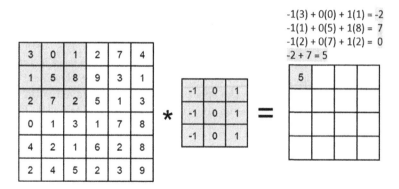

Fig. 1. Convolution process.

The convolution process is performed iteratively until it manages to go through and detect all the pixels of the image, the mathematical expression for this process is the following (Eq. 1) [15]:

$$\sum_{i=0}^{n}\sum_{j=0}^{n} f(i,j)h(x-i,y-j) \tag{1}$$

The pooling operation is responsible for carrying out a reduction of the volume in the data, this with the objective of reduce the work of analysis of the subsequent layers of the network, performs operations on small regions of the image of input and accumulates the elements of the feature layers [4]. There are different types of pooling, but the most used is the max-pooling (Eq. 2):

$$P(i,j) = max_{n,m=1,...,k}A[(i-1)p+n] \tag{2}$$

The perceptron is an artificial neuron that performs binary calculations, it is considered the simplest architecture for the linear classification in neural networks. The perceptron is defined in Eq. 3; the input neuron layer is used to capture the feature vector x, y produces output neurons the value of function [17,18].

$$\sum_{i=0}^{n} w_i x_i \tag{3}$$

Between neurons that form an artificial neural network there is a set of connections that unite them, each neuron transmits signals to others to which they are attached to its output, for each output of a neuron is associated a function of activation, in this case, the activation functions are used to refine the features extracted from images and based on this, an efficient classification can be made, they are rules that give the effect of the inputs in the activation of the unit, they are usually non-decreasing functions of the total entries [4] (Eq. 4):

$$y_k^{t+1} = F_k(S_k(t)) = F_k(\sum_j \omega_{jk}^t y_j^t + \theta_k^t) \tag{4}$$

There are several activation functions, however in this work, the following was used (Fig. 2 and Eq. 5):

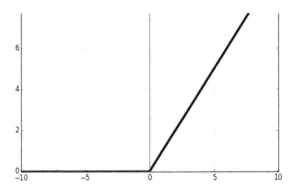

Fig. 2. RELU function.

$$max(0, z) \tag{5}$$

The RELU activation function is the most widely used currently in almost all convolutional neural networks or deep learning, returns the value 0 when the input is less than or equal to 0, otherwise will always return 1. It is used in hidden layers of the network, not in the output ones [19].

YOLO is an algorithm that transforms into pretrained models for object detection. This algorithm has gone evolving to offer users greater efficiency and precision in the detection and classification of objects. This algorithm is based on the architecture of a convolutional neural network, consisting of layers of convolution, pooling, activation functions and densely connected layers, all these layers are in charge of carrying out the corresponding analysis to the images [16].

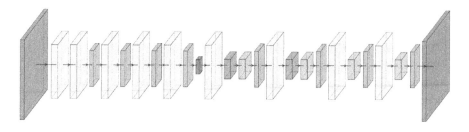

Fig. 3. Architecture of the convolutional network used (YOLOV5).

Table 1. Layers of the proposed architecture.

Name
Convolution (Conv)
BottleneckCSP (BCSP)
Spatial Pyramid Pooling (SPPF)
Upsample
Concat

The layers that are part of the proposed architecture (Fig. 3) are the following (Table 1):

The development of this work has the support of the state of art, which contains works that have made use of convolutional neural networks for detection and classification of objects. The first step to obtain results was to obtain a very large dataset equivalent to 10673 images, within of which are images downloaded from the internet supplemented with images obtained manually with a camera.

Table 2 shows the corresponding classes together with their percentages of image formats obtained.

To divide the dataset efficiently into training and validation sections, a k-fold cross-validation was used. The k-fold method consists of dividing a dataset into k subsets, each time using a different subset to validate the trained model with the other k−1 subsets [20]. To carry out the training, it was necessary to have a computer equipment that had updated and powerful components for efficient training, taking into account factors such as time and computational cost, therefore, it was chosen to use the following equipment with their respective characteristics:

- i5 12600f 6 core processor.
- 16 gb of RAM.
- 1tb HDD storage.
- Nvidia RTX 3060 graphics card with 3584 CUDA cores and 12 gb of VRAM.

In addition to this, use was also made of google colab+, which is a platform that offers the use of graphic cards to perform artificial vision tasks. The objective of the use of this tool was to save time training and performing various

Table 2. Percentage of image formats used by class

Class	Samples	%JPEG	%JPG	%PNG	%INTERNET	%MANUAL
Pliers	1040	4.9%	93.94%	1.15%	61.44%	38.55%
Padlocks	673	5.05%	94.95%	0%	87.81%	12.18%
Soldering irons	660	7.12%	91.82%	1.06%	72.57%	27.42%
Screwdrivers	1308	39.06%	59.79%	1.14%	84.48%	15.51%
Angle grinder	1142	2.10%	96.5%	1.4%	90.8%	9.19%
Axes	1018	12.77%	82.91%	4.32%	80.05%	9.19%
Wrenches	1356	45.72%	53.17%	1.1%	63.12%	36.87%
Hammers	1139	1.49%	96.75%	1.75%	44.33%	55.66%
Drills	1176	1.78%	97.36%	0.85%	45.57%	54.42%
Scissors	1161	1.11%	97.93%	0.94%	65.89%	34.1%
TOTAL	**10673**	**12.11%**	**86.51%**	**1.37%**	**73.14%**	**26.85%**

tests. For this case, it opted to purchase the pro version, which offers access to better graphic cards and more RAM. The architecture of the machine used is as follows:

- 8 core processor.
- 26 gb of RAM.
- 167 gb of storage.
- Nvidia Tesla T4 GPU with 320 Turing Tensor cores, 2560 CUDA cores and 16 gb of VRAM.

In this case, the most important components for this task are the graphic card and storage, this due to that the greater the CUDA cores and the memory of dedicated video, the greater the number of images the network will be able to analyze at the same time; regarding storage, it is important because it will be possible to use a cache system, where the network can store image data and to be able to access them at different times, preventing them from each epoch re-extract features, this translates to less training time.

2.1 Implementation

To achieve the objective of classifying the 10 classes of industrial tools, a methodology based on convolutional neural networks was used, in this section the operation and development of said methodology is analyzed, starting from the acquisition of the dataset, to the training and verification of the model. A summary and description of this methodology is shown in the Fig. 4.

Dataset Acquisition. First of all, as in any CNN configuration, it was necessary to collect a dataset large enough to train the network and for it to absorb

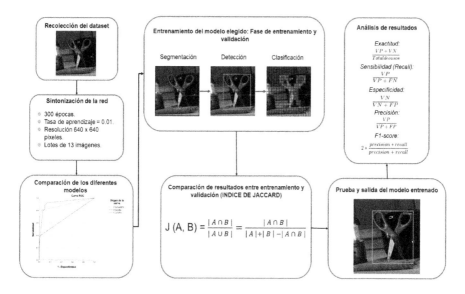

Fig. 4. Proposed methodology.

the necessary features to recognize the classes as soon as it "saw" them through a camera. The dataset was assembled from images downloaded from the internet, for this a Google Chrome extension called AllImages was used, which allows downloading all the images displayed on the screen, once the images were downloaded, they were filtered to discard those that did not work, these include images with low resolution or that were not of the required classes, additionally the dataset was complemented with images taken manually with a professional camera.

Image Labelling. Once the dataset with the filtered images was obtained, it proceeded to label the areas of interest in the images, this refers to delimiting the area where the tools appear in the images, this is done with the objective that, when the network is training, it knows which zone or pixels to analyze.

Network Tuning. Before carrying out the final training, it was necessary to tune the network so that it had a minimum margin of error. For this, the network was trained with a single class, using a k-fold cross-validation method; this was done with the objective of obtaining an optimal percentage between the images used for validation and training. After having obtained the appropriate percentage, it proceeded to experiment by training the network with different hyperparameter configurations (epochs, batch size, image resolution, learning rate) in order to obtain an optimal configuration. Subsequently, 3 different models of the YOLO algorithm were trained to verify which of them was adequate to achieve the objective of this work.

Final Training. After having obtained the optimal configuration (Percentage of training and validation, hyperparameters, YOLO model) it proceeded to carry out the final training with the images corresponding to the 10 classes of industrial tools, the results, tests and evidences are shown in the following section.

3   Results

In convolutional neural networks there are parameters such as image format, learning rate, epochs of training, the percentage of training and validation, batch size etc. Modifying these parameters may give different results when testing the trained model. A clear example of this is the image format, the PNG images usually have a 10% data loss compared to the JPG format, all these details must be to take into account when tuning the training.

For the evaluation of the efficiency of the model, use was made of the following metrics and evaluation instruments:

Confusion matrix: It is a tool that allows visualizing what types of hits and misses does a model have going through the learning process with the data. The metrics that form it are: true positives (TP), true negatives (TN), false positives (FP) and false negative (FN). From the confusion matrix, the following metrics were obtained:

Accuracy: Indicates the number of elements classified correctly compared to the total number of cases (Eq. 6)

$$\frac{TP + FN}{totalcases} \tag{6}$$

Recall: Shows the number of true positives that the model has classified according to the number total of positive values (Eq. 7).

$$\frac{TP}{TP + FN} \tag{7}$$

Specificity: Refers to the probability that the results of a test are negative if it really is (Eq. 8).

$$\frac{TN}{TN + FP} \tag{8}$$

Precision: This metric represents the number of true positives that are actually positive compared to the total number of predicted positive values (Eq. 9).

$$\frac{TP}{TP + FP} \tag{9}$$

F1-score: Allows you to combine the measurements of precision and recall on a single value. This is practical because it makes it easier being able to compare the combined performance of the precision and the sensitivity between various solutions (Eq. 10).

$$2 * \frac{precision * recall}{precision + recall} \tag{10}$$

ROC and AUC curve: These are tools that allow evaluating how good are the trained models at expressing the results graphically.

Real time video metrics were also taken into account, as they are:

FPS: It is the frequency at which a device displays images, when it comes to video, the more fps you have, the more the video will go smoothly.

Visual range: It is the optimal distance with respect to the object to detect in which the camera will capture an image with an optimal resolution that will allow to correctly detect and classify to the object.

Average prediction: It is the time it takes for the model to detect and classify an object [16].

As mentioned above, in this work it was used different versions of YOLO to make comparisons between the results and thus be able to obtain the best tuning, for this, several training sessions of 300 epochs were carried out each one and variations in learning rates, taking into account consideration the versions with more neurons (YOLOv3-SPP, YOLOV5x, YOLOv7-x) of each version of yolo (YOLOv3, YOLOv5, YOLOv7).

It is important to mention that these trainings were made with a single class, specifically scissors, to save training times, based on the results obtained more tests will be done. Table 3 shows the obtained values:

Table 3. Training tuning.

Model	Rate	Accuracy	Specificity	F1-score
YOLOv3-SPP	.01	.88	.96	.87
YOLOv3-SPP	.02	.89	.96	.89
YOLOv3-SPP	.8	.59	1	.31
YOLOv3-SPP	.9	.56	1	.21
YOLOv5x	.01	.9	.88	.89
YOLOv5x	.02	.88	0.86	.88
YOLOv5x	.8	.5	1	0
YOLOv5x	.9	.0	1	–
YOLOv7x	.01	.88	.96	.87
YOLOv7x	.02	.9	.96	.9
YOLOv7x	.8	.5	1	0
YOLOv7x	.9	.5	1	0

As can be seen, the results vary depending on of the learning rate, if it is increased too much, there will be a loss of features making the model unsuitable efficient, so generally speaking, the rate of standard learning is 0.01, since it shows the best results, giving in this test a maximum F1-score of .89 (89%) and an accuracy of .9 (90%), specifically in YOLOv5x.

Tests were also carried out with different features formats of images, which are included the JPG, JPEG and PNG formats in RGB color channel and grayscale. Table 4 is presented below, where it can be seen the results obtained taking into account 300 seasons of training and the F1-score metric, this test was performed with 100 images of scissors class, since it was only searched get the best values quickly.

Table 4. Test with different images features.

Feature	F1-score
PNG	0.7
JPG	0.28
Grayscale	0.69

As can be seen in Fig. 5, the images in JPG format did not obtain the desired results since there was a loss of features when analyzing these images; on the other hand, the results corresponding to the PNG format were efficient since they were able to absorb more features and classify the images correctly; regarding grayscale, the results were also favorable, this because the analysis did not focus on the color, but on the shape of the objects, therefore when analyzing the images in grayscale, the results are equally favorable.

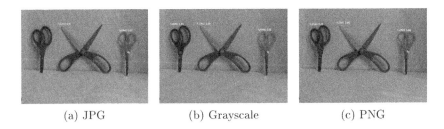

(a) JPG   (b) Grayscale   (c) PNG

Fig. 5. Results.

Once determined which configuration to use, also modified the size of the batch and of the images, these parameters considerably lengthened the training time because the more quality the image has, the more features will be able to absorb the network and the greater the batch, more images can be analyzed at the same time.

Table 5 is presented below, where you it can seen the different training sessions performed:

Table 5. Trainings performed.

Model	Size	Batch Size	Time of training
YOLOv3-SPP	640	60	4 hrs
YOLOv5x	448	25	3 days
YOLOv5x	640	20	4 days
YOLOv5x	1280	10	5 days
YOLOv7	640	25	3 days
YOLOv7x	640	8	5 days

CNN training has high computational costs, that's why it's important to have proper computers, as well as finding a proper tuning to make the time invested worth it. Exist companies that rent computer equipment which are accessed virtually via the Internet, these computers are specialized for this type of task because they offer efficient computational components for the task. As can be seen, in this case the training time depends on 2 factors: The size of the image and the batch size, from this, the following can be summarized:

- The larger the batch of images, the more images can analyze at the same time, obtaining less time of training.
- The higher the quality/size of the image, the more features will be able to detect but will increase time of training.
- The higher the quality/size of the image, the lower the batch number will be because it will occupe VRAM space of the graphic card.

Once the tuning to be used was established, it proceeded to train the different versions of YOLO, this was done with the objective of obtaining the final results of each model and so it can make a comparison between them. The results were expressed in ROC curves, where it can be observed the relationship between specificity and sensitivity, tuning used for training is as follows:

- 300 epochs of training.
- Learning rate of 0.01.
- image size of 640 × 640.
- PNG and JPG formats.
- Batch size of 13 images.

To save time, it was limited to making use only of the scissors class, which has 1161 images, this class was divided multiple times into equal parts, using a cross-validation (k-fold), leaving a part for validation and the rest for training, in addition, a small part of the images was extracted to test the model. The class was divided 6 times into 4, 5, 6, 7, 8 and 9 equal parts and the precision metric (averaged) was taken to compare results.

Table 6 shows the results:

Table 6. Cross-validation results.

Parts	Average precision
4	0.759
5	0.8652
6	0.7287
7	0.7016
8	0.636
9	0.3985

As can be seen, the best average precision is found by dividing the dataset into 5 parts, giving a distribution of 80% data for training and 20% data for validation.

This is because the more parts the data set is divided into, the more data there will be in the training section than in the validation section. Otherwise, if it is divided into fewer parts, there will be more data in the validation section than in the training section, if an optimal balance is not achieved, the model will suffer an overfitting. From this, a final training with all clases was done. After having trained the different versions of YOLO, the ROC curves were made with the results obtained, this can be seen in Table 7 and Fig. 6

Table 7. Areas under the curve of the training performed.

Model	AUC
YOLOv3-SPP	0.842
YOLOv5x	0.881
YOLOv7x	0.613

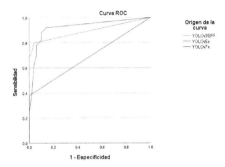

Fig. 6. ROC curves of the training performed.

As can be seen, the YOLOv5x model is more efficient than the others, having an area under the ROC curve of 0.881. From here, it will work with the YOLOv5x version

After having carried out the final training, it proceeded to evaluate the efficiency of the model with images "not seen" by the model, 100 images per class were taken to carry out the evaluation, starting from the above, the confusion matrices of each classes are presented in Table 8:

Table 8. Confusion matrices by class.

Class	TP	FP	FN	TN
Pliers	45	1	5	49
Padlocks	48	0	2	50
Soldering irons	46	0	4	50
Screwdrivers	48	12	2	38
Angle grinder	47	0	3	50
Axes	42	0	8	50
Wrenches	48	0	2	50
Hammers	46	0	4	50
Drills	48	0	2	50
Scissors	46	0	4	50

Additionally, a process was carried out to verify that the model does not have an overfit, this process consisted of taking part of the elements that were used for training as a test and passing them as input data to the model for its corresponding detection, if there is a large margin of error in the classification, then the model suffers overfitting, 100 images per class were taken to carry out the test, the results can be seen in the Table 9.

Table 9. Overfitting detection.

Correct Classification	Incorrect classification
476	24

As can be seen, the results had a minimum margin of error, this may be due to the fact that more images of certain classes are missing for the model to be able to generalize and detect them correctly.

Based on Table 8, the value of the metrics was obtained corresponding to be able to carry out the evaluation of the efficiency of the model, the results are presented in Table 10.

Table 10. Evaluation metrics by class.

Class	Accuracy	Recall	Specificity	Precision	F1-score
Pliers	0.94	0.9	0.98	0.98	0.94
Padlocks	0.98	0.96	1	1	**0.98**
Soldering irons	0.96	0.92	1	1	0.96
Screwdrivers	0.86	0.96	0.76	0.8	0.87
Angle grinders	0.97	0.94	1	1	0.97
Axes	0.92	0.84	1	1	0.91
Wrenches	0.98	0.96	1	1	**0.98**
Hammers	0.96	0.92	1	1	0.96
Drills	0.98	0.96	1	1	**0.98**
Scissors	0.96	0.92	1	1	0.96

Additionally, the results obtained from the tests carried out with the best model, as can be observe the results are favorable and efficient, fulfilling with an accuracy greater than 90% (Fig. 7):

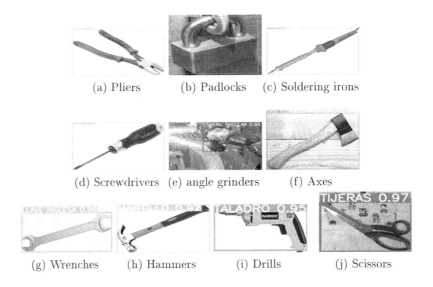

(a) Pliers   (b) Padlocks   (c) Soldering irons

(d) Screwdrivers (e) angle grinders   (f) Axes

(g) Wrenches   (h) Hammers   (i) Drills   (j) Scissors

Fig. 7. Tests performed

To obtain the tuning, different training were carried out with various models and hyperparameter configurations to determine which model gave the best result, giving as final winner the YOLOv5x version with a 98% accuracy. The metrics for the evaluation of the models are based on the objects they are able to detect rightly and wrongly, giving more emphasis to F1-score, which measures the percentage of true positives classified correctly, having a maximum value of 98%.

The value of the metrics vary in each class due to the number of classes that the network is capable of detecting and, given cases, the network can overlap these classes. This problem can be countered by adding more mixed images to the classes with this problem, in addition to this, at the time of training the resolution of the images can be increased, this is because as part of the dataset it is downloaded from the Internet the size/resolution of the images may be affected, by increasing the resolution of the images in training will also increase the computational cost, increasing training time but giving better results.

Additionally, tests were carried out in real time where the values were experimented and obtained through the metrics in real time, shown in the Table 11:

Table 11. Real-time metrics.

Métric	Average
FPS	30 fps
Average prediction	27.7 ms
Visual range	1.5–2 m

4 Conclusion

In all classes the training with images was carried out 640×640 in size in various formats (PNG, JPG AND JPEG) with a learning rate of 0.01. According the results, it is shown that the proposed model presents variations in their evaluation metrics, this due to the different number of images that were implemented by class. Table 12 is presented below, which contains the average values of the model:

Table 12. Average metrics.

Métric	Average
Accuracy	95.1%
Recall	92.8%
Specificity	97.4%
Precision	97.8%
F1-score	95.1%

As can be seen, in most of the metrics the value of 95% is exceeded, with respect to the recall metric, its value is lower than the others because in certain classes there is not a sufficient number of images to "identify" certain objects. The results of this work are better than several works in the state of the art, this may be due to the fact that the YOLO algorithm has evolved over time, offering greater efficiency for each version that comes out.

The convolutional neural networks present better performance when the images are correctly tagged and there is an intensity of the pixels sufficiently decisive, these tasks must be performed independently of the work carried out by this type of neural networks.

4.1 Limitations and Challenges

In CNN training, something that can be laborious is the collection of the dataset, this is the case in this work. It is important that the dataset contains only the elements that the model needs for its correct training, for this it is necessary to carry out a complete filtering of images in search of collecting those that have good resolution or that contain the necessary elements to analyze and discard the images that does not meet these conditions. This was a very time consuming task, however, based on the results, the process was fine.

Another task that required time is tuning the model; it is necessary to carry out many trainings in search of finding a suitable hyperparameter configuration, this in order to find the best results. This task also requires a decent computer equipment, since the trainings require high computing power; the better capacity the components have, the better results will be obtained.

Once these stages were overcome, only the results had to be obtained, however these were quick tasks and did not present great difficulties.

4.2 Future Works

This leaves as future work to improve the efficiency of the model by adding more images to the dataset and accurately labeling the areas of interest, in addition to designing a physical architecture for the detection and classification of tools. Furthermore, it should be mentioned that the YOLO algorithm is constantly being developed and updated, and it is possible to increase the detection accuracy by training more current models correctly tuned, similarly, better results could be obtained by training the model with better equipment, which contains components with more computing power and analytical capacities.

Acknowledgements. This work was supported by the Tecnológico Nacional de México/Instituto Tecnológico de Tapachula trough the project entitled "Delimitación de masas sólidas malignas en mamografías mediante un algoritmo de nodos conectados con el menor angulo polar"

References

1. Cameron: Automatización de procesos: beneficios para el mundo empresarial (2019)
2. Cognex: Introduction to computer vision, p. 3 (2016)
3. Galván: Comparativa de técnicas para la prevención del sobreajuste en redes neuronales (2021)
4. Sánchez, E.G.: Introduction to convolution neural networks. Application to vision by computer, pp. 17–20 (2019)
5. Bonilla Carrión, C.: Convolutional networks, pp. 15–34 (2020)
6. Ramirez, A.V.: Detection of bud degeneration in oil palm using a convolutional neural network, pp. III–IV (2021)
7. Matuz-Cruz, M., García-Aquino, C.J., Reyes-Sánchez, E.: Methodology for measuring the opening and coverage of the forest canopy by implementing artificial vision techniques. IEEE Latin Am. Trans. **18**(12), 2138 (2021)
8. Matuz, A. de la Cruz de los Reyes, and D. M. V. ans Artemio Enríquz Espinoza: Pest detection in plant images. J. Vibr. Control 1 (2021)
9. Matuz and D. M. V. ans Jesóus Antonio Luna Álvarez: Classification of mammograms with abnormalities using convolutional neural networks, p. 1 (2021)
10. Sandoval Rodríguez-Bermejo, D.: Design aníd implementation of a system for stress detection using convolutional neural networks from thermal images, p. 1 (2019)
11. Pérez Carrasco, J.A., Serrano Gotarredona, M.C., Acha Piñero, B., Serrano Gotarredona, M.T., Linares Barranco, B.: Fast frameless convolutional neural network for digit recognitions. Int. Radio Sci. Union 1 (2011)
12. Massiris, M., Delrieux, C., Fernández Muñoz, J.Á.: Detection of personal protective equipment using YOLO convolutional neural network, p. 1 (2018)
13. Pérez, M.A.A.: RGB, HSI color spaces and their generalizations to n-dimensions, p. 36. INAOE, Tonantzintla (2009)
14. Ketkar, N., Moolayil, J.: Convolutional neural networks, p. 66 (2021)
15. Larranaga, P., Inza, I., Moujahid, A.: Topic 8. Neural Networks. Redes Neuronales, U. del P. Vasco, vol. 12, pp. 8–18 (1997)
16. Vidal González, M.: The use of the multilayer perceptron for the classification of patterns in addictive behaviors, pp. 17–19 (2015)
17. Solsona, A.V.: Facial expression detection using convolutional neural networks. Engineering Degree in Telecommunications Systems, pp. 4–6 (2018)
18. Redmon, J., Divvala, S., Girshick, R., Farhadi, A.: You only look once: unified, real-time object detection. In: IEEE Conference on Computer Vision and Pattern Recognition (CVPR), pp. 779–788 (2016)
19. Jaramillo, V.D.M.: Evaluation of machine learning models for crime prediction in the city of medellín, pp. 13–15 (2021)
20. Pérez-Planells, L., Delegido, J., Rivera-Caicedo, J.P., Verrelst, J.: Analysis of cross-validation methods for robust derivation of biophysical parameters. Revista de teledetección (44), 58 (2015)

Power- and Speed-Efficient Compressed Sensing Encoder via Multiplexed Stabilizer

David Ernesto Troncoso Romero$^{(\boxtimes)}$ ⓘ, Daniel Sergio Martínez-Ramírez, Yolanda Pérez-Pimentel, and Ismael Osuna-Galán

Departamento de Informática y Redes, División de Ciencias, Ingeniería y Tecnología, Universidad Autónoma del Estado de Quintana Roo, Campus Cancún, Av. Chetumal SM 260 MZ 21 y 16 LT 1-01, Fracc. Prado Norte, 77519 Cancún, Quintana Roo, México
david.troncoso@uqroo.edu.mx

Abstract. This paper presents a digital hardware architecture for a compressed sensing encoder that outperforms the state-of-the-art solution in terms of speed and power metrics, with an acceptable charge in the hardware cost. The proposed core can achieve, on average, an increase of 94% in the maximum sample rate for input data and a reduction of dynamic power consumption of 30% with just 18% of extra hardware utilization, as validated with post-place-and-route information from FPGA-based implementations.

Keywords: Compressed Sensing · Sub-Nyquist sampling · Decimation

1 Introduction

Digital Compressed-Sensing Encoding (DCSE) is the process of decreasing, to sub-Nyquist rates, the amount of samples per second of digital sequences, ensuring that no information is lost. This re-sampling scheme, which works for discrete-time signals that are compressible in a variety of bases or frames, has gained great popularity because it reduces the dimension of signals in a domain-blind way —i.e., there is no need to compute the sparsifying basis in the DCSE process—, and finds applications in the energy-efficient transmission of different types of digital information in wide-band communications [1], wireless body sensor networks [2], the transmission of digital images and video [3], or in vector signal analyzers [4], among others.

The DCSE process is modeled by the product $\mathbf{y} = \Phi\mathbf{x}$, where the $N \times 1$ vector $\mathbf{x}$ is the input signal, Φ is the $M \times N$ compressed sensing matrix and the $M \times 1$ vector $\mathbf{y}$ is the obtained sub-Nyquist signal, with $M < N$—the compression ratio is $C = N/M$—. We denote $x[n]$ (or $y[n]$, etc.) the n-th sample contained in $\mathbf{x}$ (or $\mathbf{y}$, etc.), starting with $n = 0$.

It has been theoretically demonstrated [5, 6] that block- or band-structured matrices guarantee stable recovery with preservation of information. The block-structured matrix Φ with $+1/-1$ entries in each block, depicted in Fig. 1 (see also [1]), is ubiquitous because the state-of-the-art standard architecture (see [2–4]) that allows performing the product $\Phi\mathbf{x}$ with such matrix, shown in Fig. 2, is simple and regular.

M. F. Mata-Rivera et al. (Eds.): WITCOM 2023, CCIS 1906, pp. 44–50, 2023.
https://doi.org/10.1007/978-3-031-45316-8_4

+1 / −1 entries in every ($P \times Q$) block

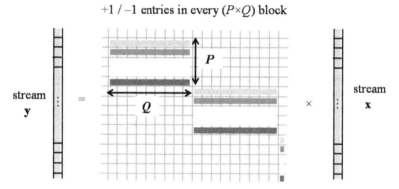

Fig. 1. Structure of compressed sensing matrix Φ.

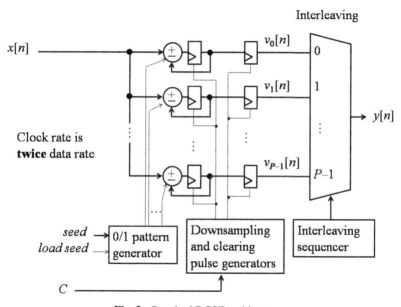

Fig. 2. Standard DCSE architecture.

The architecture consists of a generator of P 0/1 patterns controlling the sign of P parallel Adder-subtractor Accumulation Units (AAUs) that process chunks of Q samples in an accumulate-and-dump form, where P and Q are related via $C = Q/P$. In the scenario where it is necessary to maximize the quality of the recovered signal, every block of Φ must be densely populated, meaning that the architecture must allow streaming processing without missing any sample from **x**.

The problem of the standard architecture is that, to achieve such characteristic, the AAUs have to be clocked at twice the sample rate of the input data, such that their registers can be cleared every ($2Q-1$)-th clock cycle under disciplined synchronous processing

—recall that an accumulator becomes unstable if it is not periodically cleared—. Thus, its maximum frequency of operation can not be fully leveraged, since data can run, at most, only at a half of such limit. Clocking the system at the input sample data rate would introduce all-zero columns in Φ every time registers are cleared, which is against the aforementioned scenario and may even make the sensing matrix to lose its stable acquisition properties (see [5])—.

To solve the aforementioned problem, we propose an approach where: 1) we make sample data rate and clock rate equal, i.e., we take full advantage of the maximum frequency of operation of the system, and 2) we operate the AAUs without periodically clearing their registers. This solution comes from a proper multi-rate model for the DCSE process.

2 Proposed Scheme

From the structure of Φ and from the standard architecture we have that every sample in $\mathbf{y}$ is obtained by a finite summation of Q non-zero-scaled samples from $\mathbf{x}$, where the $(P \times n + i)$-th sample in $\mathbf{y}$ is computed at the i-th branch, i.e.,

$$y[P \cdot n + i] = v_i[n], \quad for \quad i = 0, 1, \ldots, P - 1, \tag{1}$$

$$v_i[n] = \sum_{k=0}^{Q-1} u_i[Q \cdot n - k], \tag{2}$$

where $v_i[n]$ is the n-th sample of the signal $\mathbf{v}_i$, generated at the i-th branch of the architecture (see Fig. 2), and $u_i[n]$ is the n-th sample of the signal $\mathbf{u}_i = \mathbf{p}_i \circ \mathbf{x}$, obtained by point-wise product (denoted by $\circ$) of the i-th $+1/-1$ sequence $\mathbf{p}_i$ with the input sequence $\mathbf{x}$ (the $+ 1/-1$ sequences $\mathbf{p}_i$ are implicitly generated by 0/1 pattern generator in the architecture, upon performing the sign changes in the AAUs).

From (2) we have that $\mathbf{v}_i$ is obtained via decimation of $\mathbf{u}_i$, i.e., Finite Impulse Response (FIR) filtering before downsampling by Q, where the FIR filter has the transfer function

$$H(z) = \sum_{k=0}^{Q-1} z^{-k}. \tag{3}$$

For this type of decimator, two solutions exist to make equal the sample rate of input data and the clock rate of the system [7, 8].

The first solution, from [7], consists in using two parallel AAUs in every branch —2P parallel AAUs in total—, where one of the AAUs would process the input stream, while the register of the other one is cleared. However, we prefer the second one, from [8], where the geometric series equivalence

$$\sum_{k=0}^{Q-1} z^{-k} = \frac{1 - z^{-Q}}{1 - z^{-1}}, \tag{4}$$

is used to preserve the regularity of the filter and, by multi-rate identities, the FIR block $1-z^{-Q}$ is moved after the downsampler. This equivalence results in the Cascaded Integrator-Comb (CIC) core, popular in recent wide-band multi-standard receivers [9, 10].

Figure 3a shows the resulting multi-rate model, where the construction of the signal $\mathbf{u}_i = \mathbf{p}_i \circ \mathbf{x}$ has been excluded for simplicity. By multi-rate identities, the P FIR blocks $1-z^{-1}$ can be moved after the interleaver as a single filter $1-z^{-P}$, resulting in the multi-rate model of Fig. 3b. This case is better because it employs only one arithmetic unit instead of using P parallel arithmetic units while the computational complexity remains the same, since in both cases the workload due to these FIR blocks is a subtraction per output sample.

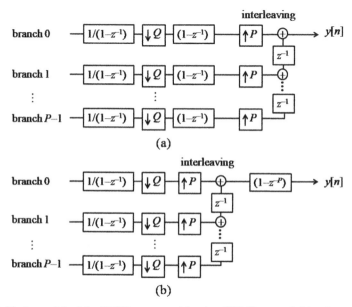

Fig. 3. Multirate model of the DCSE process: (a) using CIC filters and (b) using a hardware-efficient equivalent.

Finally, the proposed architecture can be easily derived from the model in Fig. 3b, just using pipelined AAUs instead of classic integrators in order to embed the product $\mathbf{p}_i \circ \mathbf{x}$ into these units (with this, we also take advantage of inherent pipelining). Our architecture is presented in Fig. 4, where the extra hardware elements in the standard system are highlighted in black lines.

The FIR block $1-z^{-P}$ that we have added is a stabilizer for the AAUs that allows to process data uninterruptedly. Since there is no need to set a finer time resolution for clearing AAUs, the clock rate and input sample data rate can be equal. Thus, in comparison with the standard system, we can almost double the maximum rate to process data with an acceptable increase of hardware complexity.

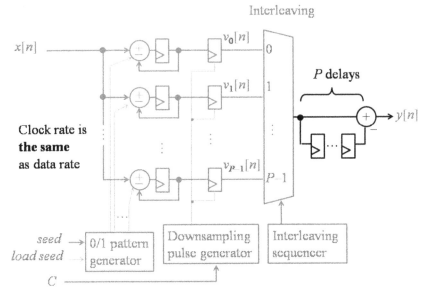

Fig. 4. Proposed modification to the standard DCSE architecture.

3   Discussion of Results

We first compare the standard and proposed architectures using the setting from [2], i.e., $P = 50$ and $Q = 500$ ($C = 10$), 8-bit input data and 10-bit output data. In that scenario, the 0/1 pattern generator is designed with two Linear Feedback Shift Registers (LFSRs), respectively 50-bit and 15-bit wide.

The synthesis of the aforementioned architectures has been carried out with Quartus Prime 18.0 Lite Edition using the EP4CE115F29C7 FPGA chip, popular in academic community, as target platform. TimeQuest Timing Analyzer was employed for the estimation of maximum frequency of operation using the 85C model, i.e., the worst-case scenario. Power Play Power Analyzer was employed to estimate power consumption, and a test signal with 80 MHz of sample rate was used as input to both cores for an estimation with high level of confidence, adding to the power analysis the Value Change Dump (VCD) data generated with ModelSim 10.5b Altera Starter Edition. The aforementioned signal rate was chosen in order to fit the maximum sample rate of input data supported by both architectures.

The test signal was randomly generated with $N = 1024$ samples, sparse in the Discrete Cosine Transform (DCT) domain with sparsity value $K = 32$. After the place-and-route tasks performed by the synthesizer, the maximum sample rate for input signal is 177.8 MHz in the proposed system, and 95.9 MHz in the standard system, which represents a great enhancement of about 85%. The estimated power consumptions due to the switching activity of the systems, i.e., dynamic power consumptions, are, respectively, 31.15 mW and 44.85 mW, i.e., we have 30% of reduction. The aforementioned advantages come with a very acceptable cost: the proposed core uses 2348 FPGA's Logic

Elements (LEs) with 816 bits of on-chip memory, against 1966 LEs used by the standard system. This represents 19.4% extra LEs, and just 0.02% of the total memory of the chip.

For a more complete information, we have build similar cores, with $P = \{4, 8, 16, 32, 64\}$ and $C = 10$. Table 1 summarizes, for the proposed system and the standard system, the maximum sample rate for input signal, the dynamic power consumption and the hardware utilization.

Table 1. Power consumption, maximum input data rate and hardware utilization for the standard and proposed architectures.

		Power consumption (mW)	Maximum input data rate (MHz)	Hardware utilization (LEs)
$P = 4$	Standard	12.3	136.3	178
	Proposed	7.8	281.1	209
$P = 8$	Standard	19.4	131.4	323
	Proposed	11.7	263.7	385
$P = 16$	Standard	23.1	121.9	640
	Proposed	16.5	234.8	730
$P = 32$	Standard	35.8	112	1279
	Proposed	29.4	222.5	1500
$P = 64$	Standard	67.1	104.1	2582
	Proposed	46.7	182.4	3091

Figure 5 shows the percentage of improvement in maximum sample rate for input data, and percentage of reduction of dynamic power consumption, which are, on average, 94.7% and 30.5%, respectively, as well as the percentage of increase in LEs utilization, which is, on average, 17.5%. Use of memory in the chip is 0.03% in the worst case ($P = 64$), which is negligible.

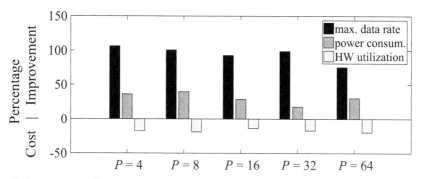

Fig. 5. Percentage of improvements and costs of proposed DCSE cores with reference to the standard DCSE equivalents.

4 Conclusion

We have shown how the AAUs of the standard DCSE architecture can work uninterruptedly via a simple FIR stabilizer. With this, clock rate of the system and sample rate of input data can be the same, thus taking full advantage of the maximum frequency of operation of the system. The proposed scheme was derived by modelling the DCSE process as a multi-rate system, and inheriting from literature equivalent multi-rate filters. The proposed scheme is applicable when disciplined synchronous methodology is employed to design digital encoders, which is necessary, for example, on FPGA platforms. The resulting system implements the product with block-structured acquisition matrices having dense entries in every block, where input samples must not be missed.

References

1. Troncoso-Romero, D.E.: Analog-to-Information conversion by encoded multi-cosets. Int. J. Electron. Lett. **8**(3), 319–328 (2020)
2. Chen, F., Chandrakasan, A.P., Stojanovic, V.M.: Design and analysis of a hardware-efficient compressed sensing architecture for data compression in wireless sensors. IEEE J. Solid-State Circuits **47**(3), 744–756 (2012)
3. Frigo, G., Narduzzi, C.: Characterization of a compressive sensing preprocessor for vector signal analysis. IEEE Trans. Instrum. Meas. **65**(6), 1319–1330 (2016)
4. Pudi, V., Chattopadhyay, A., Lam, K.-Y.: Efficient and lightweight quantized compressive sensing using μ-law. In: Maloberti, F., Setti, G. (eds.) Proceedings of the IEEE International Symposium on Circuits and Systems (2018)
5. Castorena, J., Creusere, C.D.: The Restricted Isometry Property for banded random matrices. IEEE Trans. Sig. Process. **62**(19), 5073–5084 (2014)
6. Eftekhari, A., Yap, H.L., Rozell, C.J., Wakin, M.B.: The Restricted Isometry Property for random block diagonal matrices. Appl. Comput. Harmon. Anal. **38**(1), 1–31 (2015)
7. Kline, R.B.: Digital filtering. US Patent no. 5051981 (1991)
8. Hogenauer, E.: An economical class of digital filters for decimation and interpolation. IEEE Trans. Acoust. Speech Sig. Process. **29**(2), 155–162 (1981)
9. Troncoso-Romero, D.E.: Efficient CIC-based architecture with improved aliasing rejection and reduced computational complexity. Electron. Lett. **52**(15), 1294–1295 (2016)
10. Troncoso-Romero, D.E.: Simplifying zero rotations in Cascaded Integrator-Comb decimators. IEEE Sig. Process. Mag. **40**(3), 50–58 (2023)

Classical Artificial Neural Networks and Seismology, Basic Steps for Training Process

Israel Reyes-Ramírez$^{(\boxtimes)}$ ⓘ, Eric Gómez Serrano ⓘ,
Octavio Sebastián Hernández Pérez-Riveroll ⓘ, Álvaro Anzueto Ríos ⓘ,
and Jorge Fonseca Campos ⓘ

Instituto Politécnico Nacional - UPIITA, 07340 CDMX, Mexico
{ireyesr,aanzuetor,jfonsecac}@ipn.mx,
{egomezs1300,ohernandezp1600}@alumno.ipn.mx

Abstract. The reliable detection of a seismic even is still an open task due to the complexity of the phenomenon. In addition, the same event is measured with quite different characteristics depending on the site of monitoring, partly due to the seismic signal being mainly the superposition of waves that propagate in multiple directions from their hypocenter, undergoing different attenuation phenomena, reflection, etc. The study of seismic detection has become relevant in the construction of early warning systems in cities. In this work, the application of artificial neural networks for the recognition of records from seismic and non-seismic events is presented. The seismograms and the non-seismic records were used to construct the spectrogram, treated as an RGB image and become the input data for neural networks training-test processes. Three well-known neural networks architectures were used in this study: "ALEXNET, RESNET18, and VGG16". They are based on convolutional neural networks and were specially constructed for image recognition. Given the characteristics of the images used, and the size of the dataset available, our results show that the three architectures are highly recommended for the proposed application. The data reported for the neural architectures show that it is possible to recognize the frequency elements that conform to a seismic signal. For its final implementation in real-time automatic seismic monitoring for early warning systems, it is proposed to evaluate which of the three architectures consumes less computational resources and presents less response time.

Keywords: Seismicity · Artificial Neural Networks · Early Warning Systems

1 Introduction

Seismic events are phenomena that occur without warning around the world. Its preparation mechanisms are not evident even in seismically active regions. In

Supported by COFAA-IPN, EDI-IPN AND CONAHCYT-MEXICO.

M. F. Mata-Rivera et al. (Eds.): WITCOM 2023, CCIS 1906, pp. 51–63, 2023.
https://doi.org/10.1007/978-3-031-45316-8_5

particular, Mexico is on the list of the countries most prone to earthquakes in the world since it is located in one of the most active seismic zones in the world, called the Circumpacific Belt or also known as the "Ring of Fire". In this area, some records show between 80% and 90% of the planet's annual seismic energy release.

The most reliable way that society has to react to these events is through continuous monitoring of ground vibrations, and from this, implement automatic detection systems that allow early warnings to be triggered to the population. While in its early days, earthquake detection was reserved for specialists in the field with high-end instruments and well-developed survey techniques, today, low-cost sensors and portable data processing devices make monitoring within reach of professionals in other branches of knowledge [11,13,23], hobbyists with an interest in the subject, among others.

On the other hand, while traditional analysis techniques for early detection of earthquakes are still valid today, with the processing capacity of personal computing devices, artificial intelligence techniques have been popularized in different disciplines, including seismology [2,18,19]. An important branch of this is the Artificial Neural Networks (ANN), which require a training and testing stage regarding the phenomenon of interest, whether or not it is present in the records available. During these stages, the quality of the data and the certainty of the presence or absence of the phenomenon is crucial, for which reason it is necessary to have well-refined databases that, through other techniques, have accurately selected the training data.

Many of the data from seismic records have standards that allow them to make uniform both their visualization and their processing. In the language of seismicity, an earthquake is visualized through its waveform called seismogram, which is a two-dimensional graphic representation of the acceleration, velocity, and/or displacement suffered by the ground at a specific monitoring point in one, two, and/or three spatial directions. The study and interpretation of the waveforms lead specialists to determine the seismic event's intensity and point of origin. With an adequate treatment of said graphs and the event information, neural networks have been trained for the identification and classification tasks [12,21,24,25]. In addition, the recorded waveforms are also usually analyzed through their frequency components, for example, through their Fourier series decomposition. The continuous observation of its frequency components is usually analyzed using a Fourier spectrogram, which also has its 2D representation and has been used to train neural networks [12,24].

Therefore, if the objective of detecting seismic events in progress for the eventual implementation of an early warning system is set, it is important to become familiar with seismic records, their formats, and their typical representations, as well as with the implementation of neural networks to have an optimal coupling between both themes for future implementation in real-time.

Three works were the basis of this study: First, Wang et al. developed a seismic detector based on two ANN they have designed. Their input data came from the recursive STA/LTA time series and spectrograms constructed of the original waveform of seismograms. Their results, as they said, show that the *ANN*-based detectors are better than the conventional algorithms [24]. Second, Zhu *et al.* proposed a seismogram discriminator base on *CNN ResNet*. They consider Three-component seismic waveforms as input images for training and testing *ResNet* to distinguish between good and poor seismic records. They report that their seismogram discriminator achieves an accuracy of 95% [25]. And third, Ren *et al.* propose a method for the identification natural earthquakes event and unnatural events such as explosions and collapse. The method is based on *CNN AlexNet*. The input image data was constructed from events waveform. They report that the automatic identification accuracy of natural earthquakes, explosions, and collapses was 90%, 80%, and 85%, respectively [21].

In the present work, the training of an *ANN* with records of seismic events and noise is addressed. Specifically three well known AlexNet [15], ResNet18 [6] and VGG16 [22] *ANN* architectures were selected. Seismic signals are provided from a reliable database provided by the Geophysical Institute of the National Polytechnic School of Ecuador [9], as well as environmental noise records were taken from the global network of Raspberry Shake seismometers open platform [20].

2   Seismic Signals

When an earthquake occurs, the energy released by the phenomenon propagates through the earth's crust in the form of mechanical waves. These waves propagate in multiple directions from their hypocenter, undergoing different attenuation phenomena, reflection, superposition, etc. They are detected using motion sensors installed at a specific point of the earth's surface. These records, commonly called *Seismograms*, are the record of the Earth's movement, whether in displacement, speed, or acceleration, as a function of time. Its appearance (see Fig. 1 above) reflects the combined effects of the source, the propagation path, the characteristics of the recording instrument, and the ambient noise due to the specific conditions of the installation site [16].

Each data channel of a seismic wave consists of a series of samples (signal amplitude values) for the three spatial directions, that are normally equally spaced in time (sample interval). Each data channel is headed by information with at least the station and component name, but often also the network and location code [5]. The Standard for the Exchange of Earthquake Data (*SEED*), is an international standard format for the exchange of digital seismic data primarily intended for archiving and exchanging raw earth motion data. The format is maintained by the International Federation of Digital Seismograph Networks (*FDSN*) and is documented in the *SEED* Manual (PDF format) [10]. *MSEED* is the subset of the *SEED* norm used for time series data. Very limited metadata for time series is included in *MSEED* beyond time series identification and simple health status indicators. In particular, geographic coordinates, response/scale information, and other information necessary to interpret the data values are not included [8].

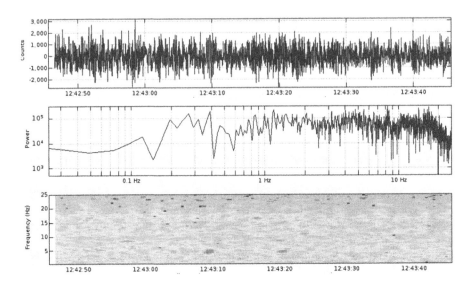

Fig. 1. Example of a record taken from Raspberry Shake, showing nonseismic noise. Above the signal. In the middle the power spectrum of all the record. Bottom the spectrogram for the record, where it is observed the sliding window used to construct them. The plots were made using *SWARM* software.

3   Frequency Analysis

Because the seismogram is a superposition of waves, its analysis typically involves decomposition into Fourier series. To implement it numerically, different algorithms are available in the literature for its implementation.

Fourier transform decomposes a time series $\{x_n\}$ in a summation of sinusoidal waves with well-determined frequency. In the discrete domain, the transformation is given by:

$$x_k = \sum_{n=1}^{N} X_n e^{-i2\pi kn/N}, k = 1, 2, ..., N/2 \qquad (1)$$

where the Fourier coefficients X_k are associated with frequencies $f_k = k/N$.

Based on the principle that the frequency content of a seismic and a non-seismic event are intrinsically different, using the frequency spectrum calculated from the fast Fourier transform in sliding windows of the original seismogram signal is proposed. The moving window of the spectrum is calculated continuously in 2-minute windows overlapping the windows by 25pc. Thus, The spectrogram consists of a two-dimensional image that includes temporal and frequency information (see Fig. 1 below and 2 below) [1].

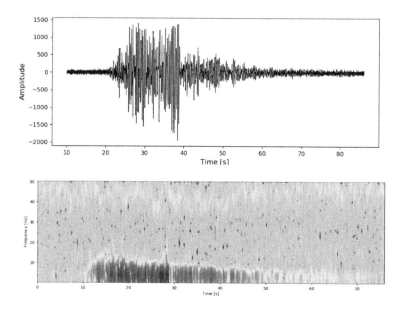

Fig. 2. Example of seismic record. Above it is shown the seismic waveform. Below is the representation of the spectrogram constructed from it.

4   Artificial Neural Networks

Artificial Neural Networks (*ANN*) is a method of artificial intelligence to process information in a very similar way to what the human brain would do, imitating the way in which biological neurons work. They are composed of an input layer, one or more hidden layers, and an output layer. These layers are made up of nodes, or artificial neurons, that are connected to each other and have an associated threshold and weight (see Fig. 3). Neural networks rely on data to learn and improve their accuracy over time [17].

The way in which an *ANN* improves its processing is through network training. Training is the process of teaching a neural network to perform a task. To improve its accuracy, networks depend on large amounts of known data as datasets.

4.1   Convolutional Neural Networks

Convolutional neural networks are *ANN* commonly used to solve problems requiring image processing or image recognition. Its most frequent use cases range from image classification to generating a textual description of an image's content. In particular, its inputs and outputs can be structured, which means that instead of receiving a vector of inputs, they can receive a vector (1D), a matrix (2D), or a tensor (>2D). Convolution is a mathematical operation applied to two functions to generate a third function, often interpreted as a modified or

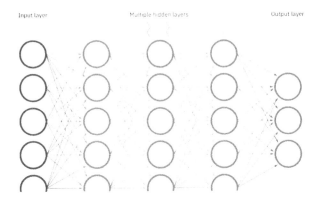

Fig. 3. Topology of a Neural Network [7]

filtered version of the original functions [3]. The convolution between the functions f and g is represented as follows:

$$[f * g](t) = \int_{-\infty}^{\infty} f(\tau)g(t - \tau)\, d\tau = \int_{-\infty}^{\infty} g(\tau)f(t - \tau)\, d\tau \qquad (2)$$

For functions of a discrete variable x, that is, arrays of numbers, it is represented as follows:

$$(f * g)[n] = \sum_{k=-\infty}^{\infty} f[k]g[n - k] = \sum_{-\infty}^{\infty} g[k]f[n - k] \qquad (3)$$

5 Application of the Proposed Neural Networks to Seismic and Non-seismic Spectrograms

It is essential to have a large enough data set to train the neural network properly. Since the main objective is the detection of earthquakes, a dataset composed of seismic and non-seismic spectrogram images is required. The type of learning used in convolutional neural networks is supervised learning, which implies that the data must be correctly labeled.

The dataset of seismic signals was obtained thanks to the collaboration with the Geophysical Institute of the National Polytechnic School of Ecuador [9]. On the other hand, non-seismic signals were collected through the network of Raspberry Shake [20] devices.

For the elaboration of the datasets, 500 seismograms were taken for constructing their spectrogram images and 500 non-seismic intervals of around 3 min were also taken for constructing the corresponding spectrogram images. The purpose of doing it this way is to ensure fair training and testing for the neural network.

As it is mentioned above, non-seismic records taken from Raspberry Shake [20] are in *MSEED* format. The RBshake system is an open platform where the user can visualize and/or download records for the past 24hrs or build a specific data request for a particular station shown in an interactive map.

Colab Google product in addition to *Tensorflow* are used to build the training module and test module for the three *ANN* architectures selected in this study named AlexNet, ResNet18, and VGG16. All of them are convolutional neural networks, and the earthquake event and noise records spectrograms were transformed into an RGB image format file.

5.1 AlexNet Assessment

For evaluating the first neural network, it is proposed to start with the pioneer convolutional neural network named AlexNet. AlexNet is a convolutional neural network designed for deep learning and image classification. It consists of several convolutional layers, pooling layers, and fully connected layers, in addition to using techniques such as ReLU (Rectified Linear Unit) as an activation function, dropout regularization, and optimization with the stochastic gradient descent algorithm.

Figure 4 illustrates the connection among the convolutional, fully connected, and output layers of the AlexNet.

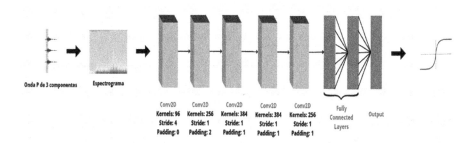

Fig. 4. Neural network model for AlexNet

This architecture is especially known for its ability to process large-scale images and its ability to handle large amounts of data, contributing significantly in time reduction for deep learning and computer vision applications [15]. Among the parameters described in Table 1, AlexNet uses a ReLU activation function and a Max-pooling of 3×3 with the stride of 2, for all its Convolutional Layers (CL).

The configuration used to train the AlexNet was as follows: 80% of the dataset was used for training and 20% was reserved for testing. All images were resized to 64×64 pixels. The Categorical Cross-Entropy Loss function [4] was applied and the Adam optimizer [14] was used with a learning rate of 0.001 with 50 training epochs. By training the AlexNet with the proposed dataset, a loss of 3% and an accuracy of 100% in training were achieved. During validation, the

Table 1. Setting for AlexNet's Convolutional Layers

Layer	Filter	Stride	Padding
CL 1	96 kernels of 11×11	4	0
CL 2	256 kernels of 5×5	1	2
CL 3	384 kernels of 3×3	1	1
CL 4	384 kernels of 3×3	1	1
CL 5	256 kernels of 3×3	1	1

loss resulted in 4.8% and an accuracy of 99%, as shown in Fig. 5. The recall, precision and F1-Score metrics were calculated, with a value of 99.41%.

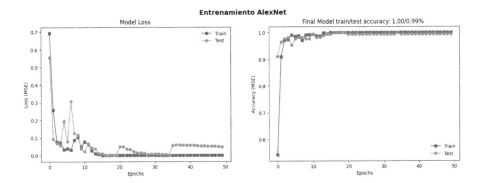

Fig. 5. Training loss graph for AlexNet

5.2 ResNet Assessment

For the evaluation of the second neural network, it is proposed to use ResNet18, which is a deep CNN architecture, designed for deep learning and image classification too. It is a variant of the ResNet architecture, introduced by Kaiming He et al. in 2015. The number "18" indicates that the network has 18 layers with trainable parameters [6].

ResNet18 is based on the idea of residual connections, which allow the network to learn identity functions more easily, thus mitigating the gradient problem in deep networks. The architecture of ResNet18 consists of an Input Layer which consists of a convolutional layer with 64 kernels of 7×7, stride of 2, and padding of 3, followed by a Batch Normalization layer and a ReLU activation function. A max-pooling layer with a kernel size of 3×3 and a stride of 2. In addition, a residual convolutional blocks settings are described as follows (Table 2):

For each block, the residual connection is made through a direct connection between the start and the end of the block, and a 1×1 convolutional layer to

Table 2. Setting for ResNet's Convolutional Layers.

Block	Layers	Filters
1	2	64 kernels
2	1	128 kernels
3	1	256 kernels
4	1	512 kernels

adapt the dimensions if it is necessary. For the output layer, the Global Average Pooling layer reduces the spatial dimensions to 1×1. Fully Connected layer with as many output units as classes have the classification problem, and Softmax activation function to obtain the probabilities of each class.

Figure 6 shows the relationship among the input layer, the pooling layers, the residual blocks, and the output layer of the ResNet18 neural network.

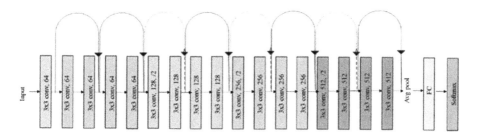

Fig. 6. Resnet18 neural network model

The configuration used to train the *ResNet18* was as follows: 80% of the database was used for training and 20% was reserved for testing. All images have been resized to 64×64 pixels. The Categorical Cross-Entropy Loss function [4] was applied and the Adam optimizer [14] was used with a learning rate of 0.001. When training the *ResNet18* with the existing database, a loss of 9% and an accuracy of 97.16% were achieved in the training. During the validation, it turned out to be a loss of 3% and an accuracy of 97.77%, as shown in Fig. 7. The recall, precision, and F1-Score metrics were calculated, with a value of 98.82%.

5.3 VGG Assessment

For the evaluation of the third neural network, it is proposed to use the VGG16 which is a CNN model that was presented by the Visual Geometry Group (VGG) at the University of Oxford in 2014 [22].

The VGG16 model consists of 16 layers with weights, hence its name. These 16 layers consist of 13 convolutional layers, followed by 3 fully connected layers.

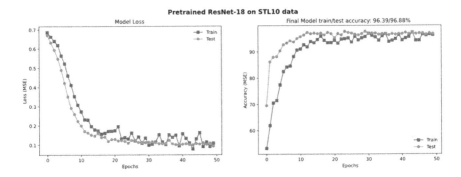

Fig. 7. Left graph: training and test loss, right graph: test and training precision

The VGG16 design uses small 3×3 convolutions on all convolutional layers, with a stride of 1 and padding of 1 to maintain spatial dimensions across layers. It also uses a 2×2 Max-pooling layer with a step of 2 to halve the spatial dimensions after each block of convolutional layers. Following is a detailed description of the VGG16 architecture (Table 3):

Table 3. Configuration for VGG blocks

Block	filters	CL
1	64 kernels	2
2	128 kernels	2
3	256 kernels	3
4	512 kernels	3
5	512 kernels	3

For each block, the Max-pooling Layer halves the spatial dimensions. The Flatten Layer transforms the 3D output into a single dimension. First and Second fully connected layers (Dense) each with 4096 neurons. Finally, the Output layer is a fully connected layer (Dense) with the number of neurons equal to the number of classes of this paper, normally a softmax activation function is used in this layer for multiclass classification.

In all convolutional and fully connected layers, the ReLU (Rectified Linear Unit) activation function is used to introduce nonlinearity into the model.

Figure 8 shows the relationship between the input layer, the pooling layers, the convolutional blocks, and the output layer of the VGG16 neural network.

The configuration used to train the VGG16 neural network was the following: 80% of the database was used for training and 20% was reserved for testing. All images have been resized to 118×118 pixels. The Categorical Cross-Entropy Loss function [4] was applied and the Adam optimizer [14] was used with a learning rate of 0.001 with 50 epochs.

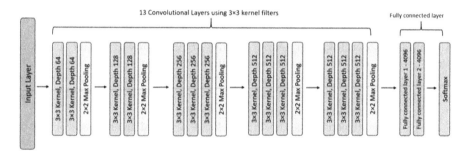

Fig. 8. VGG16 neural network model

For the training of the VGG16, pre-trained weights from the ImageNet competition were used and with the existing database, the fully connected layers were trained, with this a loss of 3% and an accuracy of 98% were achieved in the training. During validation, a loss of 1% and an accuracy of 99% resulted, as shown in Fig. 9. The recall, precision, and F1-Score metrics were calculated, with a value of 98.82%.

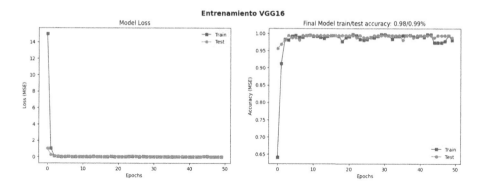

Fig. 9. Training and validation accuracy plot

Finally, after evaluating the three CNNs, taking into account their own configurations, as well as the characteristics of the image format used for each one, the evaluation metrics obtained are shown in Table 4.

Table 4. Performance for the three *CNN* selected

Model	Precision	Recall	F1-Score
AlexNet	0.9941	0.9941	0.9941
ResNet18	0.9882	0.9882	0.9882
VGG16	0.9882	0.9882	0.9882

6   Concluding Remarks

An application of well-known neural network architectures to seismic and non-seismic event records was presented. Training and testing with real seismic data can be potentially useful in real-time seismology. The implemented architectures were AlexNet, ResNet18, and VGG16. They are based on convolutional neural networks and were designed for image recognition.

To use seismic records as the input of the artificial neural networks, the standardized seismic file format MSEED was first decoded, then its frequency components were analyzed together with the temporal information through the construction of the spectrogram of the time window considered. The spectrogram is a 2D image and is used as the input for the neural networks.

Given the characteristics of the images used, and the size of the dataset available, the three architectures are highly recommended for the proposed application. For its final implementation in real-time, it is proposed to evaluate which of the three architectures consumes less computational resources and presents less response time.

Acknowledgments. This work was partially supported by CONAHCyT, México. We also thanks COFAA-IPN and EDI-IPN.

References

1. Allen, J., Rabiner, L.: A unified approach to short-time Fourier analysis and synthesis. Proc. IEEE **65**(11), 1558–1564 (1977). https://doi.org/10.1109/PROC.1977.10770
2. Arrowsmith, S.J., Trugman, D.T., MacCarthy, J., Bergen, K.J., Lumley, D., Magnani, M.B.: Big data seismology. Rev. Geophys. **60**(2), e2021RG000769 (2022)
3. Berzal, F.: Redes neuronales & deep learning: Volumen I. Independently published (2018)
4. Chen, C.H., Lin, P.H., Hsieh, J.G., Cheng, S.L., Jeng, J.H.: Robust multi-class classification using linearly scored categorical cross-entropy. In: 2020 3rd IEEE International Conference on Knowledge Innovation and Invention (ICKII), pp. 200–203 (2020). https://doi.org/10.1109/ICKII50300.2020.9318835
5. Havskov, J., Ottemoller, L.: Routine Data Processing in Earthquake Seismology: With Sample Data, Exercises and Software. Springer, Dordrecht (2010). https://doi.org/10.1007/978-90-481-8697-6
6. He, K., Zhang, X., Ren, S., Sun, J.: Deep residual learning for image recognition. In: Proceedings of the IEEE Conference on Computer Vision and Pattern Recognition, pp. 770–778 (2016)
7. IBM Cloud Education: Neural networks (2020). https://www.ibm.com/cloud/learn/neural-networks
8. Incorporated Research Institutions for Seismology: mseed. https://ds.iris.edu/ds/nodes/dmc/data/formats/miniseed/
9. Instituto Geofísico - EPN: Descarga de datos. https://www.igepn.edu.ec/descarga-de-datos
10. International Federation of Digital Seismograph Networks: Seed reference manual. http://www.fdsn.org/pdf/SEEDManual_V2.4.pdf

11. Kafadar, O.: A geophone-based and low-cost data acquisition and analysis system designed for microtremor measurements. Geosci. Instrum. Methods Data Syst. **9**(2), 365–373 (2020)
12. Khan, I., Choi, S., Kwon, Y.W.: Earthquake detection in a static and dynamic environment using supervised machine learning and a novel feature extraction method. Sensors **20**(3), 800 (2020)
13. Khan, I., Kwon, Y.W.: P-detector: real-time P-wave detection in a seismic waveform recorded on a low-cost MEMS accelerometer using deep learning. IEEE Geosci. Remote Sens. Lett. **19**, 1–5 (2022)
14. Kingma, D.P., Ba, J.: Adam: a method for stochastic optimization (2017)
15. Krizhevsky, A., Sutskever, I., Hinton, G.E.: ImageNet classification with deep convolutional neural networks. In: Advances in Neural Information Processing Systems, vol. 25 (2012)
16. Kulhanek, O., Persson, L.: Seismogram interpretation. Geophysics **157**, 2303–2322 (2011)
17. McCulloch, W.S., Pitts, W.: A logical calculus of the ideas immanent in nervous activity. Bull. Math. Biophys. **10**, 115–133 (1943)
18. Mousavi, S.M., Beroza, G.C.: Deep-learning seismology. Science **377**(6607), eabm4470 (2022)
19. Mousavi, S.M., Beroza, G.C.: Machine learning in earthquake seismology. Annu. Rev. Earth Planet. Sci. **51**, 105–129 (2023)
20. Raspberry Shake, S.A.: How it works. https://raspberryshake.org/about/technology/
21. Ren, J., Zhou, S., Wang, J., Yang, S., Liu, C.: Research on identification of natural and unnatural earthquake events based on AlexNet convolutional neural network. Wireless Commun. Mob. Comput. **2022**, 6782094 (2022)
22. Simonyan, K., Zisserman, A.: Very deep convolutional networks for large-scale image recognition. arXiv preprint arXiv:1409.1556 (2014)
23. Soler-Llorens, J.L., et al.: Design and test of Geophonino-3D: a low-cost three-component seismic noise recorder for the application of the H/V method. Sens. Actuators, A **269**, 342–354 (2018)
24. Wang, J., Teng, T.L.: Artificial neural network-based seismic detector. Bull. Seismol. Soc. Am. **85**(1), 308–319 (1995)
25. Zhu, H., Sun, M., Fu, H., Du, N., Zhang, J.: Training a seismogram discriminator based on ResNet. IEEE Trans. Geosci. Remote Sens. **59**(8), 7076–7085 (2020)

Fractals and Wavelet Fisher's Information

Julio César Ramírez Pacheco[1]($\boxtimes$) (ID), David Ernesto Troncoso Romero[1],
Homero Toral Cruz[2], and José Antonio León Borges[1]

[1] Universidad Autónoma del Estado de Quintana Roo, Av. Chetumal, Fracc. Prado
Norte, 77519 Cancún, Quintana Roo, Mexico
`juliocr@uqroo.edu.mx`

[2] Universidad Autónoma del Estado de Quintana Roo, Blvd. Bahía s/n, Del Bosque,
77019 Chetumal, Quintana Roo, Mexico

Abstract. Fisher's information measure (FIM) allows to study the complexities associated to random signals and systems and has been used in the literature to study EEG and other physiological signals. In this paper, various time-domain definitions of Fisher's information are extended to the wavelet domain and closed-form expressions for each definition are obtained for fractal signals of parameter α. Fisher information planes are computed in a range of α and based on these, characteristics, properties, and the effect of signal length is also identified. Moreover, based on this, a complete characterization of fractals by wavelet Fisher's information is presented and the potential application of each definition in practical fractal signal analysis is also highlighted.

Keywords: Fractals · complexity · Fisher information

1 Introduction

Fractals are used to model numerous phenomena such as human gait [1], human gaze [2], heart-beat dynamics [3,4] in a variety of fields such as economy [5], finance [6], physics [7,8], computer networking [9] among others [10,11]. From the early developments of Mandelbrot [12] to the recent applications in thin films, fractal analysis has undergone many significant advances including a variety of estimation procedures and more elaborate methods of analysis which include a combination of time, frequency and time-scale approcahes [13–15]. Fractal processes are usually described by a single parameter, the Hurst parameter H or its associaed parameter α, which controls its behaviour, e.g., stationarity/nonstationarity, long-memory/short-memory, etc. The Hurst parameter is not only of theoretical but also of practical importance since its estimated value indicates not only healthy or unhealthy traits in humans but also increased delays in computer networking applications. Therefore, an important research area within fractal analysis is the accurate and efficient estimation of the Hurst parameter H. Many techniques for estimating fractality have been proposed in the literature including detrended fluctuation analysis (DFA) [16–19], rescaled range (R/S) Statistic, wavelet-based techniques [20,21] among others. For an

M. F. Mata-Rivera et al. (Eds.): WITCOM 2023, CCIS 1906, pp. 64–72, 2023.
https://doi.org/10.1007/978-3-031-45316-8_6

in-depth review of the many methodologies employed in the estimation of the Hurst parameter H, please refer to [22–26]. Fractals have also been characterized by wavelet-based information tools such as wavelet entropy, wavelet Tsallis entropies and Fisher's information which can be employed as part of more robust analysis/estimation procedures. The main motivation for using information theory quantifiers is to characterize the complexities associated to fractal signals in the time-scale domain. For instance, it has been shown that entropic values are higher for slightly correlated fractal and lower for strongly correlated ones. Based on this, the main motivation of the present article is to extend the time-domain definitions of the Fisher's information measure to the wavelet domain, obtain closed-form expressions of each for fractals and to completely characterize their complexities based on the computation of Fisher's information planes. To fullfill the objectives, the following article is organized as follows. Section 2, provides a brief overview of fractals and their wavelet analysis. Section 3 extends Fisher's information to the wavelet domain, obtains closed-form expressions and computes Fisher information planes for fractal signals. Section 4 discusses the Fisher information planes and identifies potential application for fractal signals analysis and finally Sect. 5 concludes de paper.

2   Fractals and Fisher's Information

Fractal Signals

Fractal processes have been observed in numerous fields of science and technology. They are characterized by *self-similarity* and power-law or $1/f^\alpha$ power spectrum. *Self-similarity* understood in this article as invariance of statistical properties under proper scaling of time and space, i.e.,

$$X(at) \stackrel{d}{=} a^{-H} X(t), \tag{1}$$

where $X(t)$ is a real-valued random signal and $t, a \in \mathbb{R}$. Fractals also have $1/f^\alpha$ behaviour meaning that their spectral density function (SDF) behaves as a power-law in a range of frequencies, i.e.,

$$S_X(f) \sim c_f |f|^{-\alpha}, \ f \in (f_a, f_b) \tag{2}$$

where c_f is a constant and f_a and f_b represent the lower and upper frequencies upon which the power-law holds. When $\alpha \in (-1, 1)$, the process is stationary while for $\alpha \in (1, 3)$, process is regarded as non-stationary. Many stochastic models are fractals such as the popular fractional Brownian motion (fBm), fractional Gaussian noise (fGn), pure-power-law models and fractional ARIMA signals. For more details on the definitions, properties and estimators of *fractals* signals please refer to [27–29].

Wavelet Analysis of Fractal Signals

Wavelets and wavelet transforms play an important role in the analysis, estimation and modeling of fractals [20, 30–32]. As a matter of fact, estimators based on wavelet transforms are recognized as the more efficient non-parametric estimators of α, by far, the principal parameter characterizing fractal signals. Let $X(t)$ be a fractal process with SDF satisfying Eq. 2, the discrete wavelet transform (DWT) of $X(t)$, at time $k \in \mathbb{Z}$ and scale $j \in \mathbb{Z}$ is defined as,

$$d_x(j, k) \triangleq 2^{-j/2} \int X(t)\psi(2^{-j}t - k)dt,$$

for some dilated and translated mother wavelet $\psi(t)$. The family of functions $\psi_{j,k}(t) \triangleq 2^{-j/2}\psi(2^{-j}t-k)$ form an orthonormal set and thus any function $X(t) \in \mathcal{L}_2(\mathbb{R})$ (of finite energy) can be represented as $X(t) = \sum_j \sum_k X(t)d_X(j, k)$. For fractal processes, the variance of wavelet coefficients, $\mathbb{E}d_X^2(j, k)$ is called the wavelet spectrum or wavelet variance and is of primary importance since for fractal signals they satisfy the following relation,

$$\mathbb{E}d_X^2(j, k) \sim 2^{j\alpha}C(\psi, \alpha), \tag{3}$$

where $C(\psi, \alpha) = c_\gamma \int |f|^{-\alpha}|\Psi(f)|^2 df$ and $\Psi(f)$ is the Fourier integral of the mother wavelet $\psi(t)$ at Fourier frequency f. The importance of the wavelet spectrum resides in its ability to estimate α [21, 33, 34] and to construct from such a representation probability mass functions (pmf) which would allow a deeper understanding of their dynamics and nature [35–37]. Indeed, estimation from such wavelet spectrum representation has been shown to be robust to periodicities and trends of polynomial nature. Probability functions (pmf) can also be obtained by wavelet transforms [35], e.g., a wavelet spectrum-based pmf is given by,

$$p_j = \frac{(N_j)^{-1} \sum_k \mathbb{E}d_X^2(j, k)}{\sum_{i=1}^{\log 2(N)} (N_i)^{-1} \sum_k \mathbb{E}d_X^2(j, k)}, \tag{4}$$

where N_j represents the number of wavelet coefficients at scale j. Based on this, the pmf for fractal signals of parameter α and of length N is determined by direct application of Eq. 3 to Eq. 4 which results in the following relation,

$$p_j = 2^{(j-1)\alpha} \frac{1 - 2^\alpha}{1 - 2^{\alpha M}}, \tag{5}$$

where $M = \log 2(N)$. Numerous information theory quantifiers have been proposed based on this pmf such as wavelet entropy, wavelet Tsallis q-entropy among others. The paper extends many Fisher's information definitions to the wavelet domain or time-scale domain and obtains specific relations for fractal signals of parameter α.

3   Wavelet Fisher's Information Definitions

Fisher's information measure (FIM) has recently been applied to several problems in physics and engineering [38–40]. For instance, FIM has been employed for the detection of changes in non-linear dynamical systems [38], detection of epileptic seizures in EEG signals [39] and for the analysis of geoelectrical signals [40]. Let $X(t)$ be a signal with associated probability density function (PDF) $f_X(x)$. The Fisher's information of $X(t)$ is traditionally defined using the following relation,

$$I_X = \int \left(\frac{\partial}{\partial x} f_X(x) \right)^2 \frac{dx}{f_X(x)}. \tag{6}$$

Fisher's information, I_X is non-negative and yields large (possibly infinite) values for smooth (ordered) random signals and small (~ 0) values for random (disordered) signals. In a similar manner, Fisher's information is large for narrow PDFs and small for wide (or flat) PDFs. Based on this, Fisher's information is expected to be small for Gaussian white noise which is uncorrelated and large for correlated fBm.

Fisher's Information Definitions

Sánchez-Moreno and co-workers [41] studied several altenative definitions of Fisher's information and compute the Fisher's information for some discrete densities using these definitions. According to their work, Fisher's information can be defined, in continuous time, in the following equivalent ways,

$$\mathcal{I}(p) = \int_a^b \frac{(p'(x))^2}{p(x)} dx = 4 \int_a^b \left(\frac{d}{dx} \sqrt{p(x)} \right)^2$$

$$= \int_a^b p(x) \left(\frac{d}{dx} \ln p(x) \right)^2 \tag{7}$$

For discrete distributions, and based on the forward discretization operator, Fisher's information can be defined as,

$$\mathcal{I}_1(p) = \int_a^b \frac{(p'(x))^2}{p(x)} dx = \sum_{j=0}^{N-1} \frac{(p_{j+1} - p_j)^2}{p_j} \tag{8}$$

$$\mathcal{I}_2(p) = 4 \int_a^b \left(\frac{d}{dx} \sqrt{p(x)} \right)^2 = 4 \times \sum_{j=0}^{N-1} \left(\sqrt{p_{j+1}} - \sqrt{p_j} \right)^2 \tag{9}$$

$$\mathcal{I}_3(p) = \int_a^b p(x) \left(\frac{d}{dx} \ln p(x) \right)^2 = \sum_{j=0}^{N-1} p_j \left(\ln \frac{p_{j+1}}{p_j} \right)^2 \tag{10}$$

Although equivalent, these different definitions may experience different values for discrete distributions and therefore a more detailed analysis is necessary in order to select the one which is best suited for a particular distribution. In this work, based on the wavelet spectrum-based pmf and the Fisher's definitions, closed form expressions of Fisher's information are computed for fractal signals of parameter α.

Wavelet Fisher's Informations

By using the wavelet spectrum-based pmf given in Eq. (5) and applied to Eqs. (8)–(10), the following relations are obtained,

$$\mathcal{I}_1(p) = \frac{1 - 2^{\alpha(N-1)}}{1 - 2^{\alpha N}} \times (2^\alpha - 1)^2 \tag{11}$$

$$\mathcal{I}_2(p) = 4 \times \frac{1 - 2^{\alpha(N-1)}}{1 - 2^{\alpha N}} \times \left(2^{\alpha/2} - 1\right)^2 \tag{12}$$

$$\mathcal{I}_3(p) = \frac{1 - 2^{\alpha(N-1)}}{1 - 2^{\alpha N}} \times (\ln(2^\alpha))^2 \tag{13}$$

Equations (11)–(13) represent the wavelet Fisher's information for the different definitions given above. In the following, information planes are constructed from these an potential applications identified.

Wavelet Fisher's Information Planes

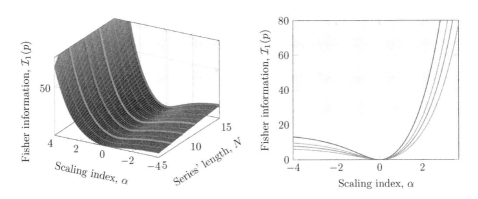

Fig. 1. Wavelet Fisher's information for $\mathcal{I}_1(p)$. Left plot displays the Fisher's information plane for $\alpha \in (-4, 4)$ and length $N \in (5, 15)$. Right plot shows 2D slices for lengths $N = \{7, 9, 11, 15\}$ from which the effect of signal length can be visualized.

In the following, Fisher's information planes for each definition are computed. Figure 1 shows the Fisher's information for Eq. (11). Left plot shows the plane for varying α and N and right plot displays the dependence on signal length which is, in this case, slightly dependent on signal length. Fisher's information are 0 for white noise, increasing for correlated processes and decreasing for uncorrelated ones. In addition, the Fisher's information from this definition is not symmetrical at $\alpha = 0$. Figure 2 displays the wavelet Fisher's information plane for Eq. (12).

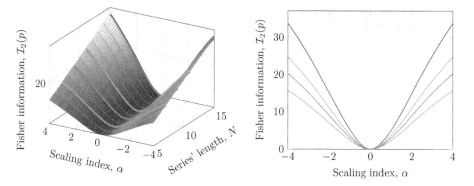

Fig. 2. Fisher's information plane for $\mathcal{I}_2(p)$. Left plot displays the Fisher information for $\alpha \in (-4, 4)$ and $N \in (5, 15)$. Right plot are 2D slices of the left plot, particularly for $N = \{7, 9, 11, 15\}$ to visualize the signal length' effect.

As in the previous figure, left plot displays the Fisher's information dependence on α and N and right plot, the effect of the signal length N. From this plot note that unlike $\mathcal{I}_1(p)$, $\mathcal{I}_2(p)$ is symmetric at $\alpha = 0$, as in the previous case, is increasing for correlated signals and decreasing for uncorrelated ones. Figure 3 displays the wavelet Fisher's information plane for $\mathcal{I}_3(p)$. Like previous definitions, Fisher's information is decreasing for uncorrelated fractals, increasing for correlated ones and is not symmetrical at $\alpha = 0$. Like $\mathcal{I}_1(p)$, $\mathcal{I}_3(p)$ is slightly dependent on N but unlike $\mathcal{I}_1(p)$, their values are more stressed at uncorrelated fractals.

4   Discussion and Applications

Figures. 1, 2 and 3 presented the wavelet Fisher's information for fractal signals within the $-4 \leq \alpha \leq 4$ range. Note that $\mathcal{I}_1(p)$ si asymmetrical with prominent values for $\alpha > 0$, therefore a potential applications for these Fisher information measure is in the classification of fractal signals as correlated or non-correlated. For instante, a possible classification criterior could be if $\mathcal{I}_1 \gg 15$ then the process is regarded as a fractal correlated processes whereas if $\mathcal{I}_1 < 15$ then the process is uncorrelated. The Fisher information of Fig. 2 has the special property of being symmetrical at $\alpha = 0$ and therefore a possible application of this measure is in the detection of white noise traits within a fractal signal. Note that for white noise, the signal has zero Fisher's information while for correlated and uncorrelated fractals the Fisher's information is nonzero. Figure 3 is the

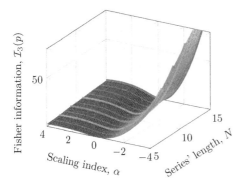
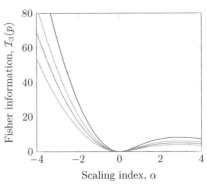

Fig. 3. Wavelet Fisher's information plane for $\mathcal{I}_3(p)$. Left plot shows Fisher's information plane for $\alpha \in (-4, 4)$ and $N \in (5, 15)$. Right plot display slices for $N = 7, 9, 11$ and 15 to stress the dependence on signal length N.

Fisher's information for $\mathcal{I}_3(p)$. Note that in a similar fashion as $\mathcal{I}_1(p)$ is asymmetrical, however, the values of the Fisher's information are more prominent for uncorrelated fractal while for the first definition are for correlated ones. The applications, as with the first definition are in the classification of correlated and uncorrelated fractals. Fisher's information for all definitions are decreasing for uncorrelated fractals, zero for completely random fractals ($\alpha = 0$) and increasing for correlated fractals ($\alpha > 0$).

5   Conclusions

In this article, the extension of three equivalent definitions of Fisher's information to the wavelet or time-scale domain were obtained. Closed-form extensions for each definition were computed for fractal signals of parameter α and based on them, Fisher information planes were obtained in order to characterize and highlight potential applications for fractal signal analysis. Fisher's information were decreasing for uncorrelated fractals, increasing for correlated ones and zero for white noise processes ($\alpha = 0$). Fisher's information can be used for the classification of correlated and uncorrelated fractals and for highlighting white noise traits in fractals.

References

1. Goldberger, A.L., Amaral, L.A., Hausdorff, J.M., Ivanov, P.C., Peng, C.K., Stanley, H.E.: Fractal dynamics in physiology: alterations with disease and aging. Proc. Nat. Acad. Sci. **99**(suppl 1), 2466–2472 (2002)
2. Stephen, D.G., Anastas, J.: Fractal fluctuations in gaze speed visual search. Attention Percept. Psychophys. **73**(3), 666–677 (2011)
3. Ducharme, S.W., van Emmerik, R.E.: Fractal dynamics, variability, and coordination in human locomotion. Kinesiol. Rev. **7**(1), 26–35 (2018)

4. Sen, J., McGill, D.: Fractal analysis of heart rate variability as a predictor of mortality: a systematic review and meta-analysis. Chaos Interdisc. J. Nonlin. Sci. **28**(7), 072101 (2018)
5. Frezza, M.: A fractal-based approach for modeling stock price variations. Chaos Interdisc. J. Nonlin. Sci. **28**(9), 091102 (2018)
6. Bu, L., Shang, P.: Scaling analysis of stock markets. Chaos Interdisc. J. Nonlin. Sci. **24**(2), 023107 (2014)
7. Gilmore, M., Yu, C.X., Rhodes, T.L., Peebles, W.A.: Investigation of rescaled range analysis, the Hurst exponent, and long-time correlations in plasma turbulence. Phys. Plasmas **9**(4), 1312–1317 (2002)
8. Peng, X.: A discussion on fractal models for transport physics of porous media. Fractals **23**(03), 1530001 (2015)
9. Beran, J., Sherman, R., Taqqu, M.S., Willinger, W.: Long-range dependence in variable-bit-rate video traffic. IEEE Trans. Commun. **43**(2/3/4), 1566–1579 (1995)
10. Zhang, C., Cui, H., He, Z., Lin, S., Degang, F.: Fractals in carbon nanotube buckypapers. RSC Adv. **6**(11), 8639–8643 (2016)
11. Fernandes, M.A., Rosa, E.A.R., Johann, A.C.B.R., Grégio, A.M.T., Trevilatto, P.C., Azevedo-Alanis, L.R.: Applicability of fractal dimension analysis in dental radiographs for the evaluation of renal osteodystrophy. Fractals **24**(01), 1650010 (2016)
12. Mandelbrot, B.B., Wallis, J.R.: Noah, Joseph, and operational hydrology. Water Resour. Res. **4**(5), 909–918 (1968)
13. Eke, A., et al.: Physiological time series: distinguishing fractal noises from motions. Pflügers Archiv **439**(4), 403–415 (2000)
14. Eke, A., Herman, P., Kocsis, L., Kozak, L.R.: Fractal characterization of complexity in temporal physiological signals. Physiol. Meas. **23**(1), R1 (2002)
15. Delignieres, D., Ramdani, S., Lemoine, L., Torre, K., Fortes, M., Ninot, G.: Fractal analyses for short time series: a re-assessment of classical methods. J. Math. Psychol. **50**(6), 525–544 (2006)
16. Peng, C.K., Buldyrev, S.V., Havlin, S., Simons, M., Stanley, H.E., Goldberger, A.L.: Mosaic organization of DNA nucleotides. Phys. Rev. E **49**(2), 1685 (1994)
17. Lin, T.-K., Fajri, H.: Damage detection of structures with detrended fluctuation and detrended cross-correlation analyses. Smart Mater. Struct. **26**(3), 035027 (2017)
18. Kwapień, J., Oświȩcimka, P., Drożdż, S.: Detrended fluctuation analysis made flexible to detect range of cross-correlated fluctuations. Phys. Rev. E **92**(5), 052815 (2015)
19. Ferreira, P.: What detrended fluctuation analysis can tell us about NBA results. Phys. A **500**, 92–96 (2018)
20. Abry, P., Veitch, D.: Wavelet analysis of long-range-dependent traffic. IEEE Trans. Inf. Theory **44**(1), 2–15 (1998)
21. Stoev, S., Taqqu, M.S., Park, C., Marron, J.S.: On the wavelet spectrum diagnostic for Hurst parameter estimation in the analysis of internet traffic. Comput. Netw. **48**(3), 423–445 (2005)
22. Serinaldi, F.: Use and misuse of some Hurst parameter estimators applied to stationary and non-stationary financial time series. Phys. A **389**(14), 2770–2781 (2010)
23. Taqqu, M.S., Teverovsky, V., Willinger, W.: Estimators for long-range dependence: an empirical study. Fractals **3**(04), 785–798 (1995)
24. Gallant, J.C., Moore, I.D., Hutchinson, M.F., Gessler, P.: Estimating fractal dimension of profiles: a comparison of methods. Math. Geol. **26**(4), 455–481 (1994)

25. Pilgram, B., Kaplan, D.T.: A comparison of estimators for 1f noise. Phys. D Nonlin. Phenom. **114**(1–2), 108–122 (1998)
26. Stadnitski, T.: Measuring fractality. Front. Physiol. **3**, 127 (2012)
27. Beran, J.: Statistics for Long-Memory Processes. Chapman & Hall, Boca Raton (1994)
28. Percival, D.B.: Stochastic models and statistical analysis for clock noise. Metrologia **40**, S289–S304 (2003)
29. Lee, I.W.C., Fapojuwo, A.O.: Stochastic processes for computer network traffic modelling. Comput. Commun. **29**, 1–23 (2005)
30. Veitch, D., Abry, P.: A wavelet based joint estimator of the parameters of long-range dependence. IEEE Trans. Info. Theory **45**, 878–897 (1999)
31. Soltani, S., Simard, P., Boichu, D.: Estimation of the self-similarity parameter using the wavelet transform. Signal Process. **84**, 117–123 (2004)
32. Pesquet-Popescu, B.: Statistical properties of the wavelet decomposition of certain non-gaussian self-similar processes. Signal Process. **75**, 303–322 (1999)
33. Abry, P., Goncalves, P., Levy-Vehel, J.: Scaling, Fractal and Wavelets. Wiley, Hoboken (2009)
34. Flandrin, P.: Wavelet analysis and synthesis of fractional Brownian motion. IEEE Trans. Info. Theory **38**, 910–917 (1992)
35. Zunino, L., Perez, D.G., Garavaglia, M., Rosso, O.A.: Wavelet entropy of stochastic processes. Phys. A **379**, 503–512 (2007)
36. Perez, D.G., Zunino, L., Martin, M.T., Garavaglia, M., Plastino, A., Rosso, O.A.: Model-free stochastic processes studied with q-wavelet-based information tools. Phys. Lett. A **364**, 259–266 (2007)
37. Kowalski, A.M., Plastino, A., Casas, M.: Generalized complexity and classical-quantum transition. Entropy **11**, 111–123 (2009)
38. Martin, M.T., Perez, J., Plastino, A.: Fisher information and non-linear dynamics. Phys. A **291**, 523–532 (2001)
39. Martin, M.T., Pennini, F., Plastino, A.: Fisher's information and the analysis of complex signals. Phys. A **256**, 173–180 (1999)
40. Telesca, L., Lapenna, V., Lovallo, M.: Fisher information measure of geoelectrical signals. Phys. A **351**, 637–644 (2005)
41. Sánchez-Moreno, P., Yánez, R.J., Dehesa, J.S.: Discrete densities and fisher information. In: Proceedings of the 14th International Conference on Difference Equations and Applications. Difference Equations and Applications, pp. 291–298

Firewall System for the Internet of Things

Martín Roberto Flores Eslava[1], Juan Carlos Herrera Lozada[1],
Miguel Hernández Bolaños[1], and Jacobo Sandoval Gutiérrez[2]([⊠])

[1] Centro de Innovación y Desarrollo Tecnológico en Cómputo, IPN, Mexico City,
Mexico
{jlozada,mbolanos}@ipn.mx
[2] Universidad Autónoma Metropolitana, Lerma de Villada, Mexico
j.sandoval@correo.ler.uam.mx

Abstract. The Internet of Things is a new technology in development
because its manufacture and consumption in objects as simple as light
bulbs and sensors are becoming widespread. However, due to the need to
reduce their cost and be affordable to users, most devices have stopped
working on security. The previous has motivated the subsequent investigation to find intermediate solutions to protect information security,
improving cybersecurity. Therefore, the objective of the present investigation was to experiment on an Internet of Things platform with commercial devices, following the standard settings, to find the risks and
be able to propose a solution. The methodology was to build the IoT
network, perform ARP and DNS attacks to obtain sensitive information,
then add a firewall to prevent the attack. The vulnerabilities could be
found using ESP8266, a Wi-Fi spotlight, a Raspberry in the specialized
hardware and software for attacks, and the solution with Raspberry as
AP. The contribution is to have shown that cybersecurity technologies
can and should be considered more formally; on the contrary, if we do
not minimize the risk, we could suffer repercussions.

Keywords: Cybersecurity · Firewall · Internet of Things

1 Introduction

The Internet of Things (IoT) is an intelligent network of devices, such as sensors,
light bulbs, refrigerators, and cameras, which can connect to the Internet and
communicate with each other using a physical or virtual manager and thus make
decisions without human interaction [1]. Therefore, this technology requires protocols with certain robustness [2], such as MQTT [3], XMPP [4], AMQP [5,6],
and CoAP [6].

Since the beginning of the massive Internet, firewalls have been present to
provide reliability to network users. These devices protect and control data traffic
within the network with better strategies than just packet filtering [7]. A firewall
is a software tool, hardware, or network variant dedicated to network security
[8]. This tool monitors incoming and outgoing data traffic and decides to let it

M. F. Mata-Rivera et al. (Eds.): WITCOM 2023, CCIS 1906, pp. 73–85, 2023.
https://doi.org/10.1007/978-3-031-45316-8_7

through or block it, thus protecting the network. This work is done using control policies programmed by an administrator [9]. Some references are in software such as IPCop [10], commercial hardware such as Qotom, ShareVDI, and Vnopn, or the new generation for protection in the cloud [11], where efficiency depends on paid support [12]. Therefore, the Internet of Things, as part of Industry 4.0, is susceptible to cyber-attacks by exploiting vulnerabilities in the existing protocols [13]. Thus attackers could achieve the goal of hijacking databases, monitoring the keyboard to steal sensitive data, or even taking control of the system [14]. The IoT reports an increase in the number of attacks on these devices every year due to two factors: the number of devices on the market is increasing. The second is the poor security robustness of the designs of these devices. In the first half of 2019 alone, 105 million attacks were reported, when in the same period of 2018, 12 million had been reported, i.e., a 900% increase in attacks on embedded systems used for IoT, of which 39% were of the DoS (Denial of Service) type employing a BOTNET called MIRAI [15].

The cost of security applied to Internet of Things devices is a topic that has been exposed [9,16]. Where the economic factor is considered as the objective of its design, i.e., one motivation is the high cost of encryption protocols in the communication between a device and the cloud, which leaves low-cost devices used in the home network susceptible to attacks. Solutions developed so far, such as a mini-firewall [17,18], horizontal port scanning [19], data traffic preprocessing [20], or implementations of new methods in hardware systems [21], do not yet achieve a definitive solution.

Due to the above, the research's objective was to analyze the vulnerabilities of tools and devices marketed on an industrial scale and used by any user to determine the risks and possible cybersecurity solutions. The method used was to acquire commercial Internet of Things devices, propose common attacks to determine the vulnerability and finally design and implement the solution. The results showed the advancement of technology and the ease of using these devices without specialized knowledge; however, ease of use increases security vulnerability. The proposed solution managed to protect the vulnerable. However, it is not so accessible for a massive implementation in the Internet of Things and Industry 4.0.

An essential contribution of the research conducted is focused on industrial developers, integrators, and users. For developers, it is important to continue thinking about security schemes or to provide a more detailed explanation of potential risks. For integrators, it is a medium-term opportunity to create business-oriented new technology markets, and, finally, users should be aware that so far that a more secure device involves a more significant investment in infrastructure and maintenance of a probable service needed for the future.

2   Method

2.1   Proposed Architecture

The conventional architecture of the connections of devices (things) connected to the modem/router is made through the gateway for these devices to connect to the Internet. In this architecture, the devices depend on the security the manufacturer has integrated to defend against attacks. To prevent security from being provided by a third party, Fig. 1 shows an improved architecture that consists of creating a firewall that can wirelessly transmit the Internet signal, i.e., an access point (AP) capable of protecting the devices for the Internet of Things.

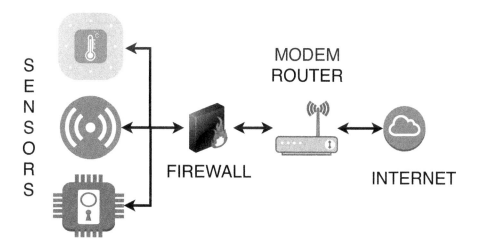

Fig. 1. Proposed architecture.

Operationally, the architecture diagram would use the tools shown in Fig. 2, where the attacks are performed on both the Gateway and the proposed Firewall, and the latter will seek to mitigate the attack so that the information on the Internet of Things devices is kept private. The attacks are of the ARP Poisoning or DNS Spoofing type.

2.2   Attack

Considering that one of the most dangerous attacks is MIM (Man-in-the-Middle), this paper will focus on this attack to protect unencrypted information in the MQTT protocol. The Address Resolution Protocol (ARP) security was breached to achieve the MIM attack. This protocol contains tables with information on the network's IP addresses and the MAC addresses associated with each IP. Each computer has a cache memory assigned to store the address table to save

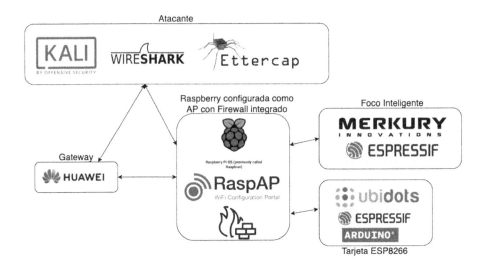

Fig. 2. Operational diagram.

time when searching. In case there is no device in this list, a message is sent to the broadcast MAC address, which is FF:FF:FF:FF:FF:FF asking for the information about this new device, which responds with its MAC address [15].

When ARP security is breached using ARP Poisoning, the phenomenon is generated with a third party in the network, placed in the middle of the communication. The "Attacker" device launches data requests to both the PC and the Gateway. When the Gateway asks for the MAC address associated with the IP address (e.g., 192.168.1.64), the Attacker responds with its MAC address which is 00:00:00:00:00:00, which is false, but this causes the Gateway to update its data in its address table with the new information. Similarly, when the PC asks for the MAC address associated with the IP (e.g., 192.168.1.254), the Attacker responds with its MAC address which is 00:00:00:00:00:00, causing the PC to update its data in the address table as well. Then, the Attacker, by causing both the PC and the Gateway to save its MAC address as the property of the IP addresses (e.g., 192.168.1.64 and 192.168.1.254), forces the information transmitted between these devices to pass through the Attacker so that it can monitor this data and steal information that is not encrypted. The following materials and software will be necessary to see ARP Spoofing or ARP Poisoning reflected.

2.3   Test Platform

A Raspberry Pi 3B+ with the Raspbian operating system and a second Raspberry Pi 3B+ with the Kali operating system were used. Also, the MERKURY brand lamp for IoT model MI-BW905-999W is supported by an application called GEENI; The server of this platform is tuya.com. The ESP8266 embedded system is a device developed by the company ESPRESSIF with WiFi capability. Figure 3 shows the devices.

Fig. 3. Devices

2.4   Software Tools

An Ubidots account was used to provide engineering services and as a private cloud. In this platform, It can mount the Internet of Things devices and thus have the ability to monitor and control the equipment through the Internet network. This service has a cost, but for educational purposes is a free service with some limitations, among which is the number of publications in a day, which are only 4000. Raspbian OS is an official operating system for the platform by the Raspberry Pi Foundation. The AP mode on Raspberry Pi is a project with a graphical interface to make interacting with the software more accessible. The terminal configuration and the graphical software work on the same HOSTAPD (Host Access Point Daemon) software, with which a network card can be enabled as an access point.

Kali Linux is an operating system that evolved from Back-Track Linux. Offensive Security developed both. Kali was developed so that the user can test the security of their systems using actual attacks and thus know how vulnerable they are to an attack, making their security more robust. Wireshark was developed as protocol analysis software, allowing visualization of all the traffic on the local network. Ettercap is software created explicitly for MIM attacks with its Spoofing tool. This tool allows us to monitor the local network. The LanScan application is software to analyze the local network and thus obtain information such as the IP address and MAC address of the devices connected to the network.

Anti-ARP Poisoning is software to detect an attacker of such protocol. The software has two options to stop the attack, defensive or offensive. The defensive mode disconnects the device from the local network, preventing any leakage of unencrypted information. In the same way as the previous idea, the offensive mode disconnects the device from the local network, but after that, launches a counter-attack with AirCRACK.

3   Experiments

For the demonstration of the present work, four experiments were carried out. Experiments 1 and 2 test the operation in an ideal environment, then the stage of attacks with Kali Linux in experiment 3, which it considered the most critical stage because it can observe the vulnerability of the security of the Internet of Things systems, and the information that can be obtained after a MIM attack. Finally, in experiment 4, the attack was stopped by using a firewall to protect our devices.

3.1   Experiment 1

The device was connected to the Internet with the MERKURY WiFi spotlight and the GEENI application after the security password was entered with a smartphone. The procedure described above only allows us to visualize the interaction with the smartphone application. However, it does not expose the processes carried out to establish a connection with the server. Figure 4 shows the configuration mechanism.

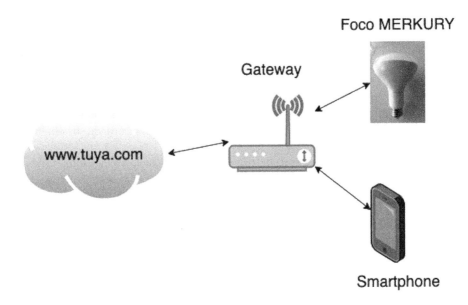

Fig. 4. MEKURY bulb connection diagram

3.2   Experiment 2

Using the ESP8266 development board, a sample program published on the official Ubidots website was made. The procedure uses the MQTT protocol for message publishing and additionally requires a computer for its configuration using the Arduino software. As shown in Fig. 5.

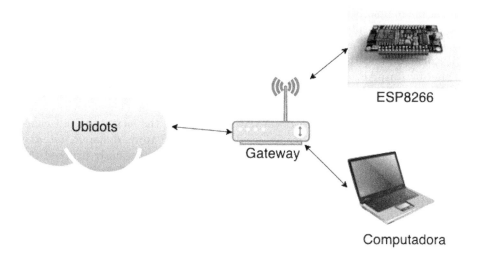

Fig. 5. ESP8266 board connection diagram

3.3 Experiment 3

Returning to experiment 2 performed in an ideal way, the ESP8266 card is attacked. For this, we need to remember the IP assigned to both the card and the Gateway IP, and for this, we will use LanScan. Obtaining the IP of the ESPRESSIF card is 192.168.1.84, and of the Gateway, it is 192.168.1.254. The above IPs as targets of the attack using the Raspberry with the Kali operating system, and an ARP Spoofing attack is implemented. To execute such an attack, we use the Ettercap software. When starting the software, we select the internal wireless NIC of the Raspberry Pi 3B+ and the corresponding targets.

3.4 Experiment 4

Similarly, to start with the attack on the MERKURY bulb, the local network's information is analyzed with LanScan to have the IP address that will later be one of our targets; in this case, the bulb is 192.168.1.87. With this, we already have our targets to attack. The Etter software startup procedure is the same as in experiment 3; therefore, the results are similar.

3.5 Experiment 5

In this experiment, the firewall is used to protect the information of the devices. Then, the Raspberry with Raspbian is configured as AP. The Hotspot creates the network with Raspberry as an access point, and we place a network name. After the configuration, it is necessary to contextualize the attack. This attack is developed when an attacker manages to break the modem security and generates an attack from within the network. First, we will attack the Raspberry Pi with the Raspbian operating system without any protection. We need the IP address assigned to the Raspberry Pi by the Gateway. The IP is 192.168.1.70; likewise, we need the IP of the Gateway, which is 192.168.1.254. Considering this variant, the ESP8266 card and the MERKURY bulb are already connected to the network created by RaspAP.

Finally, once the MIM attacks in the last experiments are completed, we attempt to protect the network. To protect the Internet of Things devices with a Raspberry Pi as a firewall, we will rely on removing the factory default characteristics in the cache memory assigned for the ARP to be dynamic, i.e., the data of interest is kept fixed or static. To recapitulate, previously exposed the type of security with which the modem cannot return static data from memory for ARP, this configuration will be carried out in the Raspberry.

For the second solution, the shARP software is used in the Firewall. With this tool, we will avoid any information leakage during an attack since, when it detects it, it disconnects our device from the local network, thus preventing any data from being leaked. The shARP software will be launched in its defensive mode and remain on standby for any anomalous activity. The MAC address of our device and its IP address would not be displayed, so the device is the Gateway.

4   Results and Discussion

In experiment 1, the operation of the device, as well as its interaction with the GEENI application, is correct. The smart spotlight can change from a cold to a warm shade, as well as the light intensity through the application, in addition to remote switching on and off. In experiment 2, the program works correctly, i.e., it connects to the network and the Ubidots server and then starts publishing the messages. During its operation stage, a network analysis was performed with LanScan, finding that the IP address assigned by the gateway is 192.168.1.84 with MAC address F4:CF:A2:4D:31:35. It also confirms that the manufacturer of the NIC is the company ESPRESSIF.

For experiments 3 and 4, we observed the effects of the ARP Poisoning attack. We must know the attacker's information, which is a Raspberry Pi 3B+ with the integrated Kali Linux operating system. With IP address 192.168.1.82 and its NIC has MAC address B8:27:EB:E9:96:0F. Given the attacker's information, we observe the data flow in Wireshark after the attack. The first step is that, since the raspberry is a device on the local network, the Gateway asks for the device with the address 192.168.1.82, which is the raspberry, to which the raspberry responds with its respective MAC address, which is B8:27:EB:E9:96:0F. After this, the attacker will start to send ARP Request packets to the broadcast address (remember that it is FF:FF:FF:FF:FF:FF). After finishing the period of the attack, we found the result. After introducing filtering by the protocol in Wireshark to display only the information of the MQTT protocol, we obtained the packets of confidential information about the TOKEN of our device, which is a unique and private code that the Ubidots platform assigns to each Internet of Things device mounted on its platform, as shown in Fig. 6.

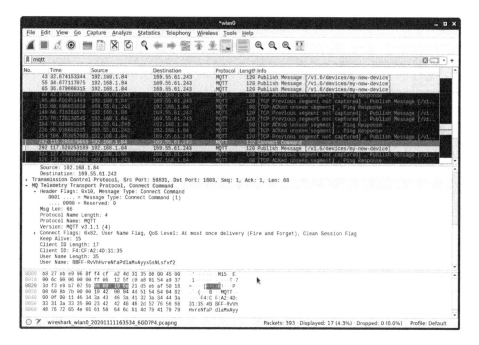

Fig. 6. Data traffic

In the experiment with the spotlight, the same phenomenon occurred previously with the ESP8266 card, but in this case, with the MERKURY spotlight. Initially, the Gateway asks for the device with the address 192.168.1.82, which, remembering the previous case, is the Raspberry with Kali, which responds with its MAC address. Subsequently, Raspberry asks for the devices with IP addresses 192.168.1.87 and 192.168.1.254, which are the bulb and the Gateway, respectively.

The results of experiment 4 show a defensive solution. We can visualize in Fig. 7 that no confidential data can be seen anymore.

The results of experiment 5 show a solution as an attack. Upon detecting the attack with the help of shARP, the firewall would disconnect from the local network to protect the data. Figure 8 shows the reaction of the Raspberry after the attack. Since the firewall disconnects from the local network, it loses contact with the outside and connection with the Ubidots server. When trying to visualize the packets that Wireshark captured, it can be seen that after filtering by protocol so that only those under MQTT are projected, the detection and disconnection of the firewall were so effective that the Wireshark software was able to detect and disconnect the firewall. So effective that the Wireshark software did not have a chance to capture any packets.

The bulb on ideal conditions works correctly and meets the expectations of value for money, but when reading the terms and conditions of use of tuya.com services, it mentions critical events. The first is that the server considers the

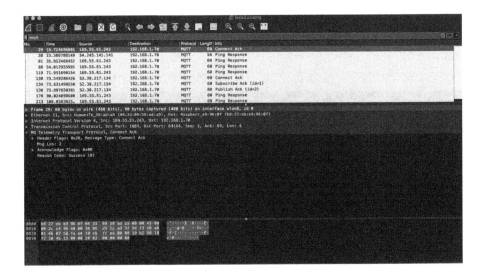

Fig. 7. Result of the defensive system

possibility of the saturation of its platform by misuse of the same, that is, considering the possibility of an attack, and that the attacker can obtain the credentials of the product, could saturate the capacity of the services offered for the MERKURY bulb. The second important idea is that causing possible damage to the platform by saturation of services would imply a legal consequence or even compensation. The third is that the platform requests that users who have had security breaches and, for some reason, their credentials have been stolen contact them, as they are still responsible for using them. In other words, tuya.com is so aware of the lack of culture to protect one's information and even profit from it.

The ESP8266 board satisfactorily achieves its goal of providing access to a low-cost, high-functional board. It is also very well supported by the maker community in the world. The problem with this device lies in its popularity and the few projects that put security as the primary point, besides the fact that the embedded system is so powerful that they could even make an IP camera on their own. Under an attack, this innocent amateur device could become a camera that alerts other people whether the people are at home or not. A typical scenario where the user's objective is the functionality of his project and not the security, as the example used in this work allows us to glimpse how vulnerable we are by not having the culture of protecting our projects no matter how simple they are. The worst thing is that few higher education curricula propose using technologies applied to the Internet of Things, where the basic subjects include data management and protection in the network; therefore, educational institutions are also responsible for the lack of culture in this area.

In the Merkury bulb, there is an information encryption problem since the product ID, user name, and password can be observed; all this information is

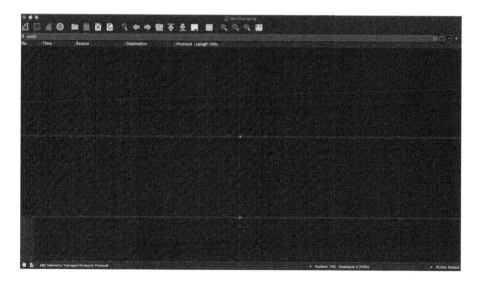

Fig. 8. Wireshark during Firewall attack

associated with the WiFi bulb, which can be considered as a security breach of the device since such data could take control of the device. The HOOBS organization currently exploits the security flaw, as it can manage devices indiscriminately with its platform.

5 Conclusions

From the proposed solutions, it can be seen that the choice of the embedded system for realizing the Firewall is correct, as it meets the project's needs very well. By statically placing the IP addresses for a specific MAC address, it can be seen that the solution to data protection, even for commercial devices, can be simple. On the other hand, the second solution is a slightly more aggressive option, and perhaps not very functional, from the point of view that the Firewall performs a disconnection when detecting the attack. The Internet of Things device is no longer in the cloud, but it is much more effective considering that it does not give Wireshark time to catch any packet. The important thing about both solutions is that they are affordable.

This paper allows us to make two observations. Protecting our devices on the local network should be a basic need since this is not a priority for Internet service providers; therefore, a small firewall at home or for small businesses can solve many security problems. The professionals in charge of the projects, at least in computer science areas, should consider the lack of interest in protecting data on the network. As a result, we have individual projects who indiscriminately buy Internet of Things devices that do not guarantee robustness in the security of the protocols on which they work.

It would be convenient to conduct studies with data processing or light encryption methods to reduce vulnerability in future work.

References

1. Singh, S., Singh, N.: Internet of things (IoT): security challenges, business opportunities reference architecture for e-commerce. In: 2015 International Conference on Green Computing and Internet of Things, pp. 1577–1581. IEEE (2015)
2. Tournier, J., Lesueur, F., Le Mouël, F., Guyon, L., Ben-Hassine, H.: A survey of IoT protocols and their security issues through the lens of a generic IoT stack. Internet Things **16**, 100264 (2020)
3. Yuan, M.: Getting to know MQTT, IBM Developer. https://developer.ibm.com/articles/iot-mqtt-why-good-for-iot/. Accessed 12 July 2023
4. Bansal, M., Priya.: Application layer protocols for internet of healthcare things (IoHT). In: 2020 Fourth International Conference on Inventive Systems and Control, pp. 369–376. IEEE (2020)
5. Glaroudis, D., Iossides, A., Chatzimisios, P.: Survey, comparison and research challenges of IoT application protocols for smart farming. Comput. Netw. **168**, 107037 (2020)
6. Naik, N.: Choice of effective messaging protocols for IotT systems: MQTT, COAP, AMQP and HTTP. In: 2017 IEEE International Systems Engineering Symposium, pp. 1–7. IEEE (2017)
7. Gold, S.: The future of the firewall. Netw. Secur. **2011**(2), 13–15 (2011)
8. Abie, H.: An overview of firewall technologies. Telektronikk **96**(3), 47–52 (2000)
9. Haar, C., Buchmann, E.: FANE: a firewall appliance for the smart home. In: 2019 Federated Conference on Computer Science and Information Systems, pp. 449–458. IEEE (2019)
10. Sharma, R., Parekh, C.: Firewalls: a study and its classification. Int. J. Adv. Res. Comput. Sci. **8**(5), 1979–1983 (2017)
11. Soewito, B., Andhika, C.: Next generation firewall for improving security in company and IoT network. In: 2019 International Seminar on Intelligent Technology and Its Applications, pp. 205–209. IEEE (2019)
12. Messmer, E.: What you should know about next generation firewalls? Network World. https://www.networkworld.com/article/2195863/what-you-should-know-about-next-generation-firewalls.html. Accessed 12 July 2023
13. Yang, G.: Introduction to TCP/IP network attacks. In: Department of Computer Science Iowa State University (1998)
14. Liu, S., Cheng, B.: Cyberattacks: why, what, who, and how. IT Prof. **11**(3), 14–21 (2009)
15. Demeter, D., Preuss, M., Shmelev, Y.: IoT: a malware story. https://securelist.com/iot-a-malware-story/94451/. Accessed 13 July 2023
16. Gupta, N., Naik, V., Sengupta, S.: A firewall for internet of things. In: 9th International Conference on Communication Systems and Networks, pp. 411–412. IEEE (2017)
17. De Almeida, F., Ribeiro, A., Ordonez, E.: An architecture for self-healing in internet of things. In: The Ninth International Conference on Mobile Ubiquitous Computing, Systems, Services and Technologies, pp. 76–81. IARIA (2015)
18. Raza, S., Wallgren, L., Voigt, T.: SVELTE: real-time intrusion detection in the internet of things. Ad Hoc Netw. **11**(8), 2661–2674 (2013)

19. Shirali-Shahreza, S., Ganjali, Y.: Protecting home user devices with an SDN-based firewall. IEEE Trans. Consum. Electron. **64**(1), 92–100 (2018)
20. Ray, A.K., Bagwari, A.: IoT based smart home: security aspects and security architecture. In: 9th International Conference on Communication Systems and Network Technologies, pp. 218–222. IEEE (2020)
21. Ezzati, S., Naji, H., Chegini, A., Mehr, P.: A new method of hardware firewall implementation on SoC. In: 2010 International Conference for Internet Technology and Secured Transactions, pp. 1–7. IEEE (2010)

Multimedia Technology and Smart Cities; an Inevitable Combination of Urban Progress

Hugo Isaac Galván Alvarez(✉) ⓘ, Hector Hugo Zepeda Peñaⓘ,
María del Consuelo Cortes Velázquezⓘ, and Claudia Patricia Figueroa Ypiñaⓘ

Universidad de Guadalajara, 48280 Puerto Vallarta, Mexico
{hugo.galvan,hector.zepeda,maria.cortes,
claudia.fypina}@academicos.udg.mx

Abstract. The abstract Multimedia technology plays a crucial role in the development of smart cities, integrating multimedia systems such as sensors, cameras, mobile applications, augmented reality, along with cloud computing, cybersecurity, big data, and the Internet of Things. This combination allows for improving the effectiveness of public services, citizen participation, and the overall quality of life in society. The purpose of this research was to identify through a systematic literature review, the benefits, challenges and issues related to multimedia technology in the construction of smart cities. The consulted sources of information included scientific articles, research projects, case studies, and electronic books. Among the results, the key opportunities for urban development exposed through the effective adoption of digital technologies, as well as innovative solutions that promote an inclusive, sustainable and well-being environment for citizens.

Keywords: Multimedia Technology · Smart Cities · Digital Technology · Sustainable Environment · Social Inclusion and Well-being

1 Introduction

In the current globalized environment, each day over 180,000 people relocate to a city to live. The Organization for Economic Cooperation and Development (OECD) estimates that by 2025, 70% will live in urban centers. In this regard, cities consume over 75% of the world's energy production and generate 60% of waste, aiming for strategic recycling and undergoing digital transformation to address global challenges [1].

Cities in recent years have undergone tremendous growth and transformation due to rapid urbanization and the integration of cutting-edge technologies. The implementation of technological solutions in cities has given rise to the term "smart city," referring to a city that employs digital technologies to enhance the quality of life for its inhabitants and increase the efficiency of its services [2].

The construction of smart cities has become a global trend and considered an inevitable process in urban development. However, for its implementation, it is necessary to incorporate and adopt advanced digital technologies to improve resource management, enhance the quality of life for residents, address urban deficiencies, increase the efficiency of public services, and promote environmental sustainability [3].

M. F. Mata-Rivera et al. (Eds.): WITCOM 2023, CCIS 1906, pp. 86–97, 2023.
https://doi.org/10.1007/978-3-031-45316-8_8

In this context, digital transformation and the convergence of technological solutions represent an innovative and visionary response to the rapid growth of urban population, aiming to harness the potential of multimedia technology to create efficient and connected environments. These technologies include cloud computing, the Internet of Things, waste management, the transportation industry, security, cybersecurity, artificial intelligence, Blockchain, biometrics, big data, and georeferencing [4].

1.1 Smart Cities

Since the birth of the Smart City concept, its definition and application have closely linked to technological advancements and the deployment of various solutions or tools to enhance management, environmental sustainability, and the quality of life for its inhabitants [5].

There are different concepts for cities that categorized based on the degree, capacity, and adoption of technology. Three categories identified.

Digital Cities. That integrate digital technology into basic infrastructure and services.

Smart Cities. Built upon Digital City infrastructure, including smart buildings, transportation systems, schools, spaces, and public services, integrated into smart urban systems.

Sustainable Smart Cities. Deploy smart urban systems focused on socio-economic development, improving the quality of life for residents, and addressing social issues affecting environmental sustainability [6].

According to the literature review, there is a wide diversity of conceptualizations regarding the term "smart cities". In this sense, the definition depends on the perspective from which is approached, leading to a multitude of interpretations [7].

A smart city is the holistic vision of a city that applies digital technologies to enhance the quality of life and accessibility for its residents, ensuring sustainable economic, social, and environmental development [8]. Additionally, smart cities emerge from collaborative technologies such as digital platforms, the Internet of Things, social networks, Blockchain, data science, and artificial intelligence [9]. It also considered that the purpose of smart cities is to increase efficiency, accessibility, or sustainability through the implementation of digital technology [10].

If we consider a Smart City as one where technologies, information, and citizenship converge to optimize all its resources, increase citizens' quality of life, and improve the environment [11]. Similarly, a smart and sustainable city utilizes information and communication technologies to enhance the quality of life, operational efficiency, urban services, and competitiveness, while also ensuring the satisfaction of citizens' economic, social, and environmental needs [12]. Therefore, a smart city is one that connects its inhabitants to public services through technological infrastructure and the efficient use of applications and multimedia resources [13].

Finally, it is relevant to specify that the United Nations define smart cities as those that use technology as a tool to optimize urban efficiency and its economy, as long as it serves to improve the quality of life for citizens and protect nature [14].

1.2   Importance of Smart Cities

The United Nations (UN) states that by 2050, 68% of the global population will inhabit urban areas, meaning they will live in cities. As a result, cities will need to meet an increasingly high demand for resources, coupled with population growth, environmental changes, and dissatisfaction with public policies and services [15].

In 2015, the UN mentioned that even though cities occupy only 3% of the Earth's surface, they produce 80% of the world's gross domestic product (GDP). Additionally, they account for over 60% of energy consumption and 75% of carbon emissions (United Nations, 2015). Cities have gained immense significance due to Sustainable Development Goal (SDG) 11, which pertains to sustainable cities and communities. SDG 11 aims to make cities and human settlements inclusive, safe, resilient, and sustainable by 2030 [16].

One of the most significant aspects of smart cities is their focus on improving citizens' quality of life. Digitalized infrastructure offers efficient public services, such as transportation and waste management, contributing to a cleaner environment. Furthermore, the implementation of sensors and real-time monitoring systems allows for a quicker response to emergencies and natural disasters, safeguarding citizens' safety [17].

Sustainability is another aspect that grants importance to smart cities. With the growing concern about climate change and resource scarcity, these cities position themselves as laboratories for adopting clean energies, reducing emissions, and efficiently managing water and energy. Through data collection and analysis, cities can identify consumption patterns and design conservation strategies, thus promoting long-term environmental resilience [18].

Ultimately, the significance of smart cities lies in their ability to transform urban areas into more efficient, sustainable, and livable environments. The adoption and implementation of technology in urban management are crucial for addressing the challenges of the 21st century and laying the foundation for a future of prosperity and well-being for their citizens [19].

1.3   Characteristics of Smart Cities

Smart Cities are urban environments that use digital technologies to enhance the quality of life for their inhabitants, efficiently manage resources, and promote sustainability [20]. These cities possess various key and essential characteristics for their formation, development, and transformation.

In this regard, six main characteristics of a smart city can be identified: (1) They generate data integration that provides necessary and transparent information; (2) They optimize resource allocation; (3) They use performance indicators to measure, compare, and enhance public policies; (4) They exhibit a high degree of citizen attention and satisfaction; (5) They increase the efficiency of government processes and procedures; and (6) They involve greater citizen participation in decision-making [21].

On the other hand, basic components have been identified for the development of a smart city, which include: (1) Transparency and data management; (2) Smart Grids and distributed power generation; (3) Intelligent Waste Management; (4) Efficient economic management; (5) City security systems; (6) Efficient and effective use of digital technologies; (7) Environmental sustainability; (8) Resilience and urban planning; (9) Key connectivity; and (10) Citizen participation [22].

In this context, when we talk about a smart city, we refer to a technician, automated, just, equitable, and sustainable city, where the citizen plays a fundamental role in the city's transformation, and the implementation of efficient and innovative solutions depends on strategies structured within six dimensions described in the report City-ranking of European medium-sized cities [23].

Governance. Including open data and transparency, e-governance, analytical administrative management that involves citizen participation.

Economy. Referring to business innovation, personal and professional entrepreneurship, and promotion of creative talent focused on innovation, productivity, and competitiveness.

Citizenship. Involving continuous training and education, opportunities for education and work, integration, and collective collaboration to form an educated, inclusive, and active society.

Mobility. Consisting of route planning systems, non-motorized transportation management, traffic control and optimization, as well as an integrated transportation system that promotes efficient urban connectivity.

Environment. Comprising the reduction of gases and pollutants, waste management, water and energy management to reduce environmental impact.

Quality of Life. Addressing the promotion of culture and tourism, city identity, security and emergencies, as well as health, well-being, and accessibility for an improved quality of life.

1.4   Smart Cities in the World

According to the ranking from the Institute of Higher Business Studies (IESE) at the University of Navarra in Spain, it was revealed that by 2022, the countries and their most important cities in the international development of smart city initiatives are as follows: United Kingdom (London), United States (New York, Boston, San Francisco, Washington, Chicago), France (Paris), South Korea (Seoul), Japan (Tokyo), Germany (Berlin), Netherlands (Amsterdam), Canada (Toronto), Switzerland (Zurich), Australia (Melbourne), China (Shanghai, Taipei, Beijing), and Spain (Barcelona). On the other hand, in Latin America, we have: Colombia (Medellin, Bogota, Cali), Ecuador (Guayaquil), Venezuela (Caracas), Peru (Lima), Bolivia (La Paz, Santa Cruz), Brazil (Salvador, Brasilia, Belo Horizonte, Rio de Janeiro, Sao Paulo, and Curitiba), Paraguay (Asuncion), Uruguay (Montevideo), Argentina (Cordoba, Rosario, and Buenos Aires), Chile (Santiago), and Mexico (Mexico City, Queretaro, Tequila, GDL, Monterrey, and Leon). These rankings highlight indicators describing the reality of cities in terms of sustainability and quality of life for their residents [24].

1.5 Multimedia Technology

Multimedia technology constitutes a new form of communication that employs the combination of different media or formats within a single environment. Its evolution are linked to the development of computers, audiovisual media, and telecommunications [25]. Below, various definitions of multimedia presented, which have transformed the nature of information and communication.

Etymologically, the term "multimedia" comes from the Latin words "multus" and "media," referring to the combination of multiple media, formats, and content to convey messages or information [26]. Likewise, multimedia technology focuses on the convergence of various forms of media in a single interactive digital environment. This convergence involves the integration of visual, auditory, and often interactive elements into a unified experience to achieve a greater impact on the comprehension of messages or data [27].

In this context, multimedia utilized in both analog and digital settings, meaning they are resources or information contained within multiple media that can sold, transmitted, presented, or received [28]. Furthermore, multimedia technology can range from simple applications, such as slide presentations, to more complex environments, such as 3D simulations and virtual environments [29].

Ultimately, multimedia is a term that pertains to the combination and integration of different types of media, such as text, images, sound, and video, using computer tools and systems. This combination enables the creation of interactive experiences and content, which can applied in fields such as education, entertainment, communication, and design [30].

1.6 Characteristics of Multimedia Technology

The main characteristic of multimedia is the possibility to enhance user experience, making communication between people more direct and straightforward [31]. On the other hand, multimedia technology has four basic characteristics: (1) Interactivity, user's action and reaction with content, tools, or applications; (2) Data branching; (3) Transparency, enabling intuitive use of the system or content; and (4) Navigation, the ability to move through information in an appropriate and effective manner [27].

Additionally, other features include interactivity, connectivity, hypermedia, and its ability to mix and use analog and digital formats such as text, audio, sound, animation, video, images, and graphics [32]. Multimedia technology is present in all fields of society, its application in social infrastructure promotes inclusion, efficiency, and innovation [26], spanning various fields including: (1) Entertainment and media; (2) Education and training; (3) Advertising and digital marketing; (4) Communication and social networks; (5) Design and creativity; (6) Medicine and sciences; (7) Architecture; (8) Tourism and travel; (9) Industry and manufacturing; (10) Telecommunications; (11) Finance and economics; (12) E-commerce and electronic business; and (13) Government.

1.7 Multimedia Technology in the Development of Smart Cities

Multimedia technology plays an essential role in the development of smart cities by transforming the way society communicates and functions. It seeks to improve the quality of life for its residents by leveraging technology to efficiently manage resources, provide advanced services, and promote citizen participation [33].

Government-proposed smart city projects have objectives related to increased efficiency, sustainability, citizen participation, and the enhancement of public services. The convergence of multimedia technology with urban sustainability places digital innovation, economy, and urban growth at the core of efforts to create sustainable smart cities. Furthermore, multimedia technology enables the creation and exchange of content through platforms or applications where information shared among cities and leaders for decision-making [34].

The growing interest in the development of smart cities proposes a new citizen-centered, technology-oriented approach that fosters sustainability, innovation, and collaboration [35].

Among the multimedia technologies that are central to the digital movement are the Internet of Things, sensors, big data, cloud platforms, smart city applications, Blockchain, biometrics, georeferencing, virtual reality, augmented reality, Web 4.0, 5G technology, cybersecurity, and artificial intelligence [36].

Despite the benefits that multimedia technology offers to smart cities, its implementation comes with significant challenges. The collection and management of large amounts of data require a robust and secure infrastructure, as well as privacy policies and data protection measures to safeguard citizens' sensitive information. Additionally, the digital divide can hinder equal access to multimedia tools, excluding certain social groups from the benefits of technology. It is essential to ensure that all communities have access to these innovations to truly make the smart city inclusive and equitable [37].

Finally, multimedia technology drives the transformation of smart cities by enabling data capture and analysis, citizen participation, and visualization of urban projects. As technology continues to evolve, it expected that smart cities would increasingly harness the potential of multimedia technology to create more efficient, sustainable, and appealing urban environments for their residents [38].

1.8   Multimedia Solutions in Smart Cities

Among the chosen strategies to implement smart cities, on one hand, their objectives are to promote hard infrastructures, efficiency, and technological advancements, provide efficient services to citizens, and increase collaboration among diverse social and economic actors to promote new business models within the public and private sectors [39].

On the other hand, enhancing soft infrastructure, emphasizing inclusion, citizen empowerment (knowledge, participation, inclusion, social and human security), among others, in such a way that cities aim to enhance their local competitiveness through innovation, improvement of public services, increased quality of life for citizens, and respect for the environment [40].

Multimedia solutions for the development of smart cities encompass a wide range of technologies and applications that enhance citizens' quality of life, operational efficiency, access to economic opportunities, urban sustainability, and ubiquitous connectivity [41]. Among them are.

Interactive Digital Screens and Signage. To provide real-time information about events, public transportation, traffic routes, security alerts, local news, and more.

Augmented Reality and Virtual Reality. To enhance the urban experience.

Multimedia Surveillance and Security Systems. To automatically detecting suspicious activities, monitor traffic, and provide a swift response to emergencies, thus improving public safety.

Multimedia Citizen Engagement Platforms. Enabling citizens to interact with the government and participate in decision-making.

Interactive 3D Mapping and Visualization. Allowing citizens to explore the city from various perspectives.

2 Method

Because the purpose of the research was to identify the benefits, challenges, and drawbacks of multimedia technology in the construction of smart cities through a systematic literature review, it declared as a descriptive investigation because it focuses on describing an object, event or phenomenon [42]. It is a documentary bibliographic research, as data and information collection were done through bibliographic materials where the terms "smart cities" and "multimedia technology" are implemented, as published in articles in peer-reviewed and indexed journals, electronic and physical books, thesis or dissertation documents, publications in news articles, and publications from recognized institutions or organizations [43]. Lastly, it employed a non-experimental sequential research design since it does not seek to alter the reality of the study variable; its purpose is solely to characterize the challenges and drawbacks of multimedia technology for smart cities [44].

An exploratory and analytical technique used for the search and collection of information based on systematic literature review procedures concerning multimedia technology and its relationship with smart cities [43]. Keywords such as "smart cities" were combined with "multimedia technology," "development," and "relationship."

For analyzing information from various bibliographic sources, the document title, thematic dimension, publication year, and publication type considered. Three stages implemented for this methodology phase.

Conceptualization. In the identified useful bibliographic sources, the main definitions of multimedia technology and smart cities, along with other related terms regarding challenges, drawbacks, and trends in smart city development, obtained. This stage also highlighted innovative strategies and solutions of multimedia technology.

Development. The contents organized and classified based on smart city characteristics, dimensions, axes, and benefits of multimedia technology. Technologies, infrastructure, and resources linked to smart city best practices also evaluated.

Learning. Findings and specific points identified through bibliographic analysis, and recommendations regarding the services and solutions that multimedia technology offers for smart city development provided starting from this stage.

3   Results

The present research yielded the result that, for the development of smart cities, a series of requirements are inevitable for their proper functioning. Research on multimedia technology and its relationship with the development of smart cities allows for the identification of technological design, innovative strategies, and solutions used to enhance the quality of life and well-being in cities.

Through literature review and data collection, patterns and trends in the implementation of multimedia technology in smart cities worldwide are recognized. Upon analyzing the results, approaches to implementing multimedia technology, digital technologies, and technological solutions for urban services management highlighted. These services are available to citizens and focused on sustainable development, public transportation, electricity, medical services, clean water, and public safety, among others.

In accordance with the results of the literature review, the convergence between multimedia technology and smart cities reveals several aspects or categories of services that are key opportunities for development, including the following.

Urban Mobility. Focused on real-time traffic management through applications and the management of transportation modes via digital platforms such as Waze or Google Maps, MoveUs Project, or MARTA [45].

Energy Efficiency and the Environment. Emphasizing the creation of the smart electrical grid or Smart Grids, intelligent water management to address water scarcity, and waste management for environmental care [45].

Building and Public Infrastructure Management. Through in-home technology for controlling heating, lighting, energy consumption, water administration, and waste control in non-residential buildings such as schools, hotels, malls, hospitals, and universities. Additionally, home automation, technology applied to household control and automation [45].

Governance and Citizenship. Including E-Government for online administration of government processes and procedures like tax payments and public services. Additionally, online citizen engagement such as Smart Cards or identity cards in mobile applications, and open data with platforms for open and public data available to citizens [46].

Public Safety. Involving the development of emergency services such as firefighting, police, hospitals, or video surveillance systems [46].

Health. Through the implementation of innovative solutions like telemedicine, tele monitoring, the use of biometric sensors for medical tracking and treatment, along with citizens' medical histories stored in a global database [46].

Educational and Cultural Formation. With the migration of educational services to the technological realm, bolstering distance education, E-Learning, telecommuting or home office work, virtual tourism, inclusive entertainment systems, as well as the use of virtual and augmented reality to enhance citizens' experiences [46].

E-Commerce. Characterized by the evolution of platforms and payment methods to address citizens' needs and improve mobility within urban areas [45].

The literature search demonstrates that the adoption of digital technologies, including multimedia technology, plays a crucial role in the transformation of contemporary society, stemming from two fundamental aspects: technological advancement and urban development. Smart cities are urban environments that utilize information and communication technologies to enhance operational efficiency, citizens' quality of life, and environmental sustainability. This convergence brings forth challenges for the development of smart cities.

In this regard, the challenges of multimedia technology in the development of smart cities can specified as follows.

Massive Data Management. Smart cities generate a vast amount of multimedia data, such as images, videos, and audio. The challenge lies in efficiently managing and processing this data to extract useful and relevant information [47].

Platform Integration. Multimedia technology originates from diverse sources and devices, which can hinder the integration and creation of unified platforms for analysis and decision-making in smart cities [47].

Privacy and Security. Capturing and utilizing multimedia data can raise concerns regarding citizens' privacy. It is essential to find ways to ensure data security and privacy while harnessing the benefits of multimedia technology [48].

Universal Accessibility. Ensuring that multimedia data is accessible to all individuals, including those with disabilities, is a significant challenge. This entails the need to develop tools and technologies that enable accessibility to various types of multimedia content [48].

Data Quality and Reliability. The quality of multimedia data can vary, directly affecting the usefulness of the obtained information. Ensuring the accuracy and reliability of multimedia data in a dynamic urban environment is a significant challenge [47].

On the other hand, among the challenges of multimedia technology in the development of smart cities [49, 50], the following stand out.

Network Infrastructure. Managing real-time and extensive multimedia data requires a robust and high-speed network infrastructure. Deploying this infrastructure in an existing city can be costly and complex [49].

Real-Time Analysis and Processing. Multimedia technology in smart cities demands the ability to analyze and process data in real-time for timely decision-making. This requires algorithms and systems capable of efficiently processing large volumes of data [49].

Interoperability. Different devices and systems generate multimedia data in diverse formats. Achieving interoperability between these systems for integrated analysis and coordinated decision-making is a technical and standards challenge [50].

Energy Load. Capturing, transmitting, and processing multimedia data can consume a significant amount of energy. In the context of sustainability in smart cities, finding ways to reduce this energy load is essential [50].

Citizen Participation. Multimedia technology can used to involve citizens in decision-making and city improvement. However, ensuring effective and equitable participation of all societal groups is a challenge that requires addressing technological and social barriers [50].

These challenges illustrate the complexity and importance of multimedia technology in the development of smart cities, as well as the need for innovative and collaborative solutions to overcome them, all with the aim of optimizing the quality of life for the citizens living within them, all alongside multimedia technology.

4 Conclusion

The literature review on multimedia technology and smart cities allowed for critical reflection on key opportunities for urban development through the effective adoption of digital technologies, in addition to identifying the benefits, challenges, and hurdles of multimedia in the construction of innovative solutions that drive an inclusive, sustainable, and well-being-oriented environment for citizens.

The conceptual model of a sustainable smart city supported by an innovation ecosystem for creating social value, where placing the citizenry at the heart of its development considered an ideal aspect, enriched by the implementation of technological platforms and digital services that support intelligent urban management.

The construction of smart cities has become an inevitable process of urban development. However, to build a sustainable smart city, it is necessary to deal with existing urban resources in a rational manner, compensate for deficiencies in urban construction, and develop urban development plans that reasonably incorporate multimedia technology, cloud computing, the Internet of Things, and artificial intelligence into the development of a smart city.

In conclusion, multimedia technology is a fundamental pillar in the development of smart cities, as it provides innovative solutions to optimize energy efficiency, improve citizens' quality of life, and promote social participation. Its application in urban planning and resource management allows for the creation of more sustainable and resilient environments. However, to realize its full potential, it is crucial to address the challenges that its implementation entails, such as privacy protection, adequate infrastructure, inclusion, and social participation. Multimedia technology will continue to evolve, and its responsible adoption will shape the course of smart cities that foster prosperity and well-being.

References

1. Segura, O., Hernández, J.: Aspectos conceptuales y metodológicos para la construcción de un índice de Ciudades Inteligentes y Sostenibles. CINPE, Costa Rica (2021)
2. Delgado, M., Delgado, T.: Sistematización sobre ciudades inteligentes con énfasis en ecosistemas de innovación para la creación de valor público. Innovar. **33**, 89 (2023)
3. Cabello, S.: El camino de desarrollo de las ciudades inteligentes: una evaluación de Bogotá, Buenos Aires, Ciudad de México y São Paulo. Documentos de Proyecto, CEPAL, Chile (2022)

4. Núñez, G.: Ciudades inteligentes: una revisión de tendencias tecnológicas para su imple-mentación. Telamatique **22**(1), 13–23 (2023)
5. Rózga, L., Ryszard, E., Hernández, R.: El concepto de ciudad inteligente y condiciones para su implementación en las ciudades de Latinoamérica más importantes (2019)
6. Estévez, E.C., Janowski, T.: Gobierno digital, ciudadanos y ciudades inteligentes. Bit & Byte **2** (2016)
7. Casas, J., Carrillo, A., Rodríguez, R.: Ciudad inteligente: una aproximación epistemológica. RUIIEC-UNAM (2018)
8. Ramírez, R.: Entre catedrales y censores: camino hacia la digitalización metropolitana de Barcelona. México INFOTEC-CONACYT (2016)
9. Komninos, N., Panori, A., Kakderi, C.: Smart Cities Beyond Algorithmic Logic: Digital Platforms, User Engagement and Data Science. Edward Elgar Publishing (2019)
10. Zook, M.: Crowd-sourcing the smart city: using big geosocial media metrics in urban governance. Big Data Soc. **4**(1) (2017)
11. Marban, A.: Smart cities y servicios públicos urbanos: el futuro de Castilla y León como smartland. Universidad de Valladolid (2018)
12. United Nations Economic Commission for Europe [UNECE]: Guidelines for the development of a smart sustainable smart city action plan. https://unece.org/DAM/hlm/documents/Pu-bli cations/Guidelines_for_SSC_City_Action_Plan.pdf Accessed 30 July 2023
13. CONUEE. ¿Qué son las ciudades inteligentes? https://www.gob.mx/conuee/articulos/que-son-las-ciudades-inteligentes. Accessed 08 Oct 2023
14. Organización de las Naciones Unidas (ONU): ¿Sabes qué son las ciudades inteligentes? https://www.un.org/sustainabledevelopment/es/2016/10/sabes-que-son-las-ciudades-inteli gentes. Accessed 18 July 2023
15. Rodríguez, R.: Desafíos constitucionales de las ciudades inteligentes. CES Derecho **12**(2), 3–22 (2021)
16. Lagos, G., Benavides, L., Marín, D.: Ciudades inteligentes y su importancia ante el covid-19. Qualitas **23**(23), 101–115 (2021)
17. Alvarado, R.: Ciudad inteligente y sostenible: hacia un modelo de innovación inclusiva. PAAKAT: revista de tecnología y sociedad **7**(13) (2018)
18. Segura, B., Hernández, J., López, M.: Ciudades inteligentes y sostenibles estado del arte. CINPE, Costa Rica (2019)
19. Fonseca, I., Prata, A.: Las ciudades inteligentes en Portugal. In: XI International Greencities Congress, pp. 267–278 (2021)
20. Sikora, D.: Factores de desarrollo de las ciudades inteligentes. Revista Universitaria de Geografía **26**(1) (2017). Universidad Nacional del Sur Bahía Blanca, Argentina
21. Bouskela, M., Casseb, M., Bassi, S., De Luca, C., Facchina, M.: La ruta hacia las Smart Cities, Migrando de una gestión tradicional a la ciudad inteligente. Banco Interamericano de Desarrollo (2016)
22. Alvarado, R.: Ciudades inteligentes y sostenibles: una medición a cinco ciudades de México. Revista de alimentación contemporánea y desarrollo regional **30**(55) (2020)
23. Copaja, M., Esponda, C.: Tecnología e innovación hacia la ciudad inteligente. Avances, perspectivas y desafíos. Bitácora Urbano Territorial **29**(2), 59–70 (2019)
24. Instituto de Estudios Superiores de la Empresa (IESE): Índice IESE cities in motion 2022. https://media.iese.edu/research/pdfs/ST-0633.pdf. Accessed 10 Aug 2023
25. Li, Z.-N., Drew, M.S., Liu, J.: Fundamentals of Multimedia. Springer, New York (2016). https://doi.org/10.1007/978-3-030-62124-7
26. Banerji, A., Mohan, A.: Multimedia Technologies. Tata McGraw Hill, New Delhi (2010)
27. Hernández, A.: Los desafíos de la docencia universitaria. Educación **26**(2), 117–124 (2002)
28. Parekh, R.: Principles of Multimedia. Tata McGraw Hill Education, India (2013)

29. Costello, V.: Multimedia Foundations; Core Concepts for Digital Design. Focal Press. Inglaterra (2013)
30. Área, M.: Introducción a la tecnología educativa. Universidad de la Laguna, España (2009)
31. Pagani, M.: Encyclopedia of Multimedia Technology and Networking, 2nd edn. Editorial IGI Global (2013)
32. Savage, T.M., Vogel, K.E.: An Introduction to Digital Multimedia, 2nd edn. Editorial Jones & Bartlett Learning (2014)
33. Molina, C., Gallegos, C., Frantz, R.: Ciudades y gobiernos inteligentes. http://gca.unijui.edu.br/publication/ac4395adcb3da3b2af3d3972d7a10221.pdf. Accessed 30 July 2023
34. Gutiérrez, K.: La importancia actual de la innovación en el desarrollo de productos multimedia. Universidad Militar Nueva Granada. http://hdl.handle.net/10654/32625. Accessed 12 Aug 2023
35. San Salvador, R., Villatoro, F., Miranda, G.: Ciudades inteligentes, ciudades sabias; por una gobernanza democrática y colaborativa. Ed. Los libros de la catarata. España (2022)
36. Naím, M.: ¿Cómo serán las ciudades del futuro? El Tiempo. https://www.eltiempo.com/vida/ciencia/sokwoo-rhee-habla-sobre-la-ciudades-del-futuro-con-moises-naim-505634. Accessed 10 Aug 2023
37. Guerra, B.: Ciudades inteligentes, más que tecnología. Cultura Económica **38**(100), 39–65. https://doi.org/10.46553/cecon.38.100.2020.p39-65. Accessed 31 July 2023
38. Erazo, L.: La evolución de la urbe hacia las ciudades inteligentes. UDA AKADEM (1), 58–69. https://doi.org/10.33324/udaakadem.vi1.131. Accessed 31 July 2023
39. Marsal, M., Colomer, J., Meléndez, J.: Lessons in urban monitoring taken from sustainable and livable cities to better address the Smart Cities initiative. Technol. Forecast. Soc. Change **90**, 611–622 (2015)
40. Angelidou, M.: Smart city policies: a spatial approach. Cities. https://doi.org/10.1016/j.cities.2014.06.007. Accessed 07 Aug 2014
41. Cabello, S.: El camino de desarrollo de las ciudades inteligentes, una evaluación de Bogotá, Buenos Aires, Ciudad de México y Sao Paulo. ELAC-CEPAL (2022)
42. Guevara, G., Verdesoto, A., Castro, N.: Metodologías de investigación educativa (descriptivas, experimentales, participativas, y de investigación-acción). RECIMUNDO **4**(3), 163–173 (2020)
43. Arias, F.: El proyecto de investigación. Ed. Episteme 7ma. Venezuela (2016)
44. Canese, M., Estigarribia, R., Ibarra, G., Valenzuela, R.: Aplicabilidad del Diseño Exploratorio Secuencial para la medición de habilidades cognitivas: una experiencia en la Universidad Nacional de Asunción, Paraguay. Arandu UTIC **7**(2) (2021)
45. Caicedo, C., Amaya, F.: Revisión sistemática de la literatura sobre ciudades inteligentes y tecnologías de servicios urbanos 2012–2021. Pentaciencias **4**(3), 215–235 (2022)
46. Calcedo, J.: Los servicios de una ciudad inteligente: Smart Cities. Universidad Pontificia Colmillas, España (2020)
47. Esposti, D.: El futuro de las ciudades digitales: retos, oportunidades y prospectivas. BARATARIA (27), 32–45. https://doi.org/10.20932/barataria.v0i27.539. Accessed 28 July 2020
48. Torre, L.: Ciudades inteligentes y conectividad digital. http://digital.casalini.it/5248504. Accessed 12 Aug 2022
49. Soto, J., Martínez, M.: Aplicando STEAM e un ambiente de Ciudades Inteligentes con Internet de las Cosas como Metodología de Aprendizaje Basada en Proyectos. Innovación y Buenas Prácticas Docentes **8**(2), 68–77 (2019)
50. Fernández, J.: Ciudades Inteligentes: La mitificación de las nuevas tecnologías como respuesta a los retos de las ciudades contemporáneas. Economía Industrial (n. 395), 17–28 (2015)

Air Quality Measurement System Using Open Hardware and IoT

Rodrigo Vázquez-López[1]🆔, Juan Carlos Herrera-Lozada[2]🆔,
Jacobo Sandoval-Gutiérrez[1(✉)]🆔, Mauricio Olguin-Carbajal[2]🆔,
and Miguel Hernández-Bolaños[2]🆔

[1] Universidad Autónoma Metropolitana, Mexico City, Mexico
rvazquez@cua.uam.mx, j.sandoval@correo.ler.uam.mx
[2] Centro de Innovación y Desarrollo Tecnológico en Cómputo, Instituto Politécnico Nacional, Mexico City, Mexico
{jlozada,molguinc,mbolanos}@ipn.mx

Abstract. In worldwide cities such as Mexico City, the overcrowding of people in well-defined areas causes a series of health problems. Air pollution is one of the causes, so governments finance fixed air quality measurement stations in strategic points of the city. However, they are not enough for such complex cities. The research aims to develop an affordable and valuable system for society. The design takes the best of several Internet of Things technologies and systems, resolves incompatibility, minimizes costs, and tests with two public interest situations. The results show the behavior in days of environmental contingency and its uninterrupted operation for a reduced cost of USD$ 250 that can be visited on the web.

Keywords: Air quality · Internet of Things · Embedded Systems · Pollution

1 Introduction

The health effects caused by exposure to environmental pollution are a serious worldwide problem. The World Health Organization estimates that air pollution is the cause of 4.2 million premature deaths [17]. In addition, the WHO found evidence of adverse health effects regarding short-term exposure to particles less than 2.5 microns ($PM_{2.5}$) [4].

In Latin America, cities such as Bogotá [8] and Temuco [5] are urban centers classified with high pollution. In Lima, in 2012 alone, it is estimated that there were approximately 2330 deaths attributable to an increased level of $PM_{2.5}$ [10]. In the case of Mexico, for example, studies have found that during the dry heat season, ozone alerts are triggered in the capital due to temperature inversions [20].

In 1986 Mexico City established an air quality stations network [12]. The network has approximately forty stations surrounding of the metropolitan zone

M. F. Mata-Rivera et al. (Eds.): WITCOM 2023, CCIS 1906, pp. 98–121, 2023.
https://doi.org/10.1007/978-3-031-45316-8_9

[19]. Figure 1 shows a station distribution map where some places have no measuring systems, so the stations do not cover all territory. Particularly, if the condominium zones generate high levels of pollutants and there are no air quality stations, a health risk could be present for all people due to overcrowding [22].

Fig. 1. Location of air quality monitoring stations in Mexico City; data updated in March 2021.

The problem has two possible solutions. The first option requires waiting for government funding. The second option invites the population to care for their health and look for alternative, more accessible, and understandable technologies. Technology can be purchased, replicated, and adapted to a particular region's conditions.

1.1   Related Work

The search began with cases applied to pollution employing the Internet, followed by the study of each element that makes up the technology, regardless of whether they have the same application.

Duangsuwan et al. [6] sstudied smart sensors for air quality in Bangkok city. Gugliermetti and Astiaso Garcia [11] proposed a new method of analyzing indoor air quality with a low-cost device designed for seniors or people with different abilities. These articles focused on introducing the importance of improving sensors for future applications and lowering the cost for future applications. Trejo et al. [21] studied the behavior of different PM low-cost sensors. Other papers have taken up the ideas and developed systems along with IoT. For example, Kumar and Jasuja [14] presented a real-time air quality monitoring system oriented around the IoT. They designed an architecture based on operations on the Raspberry Pi microcomputer. Alshamsi et al. [3] developed an air quality monitoring system using the Waspmote microcontroller as its main component. The researchers show greater importance to the processing system in these two papers. Accordingly, processing system hardware must also consider the environmental operating conditions, as Raghudathesh et al. [18] present an intelligent system focused on managing poultry farms using an embedded system.

Other authors have shown the importance of making compatible and robust links between layers concerning the IoT communication system. Vimos and Sacoto-Cabrera [23] made a communication proposal with OPC UA for a sensor network under the IoT paradigm. This solution solves the compatibility between different technologies at the software level. Kadri et al. [13] researched the construction of wireless sensor networks for pollutant measurement in open spaces. While Abraham and Li [1] focused their development on indoor-measurement, Luo et al. [15] developed a monitoring system based on a ZigBee network. These articles, in particular, solve the problem of distances with a device with its closed protocol. Other works developed, e.g., combined with similar systems such as Gehlot et al. [9], focused on measuring equipment development using open architecture platforms such as Arduino for monitoring air and water quality using XBee technology.

Another problem in IoT is the use of information; it can be from data processing cases or decision-making processes. Enigella and Shahnasser [7] focused on the real-time analysis of the variables measured using statistical tools. Alowaidi et al. [2] took better decision-making about the best area to inhabit from the relationship between noise and environmental pollution. In summary, the IoT is considered into subsystems ranging from the sensor, processing, communication, application, site conditions, cost, and additional specifications the problem requires.

This research hypothesizes that it is possible to develop a system for measuring environmental pollution using sensors with low cost, open architectures, and incorporating technology from the Internet of Things (IoT) to report the occurrences of high pollution in areas with high overcrowding of people, such as building apartments and places where the scope of systems of fixed measurement stations of the city is restricted, thus improving the coverage and reporting of possible health risks.

The IoT paradigm will allow, in addition to communication schemes, to perform data analysis to record behavior and make decisions. In addition, the information is available from any platform that connects to the Internet.

The structure of this paper is as follows: Section 2 explains the system design, Sect. 3 describes the experimental conditions, Sect. 4 presents the result with a discussion, and finally, the conclusion is in Sect. 5.

2   System Design

2.1   Architecture

Figure 2 shows the proposed architecture, which is composed of the following elements: one or more air quality stations, a hub, an IoT Server, and several IoT applications. The air quality stations are portable devices that contain pollution and weather sensors. The station calculates averages for each variable and sends it to the hub using wireless communication. The hub is responsible for receiving data from all air quality stations, storing locally, and performing the computation of the Air Quality Index. Additionally, the hub is connected to the IoT network and sends the resulting data to the IoT Server.

The IoT network selected uses the MQTT communication protocol, a lightweight data transfer protocol based on the publish-subscribe model. In this model, an IoT device generates and publishes data on one or different topics inside a Broker server. On the other hand, the consumer device or application is subscribed to the related topics to access data. This way, one or more IoT applications are connected to the MQTT broker to receive real-time values generated by one or more air quality stations.

In the next section, the operation of each module and the design criteria are described in detail.

2.2   Air Quality Station

Figure 3a shows the elements that compose the air quality station. There are divided into six different categories:

- Air quality sensors: we selected low-cost air quality sensors complying with Mexico City air quality standards and their certifications. For this purpose, the following pollutants were used as criteria: $PM_{2.5}$, PM_{10}, O (ozone), CO (carbon monoxide), and UV radiation.
- Weather sensors: temperature, humidity, and barometric pressure low-cost sensors. Table 1 summarizes the main characteristics of the sensors used.
- Positioning sensor: a Global Positioning Sensor (GPS) was included in reporting the real-time coordinates and altitude where the station was collocated.

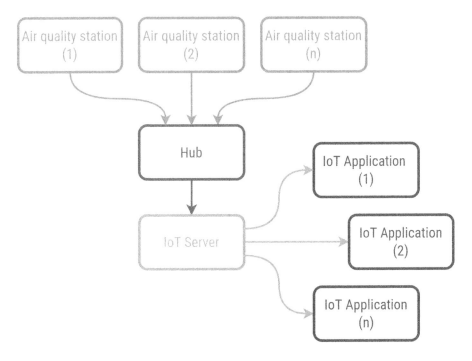

Fig. 2. Proposed system's architecture

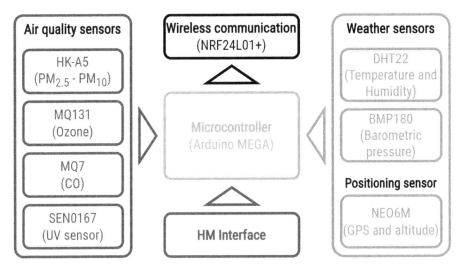

Fig. 3. A general diagram showing the elements of the air quality station module.

Table 1. Characteristics of the low-cost selected sensors

Sensor	Characteristics	Range
MQ-131	Analog electrochemical gas sensor sensitive to O_3 and other gases	10 to 1000 ppm
MQ-7	Analog electrochemical gas sensor sensitive to CO and other gases	20 to 2000 ppm
HK-A5	Digital $PM_{1.0}$, $PM_{2.5}$ and PM_{10} laser dust particle sensor	0 to 999 µg/m^3
SEN0167	Analog UV radiation sensor	0 to 11 UV Index
DHT-22	Digital temperature and humidity sensor	0 to 100 %RH, -40 to $+125$ °C
BPM-180	Digital barometric pressure sensor	300 to 1100 hPa
NEO6M	Global positioning system (GPS)	N/A

- Wireless communication: The wireless communication sends data from the air quality stations to the hub. For this purpose, a low-cost NRF24L01+ transceiver was selected, which allows sending and receiving data at speeds of up to 2 Mbps with distances of up to 1000 m in line of sight using the radio frequency spectrum.
- HM interface: a Human-Machine Interface used to report the status of the sampling process and show the last measurement values. Additionally helps users to report the correct arrival of the data packets to the hub, battery status, and update some configuration parameters.
- Microcontroller: we selected an Arduino MEGA development board due to the number of programming resources available. It provides 54 digital inputs/outputs, a 16-bit analog to digital converter (ADC) with 10 bits of resolution, two UARTs for serial communication, and hardware support for SPI and I^2C protocols.

The algorithm of the data acquisition process was implemented using a Finite State Machine (FSM). The FSM sampling sensor data every two seconds and calculates the averages for each variable every 5 min. The resulting averages are packed and sent to the hub. In addition, the FSM is also in charge of updating and controlling the information displayed on the HM interface.

Finally, the station was powered by two 18650 Li-On batteries with 3500 mAh to make the device portable and mobile. Also, it supports a 9V DC power supply. Figure 4 shows the prototype of the air quality station.

2.3   Air Quality Index Computation

The air quality index is one of the mechanisms that inform the population about pollution levels. In Mexico City, the calculation of the air quality index is based on the NADF-009-AIR-2017 [16] standard, which defines the following criteria for pollutants: O_3, NO_2, SO_2 and CO (expressed in units of parts per million), as well as $PM_{2.5}$ and $PM_{2.5}$ (expressed in units of $µg/m^3$). The calculation of the index is done by means of the equation.

Fig. 4. A prototype of an air quality station.

$$I = \alpha(c - CP_{low}) + I_{low} \tag{1}$$

where I is the computed air quality index and is evaluated for each of the criteria pollutants. For the other hand, α is a constant of proportionality and its dependent of the evaluated pollutant and its concentration, c is the measured value of the concentration of a pollutant reported by an air quality station, CP_{low} is the lower cut-off point and I_{low} is the value of the index in the corresponding interval. Values of α, CP_{low} and I_{low} were calculated previously by the government agencies and were available in the apendix of NADF-009-AIR-2017 standard. Tables 2 and 3 shown the values of α, CP_{low} and I_{low} for O_3, $PM_{2.5}$ and PM_{10} pollutants.

2.4   Hub

We selected a Raspberry Pi 3B+ microcomputer (RPi) as a hub. The RPi is a small single-board computer with a 64-bit ARM Cortex A53 quad-core microprocessor, 1 GB of RAM, wireless network card, and 40-pin GPIO. It requires an operating system installed into a microSD. We selected Ubuntu Server as the operating system, a GNU/Linux distribution.

Table 2. Table of O_3 parameters

O_3			
c (1 hr avg)	CP_{low}	I_{low}	α
0.000–0.070	0.000	0	714.29
0.071–0.095	0.071	51	2041.67
0.096–0.154	0.096	101	844.83
0.155–0.204	0.155	151	1000
0.205–0.404	0.205	201	497.49
0.405–0.504	0.405	301	1000
0.505–0.604	0.505	401	1000

Table 3. Table of $PM_2.5$ and PM_{10} parameters

$PM_{2.5}$				PM_{10}			
c (24 h avg)	CP_{low}	I_{low}	α	c (24 h avg)	CP_{low}	I_{low}	α
0–40	0	0	1.2500	0.0–12.0	0.0	0	4.1667
41–75	41	51	1.4412	12.1–45.0	12.1	51	1.4894
76–214	76	101	0.3551	45.1–97.4	45.1	101	0.9369
215–354	215	151	0.3525	97.5–150.4	97.5	151	0.9263
355–424	355	201	1.4348	150.5–250.4	150.5	201	0.9910
425–504	425	301	1.2532	250.5–350.4	250.5	301	0.9910
505–604	505	401	1.0000	350.5–500.4	350.5	401	0.6604

Figure 5 describes the hub's operation and divides it into hardware and software layers. The hardware layer consists of an NRF24L01+ radio transceiver connected to the RPi GPIO pins. The radio is responsible for receiving and reading all data packets from one or more air quality stations. On the other hand, the software layer is responsible for processing the information received by the hardware layer performing the following tasks:

1. Data reading and reconstruction logic implement the necessary algorithms to reconstruct and handle the data packets from different stations.
2. Data storage logic implements the necessary logic to access the local database system and storage data.
3. Air quality index computation, when data are ready, implements the algorithm to compute the air quality index and storage values.
4. IoT network connection logic implements the IoT client and the logic for sending data through the MQTT protocol.

The software layer was implemented using NodeJS, which is a runtime environment for JavaScript that allows the development of network applications using the asynchronous programming model. This allows handling one or more

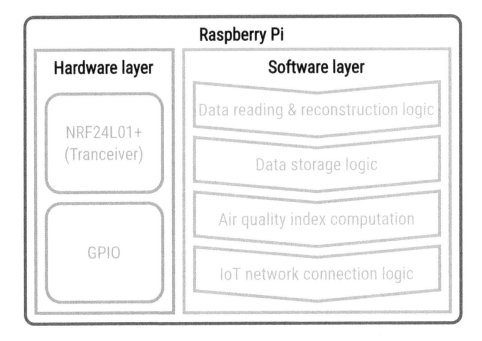

Fig. 5. Diagram of hub's components.

requests without waiting for the previous one to finish. Additionally, we selected MongoDB as a database system, which is a lightweight non-relational database system in which the data does not need to follow a schema. Figure 6 shows the finished prototype.

2.5   IoT Server

Companies such as Amazon, Google, IBM, and others offer different public and private IoT platforms and services. For this project we selected the *Flespi* platform, which is a toolkit for Telematics-oriented tools. We used the MQTT broker service for the connectivity of IoT devices.

2.6   IoT Applications

This project materialized three different types of IoT applications to consume data provided from an air quality station: a custom-designed IoT application built using NodeJS technology, a Node-RED application, and finally, a Thingspeak-based IoT.

3   Experiments

The first phase of experimentation consisted of verifying the operation of the air quality and weather sensors, the reception of data by the hub, and their correct

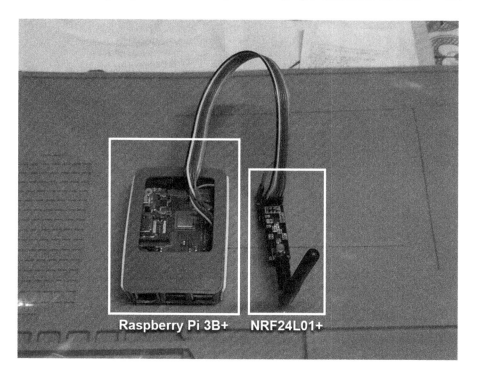

Fig. 6. Prototype of hub using a raspberry pi 3B+ microcomputer.

sending to the IoT applications. The second phase consisted of comparing some of the results obtained during the trial period with data from the environmental pollution monitoring stations in Mexico City. Finally, the last step reached a regular operation by one month in second place without overcrowding.

3.1 Experiment A. Initial Test

The objective of the first experimental test was to verify each subsystem individually and, finally, as a whole. The challenge with the sensors was to achieve simultaneous operation with the power supply without disturbances and with consistency between measurements.

In the hub system, the aim was to verify the operation of the two proposed layers and the integrity of the information received by the sensors, the processing and sent to the cloud servers The total operation was to test the uninterrupted operation of the variables in three different types of IoT applications (two private and one public).

3.2 Experiment B. Critical Operation

The operation of the measurement system was tested for a period of six days. A housing unit located in the northern part of Mexico City was chosen as the test

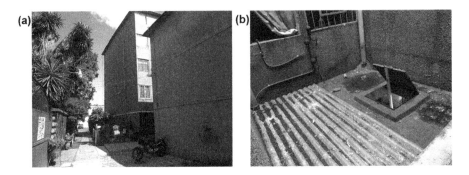

Fig. 7. Location of the second experiment in an overcrowding place. **(a)** General view of the outside. **(b)** Polluted place where air quality station were collocated.

place. This place has problems with environmental pollution and overcrowding. The Measurement system worked in a closed indoor (Fig. 7).

The trial period was from May 16 to 21, 2019. During that period, an environmental emergency was declared in Mexico City due to the poor air quality reported by the fixed stations' measurement systems.

Table 4 shows the nearest stations within a radius of 5.5 km to the experiment' site. Of the reported stations, only Camarones and Tlalnepantla have data on the pollutants O_3, PM_{10}, and $PM_{2.5}$.

Table 4. Distance between the place of the second experiment and the nearest fixed measuring stations in Mexico City Metropolitan Zone.

Station Name	Distance
Camarones (CAM)	2.60 km
Environmental Analysis Laboratory (EAL)	3.72 km
Tlalnepantla (TLA)	5.08 km

3.3   Experiment C Normal Conditions

In this experiment, the measurement system operated for more than one month. The location was in the west part outside of Mexico City. This area has free spaces, fewer environmental pollution problems, and no overcrowding. The Measurement system worked in an open outdoor as is shown in (Fig. 8).

The trial period was in June 2022. During that period, any environmental emergency was not declared by the fixed stations' measurement systems.

Table 5 shows the nearest stations within a radius of 4.5 km to the site of the experiment. San Mateo Atenco station has data on the pollutants O_3, PM_{10}, and $PM_{2.5}$. However, Xonacatlán and Metepec stations have the pollutants O_3, PM_{10}, and $PM_{2.5}$ but they are faraway (more than 10 km).

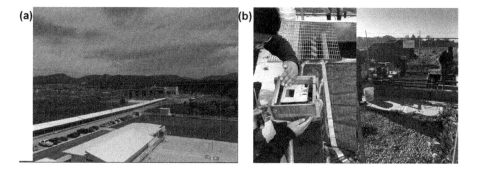

Fig. 8. Location of the third experiment in area with fewer pollution problems. (a) Areal overview of the location. (b) Place where air quality station were collocated at outdoor.

Table 5. Distance between the place of the third experiment and the nearest fixed measuring stations in Toluca Metropolitan Zone.

Station Name	Distance
San Mateo Atenco (SMA)	4.45 km
Xonacatlán (XON)	12.39 km
Metepec (MET)	10.17 km

4   Results and Discussion

The applications worked correctly because the data sent was received and processed entirely without loss. The only differences were the data sending speeds. The custom and NODE-RED applications are challenging to keep operating because the cloud service is private with a poor quality of service, while Thingspeak is more stable because the service is public. However, Thingspeak is limited to 15 s of refresh time in a basic version and limited functionalities.

Figure 9a shows the dashboard of the custom-designed application, which displays the air quality index, UV index, and real-time graphs for each pollutant with recommendations and health alerts. In addition, a map indicating the location of the stations is shown at the top of the page.

Figure 9b shows a Node-RED application, a flow-oriented programming tool that facilitates the rapid development of IoT solutions using blocks and flows. We built a basic dashboard with real-time charts and daily maximum and minimum values.

Finally, a Thingspeak-based application is shown in Fig. 9c for data collection in the cloud platform. The platform integrates data analysis using MATLAB and collects data using public and private channels. Every channel displays real-time data graphs using fields and channel data location.

The system tested the Pressure, Humidity, and Temperature variables in continuous operation from day 16 to day 21 of May 2019. The main idea was to

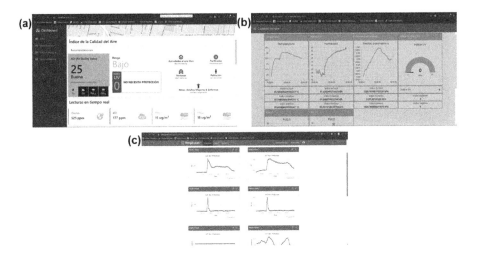

Fig. 9. IoT applications built for this project **(a)** Custom built application. **(b)** Node-RED based application. **(c)** Thingspeak based application.

verify that the system was not interrupted or disturbed by some unknown cause. The Fig. 10 shows the graphs of the temperature, humidity, and atmospheric pressure without anomaly.

Figures 11 shows a comparison of the graphs obtained with data collected by the prototype of the measurement system and the data of the Camarones (CAM) station. Unfortunately, the Environmental Analysis Laboratory (EAL) and Tlalnepantla (TLA) stations do not have available data or measure the same pollutants as the Camarones and Tlalnepantla stations. Furthermore, the Tlalnepantla station data are incomplete due to the failure and possible maintenance during the period in which the test was performed. Therefore, the only data available were those of the Camarones station.

The second experiment yields several interesting results. From the graphs, it can be observed that the levels of contamination obtained by the prototype vary from those reported at the CAM station. An example of this could be seen at the maximums peaks of the trial period. CAM station reported the maximum value of 119 $\mu g/m^3$ of $PM_{2.5}$ on May 16 at 00:00 h. On the other hand, the air quality station reported a maximum value of 214 $\mu g/m^3$ on May 16. Another relevant peaks were reported by CAM station on May 16 at 11:00 (103 $\mu g/m^3$), May 16 at 17:00 (60 $\mu g/m^3$), May 17 at 10:00 (64 $\mu g/m^3$) and May 18 at 9:00 (58 $\mu g/m^3$). On the other hand, the air quality station reported peaks on May 16 at 17:00 (186 $\mu g/m^3$), May 17 at 17:00 (123 $\mu g/m^3$) and May 19 at 22:00 (109 $\mu g/m^3$).

In the case of PM_{10} and ozone pollutants, the CAM station reported maximum peaks of 167 $\mu g/m^3$ on May 16 at 00:00 and 0.109 ppm on May 17 at 19:00 respectively, while air quality station reported values of 267 $\mu g/m^3$ on May 16

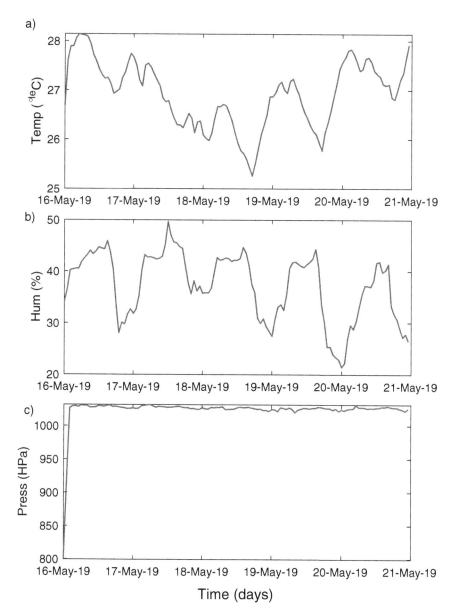

Fig. 10. Environmental data collected from May 16–21, 2019. (**a**) Temperature. (**b**) Humidity. (**c**) Environmental pressure.

at 04:00 and 0.15 ppm on May 16 at 19:00. Other PM_{10} relevant peaks that CAM station reported were 143 µg/m^3 on May 16 at 11:00, 153 µg/m^3 on May 16 at 17:00, 138 µg/m^3 on May 17 16:00 and 135 µg/m^3 on May 20 at 16:00. Also, ozone peaks were 0.103 ppm on May 18 at 14:00 and 0.105 ppm on May

20 at 13:00. Air quality station reported PM_{10} peaks of 233 µg/m^3 on May 16 at 17:00, 151 µg/m^3 on May 17 at 17:00 and 133 µg/m^3 on May 19 at 22:00. Ozone peaks were 0.117 ppm on May 16 at 19:00, 0.11 ppm on May 18 at 18:00 and 0.112 ppm on May 19 at 19:00.

Additionally, the air quality Mexican standard establishes a daily limit value for each pollutant. For example, $PM_{2.5}$, PM_{10} and ozone limit values are 45 µg/m^3, 75 µg/m^3 and 0.095 ppm respectively. These values are represented in Fig. 11 with a horizontal dotted black line. With this information, we observe that CAM station reported an interval of half of May 16 where $PM_{2.5}$ and PM_{10} values were out of limit. On the contrary, the air quality station reported for $PM_{2.5}$ pollutant May 16 and May 17 out of the limit, while in the case of PM_{10} only May 16 was out. In the case of ozone, only a few intervals of hours exceeds the limit in CAM and air quality station.

Figure 12 shows the result of the continuous Air Quality Index (AQI) computation for O_3, $PM_{2.5}$ and PM_{10} pollutants obtained by the prototype station. Mexican AQI establishes six categories to to classify air quality: good, moderate, bad, very bad, extremely bad, and dangerous. For example, ozone graph (Fig. 12a) shown intervals where AQI exceeds good category. On May 16 from 18:00 to 22:00, May 18 from 19:00 to 21:00, and May 19 from 16:00 to 21:00 raised to moderate and bad categories, while from May 17 at 18:00 to may 18 3:00 AIQ value increased only to the moderate category.

In the case of $PM_{2.5}$ and PM_{10} pollutants, we observe the influence of environmental emergency and its decrement as the days went by. $PM_{2.5}$ graph (Fig. 12b) shows May 17 from 0:00 to 12:00 where AIQ was reported as dangerous. From May 17 at 12:00 to May 18 at 6:00 AQI decreased as the extremely bad category, Next, on May 18 from 6:00 to 19:00 h, AIQ was marked as very bad and decreased to bad category from May 18 at 19:00 to May 19 at 23:00. Finally, AIQ increases fewer to very bad category from May 19 at 23:00 to May 21. For PM_{10} pollutant, AQI started on very bad category on May 17 from 0:00 to 3:00. On May 17 from 3:00 to 18:00 decreased to the bad category. Finally, AIQ decreases to moderate category from May 17 at 18:00 to May 18 at 20:00 and stays on May 19 from 5:00 to 19:00 and from May 19 at 21:00 to May 21. Only a few intervals (May 18 at 20:00 to May 19 at 5:00 and May 19 from 19:00 to 21:00) were marked as good quality.

The third experiment shown the behavior of the prototype at outside place during entirely month of June 2022. Figure 13 compares data obtained from the air quality station prototype and San Mateo Atenco (SMA) station. We selected the SMA station as the data reference because it is the nearest station to the experiment location, while Xonacatlan (XON) and Metepec (MET) are located more than 5 km away.

In this experiment, we observe maximum $PM_{2.5}$, PM_{10} and ozone peaks of 173 µg/m^3 on June 7 8:00, 509 µg/m^3 on June 30 at 8:00 and 0.094 ppm on June 26 at 15:00 reported on SMA station. On the other hand, the air quality station reported peaks of 77 µg/m^3 on June 3 at 7:00, 137 µg/m^3 on June 24 at 10:00, and 0.1049 ppm on June 6 at 16:00, respectively. Furthermore, SMA station reported another relevant peaks of $PM_{2.5}$ located at 84 µg/m^3 on June 3 at 8:00, 135 µg/m^3 on June 5 at 3:00 and 64 µg/m^3 June 11 at 9:00. PM_{10} peaks at 176 µg/m^3 on June 3 at 6:00, 193 µg/m^3 on June 5 at 3:00, 323 µg/m^3 June 7 at 8:00, 248 µg/m^3 June 7 at 16:00, 130 µg/m^3 June 8 at 7:00, 176 µg/m^3 June 8 at 17:00, 131 µg/m^3 June 13 at 9:00 and 119 µg/m^3 on June 17 at 7:00.

On the other hand, our air quality station reported peaks of $PM_{2.5}$ of 77 µg/m^3 on June 3 at 7:00, 57 µg/m^3 on June 14 at 20:00, 59 µg/m^3 on June 18 at 21:00, 58 µg/m^3 on June 20 at 14:00 and 62 µg/m^3 on June 24 at 10:00. PM_{10} peaks were located at 109 µg/m^3 June 14 at 21:00, 116 µg/m^3 June 18 at 21:00, 124 µg/m^3 on June 20 at 14:00 and 137 µg/m^3 on June 24 at 10:00. Finally, an ozone relevant peak were located with vale of 0.098 ppm at June 7 at 15:00.

Additionally, our station reported periods that exceeded daily limit values. For example, from June 4 at 4:00 to June 5 at 15:00 and from June 7 at 21:00 to June 9 at 00:00 h $PM_{2.5}$ exceed limit values. Likewise, from June 3 at 6:00 to June 6 at 14:00 and from June 7 at 20:00 to June 9 at 3:00 PM_{10} exceed the limit. Finally, ozone only exceeds the limit during two peaks.

Moreover, Fig. 14 shows the continuous AQI obtained by the prototype station. For example, ozone AQI was marked as good quality for an entire month. In the case of $PM_{2.5}$, from June 1 to June 10, AQI started in the bad category, rose to Dangerous, and variated between those categories. From June 10 to July 1 AQI variate between bad, moderate, and occasionally good categories. Conversely, PM_{10} started in the moderate category and variate between bad and moderate from June 1 to June 10. From June 10 to July 1, AQI established between moderate and good categories.

The official information pages of the fixed measurement stations present different graphs and interpretations of them. For example, the San Mateo Atenco station page shows a historical record as a type of color map. In our work, we also present a color map because we consider it essential for the general public to be able to visualize it. Figure 15 shows a comparison, and the differences are evident. The San Mateo Atenco station is located in the middle of factories with urban life, while the experimental test area was located at the city's edge and on a plain with better ventilation.

Finally, Table 6 shown average cost of the principal components that integrates the air quality station prototype. All cost are expressed on US dollars. The most expensive components were particle matter sensor (HK-A5), Arduino MEGA and Raspberry Pi boards. Total manufacturing cost is approximately $US 249 and includes one air quality station and a hub.

You can visit the air quality station at https://thingspeak.com/channels/1745957.

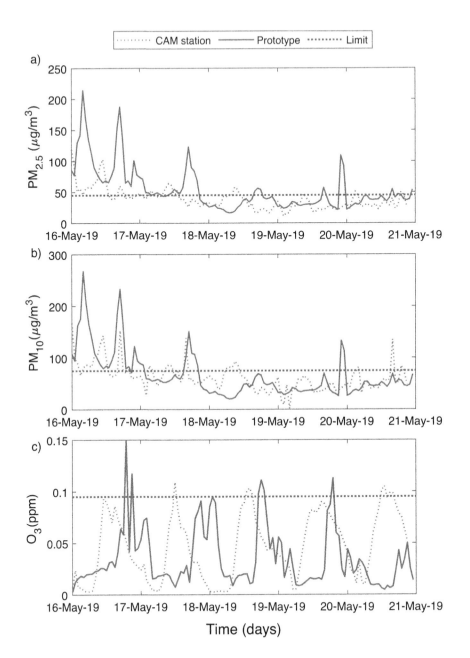

Fig. 11. Comparison between Camarones station (CAM) data and the proposed measurement system. The period of data was from May 16–21, 2019. (**a**) $PM_{2.5}$. (**a**) PM_{10}. (**c**) O_3

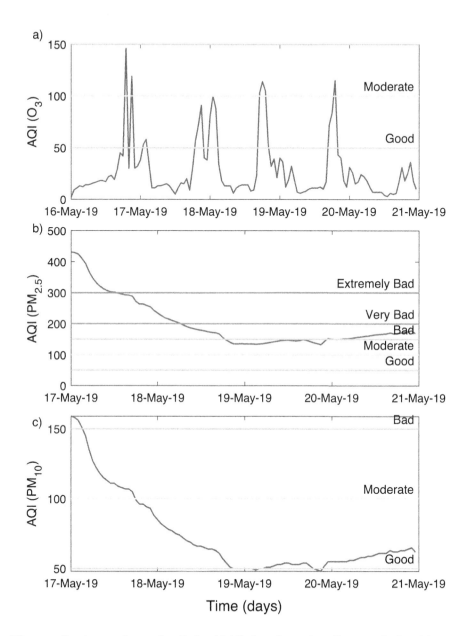

Fig. 12. Continuous Air quality Index (AQI) data for each pollutant calculated by the prototype. **(a)** O_3 one hour mobile average. **(b)** $PM_{2.5}$ 24 h mobile average. **(c)** 24 h mobile average.

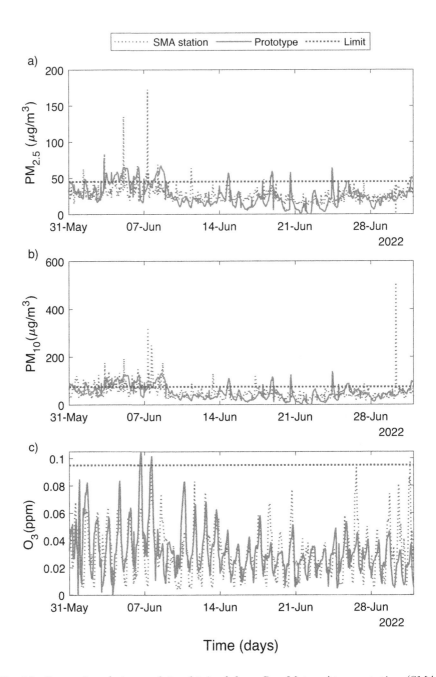

Fig. 13. Comparison between data obtained from San Mateo Atenco station (SMA) and the proposed measurement system. Data from June 2022. **(a)** $PM_{2.5}$. **(a)** PM_{10}. **(c)** O_3

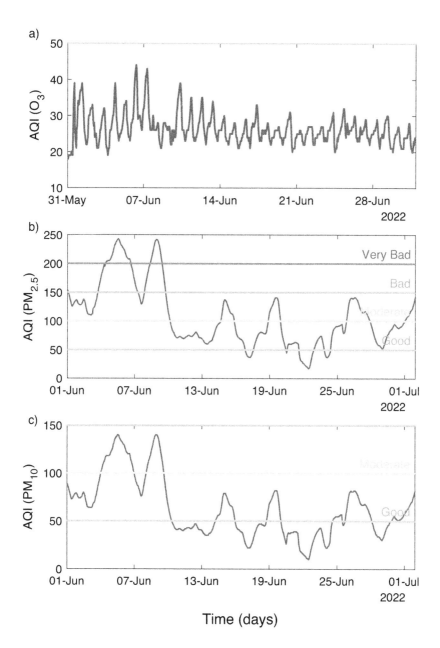

Fig. 14. Continuous Air Quality Index (AQI) data for each pollutant calculated by the prototype. (**a**) O_3 one hour mobile average. (**b**) $PM_{2.5}$ 24 h mobile average. (**c**) 24 h mobile average.

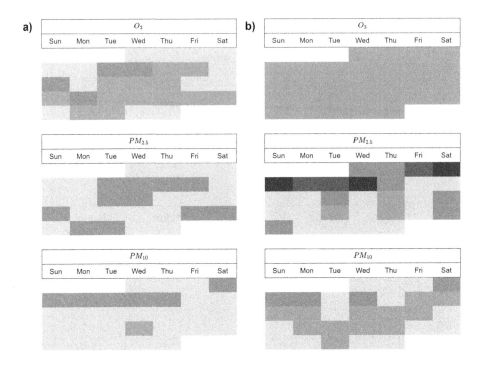

Fig. 15. Air Quality Index heat map for every day of June 2022. **(a)** Official month data from San Mateo Atenco. **(b)** Data obtained from the prototype.

Table 6. Costs of the components which are used in the air quality station and hub prototypes

Component	Cost (US$)
MQ-131	30
MQ-7	04
HK-A5	47
SEN0167	10
DHT-22	06
BMP-180	05
NEO6M	09
Arduino MEGA	35
LCD screen	11
2× NRF24L01+	10
2× 18650 batteries	12
Raspberry Pi 3B+	35
Other components	35
Total	249

5   Conclusions

The air quality system was successful. The design achieved a low cost of building and operation. The new versatile and calibrated sensors are essential to obtaining a low-cost measurement system. Another feature is the portability to be installed in outdoor or indoor spaces. The main reason for achieving portability at a low cost is due to transceivers using an open protocol. The designed hub can receive, process, and send sensor data. In addition, the hub can standardize the heterogeneous technologies that exist in the IoT.

Fixed measurement stations have the disadvantage of displaying outdated information and extensive coverage. For this reason, the proposal allows locating more stations and providing real-time access. Private cloud services show higher efficiency in quantity and response time compared to the public cloud. However, the quality of service is better in the public cloud.

From the graphs analyzed, this proposed measurement system allows for detecting abnormal values of concentrations of gases and particles in the air that circulates in areas with high population concentrations, such as urban housing areas. This system can facilitate making the appropriate decisions for improving the quality of life of the inhabitants of these areas. In addition, the record of data in punctual places can be helpful in the future.

The air quality station operated under two conditions. The first one referred to an environmental contingency detected in Mexico City. These conditions proved that some concentrations of pollutants are retained in some overcrowded spaces. On the other hand, the test in open space also had acceptable performance.

An air quality index indicator was replicated to explain the alert values that would put health at risk in a practical and simple way.

Finally, the system is a realistic solution to the problem of measuring environmental pollution with readable information and historical records at a low cost of less than USD$ 250 per system and a fee of less than USD$10/annual per cloud service if more than three stations are exceeded per account.

References

1. Abraham, S., Li, X.: A cost-effective wireless sensor network system for indoor air quality monitoring applications. Procedia Comput. Sci. **34**, 165–171 (2014). https://doi.org/10.1016/j.procs.2014.07.090
2. Alowaidi, M., Karime, A., Aljaafrah, M., El Saddik, A.: Empirical study of noise and air quality correlation based on IoT sensory platform approach. In: 2018 IEEE International Instrumentation and Measurement Technology Conference (I2MTC), pp. 1–6 (2018). https://doi.org/10.1109/I2MTC.2018.8409629
3. Alshamsi, A., Anwar, Y., Almulla, M., Aldohoori, M., Hamad, N., Awad, M.: Monitoring pollution: applying IoT to create a smart environment. In: 2017 International Conference on Electrical and Computing Technologies and Applications (ICECTA), pp. 1–4 (2017). https://doi.org/10.1109/ICECTA.2017.8251998

4. Atkinson, R., Kang, S., Anderson, H., Mills, I., Walton, H.: Epidemiological time series studies of PM2.5 and daily mortality and hospital admissions: a systematic review and meta-analysis. Thorax **69**(7), 660–665 (2014). https://doi.org/10.1136/thoraxjnl-2013-204492

5. Cursach, J.A., Rau, J.R., Tobar, C.N., Ojeda, J.A.: Estado actual del desarrollo de la ecología urbana en grandes ciudades del sur de Chile. Revista de geografía Norte Grande **52**, 57–70 (2012). https://doi.org/10.4067/S0718-34022012000200004

6. Duangsuwan, S., Takarn, A., Nujankaew, R., Jamjareegulgarn, P.: A study of air pollution smart sensors lpwan via nb-iot for thailand smart cities 4.0. In: 2018 10th International Conference on Knowledge and Smart Technology (KST), pp. 206–209 (2018). https://doi.org/10.1109/KST.2018.8426195

7. Enigella, S.R., Shahnasser, H.: Real time air quality monitoring. In: 2018 10th International Conference on Knowledge and Smart Technology (KST), pp. 182–185 (2018). https://doi.org/10.1109/KST.2018.8426102

8. Franco R., J.F.: Contaminación atmosférica en centros urbanos. desafío para lograr su sostenibilidad: caso de estudio bogotá. Revista Escuela de Administración de Negocios (72), 193–204 (2012)

9. Gehlot, A., Singh, R., Samkaria, R., Choudhary, S., De, A.: Kamlesh: air quality and water quality monitoring using XBee and internet of things. Int. J. Eng. Technol.(UAE) **7**(2), 24–27 (2018). https://doi.org/10.14419/ijet.v7i2.6.10061

10. Gonzales, G.F., et al.: Contaminación ambiental, variabilidad climática y cambio climático: una revisión del impacto en la salud de la población peruana. Rev. Peru. Med. Exp. Salud Publica **31**, 547–556 (2014)

11. Gugliermetti, L., Astiaso Garcia, D.: A cheap and third-age-friendly home device for monitoring indoor air quality. Int. J. Environ. Sci. Technol. **15**(1), 185–198 (2017). https://doi.org/10.1007/s13762-017-1382-3

12. Ine, S., Cenica, J.: Segundo informe sobre la calidad del aire en ciudades mexicanas. http://centro.paot.org.mx/documentos/ine/2do_infor_1997.pdf. Accessed 4 Jan 2023

13. Kadri, A., Yaacoub, E., Mushtaha, M., Abu-Dayya, A.: Wireless sensor network for real-time air pollution monitoring. In: 2013 1st International Conference on Communications, Signal Processing, and their Applications (ICCSPA), pp. 1–5 (2013). https://doi.org/10.1109/ICCSPA.2013.6487323

14. Kumar, S., Jasuja, A.: Air quality monitoring system based on IoT using raspberry Pi. In: 2017 International Conference on Computing, Communication and Automation (ICCCA), pp. 1341–1346 (2017). https://doi.org/10.1109/CCAA.2017.8230005

15. Luo, H., Li, W., Wu, X.: Design of indoor air quality monitoring system based on wireless sensor network. In: IOP Conference Series: Earth and Environmental Science, vol. 208. no. 1, p. 012070 (2018). https://doi.org/10.1088/1755-1315/208/1/012070

16. Secretaría del Medio Ambiente, Ciudad de México, M.: Nadf009-aire-2017. http://www.aire.cdmx.gob.mx/descargas/monitoreo/normatividad/NADF-009-AIRE-2017.pdf. Accessed 4 Jan 2023

17. World Health Organization: Ambient (outdoor) air quality and health. https://www.who.int/news-room/fact-sheets/detail/ambient-(outdoor)-air-quality-and-health. Accessed 4 Jan 2023

18. Raghudathesh, G.P., et al.: IoT based intelligent poultry management system using linux embedded system. In: 2017 International Conference on Advances in Computing, Communications and Informatics (ICACCI), pp. 449–454 (2017). https://doi.org/10.1109/ICACCI.2017.8125881

19. SEDEMA: Dirección de monitoreo atmosférico. http://www.aire.cdmx.gob.mx/. Accessed 4 Jan 2023
20. Silva-Quiroz, R., Rivera, A.L., Ordoñez, P., Gay-Garcia, C., Frank, A.: Atmospheric blockages as trigger of environmental contingencies in Mexico city. Heliyon **5**(7) (2019). https://doi.org/10.1016/j.heliyon.2019.e02099
21. Trejo, R.E.G., Rossainz, B.B., Torres, J.A.G., Zavala, A.H.: A study on the behavior of different low-cost particle counter sensors for PM-10 and PM-2.5 suspended air particles. In: Mata-Rivera, M.F., Zagal-Flores, R., Barria-Huidobro, C. (eds.) WITCOM 2022. CCIS, vol. 1659, pp. 33–50. Springer, Cham (2022). https://doi.org/10.1007/978-3-031-18082-8_3
22. Urbina, S.J.: Las condiciones ambientales urbanas como generadoras de estrés. Omnia **4**(11), 1–13 (1988)
23. Vimos, V., Sacoto Cabrera, E.: Results of the implementation of a sensor network based on arduino devices and multiplatform applications using the standard OPC UA. IEEE Lat. Am. Trans. **16**(9), 2496–2502 (2018). https://doi.org/10.1109/TLA.2018.8789574

Reduction of Energy Consumption in a WSN by Means of Quantum Entanglement

Carlos Antonio Ayala Tlalolini[1], Víctor Barrera-Figueroa[2(✉)],
and Yunia Verónica García-Tejeda[3]

[1] Instituto Politécnico Nacional, Ingeniería en Telemática, UPIITA, Av. IPN No.
2580 Col. Barrio la Laguna Ticomán, 07340 Mexico City, Mexico
cayalat1601@alumno.ipn.mx

[2] Instituto Politécnico Nacional, Sección de Estudios de Posgrado e Investigación,
UPIITA, Av. IPN No. 2580 Col. Barrio la Laguna Ticomán, 07340 Mexico City,
Mexico
vbarreraf@ipn.mx

[3] Instituto Politécnico Nacional, Academia de Ciencias Básicas, UPIITA, Av. IPN
No. 2580 Col. Barrio la Laguna Ticomán, 07340 Mexico City, Mexico
ygarciat@ipn.mx

Abstract. In this work we consider the effect of quantum entanglement regarding the reduction of energy in a wireless sensor network (WSN). Such theoretical networks are intended to use the phenomenon of quantum entanglement to reduce the overall energy consumption. As such the study allows to estimate the effective energy reduction and to compare with the energy consumption by a classical WSN.

Keywords: Quantum entanglement · Wireless Sensor Network · Energy consumption

1 Introduction

Let us consider a group of particles that somehow share spatial proximity, interact, or even were generated during an experiment. If the quantum state of each particle of the group cannot be described independently from the state of the others, even if they are far away each other, we say that the particles are entangled. The phenomenon of quantum entanglement is the key feature of quantum mechanics, it is a property that cannot be found in classical physics and has no thorough explanation in our current framework of knowledge [14].

The measurements of the physical properties of entangled particles may be correlated. These include position, momentum, spin, and polarization. For instance, if a pair of entangled particles is generated such that their total spin is zero, and the spin of one particle is, say, *up* $|\uparrow\rangle$ with respect to an axis, then

M. F. Mata-Rivera et al. (Eds.): WITCOM 2023, CCIS 1906, pp. 122–132, 2023.
https://doi.org/10.1007/978-3-031-45316-8_10

the spin of the other particle measured in the same axis is *down* $|\downarrow\rangle$. Any measurement performed on one entangled particle will affect the entangled system as a whole.

The Copenhagen interpretation of quantum mechanics establishes that the effect of measuring occurs instantly [22, p. 133]. Prior a measurement, a wave function involves all the possible outcomes, but at the moment of measuring the wave function changes suddenly and discontinuously so that the apparatus registers only one of those outcomes. It is said that the wave function has *collapsed* to the outcome registered by the apparatus. On the other hand, the many-worlds interpretation establishes that a universal wave function satisfies the same deterministic, reversible laws at all the times, and in particular there is no such a thing like a wave function collapse associated to a measurement [6]. Regardless the interpretation of quantum mechanics, all of them agree that entanglement produces correlation between the measurements, and that the mutual information between the entangled particles can be exploited, however any transmission of information at faster-than-light speed is impossible (see, *e.g.* [11,13,17,25]).

In recent years there has been a great revolution in quantum computing, which unlike traditional bit-based computing uses quantum bits also called Qubits. The impact that quantum computing exerts on today's technology is becoming increasingly apparent. Several properties distinguish the quantum computing, one of them is the superposition of states of a Qubit. Unlike classical bits, which only have one state (either ON or OFF), Qubits can have mixed states (a little OFF and a little ON, for instance). Quantum entanglement allows the state of a Qubit to modify the state of another one. The properties Qubits have lead to logic gates and therefore quantum circuits, which can be used in the construction of future quantum computers and nanoscale devices [4]. Quantum computing has recently been applied in different applications such as: detection and measurement of fields and computer security [1,12] just to mention a few.

A wireless sensor network (WSN for short) is a network formed by a large number of low-cost sensor nodes which are provided with a supply of limited power. The nodes share information with a sink node, which is in charge of gathering all the information and its processing before sending it to a base station. The energy of the nodes can be recharged once the sink node is idle [9]. The nodes can also be recharged by means other methods, for instance by wireless energy transfer and charging technologies to efficiently deliver the energy to the depleted nodes [21]. In any case, if the recharge of the nodes is frequent this could interrupt important processes in the network.

The inefficient use the energy of the network represents a problem. The aim of this work is to optimize the time life of a WSN without having to disconnect the nodes or dismantle the network to recharge the batteries, at least not so frequently. Also note that implementing a wireless energy transfer could interrupt the flow of information of the nodes to the sink, since a node will be online once its energy exceeds a certain threshold. Hence this method should also be avoided if the information possesses certain priority of transmission. Moreover, some works have considered using mobile chargers [9] or using the spanning tree construction algorithm [16]. However, in this work the phenomenon of quantum entanglement to reduce the energy consumption is propounded. Quantum entanglement has been used in magnetometry and interferometry [1], in the development of nanoscale devices [4], and in data security [12].

The use of WSNs in real-world applications is continuously increasing, so that to improve their performance, several improvement metrics can be considered. One of the most important is the lifetime and reliability of the network (see, *e.g.* [3,5,15,18]. The present work raises the possibility of using quantum entanglement to save energy in WSNs. Note that this issue has not yet addressed in the literature up to our best knowledge. Nonetheless quantum computing has been used in applications such genetic programming [24], health medicine [10], grid security [8], software security [2], security in WSNs [19], location systems [23,26]. Other engineering applications of quantum entanglement can be found in [7].

The outline of this work is as follows. In Sect. 2 we describe the network under analysis and define the Markov chains for the states of the nodes. In Sect. 3 we design an arbitrary WSN and simulate its performance according to the Markov chains previously defined. In Sect. 4 we analyze the WSN equipped by quantum entanglement in the nodes. Finally in Sect. 5 we provide some concluding comments.

2   Description of the Network

On considering the quantum entanglement in a network it is important to note that such a phenomenon does not have an equivalent in the classical world. Hence, if the nodes of a network are equipped with quantum entanglement, we have to consider that the network possesses different properties. The more relevant are superposition of states, and no-cloning principle.

Regarding the incorporation of the quantum entanglement in a WSN we can say that indeed a reduction of the energy consumption is possible. Moreover, we have the hypothesis that energy reduction does not depend on the topology of the network. Energy reduction can be achieved in linear sensor networks (LSN for short) in which nodes are located collinearly, usually with a fixed distance between nodes. Other topologies such as mesh or star topology are able to achieve energy reduction via quantum entanglement. In such networks the nodes are not located linearly but keep a regular ordering. These topologies provide extra redundancy in the interconnection of the nodes, which in turn reduces the loss of information. Finally, a network in which nodes are placed randomly are also subjected to energy reduction via quantum entanglement. This is the case of the network shown in Fig. 1.

In order to study the energy consumption in a WSN we have to consider that each node comprises a power supply, some kind of sensor, a processing subsystem, and a communication subsystem. Excluding the power supply, the rest of the components consume energy while performing their duties.

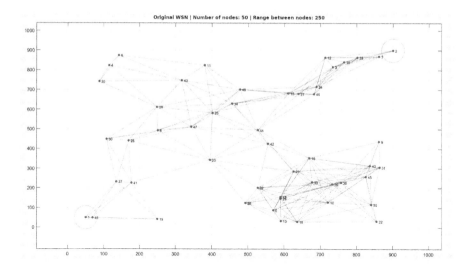

Fig. 1. A WSN with nodes placed randomly.

The sensor is responsible of sensing some physical variable. The electric signal of the sensor can be converted to a digital format if needed by an analog-to-digital converter (ADC for short). Next, the information from the sensor can be processed in a CPU of a microcontroller or microprocessor. The energy consumed by the sensor includes the sampling of the physical variable, conditioning of the electrical signal, and the analog-to-digital conversion.

The processing subsystem includes a central processing unit (CPU) of a microcontroller (MCU) or microprocessor (MPU) with certain amount of memory. This subsystem is in charge of processing the information and to provide the intelligence to the node. The energy used in processing the signals depends on the state of the CPU: active state, when the CPU processes the signals; and passive state, when the CPU is in idle state.

The communication subsystem is the main energy consumer in a node. The further away the nodes are located, the more energy is used for establishing a wireless link. The communication subsystem may consume mW to W to power the transceiver, in comparison to the μW or even nW of power used by the MCU or MPU. On this basis, we can establish the following settings for defining a Markov chain:

- The state of a node is represented by a state variable S_i, which can be either 0 (node OFF) or 1 (node ON).
- E_0 is the initial energy of a node.
- e_i is the residual energy of a node, where $0 < e_i < E_0$.
- E_{TX} is the amount of energy needed for transmitting information.
- E_{RX} is the amount of energy needed for receiving information.
- E_{sleep} is the amount of energy consumed in the Sleep mode.

- p_e is the transmission probability.
- ρ, is the probability of changing the state of the node from OFF to ON.
- If $S_i = 0 \Rightarrow S_i' = 1$, then $P_{TX} = p_e$, and $P_{RX} = 1 - p_e$.
- If $S_i = 1 \Rightarrow S_i' = 0$, then $P_{TX} = 0$, and $P_{RX} = 0$.

If the node is in the OFF state ($S_i = 0$), it can change to ON or Sleep state. Similarly, if the node is in the ON state ($S_i = 1$), it can change to OFF or Sleep state.

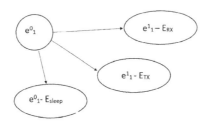

Fig. 2. Markov chain for a node in the OFF state.

Regarding Fig. 2, a node in the OFF state has the following transitions:

- $e_1^1 - E_{RX}$, in this transition the node is turned ON and is able to receive with probability $\rho(1 - p_e)$.
- $e_1^1 - E_{TX}$, in this transition the node is turned ON and is able to transmit with probability ρp_e.
- $e_1^0 - E_{sleep}$, the node remains in the sleep mode, and the state of the node does not change with probability $1 - \rho$.

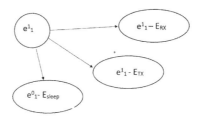

Fig. 3. Markov chain for a node in the ON state.

Regarding Fig. 3, a node in the ON state has the following transitions:

- $e_1^1 - E_{RX}$, in this transition the node remains in the same ON state and is able to receive with probability $(1 - \rho)(1 - p_e)$.
- $e_1^1 - E_{TX}$, in this transition the node remains in the same ON state and is able to transmit with probability $(1 - \rho) p_e$.
- $e_1^0 - E_{sleep}$, the node turns OFF and stay in the sleep mode.

3 Simulation and Results

The simulation was carried out using MATLAB. Let us consider a set of 50 nodes that define a topology for a WSN, as is shown in Fig. 4. Each node is associated to an index. Node 1 represents an arbitrary node, while Node 2 is a sink node. The positions of these nodes are fixed, and these nodes are chosen so that they are far away each other. The rest of the nodes are distributed randomly on a rectangle of 1000×1000 m^2. On considering this WSN as a classical network, it is equipped by the slotted ALOHA protocol, but as a modern network the nodes are equipped by quantum entanglement.

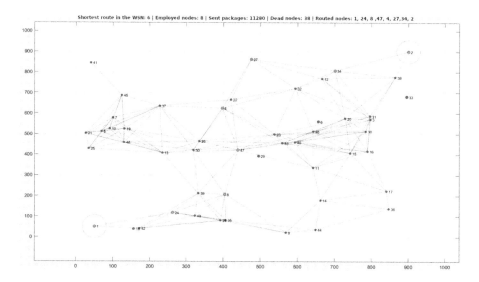

Fig. 4. Route in a WSN: packages are sent from Node 1 to the sink Node 2. (Color figure online)

The objective is to determine the energy consumption of the network in both cases: as a classical network and as a modern network. The process of transmission from Node 1 to Node 2 is defined by the flowchart of Fig. 5.

On the basis of the previous flowchart the network was simulated. Node 1 tries to transmit to a neighbor node. If the communication is not accomplished, that node is removed from the list of neighboring nodes; such a node is then called a "dead node" since it does not participate in the communication. Dead nodes are indicated by blue dots. On the other hand, if a node can be linked to a neighbor a successful transmission is indicated by a green dot, but if collision of packets occurs during the simulation that node is indicated by a red dot, as is shown in Fig. 4. These red dots are also disconnected from the networks since they could not accomplish a successful communication. The simulation consisted of sending 11280 packets. The resulting route in the network for this simulation consisted of 8 nodes, namely $1 \rightarrow 24 \rightarrow 8 \rightarrow 47 \rightarrow 4 \rightarrow 27 \rightarrow 34 \rightarrow 2$.

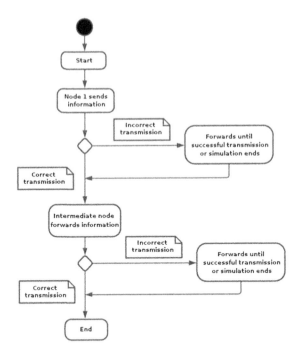

Fig. 5. Flowchart of activities for an arbitrary WSN.

The simulation shows that there exist successful tries when sending information, but also collisions when trying to reach the Node 2. Recall that E_{TX} and E_{RX} denote the energy needed for transmitting and receiving a packet, respectively. Since 8 nodes were involved in the route, the energy used to transmit a single packet to the Node 2 via the route is

$$E_{route} = e_{total} - 7E_{TX} + 7E_{RX}.$$

Note that the Node 1 transmits only, while the Node 2 (the sink) receives only, for this reason we have seven units of energy in each case. In a more general case in which κ is the number of nodes forming a route, the energy used to transmit a single packet to the Node 2 via that route is

$$E_{route} = e_{total} - (\kappa - 1)(E_{TX} + E_{RX}).$$

This is a quite ideal expression since no collisions are taken into account during the transmission. However if collisions are considered an extra amount of energy is used for retransmitting, but not so when receiving. If ι denotes the number of nodes that had collisions, the expression for the energy takes the form

$$E_{route} = e_{total} - (\kappa - 1)(E_{TX} + E_{RX}) - \iota E_{TX}.$$

On considering the leakage energy in a node, that is the energy consumed by a node that stays in the sleep mode the previous equation takes the form

$$E_{\text{route}} = e_{\text{total}} - (\kappa - 1)(E_{\text{TX}} + E_{\text{RX}}) - \iota E_{\text{TX}} - (\varrho - 1)(\kappa - 1) E_{\text{sleep}}. \quad (1)$$

where ϱ is the total number of nodes of the network.

4   Nodes Equipped by Quantum Entanglement

Now, for generating quantum entanglement between the nodes of the network, it is necessary to use the circuit of Fig. 6 for each pair of nodes. Here X and H are the corresponding logical gates in the quantum realm. By H we denote a Hadamard gate, and X is a CNOT gate [20].

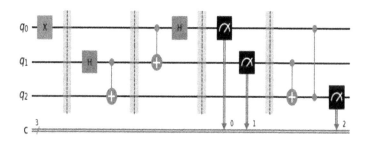

Fig. 6. Quantum circuit

Next, the teleportation was simulated by making 1024 transmissions. In this way, we obtained the 4 states and their respective probabilities, as is shown in the histogram of Fig. 7. The three binary digits in each bar of the histogram correspond to the states of the three Qubits q_0, q_1, q_2 of the previous circuit. For instance the state 100 means that q_0 is in the *up* state, while q_1 and q_2 are in the down state.

Let us assume that the nodes of the network are equipped by quantum entanglement, and suppose that we want to transmit from one node, which is referred to by *Alice*, to another node that is referred to by *Bob*. A spin emphup state $|\uparrow\rangle$ is sent via an external uniform magnetic field, which is parallel to the z axis. The corresponding Hamiltonian is given by

$$H_s = g\sigma_z,$$

where g denotes a positive constant, and σ_z is the Pauli spin matrix. The ground state of the system is the *down* state $|\downarrow\rangle$, whose eigen-energy is $-g$. The excited state of the system is the *up* state $|\uparrow\rangle$, whose eigen-energy is $+g$.

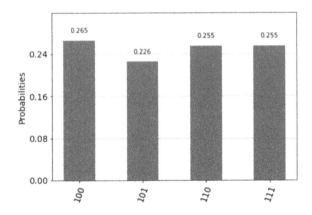

Fig. 7. Histogram of states.

A shrinking state in Alice or Bob from a Bell pair shared by Alice and Bob for QT (Quantum Teleportation) is the state of maximum entropy, whose average energy is zero. Hence, we have to provide to both Alice and Bob an average energy $+g$ to their spins for generating a Bell pair from two spins in the fundamental state via a global operation. Bob must to provide an additional energy $+g$ to its spin to receive the spin *up* from Alice by means quantum teleportation. Therefore, the total energy at the input of Bob is equal to $+2g$ whence Bob should make the respective local preparation.

Owing to the nature of the quantum teleportation protocol used in the network, the energy used to transmit a single packet in a given route is

$$E_{\text{route}} = e_{\text{total}} - (\kappa - 1)(E_{\text{TX}} + E_{\text{RX}}) - \iota E_{\text{TX}}.$$

Note that it is similar to the expression for the classical network, but the nodes of the quantum network do not fall in the sleep mode. Hence the quantum network provides an effective reduction of energy by comparing this expression with (1).

Then, one way to send the packets from the nodes of the network by incorporating quantum entanglement is by means of quantum teleportation of energy (QET for short) in spin chains using local excitations with negative energy and entanglement between ground states. It will result in preserved causality and conservation of local energy. Spin chains are made up of many one-dimensionally arranged spins. There exist short-range interactions between spins, and the Hamiltonian is obtained by summing up the terms of all local interactions. If the ground states of the spins in the chain are not degenerated and the temporal scales are short, then the dynamical evolution due to the Hamiltonian is negligible.

Let us denote the different between the largest and shortest eigen-energies by ΔE. The scale of time is assumed to satisfy

$$t \ll \frac{1}{\Delta E}.$$

By assuming this condition, it is valid to consider that the time evolution operator behaves like $e^{-iH_s t} \sim I$. In order for the previous expression to hold, the supplied energy E_{in} should be less than ΔE in the spin chain of the transmitter,

$$t \ll \frac{1}{E_{in}}.$$

5   Conclusions

As is shown in this work, using quantum entanglement in a wireless sensor network may reduce the average energy consumption. Even in the simplest network, namely a LSN, the energy consumption may be significant. The analysis of the energy consumption of such a quantum network required a slightly broader analysis, however the conclusions are fairly simple. The implementation of such a quantum property could involve several challenges.

The quantum entanglement provides security to the network due to the superposition of states. However, such a quantum technology implies a fairly significant economic expenses nowadays. For isntance, it is well-known that in order to construct a quantum computer it is necessary to keep that system at a temperature close to the absolute zero, which may represent technological and economical challenges. Notwithstanding, the advantages of incorporating quantum entanglement in a WSN could compensate for such challenges.

Some international companies already are heading for what is called "quantum supremacy". However the advantages of incorporating such technologies should be shared with all stakeholders for the sake of a commonwealth.

Acknowledgments. The authors are grateful with Professors Adriana Natalia Ramírez Salazar, Michel Galaxia Miranda Sánchez, and Mario Eduardo Rivero Ángeles.

References

1. Ahmed, Z., et al.: Quantum sensing for high energy physics. arXiv preprint arXiv:1803.11306 (2018)
2. Alyami, H., et al.: Analyzing the data of software security life-span: quantum computing era. Intell. Autom. Soft Comput. **31**(2), 707–716 (2022)
3. Cerulli, R., Gentili, M., Raiconi, A.: Maximizing lifetime and handling reliability in wireless sensor networks. Networks **64**(4), 321–338 (2014)
4. Chou, J.P., Bodrog, Z., Gali, A.: First-principles study of charge diffusion between proximate solid-state qubits and its implications on sensor applications. Phys. Rev. Lett. **120**(13), 136401 (2018)
5. Dâmaso, A., Rosa, N., Maciel, P.: Reliability of wireless sensor networks. Sensors **14**(9), 15760–15785 (2014)
6. DeWitt, B.S., Graham, N.: The Many-Worlds Interpretation of Quantum Mechanics, vol. 61. Princeton University Press, Princeton (2015)
7. Duarte, F.J., Taylor, T.S.: Quantum Entanglement Engineering and Applications, pp. 2053–2563. IOP Publishing, Bristol (2021)

8. Eskandarpour, R., Gokhale, P., Khodaei, A., Chong, F.T., Passo, A., Bahramirad, S.: Quantum computing for enhancing grid security. IEEE Trans. Power Syst. **35**(5), 4135–4137 (2020)
9. Feng, Y., Wang, Y., Zheng, H., Mi, S., Tan, J.: A framework of joint energy provisioning and manufacturing scheduling in smart industrial wireless rechargeable sensor networks. Sensors **18**(8), 2591 (2018)
10. Flöther, F.F.: The state of quantum computing applications in health and medicine. arXiv preprint arXiv:2301.09106 (2023)
11. Gupta, M., Nene, M.J.: Quantum computing: an entanglement measurement. In: 2020 IEEE International Conference on Advent Trends in Multidisciplinary Research and Innovation (ICATMRI), pp. 1–6 (2020)
12. Heigl, M., Schramm, M., Fiala, D.: A lightweight quantum-safe security concept for wireless sensor network communication. In: 2019 IEEE International Conference on Pervasive Computing and Communications Workshops (PerCom Workshops), pp. 906–911. IEEE (2019)
13. Herbert, N.: Entanglement telegraphed communication avoiding light-speed limitation by Hong Ou Mandel effect. arXiv preprint arXiv:0712.2530 (2007)
14. Horodecki, R., Horodecki, P., Horodecki, M., Horodecki, K.: Quantum entanglement. Rev. Mod. Phys. **81**(2), 865–942 (2009)
15. Katiyar, M., Sinha, H., Gupta, D.: On reliability modeling in wireless sensor networks-a review. Int. J. Comput. Sci. Issues (IJCSI) **9**(6), 99 (2012)
16. Li, Y., Zhao, Y., Zhang, Y.: A spanning tree construction algorithm for industrial wireless sensor networks based on quantum artificial bee colony. EURASIP J. Wirel. Commun. Netw. **2019**(1), 1–12 (2019). https://doi.org/10.1186/s13638-019-1496-z
17. Luck Khym, G., Jin Yang, H.: Quantum entanglement does not violate the principle of special theory of relativity. Phys. Essays **29**(4), 553–554 (2016)
18. Mahdian, B., Mahrami, M., Mohseni, M.: A method for deploying relay nodes in homogeneous wireless sensor networks using particle optimization algorithm. J. Soft Comput. Decis. Support Syst. **6**(4), 1–9 (2019)
19. Nagy, N., Nagy, M., Akl, S.G.: Quantum security in wireless sensor networks. Nat. Comput. **9**(4), 819–830 (2010)
20. Nielsen, M., Chuang, I.: Quantum Computation and Quantum Information, 10th Anniversary Cambridge University Press (2010)
21. Orumwense, E.F., Abo-Al-Ez, K.: A charging technique for sensor nodes in wireless rechargeable sensor networks for cyber-physical systems. In: 2021 International Conference on Electrical, Computer and Energy Technologies (ICECET), pp. 1–6 (2021)
22. Pauli, W., Enz, C.P., von Meyenn, K.: Writings on Physics and Philosophy. Springer, Cham (1994). https://doi.org/10.1007/978-3-662-02994-7
23. Shokry, A., Youssef, M.: Quantum computing for location determination. arXiv preprint arXiv:2106.11751 (2021)
24. Spector, L., Barnum, H., Bernstein, H.J., Swamy, N.: Quantum computing applications of genetic programming. Adv. Genet. Program. **3**, 135–160 (1999)
25. Ye, M.Y., Lin, X.M.: Energy transmission using recyclable quantum entanglement. Sci. Rep. **6**(1), 30603 (2016)
26. Zhao, J., Fu, Y., Wang, H.B.: Localization technology based on quantum-behaved particle swarm optimization algorithm for wireless sensor network. Appl. Mech. Mater. **220**, 1852–1856 (2012)

A Novel Method Based on Gunnar Farneback Method, Mathematical Morphology, and Artificial Vision for Flow Analysis in Electrochemical Reactors

Daniel A. Gutiérrez-Jiménez[1], Sebastián Salazar-Colores[1(✉)],
Fernando F. Rivera[3], and José Trinidad López-Maldonado[2]

[1] Centro de Investigaciones en Óptica (CIO), 37150 León, Mexico
sebastian.salazar@cio.mx
[2] Centro de Investigación y Desarrollo Tecnológico en Electroquímica (CIDETEQ),
76703 Querétaro, Mexico
[3] Universidad Politécnica de Querétaro (UPQ), 76240 Querétaro, Mexico

Abstract. Parallel flat plate electrochemical reactors are versatile devices that are used in a wide range of applications, including hydrogen production, organic compound synthesis, chlorine generation, wastewater treatment, and metal recovery. However, the flow dynamics within reactors are complex and can be difficult to measure. This study presents a novel analysis method for Parallel flat plate electrochemical reactors based on artificial vision techniques. The method uses a camera to capture images of the flow within the reactor, which are then processed using computer vision algorithms to extract quantitative information about the flow field. To validate the proposed method, the flow within the reactor was analyzed under three distinct configurations: empty channel, bifurcated, and canalized. The experimental results were compared with computational fluid dynamics (CFD) simulations using the mean squared error (MSE) metric. The experimental findings demonstrate the feasibility of the proposed approach.

Keywords: Parallel plate electrochemical reactor · Velocimetry · Optical flow · Gunnar Farneback · Computer Vision · Image Processing

1 Introduction

Flat plate electrodes are widely used in electrochemical processes due to their versatility, low-cost maintenance, uniform potential and current distribution, ease of constructing different electrode architectures, ability to incorporate net-like spacers or structured static mixers to improve mass transport to the electrode surface, and ease of scaling up and control [3].

- Chlorine and caustic soda production: Flat plate electrodes are used in the chlor-alkali process, which is a method of producing chlorine and caustic soda from salt water [3].

M. F. Mata-Rivera et al. (Eds.): WITCOM 2023, CCIS 1906, pp. 133–156, 2023.
https://doi.org/10.1007/978-3-031-45316-8_11

- Pharmaceutical manufacturing: Flat plate electrodes are used in the production of a variety of pharmaceuticals, including antibiotics, hormones, and vitamins [10].
- Organic and inorganic reactions: Flat plate electrodes are used in the synthesis of a variety of organic and inorganic compounds, including polymers, dyes, and catalysts [17].
- Water treatment: Flat plate electrodes are used in the treatment of wastewater, including the removal of heavy metals, organic pollutants, and pathogens [2].
- Batteries: Flat plate electrodes are used in a variety of batteries, including lead-acid batteries, nickel-cadmium batteries, and lithium-ion batteries [26].
- Fuel cells: Flat plate electrodes are used in fuel cells, which are devices that convert chemical energy into electrical energy [13].

However, recent advancements in electrochemical processes require the exploration of different reactor designs and configurations tailored to specific electrochemical processes. In the case of electrochemical reactors utilizing flat plate electrodes, the implementation of flow distributor configurations becomes essential to optimize fluid patterns and achieve competitive performance. These configurations aim to enhance mass transport distribution over the electrode surface while minimizing costs and pressure drop. For instance, Escudero et al. [9] designed flow distributors for a flat plate electrochemical reactor with a projected electrode and membrane area of $925 \, cm^2$, which improved upon their previous work [8]. Numerical and experimental studies demonstrated the uniformity of the flow field through the reaction zone, albeit at the cost of high-pressure drop, validating the numerical simulations through direct visualization, residence time distribution tests (RTD), and overall pressure drop measurements.

Marquez et al. [20] presented a study involving numerical simulations and experimental validation to evaluate the hydrodynamics of a homemade parallel plate flow electrochemical reactor. Various inlet-outlet distributor configurations were assessed, including empty channels, serpentine flow collectors, straight flow collectors, and diamond-shaped net-like spacers. Simulation studies enabled the evaluation of hydrodynamic distribution in the reaction environment with different configurations, which were subsequently validated through global RTD measurements and direct visualizations.

Although RTD and global tests are powerful techniques for elucidating hydrodynamic behavior and indirectly validating computational simulation results, the field of electrochemical reactors has also explored techniques involving local velocity measurements. Laser Doppler velocimetry (LVD) and particle imaging velocimetry have been reported, particularly in the domain of rotary mixers and gas-evolved electrochemical reactors [4,15]. These techniques rely on optical-based analysis to calculate vectorial velocity, utilizing tracer particles or measuring laser intensity losses. While suitable for measuring local velocity in transparent flow reactor vessels, these methods often require expensive infrastructure, such as high-speed cameras, high-power laser sources, and specialized software, which may limit their resolution and applicability in bench-scale reactors.

To overcome these drawbacks, it is necessary to explore alternative optical techniques, especially for velocity measurements in bench-scale electrochemical reactors where the aforementioned techniques may be susceptible to various light interferences. The utilization of computer vision algorithms emerges as a promising option for analyzing velocity measurements, leveraging well-established visualization tests. Computer vision algorithms, such as optical flow, have found extensive usage in large-scale measurements, including trajectories of urban aerial vehicles [14], control of flying robots [5], river flows [7], velocity patterns in pulsatile and constant flows in angiography [30], spatiotemporal dynamics of brain activity [1], and crystal growth velocity [23]. In the field of electrochemical reactors, to the best of the authors' knowledge, only a simple image processing method has been employed in [25] to indirectly calculate experimental RTD responses by computing time histograms through visualization tests within the reactor vessel.

In this work, we propose a novel method to visualize and analyze the local and global velocity inside electrochemical reactors. This method is entirely based on computer vision strategies, using a video of a color tracer on a plate as input. The proposed method relies on image processing techniques such as mathematical morphology opening, Ramer-Douglas-Peucker, Otsu methods and a novel standard deviation filter for data preprocessing. Gunnar Farneback's optical flow method are utilized to estimate the velocity measurements. Our results demonstrate that the proposed method is a valid alternative for conducting these analyses.

The remainder of this work is organized as follows. Section 2 presents the methodology of our research, and Sect. 3 presents the results and conclusions.

2   Proposed Method

The proposed method analyzes image sequences using a setup specifically developed for the proposed method. This section explains both the setup and the proposed method in detail.

2.1   Experimental Instrumental Setup

Flow visualizations were developed to obtain experimental velocity profiles within the parallel plate electrochemical reactor. A 1-mL volume of a colored tracer (methylene blue at a concentration of $10\,g/L$) was injected 5 cm upstream of the reactor inlet. A transparent frame was constructed using a polycarbonate sheet to visualize the flow within the filter press electrolyzer channel. The electrochemical reactor was connected to a hydraulic system comprising a 20-L PVC reservoir and a calibrated 1/15 HP, 3200 RPM magnetic centrifugal pump. The reservoir temperature was maintained at a constant 25 °C (see Fig. 1). The tracer experiments were recorded using a Nikon® D3500 camera at a flow rate of 1.2 LPM (see Fig. 3).

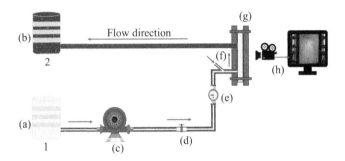

Fig. 1. Diagram of the implemented circuit for tracer visualization in the electrochemical reactor: a) Reservoir 1, b) Reservoir 2, c) Pump, d) Valve, e) Flowmeter, f) Injection point, g) Electrochemical reactor, h) Camera.

2.2 The Reactor

The electrochemical parallel plate reactor is a specialized system consisting of two parallel plates made of conductive materials that act as electrodes. This type of reactor is widely used in various electrochemical processes and experiments. When liquid is injected into parallel plate reactors, a controlled amount of liquid is introduced into the space between the plates, which is filled with an electrolytic solution or an electrolyte membrane. These liquid injections serve different purposes and have varying effects depending on the specific application. There are specific variations of the electrochemical parallel plate reactor, such as the channelized, bifurcated, and vacuum channel plate reactors, which have distinctive characteristics in terms of their design and operation. The channelized parallel plate reactor is characterized by separated and sealed plates that form individual channels between them. Each channel is used to direct the flow of the electrolytic solution or the reactant liquid through the reactor. This configuration allows for precise flow control, uniform distribution, and selective reactions in each channel. In the case of the bifurcated parallel plate reactor, the parallel plates are divided into multiple branches or bifurcations, creating parallel reaction pathways within the reactor. Each bifurcation can have different reaction properties and conditions, enabling the performance of simultaneous or sequential reactions in each branch of the reactor. On the other hand, the vacuum channel parallel plate reactor keeps the space between the plates empty of an electrolytic solution and instead uses a gas or gas mixture as the reactive medium. This design facilitates the execution of gas-phase electrochemical reactions, such as gas generation or gas absorption at the electrode interface. Figure 2 depicts an illustration of the aforementioned configurations: the channelized, bifurcated, and vacuum channel parallel plate reactors. These visual representations provide a clear understanding of the specific characteristics of each design.

Additionally, Fig. 3 presents visual examples of the liquid injections performed with these configurations. These videos effectively illustrate how a controlled amount of liquid is introduced into the space between the plates and

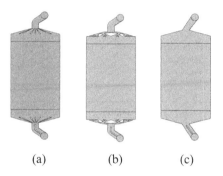

(a)   (b)   (c)

Fig. 2. Reactor configurations used in the experimentation process: a) Canalized, b) Bifurcated, c) Empty channel.

demonstrate the resulting effects and outcomes in each case. Both figures complement the preceding description by providing visual representations that enhance the comprehension of the configurations and their functioning.

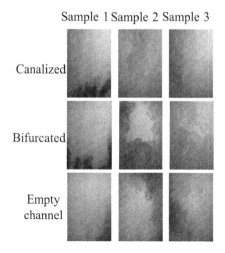

Fig. 3. Frames obtained from a video of a shot in an electrochemical reactor: tests with different configurations and a blue tracer. (Color figure online)

2.3   The Proposed Method

In this work, a method is proposed that estimates the overall velocity in each area of parallel plates using a sequence of frames as input. The frame sequence is represented by v_i, where $0 \leq i \leq n$ is the i-th frame out of a total of n frames. The general flowchart of the proposed method is shown in Fig. 4.

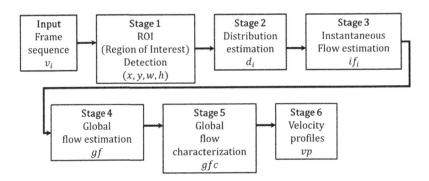

Fig. 4. Flow of the proposed method.

As shown in Fig. 4, the method consists of six main stages, which are described in detail below:

Stage 1 - Estimation of ROI Coordinates

Using the first frame of v_i, i.e., v_0 (Fig. 4 (Input)), the algorithm automatically recognizes and returns the coordinates (x, y, w, h), where x and y represent the top-left position, and w and h represent the width and height of a rectangle that encloses the region of the parallel plates, which is the region of interest (ROI).

Image normalization

Inspired by the algorithm proposed in [29], to mitigate the issues associated with illumination when binarizing an image, the frames v_i are normalized based on the maximum value among the three RGB channels across all frames of v_i, obtained using the following formula:

$$v_i' = \max_{c \in R,G,B} v_i^c \ \forall \ 0 \leq i \leq n \tag{1}$$

Morphological grayscale opening

Subsequently, to eliminate possible white artifacts caused by reflections on the frame on which the parallel plates are mounted, a morphological grayscale opening operation is performed. Morphological opening is one of the mathematical morphology operations that serves as a powerful tool for various image processing and computer vision applications. Morphology has been used for contrast enhancement, noise suppression, texture analysis, shape analysis, edge detection, and skeletonization in applications such as medical imaging [27,28], automated industrial inspection [11], image compression [24], signal analysis, geological image processing, among others. In mathematical morphology, an image is transformed by another set, known as the structuring element. The structuring element g is defined as:

$$g(s,t) \in \mathbb{R}, \forall (s,t) \in \mathbb{Z}^2 \qquad (2)$$

Dilation and erosion

Let f be the image whose pixel is represented by spatial coordinates (u,v) and let g be a structuring element whose spatial coordinate is represented by (s,t). The dilation $(f \oplus g)$ and erosion $(f \ominus g)$ of the image f by g are defined as follows:

$$(f \oplus g)(u,v) = \max_{(s,t) \in g} f(u+s, v+t) + g(s,t) \qquad (3)$$

$$(f \ominus g)(u,v) = \min_{(s,t) \in g} f(u+s, v+t) - g(s,t) \qquad (4)$$

The bright and dark details of the image are reduced through the operations of erosion and dilation. With the operators of dilation and erosion, all morphological mathematics can be extended. The opening $(f \circ g)$ of f by g is defined based on the concepts of dilation and erosion as follows:

$$f \circ g = (f \ominus g) \oplus g \qquad (5)$$

Next, the images are binarized using the Otsu thresholding method.

Otsu's thresholding method

Otsu's method [22] is based on maximizing a statistical measure called the inter-class variance. A threshold that produces the best separation between classes in terms of their intensity values will be the optimal threshold. For a two-level threshold, the optimal threshold $t*$ is chosen such that the inter-class variance $\sigma_B^2(t)$ is maximized; that is:

$$t* = max[\sigma_B^2(t)]0 \le t \le L-1 \qquad (6)$$

where L is the number of gray levels, which in our case is 256.

Edge detection
Subsequently, the edges of all binary regions are calculated using the morphological operation.

$$E = (f \oplus g) - f \qquad (7)$$

Connected Component Labeling

The Connected Component Labeling algorithm proposed in [12] is used to identify interconnected regions in an image. These regions represent continuous areas or sets of pixels that are connected to each other. In the context of eliminating small proposed regions, this algorithm helps to distinguish and isolate the edges of interconnected regions. Edges are those pixels that mark the transition between different regions. After isolating the edges, a selection criterion is applied. In this case, the region with the highest number of pixels, i.e., the region with the largest cardinality, is chosen to be retained. This prioritizes the preservation of larger and more significant regions, while discarding smaller regions that may be considered noise or insignificant details. This strategy of eliminating small proposed regions, along with the Connected Component Labeling algorithm, helps effectively segment and distinguish important regions in an image, thereby improving the analysis and understanding of the image.

Given an image v_i represented as a matrix of pixels, where each pixel has a position (u, v) and a value $v(u, v)$, the Connected Component Labeling algorithm can be summarized in the following steps:

1. Edge detection is applied to identify pixels that mark the transition between different regions.
2. Once the edges are identified, segmentation and selection of regions are performed. For this purpose, a set of interconnected regions E_i representing continuous areas in the image is defined.
3. The cardinality of each region R_i is calculated as the number of pixels it contains.
4. The region with the highest cardinality is selected as the resulting region R_{res}. Mathematically, this can be expressed as:

$$R_{\text{res}} = \arg \max_{R_i \in E_i} \text{cardinality}(R_i) \tag{8}$$

Ramer-Douglas-Peucker Algorithm

Next, the Ramer-Douglas-Peucker (RDP) algorithm [32] is used to simplify the trajectories and obtain the 4 points that define the rectangular ROI. RDP is a line simplification method that reduces the number of points that define a line. The RDP algorithm has multiple applications such as coronary artery characterization, trajectory reduction in robotics [16,18], architectural floor plan reconstruction [19], traffic sign detection [31], and compression of GPS route data [21]. The RDP algorithm is based on the search for critical points within a linear tolerance. The first baseline corresponds to the first (anchor) and last (floating) point of the original line. Then, the perpendicular distances of all intermediate points are calculated.

Let $P = \{P_1, P_2 ... P_n\}$ be a set of points representing a curve or line. Let ε be a given threshold for the maximum allowed distance between points and the linear approximation. Define a distance function between a point $P_i = (x_i, y_i)$ and a line segment defined by two points $P_j = (x_j, y_j)$ and $P_k = (x_k, y_k)$. This distance function can be calculated using the formula for the perpendicular distance from a point to a line:

$$D = dist(P_i, P_j, P_k) = \frac{|(y_i - y_j) \cdot (x_k - x_j) - (x_i - x_j) \cdot (y_k - y_j)|}{\sqrt{(x_k - x_j)^2 + (y_k - y_j)^2}} \tag{9}$$

Next, the Ramer-Douglas-Peucker (RDP) algorithm [32] is used to simplify the trajectories and obtain the 4 points that define the rectangular ROI. RDP is a line simplification method that reduces the number of points that define a line. The RDP algorithm has multiple applications such as coronary artery characterization, trajectory reduction in robotics [16,18], architectural floor plan reconstruction [19], traffic sign detection [31], and compression of GPS route data [21]. The RDP algorithm is based on the search for critical points within a linear tolerance.

The first baseline corresponds to the first (anchor) and last (floating) point of the original line. Then, the perpendicular distances of all intermediate points are calculated.

Let $P = \{P_1, P_2...P_n\}$ be a set of points representing a curve or line. Let ε be a given threshold for the maximum allowed distance between points and the linear approximation.

Define a distance function between a point $P_i = (x_i, y_i)$ and a line segment defined by two points $P_j = (x_j, y_j)$ and $P_k = (x_k, y_k)$. This distance function

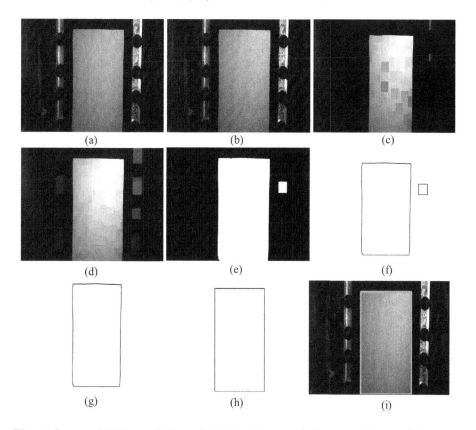

Fig. 5. Stages of ROI acquisition: a) Original image, b) Grayscale image, c) Erosion, d) Dilation, e) Otsu thresholding, f) Connected Component Labeling, g) Removal of the smallest connected component labeling, h) Ramer-Douglas-Peucker (RDP), i) ROI drawn in green color for better visualization. (Color figure online)

can be calculated using the formula for the perpendicular distance from a point to a line (Fig. 5).

Stage 2 - Estimation of the Distribution

Standard deviation, also known as the distribution standard, is a measure that indicates the variability or dispersion of a set of data. In the context of computer vision and image comparison, the standard deviation can be useful for evaluating the similarity or difference between images. When comparing two images, it is possible to calculate the distributions of pixel values in each image. The standard deviation of an image indicates how dispersed the pixel values are in relation to their mean or average value. If the distributions of the two images are similar, it is likely that the images share visual characteristics or represent the same object or scene. On the other hand, if the distributions of the two images differ significantly, this could indicate significant differences in visual characteristics between them. These differences could be due to changes in lighting, perspective, the presence of different objects, or any other factor that affects the visual appearance of the images. By using standard deviation to compare images in computer vision, a quantitative measure of their similarity or difference in terms of pixel value variability is obtained. This is useful in applications such as object recognition, object tracking, scene change detection, among others. Estimating the distribution involves calculating the difference between the standard deviation of a current image and the standard deviation of a base image. This difference is used to obtain a visual representation of the distribution of pixel values in the current image compared to the base image.

Based on the aforementioned information and through testing, we came up with the idea of normalizing the values from black to white scale and representing them with the color black, as this color is not essential for analysis in the reactor. It is worth noting that the tracer used is blue in color. By carrying out this normalization, we can analyze the shades of the color blue, ranging from white to different shades of gray, depending on the saturation of the blue color. In this way, we can discard areas or elements that are not of interest to us. The approach to achieve this is by calculating the standard deviation (Eq. (10)) for each pixel in the image along the color channels axis (axis 2). This results in a grayscale image representing the variation of intensity in the original image, as shown in Fig. 6.

$$d_i(u, v) = \sqrt{\frac{1}{channels} \sum_{i=1}^{channels} (v_i(u, v) - v_{i_{mean}}(u, v))^2} \tag{10}$$

Normalize the standard deviation image using the Eq. 11:

$$d_i n(u, v) = \left(\frac{d_{i(u,v)} - d_{i_{min}}}{d_{i_{max}} - d_{i_{min}}} \right) \times 255 \tag{11}$$

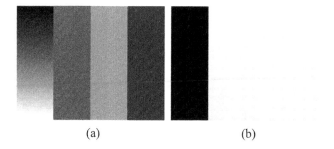

(a)   (b)

Fig. 6. Example demonstrating the functionality of the standard deviation proposed filter: a) Original color image prior to processing, b) Color image after calculating the standard deviation and applying normalization.

The resulting distribution shows how pixel values in the current image deviate from the expected values in the base image. This distribution is calculated for each color channel and ensures that it does not have negative values by setting any negative value to 0. The estimation of the distribution can be used to analyze and understand the variation of pixel values in the current image in relation to the base image. Visualizations can be generated to aid in the distribution and facilitate the analysis of changes in the image. To do this, we calculate the distribution for each frame. Starting from the first frame, d_0, we process an original image and a cropped image to obtain a combined image that we will refer to as the "cropped base image standard distribution". It is worth mentioning that this processing is done within our region of interest (ROI). These processed images should be saved in variables for subsequent visualization. Next, we obtain the total frames, d_i, to process each frame from d_0 to d_i sequentially. This way, the standard distribution between the original or current image and the cropped image is calculated. This is expressed as follows:

The total distribution is calculated by subtracting the distribution of the base image from the distribution of the current image. If any value in the total distribution turns out to be less than 0, it is adjusted to 0. Once the standard distribution of the cropped images (base image and current image) is obtained, the standard distribution of the base image is used as a reference to obtain the resulting distribution. Next, the resulting distribution is multiplied by 2 and converted to 8-bit integer values. This process is performed to adjust the scale of the distribution and convert it to a suitable format for visualization. Additionally, a JET color map is applied to enhance the visual representation (Fig. 7).

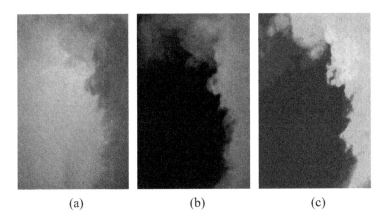

(a)   (b)   (c)

Fig. 7. Estimation of the distribution: a) Original image, b) Image with distribution estimation and normalization treatment, c) Application of JET color map to improve visualization.

Stage 3 - Estimation of Instantaneous Flow Rate

The estimation of instantaneous flow rate refers to determining the flow rate of a fluid at a specific moment. The instantaneous flow rate represents the amount of fluid passing through a point or cross-sectional area per unit of time, and it is an important measure in various fields such as hydrology, fluid engineering, and water management. Estimating the instantaneous flow rate can be done using different methods and techniques, depending on the context and data availability. By utilizing image processing and computer vision techniques, the instantaneous flow rate can be estimated from the analysis of image sequences capturing the flow. These techniques involve tracking particles or flow features in the images and estimating their velocity and displacement over time. The estimation of instantaneous flow rate in a flow can be computed using optical flow. Optical flow provides information on how points move in a sequence of images, allowing for the estimation of velocity and direction of motion.

In the stage of estimating the instantaneous flow rate, optical flow is used between two consecutive frames using algorithms such as the Farneback method [6]. These algorithms allow for the calculation of motion velocity in the form of flow vectors for each point or region of interest in the image. From these flow vectors, the magnitude of each vector is calculated, representing the velocity of motion. The magnitude is obtained as the square root of the sum of the squares of the horizontal component u and vertical component v of the flow. To perform the flow rate estimation, an area of interest is selected in the image where the flow is to be measured, in our case the ROI of an electrochemical reactor. Within this area, the magnitudes of the flow vectors are summed to obtain the instantaneous flow rate. This sum of magnitudes reflects the amount of motion in the selected area and provides an estimation of the flow rate at that specific moment. This approach based on optical flow and the summation of flow vector magnitudes allows for non-invasive estimation of the instantaneous flow rate using visual information. By leveraging the properties of optical flow and image analysis techniques, it is possible to obtain accurate real-time flow rate estimates. This information is of great importance in various fields such as hydrology, fluid engineering, and water management, where monitoring and precise flow rate measurement are crucial for decision-making and assessment purposes.

It is important to obtain the pixel intensity range before calculating optical flow in the video using optical flow techniques because it provides information about the pixel intensity range in the video. The pixel intensity range is the difference between the minimum and maximum intensity values present in the video. Knowing this range is useful for adjusting and normalizing the intensity values before performing optical flow calculation. Optical flow is based on analyzing the intensity changes between consecutive frames of a video. If the pixel intensity range in the video is very wide, there may be issues in calculating optical flow as the intensity changes could vary significantly. On the other hand, if the intensity range is more limited, it is more likely to obtain more accurate and consistent results. By obtaining the pixel intensity range before calculating optical flow, we determine the intensity range of the video and obtain the necessary minimum and maximum values for any appropriate frame adjustment or normalization before calculating optical flow. This helps to achieve more reliable and improved results in optical flow calculation. Therefore, we need to analyze the frames of the video to classify the maximum and minimum values. For this task, we will initially set the maximum value to zero and the minimum value to 255. We will iterate through all the frames, comparing the pixel values to establish the maximum and minimum values using the following logic: the minimum value of the image is compared to the current minimum value, and if it is smaller, the minimum value is updated with the new minimum value found. Similarly, the maximum value of the image is compared to the current maximum value, and if it is larger, the maximum value is updated with the new maximum value found.

Optical Flow

Optical flow in image sequences is the pattern of motion obtained from objects caused by the relative movement between the observer (camera) and the scene (recorded objects).

Motion analysis, based on image sequences, aims to extract parameters that characterize the motion of objects. These parameters are typically coefficients of equations that govern their dynamic behavior. In general, equations of different types have been used in the processing of image sequences, including linear equations (the most commonly used), non-linear equations, and polynomial equations. The estimation of motion is closely related to the temporal and spatial characteristics of the image.

Related to the temporal and spatial changes of pixel values, the motion from one image to another can be described by a displacement vector, which can go from a point on the contour of the first image to a point on the contour of the second image. There are multiple models available for this purpose. The problem of recognizing the motion of objects seen in an image sequence has been addressed using various models that attempt to describe the general characteristics of such motion. Given a set of images, the objective is to calculate the displacement of pixels between different images. For this task, we have a camera (or video camera) capturing images of a scene. In the scene, we may encounter a series of static or dynamic objects that are generally influenced by varying environmental conditions, such as light sources, shadows, reflections, and other effects, as well as challenges associated with object appearance and disappearance or occlusion between objects.

The different optical flow algorithms attempt to calculate the motion between two consecutive frames for each pixel. Thus, a pixel can be considered as $I(x, y, t)$ where I is the intensity, x and y are the coordinates (in pixel width and height, respectively), and t is the time. Additionally, (dx, dy) represents the distance that the pixel has moved in the next frame after time dt. Therefore, assuming that the intensity value of these pixels does not vary significantly:

$$I(x, y, t) = I(x + dx, y + dy, t + dt) \tag{12}$$

Approximating by Taylor series, eliminating common terms, and dividing by dt yields the following equation:

$$fxu + fyv + ft = 0 \tag{13}$$

where,

$$f_x = \frac{\partial f}{\partial x}; f_y = \frac{\partial f}{\partial y}; u = \frac{\partial x}{\partial t}; v = \frac{\partial y}{\partial t}; \tag{14}$$

This is the optical flow equation. In it, fx and fy are spatial gradients of the image, while ft is the temporal gradient. However, u and v are the unknowns to be solved and define the optical flow, representing the horizontal and vertical components with respect to the images, respectively. Therefore, since it is not mathematically possible to solve a problem with one equation and two unknowns, there are various algorithms that attempt to solve it, one of which is the Farneback method.

Farneback method

The dense optical flow algorithm proposed by Gunnar Farneback [6] aims to approximate sets of pixels belonging to the same region using quadratic polynomials in two consecutive frames. This is achieved by estimating the signal $f_1(x)$ expressed in a local coordinate system, where if_i represents the estimation of the instantaneous flow rate.

$$f_1(x) = if_i(x) = x^T A_1 x + b_1^T x + c_1 \tag{15}$$

Being A a symmetric matrix, b a vector, and c a scalar. The coefficients are approximated using the weighted least squares criterion for all pixels within a given neighborhood. The weighting consists of two components: certainty and applicability. Certainty is associated with the pixel values in the neighborhood. Additionally, outside the image, the certainty is zero, so these pixels have no impact on the flow estimation coefficient.

Applicability determines the relative weight of pixels in the neighborhood based on their position within the neighborhood, giving more weight to the central pixel and gradually decreasing radially from the central pixel. Additionally, the size of the applicability window will determine the scale of the structures captured by the expansion coefficient.

From this point, a global displacement d can be calculated, obtaining the new signal $f2$ such that:

$$f_2(x) = f_1(x - d) = (x - d)^T A_1 (x - d) + b_1^T (x - d) + c_1 \tag{16}$$

$$f_2(x) = f_1(x - d) = (x)^T A_1 (x) + (b_1 - 2A_1 d)^T (x) + d^T A d - b_1^T d + c_1 \tag{17}$$

$$f_2(x) = f_1(x - d) = (x)^T A_1 (x) + b_2^T (x) + c_2 \tag{18}$$

By equating the coefficients with $f(x)$, we obtain:

$$A_1 = A_2 \tag{19}$$

$$b_2 = (b_1 - 2A_1 d) \tag{20}$$

$$c_2 = d^T A d - b_1^T d + c_1 \tag{21}$$

This allows us to obtain a vector d for each pixel, which represents the direction and magnitude of motion in that pixel. Additionally, the estimation of the instantaneous flow rate if_i can be obtained from the contributions of the particles or features being tracked within a region of interest.

$$d = -\frac{1}{2} A^{-1} (b_2 - b_1) \tag{22}$$

In this way, using the formula of the polynomial expansion coefficient, it is possible to calculate the displacement of the vector at any point in the image, assuming that there is overlap between the regions of interest.

The total displacement can be estimated as:

$$\bar{b} = b_1 - 2A_1(\bar{d}) \tag{23}$$

We know $\overline{d}$, A_1, b_1

$$D = -\frac{1}{2}A^{-1}(b_2 + \overline{d} - b_1) \tag{24}$$

Therefore, an iterative approach can be employed, in which each successive iteration provides an improved estimate of the displacement vector. These iterations can terminate when the change in the displacement vector falls below a threshold in consecutive iterations or when a specific number of iterations is reached. Consequently, it can be stated that the region of interest in the current and previous frames aligns. Next, the Farneback algorithm is applied to obtain the displacement vector at each pixel, denoted as $v_i(x(i,j))$. The resulting vector is then converted to polar coordinates, obtaining the corresponding magnitude and angle. Finally, the obtained magnitude in each frame is globally normalized, as we now have both the magnitude and angle of the optical flow. This enables the representation of optical flow using the HSV color space.

Por lo tanto, se puede emplear un enfoque iterativo en el cual cada iteración sucesiva proporciona una estimación mejorada del vector de desplazamiento. Estas iteraciones pueden finalizar cuando el cambio en el vector de desplazamiento caiga por debajo de un umbral en iteraciones consecutivas, o cuando se alcance un número específico de iteraciones.

En consecuencia, se puede afirmar que la región de interés en los fotogramas actual y anteriores coincide.

Luego, se aplica el algoritmo de FarnerBack para obtener el vector de desplazamiento en cada píxel, denotado como $v_i(x(i,j))$. Este vector se descompone en sus componentes dx y dy. A continuación, se convierte el vector resultante a coordenadas polares, obteniendo la magnitud y el ángulo correspondientes.

Finalmente, se normaliza globalmente la magnitud obtenida en cada fotograma, ya que ahora disponemos de la magnitud y el ángulo del optical flow. Esto permite representar el optical flow mediante el espacio de color HSV.

Optical Flow Representations. In this work, two representations were chosen to visualize the optical flow, the first one based on the HSV color model.

HSV is a color model used in image processing, composed of three components: hue, saturation, and value. Hue represents the position of the color in the spectrum, saturation indicates the intensity of the color, and value represents the brightness. This model allows for the separation and individual adjustment of these components, facilitating control and manipulation of colors in an image. It is useful for selecting specific color ranges and creating intuitive color maps.

The second representation was achieved by incorporating a Jet color map to illustrate the magnitude, with arrows showing the direction of the flow. Both representations can be visualized in Fig. 8.

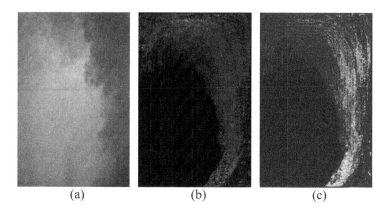

(a)   (b)   (c)

Fig. 8. Instantaneous flow visualization in a frame using the FarnerBack method: a) original image, b) Optical flow in HSV representation, c) Optical flow in color map representation.

Stage 4 - Global Flow Estimation:

In this stage, the obtained results are used to generate a sequence with the most significant magnitudes.

This process is performed iteratively for each pair of consecutive frames in the input video. The optical flow is calculated as the displacement of each pixel between the two frames, which allows us to determine the direction and magnitude of the motion.

In each iteration, a pair of consecutive frames is taken and converted to grayscale for easier processing. Then, the FarnerBack-based function is applied to the frames to calculate the optical flow between them. This function returns a matrix called gf, which has the same shape as the input frames.

The matrix gf represents the optical flow at each pixel in the image. Each element of the matrix is a two-element vector indicating the optical displacement in the horizontal (u) and vertical (v) directions for that specific pixel.

During the calculation of optical flow for each frame pair, various operations and visualizations are performed with the obtained results. For example, color maps are generated to represent the optical flow, the magnitude and angle of the flow are calculated, thresholds are applied to identify regions of interest, and the optical flow is accumulated for a global estimation.

At the end of the process, frames with the most significant magnitudes are stored in a video, allowing us to obtain a global estimation of the optical flow.

Stage 5 - Characterization of Global Flow Estimation

Global flow estimation provides a comprehensive description of motion in a video by considering optical flow across all regions and throughout the entire video. This characterization allows for thorough analysis and a comprehensive understanding of the motion patterns present in the image sequence.

When calculating global optical flow, valuable information is obtained regarding the direction and magnitude of motion at each pixel throughout the entire video. This information can be used for various purposes, such as object tracking, motion change detection, and scene dynamics analysis, among others. Characterizing global optical flow offers an overview of motion in the video, enabling the identification of common motion patterns, areas of high activity, and stable regions. Additionally, it provides quantitative measurements of motion, such as velocity and acceleration in different parts of the video.

With this characterization, it is possible to perform comparative analysis between different videos or compare them with other measurement methods, such as Computational Fluid Dynamics (CFD). To do so, the region with the highest velocity, indicated by a more intense color, often red, is selected. This allows for the normalization of values across all frames and enables the accurate and appropriate generation of velocity profiles. To carry out this process, it is necessary to decompose the image into its three color components: red, green, and blue (RGB), as this allows for greater control and processing of each color component of each frame separately. In this case, we are interested in tracking the blue component, so we will perform this operation. We will select the pixel with the highest saturation and extract the value of the blue component (P_B), which will serve as our reference pixel. With this information, we can establish the relationship between P_B and the desired maximum pixel value (P_{max}) to be used for pixel normalization in the frames, as shown in Eq. (25).

$$Multiplo = \frac{P_B}{P_{max}} \tag{25}$$

Additionally, we need to create a matrix gfc where we will store the frame with the magnitude and select the blue component of all the pixels in the gfc matrix. Next, we will divide each value of the blue component by the factor $Multiplo$. This will result in a normalized image, where the pixel values are adjusted in relation to the specified maximum value (P_B), as shown in Eq. (26).

$$gfc_{normalized} = \frac{gfc}{Multiplo} \tag{26}$$

This process is important, as if the desired maximum value is, for example, 255, the multiplication factor will be the result of dividing the value of the reference pixel by 255. Then, by dividing all pixel values in the image by this factor, the pixel values will be proportionally adjusted to be within the range of 0 to 255 (Fig. 9).

Stage 6 - Obtaining Velocity Profiles. Once the characterization of the global flow estimation is completed, we can extract its profile for analysis and compare it with the results obtained using the CFD method. At this point, we have normalized the values and selected the pixel with the maximum value. This allows us to obtain a normalized profile vp. To achieve this, we generate a sequence of values corresponding to each pixel, which can then be graphically represented as a profile in any section of the video image being analyzed (Fig. 10). To observe the result of the profile graph values, we can refer to Fig. 11.

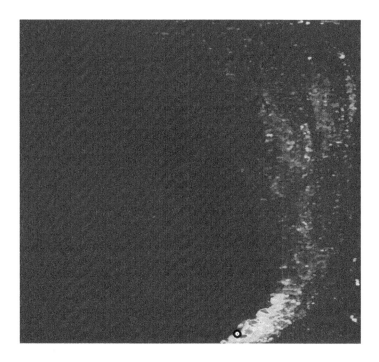

Fig. 9. Selection of pixel with highest intensity.

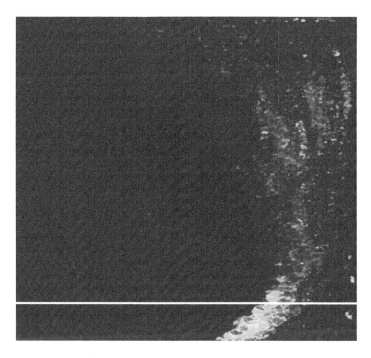

Fig. 10. Capture of profile vp in the developed system corresponding to the lower zone of the reactor.

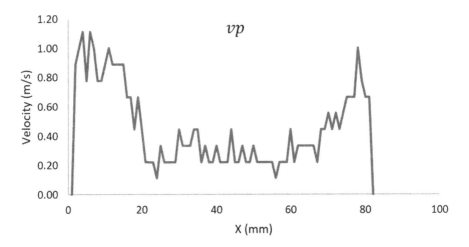

Fig. 11. Velocity profile *vp*.

3   Results

To demonstrate the outstanding feasibility and effectiveness of the proposed method, we conducted comprehensive analyses on three different reactor configurations, as illustrated in Fig. 2. Additionally, we carried out a meticulous comparison of velocity profiles at three distinct locations within the reactors, namely, at 15 mm, 65 mm, and 117 mm, using both our proposed method and a simulation obtained via Computational Fluid Dynamics (CFD).

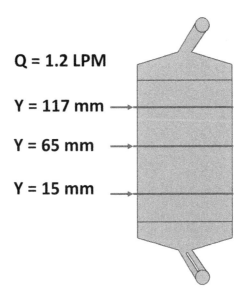

Fig. 12. Representative illustration of the measurement procedures used for the conducted comparison.

Remarkably, the results exhibited a striking resemblance in flow patterns, as clearly depicted in Fig. 12 (Fig. 13).

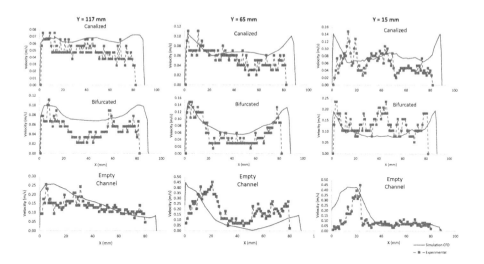

Fig. 13. Experimental velocity profiles obtained through digital image processing. These profiles were compared with those obtained through CFD simulations at a flow rate of 1.2 L/min.

To ensure a thorough quantitative assessment of the obtained results, we employed the widely accepted Mean Squared Error (MSE) metric, commonly employed in regression models and signal comparisons. The MSE serves as a robust measure to gauge the dissimilarity between an original signal and its estimated or reconstructed counterpart.

Mathematically, the MSE is computed as follows:

$$MSE = \frac{1}{n} \sum_{i=1}^{n} (x_{\text{original}_i} - x_{\text{estimated}_i})^2 \qquad (27)$$

With a focus on achieving an exemplary fit, our comprehensive analysis yielded remarkably low MSE values, signifying the remarkable accuracy and precision of our proposed method. This exceptional performance was particularly evident in obtaining velocity profiles of bifurcated electrochemical reactors, which can be vividly observed in Fig. 14. However, it is important to acknowledge the presence of qualitative disparities between the velocity magnitudes obtained from simulations and those extracted experimentally. We hypothesize that the qualitative differences observed between the simulated and experimentally obtained velocity magnitudes can be attributed not only to the complex flow phenomena within the intricate geometries of the distributors but also to the presence of noise introduced during the signal acquisition process. Factors such as lighting variations, sensor noise, and other environmental disturbances can affect the accuracy of the captured image data, leading to discrepancies in the velocity measurements.

Overall, these compelling results affirm the tremendous potential of our method in enhancing the understanding and analysis of electrochemical reactor designs.

	Mean Squared Error (MSE)		
	Y = 117 mm	Y = 65 mm	Y = 15 mm
Canalized	2.334	2.635	7.647
Bifurcated	0.575	0.520	0.594
Empty Chanel	1.979	1.015	1.920

Fig. 14. Comparison of Mean Squared Errors in velocity profile estimation vs CFD.

4 Conclusion

In this work, a novel approach was proposed for the design and analysis of electrochemical reactors, combining computational tools and experimental techniques. An innovative method involving CFD simulations, digital image processing, and data analysis techniques was employed to investigate flow distributors in single-flow electrochemical cells. This novel methodology allowed for a deeper and more accurate understanding of velocity fields in the reactors, providing valuable insights for optimizing their design and operation. By integrating different techniques and comparing experimental results with CFD simulations, a more comprehensive and reliable view of flow behavior in electrochemical reactors was achieved.

The obtained results showed a remarkable resemblance in flow patterns and good agreement with CFD simulations, supporting the effectiveness of the proposed method. However, areas for improvement were identified, and recommendations for future research were proposed, such as the implementation of deep learning techniques to enhance accuracy in velocity profile estimation.

References

1. Afrashteh, N., Inayat, S., Mohsenvand, M., Mohajerani, M.H.: Optical-flow analysis toolbox for characterization of spatiotemporal dynamics in mesoscale optical imaging of brain activity. NeuroImage **153**, 58–74 (2017). https://doi.org/10.1016/j.neuroimage.2017.03.034, https://www.sciencedirect.com/science/article/pii/S1053811917302422

2. Arenas, L., Johnson, R.: Engineering applications of flat electrodes in batteries and fuel cells. J. Power Sources **350**, 120–135 (2017)
3. Arenas, L., Smith, J.: Critical analysis of electrode materials for electrochemical applications. J. Electrochem. Sci. **25**(2), 120–135 (2020)
4. Catañeda, L.F., Rivera, F.F., Pérez, T., Nava, J.L.: Mathematical modeling and simulation of the reaction environment in electrochemical reactors. Curr. Opin. Electrochem. **16**, 75–82 (2019)
5. de Croon, G., De Wagter, C., Seidl, T.: Enhancing optical-flow-based control by learning visual appearance cues for flying robots. Nat. Mach. Intell. **3**(1), 33–41 (2021)
6. Dal Sasso, S.F., Ljubicic, R., Pizarro, A., Pearce, S., Maddock, I., Manfreda, S.: Image-based velocity estimations under different seeded and unseeded river flows. EGU General Assembly 2023 (2023)
7. Eltner, A., Sardemann, H., Grundmann, J.: Flow velocity and discharge measurement in rivers using terrestrial and unmanned-aerial-vehicle imagery. Hydrol. Earth Syst. Sci. **24**(3), 1429–1445 (2020)
8. Escudero González, J., Alberola, A., Amparo López Jiménez, P.: Redox cell hydrodynamics modelling-simulation and experimental validation. Eng. Appl. Comput. Fluid Mech. **7**(2), 168–181 (2013)
9. Escudero-González, J., Amparo Lopez-Jimenez, P.: Redox cell hydrodynamic modelling: towards real improved geometry based on CFD analysis. Eng. Appl. Comput. Fluid Mech. **8**(3), 435–446 (2014)
10. Gleede, M., Johnson, E.: Large-scale synthesis of organic compounds using flat electrodes. J. Chem. Eng. **15**(3), 250–265 (2019)
11. Hashim, H.S., Abdullah, S.N.H.S., Prabuwono, A.S.: Automated visual inspection for metal parts based on morphology and fuzzy rules. In: 2010 International Conference on Computer Applications and Industrial Electronics, pp. 527–531 (2010). https://doi.org/10.1109/ICCAIE.2010.5735137
12. He, L., Ren, X., Gao, Q., Zhao, X., Yao, B., Chao, Y.: The connected-component labeling problem: a review of state-of-the-art algorithms. Pattern Recogn. **70**, 25–43 (2017)
13. Hereijgers, J., Schalck, J., Breugelmans, T.: Mass transfer and hydrodynamic characterization of structured 3d electrodes for electrochemistry. Chem. Eng. J. **384**, 123283 (2020)
14. Honegger, D., Greisen, P., Meier, L., Tanskanen, P., Pollefeys, M.: Real-time velocity estimation based on optical flow and disparity matching. In: 2012 IEEE/RSJ International Conference on Intelligent Robots and Systems, pp. 5177–5182 (2012). https://doi.org/10.1109/IROS.2012.6385530
15. Hreiz, R., Abdelouahed, L., Fuenfschilling, D., Lapicque, F.: Electrogenerated bubbles induced convection in narrow vertical cells: PIV measurements and Euler-Lagrange CFD simulation. Chem. Eng. Sci. **134**, 138–152 (2015)
16. Iturrate, I., Østergaard, E.H., Rytter, M., Savarimuthu, T.R.: Learning and correcting robot trajectory keypoints from a single demonstration. In: 2017 3rd International Conference on Control, Automation and Robotics (ICCAR), pp. 52–59. IEEE (2017)
17. Lacasa, M., Thompson, D.: Environmental applications of flat electrodes in water treatment. Environ. Eng. J. **40**(4), 300–315 (2019)
18. Liang, C.J., Kamat, V.R., Menassa, C.C., McGee, W.: Trajectory-based skill learning for overhead construction robots using generalized cylinders with orientation. J. Comput. Civil Eng. **36**(2), 04021036 (2022)

19. Lv, X., Zhao, S., Yu, X., Zhao, B.: Residential floor plan recognition and reconstruction. In: Proceedings of the IEEE/CVF Conference on Computer Vision and Pattern Recognition, pp. 16717–16726 (2021)
20. Marquez-Montes, R.A., Collins-Martinez, V.H., Perez-Reyes, I., Chavez-Flores, D., Graeve, O.A., Ramos-Sánchez, V.H.: Electrochemical engineering assessment of a novel 3d-printed filter-press electrochemical reactor for multipurpose laboratory applications. ACS Sustain. Chem. Eng. **8**(9), 3896–3905 (2020)
21. Miller, A., Moore, A., Leonard, G.: From generalisation to segmentation: Douglas-peucker-ramer and movement data. Geocomputation 2019 (2019)
22. Otsu, N.: A threshold selection method from gray-level histograms. IEEE Trans. Syst. Man Cybern. **9**(1), 62–66 (1979)
23. Pardo, J.M., Moya-Albor, E., Ortega-Ibarra, G., Brieva, J.: Freezing front velocity estimation using image processing techniques. Measurement **151**, 107085 (2020). https://doi.org/10.1016/j.measurement.2019.107085, https://www.sciencedirect.com/science/article/pii/S0263224119309510
24. Pourasad, Y., Cavallaro, F.: A novel image processing approach to enhancement and compression of x-ray images. Int. J. Environ. Res. Public Health **18**(13), 6724 (2021)
25. Rivera, F., Hidalgo, P., Castañeda-Záldivar, F., Terol-Villalobos, I., Orozco, G.: Phenomenological behavior coupling hydrodynamics and electrode kinetics in a flow electrochemical reactor. Numerical analysis and experimental validation. Chem. Eng. J. **355**, 457–469 (2019)
26. Rivera, F.F., Miranda-Alcántara, B., Orozco, G., de León, C.P., Arenas, L.F.: Pressure drop analysis on the positive half-cell of a cerium redox flow battery using computational fluid dynamics: mathematical and modelling aspects of porous media. Front. Chem. Sci. Eng. **15**(2), 399–409 (2021)
27. Román, J.C.M., Legal-Ayala, H., Noguera, J.L.V.: Applications of multiscale mathematical morphology to contrast enhancement and images fusion. In: 2020 15th Iberian Conference on Information Systems and Technologies (CISTI), pp. 1–7. IEEE (2020)
28. Rondón, C.V.N., Carvajal, D.A.C., Casadiego, S.A.C., Delgado, B.M., Ibarra, D.G.: Una aproximación a la detección de bordes en imágenes médicas mediante análisis de histograma y gradiente morfológico. Ingeniería Competitividad: Revista Científica Tecnológica **24**(2), 1–18 (2022)
29. Salazar Colores, S., Garduño Aparicio, M., Moya Sánchez, E.U., Lopez Torres, C.V., Ramos Arreguín, J.M.: Dark channel applied for reduction of the effects of non-uniform illumination in image binarization. Comput. Sist. **23**(2), 409–416 (2019)
30. Shields, A., Nagesh, S.V.S., Ionita, C., Bednarek, D.R., Rudin, S.: Characterization of velocity patterns produced by pulsatile and constant flows using 1000 fps high-speed angiography (HSA). In: Gimi, B.S., Krol, A. (eds.) Medical Imaging 2021: Biomedical Applications in Molecular, Structural, and Functional Imaging, vol. 11600, pp. 342–359. International Society for Optics and Photonics, SPIE (2021). https://doi.org/10.1117/12.2580888
31. Vennelakanti, A., Shreya, S., Rajendran, R., Sarkar, D., Muddegowda, D., Hanagal, P.: Traffic sign detection and recognition using a CNN ensemble. In: 2019 IEEE International Conference on Consumer Electronics (ICCE), pp. 1–4. IEEE (2019)
32. Zhao, L., Shi, G.: A method for simplifying ship trajectory based on improved Douglas-Peucker algorithm. Ocean Eng. **166**, 37–46 (2018)

Search Space Reduction in Road Networks for the Ambulance Location and Allocation Optimization Problems: A Real Case Study

Miguel Medina-Perez[✉] [iD], Valeria Karina Legaria-Santiago[iD],
Giovanni Guzmán[iD], and Magdalena Saldana-Perez[iD]

Centro de Investigación en Computación, Instituto Politécnico Nacional,
Juan de Dios Bátiz, 07738 México City, Mexico
{jmedinap2022,vlegarias2019}@cic.ipn.mx, {jguzmanl,amsaldanap}@ipn.mx

Abstract. One particular problem with ambulance location is when, after a disaster, there are no fixed bases for all the available ambulances, and the entity in charge must assign them a temporal location to efficiently provide emergency medical care. Most of the ambulance location problems are modeled as extensions of the set covering problem or the location problem. However, there is no efficient algorithm that can solve them in polynomial time, given that their solutions cannot be applied in emergency environments since they require a quick response. This paper describes a proposal to allocate temporary ambulance bases on streets that meet specific requirements. The contribution of this work is a methodology to reduce the search space of possible locations, simplifying the graph as much as it cans, and thereby will reduce the execution time when an algorithm to determine the locations is applied. The proposal includes a mathematical model integrated with two objective functions; one to minimize the distance between bases and demand points and the other to minimize the number of ambulance bases. This article presents the results of the methodology to reduce the search space, applied in a real-based study case, from 2017 when the strongest earthquake in Mexico's history, collapsed several buildings in Mexico City. The emergency demand locations are carried out using Geospatial Information Systems (GIS) from an open-source platform. The methodology uses data prepossessing and an optimization algorithm to obtain the best available locations to reach the emergency demand points.

Keywords: Ambulance location problem · P-median problem · Optimization · Geographic information systems · Disasters

1 Introduction

International Federation of Red Cross and Red Crescent Societies (IFRC) defines disasters as "serious disruptions to the functioning of a community that exceeds

M. F. Mata-Rivera et al. (Eds.): WITCOM 2023, CCIS 1906, pp. 157–175, 2023.
https://doi.org/10.1007/978-3-031-45316-8_12

its capacity to cope using its own resources" [1]. According to The Pan American Health Organization (PAHO) and the World Health Organization (WHO), one of the worst natural disasters that can occur in an urban area is a major earthquake. During the last decades, earthquakes caused nearly 750 million deaths around the world, and more than 125 million affected people, including injured people from building collapses. During or after the emergency phase of a disaster, health facilities and transportation are also affected, thereby disrupting delivery service and access to care [2,3].

In 2017, Mexico experienced the largest earthquake in 100 years [4,5], and there was no national protocol in place for medical services to respond during the disaster [7]. However, 32 years earlier, in 1985, one of the deadliest earthquakes in the country's history had occurred [6]. During the disaster, the time response had a mean of 46 min with around 290 ambulances in service. 25 of them belonged to the public sector, for the attention of more than 8 million people in Mexico City. It is worth mentioning that 25 million people pass daily through the city. Until 2019, the government recognized the deficiencies of ambulance service and began strategies to increase units, to unify the service response, and to improve communication for coordinated operations [8–11].

Therefore, in this paper, we study the real case of the 2017 Mexico earthquake and propose a reduction in the search space of the possible streets for temporal ambulance location bases. To do this, the modeling of the problem uses a p-median problem, where multiple conditions of the real case were considered. The implementation required Open Street Maps for data acquisition, QGIS for mapping, and a Python environment for programming the algorithms.

The presentation of this work includes seven sections, considering the previous Introduction. Section 2 mentions the Theoretical Background and the state of the art. Section 3 describes all the considerations and the equations for the Mathematical Model. Section 4 explains the Methodology. Section 5 reports the Results. Section 6 presents the Conclusions of the work. Finally, Sect. 7 shows our suggestions for future work.

2   Theoretical Background

2.1   Location Problems

Location problems are used to optimally allocate facilities or service centers, maximizing or minimizing functions to reduce costs, times, or distances to reach end users. An application of this type of problem is in emergency services, particularly ambulances, due to the quickness with which they must act in disaster care. The simplest form of multiple facility locations is the p-median problem (1) and the maximum covering problem (6).

P-Median Problem: "This location problem consists of a set F of m facilities, a set C of n clients, and a matrix D of dimension nxm for the distances d_{ij} between each client $i \in C$ and the facility $j \in F$. Its aim is to determine the optimal location of the p facilities and allocation of clients to each facility in such a way that the total cost is minimized. The objective function of the model is defined in (1) which minimizes the summary of the d_{ij} distances for each client or demand location. (2) makes sure that each client is assigned to a facility; (3) makes sure that each client is attended by precisely one facility; (4) indicates that p facilities must be assigned, and(5) indicates the variable domain (binary)" [12]. As the location problems, the p-median problem also has NP-hard computational complexity, which implies that cannot be solved for large problems optimally.

$$\text{Minimize } f = \sum_{i=1}^{n} \sum_{j=1}^{m} d_{ij} x_{ij} \tag{1}$$

$$s.t. \sum_{j=1}^{m} x_{ij} = 1, \quad \forall i, \tag{2}$$

$$x_{ij} \leq y_j, \quad \forall ij, \tag{3}$$

$$\sum_{j=1}^{m} y_j = p, \tag{4}$$

$$x_{ij}, y_j \in 0, 1 \tag{5}$$

Maximum Coverage Problem: It is a specific instance of a Set Coverage Problem, and its goal is to choose a set of p facilities to maximize the coverage of elements. The Y_i decision variable indicates if the node i is attended by a facility. Therefore, the objective function (6) is to maximize the demand-weighted sum of the nodes attended by the sited facilities. The decision variable X_j denotes the decision to locate (or not) a potential facility site j. Constraint (7) explains if a demand node is covered at least by one sited facility, with N_i as the set of potential facilities that suitably cover demand node i. The variable a_i represents the cost of assigning demand point i to facility j, it can also be seen as the population to be served at demand node i. Equation (8) indicates that the sum of the facility siting decision must be equal to the p facilities to be located. Equation (9) specifies the binary domain of the variables: X_j takes a value of 1 if the potential facility site j is selected, 0 otherwise; Y_i takes a value of 1 if the demand node i is suitably covered at least by one sited facilities and 0 otherwise [13, 14].

$$\text{Maximize } f = \sum_{i \in D} a_i Y_i \tag{6}$$

$$s.t. \sum_{j \in N_i} X_j - Y_i \leq 0 \, \forall i \in D, \tag{7}$$

$$\sum_{j} X_j = p, \tag{8}$$

$$x_i, y_j \in 0, 1, \tag{9}$$

2.2   Ambulance Location Problem

The ambulance location problem (ALP) is treated in various works as an extension of The Set Covering Problem [15,16], which is a combinatorial problem that aims to find the smallest number of subsets that cover all the elements of the universe. While others use the p-median problem to model their problems [17].

For the ALP, the goal is to find the best distribution of ambulances to maximize coverage and minimize response times. Variations over location problems are proposed depending on the specific attends to be solved. Under disaster environments, facility locations often deal with limited facility resources, demand saturation, and uncertain and insufficient units for demand points [13].

2.3   NP-Hard Problems

Computational complexity theory classifies problems based on the difficulty of finding a solution using the available computational resources. Complexity theory proposes a formal criterion for what it means to be feasible decidable, i.e. "it can be solved by a conventional Turing machine in a number of steps which is proportional to a polynomial function of the size of its input" [18]. The complexity in time and space is defined in terms of the worst-case time and space complexity of the most efficient algorithm for deciding.

NP-hard problems manage real-world problems and they are known for their difficulty to solve them optimally in a reasonable time, as the problem size increases. The trouble is that as the search space of the problem increases, the time required to find the optimal solution grows exponentially. Therefore, their difficulty is at least as hard as the hardest problem in NP, which is solved in non-deterministic polynomial time.

NP-hard problems often require exploring a large number of possible solutions, but that makes them computationally challenging. To face them, approximation solutions or heuristic algorithms are used to find acceptable solutions within a reasonable time, although there is no guarantee to be optimal.

2.4   Greedy Algorithms

"Algorithms for optimization problems typically go through a sequence of steps, with a set of choices at each step" [19]. Greedy algorithms solve problems by making the choice that looks best at the current step. They are characterized by being simple and efficient algorithms, although it is not guaranteed to always reach the optimal result. It makes a locally optimal choice to optimize some underlying criterion. One of the most representative applications of a greedy algorithm is used to find the shortest paths in a graph [19,20].

2.5   State of the Art

Location problems are known to be NP-hard [15], which means that finding optimal solutions for them can be computationally challenging due to the complexity of the solution space. Consequently, due to computational limitations, it is often not feasible to achieve optimal solutions. However, metaheuristics offer a practical approach to tackle these problems by leveraging optimization techniques that can efficiently analyze extensive data sets and generate solutions that are either optimal or close to optimal within a reasonable timeframe.

Many works around the optimal location for facilities, warehouses, or emergency services, adopt location problems and extend them to their specific conditions. Mohri et al. [16] used an ALP for covering inherently rare and random road crashes. They adopted a covering problem with edge demand and propose an edge maximal covering location problem with partial coverage of the facilities on the edges. They applied their model to a real case using the Mashhad network, one of the more populated cities in Iran. The results were compared in two cases, one with random crashes and the second with real observed crashes. Random crashes were created by using an Empirical Bayes (EB) method. They considered the demand for road crashes and also possible administrative problems. Therefore, the stations were prioritized so the policymakers could choose the best option considering budget or other restrictions.

Barojas-Payán et al. [12] focused on determining the optimal location of pre-positioned warehouses to provide emergency supplies efficiently to people affected by a natural disaster. The purpose of that work was to develop a support tool for timely and efficient decision-making during hydro-meteorological natural phenomena. Their mathematical model integrated two elements: one based on the optimal locations of the warehouses to satisfy the highest number of people, and the other for the establishment of the inventory levels in those facilities. The authors attached two conditions two the model. First, the locations could not be impacted by the natural phenomenon and second, the location had to reach a minimum covered distance. The model was evaluated with data from two real scenarios. The results showed a variety of distance feasibility and exposed how they affect location decisions.

In another work, the research group of Barojas-Payán et al. [17] proposed a hybrid capacities multi-facility location model. The model identified multiple feasible locations for the warehouses according to the specific needs of the affected people. In contrast with [16], evaluating the suitability of the location returned by the model was beyond the scope. Instead, the relevance of this work was focused on the development of a hybrid model by integrating two heuristic methods and two exact methods. The model integrated a p-median algorithm, the metaheuristics of the nearest neighbor algorithm, and a Greedy Randomized Adaptative Search Procedure (GRASP) algorithm, for the identification of suitable locations of warehouses. In addition, the hybrid model also used the continuous review (q, R) inventory model with uncertain demand for establishing the economic lot size for each product, the reorder point, safety stock, and shortage.

3   Mathematical Model

Proposals for modeling the ambulance location problem are based on specific circumstances about the geographic zone studied in each paper; furthermore, some facts are assumed about the operation and coordination of the emergency medical services involved in that particular location, so it is not always possible to apply the same model for regions with different characteristics and different information available. In most of the literature about the ambulances location and allocation problems, it is assumed that the possible locations of temporary bases (PLTB) are known, and the optimization problem consists in deciding which of them is the best based on an objective function, nevertheless, these possible locations are not always known.

When there are not enough predefined sites for locating fleets of ambulances, the solution in practice is to use the road network, for example, using the streets nearest to the demand points. If this solution is translated directly to the ambulance location problems in the literature, this would imply a combinatorial optimization problem where the search space is every road network segment or every possible intersection in the road network; for the case study of Mexico City, this means a search space of $129,442!$ combinations. This translation of the problem is not suitable for real-world implementation, so the first procedure needed to solve the problem is to obtain all the PLTB. Based on practical considerations and using information that is available from open voluntary data sources (Open Street Maps), it is possible to adjust the model for similar situations in different regions where this data is available.

Previous to defining the mathematical model, the following assumptions are considered:

1. All possible locations of temporary bases have a finite capacity that is proportional to their length.
2. Localization of demand points is known, and all of them have a high probability of having at least one patient requiring medical assistance.
3. The destination hospital for each patient is always the nearest one with availability, so the route from the demand point to the hospital does not belong to the optimization problem.
4. The medical assistance service is heterogeneous, so multiple services (public and private) must be capable of incorporating their vehicles into the response plan, even if they are not familiar with it.
5. The estimated number of patients for each demand point is not known in this proposal, so all of them are considered with the same priority.
6. Speed limits over the road network are not considered for calculating travel distances, since ambulances are allowed to violate these limits.
7. All ambulances are considered of the same type, so the kind of injuries of the patients is not part of the optimization problem in this proposal.

Based on the data available from public repositories about the road network and about the casualties in our case study, the next nomenclature and definitions are defined:

- $G_r = \{V_r, E_r\}$: Directed homogeneous graph, represents the road network. Each vertex $v \in V_r$ is a join between highways and each edge $e \in E_r$ is a highway.
- $G = \{V, E\}$: Complete bipartite heterogeneous graph, it is a simplification of the graph G_r, where each vertex $v \in V$ is either a demand point $d_i \in D$ or a PLTB $b_i \in B$, such that:

$$V = D \cup B, D \cap B = \emptyset$$

And each edge represents the minimum distance between each pair of vertex $(b_i, d_j) \; \forall i \in B, j \in D$ given the topology of graph G_r.
- D: Set of all demand points.
- B: Set of all PLTB, it represents the decision variable.
- L: Set of maximum capacities of each corresponding edge, this is, l_i is the maximum number of ambulances allowed in the base b_i.
- C: Origin - destination weight matrix, where c_{ij} is the cost of travel from the base b_i to the demand point d_j.
- M: Boolean matrix that indicates whether a demand point d_j is covered by the base b_i.
- α: is the maximum number of available ambulances.

Having this information, the proposed model of the location problem consists of a variant of the p-median problem, where there are two main objectives: f_1, f_2, and four constraints.

$$Minimize \; f_1 = \sum_{i \in B} \sum_{j \in D} c_{ij} m_{ij} \tag{10}$$

$$Minimize \; f_2 = \sum_{i \in B} b_i \tag{11}$$

Subject to:

$$m_{ij} = \begin{cases} 1, & \text{if } b_i = 1 \text{ and } c_{ij} < c_{hj} \; \forall b_h \in B | b_h = 1 \text{ and } h \neq i \\ 0, & \text{otherwise} \end{cases} \tag{12}$$

$$\sum_{i \in B} m_{ij} = 1, \forall j \in D \tag{13}$$

$$\sum_{i \in B} l_i \geq \alpha \tag{14}$$

$$b_i \in \{0, 1\} \tag{15}$$

The Eq. 10 defines the objective of the classical p-median problem, where the target is to minimize the cost between each PLTB and its covered demand point. The purpose of the second objective function (Eq. 13) is to minimize the number of PLTB in use, since in practical situations, having multiple fleets of ambulances along the city requires a bigger coordination between different medical assistance services.

The first constraint (Eq. 12), just defines m as a boolean matrix and sets the temporary base that covers each demand point as the nearest one in use (where $b_i = 1$). The second constraint (Eq. 13) ensures that each demand point is covered by only one temporary base in use. The third constraint (Eq. 14) ensures that the sum of the capacities of all temporary bases in use is enough to locate all the ambulances available to cope with the situation. Finally, the last constraint just ensures that the set of PLTB is boolean, where 1 means that the base is in use, and 0 is the opposite.

3.1   Dynamic Version of the Proposed Model

As mentioned before, the problem in this proposal is considered a static problem, when there is a set of demand points that needs to be assisted, but this will always change over time, meaning that some demand points will be fully covered (with no more victims left), and some other demand points could arise.

An additional proposal to adapt the mathematical model to a dynamic situation is to add another objective that takes as input the previous solution. In this way, a period could be defined to find another solution, but starting the search with no prior information could lead to very different solutions that would require a significant movement of vehicles and personnel. Using the previous solution as the initial solution for the next iteration could be useful, but depending on the new data (new state of demand points) and the algorithm used, this does not guarantee to get an optimal solution that is similar to the previous one.

To achieve a similar solution, it is necessary to define similar first; in this context, similar could be defined in two ways: All the PLTB used in the solution B_{t+1} found at the period $t + 1$ can be reached from the previous solution B_t at period t within a certain interval of time or distance Δ; this means that the new solution is close to the previous one, based on a predefined parameter; for example 5 min or 500 m.

This similarity can be evaluated by the function f_A in Eq. 16

$$Minimize\ f_X = \sum_{i \in B_t} \sum_{j \in B_{t+1}} s_{ij} g_{ij} \tag{16}$$

Subject to:

$$g_{ij} = \begin{cases} 1, & \text{if } b_{t,i} = 1 \text{ and } s_{ij} < s_{i,h} \forall b_{t+1,h} \in B_{t+1} | b_{t+1,h} = 1 \\ 0, & \text{otherwise} \end{cases} \tag{17}$$

$$\sum_{i \in B_t} g_{ij} = 1, \forall j \in B_{t+1} \tag{18}$$

$$s_{ij} g_{ij} \leq \Delta\ , \forall g_{ij} \neq 0 \tag{19}$$

where s_{ij} is the square matrix origin-destination from the point $b_i \in B_t$ to all other points $b_j \in B_{t+1}$.

In this case, the constraint in Eq. 17 guarantees that ambulances located at PLTB in B_t are relocated at the nearest PLTB in the new solution B_{t+1}. Notice that the value of this objective is 0 when both solutions are the same, and the graph of the problem is not bipartite since it considers all possible connections between vertices in B.

The constraints from Eqs. 18 and 19 ensure that all ambulances travel to only one base in the new solution and that all movements require less than Δ units, respectively. Finally, the other way of defining similarity between solutions is to use the hamming distance, so the other possible objective to minimize for the dynamic version is defined by Eq. 20.

$$min\ f_Y = hamming(B_t, B_{t+1}) \tag{20}$$

where hamming is defined as:

$$hamming(A, B) = \sum_{i=1}^{n} (A_i \neq B_i) \tag{21}$$

Implementing this objective function requires fewer resources compared to Eq. 16 since it doesn't involve distance computation or constraints. With f_X the optimization algorithms to solve the problem would try to move as little as possible from one solution to the next one over time, and with f_Y will try to continue using the same PLTB from the previous solution.

Once the mathematical problem is defined, real data needs to be obtained from the case study. In this case, the data is partially available, for example, the shortest path between any pair of points in the city can be obtained using multiple software tools; the road network can be obtained from open-source repositories and the demand points are available from official repositories; nevertheless, the PLTB is not known, so the following methodology is proposed in order to generate the data.

4   Methodology

Figure 1 shows the methodology of this work, where the main steps involved data acquisition, cleaning data to obtain the graph of interest, and the procedures to find the PLTB. Following subsections explain in detail each one of the steps.

4.1   Data Acquisition

Open Street Maps (OSM) [21] is a free online mapping platform to upload and download collaborative data from the map of the entire world. The level of detail corresponds to the quality of the information uploaded voluntarily by users. As the first step of the methodology, the directed homogeneous graph G_r is constructed with the roadways of Mexico City, Mexico, downloaded from

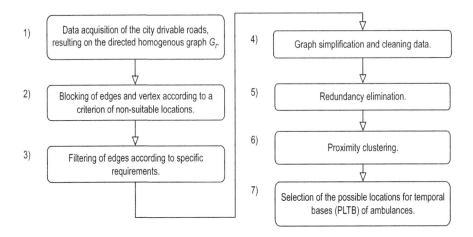

Fig. 1. Methodology to find the possible locations of temporary bases.

OSM. The edges represent all kinds of drivable roads, and the vertex represents intersections between edges.

To allocate ambulances based on the street, it is not efficient to consider residential roads due to their limited accessibility to multiple demand points. Therefore, the initial step is to exclude all residential streets from G_r.

4.2 Blocking of Edges and Vertex

In this case study, the demand points correspond to the locations of the buildings that collapsed during an earthquake. These points are considered unuseful for being one of the PLTB due to the danger of being a risk area. Therefore, those points were added to the list of blocking vertices to be excluded from consideration in the PLTB.

As this work studies a real-based case of disaster, the demand points were obtained from the records of the Open Data Portal of Mexico City [22]. After the 2017 earthquake, many buildings collapsed instantaneously, while others collapsed after a few hours. At that time, the government published a website where the location of the collapses could be requested through an API REST; currently, that data is available as a single shape file with a point layer containing the location of the buildings that collapsed, their address, and some other attributes.

At the moment of this paper, the data included all the collapses registered during this earthquake. However, in a real-time application, the location of the collapse could be added to the block vertex list as soon as the information is updated.

Edges touching blocking vertex are also unsuitable, so the PLTB had at least one edge of separation distance from a demand point.

Other important unsuitable locations are the highways where the hospitals are, as this would cause difficulties to reach the patients. Data of the active hospitals in Mexico City was obtained from the same website [22].

Unsuitable edges were registered and resumed in the next step.

4.3   Filtering of Edges According to Specific Requirements

There were three requirements for the consideration of a road as one PLTB.

- Edges with at least three lanes.
- Not be a link road.
- If the road data does not have the lane numbers nor specify if it is a link (as it comes from voluntary data), then the road must be at least a secondary road.

Roads that did not meet the above requirements or were marked as unsuitable in the previous step were filtered from the G_r graph.

4.4   Graph Simplification and Cleaning Data

Filtering of edges generates two types of vertex that can be deleted to simplify the G_r graph:

- Isolated vertices, i.e., vertices with no edges connecting them to the G_r graph.
- Vertices that remains between two edges with the same direction but with no more edges than those of the union. Since these vertices have the same direction, the graph can be simplified by deleting and replacing them with a single edge connecting the two original edges.

4.5   Redundancy Elimination

In the previous steps, the graph has been explored in terms of the edges, since these are the real possible locations for the ambulances; however, as they would be arranged in a queue over the road, the position from which the distance must be calculated to the demand points is the terminal node of the edge; this means the vertex v of the edge (u, v).

Based on this idea, it is possible to have overlapped PLTB in road intersections, mainly due to two-way streets. These overlapped points need to be merged in order to have only one PLTB in these intersections, but considering that its capacity and accumulated length is the sum of all edges that contain that vertex. Visiting all vertices once and using a dictionary is enough to avoid this problem; if one vertex was already visited, add the capacity, length, and original edge name to it and maintain the vertex as a single instance. At the end of this step, the edges (highway segments) $(a, v), (b, v), (c, v), (d, v)$ are considered as a single PLTB v.

4.6   Proximity Clustering

At this step, there are no overlapping points, although there are vertices close to
other vertices that can be visited in a small period. Therefore, considering them
as separate PLTB would not be appropriate. A greedy algorithm is proposed to
simplify the graph by avoiding vertices that are very close to other vertices as
follows:

1. Define the set of all vertices V
2. Define an empty list of clusters.
3. Define the allowed distance λ or time for connectivity (e.g. 1 min or 100 m).
   For this case was considered 1 min at 20 Km/h.
4. Choose randomly one vertex v to start exploring
5. Perform depth-first search starting from v but just in the opposite direction
   (visit nodes that can reach v). During this step, only consider neighbors that
   can be visited from its predecessors without violating λ.
6. Identify the deepest node d, such that exist a sequence of vertices from d
   to u, where each edge of the sequence don't violates λ individually. (it does
   not matter if the sum of the sequence is higher than λ.
7. Starting from d, perform a breadth-first search, with the following considerations:
   – Only visit and maintain neighbors that can be visited from the vertex d
     without violating *lamba* if they have a degree equal to or lower than their
     predecessors.
   – If there is a vertex that can be visited but violates λ or has a higher
     degree, append to a list p of pending clusters.
8. When there are no more vertices to visit from d as starting point, create a list
   g of vertices connected to d. That is a cluster where d is the representative
   vertex of all other vertices in g.
9. Append g to the list of clusters.
10. Combine information of vertices in g and append it to v.
11. Mark all vertices in g as clustered and remove them from V
    – If p is not empty: Take the first vertex in p, make it $= d$ and go to 7.
    – else:
      • if V is not empty: Take another vertex from V, make it $= v$ and go
        to 5
      • else: Finished, return the list of clusters.

It can be seen that this algorithm does not guarantee the best solution but
prioritizes the degree of the node to be the most representative vertex of its
cluster, so in each sub-graph found in V based on the proximity λ, it is more
probable to group vertices with its neighbor with a higher degree hence, creating
larger clusters.

4.7 Selection of the Possible Locations for Temporal Bases (PLTB) of Ambulances

The last step is to discard PLTBs that are unsuitable due to external reasons such as traffic over the highways, damaged infrastructure, or other risks generated by the disaster. In this case, no more PLTBs were discarded.

After the proposed methodology, optimization algorithms could be applied to solve the optimization problem and find a good solution in an acceptable time.

5   Results

Following the proposed methodology, results were obtained and presented in this section.

In the earthquake of 2017, there were 38 buildings collapsed, represented as the demand points in the mathematical model (the yellow diamond symbol in Fig. 2, Fig. 3, and Fig. 4). At the beginning of the disaster, the authorities did not know how many people were injured and going to need an ambulance. Therefore, all the demand points need to be treated with equal prioritization, as that information is unknown. Then, the 290 available ambulances need to be allocated at strategic locations to cover the demand points and reach them efficiently.

In 2017, the Mexico City road network had 129,442 intersections that could serve as PLTB, that is 129,442! combinations of possible locations of temporary bases. That will require a significant amount of time to find an acceptable solution, time that is highly valuable for making decisions in emergencies.

After applying the proposed constraints to reduce the search space in steps 2 and 3 of the methodology, the graph was reduced to 111,555 locations; one segment of this graph can be seen in Fig. 2, where the blue lines represent the edges and blue diamonds represent the vertices; it can be seen that this graph does not contain all the roads from the background map.

In step 4 of the methodology, the graph was simplified deleting the isolated vertices and those that belong to the same road and are not a road intersection. After this step, the resulting vertices represent the set V of suitable locations; this is 4,523 PLTB. The result of this step is illustrated with black diamonds for the map region in Fig. 2.

Step 5 (redundancy elimination) deleted all the overlapped PLTB; since the points were overlapping result is not graphically visible but it is computationally effective. This step reduces the set V to 3,669 locations.

Finally, the proximity clustering allowed us to reduce the closer points to just one. For example, roundabouts could be, in some cases, one point for each street connection, but after this step, all of them were reduced to one since their coverage is practically the same, and there is no significant difference in considering one more than another. This reduction is illustrated with magenta points in Fig. 2, where there was more than one black point as the possible option on the roundabouts, but then the proximity clustering left only one in two of

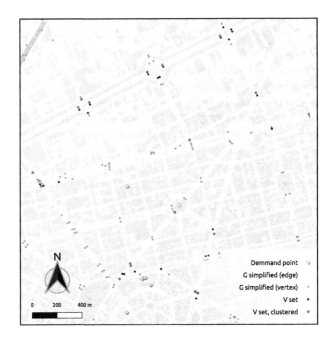

Fig. 2. Comparison of the PLTB obtained after steps 3, 4, 5 and 6.
© Mapbox ©OpenStreetMap

the roundabouts. This allows us to reduce the search space to 2,069 PLTB (see Fig. 4).

Figure 3 shows the resulting PLTB from the same region shown in Fig. 2, where the size of the marker represents the capacity of the PLTB based on the length of the road segments and the average size of an ambulance (6 m in this case).

These reductions in the search space could allow a heuristic or an approximation algorithm to achieve a prompt response and effectively allocate the 290 ambulances to cover the 38 demand points.

Table 1 shows the search space reduction in each step as mentioned before. The most influential step of the methodology was to simplify the graph after discarding edges based on the previously proposed criteria.

Table 1. Reduction of the search space in the optimization problem

Methodology Step	Result	Search space size
1	G_r obtained from OSM	$129,442!$
3	G_r simplified by unsuitable locations	$111,555!$
4	V set	$4,523!$
5	V set simplified by overlaps	$3,669!$
6	V set simplified by proximity in G_r simplified	$2,069!$

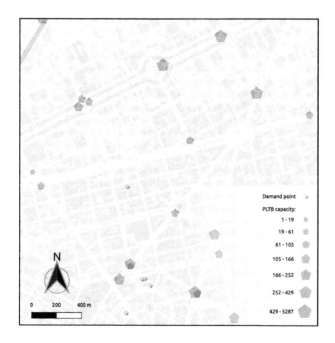

Fig. 3. Visualization of the PLTB capacities based on their length after proximity clustering. ©Mapbox ©OpenStreetMap

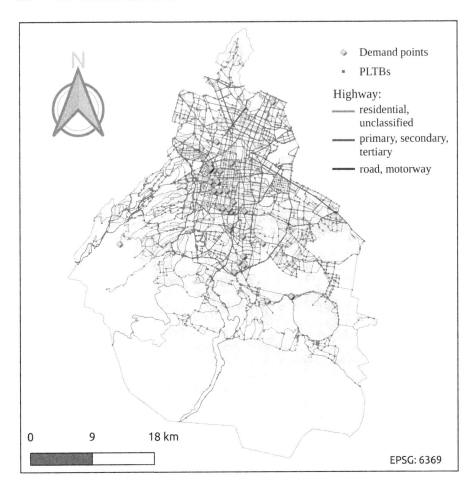

Fig. 4. Localization of PLTB and demand points in the study case.
©Mapbox ©OpenStreetMap

6   Conclusions

In real-case applications, it is not always possible to consider the whole road network to locate ambulances due to the need for a timely decision-making process; this is particularly critical in emergencies where delays in obtaining a response can lead to tragic consequences. The methodology proposed in this study involved reducing the possible location of temporary bases primarily through physical and logical constraints inherent to the problem (road size, number of lanes, road type, etc.) and subsequently employing computational methods and algorithm design.

The proposed methodology successfully reduced the initial pool of 129,442 potential locations for ambulance bases in Mexico City (which includes alleys, residential streets, and highways, among others) to just 2,069 points within the network. This reduction focused on selecting roads with sufficient capacity to place ambulances without interrupting the traffic of other vehicles.

The final locations are suitable options to assign the ambulance bases, allowing to translate location and allocation problems to places without predefined bases for ambulance fleets after disaster situations. The resulting locations represent a smaller search space than using the whole road network for the optimization problem presented in the mathematical model, which makes it highly relevant in emergency scenarios.

The biggest reduction was mainly due to data treatment and data reduction techniques, while proximity clustering was responsible for 1% search space reduction.

All data used in this paper was obtained from public repositories and voluntary data available for many countries; the methodology of the search space reduction is applicable for all regions with access to OSM road network data. Besides the methodology, the optimization problem proposed remains on simple assumptions found in many other countries, so it can be used as a base for formulating the optimization problem of locating ambulances after a disaster in other regions with similar characteristics.

7   Future Work

This methodology was proposed as a basis for obtaining meaningful data for solving optimization problems from real life, nevertheless, there are many other considerations that could potentially improve it. The use of isochrones from the PLTB can be implemented in order to validate the coverage of the city. Other relevant aspects to consider in a dynamic model are updating the real demand of the points, the traffic or obstructions over the highways, and damaged infrastructure that could generate risk in the temporary ambulance bases; these aspects needs further research about its estimation.

Acknowledgments. This work was partially sponsored by the Instituto Politécnico Nacional (IPN), Consejo Nacional de Ciencia y Tecnología (CONACYT) under grant 1183927, 960525, and the Secretaría de Investigación y Posgrado (SIP) under grants 20230454 and 20230901. Additionally, we are thankful to the reviewers for their invaluable and constructive feedback that helped improve the quality of the paper.

References

1. IFRC What is a disaster? https://www.ifrc.org/our-work/disasters-climate-and-crises/what-disaster. Accessed 2 June 2023
2. Pan American Health Organization Earthquakes. https://www.paho.org/en/topics/earthquakes. Accessed 5 June 2023
3. World Health Organization Earthquakes. https://www.who.int/health-topics/earthquakes#tab=tab_1. Accessed 5 June 2023

4. Centro Nacional de Prevención de Desastres El sismo de mayor magnitud en casi cien años en México. Sismo de Tehuantepec, 7 de septiembre de 2017. https://www.gob.mx/cenapred/articulos/el-sismo-de-mayor-magnitud-en-casi-cien-anos-en-mexico-sismo-de-tehuantepec-7-de-septiembre-de-2017. Accessed 5 June 2023
5. UNAM Estadísticas de sismicidad. http://www.ssn.unam.mx/sismicidad/estadisticas/. Accessed 5 June 2023
6. Forbes Los 8 sismos más devastadores en la historia de México. https://www.forbes.com.mx/los-8-sismos-mas-catastroficos-en-la-historia-de-mexico/. Accessed 5 June 2023
7. Sánchez Camarena, C.A., et al.: Sismo 19 de septiembre de 2017: respuesta médica en la zona cero, lecciones aprendidas. Special Article. Acta Méd. Grupo Ángeles **17**(4), 428–432 (2019)
8. CEFP Caracterización del Mercado Laboral en México. https://www.cefp.gob.mx/publicaciones/presentaciones/2018/eno1/09_CdM.pdf. Accessed 5 June 2023
9. C5, Fortalecimiento del sistema de ambulancias de la Ciudad de México (2022). https://www.c5.cdmx.gob.mx/storage/app/media/Boletin/2022/APHmedios21Feb2022.pptx. Accessed 5 June 2023
10. Noticias telemundo Las ambulancias en CDMX y los problemas del sistema de salud llegan al cine. https://www.telemundo.com/noticias/2020/03/05/entre-la-vida-la-muerte-y-el-lucro-las-ambulancias-en-ciudad-de-mexico-tmna3712049. Accessed 5 June 2023
11. Corriente alterna Ambulancias irregulares: lucrar con la vida en la CDMX. https://corrientealterna.unam.mx/derechos-humanos/ambulancias-irregulares-lucrar-con-la-vida-en-la-cdmx/#:~:text=Deacuerdoconlosreportes, porcada31milhabitantes. Accessed 5 June 2023
12. Barojas-Payán, E., Sánchez-Partida, D., Gibaja-Romero, D.E., Martínez-Flores, J.L., Cabrera-Rios, M.: Optimization model to locate pre-positioned warehouses and establish humanitarian aid inventory levels. In: Sánchez-Partida, D., Martínez-Flores, J.-L., Caballero-Morales, S.-O., Cano-Olivos, P. (eds.) Disaster Risk Reduction in Mexico, pp. 169–192. Springer, Cham (2021). https://doi.org/10.1007/978-3-030-67295-9_8
13. Zheng, Y.J., Chen, S.Y., Ling, H.F.: Evolutionary optimization for disaster relief operations: a survey. Appl. Soft Comput. **27**, 553–566 (2015)
14. Murray, A.T.: Maximal coverage location problem: impacts, significance, and evolution. Int. Reg. Sci. Rev. **39**(1), 5–27 (2016)
15. Toregas, C., Swain, R., ReVelle, C., Bergman, L.: The location of emergency service facilities. Oper. Res. **19**(6), 1363–1373 (1971)
16. Mohri, S.S., Haghshenas, H.: An ambulance location problem for covering inherently rare and random road crashes. Comput. Ind. Eng. **151**, 1–13 (2021)
17. Barojas-Payán, E., Sánchez-Partida, D., Caballero-Morales, S.-O., Martínez-Flores, J.-L.: A hybrid capacitated multi-facility location model for pre-positioning warehouses and inventories in regions at risk in Mexico. In: Sánchez-Partida, D., Martínez-Flores, J.-L., Caballero-Morales, S.-O., Cano-Olivos, P. (eds.) Disaster Risk Reduction in Mexico, pp. 193–221. Springer, Cham (2021). https://doi.org/10.1007/978-3-030-67295-9_9
18. Dean, W.: Computational Complexity Theory (Stanford Encyclopedia of Philosophy) (2016). https://plato.stanford.edu/entries/computational-complexity/. Accessed 13 July 2023
19. Cormen, T.H., Leiserson, C.E., Rivest, R.L., Stein, C.: Introduction to Algorithms, 3rd edn. MIT Press, Cambridge (2009)

20. Kleinberg, J., Tardos, É.: Algorithm Design, 1st edn. Pearson, USA (2006)
21. OpenStreetMaps About. https://www.openstreetmap.org/about. Accessed 8 June 2023
22. Portal de Datos Abiertos de la Ciudad de México Homepage. https://datos.cdmx.gob.mx/. Accessed 8 June 2023

Development of a Web-Based Calculator to Simulate Link Budget for Mobile Communications Systems at Urban Settlements

G. E. Casillas-Aviña[1] , C. A. López-Balcázar[1] , G. A. Yáñez-Casas[1,2] ,
J. J. Hernández-Gómez[2(✉)] , J. M. Arao-Quiroz[3], and M. F. Mata-Rivera[1]

[1] Instituto Politécnico Nacional, Unidad Profesional Interdisciplinaria en Ingeniería y Tecnologías Avanzadas, Mexico City, Mexico
[2] Instituto Politécnico Nacional, Centro de Desarrollo Aeroespacial, Mexico City, Mexico
jjhernandezgo@ipn.mx
[3] Instituto Politécnico Nacional, Escuela Superior de Ingeniería Mecánica y Eléctrica Unidad Zacatenco, Mexico City, Mexico

Abstract. Cellular wireless networks have taken a preponderant role in modern society. With the emergence of 5G and 6G connections, the potential that they may unleash could transform the face in which mankind and machines work together. However, current 5G links are still scarce compared with the total amount of cellular users worldwide, and 6G is still in development phase. In this sense, 2G–4G links still dominate the market, with large physical infrastructures bearing transmissions ranging from 800 to 2,000 MHz. Thus, it is still important to provide reliable link budgets within such a frequency range in order to guarantee stability and quality of service. Despite there are many software-based calculators that provide a tool for link budgeting of cellular connections, they may be cumbersome to use, they could be of payment, they do not necessarily pose the used models as well as their range of validity, among other issues. The present work consists of the design and implementation of a calculation software tool for the construction of the link budget based on radio communications. The tool aims to offer ease of use, flexibility, accuracy, and accessibility in the area of communication systems, to obtain reliable and adequate link budget parameters, prior to the construction and commissioning of the real communications system. The software contains calculation options such as: conversion and display of basic measurement units for radio frequency links, Link Budget calculation, free space loss calculation applied to open environments, simulation and calculation of parameters for the design of communication systems, simulation of statistical models of wave propagation, among others. The software has a web-based friendly-user interface which can be used in any device and under any operating system, is modular and use generic processes, so it does not depend on specific transmission equipment.

© The Author(s), under exclusive license to Springer Nature Switzerland AG 2023
M. F. Mata-Rivera et al. (Eds.): WITCOM 2023, CCIS 1906, pp. 176–198, 2023.
https://doi.org/10.1007/978-3-031-45316-8_13

Keywords: Link Budget · Propagation Models · Cost231 Walfisch Ikegami · Wireless communication system · Web-based application software · React framework · Path loss model · Cellular networks · 800–2000 MHz

1 Introduction

Nowadays, wireless communications systems have become a medullary part of the modern society [1–3]. The range of applications of wireless communications range from 2G-6G cellular connections [4–7], Internet of Things (IoT) applications [8–11], microwave links [12–14], satellite communications [15–17], among many others. There are several factors that must be taken into account to design a successful wireless link, and they heavily rely in the frequency band to be used. Very relevant factors are the geographical zone (its topography, obstacles, etc.), the required transceivers, the communication protocol to be implemented, the propagation medium, the required coverage, among many others.

One typical approach to estimate the losses between the transmitter and the receiver, i.e. the attenuation that the power of the transmitted electromagnetic waves is to undergo in different propagation scenarios is through the establishment of propagation models, or path loss models, which in most cases have an experimental basis [18–20]. Although propagation models are aimed to simplify the computation of the losses in certain conditions, it is to be remarked that such models are of limited application as they should only be used in scenarios that are similar to the ones from where they were derived and tested.

One of the first path loss models was posed by Okumura in 1968 [21], which is an empirical model that considers the propagation frequency, the height of transmitting and receiving antennas, the distance between antennas, as well as buildings of different heights. It was the result of assessing losses experimentally in many Japan cities in the 1960's. Further propagation models includes the well-known Hata (1980) [22], Walfisch-Bertoni [23] and Ikegami et al. (1991) [24] models, as well as combinations of them. Thus, if the propagation environment changes, the propagation model should as well change. In this sense, there are plenty of specific path loss models adapted to as much propagation scenarios as it can be imagined. For instance, [18] assess typical models in both urban and rural environments; [20] adapts some models to indoor propagation environments; [25] reviews propagation models adapted to high altitude mountainous areas for 2.6 GHz propagation; in [26,27] they adapt propagation models to forestry environments; [28] study propagation models in coastal environments and; [29] studies path loss in UAV air-terrestrial links for farming purposes. Moreover, there has been much research in the effects of many direct and indirect phenomena in propagation models. For example, [30] studies the attenuation due to rain in short-range millimetric links; [31] studies he impact of tropical climate in 28 GHz propagation; [32] studies the effects of solar radio Emissions on outdoor propagation models at 60 GHz bands; [33] incorporates the effects of vegetation and vehicular traffic in urban microcells; [34] reviews the impact of the presence of diffraction and specular reflectors in millimetric propagation; among many others.

In order to better assess the success of a wireless link, path loss models are applied to specific cases through the computation of a link budget [35]. Link budgeting is aimed to take into account, under certain propagation model, all the power gains and losses in propagation of the electromagnetic waves for a specific communications system, including an specific transmitter, the transmission medium and the receptor [35]. In this sense, equations used for link budgeting are to provide the received power in the receptor, as function of the transmitted power and the gains and losses provided by the system and the environment (through propagation models) [35].

Several research efforts has been done in the performance of link budgets for several applications. For instance, [36] use adaptive methods to better estimate link budget parameters; [37] performs link budget modelling for NLOS submarine optical wireless links, [38] explores link budgeting techniques for LPWAN LoRa connections; while [39] explores link budgeting for high frequency wireless conditions in extreme weather conditions. On the other side, standardisation organisms as the International Telecommunications Union (ITU) and the European Telecommunications Standard Institute have released documents on link budgeting for different wireless technologies [40, 41].

As it can be observed, the main drawback of selecting a preexisting propagation model is that in many specific situations, they can be overly simplistic and unrealistic. As the application of specific path loss models may be complicated and cumbersome, many software have been developed with the aim of easing the computation of link budgets under certain propagation models. For instance, some non-free options includes the Communications Toolbox of Matlab®/Simulink® [42] and the Keysight® ADS software [43]. However, their high costs and the fact that they act as blackboxes make them a difficult option to implement. Also, for instance, Keysight® ADS is only for the microwave range and has very specific and limited components in its catalogue. On the free access software side, there are typical options as the Pasternack [44], Huawei [45] and Radwin [46] web-based calculators. However, they have important drawbacks: 1) as they are very generic, the computation of processes like the link budget is unreliable; 2) in many occasions, the standards and models they implement is not clear; 3) most of such calculators are set up by transceivers manufacturers, so they are only specialised to such devices. The later is the case of [45], which is specialised for optic fiber Huawei equipment and [46] for Radwin radio antennas.

Some interesting developments on this field can be found in scientific literature too, which perform calculations of parameters related to radiofrequency transmission using only one or more principles. For example, [47] only takes into account the Okumura - Hata Model [22]; although their calculations are performed correctly, it does not pose the ranges within which the model is known to be effective; it also does not include its limitations (advantages, disadvantages, uses); finally, it does not include propagation losses in suburban or rural environments. Likewise, the online system of [48] calculates the transmission loss using the Okumura-Hata [22] and Walfisch-Ikegami [49] models; although it provides the used formulas, the required variables and their units, taking into account the density of the environment, the ranges of use of the models are not mentioned, and they cannot compute the propagation losses of the Okumura [50] or Walfisch-Bertoni [23] models.

In this work we develop a link budget calculation web-based software in the range of cellular communications, that is reliable, accurate, of free use, easy implementation and well-founded. As the base of our development, we consider the COST 231 Walfisch Ikegami model [51,52], which is a more updated model specifically designed for urban environments and cellular communications. As such a model is one of the most studied and updated, it will provide a robust link budget calculator. Moreover, it is implemented in free software, it have an adequate user interface, it is scalable to the parameters that requires the link budget to be calculated, the web application is compatible with any equipment, and it has proved to be accurate. This work is organised as follows: In Sect. 2 we feature theoretical background, including the basics of mobile communications systems and link budgeting, a review of the main propagation models, as well as the computational tools used for the web service. In Sect. 3 we pose the used propagation model, its adaptation for link budget calculation, as well as the development of the software calculator. Section 4 poses the results and the discussion of this research, while in Sects. 5 and 6 we pose some conclusions as well as future possible paths in which tis research could be expanded.

2 Materials and Methods

2.1 Mobile Communication Systems

The first cellular type networks began their operation in the 1980s, and since then different versions and improvements of such networks have been arisen. Since cellular communication arises as a need for users and the increasing use of mobile devices, each geographic region began to generate its technical specifications and therefore the implementation of cellular systems differed between areas [53]. These first systems are known as the First Generation (1G) of cellular systems [54,55].

The second generation (2G) of cellular systems was developed in the late 1980s and early 1990s [54,55]. They were based on digital interfaces and circuit switching, as well as the introduction of medium access techniques such as time or code division multiplexings. The two main technologies developed in this generation are Global System for Mobile (GSM) [56–58] and Code Division Multiple Access System One (CDMAOne) [59–61]. However, demand soon exceeded the capabilities of this generation.

The third generation (3G) was designed to solve the deficiencies of the second, allowing that in addition to increasing the connection capacity of mobile devices, it could also offer a greater number of services [54,55]. The 3G standard was approved in March 1992 at the International Mobile Telephone by the Year 2000 (IMT-2000) [62,63]. The main technologies included for 3G were the EDGE standard [64], Code Division Multiple Access (CDMA2000) [65–69], Wideband Code Division Multiple Access (WCDMA) [70–73] and Mobile WiMAX (World Wide Interoperability for Microwave Access) [74–78].

The fourth generation (4G) is defined in the IMT-Advanced standard [79]. The physical and logical capacities of this generation far exceed previous ones, since properties such as bandwidth, data transmission speed, quality of service, among others, have increased significantly. In this generation, technologies such as LTE (Long Term Evolution) [80,81], a new version of WiMAX [82,83], and the introduction of technologies for low-power systems, such as LTE-M [84–87] and NB-IoT [88–91], were considered.

In general, the operating frequencies of such generations of cellular systems range from 800–2000 MHz. Although there are new generations of "celullar" such as 5G and the emerging 6G, their operating frequencies are beyond the 3.4 GHz and up to the subterahertz [92,93]. Such frequencies lie beyond those used in this work.

2.2   Propagation Models

Propagation models aim to model the behaviour of signals in a defined environment, focusing on physical characteristics such as input and output signal power, link losses, antenna gains, among others. As mentioned in Sect. 1 the propagation models are a statistical approximation, based on experiments that allow to model of these parameters prior to the installation and final testing of a communications system. The propagation models, in addition to the theory and experimental results that they include, also define a methodology for calculating the link budget, that is, the particular form of the budget equations, depending on the model used.

The Okumura Model. The Okumura model is an empirical propagation model used to calculate losses in urban environments, taking into account measurements obtained in different cities in Japan [50]. A characteristic that propagation models share in their structure are the initial parameters. In Table 1, the main parameters of Okumura model are presented.

Table 1. Okumura model parameters [21].

Parameter	Value	Unit
Operating frequency	150–1,920	MHz
Transmitting antenna height	30–1,000	m
Receiving antenna height	3–10	m
Distance between antennas	1–100	km

An important result from this model is that it allowed obtaining the average attenuation curves relative to the free space losses as a function of the operating frequency and the distance between the mobile device and the base station. It is worth mentioning that the advantages of the Okumura model lie around the fact that it is a simple and useful model when it comes to irregular scenarios, that is, urban areas with buildings of different heights and high density of users [21].

The Hata Model. The Hata model is the result of a multiple regression analysis applied to the normalised propagation curves obtained in the Okumura model. From this analysis, an experimental equation was obtained to calculate losses in urban environments with a high density of devices.

The Hata model has certain advantages such as the possibility of computationally implementing the Okumura model. Although this model has a lower operating frequency than the Okumura model, its greatest contribution is obtaining the aforementioned equation and the normalised attenuation curves. Their initial parameters can be observed in Table 2.

Table 2. Hata Model Parameters [22].

Parameter	Value	Unit
Operating frequency	100–1,500	MHz
Transmitting antenna height	30–200	m
Receiving antenna height	1–10	m
Distance between antennas	1–20	km

The Walfisch - Bertoni Model. This propagation model has its main application in urban environments with lower density of device use than the Okumura and Hata models. Some examples of application scenarios can be residential areas, internal networks of shops or small industrial complexes [23].

The idea of this model is to build the line of sight (LoS) above the obstacles (mainly buildings). The signals that reach the mobile devices are the result of the diffraction that they suffer when encountering the highest parts of the buildings, so the calculation of the losses does not directly take into account the rest of the signals generated in the building, or those that may interfere with the transmission. The parameters used in this model can be seen in the Table 3.

Table 3. Walfisch - Bertoni model parameters [23].

Parameter	Value	Unit
Operating frequency	0.3–3.0	GHz
Distance between antennas	0.2–5.0	Km

This model does not necessarily require the height of the transmitting and receiving antennas, since they do not need to be in a fixed position; it only requires the distance between them. In fact, one of the advantages of this model, in addition to not requiring the height of the antennas, is that instead of obtaining attenuation curves empirically, it seeks to generalise the experimental results of previous models through analytical methods, so this model requires less specific technical parameters of the area and of the transmission devices, such that it allows a random distribution of the buildings, without necessarily knowing where they are or how many there are. The restriction is that the height of the transmitting antenna should greater than the average height of the buildings [23].

The Ikegami Model. One of the main considerations on which the Ikegami model rests is that it is a theoretical development, that is, the definition of this model is not based on experimental processes. An advantage is that the model is much more general than those that are totally empirical. However, it can lead to certain inaccuracies as it is not connected to a specific environment [94].

Despite the above, the Ikegami model is applicable in case of having specific parameter values, such as the operating frequency (usually 200–800 MHz), as well as the non-consideration of environmental phenomena and characteristics of the geographical area [94].

The Walfisch - Ikegami Model. This model is a combination of the Walfisch and Ikegami methods already described in Sects. 2.2, including some corrections and empirical adjustments to the parameters used in each model.

It must be taken into account that the model is statistical and not deterministic, since the topography of the place is not taken into account and therefore it is effective only in urban terrain without disturbances in the terrain. In turn, it makes it possible to evaluate the loss of propagation whether or not there is a LoS between the receiving antenna and the mobile receiver. The ranges in which this model is applicable are [95]. The main parameters of the model are shown in the Table 4.

Table 4. Walfisch-Ikegami model Parameters [95].

Parameter	Value	Unit
Operating frequency	800–2,000	MHz
Transmitting antenna height	0.2–5	Km
Receiving antenna height	4–50	m
Distance between antennas	1–3	m

2.3   Radio Communication Link Budget

According to [96], the link budget is defined as a method for calculating the effectiveness of a cellular communications link, taking into account the physical and geographic parameters of the environment and the devices used in the communications system.

Commonly, to calculate this budget, the gains and losses of the antennas and the attenuation due to the medium must be taken into account. Generally, the link budget calculation takes into account the following parameters [97]:

- Output Power P_{Tx},
- Transmitting antenna gain G_{Tx},
- Transmission Loss L_{Tx},
- Losses in free space L_{Fs},
- Miscellaneous Losses L_M,
- Gain in the receiving antenna G_{Rx} and
- Losses in the receiving antenna L_{Rx}.

These parameters are used to obtain the power received at the receiving antenna, so that if the estimated received power is high enough with respect to the sensitivity of the receiver, the link will be useful enough to send information. Equation 1 is used to calculate the received power.

$$P_{Rx} = P_{Tx} + G_{Tx} - L_{Tx} - L_{Fs} - L_M + G_{Rx} - L_{Rx} \qquad (1)$$

2.4   React Framework

React.js [98] is an open-source front-end development framework built on the JavaScript language, which was first released by Facebook (now Meta) back in May 2013 [99]. Thanks to the growing popularity of web pages as a means of disseminating information, the need to generate user-tailored content over static pages became a priority [100]. In response to this need, multiple development frameworks were created, some of them being AngularJs [101], EmberJs [102] or Backbone.js [103].

Many of the web development frameworks take advantage of existing templates, that are elements within the HTML code that are not rendered when the page loads, but that will later be loaded and altered by means of JavaScript. However, these templates have all the abstract elements predefined to be used in the creation of a user interface. As a solution to this, React proposes developing with components in mind, which are abstract units that are part of the constitution of a user interface, ranging from a field within a form, to a complete web page [99].

The first time the web is accessed, React compiles all the components that make up the page and proceeds to render them on the user's screen. If any of the components need to update the information it presents or its state, there is no need to recompile the entire page and re-render, as each component has its own rendering function [99]. To keep components updated as their information or state changes, React implements elements called *hooks*, being these pre-built functions within the framework that allow storing information about the state of components in the front-end and exchange information between components, these functions always start with the keyword "use" [104].

The first type of *hooks* are status hooks, which store information generated by user input (components within a form being an example). Within this category of *hooks* we find "useState", which declares the state of a variable that can be updated directly, and "useReducer", which does the same thing as the previous *hook*, but which implements logic for updating that data for validation or preprocessing. The second type is the context *hook*, which allow information to be sent from larger components to the minimum units that make them up. A good example of this is the use of a light or dark theme within our website; the main *hook* is used with the "useContext" keyword. Another type of *hooks* are the reference ones, which represent information that is not visible to the user and therefore do not need to re-render the state of a component, the main *hook* being the "useRef" mainly used to store references to the DOM (Document Object Model). For synchronisation and work with external systems to the main website, we implement "useEffect" *hook*, which allow us to store the connection status with *web sockets*, animations and widgets created with another framework or development library [104].

2.5 Tailwind CSS Library

An essential part of any web application is the user interface, which can be cumbersome to build since you have to worry about it being functional, attractive to the end user and adaptable to a large number of devices. The functionality problem is addressed through development frameworks (with React.js being selected for this work). In the case of the styling of the pages and how well they adapt to different devices with different resolutions (a concept known as *responsiveness*) is addressed through CSS (Cascade Style Sheet) libraries [105]. Currently, within the main CSS libraries we can find Bootstrap [106], Foundation [107], Bulma [108], Skeleton [109] or Tailwind [110], the latter being the one selected for the development of the calculator.

Adam Wathan [111] released the first version of Tailwind on November 1, 2017, being a library focused on the creation of utilities that allow to speed up the construction of user interfaces (an example of this being classes that allow changing the layout of containers, or centring the content). Among its main benefits we can find existing classes to style components when the mouse is over them (*hover event*), when they are clicked (*focus event*); On the other hand, we can develop our website with responsive design as a priority, we can also easily change from light to dark theme thanks to the pre-built classes, reuse styles and create custom ones [112].

3 Development

3.1 Cost231 Walfisch Ikegami Model

This model takes characteristics of the most widely used models in the design of cellular communications links, resulting in a semi-empirical model. This model is especially useful and efficient in urban environments. In particular, it is a statistical and deterministic combination of how communications behave in the frequency ranges of 800 to 2,000 MHz [51, 113]. Among the parameters considered by this model are [52]:

1. Operating frequency [MHz],
2. Distance between transceivers [m],
3. Height of antennas [m],
4. Attenuation in free space [dB],
5. Diffraction attenuation (ceilings) [dB],
6. Diffraction attenuation (obstacles) [dB],
7. Attenuation per path [dB] and
8. Urban orientation effects [dB].

As determined by the general theory of link budget calculation, the Cost231 Walfisch Ikegami model follows a mathematical structure to calculate the variables required in different link conditions.

Table 5. Cost231 Walfisch Ikegami equations [52].

Variable	Parameter	Equation
Loss (considering LoS)	P_{LOS}	$P_{LOS} = 42.64 + 26log_{10}(d) + 20log_{10}(f)$
Loss (Not considering LoS)	P_{LOS}	$P_{LOS} = L_0 + L_{rts} + L_{msd}$
Free space loss	L_0	$L_0 = 32.45 + 20log_{10}(d) + 20log_{10}(f)$

Table 5 shows the main variables that the model calculates. These calculations do not consider attenuations inherent to the zone and only consider distances and frequencies, so the calculation becomes simpler. The model allows to calculate different types of loss due to other circumstances, such as diffraction loss from ceilings

$$L_{rts} = -16.9 - 10log_{10}(\omega) + 10log_{10}(f) + 20log_{10}(h_b - h_r) + L_{ori}$$

and obstacle diffraction loss

$$L_{msd} = L_{bsh} + K_a + K_d log_{10}(d) + K_f log_{10}(f) - 9log_{10}(B).$$

The above expressions give an idea that this model is hybrid, as it includes both empirical and analytical parameters. The rest of the expressions that comprise the [52] model are listed below.

1. $L_0 = 32.45 + 20log_{10}(d) + 20log_{10}(f)$.
2. $L_{rts} = -16.9 - 10log_{10}(\omega) + 10log_{10}(f) + 20log_{10}(h_b - h_r) + L_{ori}$, taking into account that ω is the width of the building where the mobile antenna is, where

(a) $L_{ori} = \begin{cases} -10 + 0.35\alpha & \text{if } 0 < \alpha < 35° \\ 2.5 + 0.0755(\alpha - 35) & \text{if } 35 < \alpha < 55 \\ 4 - 0.0114(\alpha - 55) & \text{if } 55 < \alpha < 90. \end{cases}$

3. $L_{msd} = L_{bsh} + K_a + K_d log_{10}(d) + K_f log_{10}(f) - 9log_{10}(B)$, where B is the average of the distances between buildings, d is the distance between stations, and where

(a) $L_{bsh} = \begin{cases} -18log(1 + h_t - h_b) & \text{if } h_t > h_b \\ 0 & \text{if } h_t \le h_b, \end{cases}$

(b) $K_a = \begin{cases} 54 & \text{if } h_t > h_b \\ 54 - 0.8(h_t - h_b) & \text{if } h_t < h_b; d_{km} \ge 0.5km \\ 54 - 1.6(h_t - h_b)d & \text{if } d_{km} < 0.5km, \end{cases}$

(c) $K_d = \begin{cases} 18 & \text{if } h_t > h_b \\ 18 - 15\frac{h_t - h_b}{h_b} & \text{if } h_t \le h_b \end{cases}$

and

(d) $K_f = \begin{cases} -4 + 0.7(\frac{f_{MHz}}{925-1}) & \text{if medium size city} \\ +1.5(\frac{f_{MHz}}{925-1}) & \text{if downtown.} \end{cases}$

The equations corresponding to the complete model were considered in the application developed in this work. The Cost231 Walfisch Ikegami model offers a complete model, since being developed through three different models, each with its own vision and context, a model is obtained that combines the theoretical and practical, unlike other models that are focus on a single aspect.

3.2   Link Budget Software Calculator

Looking for the software tool to be useful and accessible, a web application was developed to solve multiple requirements related to the calculation of the radio communication link budget. Figure 1 shows the corresponding mockup, the which follows a two-column layout.

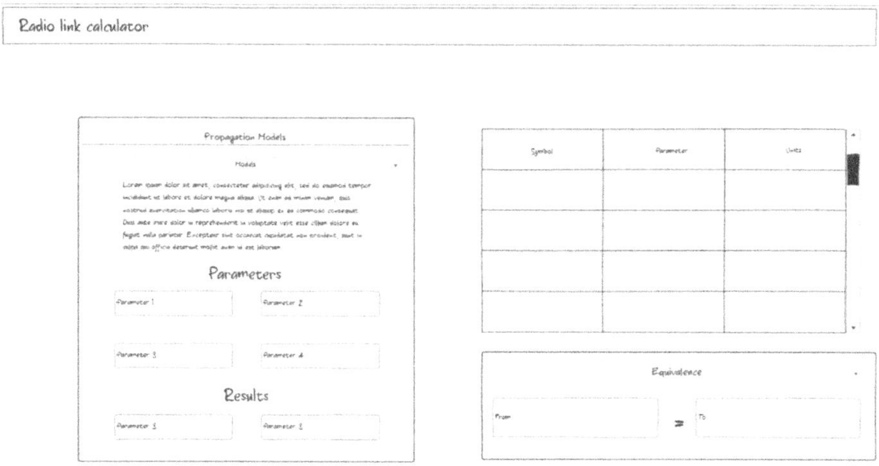

Fig. 1. Mockup for web view of the calculator.

The first column presents the graphical interface for calculating the link budget using the Cost 231 Walfisch Ikegami model. This section has a selector component that allows choosing the propagation model, then there is a descriptive text about the propagation model presented, followed by the block of parameters used within the model. Finally, a section for the presentation of results is placed.

In the second column, there is a dictionary that includes the most commonly used units in radio communications, which begins with a header that includes three parameters to display. In the lower right part of the dictionary, a unit converter is displayed that serves as a query tool, giving the possibility of choosing which conversion to perform and the units involved in it.

The design takes into account the use of the minimum number of decorative elements, seeking to simplify its use. Thanks to the use of the React.js framework [98,104], all the functionality can be kept in a single window, reducing the number of events required to access the utilities of the calculation tool, resulting in a comfortable and highly efficient user experience.

4   Results and Discussion

4.1   Web Application

As described in Sect. 3.2, the mockup presents a preview of the final application. Each section of the final web application is described in detail in what follows.

The first part of the link budget calculation is shown in Fig. 2. The component has rounded edges, a propagation model selector, then an overview of the model used along with the first block of parameters needed for the calculation, each parameter having a custom units modifier. It should be noted that for the version of the software described in this work, only a single propagation model was

implemented, as this is a work in progress. However, other path loss models can
be added straightforwardly.

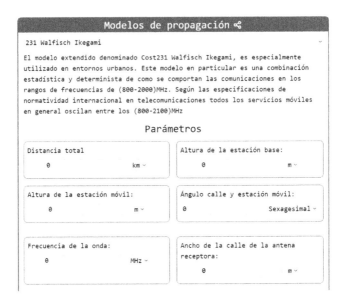

Fig. 2. Propagation model section.

The second part of the calculation component is shown in Fig. 3, which contains a button to add buildings, text fields to enter the height of each building
and a button to delete any particular building. At the bottom of these elements,
there is the collection of text fields to enter the distance between buildings, which
can be dynamically modified.

Fig. 3. Buildings section.

In the last section of the component, shown in Fig. 4, there is a button for the
calculator to process the input values and display them in the results section.

The results obtained correspond to the reception power when there is a LoS between the antennas and when it does not exist.

Fig. 4. Results section.

Figure 5 displays the unit dictionary and a unit converter that serves as a query and reference for users of the application. In the design of radio frequency links it is common to use different units for the same parameter, depending on the manufacturer, operator or developer.

Symbol	Parameter	Units
PTx	Potencia de transmisión	dB
PRx	Potencia de recepción	dB
λ	Atenuación	dB
GTx	Ganancia de antena transmisora	dB
GRx	Ganancia de antena receptora	dB
α	Longitud de onda	m/s
Aef	Área efectiva	m^2
h	Altura	m

Tiempo y frecuencia

1000	=	1
Milisegundos [ms]		Hercio [Hz]

Fig. 5. Measurement units dictionary and converter.

It should be noted that although in this paper the calculation of the link budget is presented using the Cost231 Walfisch Ikegami model, however, the software tools used and the complete conception of the tool allow the inclusion of other propagation models, which can take into account in its equations different types of losses and conditions.

4.2   Study Case

In order to validate the operation of the software, the results were compared between a link budget calculation case already documented, with respect to the results obtained through the developed application.

Using the experimental values obtained in [114] by means of a computational simulation of losses using the Cost 231 Walfisch Ikegami model, a summary of the results obtained by [114] can be observed in Table 6.

Table 6. Parameters of the model for the case of study, obtained from [114].

Parameter	Experiment 1	Experiment 2	Experiment 3
Distance between Tx and Rx (km)	1	2	3
Base station height (m)	30		
Mobile station height (km)	3		
Street orientation angle (°)	30		
Operating frequency (MHz)	900		
Street width (m)	25		
Average building height (m)	15		
Average building distance (m)	50		
Losses (dB)	**110**	**122**	**128**

For the verification experiment, the parameters of the base case were taken as input into the developed web-based calculator. The values obtained are shown in the Table 7.

Table 7. Losses obtained using the developed calculation tool.

Parameter	Experiment 1	Experiment 2	Experiment 3
Distance between Tx and Rx (km)	1	2	3
Base station height (m)	30		
Mobile station height (km)	3		
Street orientation angle (°)	30		
Operating frequency (MHz)	900		
Street width (m)	25		
Average building height (m)	15		
Average building distance (m)	50		
Losses (dB)	**117**	**128**	**135**

A difference between the values obtained by the calculation tool and the reference computational simulation is observed. In this case, this discrepancy may be due to the fact that in the original experiment numerical adjustments made to benefit the results required for that experiment. This is common, since the link budget is made based on parameters and specific geographic areas [114].

5   Conclusions

In this work we developed a novel web-based link budget calculator considering the Cost 231 Walfisch Ikegami model for urban environments in the 800–2,000 MHz frequency band of cellular wireless networks, which allows the application to yield adequate and reliable accuracy of results. The use of software tools for simulation and design of communications systems is essential, since physically implementing a communications system implies the use of relatively high economic and infrastructure resources, depending on the type of system.

Because software tools are essential, it is vital to have applications that are useful, accessible and suitable for design. In the present work the philosophy of developing an application that allows users to carry out for link design is followed.

Although there are various propagation models available for the calculation of link budget in the same frequency range, we implemented the Cost 231 Walfisch Ikegami model because is one of the most studied and updated models for 2G–4G cellular wireless networks at urban environments. Nevertheless, the modularity of the full-stack application allows to add additional path loss models if necessary.

In this sense, the developed application allows to perform the link budget with the aforementioned model, as it is one of the essential processes in the design of radio frequency systems.

As reported in Sect. 4.2, the calculation precision of the implemented model is adequate, since the result provided by the application is corroborated with results already documented in scientific literature, with a small value lag. This lag is attributed to the way of implementation of the reference case.

The application is accessible, it is completely developed with free software tools, and because it is a web application, it is highly compatible with any computer where it is run. The design and implementation of the application is scalable, as other functions can be implemented without the need to modify the original design model.

In terms of advantages regarding the use of commercial applications or free online developments, the calculator proposed in this paper has a solid scientific and theoretical foundation, since its development is based on the Cost231-Walfisch-Ikegami model theory, therefore that the accuracy of their results are reliable. It should be noted that in the case of needing to scale the tool or extrapolate it to other models, it is possible, and the base theory would be used to continue providing precision to the resulting calculations.

The research in which the proposed software tool is embedded is in progress, so for the moment it is only available in development mode; however, it is intended to take it to production mode once the investigation is completed.

6   Future Work

This research can be extended in the following pathways:

- To perform experimental tests to verify the resulting link budget.

– To include the implementation of different propagation models in the software.
– To include different operating frequencies in the software.
– To determine a specific case study to test the software.
– To consider other communication systems that require the calculation of a link budget.
– To increase the options available in the graphical interface of the software.
– To include graphic tools for visualising results.

Acknowledgements. The authors acknowledge partial economical support by projects 20230476, 20231067, 20230592, 20230593, 20231370 and 20230035, as well as EDI grant, provided by Secretaría de Investigación y Posgrado, Instituto Politécnico Nacional.

References

1. Garg, M., et al.: A review on Internet of Things: communication protocols, wireless technologies, and applications. In: Dhar, S., Do, D.T., Sur, S.N., Liu, H.C.M. (eds.) Advances in Communication, Devices and Networking. LNEE, vol. 902, pp. 265–278. Springer, Singapore (2023). https://doi.org/10.1007/978-981-19-2004-2_23
2. Avşar, E., Mowla, M.: Wireless communication protocols in smart agriculture: a review on applications, challenges and future trends. Ad Hoc Netw. **136**, 102982 (2022)
3. Ramalingam, S., Shanmugam, P.: A comprehensive review on wired and wireless communication technologies and challenges in smart residential buildings. Recent Adv. Comput. Sci. Commun. **15**(9), 1140–1147 (2022)
4. Rawat, A., Yadav, D., Tiwari, M.: A review on mmWave antennas for wireless cellular communication. In: Proceedings - 7th International Conference on Computing Methodologies and Communication, ICCMC 2023, pp. 1009–1015 (2023)
5. Lian, B., Wei, Z., Sun, X., Li, Z., Zhao, J.: A review on rainfall measurement based on commercial microwave links in wireless cellular networks. Sensors **22**(12), 4395 (2022)
6. Abbas, Z., Yoon, W.: A review of mobility supporting tunneling protocols in wireless cellular networks. Int. J. Adv. Comput. Sci. Appl. **13**(2), 24–32 (2022)
7. Raja, S.K.S., Louis, A.B.V.: A review of call admission control schemes in wireless cellular networks. Wireless Pers. Commun. **120**(4), 3369–3388 (2021). https://doi.org/10.1007/s11277-021-08618-6
8. Nayak, D.S., Akshaya Krishna, N., Shetty, S., Naik, S.D., Sambhram, V., Shetty, K.: Review on application of wireless technology using IoT. In: Joby, P.P., Balas, V.E., Palanisamy, R. (eds.) IoT Based Control Networks and Intelligent Systems. LNNS, vol. 528, pp. 161–170. Springer, Singapore (2023). https://doi.org/10.1007/978-981-19-5845-8_12
9. Pamarthi, S., Narmadha, R.: Literature review on network security in Wireless Mobile Ad-hoc Network for IoT applications: network attacks and detection mechanisms. Int. J. Intell. Unmanned Syst. **10**(4), 482–506 (2022)
10. Bhardwaj, B., Vanita, Kumar, S.: Application of IoT in 5G wireless communication: a detailed review. In: Luhach, A.K., Jat, D.S., Hawari, K.B.G., Gao, XZ., Lingras, P. (eds.) ICAICR 2021. CCIS, vol. 1575, pp. 269–279. Springer, Cham (2022). https://doi.org/10.1007/978-3-031-09469-9_23

11. Singh, M.: A review on IoT traffic wireless sensor network. In: CEUR Workshop Proceedings, vol. 3058 (2021)
12. Neeraj Krishna, N., Padmasine, K.G.: A review on microwave band pass filters: materials and design optimization techniques for wireless communication systems. Mater. Sci. Semicond. Process. **154**, 107181 (2023)
13. Zhu, X., Jin, K., Hui, Q., Gong, W., Mao, D.: Long-range wireless microwave power transmission: a review of recent progress. IEEE J. Emerg. Sel. Top. Power Electron. **9**(4), 4932–4946 (2021)
14. Tsitsos, S.: Advances on microwave ceramic filters for wireless communications (review paper). Int. J. Electr. Comput. Eng. **8**(5), 2762–2772 (2018)
15. Lakew, D., Tran, A.T., Masood, A., Dao, N.N., Cho, S.: A review on satellite-terrestrial integrated wireless networks: challenges and open research issues. In: International Conference on Information Networking, pp. 638–641 (2023)
16. Choudhary, A., Agrawal, N.: Inter-satellite optical wireless communication (IsOWC) systems challenges and applications: a comprehensive review. J. Opt. Commun. (2022)
17. Sohraby, K., Minoli, D., Occhiogrosso, B., Wang, W.: A review of wireless and satellite-based M2M/IoT services in support of smart grids. Mob. Netw. Appl. **23**(4), 881–895 (2018). https://doi.org/10.1007/s11036-017-0955-1
18. Maurya, G., Kokate, P., Lokhande, S., Shrawankar, J.: A review on investigation and assessment of path loss models in urban and rural environment. In: IOP Conference Series: Materials Science and Engineering, vol. 225 (2017)
19. Kurt, S., Tavli, B.: Path-loss modeling for wireless sensor networks: a review of models and comparative evaluations. IEEE Antennas Propag. Mag. **59**(1), 18–37 (2017)
20. Oni, O., Idachaba, F.: Review of selected wireless system path loss prediction models and its adaptation to indoor propagation environments. In: Lecture Notes in Engineering and Computer Science, vol. 2228, pp. 562–567 (2017)
21. Okumura, Y., et al.: Field strength variability in VHF and UHF land mobile service. Rev. Electr. Commun. Lab. **16**, 825–873 (1968)
22. Hata, M.: Empirical formula for propagation loss in land mobile radio services. IEEE Trans. Veh. Technol. **29**(3), 317–325 (1980)
23. Walfisch, J., Bertoni, H.: A theoretical model of UHF propagation in urban environments. IEEE Trans. Antennas Propag. **36**(12), 1788–1796 (1988)
24. Ikegami, F., Takeuchi, T., Yoshida, S.: Theoretical prediction of mean field strength for urban mobile radio. IEEE Trans. Antennas Propag. **39**(3), 299–302 (1991)
25. Li, H., He, X., He, W.: Review of wireless personal communications radio propagation models in high altitude mountainous areas at 2.6 GHz. Wireless Pers. Commun. **101**(2), 735–753 (2018). https://doi.org/10.1007/s11277-018-5713-6
26. Azevedo, J., Santos, F.: A model to estimate the path loss in areas with foliage of trees. AEU-Int. J. Electron. Commun. **71**, 157–161 (2017)
27. Kurnaz, O., Helhel, S.: Near ground propagation model for pine tree forest environment. AEU-Int. J. Electron. Commun. **68**(10), 944–950 (2014)
28. Basyigit, I.: Empirical path loss models for 5G wireless sensor network in coastal pebble/sand environments. Int. J. Microw. Wireless Technol. **14**(9), 1222–1231 (2022)
29. Duangsuwan, S., Maw, M.: Comparison of path loss prediction models for UAV and IoT air-to-ground communication system in rural precision farming environment. J. Commun. **16**(2), 60–66 (2021)

30. Budalal, A., Islam, M.: Path loss models for outdoor environment-with a focus on rain attenuation impact on short-range millimeter-wave links. e-Prime - Adv. Electr. Eng. Electron. Energy **3**, 100106 (2023)

31. Daho, A., Yamada, Y., Al-Samman, A., Abdrahman, T., Azmi, M., Arsad, A.: Proposed path loss model for outdoor environment in tropical climate for the 28-GHz 5G system. In: 2021 1st International Conference on Emerging Smart Technologies and Applications, eSmarTA 2021 (2021)

32. Sulyman, A., Seleem, H., Alwarafy, A., Humadi, K., Alsanie, A.: Effects of solar radio emissions on outdoor propagation path loss models at 60 GHz bands for access/backhaul links and D2D communications. IEEE Trans. Antennas Propag. **65**(12), 6624–6635 (2017)

33. Khan, M., Manzoor, K., Mughal, M.: Path loss prediction model incorporating the effects of vegetation and vehicular traffic in URBAN microcell. In: Proceedings - 4th IEEE International Conference on Emerging Technologies 2008, ICET 2008, pp. 152–155 (2008)

34. Al-Dabbagh, R., Al-Aboody, N., Al-Raweshidy, H.: A simplified path loss model for investigating diffraction and specular reflection impact on millimetre wave propagation. In: Proceedings of the 2017 8th International Conference on the Network of the Future, NOF 2017, pp. 153–155 (2017)

35. Khaleel, W.: Design Link Between Earth Station and Satellite System, vol. 1, 1st edn. Lambert Academic Publishing (2020)

36. Al-Hattab, M., Takruri, M.: Adaptive method to estimate link budget parameters in wireless networks. In: 2022 9th International Conference on Internet of Things, Systems, Management and Security, IOTSMS 2022 (2022)

37. Samaniego-Rojas, P., Salcedo-Serrano, P., Boluda-Ruiz, R., Garrido-Balsells, J., García-Zambrana, A.: Novel link budget modelling for NLOS submarine optical wireless links. In: Optics InfoBase Conference Papers (2022)

38. Ponce, K., Inca, S., Diaz, D., Nunez, M.: Towards adaptive LoRa wireless sensor networks: link budget and energy consumption analysis. In: Proceedings of the 2021 IEEE 28th International Conference on Electronics, Electrical Engineering and Computing, INTERCON 2021 (2021)

39. Weng, Z.K., et al.: Millimeter-wave and terahertz fixed wireless link budget evaluation for extreme weather conditions. IEEE Access **9**, 163476–163491 (2021)

40. Jones, R.: Handbook on Satellite Communications (HSC) (1985)

41. European Telecommunications Standard Institute: Fixed radio systems; point-to-point equipment; derivation of receiver interference parameters useful for planning fixed service point-to-point systems operating different equipment classes and/or capacities. Technical report, ETSI TR 101 854, European Telecommunications Standard Institute (2005)

42. The MathWorks Inc.: Communications Toolbox - MATLAB (2023). https://www.mathworks.com/products/communications.html. Accessed 01 June 2023

43. Keysight Technologies: PadthWave Advanced Design System (ADS): Keysight (2023). https://www.keysight.com/us/en/products/software/pathwave-design-software/pathwave-advanced-design-system.html. Accessed 02 June 2023

44. Pasternack: Link Budget Calculator (2023). https://www.pasternack.com/t-calculator-link-budget.aspx. Accessed 04 June 2023

45. Huawei: "pon link budget calculator" (2021). https://info.support.huawei.com/AccessInfoTool/PON_Budget_Tool/index?language=en&domain=0

46. Radwin: Radwin Link Budget Calculator (2021). http://tools.radwin.com/planner/

47. RF Wireless World: Hata model path loss calculator: Hata model path loss formula (2012). https://www.rfwireless-world.com/calculators/Hata-model-path-loss-calculator.html
48. Gütter, D.: CANDY - Tools - Simple outdoor wave propagation models (2013). http://www.guetter-web.de/mini-tools/candy-prop-outdoor.htm#wi231los
49. Cost Final Report: COST 231 Walfisch-Ikegami Model (2012). http://www.lx.it.pt/cost231/
50. Bordón L'opez, R., Alonso Quintana, R., Montejo Sánchez, S.: Evaluación de modelos de propagación de canal inalámbrico. Revista Cubana Ingeniería **3**(1), 55 (2012)
51. Alqudah, Y.A.: On the performance of Cost 231 Walfisch Ikegami model in deployed 3.5 GHz network. In: 2013 The International Conference on Technological Advances in Electrical, Electronics and Computer Engineering (TAEECE), pp. 524–527 (2013)
52. Harinda, E., Hosseinzadeh, S., Larijani, H., Gibson, R.M.: Comparative performance analysis of empirical propagation models for LoRaWAN 868 MHz in an urban scenario. In: 2019 IEEE 5th World Forum on Internet of Things (WF-IoT), pp. 154–159 (2019)
53. Hill, G.: The Cable and Telecommunications Professionals' Reference: PSTN, IP and Cellular Networks, and Mathematical Techniques. Taylor & Francis (2012). https://books.google.com.mx/books?id=Oi14kDFRl6cC
54. Del Peral-Rosado, J., Raulefs, R., López-Salcedo, J., Seco-Granados, G.: Survey of cellular mobile radio localization methods: from 1G to 5G. IEEE Commun. Surv. Tutor. **20**(2), 1124–1148 (2018)
55. Sasibhushana Rao, G., Rao, C., Satya Prasad, K.: Performance analysis of 4G (OFDMA), 3G,2G and 1G cellular systems. Int. J. Appl. Eng. Res. **10**(15), 35753–35756 (2015)
56. Barik, D.K., Mali, S., Ali, F.A., Agarwal, A.: Design and analysis of RF optimization in 2G GSM and 4G LTE network. In: Mishra, M., Sharma, R., Kumar Rathore, A., Nayak, J., Naik, B. (eds.) Innovation in Electrical Power Engineering, Communication, and Computing Technology. LNEE, vol. 814, pp. 11–18. Springer, Singapore (2022). https://doi.org/10.1007/978-981-16-7076-3_2
57. Yuwono, T., Wibisono, N.: Analysis and improvement of handover failure in 2G GSM network. In: Proceedings - ICWT 2016: 2nd International Conference on Wireless and Telematics 2016, pp. 122–126 (2017)
58. Yuwono, T., Ferdiyanto, F.: RF measurement and analysis of 2G GSM network performance case study: Yogyakarta Indonesia. In: 2015 IEEE International Conference on Smart Instrumentation, Measurement and Applications, ICSIMA 2015 (2016)
59. Hirai, S., Arakawa, N., Ueno, T., Hamada, H., Kamei, K.: A chip antenna for CDMAOne mobile phones. Furukawa Rev. **25**, 28–31 (2004)
60. Hitachi: CDMAOne cellular phone. Hitachi Review Special Issue, 28 (2001)
61. Barrick, M.: Fine-tuning test methods for CDMAOne handsets. Microwaves RF **39**(4), 84–90 (2000)
62. Dixit, Y., Muhammed, S.: Performance trade-offs of a software defined radio for 2G and 3G cellular mobile communication standards. In: First International Conference on Communication System Software and Middleware, Comsware 2006 (2006)
63. Goodman, D., Myers, R.: 3G cellular standards and patents. In: 2005 International Conference on Wireless Networks, Communications and Mobile Computing, vol. 1, pp. 415–420 (2005)

64. Pribylov, V., Rezvan, I.: On the way to 3G networks: the GPRS/EDGE concept. In: Proceedings of the 4th IEEE-Russia Conference - 2003 Microwave Electronics: Measurements, Identification, Applications, MEMIA 2003, pp. 87–98 (2003)

65. Zhang, W., Chen, S.H., Su, J.S., Chen, P.X.: Traffic measurement and analysis in CDMA2000 3G core network. Tongxin Xuebao/J. Commun. **32**(9A), 123–127 (2011)

66. Lu, J., et al.: On the beyond 3G evolution of CDMA2000 wireless cellular networks. In: Proceedings - 2007 IEEE Radio and Wireless Symposium, RWS, pp. 495–498 (2007)

67. Saugstrup, D., Henten, A.: 3G standards: the battle between WCDMA and CDMA2000. Info **8**(4), 10–20 (2006)

68. Hsu, L., Derryberry, R., Pi, Z., Niva, I.: 3G evolution: CDMA2000®1xEV-DV forward and reverse links. In: Proceedings - 2004 Global Mobile Congress, pp. 041–046 (2004)

69. Parry, R.: CDMA 2000 1xEV-DO: a 3G wireless internet access system. IEEE Potentials **21**(4), 10–13 (2002)

70. Yuwono, T., Putra, A.: Drive test and analysis of 3G WCDMA system using binning technique case study: Yogyakarta Indonesia. Adv. Sci. Lett. **23**(2), 1344–1346 (2017)

71. Joyce, R., Zhang, L.: The effectiveness of low power co-channel lamppost mounted 3G/WCDMA microcells. In: 20th European Wireless Conference, EW 2014, pp. 118–123 (2014)

72. Skoutas, D., Skianis, C.: Enhancing the high speed downlink packet access operation of 3G WCDMA systems. Wireless Commun. Mob. Comput. **14**(1), 115–127 (2014)

73. Al-Qahtani, S., Mahmoud, A.: A prioritized uplink call admission control algorithm for 3G WCDMA cellular systems with multi-services. In: IEE Conference Publication, pp. 173–177, No. 2005 in 11182 (2005)

74. Tan, W.K., Li, H.Y.: Mobile service: an empirical study of the behavior of 2/2.5G and 3G subscribers and implications to roll-out of WiMAX network. In: Proceedings - International Conference on Management and Service Science, MASS 2009 (2009)

75. Shahid, M., Shoulian, T., Shan, A.: Mobile broadband: comparison of mobile WiMAX and cellular 3G/3G+ technologies. Inf. Technol. J. **7**(4), 570–579 (2008)

76. Jaeho, J., Jinsung, C.: A cross-layer vertical handover between mobile WiMAX and 3G networks. In: IWCMC 2008 - International Wireless Communications and Mobile Computing Conference, pp. 644–649 (2008)

77. Murawwat, S., Ahmed, K.: Performance analysis of 3G and WiMAX as cellular mobile technologies. In: 2nd International Conference on Electrical Engineering, ICEE (2008)

78. Gozalvez, J.: WiMAX recognized as an IMT-2000 3G technology [mobile radio]. IEEE Veh. Technol. Mag. **2**(4), 53–59 (2007)

79. Matt, B., Li, C.: A survey of the security and threats of the IMT-advanced requirements for 4G standards. In: 2013 IEEE Conference Anthology, ANTHOLOGY 2013 (2013)

80. Deka, S., Sarma, K.: Joint source channel coding and diversity techniques for 3G/4G/LTE-A: a review of current trends and technologies. In: Research Anthology on Recent Trends, Tools, and Implications of Computer Programming, pp. 1–26 (2020)

81. Kumar, T., Moorthi, M.: Review on 4G antenna design for LTE application. In: Proceedings of the 3rd IEEE International Conference on Advances in Electrical and Electronics, Information, Communication and Bio-Informatics, AEEICB 2017, pp. 476–478 (2017)
82. Faheem, M., Zhong, S., Minhas, A., Azeem, B.: Ultra-low power small size 5.8 GHz RF transceiver design for WiMAX/4G applications. J. Beijing Inst. Technol. (Eng. Ed.) **28**(1), 103–108 (2019)
83. Sreeja, T., Jayakumari, J.: Design and analysis of compact T shape slotted patch antenna for 4G WiMAX applications. Int. J. Enterp. Netw. Manag. **9**(1), 1–10 (2018)
84. Medina-Acosta, G., et al.: 3GPP release-17 physical layer enhancements for LTE-M and NB-IoT. IEEE Commun. Stand. Mag. **6**(4), 80–86 (2022)
85. Dawaliby, S., Bradai, A., Pousset, Y.: Scheduling optimization for M2M communications in LTE-M. In: 2017 IEEE International Conference on Consumer Electronics, ICCE 2017, pp. 126–128 (2017)
86. Zhao, H., Hailin, J.: LTE-M system performance of integrated services based on field test results. In: Proceedings of 2016 IEEE Advanced Information Management, Communicates, Electronic and Automation Control Conference, IMCEC 2016, pp. 2016–2021 (2017)
87. Ratasuk, R., Mangalvedhe, N., Ghosh, A., Vejlgaard, B.: Narrowband LTE-M system for M2M communication. In: IEEE Vehicular Technology Conference (2014)
88. Abdujalilov, J., Turzhanova, K., Konshin, S., Solochshenko, A., Yakubov, B.: Analysis and improvement of the methods used for performance assessing of 4G network with NB-IoT technology for three scenarios of spectrum use in the 900 MHz range. In: 2020 International Conference on Information Science and Communications Technologies, ICISCT 2020 (2020)
89. Janakieska, M., Latkoski, P., Atanasovski, V.: Signaling in 4G/5G with NB-IoT support in 5G Option 3. In: 2020 55th International Scientific Conference on Information, Communication and Energy Systems and Technologies, ICEST 2020 - Proceedings, pp. 54–57 (2020)
90. Del Peral-Rosado, J., Lopez-Salcedo, J., Seco-Granados, G.: Impact of frequency-hopping NB-IoT positioning in 4G and future 5G networks. In: 2017 IEEE International Conference on Communications Workshops, ICC Workshops 2017, pp. 815–820 (2017)
91. Köpp, J.: NB-IoT and eMTC make 4G networks ready for the Internet of Things. Microw. J. 32 (2016)
92. McNair, J.: The 6G frequency switch that spares scientific services. Nature **606**(7912), 34–35 (2022)
93. Alhaj, N., Jamlos, M., Manap, S., Bakhit, A., Mamat, R.: A review of multiple access techniques and frequencies requirements towards 6G. In: Proceedings - 2022 RFM IEEE International RF and Microwave Conference, RFM 2022 (2022)
94. Ikegami, F., Yoshida, S., Takeuchi, T., Umehira, M.: Propagation factors controlling mean field strength on urban streets. IEEE Trans. Antennas Propag. **32**(8), 822–829 (1984)
95. Ambawade, D., Karia, D., Potdar, T., Lande, B., Daruwala, R., Shah, A.: Statistical tuning of Walfisch-Ikegami model in urban and suburban environments. In: 2010 Fourth Asia International Conference on Mathematical/Analytical Modelling and Computer Simulation, pp. 538–543. IEEE (2010)
96. Garg, V.K.: Planning and Design of Wide-Area Wireless Networks. Morgan Kaufmann (2007)

97. Ahmadi, S.: LTE-Advanced. Academic Press (2014)
98. Meta: React (2023). https://react.dev/. Accessed 07 June 2023
99. Pete, H.: Why did we build react? - react blog (2013). https://legacy.reactjs.org/blog/2013/06/05/why-react.html
100. Xing, Y., Huang, J., Lai, Y.: Research and analysis of the front-end frameworks and libraries in e-business development. In: Proceedings of the 2019 11th International Conference on Computer and Automation Engineering, ICCAE 2019, pp. 68–72. Association for Computing Machinery, New York (2019). https://doi.org/10.1145/3313991.3314021
101. Angular: Introduction to the Angular docs (2023). https://angular.io/docs. Accessed 07 June 2023
102. Ember: Ember.js Guides (2023). https://guides.emberjs.com/release/. Accessed 07 June 2023
103. BACKBONE.JS: Backbone.js (2023). https://backbonejs.org/. Accessed 07 June 2023
104. (2023). https://react.dev/reference/react
105. Bose, S.: Top 5 CSS frameworks for developers and designers (2023). https://www.browserstack.com/guide/top-css-frameworks
106. Bootstrap: Introdution bootstrap (2023). https://getbootstrap.com/docs/4.1/getting-started/introduction/. Accessed 07 June 2023
107. Foundation: Getting Started With Foundation CSS (2023). https://get.foundation/sites/docs-v5/css.html. Accessed 07 June 2023
108. BULMA: Documentation: Free, open source, and modern CSS framework (2023). https://bulma.io/documentation/. Accessed 07 June 2023
109. Skeleton: Skeleton: Responsive CSS Bilerplate (2023). http://getskeleton.com/. Accessed 07 June 2023
110. Pete, H.: Documentation - Tailwind (2023). https://v2.tailwindcss.com/docs. Accessed 07 June 2023
111. Adam, W.: Adam Wathan (2023). https://adamwathan.me/. Accessed 07 June 2023
112. Tailwind Labs Inc.: Installation - Tailwind CSS (2023). https://tailwindcss.com/docs/installation. Accessed 30 May 2023
113. Instituto Federal de Telecomunicaciones (2023). https://www.ift.org.mx/usuarios-telefonia-movil/sabias-que-la-telefonia-movil. Accessed 16 May 2023
114. Nimavat, V., Kulkarni, G.: Simulation and performance evaluation of GSM propagation channel under the urban, suburban and rural environments. In: 2012 International Conference on Communication, Information & Computing Technology (ICCICT), pp. 1–5. IEEE (2012)

Scientific Information Management System for Multidisciplinary Teams

Gomez-Miranda Pilar[1] (ID), Romero-Lujambio Jose-Fausto[2] (ID),
Aguíñiga-García Sergio[3], and Garay-Jimenez Laura-Ivoone[2](✉) (ID)

[1] Instituto Politécnico Nacional, UPIICSA, Ciudad de México, Mexico
[2] Instituto Politécnico Nacional, UPIITA, Ciudad de México, Mexico
lgaray@ipn.mx
[3] Instituto Politécnico Nacional, CICIMAR, La Paz, Baja California Sur, Mexico

Abstract. The objective of this work is to create a system that allows a group of researchers to manage scientific information derived from their research activities in a safe way to promote interdisciplinary collaboration. Design Thinking (DT) was used for the development of the system. DT is focused on the continuous interaction of end-users with the development team. Each design step is centered on understanding user needs and motivations. The system implementation was done under the Scrumban methodology, using edge computing, microservices in the cloud, and artificial intelligence elements for information search. It was subdivided into two stages of development, with end-user feedback in each stage. The validation of the system was carried out with 16 researchers participating in a multidisciplinary project. The system lets each researcher control the information they share with their work leader, which, under a modular scheme, gives access to the publications to the other module members or modules. Users publish and consult shared documents and databases, and the system allows them to view, filter, calculate statistics, graph, and download the information. The system is available as a web application for this research group. However, it can be replicated to be used by other collaborative groups that seek levels of controlled access and portability of information within a secure environment, that is not constrained to a particular choice of hardware or operating system.

Keywords: Collaborating platforms · Multidisciplinary research · Design thinking · information manager

1 Introduction

Multidisciplinary research groups must share data, preliminary results, and background information, collaborate, and perform data and information analysis. The collaboration allows the research team to analyze preliminary integrated results and monitor products, providing continuity to the investigation and guiding the decision-making processes.

Information systems available on the Web such as OceanExpert - A Directory of Marine and Freshwater Professionals, Climatic Research Unit - Groups and Centres [1] or The Brain Function Research Group (BFRG) [2] are examples of how the Internet

© The Author(s), under exclusive license to Springer Nature Switzerland AG 2023
M. F. Mata-Rivera et al. (Eds.): WITCOM 2023, CCIS 1906, pp. 199–215, 2023.
https://doi.org/10.1007/978-3-031-45316-8_14

is a mean of communication and dissemination of information [3]; they have generated value by being able to consult and use the information according to the purpose pursued. These information systems available on the Web platform create social networks that can interact and share information [4], achieving the dissemination of information. Information management aims to collect updated information, carry out processes, and generate new knowledge generated by interested parties through systems with algorithms and functions that receive, manage, and transform information, execute actions of integration and segmentation, and provide information to users using technologies such as edge computing or cloud services.

However, each multidisciplinary group had to prepare their work in closed interactive sessions to share with the rest of the group and then share it with the world. In this sense, a research group composed of members of six academic units and research centers in the National Polytechnique Institute with different academic profiles proposes a multidisciplinary project named "Ecogeochemical modeling of coastal systems towards comprehensive health.". Each module has a unique goal that contributes to the global objective. Module I studies the ecosystem disturbances due to natural impacts and anthropic in the coastal lagoons of Mexico; Module II determines the biogeochemistry of the principal elements and traces in coastal systems; Module III is doing an ambispective analysis of the health of the workers and their families of the Fishermen's Cooperative, and module IV looking for multidimensional biogeochemical models with time series associated with anthropogenic contamination of marine organisms for human consumption and possible effects on health.

The magnitude of the project requires an information system that allows each modules to manage the research products obtained, share results, analyze the data, and promote collaborative synergy in a safe way. Each researcher also requires a system where he can manage the research products obtained, share results, analyze the gathered data, without using costly commercial systems.

Thus, this document describes the development of the Scientific Information Management System (SIGIC) that was developed to support the scientific community in the management of products and information generated from the investigations of each module of the multidisciplinary project.

2   Methodology

Constant complaints from the final user that give up using a specific software or platform for collaborating are associated with lacking a focused solution, the requirements changed during the design and implementation, or the final system being too complex to learn. So, software designers are migrating to the methodology named Design Thinking (DT), as proposed and used by International Business Machines Corp. (IBM) [5], which is considered a framework of good practices for software development. It focuses on the user and identifying their user experience needs for interface and functionality.

Then, the agile techniques Scrum [6] and Kanban were used for the system implementation. They promote collaborative work of the development team and frequent user feedback based on iterative cycles called sprints [7]. It is carried out through planning meetings, assignment of activities, monitoring, delivery, and reviews of the artifacts [8]. At the end of each sprint, executable deliveries are presented to the user.

The stages that make up DT [9] are a) Empathy, which focuses on understanding the environment and user needs and putting oneself in their place to detect the system requirements accurately. Information-gathering tools such as meetings, interviews, observation, and surveys are used. b) The next stage is the definition of the problem to be solved, which is carried out with the "Point of View" (POV) technique that lets designers always focus on the detected findings, the interests, and the needs of the user, which are carefully analyzed to determine the best final requirements definition called stories. c) The third phase is designing and developing a solution prototype with the requirements, and technical and functional feasibility, which the user evaluates and provides feedback. d) The next stage is the tests along the implementation of the created stories, which validate that the system's requirements and functionalities comply with the specifications. They are carried out with the user. The user's interaction with the system confirms understanding of the requirements or, where appropriate, the suitable adjustments are considered.

2.1 Gathering of Requirements

Meetings and personalized interviews were held with the researchers, questionnaires were applied, and empathy maps and the roadmap were created.

Using the empathy map gives the designer an idea of the user activity, how he feels about it, and how he perceives his activity; Fig. 1 shows an example of an empathy map. Each user type (role) is identified and detailed. Then, as is shown in Fig. 1, pain points (red highlight), improvement opportunities (green highlight), and challenges (blue highlight) are identified, taking into account three aspects: What does he do?, What does he think?, and what does he feel?; With this information, the requirements divided in pain points, opportunities and challenges are obtained and weighted and a need statement generated.

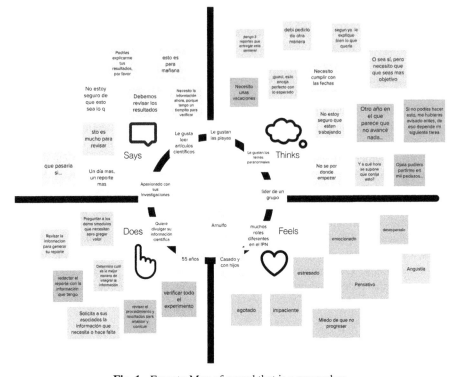

Fig. 1. Empaty Map of a used that is a researcher.

2.2   Design Process

The functionalities the researchers identified were integrated into a road map where the designers show how the system is expected to work (Fig. 2).

The designers analyzed the need statement, and a brainstorming technique was used to generate possible solutions out of the box (big ideas). Then, ideas were grouped by similarity and prioritized according to the importance and feasibility assigned by the designers (Fig. 2). Finally, the solution with a higher weighting was integrated into a road map and defined how the system could provide increased functionality, including less weighted solutions.

At this point of the design, feedback from researchers is required. With the adjustment recommended, Hills were created considering who does the action (who), how it will be done (How), and the benefit of doing it in the system (wow factor).

Besides, it was identified how the system could provide increased functionality, including less weighted solutions in the subsequent implementation in a timeline experience chart based in the road map (Fig. 3).

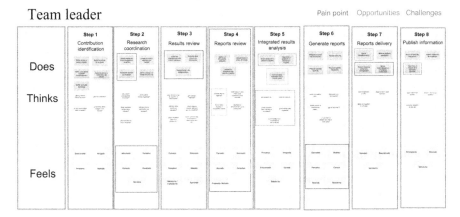

Fig. 2. User experience into the research process with pain points, opportunities, and challenges.

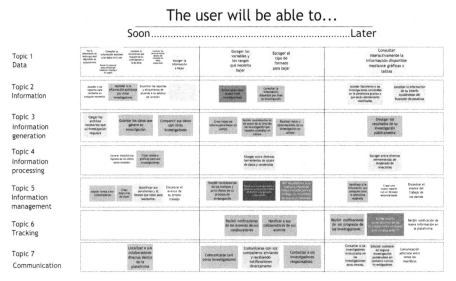

Fig. 3. Timeline of the user experience according to identified needs, their priority, and the incremental development stage.

2.3 Prototyping and Design Documentation

After researchers agree with what is expected of the system. The implementation team conformed by designers and programmers collaborated with the product owner to generate the backlog of user stories to be implemented. A preliminary UI/UX design prototype was enacted as a visual aid to the proposed features that directly correspond to the aforementioned stories. The tool used to design this prototype has been Figma®, a

collaborative design Tool [10]. Also, in order to aid the design logic of the user's interactions with the system user case and package diagrams were created using the Unified
Modelling Language (UML).

With the prototype, researchers could interact with the proposed system and feedback
to the implementation group. On the other hand, the Implementation team could analyze
the proposed solution, prioritise the stories, create group related stories into epics as
deemed necessary, and define the minimum viable product (MVP) that provides the
usability, reliability and functionality required.

2.4 Implementation

Now, once the system to be developed has been defined, we move on to the next stage
of the methodology. The logic design and work environment definition.

On one hand, the structure, languages, tools, and resources are selected based on the
functionality defined in the stories and the dynamic prototype. On the other hand, the
written acceptance criteria are associated with each user story and were then uploaded
into Jira®. This project management tool helps the implementation team to report inci-
dences and monitor the sprints and development milestones of the collaborative work
by using of a Kanban board [11], backlog tracking, and laying out a development road
map. For version control and code integration, the GitHub platform was selected [12].
Besides, Extreme Programming (XP) techniques were adopted as a way to complement
the Agile development methodology, specifically the pair-programming technique [13].

During each development sprint, an assignment is done in Jira, and then the specific
stories were developed in parallel by the team employing different Git branches. Each
branch was thoroughly tested by each programmer in their current development branch,
in accordance with the acceptance criteria set by the product owner, and design team,
then it was reported in Jira. Progress tracking is available to the product owner. Epics
and integrations are also tracked and tested previously prior to their inclusion included
in the primary production branch. Several springs development sprints were required in
order to achieve the MVP outlined in the first stage, as shown in Fig. 4. Feedback from
researchers was given periodically.

By employing Design Thinking as the basis for Agile design and development,
it has been possible to design a system that accommodates the specific needs of the
researchers, with continuous tuning to proposed functions and user interface, enabling
the implementation team to quickly identify and fix issues that could hinder the usability
and value of the system early in development.

3 Results

The generation of the system following the methodology implies several steps and the
partial results are summarized in this section.

3.1 Gathering of Requirements

It was identified that developing an information system that allows the management of
the research team's activities and data is a recurrent need in academia due to the research

activity evolving into multidisciplinary work. So nowadays, researchers' activities and interactions are no longer in a near-closed group. They collaborate on several projects simultaneously and are active contributor in several groups. These collaborations are promoted by CONAHCyT [14], a rector in national research, based on the national development plan.

So they identified four relevant and everyday activities in this context are summarized in the Table 1.

Table 1. Relevant and everyday activities detected by the identified roles

Activities	Project module Leader	Associated	Visitor	Guest
Manage information	*	*	*	*
Visualization of research results	*	*	*	*
Collaborative work between researchers	*	*	*	
Perform automatic calculations of the data	*	*	*	*

It has been determined that the development of the system would be built on top of a scheme of users and privileges, in order to ensure the appropriate levels of privacy of research data during its lifecycle and the process of data analysis.

This user privilege-based system is based on the following identified roles:

Project Module Leader. This role pertains to the researcher, whose primary responsibility is managing team's functions in a specific academic unit or research center that makes up the multidisciplinary project. As responsible for achieving the assigned goal, he needs to browse and have access to the information, deciding what can be viewed by other researchers' teams.

Visitor Researcher: Researchers who enter as visitors want to view and download information another team had shared to be revised and compared with his research or team's results.

Associated Researcher: These researchers are temporarily part of a team but contribute valuable information about their experiments, so they must share research results and datasets with their team.

Guest: This user is a external visitor who wants to find out the new developments of this researchers group.

3.2 Design

A list of 70 stories with acceptance criteria was proposed, they were included in the backlog for the implementation, and a timeline roadmap was defined. The overall system is planned in three stages in an incremental approach. So each stage generated an MVP, but each stage was implemented in several sprints according to the scrum method, which the scrum master and the product owner supervised.

This section presents the design considering usability, reliability, and incremental functionality as a priority.

3.3 System Definition

The system has access security by registering users, and their access codes or credentials employ two-factor verification with a recovery option. Each research team has a module assigned, and they can access it anywhere. The information management of each module is the responsibility of the team's leader, who will decide and give access to generated information when they deem it appropriate, in order to ensure the privacy and access security of the research data of their team. The system has been developed as a Progressive Web Application and employs interface responsiveness that enables access to mobile devices such as tablets, smartphones, and desktop and laptop computers, irrespective of the user's choice of operating system, as long as they have access to a modern, standards-compliant web browser. Tested desktop operating systems included Windows and macOS, and mobile operating systems were Android and iOS.

Each module member will have space to manage their research's data, information, and results. The summarized functionalities researchers require and associate with each module are shown below.

The system associates the researcher's ID with his documents. They can be of the type: XLSX (Excel), CSV (text), images (JPG, PNG, WEBP), PDF, and other multimedia documents (MP3, MP4, WEBM), with a size of less than one GB.

A researcher can add documents, browse, store, and visualize his and the shared documents with his module. Also, researchers can configure, upload and view the databases generated and shared. Interactive dataset visualization includes variables' selection, filter segmentation, statistical metrics, and popular essential graphic action, such as boxplots, bar or pie charts, histograms, and linear and non-linear regression with a pair of variables. Moreover, after interacting with the dataset, it is possible to edit the metadata, delete, save, and download the newly generated information without modifying the original.

In the second MVP, the researchers request that the loaded data can be treated using Clusters, multidimensional models, discriminant analysis, distribution maps, and other statistics, in addition to being able to identify relevant variables.

Another need widely expressed by researchers is that the system could show a directory of the multidisciplinary team members available by module and in a general way. Moreover, this should provide the module information, such as name, associated researchers, goal, and shared information, by module and member.

Finally, it must be highlighted that each researcher has a profile section with their contact information, such as name, email, and username, and that they can change their password.

3.4 Prototyping and Design Documentation

The platform represented as a system package is shown in Fig. 4; it has the login, the user profile, the researcher's directory and navigation between modules options, and database, documents, and pinned (favorites) sections.

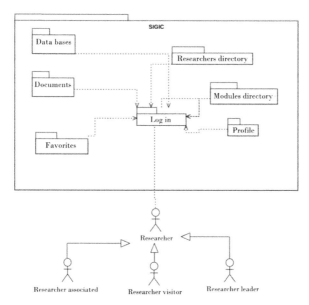

Fig. 4. System Package Diagram of SIGIC

An example of the dynamic prototyping elaborated in Figma is shown in Fig. 5. This simulation of the system's functionality gave the research possibility to feedback and the designers to glaze at the system's complexity and explain it to the programmers.

Fig. 5. Prototype of the dashboard of the researcher with his relevant information

3.5   Implementation

The logical representation between the frontend and backend of the system is shown in Fig. 6 and detailed in Fig. 7. The construction of both environments is carried out, considering the user stories and use case diagram.

Frontend: It is the user interface to interact with each system component. The language used for its development is TypeScript, supported by the Angular framework.

Backend: It is the component for processing the information received and coupling the data so the user can manage the documents and the databases. The language used is Python, using the Django framework as support.

Two either relational or non-relational databases store the data generated and uploaded by the researchers and the application's data, such as the user profiles and configurations, among other non-functional requirements. For the reference implementation, a single relational database system was employed, using two distinct information schemas, one for the platform's own metadata (users, background tasks, settings and application states and metadata of uploaded information, including a pointer to the file in the application filesystem), and another one for storing user-generated databases, as artifacts of the research process.

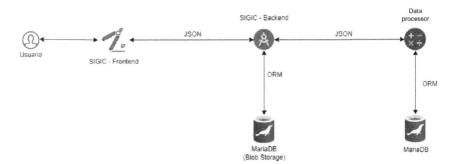

Fig. 6. General scheme of SIGIC platform.

The SIGIC Frontend component are described here.

Login: The component in charge of providing the authentication interface (login) through communication with the user manager and backend activities.

Home Screen: The component in charge of providing the user with direct access to the information they configure through communication with the backend configuration manager.

Module Browser: Component in charge of providing the user with direct access to the public or dissemination of information available on the platform through communication with the user manager.

Document Browser: The component in charge of providing the user with a document management interface through communication with the backend document manager.

Document Viewer: Provides the user with a preview of research documents and multimedia content.

File Upload: Provides the user with a means to save a local document from their computer to the platform and determine if the document should be interpreted as a raw data source.

Data Analysis and Visualization: The component in charge of providing the user with an interface for the visualization and filtering of data through communication with the Data Processor. In addition, it allows the user to keep the analysis and processing parameters used.

Directory of Researchers Component in charge of providing the user with a list of researchers registered in the platform with associated information (user profile, means of contact, and additional information configured by the researcher), this through communication with the User Manager.

Configuration: Provides the user with an interface for customizing personal information available to other users, the means to update or modify contact email addresses, and the possibility of updating their account password.

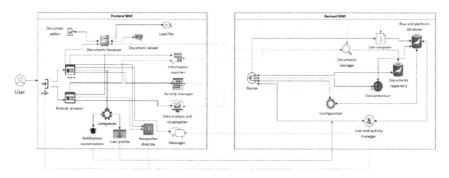

Fig. 7. Detailed scheme of frontend and backend of the SIGIC platform.

On the other hand, the SIGIC backend components are:

Router: Component in charge of linking to the Backend and Frontend for the proper functioning of the application.

Configuration Manager: Interface in charge of interpreting the input data, modifying the user's data and their notifications, and returning a response to say that the changes were made successfully.

User and Activities Manager: This interface is responsible of interpreting the input data and making the corresponding queries to the database to obtain the users' information in accordance with the specified role of the user.

Login: User search and confirmation of the registration.

Contact Information: This element looks up the contact information for the researchers.

Document Manager: This interface is responsible for interpreting the input data to perform a search for the files that can be displayed. Likewise, it is responsible for returning the found files as a response.

Data Interpreter: This interface is responsible of interpreting the input data and making the corresponding queries to the database to obtain the users' information in accordance with the specified role of the user.

Data Processor: The component in charge of carrying out all the mathematical and analysis operations available within the platform, using the input parameters to conduct the search, process them and return a result.

Raw Database: A MariaDB-compatible SQL-type database used to store the following data: Researcher-uploaded databases, storage of user and contact information, user permissions, and notification information.

Document Repository: A MariaDB database, which stores the metadata of the documents, as well as a universal unique identifier pointer (UUID) to a local or remote file system, used to store the documents, multimedia documents (images) are uploaded to the platform, serving as a file repository.

The platform implementation result is summarized in this section but access to the latest version of the system is through the link https://sigic.labips.com.mx/. The home interface presents the name of the system and welcomes the researcher, who has the options to see the purpose of the system and start to use it, see Fig. 8.

Fig. 8. Initial interface to the SIGC system.

When the researcher uses the system for the first time, they must create a new account, for which they must enter a username, password, full name with last name, and email address. It is essential to mention that the system has security measures since a confirmation email is sent when sending the user's data. If the researcher is registered, they only must enter their username and password. If they forget their login data, they can recover it. The system will email them their username and instructions for account recovery, as shown in Fig. 9.

Fig. 9. Boards for a registration request, registration confirmation, password recovery, and access to the system

Once in the system, the researcher navigates freely. The options at the top right are the following: go to favourites, the main dashboard, and exit the system. In the upper left part, direct access to the main board, with the options of access to documents, databases, a directory of researchers inscribed in the platform, access to the modules browser, and a settings page for managing the profile of each user (named "My Profile").

On the main dashboard, the researcher can start with the management of adding documents, and adding databases, see Fig. 10.

Fig. 10. User Dashboard of the system. Left image present the available menus, Right image user main dashboard.

Let us see the system's two main functions: document and database management. In document management is possible to add, view, delete, and download documents of various extensions (for example, Word, PDF, JPG, PNG, MP3, MP4, WEBP, WEBM), select one or more documents, as well it also has a favorites option in which documents that the researcher considers as such can be saved, see Fig. 11.

Fig. 11. Document management section in SIGIC.

In the database management dashboard, it is possible to store, export, and download the databases of each researcher. With the loaded databases, various analysis operations can be carried out, such as obtaining statistical data and graphs. The generated formats are PDF, CSV, MAT, XLSX, HTML, and MD, which can be downloaded. In addition, it has the functions of loading and editing the metadata of the databases and selecting, deleting, and downloading users' databases. The preview of the databases can be done through a table or in a graph.

The General Options dashboard can configure the database by selecting variables, Statistical metrics, data filters, and graphing. An example can be seen in Fig. 12. The first image is the space for the database option, the second shows a loaded database, the third shows the graph, and the last presents the obtained graph.

Finally, the functions of the researchers' directory, browsing modules, and my profile are presented.

The search for researchers is done by name, in their module, or the general list of the project members.

The system displays the environment of each module with the leader's name and the module's goal; selecting the option "more module information" displays the module's objective, the researchers that are part of the module, and the information that has been shared, see Fig. 13.

As it was mentioned, several tests were done. Nevertheless, the integrity of the system and acceptant criteria were verified before being sent to the production branch. Some examples of tests and their results are presented in the checklist in Table 2, which is the traceability matrix. The first column indicates the function identifier (ID), the second column indicates the function's name, the third column indicates the performed test; column four indicates the test result, and the last column if the result was attended and if an action is recommended.

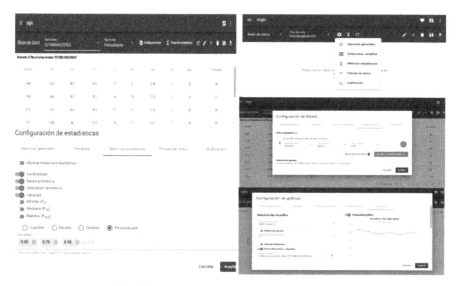

Fig. 12. Database management section in SIGIC.

Fig. 13. Directory of researchers.

Table 2. Example of the traceability matrix implementation.

ID	Description	Test	Result	Observation
RF-01	User registration	user data and password updated	Function executed correctly	None
RF-02	Validation of user's credentials	It is verified that the user receives the confirmation email	Function executed correctly	User is warning that he may receive it as a spam mail

The results of the functionality and integration tests were approved, finding functionality details corrected before the system was presented to the researchers. They considered that the system has the requested functionalities. The comments were very favorable, expressing that the interface is user-friendly and that the access and layout of the distinct components allow them to navigate the modules efficiently.

4 Conclusion

The scientific information management system (SIGIC) is a product of the research project "Multidimensional models with time series associated with anthropogenic contamination of marine organisms for human consumption and possible effects on health." The system allows researchers to manage their information product of their research work in a personal and collaborative manner. Management involves uploading articles, manuals, essays, and tables, which can be consulted by the research team or invited researchers. Invited researchers may have access to the information when the project leader considers that the research is ready for sharing.

On the other hand, researchers considered that the most valuable function is the database administrator, which allows uploading databases obtained from the research team, as the system allows viewing and configuring the data to perform the analysis through the configuration panel where statistical metrics are generated, and the results can be visually represented and graphed. It is, however, important to notice that each researcher may require the use of highly specialised software and data analysis tools that depend on very specific computing platforms, because of this, allowing researchers to include previously processed data into the system with the intent of sharing with other groups that may not have access to the specific data toolkits that would otherwise be necessitated becomes very useful and highly valuable.

Finally, the intelligent navigation function between modules was welcomed as it allows researchers access for collaboration between the investigations carried out by each team. The system currently allows the use of information available in metadata in order to provide this assistance. Future work may allow tailoring customised assistance to the researchers based on previous queries and topics of interest, as well as integration with additional software modules that could extend these capabilities.

It is concluded that the hybrid methodology implemented generates a system that covers and exceeds the requirements and expectations of the researchers. The system design enables horizontal scaling of computing resources for the database and frontend components when deployed in either cloud or hybrid environments and currently enables vertical scaling of the backend and data processing components.

Final tests were carried out by different real users with distinct roles in the system, who were given access to accompanying documentation manuals and video guides and an online meeting session for real-time feedback and support, after which it was commented by the researchers that the system seemed ready to be put into production, and the research community could begin with information management.

Researchers mentioned that accompanying the design and development process let them understand the relevance and usefulness of design thinking and Agile methodologies. Their continuous feedback and questioning enabled the development of end-user documentation that aims to reduce the learning curve of the system and increase its active usage. On the other hand, the implementation team reported that no requirements were modified, but underestimation of required effort and time was a recurrent challenge during the first stages.

As this system has been purposely designed for this specific team of research groups' needs and requirements as identified in their workflows, the system is highly specialised instead of general purpose; but because the original design considerations are basic needs that are common in this community, then this system could be reproduced for any interdisciplinary researchers' projects.

Nevertheless, it is very satisfying to say that the development of the first MVP of the first phase of the system was successfully achieved. In addition, it allowed the formation of human resources in methodologies required nowadays in the Mexican and global industry. This project also promoted collaborative work of research professors and postgraduate students, social service, and practical professions of the Academic Units of the National Polytechnic Institute of UPIICSA, UPIITA, and ESCOM.

References

1. Climatic Research Unit Groups and Centres, Ocean Expert Organization Homepage: Ocean-Expert - A Directory of Marine and Freshwater Professionals, Climatic Research Unit - Groups and Centres (uea.ac.uk). https://oceanexpert.org/. Accessed 05 June 2023
2. Brain Function Research Group Homepage. https://www.wits.ac.za/physiology/research-entities/brain-function-research-group/. Accessed 05 June 2023
3. Rodríguez Perojo, K., Ronda León, R.: El web como sistema de información. ACIMED **14**(1) (2023)
4. Chaparro, F.: Haciendo de Colombia una Sociedad del Conocimiento. In: Co-nocimiento, Innovación y Construcción de Sociedad: Una Agenda para la Colombia del Si-glo XXI. Colciencias. Santafé de Bogotá (1998). http://colombia-siglo21.net/index.html. Accessed 22 Jan 2000
5. Hildenbrand, T., Meyer, J.: Intertwining lean and design thinking: software product development from empathy to shipment. In: Maedche, A., Botzenhardt, A., Neer, L. (eds.) Software for People. MANAGPROF, pp. 217–237. Springer, Heidelberg (2012). https://doi.org/10.1007/978-3-642-31371-4_13
6. Srivastava, A., Bhardwaj, S., Saraswat, S.: SCRUM model for agile methodology. In: 2017 International Conference on Computing, Communication and Automation (ICCCA), pp. 864–869. IEEE (2017)
7. Sutherland, J.: Future of scrum: parallel pipelining of sprints in complex projects. In: Agile Development Conference (ADC 2005), pp. 90–99. IEEE (2005)
8. Canós, J.H., Letelier, P., Penadés, M.C.: Metodologías ágiles en el desarrollo de software, pp. 1–8. Universidad Politécnica de Valencia, Valencia (2003)
9. Costa Montenegro, E., Díaz Otero, F., Caeiro Rodríguez, M., Cuiñas Gómez, I., Mariño Espiñeira, P., Fernández Iglesias, M.: Evaluación de la implantación de la metodología Design Thinking en una asignatura de proyectos. In: In-Red 2016. II Congreso nacional de innovación educativa y docencia en red. Editorial Universitat Politècnica de València, July 2016
10. Figma Co. https://www.figma.com/. Accessed 20 May 2023
11. Shore Labs, Kanban Tool. https://kanbantool.com/es/metodologia-kanban. Accessed 20 May 2023
12. GitHub Inc., GitHub Platform. https://github.com/. Accessed 24 May 2023
13. Swimm team: Popular collaborative coding practices. https://swimm.io/learn/code-collaboration/code-collaboration-styles-tools-and-best-practices/. Accessed 02 June 2023
14. Congreso General de los Estados Unidos Mexicanos: Ley General en Materia de Humanidades, Ciencias, Tecnologías e Innovación. Diario Oficial de la Nación (2023)

Air Quality Prediction in Smart Cities Using Wireless Sensor Network and Associative Models

Mario Aldape-Pérez[1,2]([✉])(iD), Amadeo-José Argüelles-Cruz[4](iD),
Alejandro Rodríguez-Molina[3](iD), and Miguel-Gabriel Villarreal-Cervantes[2](iD)

[1] Computational Intelligence Section, CIDETEC, Instituto Politécnico Nacional,
07700 Mexico City, Mexico
maldape@ipn.mx
[2] Mechatronics Section, CIDETEC, Instituto Politécnico Nacional,
07700 Mexico City, Mexico
[3] Research and Postgraduate Division, Tecnológico Nacional de México/IT
de Tlalnepantla, 54070 Tlalnepantla de Baz, Mexico
[4] Computational Intelligence Section, CIC, Instituto Politécnico Nacional,
07700 Mexico City, Mexico

Abstract. This paper describes an application of Wireless Sensor Network and Associative Models to monitor and forecast air quality in Smart Cities. The modifications that were made to the Gamma Classifier provide the foundation for this proposal. The improved model proposes a different way to measure similarity between patterns in the training set, reduces pattern encoding complexity, and improves forecasting performance on atmospheric data series. Experimental results and comparisons against other time series forecasting algorithms show that the proposed associative algorithm achieves better performance and makes better air quality predictions in urban settings.

Keywords: Wireless Sensors Network · Smart Cities · Air Quality Prediction · Time Series Forecasting

1 Introduction

Urban air pollution has become a significant health issue that is getting worse, especially in emerging nations [4]. There are a variety of adverse impacts on human health that have been linked to exposure to air pollution; the severity of these effects will vary depending on a number of factors: the concentrations found in the ambient air, its physical and chemical properties, the time and frequency of exposure and the characteristics of the exposed population [3,5,13,22]. Several experimental studies, have clearly indicated that the prolonged exposure to particles that result from combustion processes and gases such as CO, NO_2 and SO_2 in ambient air is correlated with a wide variety of harmful effects (both chronic and acute), all of which have an impact on the quality of life of the

M. F. Mata-Rivera et al. (Eds.): WITCOM 2023, CCIS 1906, pp. 216–240, 2023.
https://doi.org/10.1007/978-3-031-45316-8_15

general population [2,6,7,9,23]. According to the World Health Organization (WHO), approximately 91% of the global population resides in areas where air quality exceeds WHO standards. Moreover, it is estimated that chronic respiratory diseases, lung cancer, stroke, and heart disease account for 4.2 million fatalities annually [15]. The World Health Organization (WHO) has been leading a project called the Global Platform on Air Quality and Health, which is a collaboration with over 50 different international agencies and research institutions. The goal of this initiative is to improve the capacity for air quality monitoring all around the world [16]. Nowadays, and particularly in urban settings of developing countries, it is imperative to have systems for air quality monitoring, that help authorities to establish policies to counteract the harmful effects of polluting gases on the health of the population [17]. This paper focuses on the use of wireless sensor network and associative models, to make air quality forecasting in urban settings, specifically in Zacatenco academic facilities of the National Polytechnic Institute, in Mexico City (IPN for its acronym in Spanish). To improve air quality predictions a slight modification to the original Gamma Classifier model is introduced. The proposed algorithm eliminates the limitations of the original Gamma Classifier. The proposed improvements reduce the complexity of the original Gamma Classifier algorithm, increasing forecasting accuracy in patterns represented as time series.

The remainder of this paper is as follows. In Sect. 2, previous works related to air quality predictions are presented. In Sect. 3 Associative Memories foundations as well as the hardware platform used for data acquisition and to monitor environmental parameters are described. In Sect. 4, an improved associative model is introduced. Section 5 provides details on the design of the experiments and a concise description of the dataset that was used along the experimental phase. In Sect. 6, air quality forecasting results are analysed. Finally, advantages of the proposed model, called Improved Gamma Predictor (IGP), as well as some conclusions will be discussed in Sect. 7.

2   Related Work

The Metropolitan Index of Air Quality (IMECA for its acronym in Spanish) is an analytical tool developed by the Ministry of the Environment and Natural Resources of Mexico (SEMARNAT for its acronym in Spanish) to provide the public with simple and accurate information regarding the levels of pollution, in such a way that it works as an indicator of the precautionary measures that individuals should take in atmospheric contingency. It is represented on a scale ranging from 0 to 500, with each pollutant's value indicated by the Official Mexican Standard as 100 on the scale. A value less than 100 is acceptable and poses little danger to human health. Any level above 100 poses a risk to human health; the greater the index value, the greater the contamination and risk. More information about this index and how indicators are calculated can be found in the following reference [12].

3   Materials and Methods

This section presents two associative models that form the theoretical base of the present proposal. First the theoretical background of Alpha-Beta Associative Memories is exposed and then Gamma Classifier operation details, are presented.

3.1   Associative Models

Alpha-Beta Associative Memories emerged more than a decade ago as an alternative model to perform pattern recognition tasks, they were first introduced in [19]. The mathematical basis of this supervised learning model requires two sets, set $A = \{0, 1\}$ and set $B = \{0, 1, 2\}$ which are used to define two binary operators: α and β (see Table 1). Alpha operator is used to obtain a learning matrix whose components correspond to the order relation between training patterns. The fundamentals and mathematical properties of these associative models can be consulted in [1, 21].

Table 1. Alpha and Beta Operators.

$\alpha : A \times A \longrightarrow B$			$\beta : B \times A \longrightarrow A$		
x	y	α(x, y)	x	y	β(x, y)
0	0	1	0	0	0
0	1	0	0	1	0
1	0	2	1	0	0
1	1	1	1	1	1
			2	0	1
			2	1	1

It should be noted that one of the advantages of these associative models is that they are quite robust to alterations of additive noise or subtractive noise in the training patterns set. Also they have the capacity to recover the complete fundamental set, when they are trained in auto-associative mode [20].

3.2   Gamma Classifier

This supervised learning model is based on α and β operators, taken from Alpha-Beta Associative Models, introduced in Sect. 3.1, shown in Table 1. Considering these two operators, Gamma Classifier defines a similarity operator, called Gamma Similarity [10], which takes two binary patterns $\mathbf{x} \in A^n$ and $\mathbf{y} \in A^m$; and a non-negative integer θ as input, and returns a binary number as output, according to Expression (1) and Expression (2). The following two definitions were taken from [11], and are included to explain the core concepts of Gamma Classifier. Also they are included to highlight the advantages of the proposed model, which is explained in Sect. 4.

Definition 1. *Let* $\mathbf{x} \in A^n$ *be an input binary pattern, where* $A = \{0,1\}$. *This operator* $u_\beta(\mathbf{x})$ *returns a non-negative integer number as output, according to the following expression:*

$$u_\beta(\mathbf{x}) = \sum_{i=1}^{n} \beta(x_i, x_i) \tag{1}$$

Definition 2. *Gamma similarity operator takes two binary patterns* $\mathbf{x} \in A^n$ *and* $\mathbf{y} \in A^m$; *where* $n, m \in \mathbb{Z}^+$; $n \le m$ *and a non-negative integer* θ *as input. This operator* $\gamma_g(\mathbf{x}, \mathbf{y}, \theta)$ *returns a binary number as output, according to the following expression:*

$$\gamma_g(\mathbf{x}, \mathbf{y}, \theta) = \begin{cases} 1 \ if & m - u_\beta[\alpha(\mathbf{x}, \mathbf{y}) \ mod \ 2] \le \theta \\ 0 \ otherwise \end{cases} \tag{2}$$

where mod 2 returns the remainder after division of $\alpha(\mathbf{x}, \mathbf{y})$ *by 2. This function is often called the modulo operation.*

The core of Gamma Classifier resides in the Gamma similarity operator, introduced in Definition 2, which indicates if two input patterns are similar up to a θ degree. This implies that when two input patterns are the same and the value of θ is equal to zero, Gamma similarity operator will return a value of one. This means that θ value is the one that indicates the degree of similarity between input patterns. A peculiarity of Gamma Classifier algorithm is that the fundamental set of patterns has to be encoded using Johnson-Möbius code [18]. This encoding technique converts a set of integer numbers into its binary representation (Table 2). Also this code allows the type of noise between training patterns to be preserved.

Table 2. Johnson-Möbius representation. This encoding technique converts a set of integer numbers into its binary representation, the order relation between training patterns is preserved.

Number	Johnson-Möbius representation
32	11111111111111111111111111111111
16	00000000000000011111111111111111
8	00000000000000000000000011111111
0	00000000000000000000000000000000

This means that between training patterns only additive or subtractive noise is present, eliminating mixed noise effects. As a consequence, the order relation between training patterns is preserved and therefore classification performance is improved. The details of Johnson-Möbius code algorithm, are explained in the following reference [11].

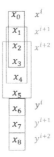

Fig. 1. Data series values represented as patterns. Each input pattern forms an associa-tion with its corresponding output pattern, so for each i, the corresponding association will be denoted as $(\mathbf{x}^i, \mathbf{y}^i)$.

Among the advantages of Gamma Classifier is that it can also be used to make predictions, in problems where data can be represented as Time Series. As it is shown in Fig. 1, this set of column vectors are used to form associations. Each input pattern (column vector) forms an association with its corresponding output pattern, so for each i, the corresponding association will be denoted as $(\mathbf{x}^i, \mathbf{y}^i)$.

4   Our Proposal

This section is divided into two parts. In the first part, a wireless sensor network is integrated to monitor air quality in urban settings in the northern part of Mexico City, while in the second, the proposed associative model is improved to make air quality predictions in Zacatenco academic facilities of the National Polytechnic Institute, in Mexico City (IPN for its acronym in Spanish).

The architecture of the proposed system consists of a wireless sensor network that communicates, using ZigBee protocol (IEEE 802.15.4 technical standard), to the local storage device as well as to the external database (Fig. 2). The external database keeps a dataset that is used to train the supervised learning algorithm.

4.1   Hardware

The Waspmote Gases 2.0 board has been designed to monitor environmental parameters such as temperature, humidity and atmospheric pressure [8]. It has the capacity to monitor some gases based on a modular architecture (Fig. 3).

The specific gases that are going to be monitored in the present work are: Carbon Monoxide – CO (Table 3), Carbon Dioxide– CO_2 (Table 4), Nitrogen Dioxide – NO_2 (Table 5) and Ozone – O_3 (Table 6). These gases are necessary to calculate the Metropolitan Index of Air Quality (IMECA for its acronym in Spanish), proposed by the Ministry of the Environment and Natural Resources of Mexico (SEMARNAT for its acronym in Spanish) to inform the population of pollution levels [12].

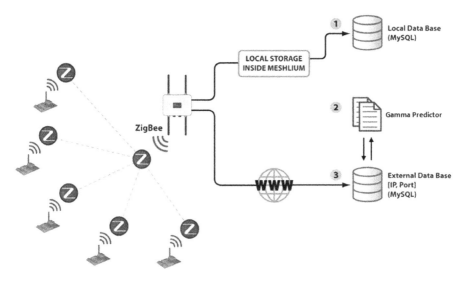

Fig. 2. System architecture.

Fig. 3. The Waspmote Gases 2.0 board has been designed to monitor environmental parameters and different types of gases [8].

Table 3. The TGS2442 is a resistive sensor sensitive to the changes in concentration of Carbon Monoxide (CO)

Carbon Monoxide (CO) Sensor – TGS2442	
Measurement range	30–1000 ppm
Resistance at 100 ppm	13.3–133 kΩ
Sensitivity	0.13–0.31 (ratio between the resistance at 300 ppm and at 100 ppm)
Supply voltage	5 V ± 0.2 V DC
Operating temperature	−10–+50 °C
Response time	1 s
Minimum load resistance	10 kΩ
Average consumption	3 mA (throughout the complete power supply cycle in one second)

Table 4. The TGS4161 sensor provides a voltage output proportional to the CO_2 concentration in the atmosphere.

Carbon Dioxide (CO_2) Sensor – TGS4161	
Measurement range	350–10000 ppm
Voltage at 350 ppm	220–490 mV
Sensitivity	44–72 mV (variation between the voltage at 350 ppm and at 3500 ppm)
Supply voltage	5 V ± 0.2 V DC
Operating temperature	−10–+50 °C
Response time	1.5 min
Average consumption	50 mA

Table 5. The MiCS-2710 is a sensor whose resistance varies in the presence of small concentrations of NO_2.

Nitrogen Dioxide (NO_2) Sensor - MiCS-2710	
Measurement range	0.05–5 ppm
Air resistance	0.8–8 kΩ (typically 2.2 kΩ)
Sensitivity	6–100 (typically 55, ratio between the resistance at 0.25 ppm and in air)
Supply voltage	1.7–2.5 V DC
Operating temperature	−30–+85 °C
Response time	30 s
Average consumption	26 mA (throughout the complete power supply cycle in one second)

Table 6. The MiCS-2610 is a resistive sensor that allows to measure the variation of the O_3 concentration between 10ppb and 1000ppb.

Ozone (O_3) Sensor - MiCS-2610	
Measurement range	10–1000 ppm
Air resistance	3–60 kΩ (typically 11 kΩ)
Sensitivity	2–4 (typically 1.5, ratio between the resistance at 100 ppm and at 50 ppm)
Supply voltage	1.95–5 V DC
Operating temperature	−30–+85 °C
Response time	30 s
Average consumption	34 mA

4.2   Improvements to Gamma Classifier

One of the main contributions of this work is based on the improvements to Gamma Classifier algorithm. The improved model proposes a different way to measure similarity between patterns of the training set, also reduces pattern encoding complexity and improves forecasting performance on atmospheric data series. The core of Gamma Classifier resides in the Gamma similarity operator, introduced in Definition 2, which indicates if two input patterns are similar up to a θ degree. Hamming distance between two input patterns of equal length is the number of positions at which the corresponding symbols are different. It measures the minimum number of substitutions required to change one pattern into the other. Considering the properties of the Hamming distance, we propose the following changes to the original Gamma Classifier algorithm.

– First step: input patterns have to be encoded using Johnson-Möbius code [18]. This encoding technique converts a set of integer numbers into its binary representation (Table 2). Also this code allows the type of noise between training patterns to be preserved.
– Second step: substitute Gamma similarity operator by using the Hamming distance between input patterns.

With these two modifications pattern complexity is reduced, forecasting performance on atmospheric data series is improved and air pollutants representation is more clear for further analysis.

4.3   Time Series Encoding

The fundamental set is the set of patterns of dimension n, that contain the measured values of some pollutant for a certain time. By dimension it is understood as the total data that each pattern contain. (Table 7).

Table 7. Data series for the fundamental set of patterns.

Index	Value
0	x_0
1	x_1
2	x_2
3	x_3
$\vdots$	$\vdots$
$k-3$	x_{n-3}
$k-2$	x_{n-2}
$k-1$	x_{n-1}
k	x_n

Atmospheric data series can be represented as k patterns of length n, according to Expression (3).

$$\mathbf{x}^k = \begin{pmatrix} x_{n-3}^k \\ x_{n-2}^k \\ x_{n-1}^k \\ x_n^k \end{pmatrix} \tag{3}$$

where $\mathbf{x}^k$ is the k-th input pattern, and x_n^k is the n-th element of $\mathbf{x}^k$ input pattern.

5   Experimental Phase

The proposed wireless sensor network, was launched in 2017 and since then it has been obtaining atmospheric data. The specific gases that were monitored are: Carbon Monoxide – CO, Carbon Dioxide– CO_2, Nitrogen Dioxide – NO_2 and Ozone – O_3. Concentration units are the same as those used in the IMECA, as explained in Sect. 2. Atmospheric data measurements obtained from each of these sensors were taken periodically (every thirty minutes) to create time series that represent the concentration of the pollutants of interest in five well-defined locations in Zacatenco academic facilities of the National Polytechnic Institute, in Mexico City (Fig. 4). Each one of the time series is composed of 17,520 points, corresponding to one year of measurements (Table 8). Datasets are available at The Computational Intelligence Laboratory at CIDETEC of IPN [14].

Table 8. Atmospheric data series of the fundamental set of patterns. Concentration units are the same as those used in the IMECA.

Sample	CO (ppm)	CO_2 (ppm)	NO_2 (ppb)	O_3 (ppb)
1	1.339	333.206	5.943	28.825
2	1.717	333.230	5.931	27.915
3	1.981	333.879	6.329	28.379
⋮	⋮	⋮	⋮	⋮
17,520	1.291	333.815	5.828	31.400

5.1   Performance Evaluation Methods

Evaluation metrics estimate different aspects of the quality of the prediction made by forecasting methods. Mean Square Error (MSE) is computed on the predicted values, according to Expression (4)

$$E_{MSE} = \frac{1}{N} \sum_{i=1}^{N} \beta \left(y_i, \widehat{y_i} \right)^2 \tag{4}$$

where y_i is the actual and $\widehat{y_i}$ is the predicted value, with N being the amount of samples considered.

Fig. 4. Locations of sensor nodes during in-field experimentation.

Fig. 5. (a) Sensor node powered by a DC power supply, (b) Sensor node with embedded storage device powered by a DC power supply.

Rooted Mean Square Error (RMSE) returns the error to the magnitude of the original values and is obtained from the MSE, according to Expression (5)

$$E_{RMSE} = \sqrt{MSE} = \sqrt{\frac{1}{N} \sum_{i=1}^{N} \beta \left(y_i, \widehat{y}_i\right)^2} \tag{5}$$

Forecasting results evaluated using MSE and RMSE will depend upon the variation magnitude among the values on individual data points for each time series (Fig. 5).

Mean Absolute Percent Error (MAPE) returns the deviation in percentage terms, according to Expression (6)

$$E_{MAPE} = \frac{1}{N} \sum_{i=1}^{N} \left| \frac{y_i - \widehat{y}_i}{y_i} \right| \qquad (6)$$

Symmetric Mean Absolute Percent Error (SMAPE) is obtained according to Expression (7)

$$E_{SMAPE} = \frac{1}{N} \sum_{i=1}^{N} \left| \frac{y_i - \widehat{y}_i}{y_i + \widehat{y}_i} \right| \qquad (7)$$

Correlation, RMSE, SMAPE and MAPE were used to evaluate and compare forecasting results of ARIMA, ARMAX, NARX and SSEST against the performance achieved by the proposed method.

6 Results and Discussion

In this section we analyse air quality predictions results achieved by each one of the compared algorithms. The specific gases that were monitored by five different sensor nodes are: Carbon Monoxide – CO (Fig. 6, Fig. 7, Fig. 8, Fig. 9, Fig. 10), Carbon Dioxide – CO_2 (Fig. 11, Fig. 12, Fig. 13, Fig. 14, Fig. 15), Nitrogen Dioxide – NO_2 (Fig. 16, Fig. 17, Fig. 18, Fig. 19, Fig. 20) and Ozone – O_3 (Fig. 21, Fig. 22, Fig. 23, Fig. 24, Fig. 25). Each one of the graphs shows the daily prediction of a specific pollutant, distributed throughout the urban environment of interest (Fig. 4).

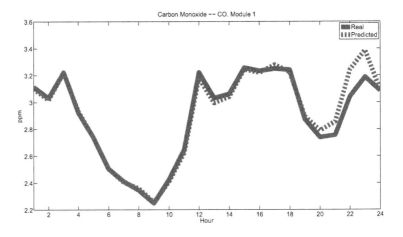

Fig. 6. Carbon Monoxide (CO) forecasting results using Module 1.

Table 9. Carbon Monoxide (CO) forecasting results obtained using Module 1.

Time Series	Model	RMSE	Correlation	SMAPE	MAPE
CO	IGP (our proposal)	**0.0642**	**0.9826**	**1.1277**	**1.1463**
	NARX	0.1897	0.8127	5.6228	5.6956
	ARMAX	0.2544	0.8824	7.2991	7.5858
	SSEST	0.2688	0.8205	8.1055	8.3537
	ARIMA	0.2315	0.8794	6.5949	6.3860

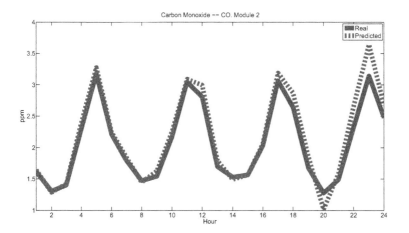

Fig. 7. Carbon Monoxide (CO) forecasting results using Module 2.

Table 10. Carbon Monoxide (CO) forecasting results obtained using Module 2.

Time Series	Model	RMSE	Correlation	SMAPE	MAPE
CO	IGP (our proposal)	**0.1667**	**0.9881**	**5.4594**	**5.5472**
	NARX	0.4476	0.8326	16.6500	17.7401
	ARMAX	0.2688	0.9437	11.0436	10.2702
	SSEST	0.3019	0.9293	12.5848	11.6274
	ARIMA	0.1992	0.9582	7.4910	7.4882

Table 11. Carbon Monoxide (CO) forecasting results obtained using Module 3.

Time Series	Model	RMSE	Correlation	SMAPE	MAPE
CO	IGP (our proposal)	**0.0771**	**0.9726**	**2.1128**	**2.1781**
	NARX	0.2065	0.6547	7.1585	7.1529
	ARMAX	0.2703	0.5508	9.5841	10.2659
	SSEST	0.3177	0.8038	10.7522	11.7555
	ARIMA	0.1969	0.7042	7.4987	7.5342

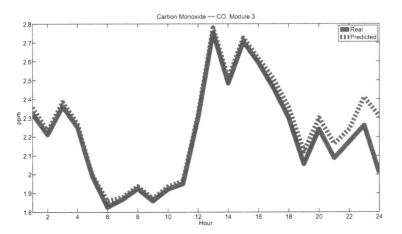

Fig. 8. Carbon Monoxide (CO) forecasting results using Module 3.

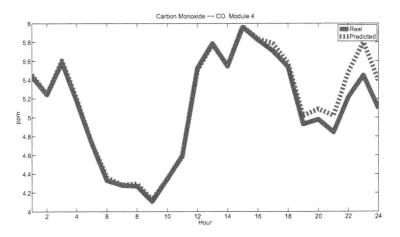

Fig. 9. Carbon Monoxide (CO) forecasting results using Module 4.

Table 12. Carbon Monoxide (CO) forecasting results obtained using Module 4.

Time Series	Model	RMSE	Correlation	SMAPE	MAPE
CO	IGP (our proposal)	**0.1413**	**0.9776**	**3.2405**	**3.3244**
	NARX	0.3962	0.7337	12.7813	12.8485
	ARMAX	0.5247	0.7166	16.8832	17.8517
	SSEST	0.5865	0.8121	18.8577	20.1092
	ARIMA	0.4284	0.7918	14.0936	13.9202

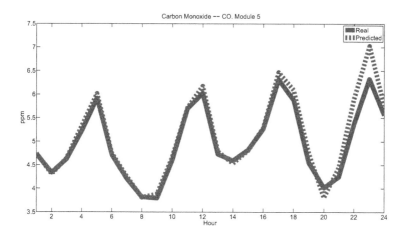

Fig. 10. Carbon Monoxide (CO) forecasting results using Module 5.

Table 13. Carbon Monoxide (CO) forecasting results obtained using Module 5.

Time Series	Model	RMSE	Correlation	SMAPE	MAPE
CO	IGP (our proposal)	**0.2309**	**0.9853**	**6.5871**	**6.6935**
	NARX	0.6373	0.8226	22.2728	23.4357
	ARMAX	0.5232	0.9130	18.3427	17.856
	SSEST	0.5707	0.8749	20.6903	19.9811
	ARIMA	0.4307	0.9188	14.0859	13.8742

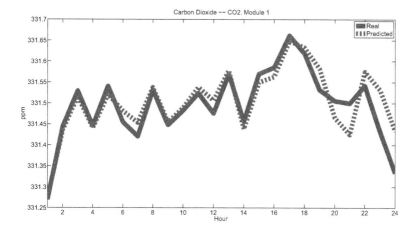

Fig. 11. Carbon Dioxide (CO_2) forecasting results using Module 1.

Table 14. Carbon Dioxide (CO_2) forecasting results obtained using Module 1.

Time Series	Model	RMSE	Correlation	SMAPE	MAPE
CO_2	IGP (our proposal)	**0.0388**	**0.8892**	**0.0084**	**0.0084**
	NARX	0.0847	0.3694	0.0217	0.0217
	ARMAX	0.1098	0.5324	0.0258	0.0258
	SSEST	0.1051	0.5910	0.0250	0.0250
	ARIMA	0.1185	0.5469	0.0312	0.0312

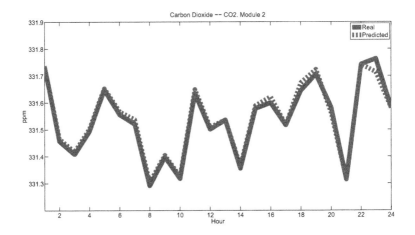

Fig. 12. Carbon Dioxide (CO_2) forecasting results using Module 2.

Table 15. Carbon Dioxide (CO_2) forecasting results obtained using Module 2.

Time Series	Model	RMSE	Correlation	SMAPE	MAPE
CO_2	IGP (our proposal)	**0.0155**	**0.9942**	**0.0023**	**0.0023**
	NARX	0.1742	0.02886	0.0429	0.0429
	ARMAX	0.1714	0.5324	0.0365	0.0405
	SSEST	0.1626	0.3502	0.0394	0.0394
	ARIMA	0.1207	0.4840	0.0285	0.0285

Table 16. Carbon Dioxide (CO_2) forecasting results obtained using Module 3.

Time Series	Model	RMSE	Correlation	SMAPE	MAPE
CO_2	IGP (our proposal)	**0.0477**	**0.9530**	**0.0086**	**0.0086**
	NARX	0.1240	0.4746	0.0317	0.0317
	ARMAX	0.0959	0.5440	0.0252	0.0252
	SSEST	0.0997	0.4170	0.0260	0.0260
	ARIMA	0.0755	0.6458	0.0184	0.0189

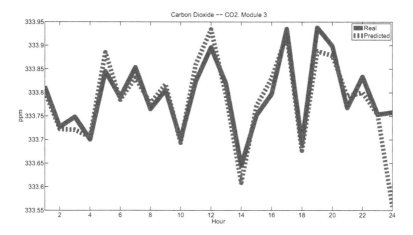

Fig. 13. Carbon Dioxide (CO_2) forecasting results using Module 3.

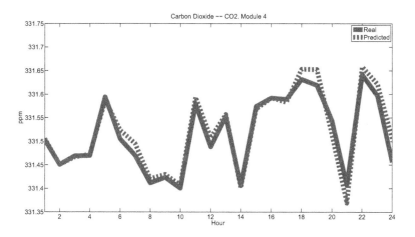

Fig. 14. Carbon Dioxide (CO_2) forecasting results using Module 4.

Table 17. Carbon Dioxide (CO_2) forecasting results obtained using Module 4.

Time Series	Model	RMSE	Correlation	SMAPE	MAPE
CO_2	IGP (our proposal)	**0.0272**	**0.9417**	**0.0054**	**0.0054**
	NARX	0.1295	0.1991	0.0323	0.0323
	ARMAX	0.1406	0.5324	0.0312	0.0332
	SSEST	0.1339	0.4706	0.0322	0.0322
	ARIMA	0.1196	0.5155	0.0299	0.0299

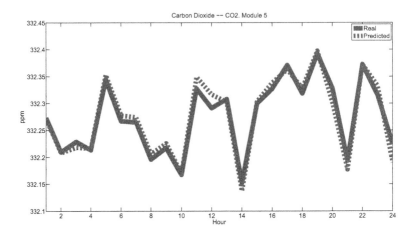

Fig. 15. Carbon Dioxide (CO_2) forecasting results using Module 5.

Table 18. Carbon Dioxide (CO_2) forecasting results obtained using Module 5.

Time Series	Model	RMSE	Correlation	SMAPE	MAPE
CO_2	IGP (our proposal)	**0.0340**	**0.9455**	**0.0064**	**0.0064**
	NARX	0.1276	0.2910	0.0321	0.0321
	ARMAX	0.1257	0.5363	0.0292	0.0305
	SSEST	0.1225	0.4527	0.0301	0.0301
	ARIMA	0.1049	0.5589	0.0260	0.0262

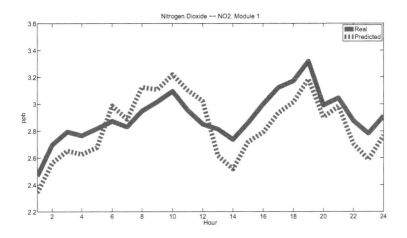

Fig. 16. Nitrogen Dioxide (NO_2) forecasting results using Module 1.

Table 19. Nitrogen Dioxide (NO_2) forecasting results obtained using Module 1.

Time Series	Model	RMSE	Correlation	SMAPE	MAPE
NO_2	IGP (our proposal)	**0.0799**	**0.9169**	**2.1403**	**2.1618**
	NARX	0.1386	0.8123	3.9851	4.0306
	ARMAX	0.4452	0.3326	13.7330	15.3520
	SSEST	0.8494	0.2896	18.6075	19.9498
	ARIMA	0.1563	0.6163	4.2784	4.2565

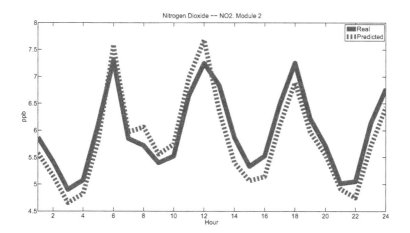

Fig. 17. Nitrogen Dioxide (NO_2) forecasting results using Module 2.

Table 20. Nitrogen Dioxide (NO_2) forecasting results obtained using Module 2.

Time Series	Model	RMSE	Correlation	SMAPE	MAPE
NO_2	IGP (our proposal)	**0.0800**	**0.9947**	**0.9584**	**0.9602**
	NARX	0.7253	0.4246	10.0418	10.2042
	ARMAX	0.7782	0.7192	11.1349	10.3981
	SSEST	0.6643	0.5175	9.7097	9.4481
	ARIMA	0.7619	0.5130	11.3423	10.9344

Table 21. Nitrogen Dioxide (NO_2) forecasting results obtained using Module 3.

Time Series	Model	RMSE	Correlation	SMAPE	MAPE
NO_2	IGP (our proposal)	**0.0812**	**0.9707**	**1.5637**	**1.5754**
	NARX	0.4428	0.6248	7.1641	7.2705
	ARMAX	0.6234	0.5367	12.6010	13.0310
	SSEST	0.7668	0.4113	14.3042	14.8407
	ARIMA	0.4705	0.5723	7.9805	7.7595

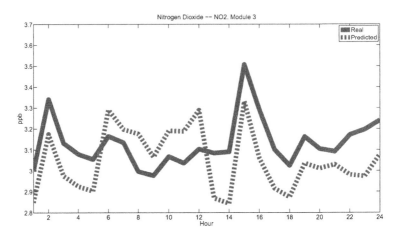

Fig. 18. Nitrogen Dioxide (NO_2) forecasting results using Module 3.

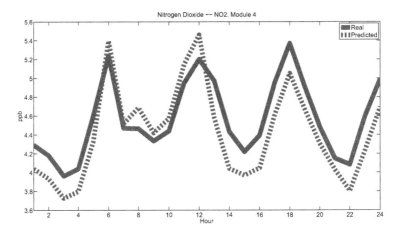

Fig. 19. Nitrogen Dioxide (NO_2) forecasting results using Module 4.

Table 22. Nitrogen Dioxide (NO_2) forecasting results obtained using Module 4.

Time Series	Model	RMSE	Correlation	SMAPE	MAPE
NO_2	IGP (our proposal)	**0.0819**	**0.9799**	**1.5851**	**1.5970**
	NARX	0.4442	0.6329	7.2039	7.3108
	ARMAX	0.6278	0.5400	12.7383	13.1845
	SSEST	0.7753	0.4142	14.4903	15.0402
	ARIMA	0.4721	0.5785	8.0233	7.8020

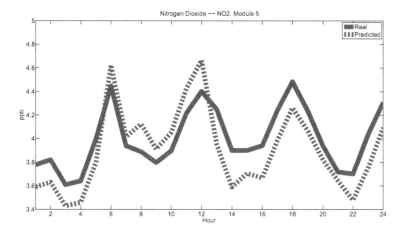

Fig. 20. Nitrogen Dioxide (NO$_2$) forecasting results using Module 5.

Table 23. Nitrogen Dioxide (NO$_2$) forecasting results obtained using Module 5.

Time Series	Model	RMSE	Correlation	SMAPE	MAPE
NO$_2$	IGP (our proposal)	**0.0807**	**0.9656**	**1.5619**	**1.5736**
	NARX	0.4377	0.6237	7.0987	7.2040
	ARMAX	0.6186	0.5321	12.5518	12.9914
	SSEST	0.7640	0.4082	14.2779	14.8197
	ARIMA	0.4652	0.5700	7.9061	7.6881

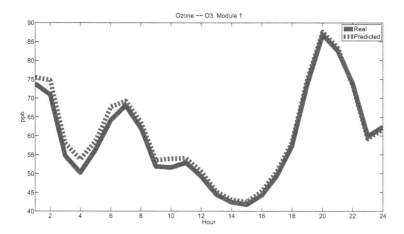

Fig. 21. Ozone (O$_3$) forecasting results using Module 1.

Table 24. Ozone (O_3) forecasting results obtained using Module 1.

Time Series	Model	RMSE	Correlation	SMAPE	MAPE
O_3	IGP (our proposal)	**1.8932**	**0.9952**	**2.6159**	**2.6646**
	NARX	12.4051	0.6725	12.6099	11.7481
	ARMAX	16.8595	0.8753	16.2998	14.4582
	SSEST	19.0765	0.7436	18.8435	17.3330
	ARIMA	11.8130	0.7152	16.6379	16.7852

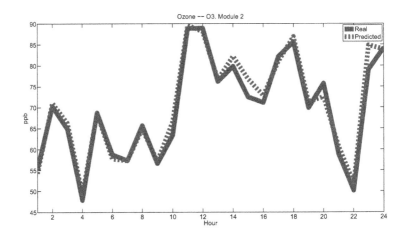

Fig. 22. Ozone (O_3) forecasting results using Module 2.

Table 25. Ozone (O_3) forecasting results obtained using Module 2.

Time Series	Model	RMSE	Correlation	SMAPE	MAPE
O_3	IGP (our proposal)	**4.3312**	**0.9564**	**3.0549**	**3.1756**
	NARX	10.9151	0.6117	13.3131	13.9853
	ARMAX	11.4197	0.6764	12.3153	11.8224
	SSEST	8.4059	0.7831	9.3959	9.2820
	ARIMA	9.7317	0.6267	11.8225	11.3096

Table 26. Ozone (O_3) forecasting results obtained using Module 3.

Time Series	Model	RMSE	Correlation	SMAPE	MAPE
O_3	IGP (our proposal)	**0.4146**	**0.9993**	**0.5735**	**0.5747**
	NARX	8.7640	0.5577	13.0514	13.0514
	ARMAX	10.1326	0.5716	14.4751	12.7148
	SSEST	10.2611	0.3735	15.9404	14.3217
	ARIMA	8.7294	0.6232	14.7024	15.7657

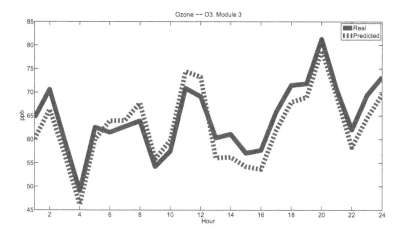

Fig. 23. Ozone (O_3) forecasting results using Module 3.

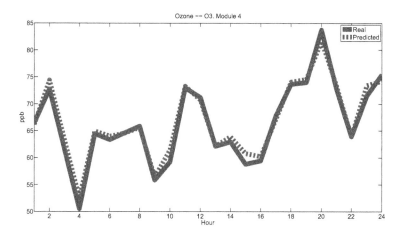

Fig. 24. Ozone (O_3) forecasting results using Module 4.

Table 27. Ozone (O_3) forecasting results obtained using Module 4.

Time Series	Model	RMSE	Correlation	SMAPE	MAPE
O_3	IGP (our proposal)	**2.3078**	**0.99725**	**3.1894**	**3.2393**
	NARX	21.1691	0.6151	25.6613	24.7995
	ARMAX	26.9921	0.72345	30.7749	27.173
	SSEST	29.3376	0.55855	34.7839	31.6547
	ARIMA	20.5424	0.6692	31.3403	32.5509

Evaluation metrics estimate different aspects of the quality of the prediction made by forecasting methods. Table 9, Table 10, Table 11, Table 12 and Table 13 show forecasting results on Carbon Monoxide – CO. Table 14, Table 15,

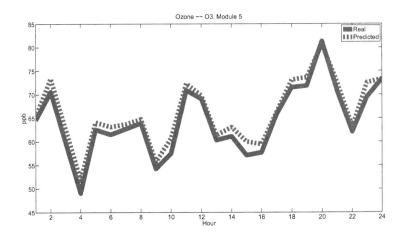

Fig. 25. Ozone (O_3) forecasting results using Module 5.

Table 28. Ozone (O_3) forecasting results obtained using Module 5.

Time Series	Model	RMSE	Correlation	SMAPE	MAPE
O_3	IGP (our proposal)	**6.2244**	**0.9758**	**5.6708**	**5.8402**
	NARX	23.3202	0.6421	25.923	25.7334
	ARMAX	28.2792	0.7758	28.6151	26.2806
	SSEST	27.4824	0.7633	28.2394	26.6150
	ARIMA	21.5447	0.6709	28.4604	28.0948

Table 16, Table 17 and Table 18 show forecasting results on Carbon Dioxide – CO_2. Table 19, Table 20, Table 21, Table 22 and Table 23 show forecasting results on Nitrogen Dioxide – NO_2. Table 24, Table 25, Table 26, Table 27 and Table 28 show forecasting results on Ozone – O_3. Each one of the tables shows the daily prediction of a specific pollutant, distributed throughout the urban environment of interest (Fig. 4). Correlation, RMSE, SMAPE and MAPE were used to evaluate and compare forecasting results of ARIMA, ARMAX, NARX and SSEST against the performance achieved by the proposed method.

7   Conclusion

In this paper the forecasting capabilities of an associative model are studied. The main result is that a novel non-linear forecasting technique based on the improved Gamma classifier associative model is introduced. Its performance to make air quality predictions in urban settings was tested. The proposed associative model outperformed previously reported techniques in terms of forecast accuracy. The wireless sensor network that was implemented meets the technical requirements to extend the platform developed by the Ministry of the Environment and Natural Resources of Mexico (SEMARNAT for its acronym in Spanish) to inform the population of pollution levels in an easy and timely manner. The results presented in this paper demonstrate associative memories potential to forecast air quality in urban settings as well as to evaluate environmental conditions in microclimates.

Acknowledgements. The authors of the present paper would like to thank the following institutions for their economical support and facilities provided to develop this work: the Secretaría de Investigación y Posgrado (SIP), the Comisión de Operación y Fomento de Actividades Académicas (COFAA), the Instituto Politécnico Nacional through project no. 20230433, the Dirección de Posgrado, Investigación e Innovación of the Instituto Tecnológico Nacional de México (TecNM) through project no. 13585.22-P and no. 14301.22-P and from the Sistema Nacional de Investigadoras e Investigadores (SNII) of the Consejo Nacional de Humanidades Ciencias y Tecnologías (CONAHCYT), México.

References

1. Acevedo-Mosqueda, M.E., Yáñez-Márquez, C., López-Yáñez, I.: Alpha-beta bidirectional associative memories: theory and applications. Neural Process. Lett. **26**(1), 1–40 (2007)
2. Ahn, J., Shin, D., Kim, K., Yang, J.: Indoor air quality analysis using deep learning with sensor data. Sensors **17**(11) (2017). https://doi.org/10.3390/s17112476, https://www.mdpi.com/1424-8220/17/11/2476
3. Benammar, M., Abdaoui, A., Ahmad, S.H., Touati, F., Kadri, A.: A modular IoT platform for real-time indoor air quality monitoring. Sensors **18**(2) (2018). https://doi.org/10.3390/s18020581, https://www.mdpi.com/1424-8220/18/2/581
4. Hao, Y., et al.: How harmful is air pollution to economic development? New evidence from PM2.5 concentrations of Chinese cities. J. Clean. Prod. **172**, 743–757 (2018)
5. Jo, B., Khan, R.M.A.: An internet of things system for underground mine air quality pollutant prediction based on azure machine learning. Sensors **18**(4) (2018). https://doi.org/10.3390/s18040930, https://www.mdpi.com/1424-8220/18/4/930
6. Kim, J., Hwangbo, H.: Sensor-based optimization model for air quality improvement in home IoT. Sensors **18**(4) (2018). https://doi.org/10.3390/s18040959, https://www.mdpi.com/1424-8220/18/4/959
7. Li, Y., Guan, D., Tao, S., Wang, X., He, K.: A review of air pollution impact on subjective well-being: Survey versus visual psychophysics. J. Clean. Prod. **184**, 959–968 (2018)
8. Libelium Comunicaciones Distribuidas S.L: The waspmote gases 2.0 board (2023). https://www.libelium.com/wp-content/uploads/2013/02/gases-sensor-board_2.0_eng.pdf
9. Lin, B., Zhu, J.: Changes in urban air quality during urbanization in China. J. Clean. Prod. **188**, 312–321 (2018)
10. López-Yáñez, I.: Theory and applications of the gamma associative classifier (in Spanish). Ph.D. thesis, Instituto Politécnico Nacional, Centro de Investigación en Computación (2011)

11. López-Yáñez, I., Sheremetov, L., Yáñez-Márquez, C.: A novel associative model for time series data mining. Pattern Recogn. Lett. **41**, 23–33 (2014)
12. Ministry of the Environment and Natural Resources of Mexico (SEMARNAT for its acronym in Spanish): Metropolitan index of air quality (IMECA) (2023). https://www.gob.mx/semarnat/. Accessed 07 Feb 2023
13. Genikomsakis, K.N., Galatoulas, N.F., Dallas, P.I., Candanedo Ibarra, L.M., Margaritis, D., Ioakimidis, C.S.: Development and on-field testing of low-cost portable system for monitoring pm2.5 concentrations. Sensors **18**(4) (2018). https://doi.org/10.3390/s18041056, https://www.mdpi.com/1424-8220/18/4/1056
14. The National Polytechnic Institute: Computational intelligence laboratory at cidetec (2019). https://www.airmx.net/. Accessed 11 Feb 2019
15. The World Health Organization (WHO): Air pollution (2023). https://www.who.int/health-topics/air-pollution#tab=tab_1. Accessed 07 Feb 2023
16. The World Health Organization (WHO): Global air pollution and health - technical advisory group (2023). https://www.who.int/groups/global-air-pollution-and-health--technical-advisory-group. Accessed 07 Feb 2023
17. Wu, L., Li, N., Yang, Y.: Prediction of air quality indicators for the Beijing-Tianjin-Hebei region. J. Clean. Prod. **196**, 682–687 (2018)
18. Yáñez, C., Felipe-Riveron, E., López-Yáñez, I., Flores-Carapia, R.: A novel approach to automatic color matching. In: Martínez-Trinidad, J.F., Carrasco Ochoa, J.A., Kittler, J. (eds.) CIARP 2006. LNCS, vol. 4225, pp. 529–538. Springer, Heidelberg (2006). https://doi.org/10.1007/11892755_55
19. Yáñez-Márquez, C.: Associative memories based on order relations and binary operators (in Spanish). Ph.D. thesis, Instituto Politécnico Nacional (2002)
20. Yáñez-Márquez, C., Díaz-de-León, J.L.: Associative memories based on order relations and binary operators (in Spanish). Comput. Sist. **6**(4) (2003)
21. Yáñez-Márquez, C., López-Yáñez, I., Aldape-Pérez, M., Camacho-Nieto, O., Argüelles-Cruz, A.J., Villuendas-Rey, Y.: Theoretical foundations for the alpha-beta associative memories: 10 years of derived extensions, models, and applications. Neural Process. Lett. **48**(2), 811–847 (2017). https://doi.org/10.1007/s11063-017-9768-2
22. Yang, T., Liu, W.: Does air pollution affect public health and health inequality? Empirical evidence from China. J. Clean. Prod. **203**, 43–52 (2018)
23. Yi, W.Y., Lo, K.M., Mak, T., Leung, K.S., Leung, Y., Meng, M.L.: A survey of wireless sensor network based air pollution monitoring systems. Sensors **15**(12), 31392–31427 (2015)

User Interface of Digital Platforms Used TDHA Patients: Case Study in Educational Environment

Diana C. Burbano G$^{(\boxtimes)}$ ⓘ and Jaime A. Álvarez ⓘ

Universidad Santiago de Cali, Cali-Valle, Colombia
diana.burbano02@usc.edu.co, jalavezs@msn.com

Abstract. Technology is a tool that has made it possible to make the world smaller, localized, and globalized, consequently, it has increased its use and appropriation in the current liquid society. In the educational context, in an educational institution in Colombia (level 9 of secondary), it is evident that the teachers of the institution are not trained to educate patients diagnosed with ADHD; consequently, this population is forgotten and treated like all students, therefore, this population is forgotten and considered outside the range of learning and causing damage on an emotional level.

The observational study is carried out through subjective measurements and direct measurements with prior informed consent. The data analysis is carried out, by recording mixed data (qualitative and quantitative) that will allow us to know the behavior in real time. The data will be analyzed from contingency tables when they are a categorical variable, using chi-square tests (parametric variables); the analysis is performed through descriptive statistics, and inferential analysis by ANOVA or T- Student test. Consequently, UI (user interface) design faces a new challenge, in which UX (user experience) in adolescents is being used constantly. Achieving good design on digital platforms, web pages, and applications will have a positive impact on digital native adolescents; allowing them to improve their alternatives of communication and social interaction. This user-focused research for special populations answers the following research question: ¿How can the UI of ADH user search reduce execution time when using digital platforms, taking the educational environment as a case study?

Keywords: User interface · digital platforms · adolescence · attention deficit hyperactivity disorder · didactic interactions

1 Introduction

Today digital platforms, are configured as an important tool for companies that want to distribute their products and services in a globalized way, as is the case of the health area, which is adopting more and more digital channels to serve young people with ADHD improving their access to educational settings. Today, technology is part of every day, and more processes are done digitally, replacing face-to-face activities, and

M. F. Mata-Rivera et al. (Eds.): WITCOM 2023, CCIS 1906, pp. 241–252, 2023.
https://doi.org/10.1007/978-3-031-45316-8_16

strengthening communication channels. Consequently, space–time conditions do not impede the carrying out of any type of operation [1]. These digital platforms aim to facilitate the execution of tasks, transforming the user's front of what is needed or demanded. In that sense, the UI becomes an important challenge in the learning processes in patients diagnosed with ADHD. The problems of contemporary educational pedagogy in patients with ADHD; propose a challenge where changes are generated in the way of reflecting, perceiving, thinking, and doing of all those who belong to the educational community, which is directed towards a cultural change that leads to the development of new ways of managing the classroom (from strategies and contents) and the institution that guides the pedagogical designs and the new work models of teachers in the new scenery.

Formulate national cyber-strategies that promote the creation of human capacities in ICT; promote research and development to facilitate access to ICTs for all, including disadvantaged, marginalized, and vulnerable groups; define national policies to ensure the full integration of ICT at all levels of education and training; strengthen the capacities of local communities, especially in rural and underserved areas, in the use of ICTs and promote the production of useful and socially significant content for the benefit of all Technological knowledge generates new learning environments that require considering aspects such as the cultural, professional, economic, psychological, and Anthropological that affect Education.

Information and communication technologies can be a tool for useful support for working with students with ADHD in the classroom, as they help the students to have greater autonomy in the learning process allowing individualized teaching, respecting learning rhythms and styles, as well as being a source of motivation that, as we mentioned earlier students with ADHD works better if behind the task there is a source of motivation [2].

The purpose of this article is to identify the digital platforms in patients with ADHD, for which the interactions of the teacher and the students in the pedagogical practices oriented to meaningful learning are analyzed.

2 State of the Matter

2.1 Education and Cognition

The relationship between education and cognition has been consolidated in the form of an indissoluble binomial that has currently been considered; The way of communication between both fields of knowledge has its historical genesis that is expressed at different moments in educational history in which essential issues in the sciences of education underlie, transversally. The inter- and transdisciplinary processes that characterize the epistemic Zeitgeist of science in the 21st century bring the challenge of a rethinking of academic and investigative identities built based on very defined limits. The overcoming of these limits between cognition and education in each of the stages. Cognitive sciences, or cognitive science, whose nomenclature varies from various sources, would be defined through the interdisciplinary study of the mind and intelligence, integrating the study of emergencies within the areas of knowledge of philosophy psychology, artificial intelligence, neuroscience, linguistics, and anthropology. Although their intellectual origins can be located in the mid-50s. [3, 4]; come from various fields to develop theories of mind based on complex representations and computational procedures, placing their origins in the creation of cognitive society.

Cognitive neuroscience is emerging today as one of the most prolific cognitive sciences of the late 21st century; Its gradual incursion into the fields of research on educational learning made it arise, around the need to integrate the brain level in the processes of construction of educational know led.

2.2 Cognitive Sciences

From the cognitive sciences, including neurosciences and their relationship with psychology, anthropology, and information sciences, innumerable contributions are made to the understanding of m-learning teaching and learning. How people learn using digital media, how information processing is carried out, how perceptual, associative, and integrative processes carried out in the brain are involved, what are the best ways to teach from the functioning of the nervous system, or as meanings are built and skills are acquired, they are some of the questions to which cognitive sciences can contribute to answering.

2.3 ADHD in Adolescence

Attention deficit/hyperactivity disorder is a frequent neurobiological condition with significant personal and social functional impairments. It has a strong genetical component, involving multiple genes which interact. Environmental and neurobiological factors thus increase genetic susceptibility and clinical heterogeneity.

The diagnosis of ADHD is complex due to his high clinical heterogeneity and the absence of a biological marker. In this review there is a description of the normal specific behavior of the adolescent and, in this context, of the challenges of the diagnosis and treatment of ADHD [5]. Neurocognitive models for ADHD point to deficits in higher cognitive functions, and executive functions (EF) necessary to direct behavior toward a goal. Recently the distinction between cold FE and hot FE has been postulated. Cold Efs correspond to the neuropsychological deficits most consistently implicated in ADHD including motor response inhibition, sustains attention, working memory, planning, and cognitive flexibility, mediated by dorsolateral and frontostriatal networks, frontoparietal [6].

2.4 Accessibility, UI/UX, Usability, and User-Centered Design

Designs under the UI/UX approach imply understanding the expectations, needs, and motivations of the users so that they are easy to use [7]. Inside the supporting methodologies are pedagogical usability, user–centered design, and thinking [8]. For this, usability works under five well-known principles (memorable, learning, success, satisfaction, and efficiency) [9]. In the second, the person is the central axis of the process to obtain an optimal design [10], and in the last one, its objective is to understand what people the design is directed at and to question the problems of daily activities in an effort to search for specific solution alternatives to problems specific [11]. Each of these elements along with accessibility, is related to the way in which the user can navigate and access the product successfully. They are key to achieving a good UI, and therefore a satisfactory UX.

2.5 Didactic Interactions and Cognitive Relationships

In the educational context of the classroom, a space organized intentionally to promote the teaching-learning process, we understand that the didactic interaction factors that occur in it are not always transferable to other educational contexts. This is due to the differences between the physical context spatial characteristics, infrastructure, materials, and the mental context representations, expectations, affects, and motivations [12] which imply that both contexts are mediating spaces. Par excellence of culture [13]. Thus, the classroom and pedagogical practices assumed a relationship of interdependence, in which it is interesting to know interactive communicative behaviors are mobilized in the teaching and learning process from didactic discourse analysis.

3 Methodology

The methodology presented is oriented according to the specific objectives; Analyze the behavior of users in adolescents with TDAH, which allows for identifying the limitations, and needs when the use digital platforms. Identify situations of use, observations are made of use activities in the case study, observational study is carried out through subjective measurements with informed consent, video recording, and field notes. The analysis of the data and recording of mixed data (qualitative and quantitative) is carried out, which will reveal the behavior in real time. Likewise, unstructured interviews are carried out to configure an empathy map.

The data analysis will be carried out through chronicles of activities with the recording of data (qualitative and quantitative); the above demonstrates showing the behavior in real- time. Likewise, unstructured interviews are carried out to configure empathy maps that allow the identification of the needs of the participants. About the second objective of identifying interaction actions in terms of execution time and effectiveness of achieving experimental protocol is proposed: based on the proposed hypothesis, there are interaction actions in terms of errors, and execution time (normalization protocols of the eye tracking team). At the end of the first stage, the registration of the participant begins with a battery of tasks in an order established randomly by the researchers.

The data will be analyzed from contingency tables when they are categorical variables, using chi-square tests (parametric variables); the analysis is performed through descriptive statistics, inferential analysis by ANOVA or T - Student test. Relation to the third objective, is to formulate a guide focused on inclusive design in patients design in patients with TDAH in educational contexts. Consequently, the design requirements are established according to the functional spheres, use, accessibility, and social interaction (usability in the design of the user interface) in order to promote user-centered design. When prototyping and validating, the content structure is defined that allows the information to be displayed in a simple orderly manner; in order to carry out an evaluation analysis of heuristics with end users and experts. Based on the above, this article proposes as a contribution a guide focused on inclusive design in patients diagnosed with TDAH in order to determine the interfaces of the digital platform in terms that are intelligible to users in educational contexts.

3.1 Research Design

In the present investigation, the study methodology mixed (qualitative and quantitative) with an alternative epistemological perspective.

Phase I:
In relation to the type of qualitative research, based on exploratory. Data collection was done in 6 months (study 2021 – 2023 A) and was developed in phases, first, the characterization of the students was carried out in correlation with the diagnoses according to the clinical history; second semi-structured interviews (question guide and recorder support, with filming) and interface capture videos were done, third, observation guides were implemented to record complementary information to the study. The data analysis follows the guidelines of the class diagram after processing the interface language on the Educat Platform.

The private educational institutions where the research is done in the face -to face modality present the following characteristics; first how much school infrastructure, mixed child population (men and women), medium–high socioeconomic level, teaching staff that articulates with the UAF (pedagogical self – training unit). The sample consisted of 21 children, the students were 13 and 14 years old. The teachers have higher education, with more than 10 years of experience, and belong to various secondary curricular areas. The participation of teachers and psychologists was voluntary and they accepted the informed consent protocol. The institution's pedagogical model is constructivist and develops DBA according to [14].

Phase II:
In the analysis of the results, two category systems were selected: social and cognitive interaction according to interaction according to [15], which 'present subcategories for the behavior of the student and the teacher [16], both linked to the achievement of student learning (Table 1).

Phase III:
In phase III, in relation to the results, the theoretical categorization and unit of analysis is carried out with the Atlas Ti software. When quantitative analysis is implemented; descriptive statistics inferential analysis by ANOVA or T- Student. The confidence interval of the data was performed using the com Brach alpha (Fig. 1).

3.2 Consent to Participate in the Study

The current provisions and ethical considerations as provided in resolution 008430 of 1993 of the Colombian Ministry of Health and law 84 of 1989 (approval certificate of

Table 1. Categories of analysis linked to the cognitive process Cuadrado & Fernandez (2008)

Categories	Description
Social frame of reference	The comments related to experiences or personal experiences of teachers and students outside their school context, are linked to the contents by area of knowledge
Specific frame of reference	Reference previous contents that are related to the new ones that allow to contextualize and give continuity to the curricular contents
Question formulation	Questions that are formulated to access the previous knowledge of their students and verify the meaning that is constructed
Meta statements	Contextualize expressions that inform the interlocutors of the actions to be carried out to facilitate their understanding of the tasks
Literal repetitions	Verbatim reproduction of student contributions
Reformulations	Way of recontextualizing their student's interventions and accentuating those parts or affirmations that are considered valid, or correcting the errors identified or their incomplete answer
Summaries	Recapitulation of their information given or done

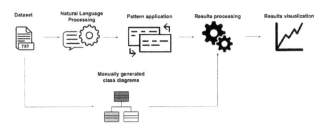

Fig. 1. Research phases Own source

the ethics committee is attached); in addition to what is stipulated in resolution 008430 it determines the low-risk category.

The document will explain to the research participants in the focus groups (unstructured interview) the nature of the study and empathy to the eye tracking protocol, its objectives, as well as the right not to participate or to suspend their participation at any time and the confidentiality of the information provided to the participants.

3.3 Data Analysis Plan

The proposed methodology is complementary (quantitative and qualitative), the analysis of the data obtained according to their nature will be performed. For the processing and analysis of quantitative data, the statistical software SPSS version 4.0 for Windows, was used. First, the descriptive statistics will be kept, including frequencies, calculation of measures of central tendency (mean, median and mode), and dissension (variance and standard deviation). The analysis is performed between differences of groups (T students test for independent samples and analysis of variance of a factor) and the degree of association or relationship between the variables (Pearson's correlation coefficient and chi-square tests).

The qualitative information collected will be analyzed with the MaxQda software, version 2018. The interviews are made recorded in audio format and subsequently transcribed and incorporated into the software for the organization and classification of data, summarizing and tabulating them (data reduction). It will be done following the inductive method, based on the information obtained, the analysis categories will arise. Therefore, following the suggested methodology, qualitative data will pass to an analytical description to extract relevant information.

4   Results

In the following session, the results of the investigation are presented about the quantitative results. Initially, a characterization of the group of students is done through a diagnostic test before using the educational software EDUCAP to compare it with a test that is done at the end of the process of using the software. The two tests were generated by academic DBA to observe the satisfaction variable when strengthening the academic competencies of each student.

The results of the academic diagnostic test analysis, first the characterization of the students is established by being correlated with the clinical history (clinical diagnosis), they total test is analyzed (the time it took the students to develop), and behavior analysis. At the end of the period, the qualification of the test is in charge of the teacher of the educational institution.

When carrying out the analysis, the results of each unit are grouped into three ranges or groups according to the qualifications obtained: group No. 1 (low), group 2 (medium), and group No. 3 (high).

The first unit evaluated was mathematics with an estimated time of 3 min in its development, having the following findings: 70% of the students presented deficiencies in the development of mathematical operations and mathematical logic, being in the group they are classified into group II and group III. The second unit evaluated is Spanish and literature, it has an estimated development time of 20 min as a complement to critical reading; in the performance results, a classification in group II is evidenced and the rest in 20% in group I.

The third unit evaluated is drawing, which has an estimated time of 40 min in this subject gross and fine motor skills, creativity, and imagination are evaluated. The group was characterized because half of the group is in group III, that is their results were high and the rest were classified in group I, low when referring to children who have problems deciding what to draw, how to Doi it? Group I.

The result of the analysis of the behavior in real- time, in the DBA of mathematics in the students the subject of mathematical logic is evidenced and the principles of factorization present a greater degree of difficulty, for this reason, they require more time in solving problems; on this issue reflect a marked feeling of frustration.

4.1   Interface Design Test Results vs. Educational Software Product Results

With the design of the interface in the educational platform in the educational platform in the Spanish unit and critical reading, it was possible to reduce the number of students who were at a basic knowledge level (group I) as well as the number of students who belong to group II (medium knowledge). This is reflected in the displacement of the sample towards group III, with a high level of knowledge, evidencing an improvement in the academic performance of the unit.

The use of software in the drawing unit, an exponential improvement was evidenced, managing to eliminate the students of group I, displacing groups II, and III, it is inferred that there is a positive response in the interface design, improving academic performance of the students.

In the mathematics unit, a notable improvement of the children from Group I to Group III was evidenced, demonstrating an improvement in academic performance, group II decreased the number of members and is located in Group III at this level. They develop improvement plans to improve their learning outcomes.

In the general analysis of the results of the diagnostic test vs. interface design, it was evidenced that it managed to improve academic performance by placing the students in group I to group II and to a greater extent in group III. Students who are at the average level of knowledge, which requires follow-up and improvement plans in each period. In relation to group III, the progress of the students must be evaluated per period and the tools to keep them in the group must be sought. In general, all the students had good behavior toward the development of their investigation, which denotes that their motivation to learn increased. The teachers who were part of the research are professionals in education and the qualification criteria take a high score of 5.0 and a low score of 1.0.

Table 2 shows the notes of the initial evaluations and the final evaluation of the grades of students with ADHD diagnoses implementing and interface on digital educational platforms.

Table 2. Comparison between total averages final evaluation and final evaluation Own source

Student	Average initial evaluation	Final evaluación average
Student 1	22.74	35.6
Student 2	39.0	42.4
Student 3	33.75	36.7
Student 4	26.076	37.5
Student 5	32,90	40.0
Student 6	33.9	42.2
Student 7	38.4	45.6

Figure 2 show the results of the characterization of the students of the educational institution with a diagnosis of ADHD in relation to their initial and final grades (academic results).

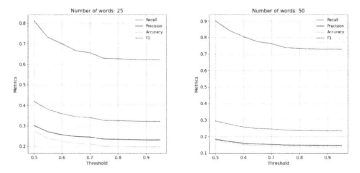

Fig. 2. Evaluations results Own source

4.2 Analysis of Quantitative Research Results

In relation to the analysis of the results in the diagnostic written test, it was found: in the time analysis, 30 min was established, however, 1 h was estimated in its resolution, finding that the units that students took the longest are math and creativity.

5 Conclusions

The present study reveals interactive activities in the interface of the Educat platform during the class sessions, in which the student is accompanied by a counseling teacher in the development of their DBA contemplated in the PIAR (ideal tool to guarantee the relevance of the teaching–learning process of students with disabilities, within the classroom respecting their learning styles and rhythms - inclusive education) [17].

The psycho-pedagogical orientations generate conditioning factors in the learning results; learning by doing from previous knowledge, new knowledge is appropriated; that is, learning from constructive mistakes.

The articulation of the categories of cognitive behavioral analysis as constructs that link cognition, behavior, and learning results (PIAR) [16] is defined as didactic interactions, which emerge and are configured as interrelation actions develop [18].

It is necessary to point out the predominance of a greater number of cognitive interactions over behavioral ones [19]. The author refers to "the interaction structures there are instantaneous intentions" which is interpreted through the present study. In the observed teaching pedagogical practices, cognition is more relevant than behavior.

Cognitive categories in teacher participation - student identifies the pedagogical activities: formulation of the forum-type question (H5P activities on the platform), literal repetitions, illustrative gestures of literary figures, workshops with real-time feedback, among others.

The emerging categories of the qualitative analysis unit reflect a relationship between communicative mechanisms and cognitive theory in students with ADHD and the unidentified categories are PIR (comprehensive recovery plan). The behavioral category identified by the teachers presents the following methodological strategies: collaborative – cooperative learning, problem–based learning (ABP), and formulation of questions. The results show a higher frequency of intervention by teachers regarding student participation, which correlated with what was stated by the author [20].

ADHD prevalence figures are higher in boys than in girls, this is due to the presentation of hyperactive–impulsive behavior; longitudinal follow-up studies show that the disorder persists into adulthood in more than 50% of cases [21].

The role of the student acts as an autonomous subject and responsible for his knowledge [22]. Technological mediations achieve the active participation of the student in achieving their learning, in this sense, the interface design in educational platforms offers real learning that allows broadening their horizons and places of learning. Technological mediations achieve the active participation of the student in achieving their learning, in this sense the interface design in educational platforms offers real learning that allows broadening the horizons and places of learning [23].

An additional comparative analysis with existing studies in the state of the art; address different aspects related to the user interface in platforms aimed at patients with ADHD from the perspective of the user experience to the effectiveness of the treatment. Below is a profile of each of the characteristics considered for the user and their use to lower if one may be suffering from TDAH symptoms The author [24], to characterize and quantify user behaviors that may be relevant to TDAH symptoms, the short version of the adult TDAH self – report scale – v 1-1 (ASRS v 1.1.) is used. It is estimated that four or more positive answers suggest the presence of symptoms compatible with TDAH in adults. To mitigate false positive results, a key question has been included to rule out disorders other than TDAH. The result of the behavior evaluation is positive or negative.

Research on TDAH has focused mainly on the cognitive aspects, leaving the study of the affective deficiencies of the disorder in the background. In this context, various studies have affirmed that these affective deficiencies are also important for the adequate diagnosis and treatment of TDAH [25–28]. Specifically, these studies indicate that children, adolescents, and adults with TDAH present a primary dysfunction of emotional stimuli. In addition, these people have a significant disability to control their emotions, specifically the negative ones such as aggressiveness, depression, sadness, anger, and frustration.

In the present investigation the following characteristics were presented: cognitive deficiencies such as emotional ones, a recent model, known as the Dual Pathway Model, establishes that in TDAH there are separate pathways for cognitive deficits and motivational deficits. A person with TDAH is deficient in either or both of these pathways [29].

This research provides quality learning processes to people with attention problems, specifically adults with TDAH. This is because these individuals may find education with a traditional learning model difficult to follow and may find virtual learning an alternative to further their education. Therefore, the research was carried out from a user model that considers some deficient features [30] in TDAH, which can be used to infer whether a specific student may have TDAH symptoms. The work presented in this document may be the first step in providing personalized learning resources for students with TDAH.

5.1 Future Work

The creation of a data set of user stories in ADHD patients regarding interface interaction is being considered as minimum expected products in new proprietary knowledge products to mitigate risks to the validity of the experiments.

The attributes and methods of the possible classes could be detected, as well as the existing relationships between them. The social interaction between teacher and student in relation to the pedagogical usability of the interface in the educational application.

This research has been funded by Direccion General de Investigaciones of Universidad Santiago de Cali under call No. 02-2023.

References

1. Duarte, C., Coelho, J., Matos, E., Gomes, G.: Designing a Facebook Interface for Senior Users. Sci. World J. (2014)
2. Gonzalez, N.R.: Tratamiento del TDAH. atraves del uso de las TIC en la educacion: Revision Bibliografica. Escuela de doctorado y estudios de posgrado. Universidad de la Laguna, España (2020)
3. Gardber, H.: The Minds New Science: A History of the Cognitive Revolution. Basic Books, New York (1985)
4. Thagard, P.: Introduction to Cognitive Science. Katz Editores, Buenos Aires (2008) (1996)
5. E. R. B.: Attentio deficit/Hyperactivity disorder in adolescents. Rev. Med. Clin. Condes. 26(1), 52–59 (2015)
6. Rubia, K.: Cool inferior frontostriatal dysfunction in attention - deficit hyperactivity disorder versus hot ventromedial orbitofrontal - limbic dysfunction in conduct disorder: a review. Biol. Psychiatry (2011)
7. Jeff, G., Josh, S.: Lean UX: Designing Great Products with Agile Teams. The Lean Series (2021)
8. Escobar Estrada, C.A.: La adaptacion del diseño UX de los e-commerce a los consumidores limeños. Rev. Tecnol., Lima (2022)
9. Ramírez-Acosta, K.: Interfaz y experiencia de usuario: parametros importantes para un diseño efectivo. Rev. Tecnol. En marcha 30, 49–54 (2017)
10. Mushthofa, D., Sabariah, M.K., Effendy, V.: Modelling the user interface design pattern for designing Islamic e-commerce website using user centered design. AIP Conf. Proc. 1977(1), 020022 (2018)
11. Márquez, B.L.V., Hanampa, L.A.I., Portilla, M.G.M.: Design Thinking aplicado al diseño de experiencia de usuario. Innov. Softw. (2021)
12. Coll Salvador, C., Sánchez Miguel, E.: El analisis de la interaccion alumno - profesor: lineas de investigacion. Revista de educación 346, 15–32 (2008)
13. Villalta Páucar, M.A., Assael Budnik, C., Martinic Valencia, S.: Conocimiento escolar y procesos cognitivos en la interaccion didactica en la sala de clase. Perfiles educativos 35(141), 84–96 (2013)
14. Ministerio de Educación Nacional: Viceministerio de educacion Preescolar, Basica y Media. Decreto 1421–2017. Informacion general del estudiante (2017)

15. Cuadrado, I., Fernandez, I.: Adaptaciones cognitivo - linguisticas del profesor a los comportamientos comunictaivos de los alumnos. Revista de educacion (345), 301–328 (2008)
16. Velasco, A.: Un sistema para el analisis de la interaccion en el aula. Revista Iberoamericana de Educacion **42**(3), 1–12 (2007)
17. El Ministerio de Educación Nacional: Decreto 1421 de 2017 (2017)
18. Villalta Páucar, M.A., Martinic Valencia, S.: Modelo de estudio de la interaccion didactica en la sala de clase. Investigacion Postgrados **24**(2), 61–76 (2009)
19. Velasco, A.: Un sistema para el analisis de la interaccin en el aula. Revista Iberoamericana de Educacion **12**(42), 1–12 (2007)
20. Velasco, A., Alonso, L.: Sobre la teoria de la educacion dialogica. Revista Educere **12**(42), 461–470 (2008)
21. Faraone, S.V., Biederman, J., Mick, E.: The age - dependent decline of attention deficit hyperactivity disorder: a meta - analysis of follow-up studies. Psychol. Med. (2006)
22. Lopes, A., Gomes, N.: Experimentar con TIC en la formacion inicial de profesores. Educativo siglo XXI **36**(3), 255–274 (2018)
23. Minguell, M.E., Ferrés, J., Cornellas, P., Regás, D.C.: Realidad aumentada y codigos QR en educacion. Tendencias emergentes en educacion con TIC: Asociacion Espiral, educacion y Tecnologia 135–156 (2012)
24. Daigre, C., et al.: Cuestionario autoinformado de cribado de TDAH ASRS - V 1.1 en adultos en tratamiento por transtornos. Actas Esp Psiquiatr. **37**(6), 299–305 (2009)
25. Barkley, R.: Inhibicion conductual, atencion sostenida y funciones ejecutivas: construccion de una teoria unificadora del TDAH. Psychol Bull. **121**, 65–94 (1997)
26. Nicolau Palou, R.: TDAH: el control de las emociones. Funadacion ADANA, problemas asociados al TDAH. Revista de psicologia y psiquiatria infantile **37**(1), 51–87 (2002)
27. F. M. B. S. R. H. a. a. Reimherr: Desregulacion emocional en adultos con TDAH y respuesta a atomoxetina. Psiquiatria biologica **58**, 125–131 (2005)
28. Sonuga-Barke, E.: El modelo de doble via del TDAH: una elaboracion de las caracteristicas del neurodesarrollo. Revisiones de neurocien y biocomportamiento **27**(7), 593–604 (2003)
29. Sonuga-Barke, E.: El modelo de doble via del TDAH: una elaboracion de las caracteristicas del neurodesarrollo. Revisiones de neurociencia y biocomportamiento **27**(7), 593–604 (2003)
30. Valetts, L.P.M.: Indicadores de sintomas de TDAH en contexto de aprendizaje virtual utilizando tecnicas de aprendizaje automatico. Rev. EAN. version en linea. Scielo. (2015)
31. Li, Z., Bouazizi, I.: Light Weight Content Fingerprinting for Video Playback Verification in MPEG DASH. Samsung Research America (2013)
32. Muller, C., Lederer, S., Rainer, B., Waltl, M., Grafl, M., Timmerer, C.: Open source column: dynamic adaptive streaming over HTTP toolset. ACM SIGMM Rec. **16**(9) (2013)
33. Timmerer, C., Griwodz, C.: Dynamic adaptive streaming over HTTP: from content creation to consumption. In: MM 2012, 2 Noviembre 2012

Recognition of Pollen-Carrying Bees Using Convolutional Neural Networks and Digital Image Processing Techniques

Josué Emmanuel Pat-Cetina[1,2] , Mauricio Gabriel Orozco-del-Castillo[1(✉)] ,
Karime Alejandra López-Puerto[1] , Carlos Bermejo-Sabbagh[1] ,
and Nora Leticia Cuevas-Cuevas[1]

[1] Departamento de Sistemas y Computación, Tecnológico Nacional de México/IT de
Mérida, Mérida, Yucatán, Mexico
{mg16081527,mauricio.od,karime.lp,carlos.bs,nora.cc}@merida.tecnm.mx,
mauricio.orozco@itmerida.edu.mx
[2] AAAI Chapter of Mexico (AAAIMX), Mérida, Mexico

Abstract. The accurate classification of bees into pollen-carrying and
pollen-free categories plays a crucial role in various aspects of bee
research and management, avoiding economic losses in the bee-keeping
sector and a reduction in pollinations of ecosystems. Although beekeepers
can identify when pollen-free bees enter other hives and initiate possible
looting, the task involves a lot of resources. In this paper, we propose
a method for classifying images of bees based on their pollen-carrying
status. We present two approaches: the first method utilizes a convolutional neural network (CNN) to classify original RGB images, while the
second method enhances pollen regions in the images using digital image
processing techniques before training the CNN. The results of the classification metrics demonstrate the effectiveness of both methods, with
the second method achieving higher accuracy values and reduced loss
compared to the first one. Moreover, the image enhancement techniques
employed in the second method, including thresholding, morphological
operations, and circularity ratio calculation, contribute to improved classification performance. Additionally, we discuss the CNN architecture,
training parameters, and the significance of incorporating deep learning
techniques in bee image analysis. The proposed method exhibits potential for application across different bee species, and future work may
explore the extension of this approach to detect looting behavior.

Keywords: Convolutional neural networks · Artificial neural
networks · Digital image processing · Bee management

1 Introduction

The honey bee (*Apis mellifera L.*) is a species native to Africa, western Asia,
and Europe. It was taken to other continents for the production of honey and

M. F. Mata-Rivera et al. (Eds.): WITCOM 2023, CCIS 1906, pp. 253–269, 2023.
https://doi.org/10.1007/978-3-031-45316-8_17

pollination of crops, except in Antarctica, and it is the most used bee for those activities [1]. Beekeeping in Mexico is present in various agricultural areas of the country, and has been practiced since pre-Columbian times. Mexico is in third place of production, behind China and Argentina [13]. In Mexico there are approximately 44 thousand producers who generate direct and indirect jobs [13]. In 2013, there was an income of $164.3 million dollars from the production of honey, generating approximately 2.2 million working days and $24.9 million dollars for salary payments [13].

The attack on bee colonies by other insects, such as the Asian hornet, or even their own species, can cause economic losses in the beekeeping sector, and a reduction in pollination of ecosystems [11]. It is important to monitor the spread of the species that invade bee colonies in order to plan the actions and activities that lead to stopping their expansion. Some activities carried out to monitor invasive species include direct observations of hornets in hives and flowers, as well as the use of traps such as bottles, funnels, and sticky traps [11]. Although beekeepers can identify when pollen-depleted bees enter other hives and initiate possible looting, the task is expensive, both in terms of time and money [17]. With this in mind, technologies to automate these processes have come into focus in recent years. For instance, recognition of bees has been attempted by the detection of their buzz from audio recordings [8], detection and tracking in three dimensions of bees using real-time stereo vision [4], as well for monitoring the activity of entering and leaving the hive of honey bees [3].

Due to the growing amount of available data, data science and artificial intelligence (AI), particularly machine learning (ML), applications have become much more frequent. Digital image processing (DIP) and computer vision techniques jointly with methods of statistical analysis and inference such as regression, have managed to recognize 98.7% of bees correctly [26]. Some other more powerful ML methods have also been used for bees-related applications, such as artificial neural networks (ANNs). ANNs (described in more detail in Sect. 2.2) are models inspired by the nervous system of living beings, composed as a set of processing units called artificial neurons [19], interconnected through connections called artificial synapses [14]. A specific kind of ANNs particularly useful when dealing with images are convolutional neural networks (CNNs). This model has the capacity to imitate the way in which the visual cortex of the brain processes and recognizes images [10].

In terms of identifying attacks on bees colonies, CNNs have been particularly applied to classify images of bees into two categories: those which carry pollen and those which do not, therefore helping in the identification task automatically. The classification of bees with pollen and without pollen has been carried out using various approaches, for example shallow and deep CNNs were used to detect bees carrying pollen using a manually annotated dataset [21].

This work describes the implementation of a CNN to classify images of bees with pollen and without pollen. Using the dataset from [21], we implement our own CNN model to classify the images and compare its performance with a second model in which the original dataset was enhanced after applying different DIP techniques, particularly related to mathematical morphology.

This paper is structured as follows. In Sect. 2 we describe the computational methods employed in this work, particularly mathematical morphology in Sect. 2.1 and ML in Sect. 2.2, with a particular emphasis on ANNs and CNNs. In Sect. 3 we present the development process, particularly the data acquisition and the two separate methods, the first one using just the CNN model, and the second one using DIP techniques to emphasize aspects to enhance classification by the model. In Sect. 4 we discuss our results and present our final remarks. Finally, in Sect. 5 future lines of work are explored.

2 Materials and Methods

2.1 Mathematical Morphology

Mathematical morphology describes a set of tools used to extract components from an image, which are used to represent and describe the shape of an object [7]. The analysis of objects is based on set theory, lattice theory, functions, among others [24]. In mathematical morphology objects in an image are represented by sets, for example, in a binary image the set of all white pixels is a morphological description of the original image. Each set in the binary image is a member of a two-dimensional space Z. In mathematical morphology the so-called *structural elements* are used, which are subsets or small images that are used to find properties of interest in an image [7]. By applying structural elements, features such as edges, fills, holes, corners, portions, and cracks can be extracted [24]. The structural elements can be rectangular arrays, but they can also be disc-shaped, rhombus-shaped, etc. [7].

There are several mathematical morphology operations. One of the most commonly-known is erosion [7], which can be thought of as a contraction [9]. Given two sets A and B in a space Z, the set A represents the objects of the image that will be operated by the erosion with the structural element B. The result is a set made up of the points Z, such that the set B translated by Z, is included in the set A [7]. Dilation, on the other hand, can be described as an expansion [9]. The result of the dilation is a set made up of the displacements Z, such that sets B and A overlap by at least one element [7].

Two other mathematical morphology operations are opening and closing, processes that manipulate erosion and dilation operations to improve an image [16]. Opening is a morphological operation used to soften the contour of an object, break up narrow extensions, and remove thin bulges [7]. In contrast, the closing operation serves to enhance the smoothness of contour sections, connect narrow gaps, bridge elongated and thin separations [7], eliminate small holes, and remove internal bulges [24].

Circularity is one of the approaches to describe image regions, and it is used to measure the compactness of a region. The ratio of circularity is the ratio between the area of a region and the area of a circle that has the same perimeter, where the area of a region is given by the number of pixels in the region and the perimeter of a region is the length of its boundary. Therefore, the circularity ratio R_c is given by:

$$R_c = \frac{4\pi A}{P^2},$$

where A is the area of the region and P is the length of its perimeter. A value of 1 for R_c corresponds to a circular region, while a value of $\frac{\pi}{4}$, corresponds to a square. The circularity ratio is a measure that does not change with uniform scale or orientation changes, such as errors that can occur when resizing and rotating a digital region [7]. If the perimeter of the surface increases and the area does not change, then the ratio of circularity decreases; since irregularities appear on the surface, if the area decreases and the perimeter does not change, as in the case of an ellipse from a circle, then the circularity ratio also decreases [25]. Other measures of the region descriptors used are the average and median intensity levels, the minimum and maximum intensity values, and the number of pixels with values above and below the average [7].

2.2   Machine Learning

ML is a branch of AI that focuses on constructing models capable of extracting knowledge from data and classify, predict, or make decisions without being explicitly programmed to do so. It commonly involves the analysis of large datasets and the extraction of patterns and insights that can be used to improve future performance. ML techniques can be broadly classified into three categories: supervised, unsupervised, and reinforcement learning. Supervised learning algorithms learn from labeled examples, while unsupervised learning algorithms identify patterns and structures in unlabeled data. Deep learning (DL), a subfield of ML, utilizes ANNs with multiple layers to process and learn complex patterns from large amounts of data. By linking inputs and outputs through interconnected layers of artificial neurons, deep learning models are able to automatically extract hierarchical representations and achieve remarkable performance in tasks such as image recognition, natural language processing, and speech recognition. DL has made significant progress in solving AI problems, working with high-dimensional data, and has been applied in various fields such as science, business, and government, encompassing diverse tasks [12].

Artificial Neural Networks. An ANN is a supervised ML method [15]. It is a system made up of many simple elements called neurons, which are interconnected to process information and respond dynamically to external stimuli [18]. The structure of ANNs was developed based on known models of the nervous system and the human brain [14], aiming to emulate their behavior characterized by learning from experience and acquiring general knowledge from a dataset [6]. A neuron conducts electrical impulses generated by chemical reactions under specific operating conditions and consists of three parts: 1) dendrites, which continuously acquire stimuli from several connected neurons; 2) the cell body, or soma, which processes the information from the dendrites to produce a potential activation indicating whether the neuron sends an electrical impulse along its axon; and 3) the axon, which terminates with branches called *synaptic terminals*, forming connections that transmit impulses from one neuron's axon to the dendrites of other neurons. Since there is no physical contact between the neurons at the synaptic junction, neurotransmitters released in the junction weigh the transmission from one neuron to another [14].

Convolutional Neural Networks. CNNs were developed in the 1980s but were forgotten due to their impracticality in real-world applications. They have since been revived and gained prominence since 2012. CNNs are a type of deep ANN used for image recognition and computer vision tasks [10]. They mimic the way the visual cortex of the brain processes and recognizes images [10]. CNNs process data composed of multiple arrays, such as images composed of three 2D arrays representing the intensity of the three RGB color channels for each pixel [12]. A CNN is broadly composed of two stages: the first one extracts features from an input image, such as gradients, edges, or spots [27], and the second one classifies the image based on the extracted features [10].

3   Development and Results

In this section we describe the methodology employed from the data acquisition to the development and analysis of two methods to classify the images of bees that carry pollen and those that do not: 1) a CNN model trained with the original images, and 2) a CNN model trained with images enhanced with a set of DIP techniques.

3.1   Data Acquisition

A set of images of bees that correspond to the species *Apis Mellifera* was obtained from [21]; data were originally collected from videos captured at a hive entrance. The set consists of 714 RGB images, of which 369 images correspond to bees with pollen and 345 without pollen, measuring 180×300 pixels each. Along with the dataset, a csv file containing the name of each image and the category to which it corresponds was also downloaded. A set of these images is shown in Fig. 1.

Method 1: CNN with Original Images. In the first method, we developed a CNN to classify images of bees based on whether they are carrying pollen or not. The images used in the study were in the standard RGB format, represented as 8-bit integers. In this format, the color values range from 0 (darkest color) to 255 (lightest color). To prepare the image data for CNN training, it was necessary to label each image with the corresponding category from the dataset. Since the images were not in the same order as the dataset, categorical variables were used for labeling. Additionally, to ensure compatibility with the CNN model,

(a) Pollen-carrying bees   (b) Pollen-free bees

Fig. 1. Samples of the dataset retrieved from [21] showing 20 images of (a) pollen-carrying bees, and of (b) pollen-free bees. Notice the amber-colored lumps on the images on the left.

the color values were scaled to a range between 0 and 1 by dividing each value by 255.

The dataset was divided into three subsets: training, validation, and test sets. Random sampling was used to create these subsets, with 64% of the images assigned to the training set, 16% to the validation set, and 20% for testing the trained CNN model. The CNN architecture consisted of five convolutional modules, each using the Rectified Linear Unit (ReLU) activation function. ReLU was chosen as it allows the preservation of positive values, which helps extract image features effectively in subsequent convolutional layers, while setting negative values to zero [2]. This choice was made to avoid the limitations of other activation functions such as tanh or sigmoid, which would restrict the output values to a small range [23].

The configuration details of the convolutional modules used in the CNN are presented in Table 1. These modules play a crucial role in feature extraction and representation learning, enabling the CNN to capture relevant patterns for distinguishing pollen-carrying bees from pollen-free ones.

Within each convolutional module, a max pooling layer with a size of 2 × 2 is applied after the convolution layers. This pooling layer reduces the spatial dimensions of the filtered images by half, effectively downsampling them. The resulting feature maps are then flattened and connected to a fully connected layer comprising 32 neurons with linear activation function. Subsequently, the

Table 1. Configuration of convolution modules.

Module	Convolution Layers	Kernel	Filters
1	5	5×5	16
2	3	3×3	16
3	3	3×3	32
4	3	3×3	32
5	2	3×3	32

output is passed to a layer consisting of two neurons, responsible for calculating the probabilities corresponding to each category using the softmax function [5]. The softmax function ensures that the outputs represent the probabilities of the image belonging to either category. The training of the CNN model involves 65 epochs, a learning rate of 0.005, and a batch size of 18 images. These parameters were empirically determined to improve performance. The architecture of the CNN is illustrated in Fig. 2, showcasing the arrangement and connections of its different layers.

The accuracy and loss values corresponding to the training stage of the model are shown in Fig. 3a. Initially the accuracy is 0.5065 and the loss is 0.6914. By epoch 13, the accuracy improves to 0.6600, and the loss decreases to 0.6712, with a marginal difference between the two. Notably, by epoch 19, the accuracy significantly rises to 0.9035 while the loss decreases to 0.2713 compared to epoch 13, indicating substantial improvement. Remarkably, in epoch 65, the accuracy reaches its peak close to 1, indicating successful classification of the training data, while the loss drops to 0.0002. Unsurprisingly, validation shows a less stable behavior. In Fig. 3b, the accuracy and loss values during the model validation stage are presented. The accuracy and loss are, respectively, 0.5391 and 0.6914. By epoch 13, the accuracy increases to 0.8347, and the loss decreases to 0.6638, with relatively similar values. Notably, by epoch 65, the accuracy reaches 0.9652, while the loss further reduces to 0.2544 compared to epoch 19, indicating improved accuracy and decreased loss.

Method 2: CNN with Processed Images. In the second method, a DIP technique is employed to enhance the images with the intention to support and improve the CNN classification. This technique involves the application of segmentation techniques, morphological operations, and the calculation of circularity ratio to emphasize relevant features in the images (Fig. 4). To initiate the image enhancement process, a thresholding was proposed for an initial image segmentation. Manually, a set of pixels representing the pollen regions of the images was obtained. Using the average values of this set of RGB color samples the computed average values for the RGB colors are as follows: 178.12 for red, 151.13 for green, and 120.38 for blue. To achieve a wider range of segmentation for the images, a proposal was made to utilize two thresholds for each RGB color channel, derived from the calculation of their respective standard

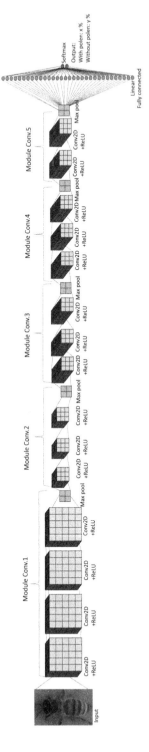

Fig. 2. The architecture of the CNN employed for RGB image classification is depicted. The input image, representing either a pollen-carrying or pollen-free bee, undergoes processing by the CNN for classification. The CNN architecture comprises five convolution modules (represented by yellow grids) followed by max pooling layers (represented by orange grids). These modules extract essential features from the input image. The flattened feature maps are subsequently connected to a fully connected layer (depicted by green neurons). Finally, the fully connected layer is linked to two output neurons employing the softmax function, facilitating the determination of the input image's class. (Color figure online)

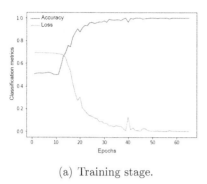
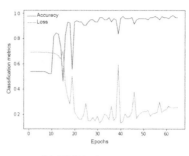

| (a) Training stage. | (b) Validation stage. |

Fig. 3. Classification metrics in the training and validation stage. Both graphs show the accuracy values in orange, and loss in blue. The x axis shows the epochs and the y axis shows the values of the classification metrics. (a) Accuracy and loss values in the training, (b) accuracy and loss values in the validation of the first method. (Color figure online)

deviations. The calculated standard deviation values are 27.84 for red, 27.45 for green, and 29.86 for blue. For each RGB color channel, the first threshold, denoted as T_1, is computed as $T_1 = \mu_{\mathbf{C}} - 2\sigma_{\mathbf{C}}$, i.e., the average minus two times its standard deviation, while the second threshold, denoted as T_2, is computed as $T_2 = \mu_{\mathbf{C}} + 2\sigma_{\mathbf{C}}$, i.e., the average plus two times its standard deviation, where μ denotes the mean and σ the standard deviation of a sample of RGB values for a given $\mathbf{C}$ channel. This approach was adopted to enable effective segmentation of multiple pollen regions within the images, as using a single standard deviation value yielded undersegmentation, and using more than two, oversegmentation of the pollen bodies. These values are shown in Table 2.

Table 2. Statistical parameters of the RGB values of the pollen samples and the calculated threshold values.

Color channel	Mean	Standard Deviation	T_1	T_2
Red	178.12	27.84	122.43	233.80
Green	151.13	27.45	96.21	206.04
Blue	120.38	29.86	60.65	180.11

For all three color channels, the respective segmented image $g(x,y)$ is given by:

$$g(x, y) = \begin{cases} 1, & \text{if } T_1 < f(x, y) < T_2 \\ 0, & \text{if } T_1 > f(x, y) \text{ or } f(x, y) > T_2 \end{cases} \tag{1}$$

The result of this operation makes it possible to segment those areas with values similar to those of the mean color of the pollen. When performing the thresholding, it was observed that there are segmented regions in the image that do not correspond to pollen, particularly the bees' stripes, since their color is similar to that of pollen. The second column of Fig. 4a shows the result of a thresholded image of a pollen-carrying bee, and that of Fig. 4b shows the result of a thresholded image of a pollen-free bee.

To eliminate the areas that do not correspond to the pollen, the morphological opening operation was applied, using a circular structural element of radius 6. The result of this operation allows removing the thin areas of the image, such as the stripes of the bee's body, and soften the outline of the pollen. Most of the stripes on the bee's body were removed, but some still remained. The third column of Fig. 4a shows the result of opening the image of a pollen-carrying bee, and that of Fig. 4b shows the result of opening an image of a pollen-free bee. The pollen area has a nearly circular shape, while the non-pollen regions have a more elongated and not quite circular shape.

To eliminate the areas which do not correspond to pollen, it was proposed to calculate the circularity ratio R_c, and thus establish a value to discard those non-circular areas of the binary images. The value of R_c was determined empirically, trying to find regions that are somewhat circular. The value set for R_c was 0.6, therefore regions of the binary image that have R_c greater than 0.6 are kept in the image, and regions that have R_c less than 0.6 are discarded. The result of applying this operation makes it possible to remove the areas that are not circular, such as the fringes of the bee's body, and to preserve the rounder areas that correspond to the bee's pollen. The fourth column of Fig. 4a shows a pollen-carrying bee, whose areas were not discarded because the R_c value was not less than 0.6, and the Fig. 4b shows how these zones disappeared for the pollen-free bee, since the value of R_c was less than 0.6.

To emphasize the images of the bees, the average of the RGB colors that was calculated from the pollen (Table 2) is used in such a way that the position (x, y) of the binary image that has a value equal to 1, will have the average value of the RGB colors of the pollen in the original image (last column of Fig. 4a), otherwise the color of the original image is preserved (last column of Fig. 4b). The described process (Fig. 4) was carried out with the entire set of images to emphasize the pollen on those bees carrying it.

To prepare the image data for the CNN model, the color values are normalized to be between 0 and 1 by dividing them by 255. The dataset is then divided into three subsets: 64% for training, 16% for validation, and 20% for testing. These subsets are randomly selected to ensure representative samples. The CNN architecture used in this method is the same as the one employed in the first method. It consists of five convolution modules, each utilizing the ReLU activation function. After the convolution layers, a 2×2 max pooling layer is applied to downsample the images. The filtered images are then flattened and connected to a layer of 32 fully connected neurons with the linear activation function. This layer is further connected to a final layer of two neurons using

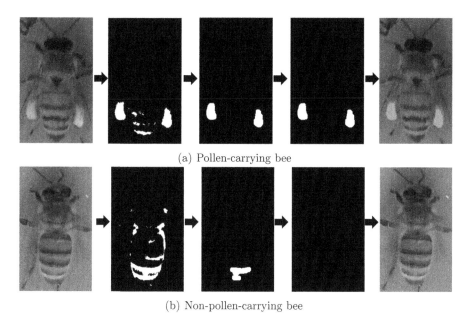

(a) Pollen-carrying bee

(b) Non-pollen-carrying bee

Fig. 4. The proposed process for image enhancement and segmentation of bee images, both for (a) pollen-carrying bees, and (b) pollen-free bees. From left to right, the original image of a bee, the image after thresholding, which separates the foreground (pollen-carrying regions) from the background, the image after applying the opening operation to remove noise and smooth the regions, the image after filtering to remove areas with circularity below 0.6, refining the pollen-carrying regions, and finally the enhanced image obtained by combining the binary areas from the filtering step with the original image, highlighting the pollen-carrying regions. The process effectively enhances the visibility and segmentation of the pollen-carrying areas in bee images.

the softmax function, which calculates the probabilities of an image corresponding to a bee with or without pollen. The CNN is trained for 50 epochs using a learning rate of 0.005 and a batch size of 18 images. The CNN architecture is depicted in Fig. 5. The specific parameters of the CNN were determined through empirical experimentation.

Figure 6a displays the accuracy and loss values throughout the training phase of the model. In the initial epoch, the accuracy value is 0.5153, accompanied by a loss value of 0.6940. By epoch 13, the accuracy increases to 0.7258, and the loss decreases to 0.6216. Notably, in epoch 18, the accuracy significantly improves to 0.9188 compared to epoch 13, while the loss decreases to 0.2397. Eventually, in epoch 50, the model achieves a perfect accuracy of 1, signifying successful classification of the training data.

With respect to the validation stage (Fig. 6b), initially, the accuracy is 0.5652, and the loss is 0.6892. A notable improvement is evident by epoch 13, when accuracy reaches 0.8608 and loss 0.5658. Further progress is observed in epoch 18, with the accuracy climbing to 0.8869 and the loss declining to 0.2051. By

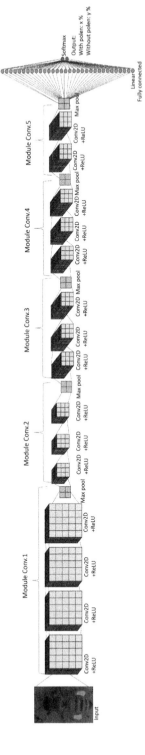

Fig. 5. The CNN architecture employed for classifying processed bee images. The image depicts a bee with pollen, which is fed into the CNN for classification into pollen-carrying or pollen-free categories. The architecture consists of five convolution modules represented by yellow grids, followed by max pooling layers depicted by orange grids. Subsequently, a fully connected layer is illustrated with green neurons, which are further connected to two output neurons utilizing the softmax function. This configuration enables the determination of the image's corresponding class. (Color figure online)

epoch 50, the accuracy achieves a steady state at 0.9478, accompanied by a loss value of 0.2204. Overall, the accuracy and loss values indicate a strong performance.

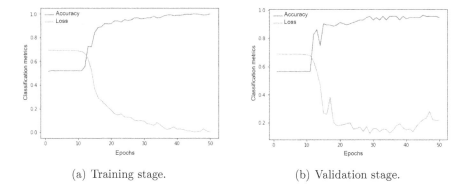

(a) Training stage.   (b) Validation stage.

Fig. 6. Classification metrics in the training and validation stage. Both graphs show the accuracy values in orange, and loss in blue. The x axis shows the epochs and the y axis shows the values of the classification metrics. (a) Accuracy and loss values in the training, (b) accuracy and loss values in the validation of the second method. (Color figure online)

4 Discussion and Conclusions

This work presents a comprehensive process for effectively classifying images of pollen-carrying bees and pollen-free bees. Initially, we utilized a dataset collected from videos captured at a hive entrance [20,21] as the foundation for developing two distinct methods to classify these bee images. A CNN was created and trained using images of pollen-carrying and pollen-free bees. Both methods utilized this trained CNN to compare their classification performance and determine the more effective approach. The classification metrics, including accuracy and loss, are presented in Table 3.

In the first method, we directly used the original RGB images of pollen-carrying and pollen-free bees for classification. The CNN yielded promising results, achieving an accuracy of 0.9230 and a loss value of 0.6861 during the testing stage.

The second method proposed a novel approach to enhance the identification of pollen-carrying bee images. The process involved several image enhancement techniques, including pollen area segmentation using the thresholding technique, application of morphological operations to eliminate irrelevant areas, and utilization of the circularity ratio to refine pollen detection. These emphasized images were then used to train the CNN. In the testing stage, the second method demonstrated improved performance, with an accuracy value of 0.9510 and a reduced loss value of 0.5707. The increased accuracy in the second method can be attributed to the effectiveness of the DIP techniques in emphasizing pollen regions and subsequently enhancing the CNN's ability to correctly identify and classify them.

Comparing the two methods, we observed that method 1 performed better for the validation set, while method 2 outperformed it in the test set, increasing accuracy from 0.9230 to 0.9510 and decreasing loss from 0.6861 to 0.5707. This suggests that the application of DIP techniques could be highly beneficial in improving the overall accuracy of CNN models.

Our findings demonstrate the capability of CNNs to effectively classify images of pollen-carrying and pollen-free bees. Furthermore, by incorporating DIP techniques to emphasize relevant features, such as pollen zones, the accuracy of the classification process can potentially be significantly enhanced. Overall, this study provides a solid foundation for future research and opens up opportunities to advance the field of bee image analysis.

Table 3. Classification metrics of the test stage of the two methods, particularly accuracy and loss test values.

Method	Accuracy	Loss	Stage
CNN	1	0.002	training
CNN	0.9652	0.2544	validation
CNN	0.9230	0.6861	test
DIP+CNN	1	0.0024	training
DIP+CNN	0.9478	0.2204	validation
DIP+CNN	0.9510	0.5707	test

5   Future Work

Future work in bee image analysis should consider the advantages and disadvantages of using CNNs and DIP techniques. While the proposed method primarily focuses on honey bees, its applicability can be tested with other bee species, such as melipona bees. To further enhance the classification performance, improvements can be made to the image enhancement techniques by adjusting parameters, including the type and size of structural elements used in operations like opening. Fine-tuning the CNN's batch size and training epochs could also lead to improved classification results.

Although this work employed a CNN for image classification, exploring alternative ML methods for feature extraction and classification, such as nearest neighbor or Bayesian classifiers, presents an intriguing avenue for future research [22]. Comparing the performance of these alternative methods with the CNN approach would provide valuable insights into their effectiveness in the context of bee image classification.

While the proposed method does not directly address the detection of looting in bee colonies, the accurate classification of bees into pollen-carrying and pollen-free categories opens up possibilities for automatic counting. This data can be utilized in future research to develop methods for looting detection [22]. Investigating correlations between pollen-carrying behavior and other factors associated with looting could pave the way for identifying and analyzing looting events.

Future work should focus on expanding the applicability of the proposed method to other bee species, refining the image enhancement techniques, exploring alternative classification algorithms, and investigating the potential link between pollen-carrying classification and looting detection. These endeavors will contribute to advancing the field of bee image analysis and provide valuable insights for various research applications. Additionally, addressing concerns regarding the generalizability of results by incorporating a wider range of bee species and populations in the dataset is crucial. Furthermore, accounting for variations in image quality and potential artifacts that may impact classification accuracy should be carefully considered. It is important to recognize the subjectivity inherent in image enhancement techniques and address potential variations in the enhancement process and their impact on classification results.

Acknowledgements. This work was supported by projects 13933.22-P and 14601.22-P from Tecnológico Nacional de México/IT de Mérida.

References

1. Agüero, J.I., Rollin, O., Torretta, J.P., Aizen, M.A., Requier, F., Garibaldi, L.A.: Impactos de la abeja melífera sobre plantas y abejas silvestres en hábitats naturales. Ecosistemas **27**(2), 60–69 (2018). https://doi.org/10.7818/ECOS.1365. https://revistaecosistemas.net/index.php/ecosistemas/article/view/1365
2. Barrera, G.M., Ordiales, H.: Transferencia de estilo entre audios mediante redes neuronales. Revista Digital del Departamento de Ingeniería e Investigaciones Tecnológicas de la Universidad Nacional de la Matanza **4**(1), 12 (2019). https://www.researchgate.net/publication/336221120_TRANSFERENCIA_DE_ESTILO_ENTRE_AUDIOS_MEDIANTE_REDES_NEURONALES_STYLE_TRANSFER_BETWEEN_AUDIOS_USING_NEURAL_NETWORKS
3. Chen, C., Yang, E.C., Jiang, J.A., Lin, T.T.: An imaging system for monitoring the in-and-out activity of honey bees. Comput. Electron. Agric. **89**, 100–109 (2012). https://doi.org/10.1016/j.compag.2012.08.006. https://www.sciencedirect.com/science/article/abs/pii/S0168169912002074
4. Chiron, G., Gomez-Krämer, P., Ménard, M.: Detecting and tracking honeybees in 3D at the beehive entrance using stereo vision. EURASIP J. Image Video Process. (59), 1–17 (2013). https://doi.org/10.1186/1687-5281-2013-59. https://jivp-eurasipjournals.springeropen.com/articles/10.1186/1687-5281-2013-59
5. Cortés, E., Sánchez, S.: Deep learning transfer with AlexNet for chest X-ray COVID-19 recognition. IEEE Lat. Am. Trans. **100** (2020). https://latamt.ieeer9.org/index.php/transactions/article/view/4336

6. Flórez López, R., Fernandez, J.M., Fernández Fernández, J.M.: Las redes neuronales artificiales. Netbiblo, S.L., León, 1 edn. (2008). https://books.google.com.
   mx/books?id=X0uLwi1Ap4QC&dq=redes+neuronales+artificiales&lr=&hl=es&
   source=gbs_navlinks_s https://books.google.com.ec/books?id=X0uLwi1Ap4QC
   &printsec=frontcover&dq=las+redes+neuronales+tienen+una+importante+capa
   cidad+para+detectar+
7. Gonzalez, R.C., Woods, R.E.: Digital Image Processing, 3rd edn. Pearson Prentice
   Hall, New Jersey (2007). https://dl.acm.org/citation.cfm?id=1076432
8. Heise, D., Miller-Struttmann, N., Galen, C., Schul, J.: Acoustic detection of bees in
   the field using CASA with focal templates. In: Proceedings of the 2017 IEEE Sensors Applications Symposium, SAS 2017, p. 5. Institute of Electrical and Electronics Engineers Inc., Glassboro (2017). https://doi.org/10.1109/SAS.2017.7894089
9. Khosravy, M., Gupta, N., Marina, N., Sethi, I.K., Asharif, M.R.: Morphological
   filters: an inspiration from natural geometrical erosion and dilation. In: Patnaik, S.,
   Yang, X.-S., Nakamatsu, K. (eds.) Nature-Inspired Computing and Optimization.
   MOST, vol. 10, pp. 349–379. Springer, Cham (2017). https://doi.org/10.1007/978-
   3-319-50920-4_14
10. Kim, P.: MATLAB deep learning. In: MATLAB Deep Learning, chap. 6, 1 edn.,
    pp. 121,147. Apress, Berkeley (2017). https://doi.org/10.1007/978-1-4842-2845-6
11. Laurino, D., Lioy, S., Carisio, L., Manino, A., Porporato, M.: Vespa velutina: an
    alien driver of honey bee colony losses. Diversity **12**(1) (2020). https://doi.org/10.
    3390/D12010005
12. Lecun, Y., Bengio, Y., Hinton, G.: Deep learning (2015). https://doi.org/10.1038/
    nature14539. https://www.nature.com/articles/nature14539
13. Magaña, M.Á.M., Sanginés García, J.R., Lara y Lara, P.E., De Lourdes Salazar
    Barrientos, L., Morales, C.E.L.: Competitividad y participación de la miel mexi-
    cana en el mercado mundial. Revista Mexicana De Ciencias Pecuarias **8**(1), 43–52
    (2017). https://doi.org/10.22319/rmcp.v8i1.4304
14. Nunes da Silva, I., Hernane Spatti, D., Andrade Flauzino, R., Liboni, Bartocci,
    L.H., dos Reis Alves, S.F.: Artificial Neural Networks, vol. 6, , 1 edn. Springer, Sao
    Paulo (2018). https://doi.org/10.1016/B978-0-444-53632-7.01101-1
15. Padilla Ospina, A.M., Medina Vásquez, J.E., Ospina Holguín, J.H.: Métodos de
    aprendizaje automático en los estudios prospectivos desde un ejemplo de la finan-
    ciación de la innovación en Colombia. Revista de Investigación, Desarrollo e Inno-
    vación **11**(1), 9–21 (2020). https://doi.org/10.19053/20278306.v11.n1.2020.11676.
    https://revistas.uptc.edu.co/index.php/investigacion_duitama/article/view/11676
16. Perlis, U.M., Jambek, A.B., Anuar, K., Said, M., Sulaiman, N.: A study of
    image processing using morphological opening and closing processes. Int. J. Con-
    trol Theory Appl. **9**(31), 15–21 (2016). https://www.researchgate.net/publication/
    314154399
17. Uroš, P., Rand'ić, S., Stamenković, Z., Pešović, U., Rand'ić, S., Stamenković, Z.:
    Design and implementation of hardware platform for monitoring honeybee activity.
    In: International Conference on Electrical, Electronics and Computing Engineer-
    ing (October), pp. 5–8 (2017). https://www.etran.rs/common/pages/proceedings/
    IcETRAN2017/RTI/IcETRAN2017_paper_RTI1_5.pdf
18. Pino Díez, R., Gómez Gómez, A., de Abajo Martínez, N.: Introducción a
    la Inteligencia Artificial: sistemas expertos, redes neuronales artificiales y com-
    putación evolutiva. Universidad de Oviedo, Oviedo, 1 edn. (2001). https://books.go
    ogle.com.mx/books?id=RKqLMCw3IUkC&dq=redes+neuronales+artificiales&lr
    =&hl=es&source=gbs_navlinks_s https://books.google.com.co/books?id=RKqLM

Cw3IUkC&lpg=PP1&dq=sistemasexpertosdefinicion&pg=PA10#v=onepage&q=
sistemasexpertosdefinicion&f
19. Rivera, J.S., Gagné, M.O., Tu, S., Barka, N., Nadeau, F., Ouafi, A.E.: Quality
classification model with machine learning for porosity prediction in laser welding
aluminum alloys. J. Laser Appl. **35**(2) (2023)
20. Rodriguez, I.F., Branson, K., Acuña, E., Agosto-Rivera, J.L., Giray, T., Mégret,
R.: Honeybee detection and pose estimation using convolutional neural networks.
Congres Reconnaissance des Formes, Image, Apprentissage et Perception (RFIAP),
pp. 1–3 (2018). https://par.nsf.gov/biblio/10095766
21. Rodriguez, I.F., Megret, R., Acuna, E., Agosto-Rivera, J.L., Giray, T.: Recognition
of pollen-bearing bees from video using convolutional neural network. In: Proceedings of the 2018 IEEE Winter Conference on Applications of Computer Vision,
WACV 2018, pp. 314–322. Institute of Electrical and Electronics Engineers Inc.,
Lake Tahoe (2018). https://doi.org/10.1109/WACV.2018.00041
22. Salah, M.: A survey of modern classification techniques in remote sensing for
improved image classification. J. Geom. **11**(1), 20 (2017). https://isgindia.org/
wp-content/uploads/2017/04/016.pdf
23. Salas,   R.:   Redes   Neuronales   Artificiales-Rodrigo   Salas.   Universidad   de   Valparaíso,   Valparaíso,   Technical   report   (2005).
https://d1wqtxts1xzle7.cloudfront.net/50358783/Redes_Neuronales_
Artificiales.pdf?1479332205=&response-content-disposition=inline
%3B+filename%3DRedes_Neuronales_Artificiales.pdf&Expires=1619480693&
Signature=csYakiIQj8LjAQrIPQU1Nw44Yt7z~juzjQlzOq1AZdchPy5wH
24. Shih, F.Y.: Image Processing and Mathematical Morphology. CRC Press, Boca
Raton (2017). https://doi.org/10.1201/9781420089448. https://www.taylorfrancis.
com/books/mono/10.1201/9781420089448/image-processing-mathematical-
morphology-frank-shih
25. Takashimizu, Y., Iiyoshi, M.: New parameter of roundness R: circularity corrected by aspect ratio. Progress Earth Planet. Sci. **3**(1), 1–16
(2016). https://doi.org/10.1186/s40645-015-0078-x. https://progearthplanetsci.
springeropen.com/articles/10.1186/s40645-015-0078-x
26. Tu, G.J., Hansen, M.K., Kryger, P., Ahrendt, P.: Automatic behaviour analysis
system for honeybees using computer vision. Comput. Electron. Agric. **122**, 10–18
(2016). https://doi.org/10.1016/j.compag.2016.01.011
27. Venkatesan, R., Li, B.: Convolutional Neural Networks in Visual Computing: A
Concise Guide, 1st edn. Taylor & Francis Group, Phoenix (2018)

Enhancing Air Quality Monitoring in Mexico City: A Hybrid Sensor-Machine Learning System

Camilo Israel Chávez Galván, Roberto Zagal, Miguel Felix Mata, Fabio Duarte, Simone Mora, Amadeo Arguelles$^{(\boxtimes)}$, and Martina Mazzarello

Av Juan De Dios Batiz S/N, Col Nueva Industrial Vallejo, 07738 Mexico City, Mexico
{alumno2022,rzagalf,mmatar,aarguelles}@ipn.mx, {fduarte,moras,
mmazz}@mit.edu

Abstract. We present and approach for monitoring and built a dataset of regional historical air quality data in Mexico City. We design a hybrid air quality network prototype that combines mobile and stationary sensors to collect street-level data on particulate matter (PM2.5 and PM10). The network is composed of mobile monitoring modules, both stationary at street level and mounted on vehicles, to capture a comprehensive sample of particulate matter behavior in specific areas. Collected data is transmitted using IoT network and processed using machine learning techniques, to generate predictive models to forecast air quality at street level. This approach is an additional improvement to current monitoring capabilities in Mexico City by providing granular street-level data. The system provides a regional and periodic perspective on air quality, enhancing the understanding of pollution levels and supporting informed decision-making to enhance public health and well-being. This research represents a solution for environmental monitoring in urban environments to know how the behavior from pollution levels in air is. The experiments show the effectiveness, and the model of forecast has an overall performance around 81% that is acceptable for the small geographical area testing. As future work is required to include a major number of nodes to collect data from a big geographical coverage and test with other models and algorithms.

Keywords: Air quality · monitoring · IoT · Machine Learning

1 Introduction

Despite decades of global efforts to combat air pollution, the progress seems to be declining due to various factors such as climate change, wildfires, and increased human consumption driven by population growth as other research indicated such as [1]. Mexico City has long been known for its high levels of air pollution [2], and while significant efforts have been made to reduce pollutant emissions, the problem persists not only in the city but also worldwide [4].

One of the most significant challenges in recent decades has been the efforts to reduce the environmental impact we create as a species by polluting our air. It is a phenomenon

M. F. Mata-Rivera et al. (Eds.): WITCOM 2023, CCIS 1906, pp. 270–288, 2023.
https://doi.org/10.1007/978-3-031-45316-8_18

that claims thousands of lives annually and increasingly affects large cities. It is no coincidence that there are more and more independent organizations and projects joining the cause to find alternatives to reduce pollution levels on our planet.

For other and, in [3] is used of low-cost air quality monitors (LCMs) and their performance in assessing particulate matter levels. It highlights the advancements in sensor technology that have made LCMs accessible for home use. The study's methodology, which involved comparing LCM measurements to reference data from various sources, is commendable.

Air pollution consists of particles and gases that can reach hazardous concentrations in both outdoor and indoor environments. The adverse effects of high pollution levels range from health risks to increased temperatures. Key pollutants that require constant monitoring include sulfur dioxide (SO_2), carbon monoxide (CO), nitrogen dioxide (NO_2), ozone (O_3), suspended particles (PM_{10}, $PM_{2.5}$), among others. According to the World Health Organization (WHO), air pollution is estimated to cause 7 million deaths globally each year, with 9 out of 10 people breathing air that exceeds WHO guidelines, disproportionately affecting poorer and developing countries [7].

According to SEDEMA [8], air quality regulations for suspended particles are categorized according to Table 1.

Table 1. Values of air quality in Mexico City.

Contaminant	Values	Quality
PM2.5/PM10	0–50	Good
PM2.5/PM10	51–100	Moderate
PM2.5/PM10	101–150	Poor
PM2.5/PM10	151–200	Very Poor
PM2.5/PM10	201–300	Extremely Poor

Similar to other densely populated cities, especially those located in valleys like Mexico City, there are challenges in controlling pollutant levels due to geographical characteristics, particularly with ozone and suspended particles. Although government efforts have gradually reduced emission levels since the 1990s, population growth has hindered further progress in recent years [7]. Currently, Mexico City has the Atmospheric Monitoring System (SIMAT) implemented to comply with regulations for controlling pollutant levels and promptly preventing risks associated with high pollutant concentrations that may endanger public health. SIMAT includes the Automatic Atmospheric Monitoring Network (RAMA), which measures sulfur dioxide, carbon monoxide, nitrogen dioxide, ozone, PM10, and PM2.5. It consists of 34 stations and the Air Quality Information Center (CICA), which serves as the repository for all data generated by the Atmospheric Monitoring System and is responsible for data validation, processing, and dissemination [8]. This network enables the creation of a pollution level map through stationary stations at specific locations. However, despite being in operation for decades, this monitoring system has not significantly evolved alongside the rapid growth and constant changes of the city.

Our research is motivated by the increasing demand for new technologies like IoT and Machine Learning in problem-solving [5], and how their implementation can greatly improve the lives of people. Inspired by the initiatives of non-governmental organizations in creating intelligent air quality monitoring systems, such as the Environmental Defense Fund in London and research like [6].

This research aims to address the limitations of the current air quality monitoring system in Mexico City by proposing the development of a hybrid network that integrates mobile and stationary sensors with IoT and Machine Learning technologies. The goal to long term is to create a scalable and accurate system capable of providing real-time, street-level data on air pollutants. Where a mobile monitoring system will be implemented using vehicles that are constantly moving around a regional area such as Zacatenco.

2   Related Work

Significant progress has been made worldwide in the monitoring of air quality in terms of PM2.5 and PM10 particles. In this section we present, some works that have involved the deployment of monitoring systems in urban areas, to measure air quality and the use of Machine learning models to predict air quality indices based on air quality data. Despite the fact of the interdisciplinary nature of air quality research involves several domains such as atmospheric chemistry, meteorology, and data science for mention some of them.

The use of monitoring stations combined with machine learning models have been studied before, like in [9] where is presented a study of monitoring pollutant levels, specifically PM2.5, PM10, and NO2, at two locations in Stuttgart is conducted using monitoring station. Machine learning is employed to simulate and predict pollutant concentrations based on meteorological, traffic, and nearby monitoring station data. But the approach does not consider the use of mobile monitoring stations.

While, in [10] The importance of investigating morphological factors that contribute to the spatial distribution of air pollution using mobile monitoring data is emphasized. They assess the nonlinear relationship between the spatial distribution of atmospheric pollutants and the morphological indicators of buildings in a high-density city. They use a mobile station of monitoring but focused on predicting the spatial variability of pollutants and the assessment of six machine learning models where neural networks have a better performance, the testing was made in Shanghai.

Continuing with the machine learning research on air quality, in [11] is shown a study, where is mentioned that there has been a significant increase in the application of ML models in air pollution research. The study is based on a bibliometric analysis of 2962 articles published from 1990 to 2021 and highlights that most publications occurred after 2017. As well as the main research topics related to the application of ML in the chemical characterization of pollutants, short-term forecasting, detection improvement, and emission control optimization. The paper is based on explore the status of ML applications in air pollution research.

For another hand, in [12] research is presented based on spatial-temporal approach combined with machine learning on air quality, they discusses air pollution management and the importance of linking pollution sources to air quality. It mentions that since weather cannot be controlled, air pollution can only be managed by planning and controlling pollution sources. It emphasizes that mathematical models that don't establish a relationship between the source and air quality don't provide guidance on how to regulate air quality. To address this, a machine learning model is used to predict the daily average concentrations of NO2 and SO2 in five different locations. Features related to weather and features related to the type and quantity of fossil fuels consumed by power plants are used as proxies for emission rates. Three different models are compared, and Model III is found to be the most accurate, showing significant improvements in pollutant concentration prediction. The paper does not consider the use of mobile stations as our proposal.

Furthermore, in [13] discusses the concern over high air pollution levels in Ho Chi Minh City (HCMC) Vietnam, and the use of machine learning algorithms to forecast air quality in the region. It is mentioned that air pollution levels have exceeded WHO standards, leading to significant impacts on human health and the ecosystem. Is described an effort to develop a global air quality forecasting model that considers multiple parameters such as weather conditions, air quality data, urban spatial information, and temporal components to predict concentrations of NO2, SO2, O3, and CO at hourly intervals. The datasets on air pollution time series were gathered from six air quality monitoring sites from February 2021 to August 2022. It concludes that the global model outperforms previous models that consider only a specific pollutant. Not mobile monitoring is treated, but forecasting is treated.

Forecasting on air quality is addressed in [15] They applied Air Quality Index (AQI) to the city of Visakhapatnam, Andhra Pradesh, India, focusing on 12 contaminants and 10 meteorological parameters from July 2017 to September 2022. Using several machine learning models, including LightGBM, Random Forest, Catboost, Adaboost, and XGBoost. Where Catboost model outperformed other models, they used air quality and meteorological datasets.

The health impacts of air pollution are treated in [14] discussing the alarming increase in air pollution due to industrialization in developing countries and its impact on hospital visits by patients with respiratory diseases, specifically Acute Respiratory Infections (ARI). The study collects data on outpatient hospital visits, air pollution, and meteorological parameters from March 2018 to October 2021. Eight machine learning algorithms were applied to analyze the relationship between daily air pollution and outpatient visits for ARI. The results indicate that, among the eight machine learning models studied, the Random Forest model performed the best. However, it was found that the models did not perform well when considering the lag effect in the dataset of ARI patients.

To conclude, air quality monitoring and prediction, especially regarding PM2.5 and PM10, represent active and evolving research and application areas worldwide. The combination of fixed and mobile sensors, machine learning models, and interdisciplinary research has significantly enhanced our capacity to understand, predict, and address air quality issues in various regions and contexts.

3 Material and Methods

This section presents the system architecture consists of a broker (Azure IoT Hub), a resource for data processing and analytics, which enables working with the stream received by the broker and processing it for storage in a non-relational database using the CosmosDB SQL API it is shown in Fig. 1.

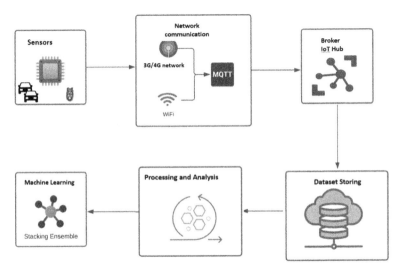

Fig. 1. System Architecture

As Fig. 1 is depicted, each module will be described as follows:

The Sensor Module: This module is responsible for sampling suspended particles (PM10, PM2.5) every hour throughout the day for the stationary station and around 300 samples per day for the mobile station. The sampling frequency for the mobile station was chosen to ensure continuous monitoring and verification of sensor data while in motion. However, this monitoring supervision could be avoided if higher-quality sensors were accessible, such an improvement can be considered for future implementations.

The Network Communications Module: This module is responsible for transmitting the samples taken by the sensor module to the network. The data is processed to determine predictive models that serve as a reference for understanding pollutant behavior.

IoT Broker: It is used to enable secure and bidirectional communication between sensors and cloud applications, enabling secure communication using a set of protocols.
Dataset Storing module: It is responsible for managing and storing the data, from its preprocessing, and for sending it to the data processing module.
Processing and Analysis Module: it is required to prepare data, cleaning and deliver the data to be sent to machine learning module.

Machine Learning module, here is trained, validated the models using the data obtained data module and graphs are generated.

The input data for this project consists of PM10 and PM2.5 levels provided by sensors on the mainboard, a GPS module providing coordinates for hourly measurements, and additional data from the sensors and package transmission time. The route was conducted with a vehicle in the Zacatenco area. Test zones can be stationary or mobile monitoring areas with vehicles that have a constant route throughout the city, as well as public areas where the module for pollutant monitoring can be installed. The monitored data includes PM10 and PM2.5 suspended particles, obtained through the network sensors.

4 Design Network Air Quality

This section is divided into two parts. The first part involves the design, installation, and operation of a sensor network to monitor air quality in the Zacatenco academic facilities of the National Polytechnic Institute in Mexico City. The second part integrates the data obtained from mobile and stationary monitoring and uses a model to predict air quality.

4.1 Design Sensor Network Hardware

This section describes the design of the monitoring stations, which includes the integration of PM2.5/PM10 sensors and a GPS module using two different base boards. It is shown in Fig. 2.

As Fig. 2 shows, one base board is used for the mobile monitoring station, which incorporates the Arduino MKR 1400 GSM board and utilizes the Message Queuing Telemetry Transport (MQTT) protocol for data transmission. The other base board is used for the stationary monitoring station, which incorporates the Arduino MKR 1010 WiFi board and utilizes the MQTT protocol. The PM2.5/PM10 sensor has the following characteristics shown in Table 2.

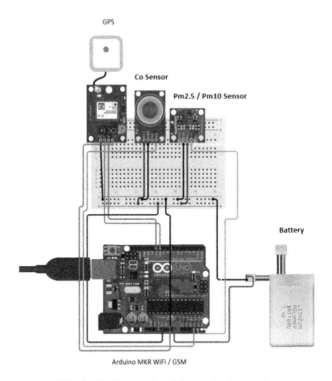

Fig. 2. Hardware of mobile monitoring station.

Table 2. Specifications of suspended Particle Sensor $PM_{2.5}/PM_{10}$

Specifications	
	Operating Voltage: 4.95 – 5.05 V
	Maximum Electrical Current: 120 mA
	Measurement Particle Diameter: 0.3–1.0, 1.0–2.5, 2.5–10(um)
	Measurement Range for Particulate Matter: 0 – 999 ug/m^3
	Standby Current: $\leq$200 uA
	Response Time: $\leq$10 s
	Operating Temperature Range: -20 – 50 C
	Operating Humidity Range: 0 – 99% RH
	Maximum Size: 65 $\times$ 42 $\times$ 23 (mm)
	MTBF (Mean Time Between Failures):$>=$ 5 years
	Fast Response
	Standard Serial Word Output
	Second-Order Multipoint Calibration Curve
	Minimum Resolution Size of 0.3 microns

4.1.1 Design Stationary Monitoring Station

The stationary monitoring station was designed to take readings of PM 2.5/ PM10 each 15 min per day. The period required by the sensors to obtain accurate samples, which is 5 s. The stationary monitoring station consists of an Arduino board, a PM2.5/PM10 suspended particles module, and a GPS module. The station is shown in Fig. 3.

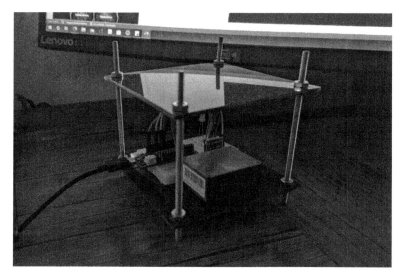

Fig. 3. Stationary station

4.1.2 Design Mobile Monitoring Station

The mobile monitoring station was designed to take readings of PM2.5/PM10 and coordinates every 5 seconds during the routes defined in testing zones. The sensor module was integrated with a module that allows the transmission of the data obtained by the sensors in real-time using either the 4G network or Wi-Fi. It is shown in Fig. 4.

The design of this monitoring station allows it to be transported in an automobile. The average sampling time during each journey was from 10 to 20 min, and it was conducted three times per day, five days a week (Monday to Friday). The integration of the sensor module with the Arduino MKR WiFi 1010 and Arduino MKR GSM 1400 boards enables the periodic transmission of data obtained by the monitoring stations using the available Wi-Fi or GSM/4G network, respectively.

Fig. 4. Mobile Monitoring station

4.2 Analysis of Air Quality Data

Data cleaning was performed to prepare the training and validation data, keeping only the relevant data for the purpose of the machine learning model, which includes the timestamp and the parameters-pm25/value and parameters-pm10/value.

The timestamp column was transformed into a date type, and the execution was performed in two phases: one with PM2.5 suspended particle values and the other with PM10 suspended particle values.

The collected data is stored as JSON documents in the Cosmos DB, a NoSQL database where T-SQL is used for queries and data processing (see Table 3).

Table 3. JSON Document Data Dictionary

Document	Variable Name	Data Type	Description
General	Timestamp	String	Event Identifier with Date and Time
	Stationid	String	Station Identifier
	Parameters	Object	Document with Event Parameters Information
	Latitude	Float	Event Coordinates
	Longitude	Float	Event Coordinates

(continued)

Table 3. (*continued*)

Document	Variable Name	Data Type	Description
Parameters	Idparameter	String	Parameter Identifier
	Value	Int	Sensor Reading Value
	Unit	Int	Sensor Reading Unit
*Obtained from IoT Hub	EventProcessedUtcTime*	String	Chain Processing Time
	PartitionId*	Int	Hub Partition ID
	EventEnqueuedUtcTime*	String	Chain Queue Processing Time
	MessageId*	null	Message ID
	CorrelationId*	null	IoT Hub Relationship ID
	ConnectionDeviceId*	String	Device ID
	ConnectionDeviceGenerationId*	String	Connection ID
	EnqueuedTime*	String	Queue Processing Time
	Id*	String	Message ID in Document

A database was provisioned for each of the monitoring stations, the data normalization used the method min-max scaler. This normalization method allows us to transform our features (i.e., the columns of our data [PM2.5/PM10]) within a minimum and maximum value (0 and 1).

The mathematical function for min-max scaler normalization is given by Eq. (1):

$$x_{scaled} = \frac{x - min(x)}{max(x) - min(x)} \tag{1}$$

The selection of model for training was based on the requirement of predicting a single dimension, in this case the suspended particles PM2.5/PM10, then we used a Long Short-Term Memory model (LSTM network and because is scientific literature has been used as in such as weather forecasts and Time Series Prediction, where LSTM is excellent for forecasting future values in time series data, due to its ability to capture long-term patterns in the data.

Long Short-Term Memory (LSTM) method, is a type of Recurrent Neural Network (RNN) that is capable of learning long-term dependencies. It was introduced by Hochreiter and Schmidhuber in 1997 [17]. All recurrent neural networks have a chain-like structure with repeated modules of a neural network. LSTM networks also have a similar structure, but the iteration module has a different structure. Instead of a single layer, it consists of four layers of neural networks that interact in a special way. The

LSTM neural network comprises an input layer, an LSTM layer, a fully connected layer, and an output layer [16], as depicted in Fig. 5.

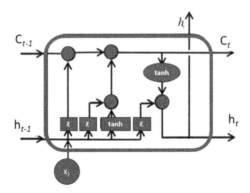

Fig. 5. LSTM representation

The LSTM model works as follows:

1) The first step is to decide which information to discard in the node state. This decision is made by the layer called the 'forget gate layer'. From the output of h_(t-1) and x_t, ranges between 0 and 1 are obtained, indicating whether the information is transmitted to the next node or discarded. A value of 1 means the information is needed, while 0 means it should be discarded.
2) The next step is to decide which new information to store in the node state. This process is divided into two sub-processes. The first is defined by the sigma function, which determines the values to be updated. The tanh function creates a vector with the new values of the candidates that can be stored in the node state.
3) The following step is to perform what was decided in the previous step. We multiply the previous state by f_t, forgetting the previously decided information, and adding the new candidates.

Finally, we decide what to send to the output. This is based on the state of our node. The sigma function determines which part of the node state to send to the output. We then force the values to be within -1 and 1 using the tanh function and multiply them by the output of the sigma function. This ensures that only the data decided in the process is sent to the output.

5   Experiments and Results

The experiments and testing took place over a two-month period spanning from October to November 2022. The configuration involved the installation of three stationary monitoring stations at distinct locations within the Zacatenco region of Mexico City, specifically at IPN Campuses UPIITA, ESCOM, and CIC, respectively. In the case of the mobile monitoring station, a predefined journey sequence was executed. This journey route covered the Zacatenco area and its adjacent avenues. The average sampling duration for each journey ranged from 10 to 20 min, and this process was repeated three times daily, from Monday to Friday. A visual representation of this route can be found in Fig. 6 on the map.

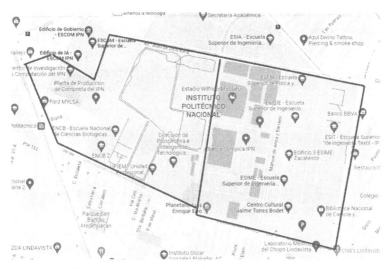

Fig. 6. Geographical area of monitoring in Zacatenco

The two stationary monitoring stations were connected to IPN Wi-Fi network, while the third mobile monitoring station was connected to the GSM/4G network. In Fig. 7 is shown the prototype sensor installation of UPIITA station.

The monitoring process at the UPIITA and ESCOM stations was meticulous, with readings captured at 15-min intervals. This effort resulted in the accumulation of a noteworthy 5,760 data points over the span of two months. This dataset shows the air quality and environmental conditions at these specific locations.

In contrast, the mobile monitoring station employed a more frequent sampling strategy, conducting readings every 5 min. This high-frequency approach led to the collection of a substantial 17,280 samples over the same two-month period. This dataset allows for a more detailed examination of air quality variations in the broader Zacatenco area, offering a comprehensive perspective on the region's environmental dynamics. For a comprehensive overview of the total samples obtained by each monitoring station, including their respective data collection periods, refer to Table 4.

Fig. 7. UPIITA station installation

Table 4. Sample data collection periods

Station ID	Location	Sample Count	Period	Duration
1	ESCOM	17280	September 30 - November 26	2 months
2	UPIITA	5760	October 7 - November 26	2 months
3	CIC	5760	October 26 - November 26	2 month

Figure 8 provides a detailed visual representation of the routes meticulously traced by our mobile monitoring station within the Zacatenco region of Mexico City. These routes were carefully selected to encompass key areas of interest, allowing us to comprehensively assess air quality and environmental conditions across this bustling urban landscape. The map in Fig. 8 not only showcases the routes but also offers essential geographical context, with reference points along the way. By charting these paths, we've been able to gather a wealth of data that contributes significantly to our understanding of air quality dynamics in the Zacatenco area.

This graphical representation allows to visualize the coverage of our mobile monitoring efforts, providing a clear picture of the regions where we have collected critical data for analysis.

As we closely examine the data, we've identified two distinct locations marked on our heat map in red color. One of these points is located at the entrance of campus ESCOM, while the other lies amidst the bustling cross avenues adjacent to the shopping center known as "Torres Lindavista". These specific locations have registered elevated levels of PM 10 and PM 2.5, making them crucial focal points for our analysis.

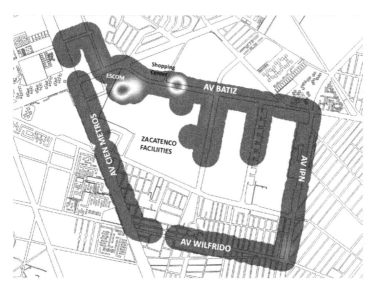

Fig. 8. Geographical area and routes of mobile monitoring in Zacatenco

In our pursuit of building a reliable model, we focused on training and validating it using data from monitoring stations that have accumulated the highest number of samples. As indicated in Table 2, our primary sources of data for model development are the Mobile and stationary monitoring station, which contributed a substantial 17,280 samples, and the second contributor with 5,060 samples.

These stations were strategically chosen due to their data records, ensuring that our model is equipped to provide accurate insights into air quality conditions, especially in areas where historical records have consistently shown heightened PM 10 and PM 2.5 levels. The utilization of these datasets allows to the model predict and address air quality concerns effectively. The Fig. 9 shows the historical behavior obtained from stationary station in UPIITA for PM10 over a 2-month period.

In reference to PM10 levels, it is essential to underscore that the 24-h average remains stable at 75 μg/m^3, in accordance with the data provided by the air quality index, accessible at http://www.aire.cdmx.gob.mx/. The fact that this value aligns with the recommended limit, as depicted in the accompanying chart, is indeed a positive indication. This implies that, daily, the air quality generally falls within acceptable standards.

Nonetheless, it is imperative to draw attention to a critical point. Towards the end of September, a notably high PM10 value was recorded. This anomaly demands a more comprehensive investigation and heightened attention. It is essential to delve deeper into the circumstances surrounding this spike to better understand the potential causes and implications for air quality management and public health in the region.

Shifting our focus to PM2.5, we have delved into an analysis of its trends, all appears in Fig. 11. This figure serves as a visual aid, enabling us to conduct a more thorough and nuanced examination of PM2.5 concentrations and their fluctuations over time.

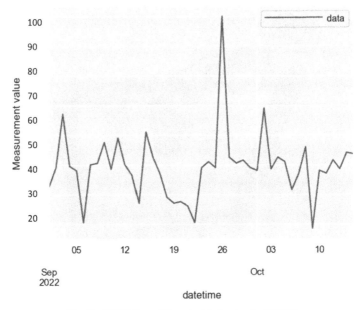

data

Fig. 9. PM10 Data Historical behavior in UPIITA

Gaining a deep understanding of the dynamics of PM2.5 is of paramount importance. These fine particulate matter particles, with a diameter of 2.5 μm or smaller, have a unique ability to linger in the atmosphere and penetrate deeply into our respiratory system when inhaled. As such, comprehending how PM2.5 levels evolve and vary over time is crucial, as it provides invaluable insights into the potential impact on air quality and, consequently, public health.

By dissecting the data represented in Fig. 10, we gain a picture of the temporal trends of PM2.5, enabling us to make informed decisions regarding air quality management strategies and health measures.

In the model training process, we have allocated 2/3 of our samples for training the model, enabling the LSTM algorithm to learn complex patterns from a sufficiently dataset.

This constitutes a critical phase in the implementation of machine learning algorithms, such as the LSTM algorithm employed in this study. The data source is from two stations with remarkable total of 17,280 samples, with the second-largest contributor providing 5,060 samples, all collected over a period of two months.

The validation phase becomes essential to assess the model's performance. We make to experiments, one using only the data form stationary station.

The separation of 1/3 of the data for this purpose allows us to verify how the model performs on unseen data and ensures it is not overfitting the training data. In Fig. 11 as can be showed the forecast was not good, the performance was around 70%.

Then, we proceed to integrate and balance all dataset and apply the LSTM therefore, with the model trained and validated, it was applied. The results are illustrated in Fig. 12.

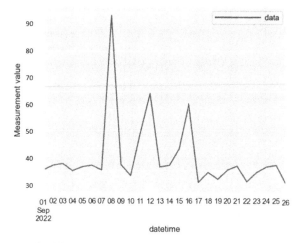

Fig. 10. PM2.5 Data Historical behavior in UPIITA

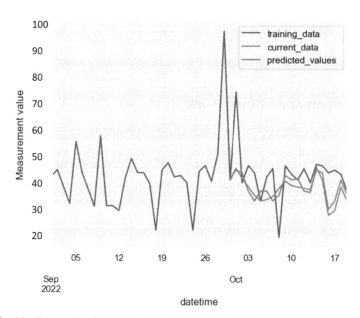

Fig. 11. Forecasting for PM10 only with data from Stationary monitoring station

The performance of LSTM was 88% for the case of PM10 as is shown in graphic. We can conclude the success of the model based on the results obtained.

Finally, the performance metrics of our model for PM10 suspended particles. With a loss of 0.008674 defined by the which indicates the percentage of error obtained by the model.

The monitoring stations fulfill the purpose of taking street-level readings every hour, 24 h a day for the stationary station, and every 5 s for daily routes for the mobile station.

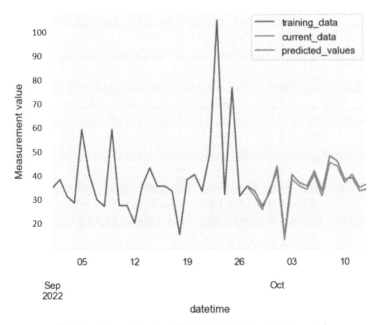

Fig. 12. Forecasting for PM10 with all datasets integrated

6   Conclusions and Future Work

The presented approach successfully demonstrates an effective method for monitoring air quality in regional areas of Mexico City. The hybrid network of mobile and stationary sensors provides a granular street-level perspective on particulate matter behavior. The combination of IoT technology and machine learning techniques proves to be valuable for data processing and generating predictive models for air quality forecasting at street level.

This research contributes to enhancing the understanding of pollution levels in urban environments, supporting informed decision-making to improve public health and well-being. While the model's overall performance is acceptable, there is room for improvement. Future work should explore additional models and algorithms to enhance accuracy. To gain deeper insights into air quality patterns, long-term data analysis should be considered to identify seasonal variations and correlations with other factors.

The presented approach represents a significant step towards improved air quality monitoring in Mexico City. It highlights the potential for using technology and data-driven methods to address air pollution challenges in urban environments. However, ongoing research and collaboration are needed to refine the system and maximize its impact on public health and environmental well-being.

While in Future work, expansion of Sensor Network, this would allow for data collection across a larger geographical coverage, providing a more comprehensive view of air quality in Mexico City.

Regarding experimenting with different machine learning models and algorithms to improve the accuracy of air quality forecasts. This may include exploring more sophisticated techniques or ensemble methods.

To better understand trends and patterns in air quality, conducting long-term data analysis could be beneficial. This could involve analyzing data over several years to identify seasonal variations, long-term trends, and potential correlations with other factors like weather patterns or traffic. Developing user-friendly data visualization tools and platforms for public outreach Making air quality data easily accessible and understandable to the public can raise awareness and drive behavior change. Continuously validating and calibrating the sensors to ensure data accuracy is crucial. Developing protocols and methodologies for sensor calibration and validation. Overall, the future work could involve refining and expanding the existing air quality monitoring system to enhance its accuracy, coverage, and impact on public health and urban well-being.

Acknowledgments. The authors want to thank God, IPN, COFAA, UPIITA-IPN, and ESCOM-IPN for their support. This work has been partially supported by the IPN SIP-20231645, 20230096, 20231156, CONAHCYT CF-2023-G-1170 and 7051 projects, and MISTI-IPN-MIT Found.

References

1. Guo, P., et al.: Ambient air pollution and markers of fetal growth: a retrospective population-based cohort study of 2.57 million term singleton births in China. Environ. Int. **135**, 105410 (2020)
2. Bravo-Alvarez, H., Torres-Jardón, R.: Air pollution levels and trends in the Mexico City metropolitan area. Urban Air Pollution and Forests: Resources at Risk in the Mexico City Air Basin, pp. 121–159 (2002)
3. Wang, Z., Delp, W.W., Singer, B.C.: Performance of low-cost indoor air quality monitors for PM2. 5 and PM10 from residential sources. Building Environ. **171**, 106654 (2020)
4. Nelson, P.F.: Environmental issues: emissions, pollution control, assessment, and management. In: The Coal Handbook, pp. 31–76. Woodhead Publishing (2023)
5. Dai, X., Shang, W., Liu, J., Xue, M., Wang, C.: Achieving better indoor air quality with IoT systems for future buildings: opportunities and challenges. Sci. Total Environ. **895**, 164858 (2023)
6. Hajmohammadi, H., Heydecker, B.: Evaluation of air quality effects of the London ultra-low emission zone by state-space modelling. Atmos. Pollut. Res. **13**(8), 101514 (2022)
7. SEDEMA. Calidad del Aire, SEDEMA, 2018. [En línea]. Available: http://www.data.sedema.cdmx.gob.mx/breatheLife/calidadAire.html
8. Gobierno de la Ciudad de México. Dirección de Monitoreo Atmosférico, [En línea]. Available: http://www.aire.cdmx.gob.mx/default.php?opc=%27ZaBhnmI=%27
9. Samad, A., Garuda, S., Vogt, U., Yang, B.: Air pollution prediction using machine learning techniques – an approach to replace existing monitoring stations with virtual monitoring stations. Atmos. Environ. **310**, 119987 (2023)
10. Huang, C., et al.: Effect of urban morphology on air pollution distribution in high-density urban blocks based on mobile monitoring and machine learning. Build. Environ. **219**, 109173 (2022)
11. Li, Y., Sha, Z., Tang, A., Goulding, K., Liu, X.: The application of machine learning to air pollution research: a bibliometric analysis. Ecotoxicol. Environ. Saf. **257**, 114911 (2023)

12. Alolayan, M.A., Almutairi, A., Aladwani, S.M., Alkhamees, S.: Investigating major sources of air pollution and improving spatiotemporal forecast accuracy using supervised machine learning and a proxy. J. Eng. Res. 100126 (2023)
13. Rakholia, R., Le, Q., Ho, B.Q., Vu, K., Carbajo, R.S.: Multi-output machine learning model for regional air pollution forecasting in Ho Chi Minh City Vietnam. Environ. Int. **173**, 107848 (2023)
14. Ravindra, K., et al.: Application of machine learning approaches to predict the impact of ambient air pollution on outpatient visits for acute respiratory infections. Sci. Total Environ. **858**, 159509 (2023)
15. Ravindiran, G., Hayder, G., Kanagarathinam, K., Alagumalai, A., Sonne, C.: Air quality prediction by machine learning models: a predictive study on the Indian coastal city of Visakhapatnam. Chemosphere **338**, 139518 (2023)
16. Meyal, A.Y., et al.: Automated cloud based long short-term memory neural network based SWE prediction. Front. Water **2**, 574917 (2020)
17. Hochreiter, S., Schmidhuber, J.: Long short-term memory. Neural Comput. **9**(8), 32 (1997)

Multi-labeling of Malware Samples Using Behavior Reports and Fuzzy Hashing

Rolando Sánchez-Fraga$^{(\boxtimes)}$, Raúl Acosta-Bermejo, and Eleazar Aguirre-Anaya

Instituto Politécnico Nacional, Centro de Investigación en Computación,
Laboratorio de Ciberseguridad, Av. Juan de Dios Bátiz, Nueva Industrial Vallejo,
Gustavo A. Madero, 07738 Mexico City, Mexico
{rsanchezf2020,racosta,eaguirre}@cic.ipn.mx

Abstract. Current binary and multi-class (family) approaches for malware classification can hardly be of use for the identification and analysis of other samples. Popular family classification methods lack any formal naming definitions and the ability to describe samples with single and multiple behaviors. However, alternatives such as manual and detailed analysis of malware samples are expensive both in time and computational resources. This generates the need to find an intermediate point, with which the labeling of samples can be speeded up, while at the same time, a better description of their behavior is obtained. In this paper, we propose a new automated malware sample labeling scheme. Said scheme assigns a set of labels to each sample, based on the mapping of keywords found in file, behavior, and analysis reports provided by VirusTotal, to a proposed multi-label behavior-focused taxonomy; as well as measuring similarity between samples using multiple fuzzy hashing functions.

Keywords: multi-label classification · malware taxonomy · malware behavior · AV labels · malware analysis

1 Introduction

The classification of malware samples into malware families is vital to malware analysis. Malware samples belonging to family feature properties that contribute toward the same goal. Malware classification provides analysts with a better understanding of how malware operates and its danger level, as well as approaches to combat against malware [38]. In recent years, malware behavior complexity, either to exploit multiple vulnerabilities, as part of a more complex attack or evade defense mechanisms, has raised the need to improve the characterization through its classification to help the development of new defense techniques. On the other hand, nowadays, the boundaries that divide a malware class from another do not exist anymore, as modern malware samples are usually built on functional modules, presenting thus, at the same time, the behavior expected from multiple malware types.

However, malware names are not clear; neither the terms related to them have a common understanding, nor the names themselves. There is no common

M. F. Mata-Rivera et al. (Eds.): WITCOM 2023, CCIS 1906, pp. 289–311, 2023.
https://doi.org/10.1007/978-3-031-45316-8_19

standard. Current use of malware names and their creation suffer from the following problems: malware families and variants have several names, one name used simultaneously for several families, malware families are conflated with their detection name, the meaning of a name can change over time; the meaning of a name can depend on the person or organization using it; sometimes, the same name is used for the family as well as the malware type; they describe distinct classes tied to specific behaviors in a strict scope; and classification algorithms are applied to already known families and on a limited amount of classes [16].

Through the classic binary classification, we can successfully identify whether a certain application is malicious or benign. However, even if it is correctly classified, we still have no idea about its specific attack chain and corresponding malicious behaviors. In other words, the detection result can hardly provide any clue for security analysts, who aim at completing the knowledge of the detected 0-day attack efficiently and further provide potential victims with alerts and emergency protections. On the other hand, family classification's focal point is classifying malware into a certain family, whose definition can tell the key malicious behavior the malware may perform and the potential hazards the malware may have [40].

Most prior methods regard malware family classification as a multiclass classification problem, where a single-family label is assigned to a malware sample. However, the construction of annotated malware datasets is challenging. First, annotating labels verified manually by skilled experts in samples of fast-evolving malware is extremely difficult because it is a time-consuming task that requires sophisticated analyses; thus, raising the need to automatize said process.

The main contributions of our study are the definition of a multi-label malware behavior taxonomy; and a process for the automatization of the multi-labeling of malware samples, using behavior reports and fuzzy hashing.

The remainder of this paper is organized as follows: Malware labeling methods and taxonomies are presented, proposed, and compared in Sect. 2. In Sect. 3, we describe existing work on the automatization of malware labeling. Section 4 describe the proposed multi-labeling process of malware samples. In Sect. 5, we discuss the properties, limitations, and future endeavors of our work. We conclude the paper in Sect. 6.

2   Malware Taxonomies

The classification terms and schemes used in the computer security field, are far from being standardized. This makes the field hard to take in, and leaves room for misunderstandings and the risk of scientific work being hampered [22]. Not only that, current malware samples exhibit multiple behaviors that are common among different classes and families; making most of the taxonomies and labeling schemes described in the literature unsuitable to identify and describe them. In this section, we describe a group of naming schemes and taxonomies that try to tackle such problems.

2.1   CARO-Like

All the anti-virus (AV) companies today name the malware they have found in their way, several of them similar to the Computer Antivirus Research Organization (CARO) naming convention established in 1991 [37]. The full name of a malware sample consists of up to four parts, delimited by points. Any part may be missing, but at least one must be present. The general format is `Family_Name.Group_Name.Major_Variant.Minor_Variant[[:Modifier]]`.

Unfortunately, the companies have not managed to agree on a common implementation. One of the bigger obstacles on the road toward a common naming scheme is money. Each company wants to show that they were the first to find a virus and also to present a cure for it. Therefore they are reluctant to share information to facilitate a common naming of malware [22]. An example of this is the Microsoft Malware Naming [34]. Their scheme uses the format shown in Fig. 1.

The five components that comprise each name, are:

- Type - Describes what the malware does on your computer.
- Platforms - Guide the malware to its compatible operating system, programming languages, and file formats.
- Family - Groups malware based on common characteristics.
- Variant letter - Used sequentially for every distinct version of a malware family.
- Suffixes - Provides extra detail about the malware, including how it's used as part of a multi-component threat.

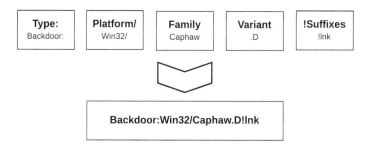

Fig. 1. Microsoft Malware Naming [34]

2.2   AVOIDIT

Work in [45] proposes a cyber-attack taxonomy called AVOIDIT (Attack Vector, Operational Impact, Defense, Information Impact, and Target). It uses five dimensions to characterize the nature of an attack, which seeks to provide, through its application, a knowledge repository used by a defender to classify vulnerabilities that an attacker can use.

The five major classifiers are:

- Attack Vector - It's defined as a path by which an attacker can gain access to a host.
- Operational Impact - Involves the ability for an attack to culminate an attack.
- Defense - Highlights several strategies a defender can employ to remain vigilant in defending against pre-attacks and post-attacks.
- Informational Impact - Describes the potential of an attack to impact sensitive information.
- Attack Target - Variety of hosts targeted by an attack.

This way, the classification of attacks results in a tuple of five elements, a class for each dimension.

2.3   A Behavior-Centric Malware Taxonomy

Part of the work in [14] was to define a behavior-centric malware taxonomy. Such taxonomy takes as a base attributes observed in previous work and extracts a set of suspicious behaviors found in their malware collection and recent literature. It defines a taxonomy with three dimensions, which are:

- Class - An attribute that describes the type of behavior observed in a malware sample.
- Suspicious Activity - This specifies the potentially malicious activity performed by a malware sample, and that caused its assignment to a certain class.
- Violated Security Principle - To make it better and simpler to understand the damage and risks that a malware sample poses to its victim.

The resulting scheme is shown in Fig. 2, which assigns a label to a malware sample that allows them to map it back to the taxonomic descriptions. Thus, a sample may be in several classes if it presents multiple behaviors. With this taxonomy, each malware sample classification produces a behavioral matrix.

2.4   Proposed Taxonomy

After studying and analyzing the most representative malware taxonomies, we have taken them as a basis and proposed a new taxonomy that helps us identify malware samples and their multiple behaviors, as well as assigning classes as labels to each one of them. the samples. Taxonomy is structured in dimensions and levels. Multiple dimensions are defined, each of which describes a different aspect of the characteristics and behaviors of a malware sample; while each level denotes a different degree of specificity about said characteristics and behaviors. Current dimensions, describe the operations of malware during execution, the types of malware it represents (according to their objectives and activity), and the platform or environment needed to be executed. An overview of the dimensions and first level of our taxonomy is presented in Fig. 3.

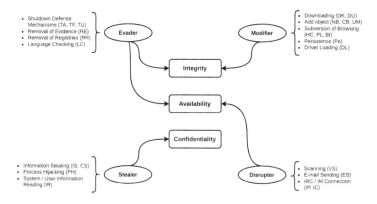

Fig. 2. Behavior-Centric Malware Taxonomy [14]

Each of the dimensions that comprise the proposed taxonomy, is briefly described below.

Classification by Platform. Classification by Platform tries to describe all those requirements that need to be met to be executed in a host and provide high-level information on such requirements for experts and those less familiar that want to run a dynamic analysis of malware samples in a controlled environment. Figure 4 shows current classes inside the platform dimension of our taxonomy.

Architecture. Sometimes malware tries to exploit vulnerabilities that are available for some processor architectures. This includes instruction sets, cache, speculative execution, and privilege levels, to name a few. A recent example of this is malware samples (or proofs of concept) that exploit the Meltdown [30] and Spectre [27] vulnerabilities. These vulnerabilities affect Intel x86, POWER, and some ARM processors.

Operating System. Classifies a malware sample by the operating system it needs to execute properly. Some malware exploits a vulnerability in the design, imple-

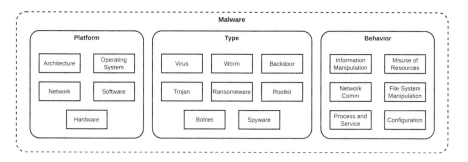

Fig. 3. Malware Taxonomy Overview

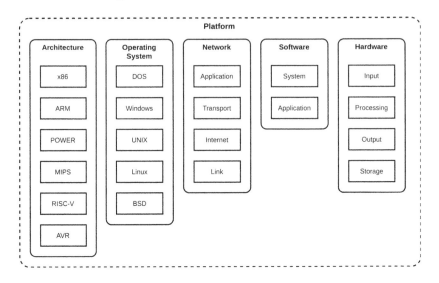

Fig. 4. Malware Taxonomy - Platform Dimension

mentation, or configuration in a kernel subsystem or bundled application of a specific version of an operating system. We took the work in [11] as a basis for our hierarchy. The first level of the taxonomy describes major OS families, while subsequent sub-levels divide them by sub-families, major versions, etc.

Network. Tries to differentiate samples by the protocols used during its network activity, if any. The hierarchy is defined by de TCP/IP model [4], which includes its layers and protocols.

Software. This part of the taxonomy describes those malware samples that exploit a vulnerability inside a specific version of installed software. Recent examples of this, are: Apache Log4j vulnerabilities that affect versions from 2.0 to 2.17 [5], a vulnerability in Chrome's Bookmark implementation before version 97.0.4692.71 [6] or Microsoft Excel remote code execution vulnerability [7].

Hardware. This category distinguishes malware by the specific hardware required for its correct execution. It includes the need for a specific microprocessor, ram modules, hard drives, routers, video cards, IoT devices, etc.

Classification by Type. With a classification by type of malware, we try to maintain part of the more conventional classification of malware and complement other dimensions. That is family-like classes according to their objective, activity, spread and infection, traits, and characteristics. Figure 5 shows current classes for the type dimension.

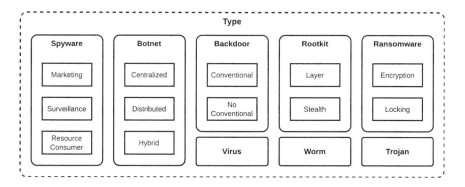

Fig. 5. Malware Taxonomy - Type Dimension

Virus. Class that describes all malware samples that, when executed, tries to replicate itself into other executables, files, boot sectors, or memory, inserting its code. If it succeeds, the infected element also executes de virus when it's executed. [10,13,47]. This kind of malware requires a host element and lays dormant in the system until it is executed o other required action is taken [29]. It can be further expanded by the type of replication and code evolution techniques it uses, which could include: monomorphic, encrypted, oligomorphic, polymorphic, and metamorphic [48].

Worm. Include all samples of a self-replicating, self-propagating, self-contained program that uses networking mechanisms to spread itself [10]. Most of them can replicate and propagate without any type of activation, allowing an extremely quickly spread [29]. Sub-classes could be defined according to the target space: internet, p2p, email, and instant messaging [39].

Backdoor. Class describing all samples that create or establish a hidden way to a computer system that can be used to bypass security policies, get access to the data it contains, allow remote access or listen for commands [35]. Could be further divided into conventional (relying on hidden parameters, redundant interfaces, exposed admin and management interfaces, redundant users, and third-party access) and unconventional (authentication and authorization between components, old users, flawed hardening, and exposed configuration data) [46].

Rootkit. Includes all malware samples that allow an adversary to access privileged software areas on a system while at the same time hiding its presence. Its purpose is to mask payloads and preserve their privileged existence on the system [8,10]. It contains two subclasses: layer and stealth. Layer refers to the operation layer of the rootkit in the system architecture, having five subclasses: application, library, kernel, hypervisor, and firmware [2,8]. Stealth describes the degree of system security compromise, having four subclasses: Type 0, Type 1, Type 2 and Type 3 [2,14,42].

Ransomware. Is a type of malicious code that blocks or limits access to a system by locking and encrypting parts of the system until a ransom is paid. There are two different types of ransomware, encryptors and lockers. The encryptors block system files by encrypting them (like Cryptolocker and WannaCry). Lockers are designed to lock users out of the system but leave the files untouched (like Winlocker) [8,35].

Trojan. All malware samples that disguise themselves as legitimate software to convince a victim to install it. Once installed, the malware can perform its malicious activity when invoked [8].

Spyware. Malware with certain behavior like advertising, collecting personal information, or changing the configuration of the system; generally without appropriately obtaining the user's consent. According to [1], spyware can be sub-categorized based on its uses and mechanisms. The categories are marketing, which includes adware and browser hijackers; surveillance, conformed by screen capture devices, key loggers, browser helper objects, layered service providers, and password stealers; and resource consumers, which profit from taking system resources (bandwidth, CPU time and storage) away from the users [49].

Botnet. Class that includes all samples that help create or manipulate a botnet, which refers to a pool of compromised computers that are under the command of a botmaster. As proposed in [33], botnet malware can be further classified by topology or Command and Control(C&C) model. Topologies can be centralized, where exists a central point (master) forwarding messages among clients (bots) and includes star and hierarchical arrangements; decentralized, where no single entity is responsible for providing C&C to bots and includes distributed (multi-server) and random (p2p) topologies; and hybrid, which is a combination of centralized and decentralized topologies [15,20,25]. We are currently evaluating the addition of a category for rally mechanisms, as noted by [33].

Classification by Operation. When a malware sample is executed, it performs a set of operations that could be viewed and considered as its behavior. With a classification by operation, we aim to provide high-level information on such operations to help with mitigation and defense mechanisms. We consider the work and definitions presented in [45,51] to construct this dimension. Figure 6 shows current classes for the operation dimension.

Configuration Manipulation. Includes all actions related to the modification of configuration parameters in any element part of the victim's system. Such an element could be a user application, operating system, library, module, or firmware.

Information Manipulation. Classifies every malware sample according to the effects of manipulation on sensitive information assets. Such effects could be distortion, the change or modification of information from the asset; disruption,

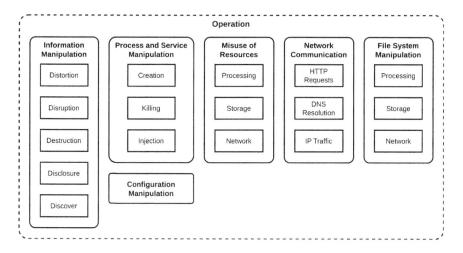

Fig. 6. Malware Taxonomy - Operation Dimension

the change or removal of access to the asset's information; destruction, deletion of an asset or removal of information from it; disclosure, which provides an unauthorized view of information from the asset; and discovery, by obtaining information not previously known, from the asset.

Misuse of Resources. Class that covers all unauthorized use of resources. Such resources include processing power, volatile and non-volatile storage, network bandwidth, and policies.

Network Communication. Include all types of network communications observed during the execution of the malware sample. Such communications are divided into HTTP requests, DNS resolutions, and all IP traffic. Other types of communications classes could be added, according to protocols and layers in the TCP/IP suite.

File System Manipulation. Classifies malware samples according to the manipulation of elements inside the file system. The manipulation includes opening, writing, deletion, or attribute change of files.

Process Manipulation. Classifies malware samples according to the manipulation of the system processes, during its execution. The manipulation includes the creation, killing, and injection of processes. We are currently evaluating the addition of services, either as a separate class or sub-classes of process manipulation.

2.5 Comparison Between Malware Classification

Finally, we present a comparison between the taxonomies described and how well can they identify a sample and describe its behavior on their own. The comparison consists of classifying a malware sample; in this case, the sample *VirusTotal_29ae18b552052271c671ba22b6fa6c9a* which is provided by VirusTotal [53]. According to their report [52], the sample is a Windows executable file and is flagged as malicious by 62 of the 71 security vendors consulted (Table 1 shows all the analysis stats).

Table 1. Analysis stats of 29ae18b552052271c671ba22b6fa6c9a by VirusTotal report

Result	# Vendors	Result	# Vendors
Harmless	0	Type unsupported	4
Suspicious	0	Confirmed Timeout	0
Malicious	62	Timeout	0
Undetected	9	Failure	0

Based on the information provided by the report, we can conclude the following statements, regarding the characteristics and behavior of the analyzed sample:

- Is listed as malicious (since >85% of the vendors flagged it as such).
- Is compiled for a machine with an Intel 386 or later/compatible processor and packed using MPRESS [32].
- The file can be downloaded via the web or as an attachment (usually thinking is benign, harmless o a valid application) or by another malicious program as part of a multi-stage attack.
- Exhibits network communication, which includes DNS resolutions, and IP traffic (TCP).
- Perform actions on the file system like opening, writing, and deleting files.
- Create/terminate process and execute shell commands.
- Open and set registry keys.
- Captures Input

With the recollected information, we proceeded to classify the sample with each of the previously reviewed taxonomies and compare them. Table 2 shows the result of each classification.

CARO-Like Naming Schemes. Some of the results using these taxonomies can be obtained from the report itself. A large part of the 71 security vendors whose results are shown in the report, follow their variant of the scheme proposed by CARO, while others only describe whether they classify the sample as malicious or not(for example Google, DeepInstinct [18] or Cynet [9]).

For example, Microsoft assigns *Trojan:Win32/Zbot.SIBE12!MTB* to the sample. As explained in Subsect. 2.1, this name contains five elements: *Trojan* (type) which by definition describes that the sample disguises as a legitimate file to be

Table 2. Classification of 29ae18b552052271c671ba22b6fa6c9a

Microsoft				
Type	Platform	Family	Variant	Suffix
Trojan	Win32	Zbot	SIBE12	!MTB
Kaspersky				
Prefix	Behavior	Platform	Name	Variant
HEUR	Trojan	Win32	Generic	-
AVOIDIT				
Attack Vector	Operational Impact	Defense	Informational Impact	Target
Social Engineering	Installed Malware [Trojan, Spyware] Misuse of Resources	Mitigation [Remove from Network, Whitelisting, Reference Advisement] Remediation [Patch System]	Distort Destruct Disclosure	Local
Behavior-Centric Taxonomy				
Evader	Disrupter	Modifier		Stealer
RemEvdRemReg	-	NewBin ChgBin UnkMut		InfStlCrdStlInfRdnPrcHjk
Proposed Taxonomy				
Platform		Type	Operation	
x86 [i386, x64] Windows [Win2000, WinXP, WinVista, Win7, Win8, Server 2008, Server 2012] Network [app [http, dns], inet [ipv4], trans [tcp]]		Trojan Spyware [Surveillance] Botnet	Info [distortion, disclosure] Config [read, set, delete] FileSystem [open, write, delete] Process [create, kill] NetAct [comm]	

downloaded; *Win32* (platform) which means the sample needs a Windows operating system running on a 32-bit architecture; t'*Zbot* (family), the meaning of which, according to Microsoft (meaning can change from vendor to vendor) is a family of trojans that can steal your personal and financial information, give malicious access and control to the system and lower your system's security [19]; *SIBE12* (variant) which indicates the order and number of existing variants; and *!MTB* (suffix) indicating its spread via email attachments and downloads when visiting websites.

On the other hand, Kaspersky, another popular AV vendor, assigned the name *HEUR:Trojan.Win32.Generic*. According to Subsect. 2.1, this means *HEUR* (prefix) meaning the sample was detected by their heuristic analyzer module; *Trojan* (behavior) assigned to all malicious programs that perform actions which are not authorized by the user [24]; *Win32* (platform) for a 32 bit Windows system to be executed; and *Generic* (name) as it was detected by the heuristic analyzer. As per Kaspersky itself, the name is assigned to all objects detected by the heuristic module, that delete, block, modify, or copy information, and disrupt the performance of computer or computer networks [23].

In general, these naming schemes group malware samples into families or behaviors that usually end up being too generic or unintuitive and descriptive names regarding their characteristics and behavior; making questionable the utility of the labels to the extent of the user's comprehension.

AVOIDIT. With this taxonomy, we can get an overview of the role of the sample during an attack, but little information on its behavior. For example, it would be difficult to classify the sample by attack vector. If we consider how we get the user to download and install the malware as an attack vector, we might select the social engineering option. The operational impact would be the installation of malware, in this case, a trojan, which, although it describes how it infects a system, does not in any way describe its possible behavior once it is inside the system; in addition, considering the findings of the report, we could also select the misuse of resources and the installation of spyware. Regarding defense, we could select any of the classes, whether we take into account removing access to the network and limiting the sending of the information collected, the YARA rules available for its detection, the information provided by the security vendors to remove the sample from the system, revert the system to a previous state, or update any installed detection software. According to the impact on the information, it could be classified within the distortion and disclosure of information.

With this example, we can rescue two important ideas. On the one hand, since the taxonomy focuses on cyberattacks, it may not be appropriate for classifying samples, which may only be part of an attack; on the other, the taxonomy seeks to fulfill the property of mutual exclusivity, but when faced with multiple behaviors, it results in an ambiguous classification.

Behavior-Centric Malware Taxonomy. With this taxonomy, we finally get a classification more focused on the description of its behavior. For the evader class, we can classify it as 'RemEvd' and 'RemReg' since it performs file and registry manipulation actions on the system; With the information found in the report, it is not clear if any network communication is command and control related, and thus, having a disruptive behavior. It gets the 'NewBin', 'ChgBin', and 'UnkMut' tags as it creates and modifies at least one executable and mutex. Finally, it is assigned the tags 'InfRdn' and 'PrcHjk' since it reads certain system configuration information and tries to modify the permissions of certain processes.

With this classification it is possible to expose the behavior of the samples, although given its nature, in some cases it may be generic; In addition, it does not provide information on the necessary characteristics of the system for its execution.

Proposed Taxonomy. With the proposed taxonomy, 39 tags have been assigned to the sample: 19 corresponding to the description of the platform, 4 to type, and 16 to the description of its operation. It was assigned the architecture tags x86 and its child tags since the executable was compiled for those architectures, the tag Windows since it is a PE exe file, and the different tags that correspond to versions of the Windows operating system that include the folders and records necessary for the proper functioning of the malware, and network communication protocol labels, according to the activity detected. For the type, Trojan, Spyware, Surveillance, and Botnet were assigned, since it is software that pretends to be non-malicious to reach the user's machine, captures user information, and sends it to an element in the internet. Finally, as part of its operation, it is assigned all those labels related to file system manipulation, process manipulation, system configuration, and network communication. With these labels, it is possible to describe the complete operation of the malware sample, during its execution.

3 Related Work

Over the last few years, some proposals for the automation of the labeling of malware samples have been presented. One of them is AVClass [43], which was the first paper that attempted the labeling of family names for all malicious files based on their AV labels. As shown in Fig. 7, labeling was conducted through token extraction and alias detection, in two phases: preparation and labeling. During the preparation phase, an analyst runs the generic token detection and alias detection modules on the AV labels of a large number of samples to produce lists of generic tokens and aliases, which become inputs to the labeling phase. The labeling phase implements the label normalization process. It takes as input the AV labels of a large number of samples to be labeled, a list of generic tokens, a list of aliases, and optionally a list of AV engines to use. For each sample to be labeled, it outputs a ranking of its most likely family names.

Time later, AVClass2 [44] was presented. AVClass2, whose architecture is shown in Fig. 7, comprises two modules: labeling and update. The labeling module takes as input the AV labels assigned by multiple AV engines to the same samples, an optional list of AV engines whose labels to use, a set of tagging rules, an optional set of expansion rules, and a taxonomy that classifies tags. For each input sample, it outputs a set of tags ranked by the number of AV engines including the tag's concept in their label. The update module takes as input the co-occurrence statistics, tagging rules, expansion rules, and taxonomy. It first identifies strong relations between tags, which generalize knowledge beyond individual samples. Then, it uses inference rules on the relations to automatically propose new tagging rules, new expansion rules, and taxonomy updates, which are then fed back to the labeling.

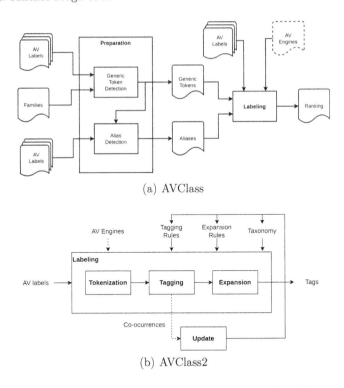

(a) AVClass

(b) AVClass2

Fig. 7. AVClass and AVClass2 architectures [43,44]

The multi-label malware dataset proposed by [3] provides API call sequences for thousands of malware samples executed in Windows 10 virtual machines and their corresponding labels to describe its malicious behavior. The creation of their dataset can be broken down into four stages: sample collection, where they recollect and filter PE samples from the VirusShare repository and non-malicious programs from the internet (and some system files); labeling malware with VirusTotal, where they download each sample's file report; analysis with CAPE sandbox, where they setup their own CAPE sandbox, run a dynamic analysis and obtain the corresponding report; and processing of all collected data, where they create a list of API calls ordered by timestamp, and the popular threat classification and categories from the VT reports which will become the set of labels for the samples.

The classification model EnDePMal is presented in [38] which uses the MaleVis dataset and also describes a procedure to assign a sequence of labels to malware samples. This procedure consists of five steps: obtain a file report from VirusTotal for a malware sample using its SHA-1 hash; submit the report to the AVClass tool and obtain the results for the four categories of the malware sample; extract the malware family names from the AVClass report based on the 41 malware family names defined by them; sort the extracted malware family names in descending order based on their number of votes; and assign a sequence of sorted malware family names to the malware sample as a sequence label.

Euphony, proposed in [17], is described as a unifier of malware labels by parsing malware labels and producing a single family per file. As input, the tool takes a collection of AV scanning reports. Then for each sample, Euphony performs the following tasks: preprocess the AV labels to derive the family name assigned by each vendor to a given sample; structure the relationship between different family names and provide the most appropriate associations between them, through the analysis of the correlation and the overlap between all family names; and bring consensus between the different vendors and outputs the most appropriate family name for a given sample.

In the paper [12], they introduce a simple multi-labeling approach to automatically tag the usual multiple behaviors of malware samples. Instead of trying to unify and reduce labels for a given malware sample, they take the classes provided by the security vendors, and taking into consideration a group of predefined expected behaviors for malware, each sample will be finally assigned with a tuple of labels aimed to gather the different potential typologies the sample corresponds to.

And Sumav [26], another automated labeling tool, assigns each file a family name based on AV labels, without prior knowledge or sample files, but the relationship between AV label tokens from the statistical data on AV labels. It generates token relationship graphs, called Sumav graphs, to search them for AV labels so that representative labels are extracted (Fig. 8).

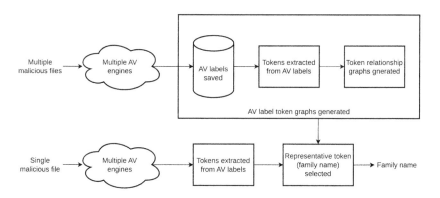

Fig. 8. Overview of Sumav operations [26].

4   Multi-labeling of Malware Samples

In this section, we describe a new multi-labeling approach to automatically label malware samples. This approach takes the reports from VirusTotal analyses, our proposed taxonomy, and previously labeled samples, to label new samples. The process of labeling involves the following steps, as shown in Fig. 9: (1) Sample processing, where we obtain all the necessary reports from VirusTotal, and calculate all sample fuzzy hashes (2) Report labeling, to extract information from the reports, search for behavior keywords, generate tokens and map them to the proposed taxonomy; and (3) Check file similarity to other samples already labeled and add their labels.

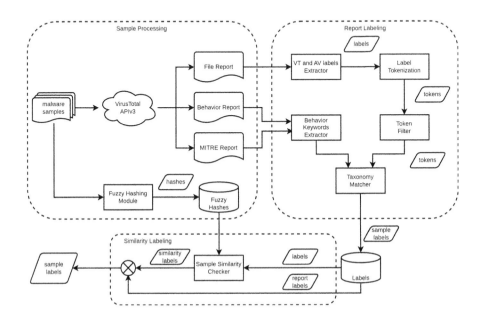

Fig. 9. Proposed multi-labeling process.

4.1   Sample Processing Phase

The sample processing phase proceeds as follows: (1) The acquisition of Virus-Total reports and (2) the calculation of the sample's fuzzy hashes.

Sample Reports. To download the file, behavior, and MITRE reports, we use VirusTotal API. First, if we don't have it, calculate the sample hash (md5, sha1, or sha256). Then we request the reports by sending the calculated hash to the appropriate endpoint. If the last sample analysis by VirusTotal is old enough, we request a new analysis and download the reports again. The reports have a JSON format. Although the API is public, you need a key and a max number of requests quota.

Sample Fuzzy Hashes. Fuzzy hashing or similarity hashing converts digital artifacts into an intermediate representation to allow efficient identification of similar objects. To be able to check the similarity between malware samples, we first need to calculate each sample hashes. As described in [28, 31, 36, 41], different hashing algorithms have their way to do calculations and use different parts of the files and are better at identifying certain types of similarities/differences than others. For that reason, we decided to use multiple hashing algorithms, which will allow us to determine which samples are similar from multiple fronts. These hashing algorithms are ssdeep, sdhash, and tlsh.

ssdeep. Creates a hash value that attempts to detect the level of similarity between two files at the binary level, by computing a signature based on context-triggered piece-wise hashes. It breaks up a file into pieces, hashes each piece, and combines the produced hashes to create a hash for the whole file. Similarity for each piece of the file can then be calculated since small chunks of the file are examined. When comparing two files, the similarity of chunks will result in a similar hash.

sdhash. Allows two arbitrary blobs of data to be compared for similarity based on common strings of binary data. There are two general classes of problems where sdhash can provide significant benefits: fragment identification and version correlation [21,41]. It uses probabilistic feature extraction to find features that are unlikely to happen randomly. The extracted features are hashed and put into a bloom filter.

tlsh. A locality-sensitive hashing algorithm, for which, given a byte stream with a minimum length of 50 bytes and a minimum amount of randomness, generates a hash value that can be used for similarity comparisons. The computed hash is 35 bytes long. The first 3 bytes are used to capture the information about the file as a whole (length, ...), while the last 32 bytes are used to capture information about incremental parts of the file.

For every sample, we calculate all three hashes and save them in a database. For all the algorithms, there is an existing tool or library we can call to calculate them.

4.2   Report Labeling Phase

The objective of this phase is to take VT reports as input and output a corresponding set of labels. The procedure is as follows. (1) We take the file report and extract the VT and AV labels (2) Take those labels and extract the tokens (3) Filter the token list (4) Take behavior and MITRE reports and search for a set of keywords and (5) We take the list of tokens and the keywords found and translate them to classes of our taxonomy.

VT and AV Label Extractor. During this stage, we extract the "popular threat classification", "last analysis stats" and "last analysis results" elements from the file report.

popular_threat_classification. We extract the suggested threat label, each value in the popular threat category, and each value from the popular thread name element.

last_analysis_stats. Contains the statistics from the responses obtained by every security vendor. We use these stats to determine if the sample is malicious or not. Since processing and labeling a sample that was not detected by most AV vendors would insert noise in the similarity labeling stage, samples that fall in this case are discarded.

last_analysis_results. We extract every non-null result element which corresponds to the labels assigned by the AV vendors.

Label Tokenization. At this stage, we extract tokens from each label extracted. To extract them, we replace elements in each label, with the character "|", using the regular expression [\/\.\,\-_\s\~\+\[\]\(\)\:\!\%\=\@\#]+ and then we split them by the same character. Each element would be added to the list of tokens.

Token Filter. Once we have our list of tokens, we filter them by applying the following rules:

1. Remove tokens that are decimal numbers only with the regex ^[0-9]+$
2. Remove tokens which are hex numbers, with regex ^[a-fA-F0-9]{3,}$
3. Remove tokens that have a digit between letters (usually indicates an id) using regex [a-zA-Z]+\d+[a-zA-Z]+
4. Remove alphanumeric tokens and all upper case, using the regular expression ^[A-Z0-9]{5,}$
5. Filter tokens that start with an R followed by digits (kind of an id for AhnLab-V3) using regex ^[rR]\d+$
6. Change tokens to lowercase
7. Filter tokens in a blacklist and small tokens without meaning (for these steps, both lists should be defined). For example, tokens like "generic", "malware", and "other", etc. should be discarded. The same applies to tokens with a length below five characters. Elements like "trj", "net", "spam", "surv" must be kept, while "aqx", "aaa", etc. discarded.
8. Discard all tokens with less than 3 occurrences in the list.
9. Remove repeated elements.

Behavior Keywords Extractor. For this step, we traverse the behavior and MITRE reports looking for keywords like "IP traffic", "DNS lookups", "files opened", "attack techniques", "MITRE attack techniques", etc., and descriptions like "Query Registry", "System Information Discovery", "Modify Registry", etc. A list is created with all those keywords found in the reports.

Taxonomy Mapping. Now that we have our list of tokens and the list of keywords, the taxonomy mapping module can use a predefined dictionary to map from both tokens and keyword lists to classes from the proposed taxonomy. Table 3 shows an example of the entries defined in the mapping dictionary.

Table 3. Example of taxonomy mapping dictionary entries.

token / keyword	platform labels	type labels	operation labels
win32	windows, x86, i386	-	-
troj	-	trojan	-
mirai	linux, n_app, h_proc, h_netcard	botnet	net, netdos
ddos	n_app, h_proc, h_netcard	-	net, netdos
zbot	windows, h_in, h_proc, h_netcard	trojan, botnet, bncent, spyware, spysurv	infodiscl, info, misres, net, netcomm
kryptik	windows	trojan, spyware	misres, config, info
ppatre	-	trojan	-

Once we have our set of labels, we store it along with the sample id and the fuzzy hashes in case they need to be used during the similarity labeling phase.

4.3   Similarity Labeling Phase

This phase consists in calculate the similarity between a malware sample and the rest of the hashes stored in the database. Each hashing algorithm defines their own similarity (or matching) function. For example, ssdeep has a matching mode, which provides the ability to match a hash against a list of hashes; and as a result, it returns an integer between 0 and 100 indicating the match score between hashes. The higher the number, the more similar the files. Sdhash has a digest comparison function, which returns a value between -1 and 100 and that should be viewed as a confidence value that indicates how certain the tool is that the two data objects have non-trivial amounts of commonality [50]. Tlsh hashes a function to calculate and return the distance between 2 hashes; where a distance score of 0 represents that the files are identical, and scores above that represent greater distance between the documents. A higher score should represent that there are more differences between the documents.

Table 4 shows the calculated similarity with all hashes, between two malware samples 1ea7af5c1214aa8ed3cccfa844785b30 (sample 1) and 1438ff0ed2c47ba6841facd5d3e4ca10 (sample 2). Both samples have similar labels assigned by security vendors and behavior; however, have different compilers and one of them is packed.

Table 4. Example of fuzzy hash comparison

	sample 1	sample 2
threat label	trojan.upatre/smnb	trojan.upatre/zbot
threat categories	trojan, downloader	trojan, downloader
family labels	upatre, smnb, fahf	upatre, zbot, waski
ssdeep score	0 (no match)	
tlsh score	223 (a lot of differences)	
sdhash score	0 (negative)	

5   Discussion and Future Work

Our study of the state of the art in terms of malware taxonomies shows a clear trend in the definition of multiple dimensions and non-exclusive classes that allow the classification of the sample and a better description of its behavior; however, it comes with some drawbacks. Currently, we have a set of around 25000 labeled samples, and the label distribution shows a considerable lack of balance between them (some classes never appear) and might require further study.

With our labeling approach, while more descriptive and useful at identifying malware samples, the fail/success relies heavily on prior knowledge; that is, the existence of file and behavior reports and the completeness of our mapping dictionaries. It is probably worth further study of the advantages and disadvantages concerning other proposals such as Sumav, which claim to have no such restrictions.

We also note the limitation of using fuzzy hashes to determine the similarity between two samples, when one is packed or obfuscated.

As future work, we can envision the following work paths: (1) Continuous labeling of malware samples. (2) The use of the labeling process described in the present work, in the construction of a multi-label classification model of malware samples. (3) Updating the taxonomy in case of finding cases of malware samples whose characteristics and behaviors cannot be correctly described, due to its current state. (4) The constant updating of the dictionaries used to map tokens and keywords to classes within the proposed taxonomy. (5) Extensive testing with possible threshold values defined in the labeling process.

6   Conclusion

The present paper describes an initial attempt to define an automated multi-labeling process for malware samples, focused on the identification and description of its behavior. The comparison with other taxonomies and labeling schemes shows that our proposal manages to describe the behavior by itself, thanks to the use of concrete concepts and less ambiguous definitions, as opposed to the use of less intuitive family names. Also, the proposal for the use of labeling through the similarity of the samples can allow labeling even when the reports do not exist or are incomplete.

Acknowledgements. This work has been supported by the CONACyT and the Instituto Politécnico Nacional.

References

1. Barwinski, M.A.: Taxonomy of spyware and empirical study of network drive-by-downloads. Technical report, Naval Postgraduate School Monterey CA (2005)
2. Bravo, P., García, D.F.: Rootkits survey. Architecture **6**, 7 (2011)
3. Carpenter, M., Luo, C.: Behavioural reports of multi-stage malware. arXiv preprint arXiv:2301.12800 (2023)
4. Cerf, V., Kahn, R.: A protocol for packet network intercommunication. IEEE Trans. Commun. **22**(5), 637–648 (1974)
5. Corporation, C.P.T.M.: CVE-2021-44832. https://cve.mitre.org/cgi-bin/cvename.cgi?name=CVE-2021-44832
6. Corporation, C.P.T.M.: CVE-2022-0101. https://cve.mitre.org/cgi-bin/cvename.cgi?name=CVE-2022-0101
7. Corporation, C.P.T.M.: CVE-2022-21841. https://cve.mitre.org/cgi-bin/cvename.cgi?name=CVE-2022-21841
8. for Cybersecurity (ENISA), E.U.A.: Glossary (2021). https://www.enisa.europa.eu/topics/csirts-in-europe/glossary
9. Cynet: Cynet autoxdr™ | cybersecurity made easy. https://www.cynet.com/
10. Dukes, C.: Committee on national security systems (CNSs) glossary. CNSSI, Fort 1322 Meade, MD, USA, Technical report, vol. 1323, pp. 1324–1325 (2015)
11. Eylenburg, A.: Operating systems: timeline and family tree. https://eylenburg.github.io/os_familytree.htm
12. García-Teodoro, P., Gómez-Hernández, J.A., Abellán-Galera, A.: Multi-labeling of complex, multi-behavioral malware samples. Comput. Secur. **121**, 102845 (2022)
13. Grance, T., Hash, J., Peck, S., Smith, J., Korow-Diks, K.: Security guide for interconnecting information technology systems: recommendations of the national institute of standards and technology. Technical report, National Inst of Standards and Technology Gaithersburg MD (2002)
14. Grégio, A.R.A., Afonso, V.M., Filho, D.S.F., Geus, P.L.d., Jino, M.: Toward a taxonomy of malware behaviors. Comput. J. **58**(10), 2758–2777 (2015)
15. Hachem, N., Ben Mustapha, Y., Granadillo, G.G., Debar, H.: Botnets: lifecycle and taxonomy. In: 2011 Conference on Network and Information Systems Security, pp. 1–8 (2011). https://doi.org/10.1109/SAR-SSI.2011.5931395
16. Hahn, K.: Naming malware: why this jumbled mess is our own fault. https://www.gdatasoftware.com/blog/malware-family-naming-hell
17. Hurier, M., et al.: Euphony: harmonious unification of cacophonous anti-virus vendor labels for android malware. In: 2017 IEEE/ACM 14th International Conference on Mining Software Repositories (MSR), pp. 425–435. IEEE (2017)
18. Instinct, D.: Deep instinct | deep learning AI cybersecurity platform. https://www.deepinstinct.com/
19. Intelligence, M.S.: Win32/zbot threat description - microsoft security intelligence. https://www.microsoft.com/en-us/wdsi/threats/malware-encyclopedia-description?name=win32%2Fzbot

20. Ismail, Z., Jantan, A., Najwadiyusoff, M., Kiru, M.: A botnet taxonomy and detection approaches. Test Eng. Manag. **88**, 3386–3408 (2020)
21. James, J.I.: Similarity comparison with sdhash (fuzzy hashing) - dfirscience. https://dfir.science/2012/09/similarity-comparison-with-sdhash-fuzzy.html
22. Karresand, M.: A proposed taxonomy of software weapons (2002)
23. Kaspersky: Heuristic and proactive detections | Kaspersky it encyclopedia. https://encyclopedia.kaspersky.com/knowledge/heuristic-and-proactive-detections/
24. Kaspersky: Trojan | kaspersky it encyclopedia. https://encyclopedia.kaspersky.com/glossary/trojan/
25. Khattak, S., Ramay, N.R., Khan, K.R., Syed, A.A., Khayam, S.A.: A taxonomy of botnet behavior, detection, and defense. IEEE Commun. Surv. Tutor. **16**(2), 898–924 (2013)
26. Kim, S., Jung, W., Lee, K., Oh, H., Kim, E.T.: Sumav: fully automated malware labeling. ICT Express **8**(4), 530–538 (2022)
27. Kocher, P., et al.: Spectre attacks: exploiting speculative execution. CoRR abs/1801.01203 (2018). https://arxiv.org/abs/1801.01203
28. Kornblum, J.: Identifying almost identical files using context triggered piecewise hashing. Digit. Investig. **3**, 91–97 (2006)
29. Latto, N.: Worm vs. virus: what's the difference and does it matter? (2022). https://www.avast.com/c-worm-vs-virus
30. Lipp, M., et al.: Meltdown. CoRR abs/1801.01207 (2018). https://arxiv.org/abs/1801.01207
31. Martín-Pérez, M., Rodríguez, R.J., Breitinger, F.: Bringing order to approximate matching: classification and attacks on similarity digest algorithms. Forensic Sci. Int.: Digit. Invest. **36**, 301120 (2021)
32. MATCODE: Mpress - free high-performance executable packer forpe32+/.net/mac-os-x. https://www.matcode.com/mpress.htm
33. Micro, T.: Taxonomy of botnet threats. Whitepaper (2006)
34. Microsoft: Malware names. https://docs.microsoft.com/en-us/microsoft-365/security/intelligence/malware-naming
35. Nieles, M., Dempsey, K., Pillitteri, V.Y., et al.: An introduction to information security. NIST Special Publication **800**(12), 101 (2017)
36. Oliver, J., Cheng, C., Chen, Y.: TLSH–a locality sensitive hash. In: 2013 Fourth Cybercrime and Trustworthy Computing Workshop, pp. 7–13. IEEE (2013)
37. Organization, C.A.R.: Naming scheme - Caro - computer antivirus research organization. https://web.archive.org/web/20150923200549/. https://www.caro.org/naming/scheme.html
38. Paik, J.Y., Jin, R.: Malware family prediction with an awareness of label uncertainty. Comput. J. (2022)
39. Pratama, A., Rafrastara, F.A.: Computer worm classification. Int. J. Comput. Sci. Inf. Secur. **10**, 21–24 (2012)
40. Qiao, Q., Feng, R., Chen, S., Zhang, F., Li, X.: Multi-label classification for Android malware based on active learning. IEEE Trans. Dependable Secure Comput. (2022)
41. Roussev, V.: Data fingerprinting with similarity digests. In: Chow, K.-P., Shenoi, S. (eds.) DigitalForensics 2010. IAICT, vol. 337, pp. 207–226. Springer, Heidelberg (2010). https://doi.org/10.1007/978-3-642-15506-2_15
42. Rutkowska, J.: Introducing stealth malware taxonomy. COSEINC Advanced Malware Labs, pp. 1–9 (2006)
43. Sebastián, M., Rivera, R., Kotzias, P., Caballero, J.: AVCLASS: a tool for massive malware labeling. In: Monrose, F., Dacier, M., Blanc, G., Garcia-Alfaro, J. (eds.)

RAID 2016. LNCS, vol. 9854, pp. 230–253. Springer, Cham (2016). https://doi. org/10.1007/978-3-319-45719-2_11

44. Sebastián, S., Caballero, J.: AVClass2: massive malware tag extraction from AV labels. In: Annual Computer Security Applications Conference, pp. 42–53 (2020)

45. Simmons, C., Ellis, C., Shiva, S., Dasgupta, D., Wu, Q.: AVOIDIT: a cyber attack taxonomy. In: 9th Annual Symposium on Information Assurance (ASIA 2014), pp. 2–12 (2014)

46. Simsolo, Y.: Owasp 10 most common backdoors. https://owasp.org/www-pdf-archive/OWASP_10_Most_Common_Backdoors.pdf

47. Stallings, W., Brown, L., Bauer, M.D., Howard, M.: Computer Security: Principles and Practice, vol. 2. Pearson, Upper Saddle River (2012)

48. Szor, P.: The Art of Computer Virus Research and Defense. Addison-Wesley Professional (2005)

49. Tripathy, S., Kapat, S., Das, S., Panda, B.: A spyware detection system with a comparative study of spywares using classification rule mining. Int. J. Sci. Eng. Res. **7** (2016)

50. Vassil Roussev, C.Q.: Quick start - the sdhash tutorial. https://roussev.net/sdhash/tutorial/03-quick.html#result-interpretation

51. VirusTotal: File behaviour. https://developers.virustotal.com/reference/file-behaviour-summary

52. VirusTotal: Virustotal - file - 2400e927b316aa75771c1597dad5. https://www.virustotal.com/gui/file/29ae18b552052271c671ba22b6fa6c9a

53. VirusTotal: Virustotal repository. https://www.virustotal.com/gui/home/upload

Computational Simulation Applied to 3.5 GHz Band Microstrip Yagi Array Antenna Design for 5G Technology Mobile Wireless Device

Salvador Ricardo Meneses González$^{(\boxtimes)}$ 🆔 and Rita Trinidad Rodríguez Márquez

Escuela Superior de Ingeniería Mecánica y Eléctrica, Unidad Zacatenco, Instituto Politécnico Nacional, Cd. de México, México
rmenesesg@ipn.mx

Abstract. The wireless communication mobile systems demand for compact and fully integrated radio frequency (RF) devices, low cost, small dimensions due to the space and volume available within the radio device is limited, and a high degree of miniaturization, capable to operate within the crowded 5G NR sub-6-GHz bands. In this way, the microstrip yagi patch antenna design, simulation, implementation, and measurement to be applied to 3.5 GHz band 5G technology is described and purpose of this work.

Keywords: 5G NR · Yagi antenna · S_{11} Parameter · 3.5 GHz band

1 Introduction

Release 15 of the 3GPP specifications for 5G NR (Next Radio) includes 26 operating bands in frequency range 1, FR1, includes all existing and new bands below 6 GHz, and three in frequency range 2, FR2, which include new bands in the range 24.25–52.6 GHz, mm-wave bands [1]. The sub-6-GHz bands are most valuables due to have favorable propagation characteristics, which differ from FR-2, above 24 GHz, given these makes use of massive MIMO, beam forming and highly integrated advanced antenna systems.

On the other hand, the 3.5 GHz frequency band (3.3 -3.8 GHz) is used in 5G commercial networks, and these have a great number of devices, which makes that this band can be considered as a globally uniform band. A serious reason for 3.5 GHz frequency band release, which is the key to further the success of the 5G technology. The 3.5 GHz range is a core spectrum band for 5G deployment, being an ideal band for this technology as it is able to provide both capacity and coverage. Actually, this matter is currently working, which are being rolled out in the world at the moment, the rollout of 5G is still underway [2].

Similarly, relative to Sub.6 GHz devices, these work on multiple channels and carry out the operation band channel selection by themselves, to perform this function, they need a sensing channel function and hold the key incorporating the IBFD (in-band-full-duplex) technology, which allows the devices to transmit and receive on the same frequency at the same time, and the self-interference cancellation (SIC) technique [3], in

M. F. Mata-Rivera et al. (Eds.): WITCOM 2023, CCIS 1906, pp. 312–322, 2023.
https://doi.org/10.1007/978-3-031-45316-8_20

addition, the device's transmitter and receiver can share a single antenna through different antenna interfaces, therefore, the antenna is fundamental part of this technology.

In this sense, various antennas have been proposed to meet the band coverage (3.3–3.8 GHz), for instance, a dual-polarized antennas, using parasitic resonators and complex structure [4], using a pair of antisymmetric L-shaped probes [5, 6] which uses two pairs of quarter-circle dipoles, or [7] a MIMO antenna formed by the periodic arrangement of bifacial and orthogonal "I" shaped metamaterials, etc., but, due to the own structure, they demand considerable space and volume.

In the same way, [8] proposes a microstrip patch antenna using FEKO simulation, which has a return loss of − 20 dB, a radiation pattern that is nearly omnidirectional, and a gain of 2.5 dBi, but only addresses the simulation process. Likewise, [9] reports three different designs of elliptical microstrip path antenna, using FR-4 as substrate, with bandwidths approximately 1 GHz and directivity approximately 4.9 dBi, similar value to the obtained by the Yagi antenna proposed in this work. Also [10] proposes a small patch antenna which directivity is 5 dBi, a simulation result, given that there is no implementation and measurements. In the same way, [11] addresses only the simulation results, a rectangular microstrip antenna 1x2 array, reporting a gain value equal to 5 dBi. On the other hand, [12] proposes a 1×8 arrays antenna, using individual slotted patches, reporting a gain value equal to approximately 6 dBi, obtained from simulation process.

As a result of different paths arriving to the antenna and given that the antenna impedance is not perfectly, antenna reflections are produced, creating a mismatch impedance and hence a stationary wave is produced (VSWR), creating interference, which is increased when waves that impact directly on the ground are reflected, that combine with the direct ray. In order to counteract this, the SIC technique is applied, which consists of the location of where the signal cancellation occurs, based on the passive and active propagation domain. The passive domain consists of apply channel separation, which introduce isolation between the transmit and receive channels, as well as, spatial beam, where the antenna is oriented to minimize the radiation beam, and in the case of use two antennas, the active domain technique, that is, the cross polarization is applied.

Figure 1 shows the passive and active self-interference cancellation techniques, in which the Yagi antenna or Yagi array is proposed to be a part of it.

In this work the Microstrip Yagi Array Antenna has been designed, simulated, and measured, obtaining a high-performance antenna, in order to operate to 3.5 GHz band to be applied to 5G technology.

This kind of antenna does not demand too much space, easy implementation, radiation pattern which main beam not so wide, bandwidth suited for their particular needs of this technology, and low cost.

The paper is organized as follows: Sect. 2 describes the Yagi antenna foundations and design, Sect. 3, the simulation, implementation and measurement, concluding the presently work with conclusions and references.

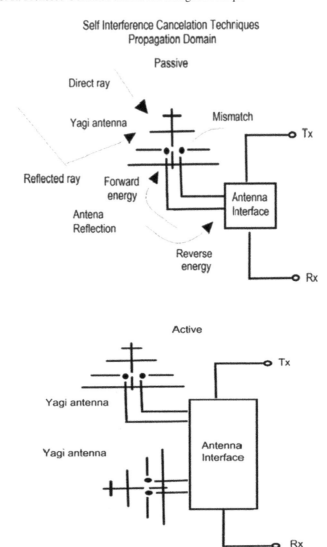

Fig. 1. Self-interference cancelation technique, passive and active respectively.

2   Antenna Design

Yagi antenna only requires a single driven element, generally, a half wave dipole, and the amplitude and phase of the other elements [13–15], parasitic elements, reflector element adjusted to cancel radiation from the backside of the array, and director elements which enhance radiation in the forward direction, are electromagnetically induced, depending upon the spacing between the driven element and these ones. A figure of merit its front-to-back ratio, which measures the capability to reduce the antenna´s response to interfering signals from directions opposite the desired direction. For that, good impedance matching characteristics are achieved, approximately equal to half wave dipole impedance and narrow beamwidth desirable to cover selected areas. Figure 2 shows the Yagi antenna basic structure based on dipoles.

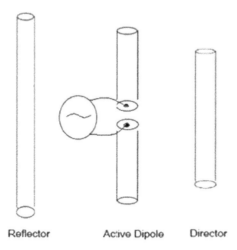

Reflector   Active Dipole   Director

Fig. 2. Yagi antenna basic structure.

For design and simulation purposes, to achieve an efficient radiation coverage, the gain value is proposed to be equal approximately to 12 dB, which is directly related to the beam width angles, θ_1 and θ_2, plane E and plane H respectively, and by the number of elements, given by expressions [16, 17]:

$$D = \frac{4\pi}{\theta_1\theta_2}; D_{dB} = 0.62n + 8.5 \tag{1}$$

n, number of elements of the array.

In this sense, due to antenna gain value, it is necessary four elements that make up the antennas array, the reflector, the active source and two directors, which lengths and spacings are given by the following:

Element Lengths:

Reflector length: $L_R = 0.51\lambda$.

Active Source: $L_{AP} = 0.5\lambda$.

Directors: $L_{D_1} = L_{D_2} = 0.45\lambda$.

Element Spacings:

Reflector - Active Source: $d_1 = 0.2\lambda$.

Active Source – Fist director: $d_2 = 0.15\lambda$.

Fist director - Second director: $d_3 = 0.2\lambda$.

Due to the central frequency value is equal to 3.5 GHz, the designed antenna dimensions are shown in Table 1.

Table 1. Designed antenna dimensions (mm).

Length	L_R	L_{AP}	L_{D_1}, L_{D_2}
	43	42	38
Spacing	d_1	d_2	d_3
	17	13	17
Patch width g	Length L_T	Width W_T	
25	150	60	

3 Simulation and Implementation

In this way, Fig. 3 shows the proposed Yagi antenna simulation which has been simulated using the Electromagnetic Field Simulation Software, CST Studio Suite [18], based on a slotted patch as active source, and the parasitic elements, square patches as reflector and directors, in order to increase a higher effective area.

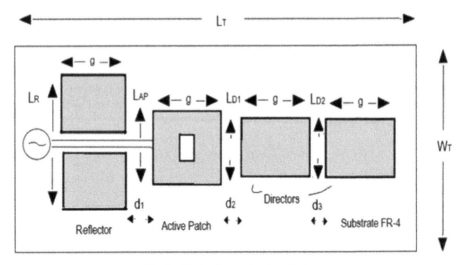

Fig. 3. Yagi antenna structure design.

Figure 4 shows the prototype antenna, it has been considered the epoxy FR-4, a thin layer of copper foil laminated to one or both sides of an FR-4 glass epoxy panel, which relative permittivity is equal to 4.4, as the substrate to serve as ground plane. The feeding line length, $\lambda/4$, in order to enable the match impedance antenna with SMA connector.

The antenna performance is evaluated through the S_{11} parameter result, known as the reflection coefficient or return loss, which value is less than or equal to -10 dB, within a designated frequency range, it means that 90% of the energy is radiated and the 10% of the energy is reflected [19].

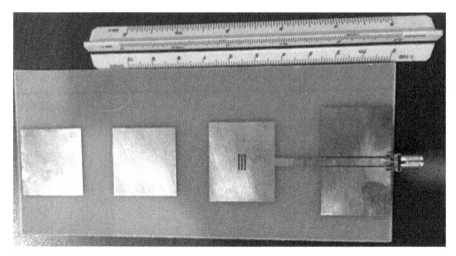

Fig. 4. Prototype antenna.

3.1 S_{11} Parameter

Figure 5 shows the S_{11} parameter simulation graphic, which shows a magnitude of -20 dB at 3.5 GHz and wideband approximately equal to 100 MHz (3.4–3.5 GHz), which is within frequency range specified for 5G technology.

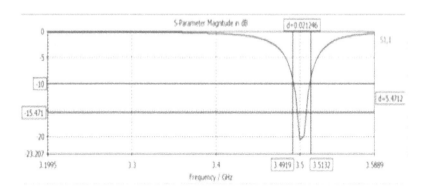

Fig. 5. S_{11} parameter simulation graphic.

In order to measure experimentally the S_{11} parameter the vector network analyzer is used. Figure 6 shows the outcome of this experimental stage, the resonance peak is ubicated at 3.5 GHz with a magnitude of -12 dB, and wide band approximately equal to 100 MHz, these results are similar to those obtained in the simulation.

Figures 7 shows the experimental test with the vector network analyzer to obtain the S_{11} parameter.

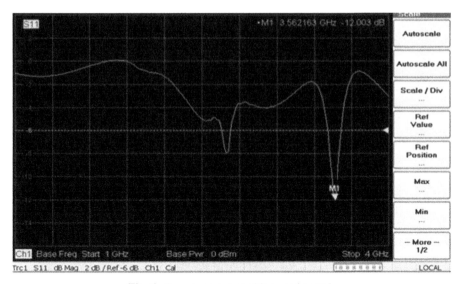

Fig. 6. S_{11} parameter graphic experimental.

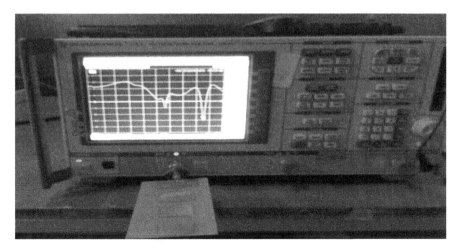

Fig. 7. Prototype antenna under vector network analyzer test.

3.2 Radiation Pattern

Radiation pattern, graphical representation of the radiated energy spatial distribution as a function of angle, which 3-D diagram simulated result is depicted in Fig. 8. Main beam is symmetrical directed towards to 0°-180° direction, as well as there are two minor secondary lobes, directed towards to 90°-270° direction and complete absence of nulls. In the same way, the simulation graphic shows 4.9 dBi in the direction of the antenna's maximum gain. This kind of radiation pattern is an asset, due to 5G device is covered by the electromagnetic radiation a greater or lesser extent in any direction rather than selected areas.

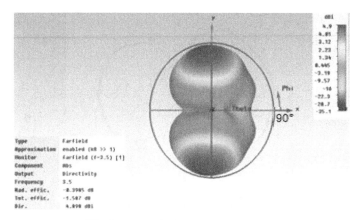

Fig. 8. 3-D radiation pattern simulation.

In the same way, to obtain the experimental radiation pattern, the prototype antenna under test in conjunction with a reference antenna are placed into the anechoic room, separately from each other, 2.5 m away, line of sight, 1.5 m above the ground, as shown in Fig. 9 [20].

Fig. 9. Prototype antenna under anechoic room test.

The transmission power is set to a value known and received signal power readings are taken when the prototype antenna rotates degree by degree rotation, which are plotted as plane E, as shown in Fig. 10, it is possible to observe that the maximum value of the received power signal is achieved approximately in 150° direction, and the minimum value is achieved in 90° direction.

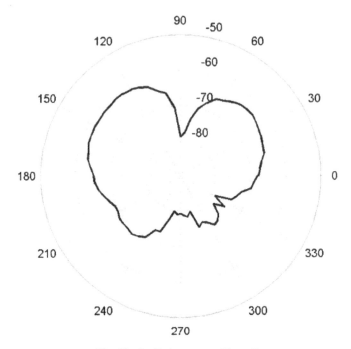

Fig. 10. Radiation pattern Plane-E.

In order to obtain the value of the antenna gain or directivity, it is possible to apply the Friss Eq. (2), [16, 17], taking the data obtained by direct measurements, we have:

$$P_{RX} = P_{TX} G_{TX} G_{RX} \left(\frac{\lambda}{4\pi r} \right)^2 \qquad (2)$$

where:
P_{TX}, Transmitted power.
P_{RX}, Received power.
G_{TX}, Transmitter antenna gain.
G_{RX}, Receiver antenna gain.
R, Separation distance between antennas.

The result is 4.7 dBi, similar to the obtained result by simulation, that is, the power transmitted in the direction of maximum radiation is 2.95 times that from an omnidirectional antenna radiating the same total power.

On the other hand, in comparison with, the value of the antenna gain by the yagi antenna is similar to the reported antennas which use different antenna structures, however, the yagi antenna is simple, four elements, one active and the rest passive, flexible and functional.

Conclusions

A four elements Yagi microstrip patch antenna, to operate in the 3.5 GHz band, for 5G technology application, is simulated, constructed, and measured. The radiation pattern shows no nulls, given the directivity value achieved and range covered, the designed antenna provides a significant efficiency, the receiver mobile will have the advantage of ensuring signal reception.

In the construction of the prototype, the susbstrate FR-4 has been used, however, the antenna parameters, the gain value, particularly, can be improved using other materials as substrate, for instance, RT duroid or Roger, which electric permittivity and loss tangent are higher than the epoxy Fr-4 characteristics.

The designed antenna is characterized by small size, flexible, cheap, easy construction, parameters as resonance frequency, bandwidth, and radiation pattern, functionality, availability for work with the Self-interference cancelation technique, passive and active, as a result of which, it can be recommended for use in 5G wireless communication devices.

References

1. Dahlman, E., Parkvall, S., Sköld, J.: 5G NR: The Next Generation Wireless Access Technology. Academic Press (2018)
2. Meroua, M., Bertin, E., Crespi, N.: 5G shortcomings and Beyond-5G/6G requirements. International Conference on 6G Networking (6GNet). Paris, France (Jul 2022)
3. Kolodziej, K.E., et al.: In-band full-duplex technology: techniques and systems survey. IEEE Trans. Microw. Theo. Techniq. **67**(7) (july 2019)
4. Wu, R., Chu, Q.: Multi-mode broadband antenna for 2G/3G/LTE/5G wireless communication. The Institute of Engineering and Technology **54**(10) (May 2018)
5. Mak, K., Lai, H., Luk, K.: A 5G Wideband Patch Antenna with Antisymmetric L-shaped Probe Feeds. EEE Transactions on Antennas and Propagation (Feb. 2018)
6. Bosong,. Q., Shenyuan, L., Yingsong, L.: A broadband dual-polarized antenna for Sub-6 GHz base station application. In: 2020 IEEE 3rd International Conference on Electronic Information and Communication Technology (ICEICT) (November 2020)
7. Wei, Z., Junwei, Q., Jiang, T.: A Low Coupling Broadband MIMO Antenna for 5G Using Meta-surface Decoupling Structure. In: Conference: 2022 IEEE International Symposium on Antennas and Propagation and USNC-URSI Radio Science Meeting (AP-S/USNC-URSI) (July 2022)
8. Ramakrishna, Ch., et al.: Design of Microstrip Patch Antenna At 3.5 GHz Frequency Using FEKO Simulation. In: 2023 Second International Conference on Electrical, Electronics, Information and Communication Technologies (ICEEICT) (April 2023)
9. Hasan, M., et al.: Design and Analysis of Elliptical Microstrip Patch Antenna at 3.5 GHz for 5G Applications. In: 2020 IEEE Region 10 Symposium (TENSYMP) (November 2020)
10. Ferdous, N., et al.: Design of a small patch antenna at 3.5 GHz for 5G application. IOP Conf. Series: Earth and Environmental Science **268**, p. 012152. IOP Publishing (2019). https://doi.org/10.1088/1755-1315/268/1/012152
11. Irfansyah, A., et al.: Design of rectangular microstrip antenna 1x2 Array for 5G communication. J. Phys: Conf. Ser. **2117**, 012028 (2021). https://doi.org/10.1088/1742-6596/2117/1/012028
12. Jamal, A.: Microstrip patch antenna arrays design for 5G wireless backhaul application at 3.5 GHz. Recent Advances in Electrical and Electronic Engineering and Computer Science Publisher: Springer (January 2021)
13. Jordan, E.C., Balmain, K.G.: Electromagnetic Waves and Radiating Systems. Prentice Hall (1968)

14. Yagi, H., Uda, S.: Projector of the Sharpest Beam of Electric Waves. Proc. Imperial Academy of Japan (February 1926)
15. Abbosh, A., Babiceanu, R.F., Al-Rizzo, H.M., Abushamleh, S., Khaleel, H.R.: Flexible Yagi-Uda Antenna for Wearable Electronic Devices. In: 2013 IEEE International Symposium on Antennas and Propagation and USNC-URSI National Radio Science Meeting, July 7–12. Lake Buena Vista, Florida, USA (2013)
16. Krauss, J., Marhefka, R.: Antennas for all applications. 3erd. Ed., Mc Graw Hill (2002)
17. Balanis, A.: Antenna Theory Analysis and Design. 3er. ed., John Wiley and Sons (2012)
18. https://www.cst.com/Academia/Student-Edition
19. Pozar, Y.D.M.: Microwave Engineering, 3rd edition. John Wiley & Sons, New York, NY, USA (2005)
20. Meneses, R., Rodríguez R.: Microstrip Antenna Design for 3.1–4.2 GHz Frequency Band Applied to 5G Mobile Devices. European J. Eng. Res. Sci, **4**(10) (October 2019)

3D Point Cloud Outliers and Noise Reduction Using Neural Networks

Luis-Rogelio Roman-Rivera[1]([✉]) [iD], Jesus Carlos Pedraza-Ortega[1] [iD],
Israel Sotelo-Rodríguez[1] [iD], Ramón Gerardo Guevara-González[2] [iD],
and Manuel Toledano-Ayala[1]

[1] Facultad de Ingeniería, Universidad Autónoma de Querétaro, Cerro de las
Campanas S/N, 76010 Santiago de Querétaro, Mexico
{lroman26,isotelo17}@alumnos.uaq.mx, toledano@uaq.mx
[2] Cuerpo Académico de Ingeniería de Biosistemas, Universidad Autónoma de
Querétaro, Cerro de las Campanas S/N, 76010 Santiago de Querétaro, Mexico
ramon.guevara@uaq.mx
https://www.uaq.mx/

Abstract. 3D point clouds find widespread use in various areas of computing research, such as 3D reconstruction, point cloud segmentation,
navigation, and assisted driving, to name a few examples. A point cloud is
a collection of coordinates that represent the shape or surface of an object
or scene. One way to generate these point clouds is by using RGB-D cameras. However, one major issue when using point clouds is the presence
of noise and outliers caused by various factors, such as environmental
conditions, object reflectivity, and sensor limitations. Classification and
segmentation tasks can become complex when point clouds contain noise
and outliers. This paper proposes a method to reduce outliers and noise
in 3D point clouds. Our proposal builds on a deep learning architecture
called PointCleanNet, which we modified by adding extra convolutional
layers to extract feature maps that help classify point cloud outliers.
We demonstrate the effectiveness of our proposed method in improving
outlier classification and noise reduction in non-dense point clouds. We
achieved this by including a low-density point cloud dataset in the training stage, which helped our method classify outliers more efficiently than
PointCleanNet and Luo, S, et al.

Keywords: Point cloud · outliers · classification · convolutional neural
networks

1 Introduction

Data representing 3D scenes and objects in the form of 3D point clouds [42, 43, 45]
play a crucial role in many computer vision research areas, such as 3D reconstruction [6] generating high fidelity textures, recovering urban building geometries
[9, 29], mapping buildings [12], indoor scene reconstruction [14], segmentation
with background removal [34], recognition tasks in robotics using scene modeling

© The Author(s), under exclusive license to Springer Nature Switzerland AG 2023
M. F. Mata-Rivera et al. (Eds.): WITCOM 2023, CCIS 1906, pp. 323–341, 2023.
https://doi.org/10.1007/978-3-031-45316-8_21

and object reconstruction [18], navigation of robotic systems in agriculture [31], estimate the height of mature rice in agronomy [30], augmented reality (AR) with applications such as robot teleoperation [22], computer-assisted surgery [33], duplicating the working scenes [41], object recognition using segmentation and extraction of features, [15,19], pedestrian detection [32], computer vision as face recognition [44], 3D navigation for pedestrians and robots [2,37], navigation of agricultural robots in the farmland [27], uncrewed aerial vehicles (UAVs) navigation [1], autonomous driving [21,40], ADAS (advanced driving assistance systems) [16] provides a better view of the environment, mapping to the environment to classify or identify static or moving objects, thus reducing the number of traffic incidents caused unintentionally by drivers. 3D scene reconstruction is an excellent alternative to decreasing mapping errors and increasing object reconstruction accuracy [45].

One of the main challenges in 3D point cloud reconstruction is the presence of noise and outliers in the data, which can be caused by various factors such as light sources, interference produced by reflective objects, and errors in depth layer information measurements at the edges of objects. These errors can significantly impact the geometry and depth of the scene or object reconstruction.

3D point cloud pre-processing to eliminate outliers and reduce noise may be needed if the point clouds are used for classification or segmentation tasks, several methodologies have emerged to attack the problem, such as robust statistical methods, methods to improve the tangent plane at each point, and tedious parameter adjustments to algorithms. Detecting outliers has been a tremendous challenge for several decades, with different methods based on distribution, depth, and clusters. Noise in point clouds can cause problems in local triangulation methods. Moreover, the models used depend more on the characteristics that appear on the scanned surface, and the noise problem is not adequately addressed [24]. Outliers in point clouds are points that have geometric discontinuities and their surface shapes can be arbitrary. Outliers are present in clouds for different reasons. Some are reflectivity in materials, the geometry of objects or scenes, sunlight and sensor limitations, among others. It is challenging to obtain point clouds without the presence of outliers. New technologies using laser sensors are alternatives and the problem with these technologies is the high cost of the sensors [20].

Machine learning algorithms are the next step in object 3D reconstruction, 3D point cloud noise reduction and outliers removal [28,45]. 3D point cloud classification and segmentation neural networks have proved to have optimal performance. Some of the most relevant algorithms are based on convolutional neural networks, such as PointNet [23] and PCPNet [8] and PointCleanNet [24].

The primary motivation for this paper is to propose a new architecture based on PointCleanNet [24]. PointCleanNet is a network different from many traditional approaches that preserve high-curvature features without requiring additional information about the underlying surface type. Our proposal uses PointCleanNet because it has proved efficient with high-density point clouds but presents low performance on non-dense point clouds. Convolutional neural networks such as PointCleanNet have proven to perform well using a local out-lier detection network that efficiently solves noise in large densely-sampled point clouds. Nevertheless, in low-density point clouds, the performance is affected. Our primary focus is to use the bases of PointCleanNet to strengthen or improve these models' state-of-the-art.

We propose a variation to a convolutional neural network architecture based on PointCleanNet [24] adding convolutional layers, applying the model to non-dense 3D point clouds to reduce outliers and noise concentration in the cloud. The primary purpose is to increase the based model accuracy and classify outliers more efficiently.

2   General Information

2.1   Devices for Depth Processing

In order to estimate the shape of an object in 3D, several methods allow us to capture shapes or objects in the environment. Furthermore, smartphones and tablets include depth sensors and technologies such as Time of Flight Camera (ToF) [10,26] and Light Detection and Ranging (LiDAR) [4,11,13,25] are becom-ing the standard for capturing depth information with alternatives in Android and iOS devices [3,36]. Triangulation methods use two cameras and a light source to capture the depth of an object. Some of these models imitate our brain's abil-ity to process images captured from two different points.

2.2   Devices and Point Cloud Preprocessing

An RGB-D camera is a sensor that provides two images: a color image rep-resented in RGB (Red, Green, Blue) format and a depth image where values represent the scene's depth. Sensor manufacturers usually apply filters to the point clouds and integrate these filters with the sensor software. It is often a black box for the users since it is impossible to modify or adjust these filters in most of the sensors. It is essential to consider the limitations of the different sensors on the market before starting to work with them.

2.3   Point Clouds, Sensors, Scenes and Objects

The primary sensor characteristics that influence the quality of point cloud reconstruction can be affected by: modulation techniques (continuous wave or pulse), measurement techniques (time of flight, phase or amplitude-based), detec-tion (coherent or direct), transmitter and receiver configurations (monostatic or bistatic) [38].

Some atmospheric conditions, such as the presence of water in the environ-ment, the presence of light from the sun or any artificial source, as well as the type of scene (indoor and outdoor), the reflectivity of the surface and the rough-ness of the material, can affect the reflection of the light on the sensor, the shape of the object, the orientation and the distance of the object from the sensor and therefore distortions can seriously affect the reconstruction of the scene [7].

2.4   PointCleanNet

PointCleanNet [24] is a simple data-driven denoising approach based on a convolutional neural network. Design with a two-stage point cloud cleaning network based on PCPNet architecture to estimate robust local features and use this information to denoise the point cloud, Fig. 1. PointCleanNet is a deep-learning algorithm that estimates the neighboring points for each coordinate.

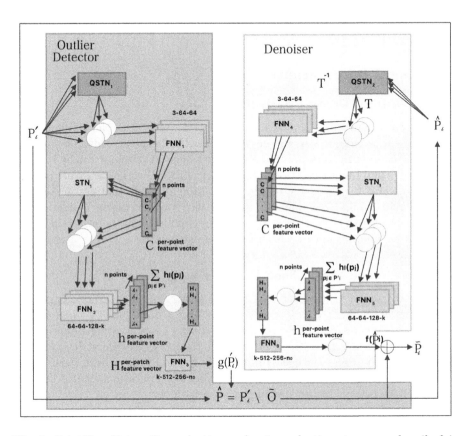

Fig. 1. PointCleanNet outlier reduction and noise reduction stages, as described in [24].

Furthermore, this allows the processing of point clouds without losing relevant features. The neighboring points are calculated using a radius, and it is computed based on the diagonal described by the maximum and minimum values of the boundary point cloud.

For outlier reduction, the neural network is based on PCPNet architecture, as shown in Fig. 2, where STN is used. They are spatial transformer networks that apply a quaternion rotation (STN1) or a full linear transformation (STN2) [8] and PointNet [23]. This network learns a set of optimization criteria that

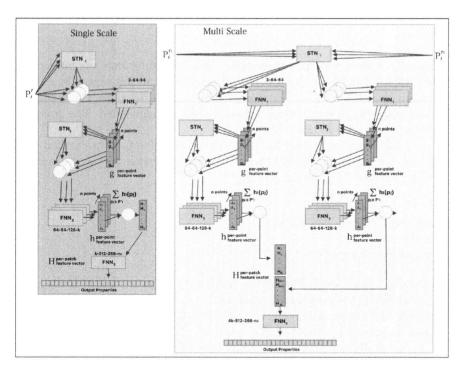

Fig. 2. The PCPNet network learns a set of point cloud characteristics in the local space of a set of points, as described in [8].

select interesting or informative points from the point cloud and uses a selection function. The PointNet architecture is observed in Fig. 2. According to Point-CleanNet, given the normalized local patch $\mathbb{P}i$, the network first applies a spatial transformer network (STN) and a quaternion spatial transformer network (QSTN), the main intention with the spatial transformer is for estimating local shape properties such as normals and curvature from raw point clouds, giving better shape details on dense point clouds.

3   Materials and Methods

The main goal was to create a data set that allows the classification of outliers on point clouds with different densities. Noisy point clouds were generated by adding Gaussian noise with a standard deviation of 0.01% of the original shape's bounding box diagonal. In total, the denoising training set contains 40 point clouds, arising from 8 levels of noise for 5 different shapes. The point cloud noise is described by Eq. 1. Where $\mathbb{P}'$ represents the 3D point cloud noise, $\mathbb{P}$ is the ideal surface sample with p_i lying on the scanned surface of the object, n_i is the additive noise and $\mathbb{O}$ is the set of outliers points present in the 3D point cloud.

$$\mathbb{P}' = \{p_i'\} = \{p_i + n_i\}_{p_i \in \mathbb{P}} \cup \{o_j\}_{o_j \in \mathbb{O}} \qquad (1)$$

$$\tilde{o}_i > 0.5 \tag{2}$$

Equation 2 represents the outlier probability $\tilde{o}$. It states that a point is added to the outlier set if the outlier probability is more significant than 0.5.

Due to the high computational requirements that 3D point cloud processing demands, a high-performance workstation is recommended. The computer requirements we used in this research are:

Low-performance computer for datasets creation: Laptop Hp Pavilion 4 Gb RAM, 500 Gb HDD, GTX1650, Rizen 7. Software needed for point cloud preprocessing and visualization purposes:

- MeshLab versión 2020.12
- Anaconda Python 3.7 64-Bit
- Jupyter notebook
- Pycharm versión 2020.1

The point cloud pre-processing was made by loading the point clouds to the GPU. For the 3D point cloud visualization, we used Meshlab [5], where a point cloud with 140 000 points usually uses 532 MB RAM.

High-performance computer: Workstation NVIDIA GeForce RTX 3060 TI. 8 GB GDDR6. 4864 CUDA Cores, AMD Ryzen 5600x, 6 Cores, 12 threads, 3.7 GHz 32MB L3 Cache, 3 MB L2 Cache, 16 GB RAM. Software characteristics:

- Docker container Linux Engine Versión 19.03.8
- Ubuntu 20.04.2 LTS
- MeshLab version 2020.12
- Pycharm version 2020.1
- Jupyter notebook
- Pycharm version 2020.1

In addition, we used Google Colab for training and inferences purposes. The Google Colab package includes the following specifications:

- K80, P100, T4 24 GB GPU 2 x vCPU
- 358 Gb disk space
- Python 3.7

3.1   PointCloud Dataset

We considered the PointCleanNet dataset methodology to create our dataset in terms of the standard deviation used for the point cloud dataset. As we can observe, the main difference between the Point CleanNet dataset and ours is low density. Our dataset has two Table 1, one dedicated to training with thirty clouds and one for testing with ten clouds.

Table 1. Datasets used for training and validation purposes.

Dataset Name	Scene Points	Point clouds
PointCleanNet Dataset	100, 000	28
Balon Dataset (ours)	15,843	40

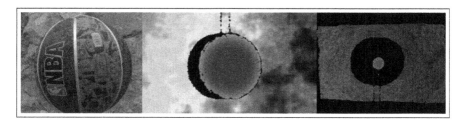

Fig. 3. The figure shows the following process to create a 3D point cloud. The heating map allows for determining the depth of the scene

The dataset contains point clouds without noise (reference or Ground-Truth) and clouds with different magnitudes of white noise and outliers. An example of a reconstructed object is in Fig. 3, where the 3D reconstruction of the Ground-Truth cloud is from left to right, the RGB image of a basketball, a basketball heating map and the 3D reconstruction. Later, the 3D reconstruction only shows the relevant basketball area for visualization purposes in Fig. 4. Later we capture the basketball and we introduce noise with different magnitudes. Moreover, we add the Gaussian noise, and then we apply our strategy to obtain the 3d reconstruction of noisy data, as can be observed in Fig. 5.

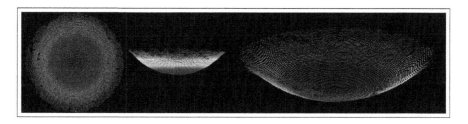

Fig. 4. 3D reconstruction of the basketball ball. A semi-sphere is obtained due to the position of the sensor wrt. basketball. The image corresponds to a point cloud with 15,843 points without noise (Ground Truth).

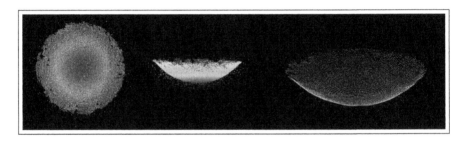

Fig. 5. This is a point cloud that corresponds to the reconstruction of our basketball with Gaussian noise with a 1×10^{-3} standard deviation.

3.2 Proposed Neural Network Architecture

The Fig. 6a) shows a basic convolutional block of one dimension. PointClean-Net proposes this block [24]. It begins with a convolutional layer in charge of extracting feature maps, and then transformations are applied to produce new feature maps. The layer Information is reduced using batch normalization by reducing the dimensionality of the feature maps and obtaining the maximum value of each of the maps to transform the patches. A shortcut layer is used to help learning significant features from higher layers.

In our proposed network in Fig. 7, we add an additional convolutional layer to this basic block see Fig. 6b), to obtain a higher significant feature extraction, which will help us to identify outliers within the cloud and the presence of noise.

The basic block in Fig. 6c) represents a basic feed-forward network (FNN) that PointCleanNet uses as an essential building block. In our proposal in Fig. 6d), a linear layer is added to provide more significant support in identifying local patterns in the point clouds. Convolutional layers (Conv1D) apply a 1D convolution on an input signal composed of several input planes, The equation representing this convolution is Eq. 3.

$$out(N_i, C_{out_j}) = bias(C_{out_j}) + \sum_{k=0}^{C_{in}-1} weight(C_{out_j}, k_i) * input(N_i, k) \qquad (3)$$

where $*$ is the valid cross-correlation operator, N_i is the batch size, and C denotes the number of channels. Furthermore, additional layers were also used for batch normalization (also known as a batch norm), Eq. 4. It is a method to make artificial neural networks faster and more stable by normalizing layer inputs by re-centering and re-scaling. The proposed architecture is shown in Fig. 7.

$$y = \frac{x - E[x]}{\sqrt{Var[X] + \epsilon}} * \gamma + \beta \qquad (4)$$

where γ and β are learnable parameter vectors of size C (where C is the input size), the mean and standard deviation are calculated per dimension over the mini-batches (a smaller sample from the actual data, which takes an iteration in the learning process). By default, the elements of γ are set to 1 and the elements of β to 0. The standard deviation is calculated using the biased estimator.

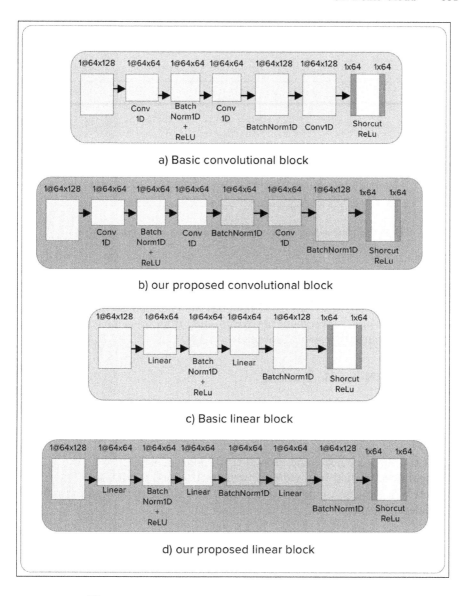

Fig. 6. Proposed convolutional and linear basic blocks.

Our proposed method starts with a convolutional layer in charge of extracting the feature map. We use feature maps to extract significant outliers and noise characteristics. After this, batch normalization reduces the output layer. This layer reduces the dimensionality of the feature maps, extracting even smaller maps and obtaining the maximum value of each map. Then, transform the patches, after which it goes through a shortcut layer, which helps to learn high-level features that may be lost during batch normalization tasks. In this way, these shortcuts are in charge of obtaining meaningful features from higher significant features from higher layers.

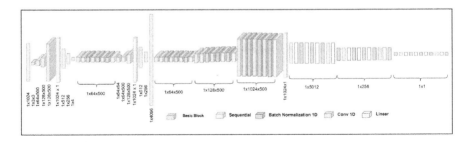

Fig. 7. Proposed network architecture based on PointCleanNet.

Convolutional layers learn local patterns from the point cloud, they take nxn dimensional feature maps and return a nxn response map. For each convolutional layer, a filter is applied, and each filter contains a response map of $[in_{maps} * maps]$ values, in_{maps} represents the feature map from previous layers and maps represent the current layer feature map.

3.3   Neural Network Training

It is essential to establish the requirements in order for the neural network to work correctly. Developing a neural network to remove outliers and noise in a point cloud involves various activities, some of which are:

- For training, use noisy and ground truth point clouds.
- The dataset should be divided between testing and validation.
- Moreover, process the point clouds for the training section and also for the validation section.

Before beginning, the training must also know which points do not correspond to the point cloud object. The dataset requires reference points that allow the calculation of the confusion matrix. The neural network can also be trained with data augmentation techniques, allowing us to achieve better model generalization.

After the training and validation dataset in Table 2 have been set, training and testing of the neural network are performed.

4   Results

4.1   Model Evaluation

When we try to reduce outliers in a point cloud, we must consider that the points being removed with the proposed model correspond to the outliers (True

Table 2. Training and validation dataset.

Dataset Name	Number of point clouds
Training	30
Test	10

Positive) and that the number of points removed erroneously is quantified (False Positive) [35]. These two metrics contribute to the Accuracy, Eq. 5, Recall, Eq. 6, F1-Score, Eq. 7; and the Mean Squared Error, Eq. 8.

$$Precision = \frac{TruePositive}{TruePositive + FalsePositive} \tag{5}$$

$$Recall = \frac{TruePositive}{TruePositive + FalseNegative} \tag{6}$$

$$F1 - Score = 2 * \frac{Precision * Recall}{Precision + Recall} \tag{7}$$

$$mse = \frac{\sum_{i=1}^{n}(y_i - y_i')^2}{n} \tag{8}$$

A proper comparison between two point clouds is crucial for guiding the training process and providing a reasonable evaluation. The confusion matrix is commonly used for performance evaluation since it may help to visualize the point clouds based on metrics used to identify biases within a ground truth 3D point cloud and the inferences of the 3D point cloud. It is essential to mention that to create the confusion matrix, we have to use a reference point cloud with highlighted outliers or noise points. The recall equation allows us to determine how many positive classes we predicted correctly, and it is in our best interest to make the recall as high as possible.

The precision equation indicates all the positive and negative classes and how many of them we have predicted correctly. In a model, it is convenient to have high precision. It may happen that when evaluating our model, we obtain a high recall and a low precision. For this case, F1-Score is a metric that allows us to compare precision and recall in a simple and correlated way.

In this paper, we also consider the Chamfer Distance as an evaluation metric. Chamfer distance is a universally acknowledged metric in various point cloud tasks [39]. Chamfer Distance is a nearest-neighbor-based method and benefits from its efficient computation and flexible applicability for point sets with different point numbers Fig. 9. Chamfer Distance between two point sets S1, and S2 is defined as:

$$d_{CD}(S_1, S_2) = \frac{1}{|S_1|} \sum_{x \in S_1} \min_{y \in S_2} \|x - y\|_2 + \frac{1}{|S_2|} \sum_{y \in S_2} \min_{x \in S_1} \|y - x\|_2 \tag{9}$$

Each point $x \in S_1$ finds its nearest neighbor in S_2 and vice versa; all the point-level pair-wise distances are averaged to produce the shape-level distance.

4.2   Cualitative Results

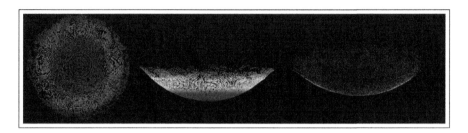

Fig. 8. Inference of a ball made with our proposed model. The three semi-spheres correspond to the same point cloud seen from different perspectives.

Inferences were made for ten 3D point clouds in Table 2 with different noise magnitudes with a standard deviation of 1% and different densities, as shown in Fig. 5. The cloud density is a function of the percentage of points removed, with lower density being those clouds from which a higher percentage were removed (Figs. 8 and 9).

Fig. 9. Point Cloud inference obtained with our PointCleanNet, the images correspond to the same point cloud after inference with our proposed model.

In the PointCleanNet model comparison in Table 4, we can see that the accuracy ranges from 10% to 82%, which shows a variation in the classification of outliers. Conversely, the results shown by the comparison Table 4 of our proposed model in Fig. 4 are more consistent. Our results show a precision of 77% in the lower limits and an upper value of up to 88%. Furthermore, results demonstrate a high consistency in the outliers classification.

We can observe that the MSE values of the proposed model are acceptable because they are below the reference threshold compared to the PointCleanNet results in Table 4. However, it is worth paying attention to F1-score and recall metrics as they may indicate a mismatch between classes (Fig. 11).

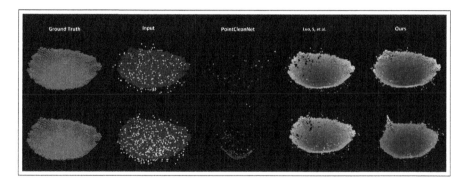

Fig. 10. Qualitative comparison on our outlier dataset.

Fig. 11. 3D point cloud inference obtained with our proposed model, the semi-spheres correspond to the same point cloud after inference.

The main task here is to reduce the outliers from the point cloud. Point-CleanNet performs poorly in the presented low-density point clouds in Fig. 10. The point clouds shown in the previous figure are the inference result made with PointCleanNet, Luo, S, et al., and our model. The first point cloud contains 10,750 points, of which 125 points are outliers with a standard deviation of 10%. The second point cloud contains 3657 points, of which 609 points are outliers with a standard deviation of 20%. We can observe that PointCleanNet, in comparison with Luo, S, et al. models and our proposal, has the worst performance in low-density point clouds. PointCleanNet accuracy is 16.3% compared to 60.6% of our method as shown in Table 4 in point clouds 3 and 9 (same presented in Fig. 10). We can also observe in Table 5, that Chamfer loss is higher in PointCleanNet with 2.5 compared to Luo, S, et al. with 0.266 and our model with 0.05. Figure 10 show how our proposal cleans outliers w.r.t. ground truth with less outliers compared with PointCleanNet and Luo, S, et al.

4.3 Quantitative Results

The following tables show the inference for nine different point clouds. The point clouds have different outliers magnitudes and different densities. Furthermore, the inferences correspond to the analysis for the point clouds listed in Table 3. The number of outliers and non-outliers can be found here for each point cloud. The primary purpose of Table 4 is to show the point at which the model performance leads to a degradation in the outlier classification. Point clouds with outliers with lower density tend to degrade model performance. On the other hand, the performance increases when the density is higher than 10,000 outliers.

In the inference described in Table 4, we can observe that the MSE values for our proposed model are lower than the PointCleanNet MSE results; there is a high percentage in the accuracy of our proposed model for outlier detection in the same point clouds. Our results indicate an appropriate classification. It is worth paying attention to F1-score metric as it may indicate a class mismatch. The increase in accuracy is shown in point cloud N°4–9 in Table 4, where we can see that the median is close to the third quantile and higher than the 80th compared to the results obtained with the PointCleanNet model.

Table 3. Inferences with low-density point clouds.

Point cloud	Total Number non-outliers	Total Number of outliers
0	15843	1584
1	15843	3168
2	10625	1062
3	10625	125
4	5296	529
5	5296	1059
6	3916	391
7	3916	783
8	3048	304
9	3048	609

A comparison of the PointCleanNet, Luo, S, et al. [17], and our model is shown in Table 5, using the Chamfer loss metric. In this comparison, we can observe that our proposed model has a lower loss concerning the results obtained with Point CleanNet and Luo, S, et al.; this is most likely due to the displacement that the point cloud has suffered once the inference has been completed, showing that our model only affects those points that are classified as outliers and not on the entire point cloud. Results show our proposal performed better with less amount of points and a bigger ratio on the amount of outliers versus inliers.

Table 4. Comparison between the PointCleanNet model and our proposed model.

Method	Number of point cloud	Precision	Sensitivity	F1-score	Accuracy	MSE
PointCleanNet	0	0.086038	0.105429	0.094752	0.81689	0.18311
	1	0.162519	0.171086	0.166692	0.71495	0.28505
	2	0.095279	0.210923	0.131263	0.74630	0.25370
	3	0.163770	0.199529	0.179890	0.69678	0.30322
	4	0.092794	0.676749	0.163209	0.36979	0.63021
	5	0.171616	0.693107	0.275112	0.39135	0.60865
	6	0.090674	0.987212	0.166093	0.10007	0.89993
	7	0.167146	0.964240	0.284906	0.19345	0.80655
	8	0.090692	1.000000	0.166302	0.09069	0.90931
	9	0.166667	1.000000	0.285714	0.16735	0.83265
Ours	0	0.091530	0.431818	0.151043	0.55879	0.44121
	1	0.164659	0.517677	0.249848	0.48198	0.51802
	2	0.091441	0.412429	0.149692	0.57423	0.42577
	3	0.171462	0.485176	0.253379	0.52345	0.47655
	4	0.096508	0.465028	0.159844	0.55605	0.44395
	5	0.170346	0.488196	0.252565	0.51849	0.48151
	6	0.100656	0.588235	0.171898	0.48549	0.51451
	7	0.170197	0.574713	0.262620	0.46223	0.53777
	8	0.091949	0.634868	0.160633	0.39827	0.60173
	9	0.162986	0.605911	0.256874	0.41619	0.58381

Table 5. Chamfer loss comparison between PointCleanNet, Luo, S, et al. and our proposed model.

Number of point cloud	PointCleanNet Chamfer Loss	Luo, S, et al. Chamfer Loss	Our Proposal Chamfer Loss
0	0.07782	0.16389	0.02181
1	0.07782	0.21744	0.02863
2	0.13977	0.20516	0.05945
3	4.55815	0.20388	0.02294
4	0.70367	0.26565	0.04464
5	0.73141	0.20699	0.02136
6	0.11121	0.18111	0.02035
7	0.15080	0.24181	0.05381
8	6.05349	0.29295	0.05481
9	2.94945	0.26633	0.05060

5   Discussion

By making inferences on the 3D point clouds, we can observe that one factor that affects the reduction of noise and outliers is the density and outliers number in the 3D point clouds. Higher outliers, such as those presented in the analysis, affect inferences, resulting in poor classification performance. The type of noise and its distribution can impair the quality of the cloud. The experiment was performed with different noise levels to test the effectiveness of the network in removing noise and outliers from the point clouds. We could conclude that the greater the noise dispersion, the more complicated it will be for the neural network to remove outliers.

In addition to the analysis with the dataset created, point clouds were used for training, validation, and inference of the neural network, and the figures used in the analysis were taken from the dataset that we created. These point clouds provided various point clouds of basketballs with different properties that allowed us to perform data augmentation to the dataset and, thus, further generalize the training of the network.

Starting with the advantages of the proposed model compared to the model proposed by PointCleanNet, we can observe that the accuracy increases considerably for some of the figures. This is due to the changes made in the network architecture. It is essential to mention that, after each iteration, the model's accuracy is determined. This was not previously done with the model proposed by PointCleanNet, which permits a model that allows classifying outliers more efficiently for some point clouds of our model.

Moreover, with the limitations, there are some point clouds in which the accuracy is considerably low. Figures with fewer points in the 3D point cloud tend to make the probability of a point being an outlier very low due to the density of the outlier clusters. One possible solution to this problem is to modify the model's sensitivity to determine whether a point is an outlier, as described in Eq. 2. Another possible solution would be to increase the number of noisy points with high dispersion in the training dataset.

6   Conclusions

The processed 3D point clouds allowed us to analyze the inferences' results and verify under what circumstances the neural network has acceptable results. For example, when the degradation of the characteristics of the figure itself is impaired, point clouds help to determine to what extent it is advisable to reduce the density of the cloud. Cloud density and noise standard deviation significantly affects the performance of the network. By making the inference on the 3D point cloud, we can observe that the noise level is one-factor affecting noise reduction and outliers. Objects in 3D point clouds with high noise dispersion are affected, resulting in the loss of features.

One of the significant advantages of using the Gaussian distribution to generate noise and outliers in the clouds is that it is unnecessary to have extensive computational resources due to its statistical nature. We observed that depending on the distribution and amount of noise in the clouds influence the network's capacity in the final classification, which makes the results easily interpreted. It is crucial to know different methods of model validation. K-fold cross is a stochastic methodology that allows us to evaluate the model with different permutations test of the dataset. In turn, the confusion matrix is a deterministic method that allows us to know the algorithm's performance in the dataset. The method lets us know the algorithm performance based on accuracy, precision, recall, F1-score, and MSE. It is worth mentioning that accuracy is advantageous when the dataset is symmetrical, i.e., when the number of False Negatives and False Positives is similar. The F1 score tends to be a good indicator when the classes have an unequal distribution. Similarly, we should pay attention to accuracy if we are interested in True Positive. On the contrary, if the metric of interest is True Positive. The metric of interest is True Negative. Then we should pay attention to specificity.

As the proposed method is applied to a 3D point cloud it has potential to be adapted as a post processing stage to reduce outliers.

In future work, we plan to explore the following enhancements to increase performance in the proposed network:

- Augmentation of the dataset using noisy point clouds with non-Gaussian distribution, e.g., point clouds of natural scenes captured with an RGBD camera.
- Propose a new architecture using transfer learning and modify only the convolution layers.
- Analyze the hyper-parameters and determine which fine-tuning methods can be used to obtain better performance.
- Downsample the point clouds in the dataset using a voxel grid filter.
- Reduce the dimensionality of the neural network using neural pruning methods.

References

1. Antonopoulos, A., Lagoudakis, M.G., Partsinevelos, P.: A ROS multi-tier UAV localization module based on GNSS, inertial and visual-depth data. Drones **6**(6), 135 (2022)
2. Chidsin, W., Gu, Y., Goncharenko, I.: AR-based navigation using RGB-D camera and hybrid map. Sustainability **13**(10), 5585 (2021)
3. Costantino, D., Vozza, G., Pepe, M., Alfio, V.S.: Smartphone lidar technologies for surveying and reality modelling in urban scenarios: evaluation methods, performance and challenges. Appl. Syst. Innov. **5**(4), 63 (2022)
4. Debeunne, C., Vivet, D.: A review of visual-lidar fusion based simultaneous localization and mapping. Sensors **20**(7), 2068 (2020)
5. Edelmers, E., Kazoka, D., Pilmane, M.: Creation of anatomically correct and optimized for 3D printing human bones models. Appl. Syst. Innov. **4**(3), 67 (2021)
6. Fu, Y., Yan, Q., Yang, L., Liao, J., Xiao, C.: Texture mapping for 3D reconstruction with RGB-D sensor. In: Proceedings of the IEEE Conference on Computer Vision and Pattern Recognition, pp. 4645–4653 (2018)
7. Giancola, S., Valenti, M., Sala, R.: A Survey on 3D Cameras: Metrological Comparison of Time-of-Flight, Structured-Light and Active Stereoscopy Technologies. Springer, Cham (2018). https://doi.org/10.1007/978-3-319-91761-0

8. Guerrero, P., Kleiman, Y., Ovsjanikov, M., Mitra, N.J.: PCPNet learning local shape properties from raw point clouds. In: Computer Graphics Forum, vol. 37, pp. 75–85. Wiley Online Library (2018)
9. Herban, S., Costantino, D., Alfio, V.S., Pepe, M.: Use of low-cost spherical cameras for the digitisation of cultural heritage structures into 3D point clouds. J. Imaging 8(1), 13 (2022)
10. Horio, M., et al.: Resolving multi-path interference in compressive time-of-flight depth imaging with a multi-tap macro-pixel computational CMOS image sensor. Sensors 22(7), 2442 (2022)
11. Kim, S., Moon, H., Oh, J., Lee, Y., Kwon, H., Kim, S.: Automatic measurements of garment sizes using computer vision deep learning models and point cloud data. Appl. Sci. 12(10), 5286 (2022)
12. Klingensmith, M., Dryanovski, I., Srinivasa, S.S., Xiao, J.: CHISEL: real time large scale 3D reconstruction onboard a mobile device using spatially hashed signed distance fields. In: Robotics: Science and Systems, vol. 4. Citeseer (2015)
13. Ko, K., Gwak, H., Thoummala, N., Kwon, H., Kim, S.H.: SqueezeFace: integrative face recognition methods with lidar sensors. J. Sens. 2021 (2021)
14. Li, J., Gao, W., Wu, Y., Liu, Y., Shen, Y.: High-quality indoor scene 3d reconstruction with RGB-D cameras: a brief review. Comput. Vis. Media 1–25 (2022)
15. Liu, Z., Zhao, C., Wu, X., Chen, W.: An effective 3D shape descriptor for object recognition with RGB-D sensors. Sensors 17(3), 451 (2017)
16. Long, N., Yan, H., Wang, L., Li, H., Yang, Q.: Unifying obstacle detection, recognition, and fusion based on the polarization color stereo camera and lidar for the ADAS. Sensors 22(7), 2453 (2022)
17. Luo, S., Hu, W.: Score-based point cloud denoising. In: Proceedings of the IEEE/CVF International Conference on Computer Vision, pp. 4583–4592 (2021)
18. Morell-Gimenez, V., et al.: A comparative study of registration methods for RGB-D video of static scenes. Sensors 14(5), 8547–8576 (2014)
19. Na, M.H., Cho, W.H., Kim, S.K., Na, I.S.: Automatic weight prediction system for Korean cattle using Bayesian ridge algorithm on RGB-D image. Electronics 11(10), 1663 (2022)
20. Ning, X., Li, F., Tian, G., Wang, Y.: An efficient outlier removal method for scattered point cloud data. PLoS ONE 13(8), e0201280 (2018)
21. Oliveira, M., Santos, V., Sappa, A.D., Dias, P., Moreira, A.P.: Incremental texture mapping for autonomous driving. Robot. Auton. Syst. 84, 113–128 (2016)
22. Pan, Y., Chen, C., Li, D., Zhao, Z., Hong, J.: Augmented reality-based robot teleoperation system using RGB-D imaging and attitude teaching device. Robot. Comput.-Integr. Manuf. 71, 102167 (2021)
23. Qi, C.R., Su, H., Mo, K., Guibas, L.J.: PointNet: deep learning on point sets for 3D classification and segmentation. In: Proceedings of the IEEE Conference on Computer Vision and Pattern Recognition, pp. 652–660 (2017)
24. Rakotosaona, M.-J., La Barbera, V., Guerrero, P., Mitra, N.J., Ovsjanikov, M.: PointCleanNet: learning to denoise and remove outliers from dense point clouds. In: Computer Graphics Forum, vol. 39, pp. 185–203. Wiley Online Library (2020)
25. Royo, S., Ballesta-Garcia, M.: An overview of lidar imaging systems for autonomous vehicles. Appl. Sci. 9(19), 4093 (2019)
26. Schneider, P., et al.: Timo-a dataset for indoor building monitoring with a time-of-flight camera. Sensors 22(11), 3992 (2022)
27. Song, Y., Xu, F., Yao, Q., Liu, J., Yang, S.: Navigation algorithm based on semantic segmentation in wheat fields using an RGB-D camera. Inf. Process. Agric. (2022)

28. Sotoodeh, S.: Outlier detection in laser scanner point clouds. Int. Arch. Photogram. Remote Sens. Spat. Inf. Sci. **36**(5), 297–302 (2006)
29. Sui, W., Wang, L., Fan, B., Xiao, H., Huaiyu, W., Pan, C.: Layer-wise floorplan extraction for automatic urban building reconstruction. IEEE Trans. Visual Comput. Graphics **22**(3), 1261–1277 (2015)
30. Sun, Y., Luo, Y., Zhang, Q., Xu, L., Wang, L., Zhang, P.: Estimation of crop height distribution for mature rice based on a moving surface and 3d point cloud elevation. Agronomy **12**(4), 836 (2022)
31. Tagarakis, A.C., Kalaitzidis, D., Filippou, E., Benos, L., Bochtis, D.: 3D scenery construction of agricultural environments for robotics awareness. In: Bochtis, D.D., Sørensen, C.G., Fountas, S., Moysiadis, V., Pardalos, P.M. (eds.) Information and Communication Technologies for Agriculture—Theme III: Decision. Springer Optimization and Its Applications, vol. 184, pp. 125–142. Springer, Cham (2022). https://doi.org/10.1007/978-3-030-84152-2_6
32. Tan, F., Xia, Z., Ma, Y., Feng, X.: 3D sensor based pedestrian detection by integrating improved HHA encoding and two-branch feature fusion. Remote Sens. **14**(3), 645 (2022)
33. Tanzer, M., Laverdière, C., Barimani, B., Hart, A.: Augmented reality in arthroplasty: an overview of clinical applications, benefits, and limitations. J. Am. Acad. Orthop. Surg. **30**(10), e760–e768 (2022)
34. Trujillo-Jiménez, M.A., et al.: body2vec: 3D point cloud reconstruction for precise anthropometry with handheld devices. J. Imaging **6**(9), 94 (2020)
35. Visa, S., Ramsay, B., Ralescu, A.L., Van Der Knaap, E.: Confusion matrix-based feature selection. In: MAICS, vol. 710, pp. 120–127 (2011)
36. Vogt, M., Rips, A., Emmelmann, C.: Comparison of ipad pro®'s lidar and truedepth capabilities with an industrial 3d scanning solution. Technologies **9**(2), 25 (2021)
37. Wang, F., et al.: Object-based reliable visual navigation for mobile robot. Sensors **22**(6), 2387 (2022)
38. Weinmann, M., et al.: Reconstruction and Analysis of 3D Scenes. Springer, Cham (2016). https://doi.org/10.1007/978-3-319-29246-5
39. Wu, T., Pan, L., Zhang, J., Wang, T., Liu, Z., Lin, D.: Density-aware chamfer distance as a comprehensive metric for point cloud completion. arXiv preprint arXiv:2111.12702 (2021)
40. Yan, Y., Mao, Y., Li, B.: SECOND: sparsely embedded convolutional detection. Sensors **18**(10), 3337 (2018)
41. Yu, K., Eck, U., Pankratz, F., Lazarovici, M., Wilhelm, D., Navab, N.: Duplicated reality for co-located augmented reality collaboration. IEEE Trans. Visual Comput. Graphics **28**(5), 2190–2200 (2022)
42. Yuan, Z., Li, Y., Tang, S., Li, M., Guo, R., Wang, W.: A survey on indoor 3D modeling and applications via RGB-D devices. Front. Inf. Technol. Electron. Eng. **22**(6), 815–826 (2021)
43. Zhang, G., Geng, X., Lin, Y.-J.: Comprehensive mPoint: a method for 3D point cloud generation of human bodies utilizing FMCW MIMO mm-wave radar. Sensors **21**(19), 6455 (2021)
44. Zheng, H., Wang, W., Wen, F., Liu, P.: A complementary fusion strategy for RGB-D face recognition. In: Þór Jónsson, B., et al. (eds.) MMM 2022. LNCS, vol. 13141, pp. 339–351. Springer, Cham (2022). https://doi.org/10.1007/978-3-030-98358-1_27
45. Zollhöfer, M., et al.: State of the art on 3D reconstruction with RGB-D cameras. In: Computer graphics forum, vol. 37, pp. 625–652. Wiley Online Library (2018)

Development and Coding of a Data Framing Protocol for IoT/LPWAN Networks Based on 8-Bit Processing Architectures

F. Ramírez-López[1] , G. A. Yáñez-Casas[1,2] , C. A. López-Balcázar[1] ,
J. J. Hernández-Gómez[2]([✉]) , R. de-la-Rosa-Rábago[2] ,
and C. Couder-Castañeda[2]

[1] Instituto Politécnico Nacional, Unidad Profesional Interdisciplinaria en Ingeniería y Tecnologías Avanzadas, Mexico City, Mexico
[2] Instituto Politécnico Nacional, Centro de Desarrollo Aeroespacial, Mexico City, Mexico
jjhernandezgo@ipn.mx

Abstract. The development of wireless communication systems has had a great increase due to the needs of digital services that are increasingly demanded by today's societies. Wireless networks have become the most used systems by an increasingly growing number of users. In this context, the same wireless networks have diversified; proof of this are the solutions known as IoT (Internet of Things) based on LPWAN networks (Low Power Wide Area Network), which are adaptable, of low cost and relatively low development complexity, which have the potential to be used in a wide type of applications. Despite the advantages that they represent and the benefits that they could provide, there are still challenges to overcome in terms of design and implementation. One of the main aspects that require attention is the development and adaptation of an information (data) encapsulation structure according to the needs of the system and the application, since such an information must be transported safely, fully and efficiently, always respecting the limitations of the communications system. This paper proposes a data framing protocol structure based on an LPWAN/IoT monitoring system, which is based on COTS components and has the function of acquiring environmental variables.

Keywords: LPWAN · Low Power Wide Area Network · sensing · environmental variables · climate change · 8-bit microcontroller · AVR architecture · datalink communications protocol · dataframe · data security · data integrity

1 Introduction

Nowadays, Internet of Things (IoT) is taking a preponderant role in the development of modern society [1,2]. Part of the current success of IoT is its incorporation to Low Power Wide Area Networks (LPWAN), which allows to extend the coverage of IoT applications to low power consumption devices and networks [3–10]. In turn, it has allowed to increase exponentially the possible applications of IoT applications, which now heavily rely in the transmission of data in real time [11]. One of the most promising applications of IoT working under the LPWAN principles is the development of sparse IoT networks with a long-range coverage [12–18].

There are several long-range LPWAN technologies that are under current use and development, such as LoRa/LoRaWAN, LTEM, MQTT, NBIoT and Sigfox [19]. Each of them may or may not consist in both the physical and the logical layer of the wireless communications system. For instance, MQTT only develops a single-layer communications protocol that sends small messages, so it can be, in principle, mounted on any physical infrastructure [19]. On the other side, NBIoT and LTEM have multi-layer protocols because they are mainly adapted to 4G physical layer. In this sense, we can talk about a set of LPWAN communications protocols that posses common features as small frames, few frames, simple security and integrity techniques (if any), as well as several identifiers for users and devices [19]. Research has been done in the development and application of LPWAN protocols [20–23].

LPWAN-based IoT networks could be potentially beneficial for applications that require to gather data at non-urban environments where there is little or no coverage of traditional wireless communications systems as 2G-5G, microwaves or Wi-Fi. A fundamental application of IoT sparse networks is the use of low power IoT devices to obtain data in remote regions that could lead to assess the impact of Climate Change at regional and global scales [24–32]. In order for IoT devices to be able to monitor climatic-related variables in order to first recognise, and later forecast, climate change, such devices should follow the low power philosophy in both its design (current consumption) and operation (under LPWANs) [33]. In order for IoT devices to accomplish low power consumption goals, they are opting for the use of small scale microcontroller architectures for the processing of the data [33–37].

For instance, [33] develops very low cost sensing nodes designed for ultra low power consumption, based on COTS components. Such nodes are able to gather the following weather variables: atmospheric pressure, environmental temperature, altitude, rain level, humidity, intensity of ultraviolet light, wind speed, concentration of methane, hydrogen, LPG gas, butane, propane, natural gas, carbon monoxide as well as ethyl alcohol, as well as the telemetry of the node (current and voltage monitoring of the system, GPS position of the node, and an MPU module). They also feature LPWAN wireless connection able to provide the gathered data to an IoT server to record and visualise data in real time on a web interface [33].

As the work [33] is focused in the development of the physical layer of the whole communications system, it implemented a very low consumption processing architecture, the AVR 8-bit microcontroller. It entails, however, the problem that such a small-scale processing units has a very small word length, and current LPWAN protocols have multi-layer communications protocols that are very lengthy (several bytes). In this sense, their implementation in such very small scale processing architecture is difficult and it entails a very high computational burden.

In this work we develop a one-layer communications protocol for IoT/LPWAN sensors systems with an 8-bit processing unit. Our development is based in the sensing nodes developed and tested by [33]. The proposed data framing structure can be adapted to different length of data, as is of variable codification [38] and it can be scaled to any number of sensors within the IoT device. We also design and implement security and integrity fields adapted to such a small scale processing architecture. Such a protocol shows to achieve a balance between the use of memory storage and processing time, since less than 10% of the 32 KB flash memory of the ATMEGA328P microcontroller was used, with processing times in the order of milliseconds. The structure of the proposed protocol is adequate to frame the information according to the data acquired, avoiding ambiguities and unnecessary generalisations.. This work is organised as follows: in Sect. 2 we pose the materials and methods required for this work, including LPWAN and IoT principles, LPWAN protocols, serial communication protocols, data security and integrity as well as 8-bit processing architectures. Section 3 features the development of this work, the design of the data frame structure as well as the design of security and integrity fields for the proposed protocol. In Sect. 4 we show the results and discussion of this research while in Sects. 5 and 6 we pose the conclusions as well as some paths that this research may follow in the future.

2   Materials and Methods

2.1   Low Power Wide Area Networks and Internet of Things Applications

Wireless communication networks make up an important portion of the total existing infrastructure of communication systems [39–41]. Currently, wireless networks are one of the most demanded transmission systems, not only in daily activities, but also in other aspects such as research and industry. Due to their extensive use, the infrastructure saturation cannot continue forever. Thus, alternatives to typical wireless communications networks have emerged in order to mitigate the inconveniences that saturation represents. infrastructure [42–44].

The aforementioned alternatives have resulted in various proposals, mainly those based on the so-called Low Power Wide Area Networks (LPWAN) [45], which are constituted by a standard that aims to present a less expensive and more versatile option. The LPWAN standard has been developed and documented by the Internet Engineering Task Force (IEFT) [46].

LPWAN communications systems consist of two phases: the first is called a private or dedicated network, in which the data acquisition devices and the so-called radio gateways exist. The dedicated network is where the designer has complete control over the use of the components within the system implementation. On the other hand, the second phase is made up of the public network (usually an IP network), where the server that places the data acquired in the cloud is located [46].

On the other hand, IoT applications encourage the use of a large number of interconnected elements through various techniques, allowing the remote and effective transmission of the data acquired through such elements, which publish their data through IP networks. One of the fundamentals of IoT applications is the possibility of interconnecting a large number of devices through various techniques, allowing the transmission of data effectively using networks based on IP networks as the final transmission system. IoT focuses its efforts on presenting open and accessible environments, where both physical and logical components of the system have a high level of compatibility and interoperability, allowing devices of a different nature to be used in the same system [47].

IoT follows the "Edge Computing" paradigm, which defines the transition from the paradigm of isolated and dedicated communications towards an environment of interaction between systems, despite the complexity that may arise [48]. Since the main idea of IoT is to interconnect both objects and users without this difference being noticed, it is an excellent application of the Edge Computing paradigm.

Since IoT presents a great opportunity for technological development, both public and private organisations have undertaken the task of designing their own proposals for both physical and logical tools that have resulted in complete technologies based on LPWAN/IoT principles. Examples of such technologies are LoRa/LoRaWAN, Sigfox, LTE-M, NBIoT, among others [19,49].

Even though each manufacturer or organisation has its own technical specifications, all LPWAN/IoT technologies share certain features, such as: operating frequencies in the 300–400 MHz and 800–900 MHz bands, communication protocols based on the structure of the User Datagram Protocol (UDP), authentication and security algorithms based on the authentication of the device or users, usually low transmission speed (kbps), use of little complex digital modulation techniques, coverage based on the geographic region and the capabilities of the transceiver and connection in the form of a star topology [50–54].

The aforementioned characteristics make LPWAN/IoT networks a flexible and adaptable opportunity for the development of ubiquitous and compatible applications, so it is of the utmost importance to explore each of its aspects, where one of the most crucial is the framing of the information to be transmitted through the LPWAN.

2.2 Low Power Communications Protocols

A simplified communications system is made up of three stages: Transmission stage, transmission medium, and reception stage. Each of these stages has two basic components that are the physical component and the logical component, regardless of the used standard or technical specification [55].

Principles of Protocols. Regarding the logical layer of a communications system, it is well known that most communication systems are organised in a stack of layers or levels, each one constituted to provide service to the previous layer and exchange information with it. The idea of layered design is to simplify and outline more clearly the data transformation process of the communications network in question. The rules for exchanging information between layers are generally called protocol. For purposes of data transmission between two points, the information is not transmitted directly from layer n of the transmitter to layer n of the receiving point. First, when sending, each layer communicates in a descending hierarchical way, until reaching the transmission medium; once the information reaches the lowest layer of the receiver, the information is transmitted upwards through the layers of this [56]. A generic schematic of a layer system is shown in Fig. 1.

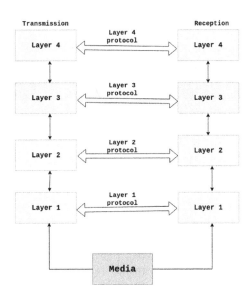

Fig. 1. Generic layer system [57].

The layered design takes into account that a physical layer must exist, so the shape of the subsequent layers is purely logical, even when they depend on the infrastructure. Immediately after the physical layer, a layer must continue where it is possible to regulate the data flow by building the frames that shape the information. Likewise, it is in this layer where the reinforcement techniques for error handling and encryption are placed. Commonly, this layer is called the link layer. The shape of the frames depends directly on the application of the communications system and the physical layer, so the fields that compose them also obey these characteristics. Despite the above, all link layer protocols contain the fields presented in Fig. 2 [56].

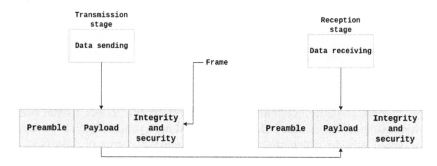

Fig. 2. Generic data link layer [57].

The preamble is generally made up of identifiers, addresses and specific information for each device in the communication system, the payload corresponds to the information to be transmitted and the security and integrity field corresponds to the techniques implemented to reinforce the frame (see Fig. 2).

In this work, the protocol proposal designed is the one corresponding to the link layer of the base communications system.

Low Power Protocols. Once the general structure of information exchange between layers in a communications system has been described, it is important to note that the number of layers and the design of the link protocol depend directly on the technology on which it is implemented. The more complex the communication system, the more complex the protocol and the greater number of layers it has. In the case of LPWANs, the protocols are particularly specific, due to the limitations of the physical layer [47].

With the increase in the number of LPWANs, various manufacturers and telecommunications operators have developed their own technical specifications for low power systems and inherent to this, specific protocols have been developed for such specifications.

In general terms, low power protocols tend to be able to support and recognise a large number of devices on the same network, which may have the ability to interchange short messages between them to ensure network functionality. Usually, the communication is implemented unidirectionally if it is necessary to save power consumption. Due to the recent implementations of low power technologies, the protocol specifications are usually regional, in such a way that the corresponding geographical regulations are respected. They implement simple security techniques and are band limited compared to other more robust communication systems [46].

The frames of low power protocols tend to have a short extension and there is usually no field nesting, unless required. Due to the above, the data transmission speeds that these systems have are in the kbps range. Among the most widely used technologies, which share similar values of the aforementioned characteristics are: Lora/LoRaWAN, Sigfox, NBIoT, LTEM, Bluetooth Low Power, among others [19].

2.3   Eigth Bit Architectures and Serial Communication Protocols

In the context of digital systems, an n bit architecture refers to the design, operation, stages, and elements that are required for a processing unit to operate in a minimal way, in which the size of the memory registers of data is n [58]. Some of the main features of a small-scale architecture like microcontrollers and microprocessors are mentioned in Table 1.

Table 1. Technical features of processing unit [59].

Characteristic	Value
Program Memory	1 KB–2 MB
#Cores	1–2
Operation Frequency	4–64 MHz
Registers length	8–32 bits
# UART Interface	1–2
# SPI Interface	1–2
# I^{2}C Interface	1–2

Serial communication protocols are used at the link layer in the transmission of information between microcontrollers and microprocessors and with other devices due to their simplicity. Among the most used are UART (Universal Asynchronous Receiver Transmitter), I^{2}C (Inter-Integrated Circuit), USART (Universal Synchronous/Asynchronous Receiver/Transmitter) and SPI (Serial Peripheral Interface) [58].

As previously mentioned, these protocols work at the link layer in the communication between devices. When implementing them in small-scale architectures, a local protocol is not usually developed, that is, a logical layer is not implemented for the transmission of information by this medium due to the following factors [60]:

– *Memory size:* We are to send information frames as small as possible, since we have limited memory.
– *Data link protocol features:* The serial communication protocol is limited by the characteristics of the architecture in which it is implemented (Baud Rate and size of the information to be sent per work cycle). A message must be distributed in memory for processing and framing before being sent, since it depends on the length of the records and the size of information that can be transmitted per work cycle. Small-scale architectures use a higher number of duty cycles, and since they are sent at a small frequency, they require more time to send the message.

– *Processing features:* In general, to guarantee the security and integrity of the information, algorithms are used that may require processing capacities and/or hardware elements that are not necessarily intrinsic to the architectures of small scale, which makes them difficult to implement.

2.4   Data Security and Integrity

The transmission of data in wireless communication systems is seriously compromised once the information is sent, since when it is transmitted by an unguided medium, it is common for the information to suffer a certain degree of corruption, so it is extremely important to provide the data structures to be sent with a certain degree of integrity and security. Such algorithms are to be presented in what follows.

Integrity Techniques (Cyclic Redundancy Check (CRC)). In general, there are many methods to achieve data integrity, for instance, Hamming codes. However there are simpler options to implement. Techniques based on CRC (Cyclic Redundancy Check) algorithms provide data integrity by verifying whether the information has been received correctly or not. One of the advantages of CRC over some other data integrity algorithm is its easy implementation and low computational demand. Thus, it is suitable for its implementation in devices such as microcontrollers for frame verification [61]. Basically, two vital aspects are required for the algorithm to work optimally. In one hand, the larger the frame size, the less likely prone to errors. On the other hand, the characteristic called chaos requires that a polynomial be selected that allows to substantially alter the result of the verification obtained, at the minimal frame change [62].

The CRC technique is based on successive divisions where three useful values are used: the divisor, the dividend, and the remainder. In this case, the frame to be transmitted corresponds to the dividend (which must have a size W), the divisor is the polynomial used G, and the remainder is the sequence left over once the division has been carried out. In general CRC consists of the following steps [62]:

1. Choose a width W, and a polynomial G (of width W).
2. Append W zero bits to the message. Call this M'.
3. Divide M' by G using CRC arithmetic. The remainder is the checksum.

At the receiver, both the polynomial size G and the dividend size W must remain the same, otherwise the original frame is assumed to have bit errors. In practice, the receiver has two options to verify if the frames were received without error. One possibility is to separate the useful information field of the frame from the field where the checksum is stored and once separated, the checksum to the useful information field is calculated and compared with the received checksum. Another possibility is to calculate the checksum without adding the sequence of zeros of size W and verify that the sum is zero [62].

Security Algorithms (Shift Cipher and Permutation Cipher). Generally, data encryption techniques are used in order to keep secure the information that is transmitted through a communications network or when exchanging sensitive data between users or groups of users. These techniques become essential when the exchange of information is done between devices, where there is no user who controls the criteria of what information can be shared and what information should not be shared. This implies that it is necessary to choose the appropriate techniques for the type of application and/or system.

The cipher algorithms, generally are defined by mathematical components. In Table 2 common elements of such a cryptosystem are shown.

Table 2. Cryptosystem mathematical components [59].

Variable	Meaning
P	Set of possible plain text
C	Set of possible cipher text
K	Set of possible Keys
$\epsilon_{P_i}(k)$	Encryption Rule
$\delta_{P_i}(k)$	Decryption Rule

The ideal cryptosystem is defined by having a big set of K, and C, in order to frustrate brute force attacks. Therefore, in 8-bit architectures we must design such a cryptosystem, but reducing the processing burden inasmuch as possible; that's because will be used the monosylabus ones [59].

The Shift Cipher is the most basic cypher algorithm, and as its name suggest, it consists of shifting a n-alphabet and changing the corresponding object of the alphabet. The metrics of the Shift Cipher has $n - 1$ possible shifts, in general this one has $P = C = K = \mathbb{Z}$. The operation of shifting is done by Eqs. (1) and (2) [59],

$$\epsilon_{P_i}(k) = (P_i + k)mod(n) \tag{1}$$

and

$$\delta_{P_j}(k) = (P_j - k)mod(n) , \tag{2}$$

where P_j is the encoding (ϵ_{P_i}) and the k value must be the same for the decoding δ_{P_j}.

On the other hand, Permutation Cipher has two alphabets in different order each one, and it only interchange the corresponding symbols in their same position. Suppose a general case of n-alphabets; it implies that $P = C = \mathbb{Z}_n$ and the $K = n!$. The encryption rule is governed by Eqs. (3) and (4) [59],

$$\epsilon_{P_i}(k) = \pi(x) \tag{3}$$

and

$$\delta_{P_j}(k) = \pi^{-1}(x) \ , \tag{4}$$

where $\pi(x)$ and $\pi^{-1}(x)$ are one of the universe of the permutations. It must be remarked that a trivial way to self-generate the permutations in a clear way does not exist. In this way, this is the main drawback of this kind of cypher; thus, the permutations must be pre-selected in a certain way, and the k value must be the same in both the forward and inverse permutations [59].

In this work, a combination of both encryption techniques is proposed in order to balance the use of computational resources, considering the limitations of the 8-bit processing architecture.

3   Development

3.1   Base Communication System

As mentioned in Sect. 1, the basic communications system on which the data framing proposal of this work is based, deals with an environmental monitoring system, based entirely on physical layer standards LPWAN/ IoT [33]. The monitoring system uses the concepts of LPWAN/IoT in the sense that all electronic elements are of low consumption and low cost. Likewise the design is scalable and its implementation is accessible and reproducible [63–65]. The Fig. 3 shows the block diagram of the base communications system.

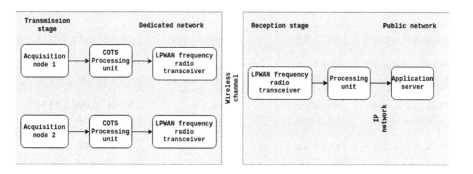

Fig. 3. Monitoring system design [33].

In order to provide redundancy and modularity, the transmission system consists of two acquisition nodes based on COTS sensors of meteorological variables. Such sensors provide readings that are acquired by the processing unit and further sent to the radio frequency transceiver to be wirelessly transmitted. Subsequently, in the reception stage, there is a mirror circuit of the transmission stage. Once the data is processed at the reception stage, it is distributed through a network based on IP (Internet Protocol) and finally it is put into an application where it can be consulted and used. A summary of the characteristics of the components used is shown in the Table 3.

Table 3. Characteristics of the electronics components considered for the hardware of this system [33].

Type	Model	Variable(s)	Range	Unit
Processing unit component				
Micro-controller	ATMEGA328P [66]	N/A	N/A	N/A
Conditioning and measure components				
Analogical multiplexer	CD4051 [67]	N/A	N/A	N/A
Analogical sensor	ACS712 [68]	Current consumption	0 to 60	A
Screen	LCD 1602A [69]	N/A	N/A	N/A
Communication components				
Radio transceiver	CC1101 [70]	Wireless transceiver	387 to 464	MHz
Acquisition node 1 sensors				
Digital sensor	BMP180 [71]	Atmospheric pressure, altitude, environmental temperature	300 to 1100 500 to 9000 −40 to +85	Pa,
Digital sensor	DHT11 [72]	Humidity, environmental temperature	0 to 90 0 to 50	%, °C
Analogical sensor	Yl-83 [73]	Rain level	0 to 100	%
Analogical sensor	ML8511 [74]	Intensity of ultraviolet light (UV)	100 to 700	mW/cm^2
Analogical sensor	PH0245S [75]	Wind speed	0 to 30	m/s
Acquisition node 2 sensors				
Analogical sensor	MQ-2 [76]	Propane, hydrogen, LPG gas	300 to 10,000	PPM
Analogical sensor	MQ-3 [77]	Ethyl alcohol	0 to 10	mg/L
Analogical sensor	MQ-4 [78]	Propane, methane (CH4), natural gas	300 to 10,000	PPM
Analogical sensor	MQ-5 [79]	Natural gas	200 to 10,000	PPM
Analogical sensor	MQ-6 [80]	Natural gas, butane, LPG gas	300 to 10,000	PPM
Analogical sensor	MQ-7 [81]	Carbon monoxide (CO)	10 to 10,000	PPM
Analogical sensor	MQ-8 [82]	Hydrogen, LPG gas, Methane (CH4)	100 to 10,000	PPM
Analogical sensor	MQ-9 [83]	LPG gas, Carbon monoxide (CO), methane (CH4)	100 to 10,000	PPM

The processing unit of the system is a microcontroller of the AVR [60] family. The ATMEGA328P is a general purpose microcontroller with 32 8-bit registers and a RISC (Reduced Instruction Set Computing) instruction set. The operating frequency is 16 MHz, with 32 Kb of flash memory and it is compatible with the I^2C protocol, in addition to other serial communication protocols [84, 85]. This architecture supports C language, assembler and in some versions, the Python programming language [66].

For the dedicated network, a radio frequency transceiver was selected which operates in the band known as Industrial, Scientific and Medical (ISM) [86], which coincides with the portion of the spectrum assigned to low power communication systems. Texas Instruments' CC1101 transceiver, which operates in two frequency ranges (300–400 MHz and 800–900 MHz), has a range of more than 200 m in open field. In addition, the transmission power can be modified by internal configuration according to the required application [70].

The first node contains 5 weather sensors, two providing digital readings and three providing analog readings. Such sensors can generally be supplied with 5 V and their current consumption is of the order of mA. On the other hand, the second node contains only analog sensors and its electrical characteristics are similar to those of node 1. The variables corresponding to each node are described in Table 3.

3.2 Data Frame Structure and Data Convention

In wireless communication between devices, the transmission medium compromises the integrity and security of the information. Besides the exposed considerations in Sect. 2.3, another reason why a logic layer is not implemented in a serial communication protocol is that the information transits on a wired medium in short distances and therefore the information does not require further treatment.

The base system case discussed in Sect. 2.3, is an example of a system where a change of transmission medium occurs, from a wired to a wireless medium. Through a serial communication protocol, the microcontroller communicates with the transceiver; the transceiver frames this information as part of the payload of its radio frequency link protocol, depending on the technical specification of the transceiver. The transceiver handshake may or may not be a standardised structure. Regarding the operation of the internal protocol of the transceiver, it is important to emphasise the following points:

- The protocol implemented by the transceiver is only at the link layer level, so the microcontroller connected to it does not receive a security or integrity check from the transceiver.
- Regardless of the means of transmission and link protocols by which the information is transmitted, it is expected that the useful information to be sent will be received with integrity. However, there is no certainty of such integrity if a proprietary protocol at the link layer level is not implemented to frame the information source.

Since the main goal of this paper is precisely to design and implement a communications protocol at the specific link layer level to frame the source of information (see Sect. 3.1), it is necessary to take into account technical features of the small-scale 8-bit processing architecture, which can be observed in the Table 4.

Table 4. Technical features of AVR architecture for protocol design [66].

Field	Value	Unit
Processing unit	ATMEGA328P	N/A
Serial protocol communication	UART	N/A
Baud Rate	9600	$Symbols/second$
Duty cycles	8	1
Operating frequency	433	MHz

The ATMEGA328P microcontroller has UART/USART, I^2C and SPI serial communication interfaces. For this work, we used UART for its simplicity, so implementing the protocol design under this interface allows it to be easily adapted under other interfaces.

For the structure of the herein developed frame, it is considered that the information to be transmitted is the information coming from the sensors of the communications system [33]. Since a balance between the required processing power and memory storage of the microcontroller, the following frame fields are considered:

- *Preamble:* Contains a set of identifiers useful in the reception stage such as destination identifier, source identifier, corresponding sensor and the acquired variable. Since the base system does not contain a large number of elements, it is proposed to store the identifiers in memory to reduce the alphabet and the size of the information to be processed later in the payload field.
- *Data payload:* Contains the value of the measured weather variable. The range of values of this field includes numerical values from -250 to 10,000 taking a resolution of 2 tenths. If such an information information were sent as floating point variables, it could generate an alphabet of 1,025,000 symbols, with a fixed length of 4 bytes, that implies larger processing capabilities and memory for security and integrity algorithms. In this sense, a data conversion is performed, from floating point to a one-dimensional array of characters, taking the ASCII standard as a reference [87], allowing to reduce the alphabet, since each of the elements take numerical values between 0 - 9, decimal point and negative sign, which makes it necessary to add one more element to indicate the end of the field since its length depends on the number of digits of the sent value.
- *Security:* Contains the defined keys and additional information for data encryption. It is important to mention that the encoding is limited to the content of the Data Payload field given the processing limitations of the microcontroller.
- *Integrity:* Contains the result of a series of logical and arithmetic operations applied to the information in the Data payload field, to verify whether the exact sent message from the origin node has been received.
- *End Frame:* Contains an identifier to indicate the end of frame.

The structure of the frame is according to the Fig. 4.

Field name	Preamble	Data payload	Security	Integrity	End Frame
Length (Bytes)	2	Variable	13	1	1

Fig. 4. Protocol frame structure.

In Sect. 4, the detailed description of the content and conformation of each of the fields of the general frame can be found.

The data to be processed to generate the integrity and security fields in the frame structure, represent a challenge due to its size when using a microcontroller of 8 bits, to process it, two memory spaces of 15 bytes length were reserved in the program memory, then the information is distributed in 8-bit sections and stored in assigned sections, in this way, it is possible to implement logical-arithmetical algorithms such as Booth's algorithm, ones and twos complements among others to process information with size greater than 8 bits.

3.3 Design of CRC for the Proposed Protocol

For the cyclic redundancy field, based on Sect. 2.4, the CRC algorithm provided by the MathWorks [88] documentation was taken as a reference. The following considerations were taken to process it in 8-bit architecture:

- *Data payload field:* In order to minimize the processing requirements of the algorithm, it was applied only to the Data payload field before being encrypted.
- *Degree polynomial divisor:* A polynomial of degree 4 of the form $x^4 + x^3 + x^2 + x + 1$ is used, for the arithmetic - logical operations of the algorithm, is represented by the number $b'11111$, so that the cyclic redundancy has 4 useful bits, allowing fewer sequential divisions [59].

Let n_i be the size of the message in bits, up to the last useful position it occupies in the memory registers. The number of times m_i that the divisor polynomial must be traversed to the left at the beginning of the algorithm is given by Eq. (5),

$$m_i = n_i - 5. \tag{5}$$

Thus, both n_i and m_i have the same size. Subsequently, when doing the divisions, the divisor is shifted to the left to have the same length in bits as the module of the previous division. When a right-shift divider overflow occurs, the overflowed bits are stored in register C. The algorithm ends when the dividend is 1, so the content of the C overflow register is the CRC, as shown in Fig. 5.

C7	C6	C5	C4	C3	C2	C1	C0
CRC3	CRC2	CRC1	CRC0	0	0	0	0

Fig. 5. Overflow register content CRC.

In case the content of the data payload is 0, the default CRC will be 0.

3.4   Design of Cypher Technique for the Proposed Protocol

It is common that in any encryption algorithm, the stage that requires the most processing is decryption, in case the decryption key is not known. However, in 8-bit systems it is imperative that a system that does not require a lot of processing is used since there is a lot of workload on the processing unit.

Since this paper focuses on an 8-bit architecture, it is proposed to use an algorithm resulting from the combination of the security techniques explained in Sect. 2.4, in order to have a robust set of keys and low processing time. The proposal for data encryption works according to the diagram shown in Fig. 6.

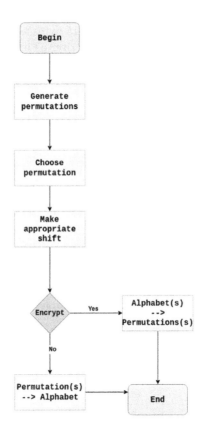

Fig. 6. Designed cypher algorithm flow chart.

By using a substitution process as the final part of the algorithm, it would be possible to use the same elements of the encryption in the decryption.

The resulting algorithm has by definition $\frac{n!}{n} = (n-1)!$ valid permutations, because when counting permutations we are also counting the shifts that are given to some predefined ordering. In general, if fewer permutations are used (n_k) and each permutation can have k shifts, it will imply that in general there will be $(n_k)(k)$ substitutions. Therefore, the used keyspace is valid.

4   Results and Discussion

4.1   Acquisition Nodes

As described in Sect. 3.1 the transmission stage of the communications system begins with the acquisition nodes, which constitute the system's information source. In Figs. 7 and 8, the block diagrams corresponding to each data acquisition node are shown.

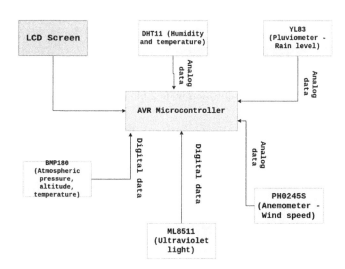

Fig. 7. Acquisition node 1 block diagram.

In general, the components that are part of each acquisition node are shown in Figs. 7 and 8. For the purposes of this work, the aspect to highlight are the variables, their type and length, that are acquired from each sensor, as they are the key for construction of the data framing protocol.

On the other hand, the use of a microcontroller as a processing unit allows maintaining low-power operating characteristics and is also one of the components that delimits the extension of the protocol.

4.2   Protocol Simulation

The sending of information was simulated using the protocol developed under the following characteristics:

- *Sensors:* A total of 15 different sensors are considered, so the assigned length for sensor identifiers is 4 bits.

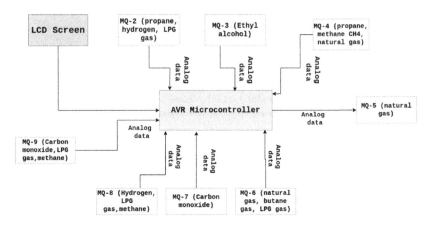

Fig. 8. Acquisition node 2 block diagram.

- *Acquisition nodes and reception modules:* It is considered to work in a network of 8 nodes and 2 receiver nodes. It is assigned a length of 4 and 2 bits respectively.
- *Variables:* A total of 35 variables from the sensors are considered, leaving a length of 6 bits for the identifiers of each variable.

Figure 9 shows the equivalent circuit for the protocol simulation. The communication between a node and a reception module take into account the characteristics mentioned for the implementation of the protocol at the software level. Two simulation tests were performed.

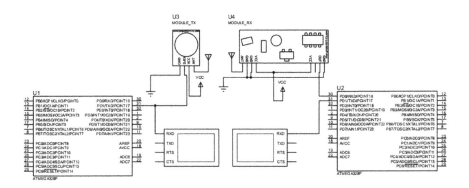

Fig. 9. Circuit simulation diagram.

Minimal Frame Transmission Simulation. We understand by minimum frame, the smallest frame that can be sent using the proposed protocol, so that it uses the smallest possible processing burden. For this protocol, this case occurs when the data payload size is 1 byte since the communication protocol serial (UART) does not allow sending less information to it, its content is $0x00$. It is important to mention that this designation minimizes the CRC processing time, which by default is $0x00$ when the data payload has that value. Since the identifier and the end-of-frame fields are stored in memory and have a fixed length, their content does not affect the required processing time. The time it takes for the transmitter to process the simulated algorithm is 23 ms.

Full System Frame Forwarding Simulation. The case in which the information of all the variables of the 15 sensors is sent from the same node was considered, so that 26 different frames are sent per transmission cycle. For the operation of the node, it was considered that the microcontroller collects the information from all the sensors, so that it processes the frames of each sensor consecutively. The memory space to store the character arrays, keys, alphabet, CRC, identifiers and other constants was 397 bytes, while the total space for algorithm processing was 2985 bytes. The time taken by the transmitter to process and send the entire data frame is 675 ms.

The algorithm used to send the frame of the entire system uses 9.16% of the microcontroller's program memory, in other words, 98.84% of the memory is available for processing other tasks.

Table 5. Protocol's processing results.

Parameter	Simulation 1	Simulation 2
Memory [Bytes]	$1,427$	$2,985$
Processing time [ms]	23	675

Table 5 shows the performance results concerning to memory allocation as well as to processing time used in both simulations. These parameters reflect the fact that the proposed protocol structure is suitable for the architecture used, since the microcontroller capabilities are not saturated.

It should be noted that the protocol proposal includes the fields corresponding to the use of security techniques and data integrity. Originally, these types of techniques are not intended to be used in small-scale architectures. Thus, both the encryption algorithm and the CRC code were adequately conditioned to avoid processing saturation in the microcontroller.

The use of a custom design for the data structure in a low power communications system, lies mainly in the physical capabilities of the system, the limitations in size, mass and therefore processing capabilities. Although there are other link layer protocols already developed for LPWAN systems, it is vital to define your own structure, if the communications system has a specific mission and characteristics.

Since the applications and variants of LPWAN systems are different and depend on who designs them, the data sent must be treated in a detailed and precise manner, so if said data were sent without any understandable structure in the context of the application, the information that the user receives may not be correct or may be corrupted during delivery.

5   Conclusions

In the present work, the design and implementation of a data framing structure for an environmental monitoring system based on low power networks (LPWAN) is proposed, adapted to a small-scale processing unit, which uses low cost COTS components and provides the data processed in the designed protocol.

One of the main criteria taken into account for the form of the frames is the used processing unit. The ATMEGA328P 8-bit microcontroller allows to maintain a low level of power consumption, so the processed data structures must be limited in a way that such electrical characteristic is preserved.

The acquisition of data from the physical monitoring system comes from different components that are not necessarily directly compatible. In this sense, the serial communication used plays a vital role, since it is not completely dependent on such compatibility. The coding of the proposed protocol makes it possible to use this generality to frame the data while not depending on the devices, which makes it extremely flexible and easy to program.

The programming of the proposed protocol, despite its simplicity, provides security and integrity to the framed information. In this sense, the use of a communications system with certain consumption and processing restrictions did not represent a hindrance to include security and integrity attributes in the structure of the frame.

When the protocol is used in the transmission of different data through the same link layer, the growth of the used memory is reduced with respect to the space initially used by the added variable. The time increases almost proportionally depending on the number of variables and the extension of each one.

When using small-scale architectures, the implementation of this protocol in the logical layer must be restricted to communications whose characteristics compromise integrity and security, such as the case proposed in this article. This is due to the fact that the space used in memory by the protocol grows dramatically with each different datalink protocol or standard to be implemented within the same system.

It should be remarked that we the larger simulated system consisted of eight sensing nodes, and it only used 2.985 KBytes of the total 32 KBytes of available memory in the ATMEGA328P microcontroller, thus showing that the implemented protocol is apt to support large IoT/LPWAN devices networks. Thus, the developed datalink protocol can be implemented in networks under different standards and can be scaled to systems that require a greater number of devices with different architectures, features, can easily better perform during processing.

6   Future Work

This research can be extended in the following pathways:

– To build networks based on radio frequency considering the data acquisition nodes herein studied.
– To reproduce the data acquisition nodes used considering in different programmable processing architectures.
– To test the protocol proposed in this work in other programmable architectures.
– To design a distributed communication scheme based on the original system.
– To propose and test different types of information sources.
– To diversify sensors and data acquisition elements.

Acknowledgements. The authors acknowledge partial economical support by projects 20230476, 20231067, 20230592, 20230593, 20231370 and 20230035 as well as EDI grant, provided by Secretaría de Investigación y Posgrado, Instituto Politécnico Nacional.

References

1. Mahmood, Y., Kama, N., Azmi, A., Ya'acob, S.: An IoT based home automation integrated approach: impact on society in sustainable development perspective. Int. J. Adv. Comput. Sci. Appl. **11**(1), 240–250 (2020)
2. Rohen, M.: IoT Driving Digital Transformation-Impact on Economy and Society. Taylor & Francis (2017)
3. Janssen, T., Koppert, A., Berkvens, R., Weyn, M.: A survey on IoT positioning leveraging LPWAN, GNSS and LEO-PNT. IEEE Internet Things J. 1 (2023)
4. Kumar, V., Yadav, P., Indrusiak, L.: Resilient edge: building an adaptive and resilient multi-communication network for IoT edge using LPWAN and WiFi. IEEE Trans. Netw. Serv. Manag. 1 (2023)
5. Sharma, S.: Getting started with LPWAN: LoRa, Sigfox and NB-IoT. In: Dhar, S., Do, D.T., Sur, S.N., Liu, H.C.M. (eds.) Advances in Communication, Devices and Networking. LNEE, vol. 902, pp. 559–568. Springer, Singapore (2023). https://doi.org/10.1007/978-981-19-2004-2_51
6. Ogbodo, E., Abu-Mahfouz, A., Kurien, A.: A survey on 5G and LPWAN-IoT for improved smart cities and remote area applications: from the aspect of architecture and security. Sensors **22**(16) (2022)
7. Andre, H., et al.: LPWAN communication in IoT network for electrical energy monitoring. In: Proceeding of the 2022 International Symposium on Information Technology and Digital Innovation: Technology Innovation During Pandemic, ISITDI 2022, pp. 32–35 (2022)
8. Zemko, L., Cicak, P.: IoT and LPWAN networks: increasing efficiency by communication planning. In: 2022 45th International Conference on Telecommunications and Signal Processing, TSP 2022, pp. 116–121 (2022)
9. Stanco, G., Botta, A., Frattini, F., Giordano, U., Ventre, G.: On the performance of IoT LPWAN technologies: the case of Sigfox, LoRaWAN and NB-IoT. In: IEEE International Conference on Communications, vol. 2022-May, pp. 2096–2101 (2022)

10. Sarath Kumar, R., Gokul Prasanth, M., Bharath Kumar, R., Abhishek, J., Ajay, D.: LPWAN for IoT. In: 2022 International Conference on Advanced Computing Technologies and Applications, ICACTA 2022 (2022)
11. Pattnaik, S., et al.: Future wireless communication technology towards 6G IoT: an application-based analysis of IoT in real-time location monitoring of employees inside underground mines by using BLE. Sensors **22**(9) (2022)
12. Olazabal, A., Kaur, J., Yeboah-Ofori, A.: Deploying man-in-the-middle attack on IoT devices connected to long range wide area networks (LoRaWAN). In: 8th IEEE International Smart Cities Conference, ISC2 2022 (2022)
13. Kaur, G., Gupta, S., Kaur, H.: Performance evaluation and optimization of long range IoT network using whale optimization algorithm. Cluster Comput. (2022)
14. Fachrizal, F.: Data transmission performance on the internet of thing (IoT) network using long range communication (LoRA). In: Proceedings of the 2nd International Conference on Computer Science and Engineering: The Effects of the Digital World After Pandemic (EDWAP), IC2SE 2021 (2021)
15. Chabi, A., et al.: A IoT system for vehicle tracking using long range wide area network. In: 2021 IEEE International Conference on Consumer Electronics-Taiwan, ICCE-TW 2021 (2021)
16. Wang, Z., Feng, L., Yao, S., Xie, K., Chen, Y.: Low-cost and long-range node-assisted WiFi backscatter communication for 5G-enabled IoT networks. Wirel. Commun. Mob. Comput. **2021** (2021)
17. Elhadi, S., Marzak, A., Sael, N.: Operating models of network protocols IoT: long-range protocols. In: Ben Ahmed, M., Rakıp Karas, İ, Santos, D., Sergeyeva, O., Boudhir, A.A. (eds.) SCA 2020. LNNS, vol. 183, pp. 1059–1070. Springer, Cham (2021). https://doi.org/10.1007/978-3-030-66840-2_81
18. Bahashwan, A., Anbar, M., Abdullah, N., Al-Hadhrami, T., Hanshi, S.: Review on common IoT communication technologies for both long-range network (LPWAN) and short-range network. Adv. Intell. Syst. Comput. **1188**, 341–353 (2021)
19. Yáñez-Casas, G., et al.: On the capacities and applications of IoT networks: LoRaWAN, LTEM, MQTT, NBIoT and Sigfox. Proc. CNIES **2021**(048), 345–349 (2021). https://www.researchgate.net/publication/357240615_On_the_capacities_and_applications_of_IoT_networks_LoRaWAN_LTEM_MQTT_NBIoT_and_Sigfox
20. Huang, C.C., Chien, Y.C., Zhang, J.C., Huang, N.F.: Reliable and delay tolerant transmission protocols for LPWAN IoT sensors. In: International Conference on Information Networking, vol. 2021-January, pp. 553–558 (2021)
21. Pham, V.D., Le, D.T., Kirichek, R.: Evaluation of routing protocols for multi-hop communication in LPWAN. In: NEW2AN/ruSMART -2020. LNCS, vol. 12525, pp. 255–266. Springer, Cham (2020). https://doi.org/10.1007/978-3-030-65726-0_23
22. Moons, B., Karaagac, A., Haxhibeqiri, J., Poorter, E., Hoebeke, J.: Using SCHC for an optimized protocol stack in multimodal LPWAN solutions. In: IEEE 5th World Forum on Internet of Things, WF-IoT 2019 - Conference Proceedings, pp. 430–435 (2019)
23. Kirichek, R., Kulik, V.: Long-range data transmission on flying ubiquitous sensor networks (FUSN) by using LPWAN protocols. In: Vishnevskiy, V.M., Samouylov, K.E., Kozyrev, D.V. (eds.) DCCN 2016. CCIS, vol. 678, pp. 442–453. Springer, Cham (2016). https://doi.org/10.1007/978-3-319-51917-3_39
24. El Maachi, S., Saadane, R., Wahbi, M., Chehri, A., Badaoui, A.: Vision of IoT, 5G and 6G data processing: applications in climate change mitigation. In: 2022 International Symposium on Intelligent Signal Processing and Communication Systems, ISPACS 2022 (2022)

25. Patel, S., Deshmukh, S.: UAV and IoT based micro UGV platform applications for forestry climate change and lunar space explorations. In: 5th IEEE International Conference on Advances in Science and Technology, ICAST 2022, pp. 564–568 (2022)
26. Singh, P., Sammanit, D., Shaw, R.N., Ghosh, A.: Comprehension of climate change with IoT-enabled CNN. In: Shaw, R.N., Das, S., Piuri, V., Bianchini, M. (eds.) Advanced Computing and Intelligent Technologies. LNEE, vol. 914, pp. 385–394. Springer, Singapore (2022). https://doi.org/10.1007/978-981-19-2980-9_30
27. Silva, R., Fava, M., Saraiva, A., Mendiondo, E., Cugnasca, C., Delbem, A.: A theoretical framework for multi-hazard risk mapping on agricultural areas considering artificial intelligence, IoT, and climate change scenarios †. Eng. Proc. 9(1) (2021)
28. Carrasquilla-Batista, A., Chacón-Rodríguez, A.: IAC-17.B5.1.2: a fuzzy logic controller with internet of things (IoT) capabilities and cots components for monitoring and mitigation of climate change effects on sensible tropical crops. In: Proceedings of the International Astronautical Congress, IAC, vol. 10, pp. 6469–6473 (2017)
29. Gonzalez, C., Espinosa, A., Ponte, D., Gibeaux, S.: Smart-IoT platform to monitor microclimate conditions in tropical regions. In: IOP Conference Series: Earth and Environmental Science, vol. 835 (2021)
30. Wang, E., Wang, F., Kumari, S., Yeh, J.H., Chen, C.M.: Intelligent monitor for typhoon in IoT system of smart city. J. Supercomput. 77(3), 3024–3043 (2021)
31. Hernandez-Alpizar, L., Carrasquilla-Batista, A., Sancho-Chavarria, L.: Monitoring adjustment based on current data of an IoT-COTS monitor for environmental chemical analysis. In: 2021 IEEE 12th Latin American Symposium on Circuits and Systems, LASCAS 2021 (2021)
32. Yuan, Z.L., Hua, Z.S., Chun, J.J.: Design of small automatic weather station monitoring system based on NB-IoT technology. Meteorol. Sci. Technol. 48(06), 816–822 (2020)
33. Ramírez-López, F., Yáñez-Casas, G., Casillas-Aviña, G., Hernández-Gómez, J., Mata-Rivera, M., Ramírez-Espinosa, S.: Simulation and implementation of an environmental monitoring system based on LPWAN/IoT. In: Mata-Rivera, M.F., Zagal-Flores, R., Barria-Huidobro, C. (eds.) WITCOM 2022. CCIS, vol. 1659, pp. 237–369. Springer, Cham (2022). https://doi.org/10.1007/978-3-031-18082-8_16
34. Chaduvula, K., Kranthi Kumar, K., Markapudi, B., Rathna Jyothi, C.: Design and implementation of IoT based flood alert monitoring system using microcontroller 8051. In: Materials Today: Proceedings, vol. 80, pp. 2840–2844 (2023)
35. Sultan, I., Banday, M.: Ultra-low power microcontroller architectures for the internet of things (IoT) devices. In: Proceedings of the 5th International Conference on Smart Systems and Inventive Technology, ICSSIT 2023, pp. 482–488 (2023)
36. Virat, A., Ashish, A., Patel, R., Dash, R.N.: Analysis and controlling of distribution transformer parameter using AVR microcontroller IoT system. In: Dash, R.N., Rathore, A.K., Khadkikar, V., Patel, R., Debnath, M. (eds.) Smart Technologies for Power and Green Energy. LNNS, vol. 443, pp. 267–280. Springer, Singapore (2023). https://doi.org/10.1007/978-981-19-2764-5_22
37. Ahmed, A., Elbhoty, M., Said, L., Madian, A.: IoT microchip AVR microcontroller's fuses and lock bits high voltage programmer. In: 2022 International Conference on Microelectronics, ICM 2022, pp. 197–200 (2022)
38. Yáñez-Casas, G.A., Medina, I., Hernández-Gómez, J.J., Orozco-del-Castillo, M.G., Couder-Castañeda, C., de-la-Rosa-Rabago, R.: High data rate efficiency improvement via variable length coding for LoRaWAN. In: Mata-Rivera, M.F., Zagal-Flores, R., Barria-Huidobro, C. (eds.) WITCOM 2020. CCIS, vol. 1280, pp. 97–115. Springer, Cham (2020). https://doi.org/10.1007/978-3-030-62554-2_8

39. Wang, C.X., et al.: Cellular architecture and key technologies for 5G wireless communication networks. IEEE Commun. Mag. **52**(2), 122–130 (2014)
40. Ahir, R.K., Chakraborty, B.: Pattern-based and context-aware electricity theft detection in smart grid. Sustain. Energy Grids Netw. 100833 (2022)
41. Junejo, A.K., Benkhelifa, F., Wong, B., Mccann, J.A.: LoRa-LiSK: a lightweight shared secret key generation scheme for LoRa networks. IEEE Internet Things J. **9**(6), 4110–4124 (2021)
42. Haider, A., Chatterjee, A.: Low-cost alternate EVM test for wireless receiver systems. In: VTS, pp. 255–260 (2005)
43. Zhao, Y., Ye, Z.: A low-cost GSM/GPRS based wireless home security system. IEEE Trans. Consum. Electron. **54**(2), 567–572 (2008)
44. Kildal, P.S., Glazunov, A.A., Carlsson, J., Majidzadeh, A.: Cost-effective measurement setups for testing wireless communication to vehicles in reverberation chambers and anechoic chambers. In: 2014 IEEE Conference on Antenna Measurements & Applications (CAMA), pp. 1–4. IEEE (2014)
45. International Telecommunication Union: Technical and operational aspects of Low Power Wide Area Networks for machine-type communication and the Internet of Things in frequency ranges harmonised for SRD operation. Technical report 1, International Telecommunication Union, Ginebra, Switzerland (2018)
46. Internet Engineering Task Force: Mission and Principles. Online (2022). https://www.ietf.org/about/mission/. Accessed 15 May 2022
47. Cirani, S., Ferrari, G., Picone, M., Veltri, L.: Internet of Things: Architectures, Protocols and Standards. Wiley (2018). https://books.google.com.mx/books?id=iERsDwAAQBAJ
48. Shuiguang, D., et al.: Dependent function embedding for distributed serverless edge computing. IEEE Trans. Parallel Distrib. Syst. **33**, 2346–2357 (2021)
49. Celebi, H.B., Pitarokoilis, A., Skoglund, M.: Wireless communication for the industrial IoT. In: Butun, I. (ed.) Industrial IoT, pp. 57–94. Springer, Cham (2020). https://doi.org/10.1007/978-3-030-42500-5_2
50. LoRa Alliance Corporate Bylaws: A technical overview of LoRa and LoRaWAN. Technical report 1, LoRa Alliance, Fermont, California, United States (2015)
51. Sigfox: Sigfox Technical Overview. Technical report 1, Sigfox, Labège, France (2021)
52. Global System for Mobile Association: LTE-M Deployment Guide to Basic Feature set Requirements. Technical report 1, GSMA, London, UK (2019)
53. Global System for Mobile Association: NB-IoT Deployment Guide to Basic Feature set Requirements. Technical report 1, GSMA, London, UK (2019)
54. ISA100 Wireless Compliance Institute: The Technology Behind the ISA100.11a Standard-An Exploration. Technical report 1, ISA100, London, UK (2021)
55. Shannon, C.E.: A mathematical theory of communication. Bell Syst. Tech. J. **27**(3), 379–423 (1948)
56. Oracle Corporation: Open Systems Interconnection (OSI) Reference Model. Online (2010). https://docs.oracle.com/cd/E19504-01/802-5886/intro-45828/index.html. Accessed 15 May 2023
57. Tanenbaum, A.S.: Computer Networks. Pearson Education India (2003)
58. Dawoud, D., Dawoud, P.: Serial Communication Protocols and Standards: RS232/485, UART/USART, SPI, USB, INSTEON, Wi-Fi and WiMAX. River Publishers Series in Communications Series, River Publishers (2020). https://books.google.com.mx/books?id=nj50zQEACAAJ

59. Stinson, D.: Cryptography: Theory and Practice, 3rd edn. Discrete Mathematics and Its Applications. CRC Press (2005). https://books.google.com.mx/books?id=FAPLBQAAQBAJ
60. Microchip Technology Inc.®: AVR MCUs® (2021). https://www.microchip.com/en-us/products/microcontrollers-and-microprocessors/8-bit-mcus/avr-mcus#. Online. Accessed May 2022
61. Schmidt, T.: CRC Generating and Checking. Microchip Technology Inc. (2021). https://ww1.microchip.com/downloads/en/AppNotes/00730a.pdf
62. Williams, R.N.: A Painless Guide to CRC Error Detection Algorithms (1993). https://ceng2.ktu.edu.tr/~cevhers/ders_materyal/bil311_bilgisayar_mimarisi/supplementary_docs/crc_algorithms.pdf
63. International Telecommunication Union: Technical and operational aspects of low-power wide-area networks for machine-type communication and the Internetof Things in frequency ranges harmonised for SRD operation. Technical report. SM.2423-0, International Telecommunication Union, Ginebra, Switzerland (2018)
64. Internet Engineering Task Force (IETF): Low-Power Wide Area Network (LPWAN) Overview. Technical report, Internet Engineering Task Force (IETF), Dublin, Ireland (2018). https://datatracker.ietf.org/doc/html/rfc8376
65. Yuksel, M.E., Fidan, H.: Energy-aware system design for batteryless LPWAN devices in IoT applications. Ad Hoc Netw. **122**, 102625 (2021)
66. Atmel Corp.: ATmega328P 8-bit AVR Microcontroller with 32K Bytes In-System. Atmel Corp., California, United States, 1st edn. (2015)
67. National Semiconductor: CD4051BM/CD4051BC Single 8-Channel AnalogMultiplexer/Demultiplexer Module. National Semiconductor, Santa Clara, United States, 1st edn. (2013)
68. Allegro MicroSystems: Fully integrated, hall effect-based linear current sensor. Allegro MicroSystems, New Hampshire, United States, 60950-1-03 edn. (2003)
69. Hitachi: Dot Matrix Liquid Crystal Display Controller/Driver. Hitachi, Tokyo, Japan, hd44780u (lcd-ii) edn. (1998)
70. Chipcon Products.: Low-Cost Low-Power Sub-1GHz RF Transceiver. Texas Instrument., Texas, United States, 6th edn. (2015)
71. Bosch: BMP180 Digital Pressure Sensor. Bosch, Gerlingen, Germany, 2nd edn. (2013)
72. Electronics, M.: DHT11 Humidity and Temperature Sensor, 1st edn. Mouser Electronics, Mansfield, Texas, United States (2019)
73. VAISALA: Yl-83 Rain Detector. VAISALA, Eindhoven, Netherlands, b01001en-b edn. (2015)
74. Keyestudio : GY-ML8511 Ultraviolet Sensor Module. Keyestudio, Ischia, Italy, 1st edn. (2013)
75. DFRobot: Wind speed sensor. Online (2022). https://wiki.dfrobot.com/Wind_Speed_Sensor_Voltage_Type_0-5V_SKU_SEN0170. Accessed 15 May 2022
76. Pololu: MQ-2 Semiconductor Sensor for Combustible Gas. Pololu, Las Vegas, United States, 1st edn. (2013)
77. Pololu: MQ-3 Semiconductor Sensor for Alcohol. Pololu, Las Vegas, United States, 1st edn. (2013)
78. Pololu: MQ-4 Semiconductor Sensor for Combustible Gas. Pololu, Las Vegas, United States, 1st edn. (2013)
79. Hanwei Electronics Co., LTD: MQ-5 Gas sensor. Hanwei Electronics Co., LTD, Beijing, China, 1st edn. (2015)
80. Pololu: MQ-6 Semiconductor Sensor for Combustible Gas. Pololu, Las Vegas, United States, 1st edn. (2013)

81. Pololu: MQ-7 Semiconductor Sensor for Combustible Gas. Pololu, Las Vegas, United States, 1st edn. (2013)
82. Hanwei Electronics Co., LTD: MQ-8 Gas sensor. Hanwei Electronics Co., LTD, Beijing, China, 1st edn. (2015)
83. Pololu: MQ-9 Semiconductor Sensor for Combustible Gas. Pololu, Las Vegas, United States, 1st edn. (2013)
84. Semiconductors, P.: AN10216-01 I2C Bus. Phillips Semiconductors, Eindhoven, Netherlands, an10216 edn. (2003)
85. Ibrahim, D.: PIC Microcontroller Projects in C: Basic to Advanced. Elsevier Science (2014). https://books.google.com.mx/books?id=xQajAgAAQBAJ
86. International Union of Telecommunications: Short-range radiocommunicationdevices measurements. Technical report, International Union of Telecommunications, Ginebra, Switzerland (2010)
87. Mackenzie, C.E.: Coded Character Sets, History and Development. Wiley (1980)
88. MathWorks América Latina: Comprobar la redundancia cíclica. Online (2019). https://la.mathworks.com/help/matlab/matlab_prog/perform-cyclic-redu ndancy-check.html

Performance Analysis of Variable Packet Transmission Policies in Wireless Sensor Networks

Isaac Villalobos[1], Mario E. Rivero-Angeles[2(⊠)], and Izlian Y. Orea-Flores[3]

[1] Massachusetts Institute of Technology, Cambridge, MA 02139, USA
villa200@mit.edu
[2] Instituto Politécnico Nacional—(CIC-IPN), 07738 Mexico City, Mexico
mriveroa@ipn.mx
[3] Instituto Politécnico Nacional—(UPIITA-IPN), 07738 Mexico City, Mexico
iorea@ipn.mx

Abstract. Wireless sensor networks are used extensively to monitor different environments and physical variables. However, in many cases, there are many nodes in the same region and given its distributed nature, these networks can suffer from corrupted data if too many transmissions occur at once. Therefore, it is important to maximize the number of successful transmissions while also minimizing the amount of energy used to transmit this data. The main component of wireless sensor networks that impacts these variables is the transmission probability. Thus, it follows that to improve successful transmission probability and to reduce energy consumption, an adequate transmission probability value should be selected. In particular, we propose the use of a transmission probability that decrease as the energy consumption increases in such a way as to reduce energy consumption towards the end of the system lifetime but that still allow the reporting of the events, i.e., packet transmissions.

To this end we propose and evaluate the system performance in terms of average energy consumption and successful packet transmission probability using different mathematical functions for the transmission probability that decrease as the energy consumption increases but do not decrease to zero, allowing sporadic transmissions towards the end of the system operation and compare them to the case of using a fix value.

Keywords: Wireless Sensor Networks · transmission probability · Energy consumption · Lifetime

1 Introduction

A wireless sensor network (WSN) is a network of infrastructure-less sensors that collect information about the surrounding system, physical, or environmental conditions [2]. The main purpose of wireless sensor networks is to deploy them across a wide area in order to retrieve specific information from each individual sensor node. The sensor nodes collect information from their designated environments, process the readings, and

M. F. Mata-Rivera et al. (Eds.): WITCOM 2023, CCIS 1906, pp. 367–379, 2023.
https://doi.org/10.1007/978-3-031-45316-8_23

then transmit the data to a central location which we will call the sink node. Wireless sensor networks are widely used in the world around us. Their current and future usage impacts many industries and disciplines. Creating more efficient WSN's and optimizing their performance would thus be a great benefit for a variety of sectors. Currently, the most popular use of WSN's is in environmental, flora & fauna, industrial, urban, military, and health applications [3]. While WSN's can be applied to almost any industry, three of the most promising sectors for advancement in the use of WSN's include military, environmental, and health applications. The military domain implemented some of the first uses of WSN's and is considered to have motivated the rise of WSN research. One of these initial applications was developed in the 90's and was known as Smart Dust [4]. This was a research effort to develop very small sensor nodes that were capable of spying and surveillance. Nowadays, the current applications of WSN's in the military are mainly combat monitoring, battlefield surveillance, and intruder detection. In the healthcare industry, WSN's are being paired with advanced medical sensors to monitor patients within a healthcare facility, hospital, or their homes. These three applications are classified as patient wearable monitoring, home assisting systems, and hospital patient monitoring. The use of WSN's in health is still relatively new meaning that the potential for growth is very promising. Environmental monitoring demands continuous reading of requested conditions. WSN's can help with monitoring these conditions in hostile or remote areas. Currently the main environmental applications of WSN's include helping with water monitoring, air monitoring, and emergency alerting. Because of their widespread use, the optimization of WSN's is in the interest of many different domains [4].

Because these networks end up processing a large amount of data, it is important to optimize them for data transmission and energy efficiency. Optimizing for data transmission means that the data packets from the sensor nodes are accurately transmitted and not corrupted in the process. We classify a successful transmission as an exit, that is one sensor node transmitting to the sink node at a given time. When more than one sensor node transmits at a given time, this causes a collision in the transmission channel and corrupts the data packets. On top of making sure the system successfully transmits data, it is also important that it be relatively energy efficient. Since most sensor nodes are battery powered and node locations are extremely variable, changing/charging these batteries is often rather complicated. Therefore, it is important to consume energy efficiently to limit the amount of sensor nodes losing power and thus having to be manually recharged. This energy consumption mainly depends on the sensor node's operations like communication and data processing. Energy efficiency is especially important when trying to scale the network to a larger region/sample size. We will calculate the energy efficiency of the WSN by measuring the lifetime of the system, that is, the number of timesteps that sensor nodes could transmit before the total energy in the system runs out. One variable that impacts both data transmission and lifetime is the transmission probability which we will refer to as τ. Specifically, we consider a slotted channel where nodes can only transmit at the beginning of the time slot. As such, nodes have to transmit with probability τ, selecting an adequate value in order to reduce both packet collisions and empty time slots. Indeed, if τ is too high for the number of nodes attempting a packet transmission, it can generate many collisions, preventing the successfully data transmissions while consuming a lot of energy in the system. On the contrary, it it is too low, many time slots would be unused and data is not conveyed to the sink node, directly affecting the reporting capabilities of the network. An exit is classified as only one node transmitting at a given time so the value of τ must be made to maximize the probability of only one node transmitting. Thus, our goal is to find a τ value or equation that will have the most exits during the lifetime of the WSN.

In the literature, it is common to consider a fix value of τ [1], usually selected according to the number of nodes in the system mainly due to its easy implementation. However, a fix transmission probability may drain the system energy when the number of nodes changes, due to malfunctions or nodes running out of energy. Also, this fix scheme does not consider the case that towards the end of the system lifetime, nodes continue to consume energy at the same rate than at the beginning of the system operation. In contrast, we propose to use an equation that depends on the residual energy of the system such that it reduces packet transmissions as energy is running low in order to extend the system lifetime, giving the opportunity to replace the batteries or replenish the area with new nodes before total energy depletion, even if data reporting its degraded but not completely stopped. We propose different mathematical expressions to calculate the value of τ to study their effects and choose the most appropriate scheme, comparing those to the fixed strategy.

A variable τ has been proposed before [1, 5], such that it adapts to the number of nodes in the system, but these schemes did not consider the residual energy of the system, but only the system throughput. Other works have focues on energy efficient transmissions schemes. For instance, in [6], the authors propose a transmission scheme to reduce energy consumption by only allowing the nodes with an adequate channel condition, avoiding transmissions that would be highly compromised by errors in the channel. In [7], the authors propose a transmission scheme in order to balance the load in the system effectively extending the system lifetime. Similarly, in [8], the authors propose a load balancing scheme but allowing direct transmissions to the sink, reducing the relay packet reception at certain nodes. Also, in [8], the authors propose a ring-based topology and calculate the transmission probability according to the sink node placement in realtion to the rings around it. In these works, the energy level in the system is not explicitly used to calculate the transmission probability.

Other works have proposed different methods to calculate the transmission probability, such as [10], where the authors propose an optimization scheme using a bio-inspired heuristic algorithm based on ant colonies. However, the optimization scheme requires much more energy and resources than the use of a direct mathematical expression to calculate τ. In [11], the authors propose a game theory-based optimization algorithm to calculate the transmission probability depending on the energy level of the nodes and the importance of their packets when energy harvesting capacities are enabled. In [12] a game theoretic MAC protocol is proposed using auto degressive backoff mechanisms. Again, the optimization problem requires much more procedures, memory and energy compared to a simple mathematical expression as in our proposal.

Other approaches to optimization include using a clustered-based WSN and varying the transmission probability of the system based on the number of sensor nodes [1]. While many wireless sensor networks implement cluster-based architecture in their design, (i.e., sensors in the same region transmit to a cluster node and then the cluster nodes transmit to the sink node) we did not include cluster-based wireless sensor networks in our experiment design. Instead, we analyzed a system where all the sensor nodes in the WSN transmit directly to the sink node. Thus, in the lifecycle of our WSN, sensor nodes have two states that they can be in. They can either be actively transmitting data to the sink node, or they can be idle. We created a simulation of this WSN in python3. It takes in a set number of sensor nodes and runs the network with a value of τ set by the user. The simulation then counts exits and lifetime until the energy of the system runs out.

The rest of the paper is organized as follows: We first describe the basic system operation in Sect. 2. In Sect. 3 we describe a WSN using a fix packet transmission probability. Then, in Sect. 4 we explain the different mathematical expressions to calculate a variable value fo the packet transmission probability that depends on the residual energy of the system and provide performance metrics using the equations with better results in terms of the number of successful packet transmissions. We end the paper with the main conclusions of our work.

2 System Model

2.1 Setting up the Model

In this section we describe the process for simulating the WSN in python3. The simulation requires the initial values of the following variables: number of nodes in the system (N), initial total energy per node (E_0), the total system energy I, the energy use of a node transmitting (E_x), and the energy use of a node being idle (E_i). E_0 was set to 50 energy units which can be converted to joules depending on the specific capabilities of the nodes. Specifically, we normalized the energy consumption such that the transmission of a packet consumes 1 energy unit, i.e., $E_x = 1$ energy unit. As such, when a commercial node is used and depending on the packet size, the energy required to transmit that packet is equivalent to 1 energy unit in our model. Since E is the total system energy, we calculated this as $E = (NxE_0)$ which ends up being 500 energy units with our given inputs. E_i was set as 0.01 energy units.

We use the Slotted ALOHA (S-ALOHA) random access protocol to transmit the packets from the nodes to the sink. The reason for this is its simplicity and efficiency in the sense that a node simply waits for the beginning of the time slot to transit without the need to sense the channel before (as in Carrier Sense Multiple Access {CSMA} schemes), which in turns, also reduces energy consumption compared to Carrier Sense-based protocols. Additionally, the different mathematical expressions used for setting the value of τ in the S-ALOHA protocol, can also be used in CSMA-based protocols.

The system starts with energy E, as stated above, and the simulation ends when the energy in the system is 0. In every time slot, the N nodes decide, with probability τ, if they transmit a packet or not, consuming in that time slot a certain amount of energy given by the number of transmissions.

2.2 Implementing Our Design

Our model is composed by several functions. Specifically, we use five different functions, two of which being helper functions. The helper functions included a function that calculates the probability of n nodes transmitting, P(n), and one that calculates the new system energy when n nodes transmit. The probability function code was implanted in the following way:

```
Def Probability(
Input: N, n, tau
Output: Returns P, the probability of n nodes transmit-
ting.
```

Runs a for-loop through the range [0, n], adding P(n) to P for each iteration:

$$P(n) = (C_n^N \times \tau^n \times (1 - \tau)^{N-n}) \tag{1}$$

)

Equation (1) describes the probability of n nodes transmitting at a time slot.. Thus, the equation gives the probability of n nodes transmitting and (N-n) nodes remaining idle. The function that calculates the new system energy was executed as follows:

```
Def Calc_New_Energy(
Input: E_t, n
Output: Returns a changed E_t
```

Calculates the change of energy (ΔE) and subtracts this value from the system energy E_t:

$$\Delta E = (E_x \times n) + (N - n) \times E_i \tag{2}$$

)

Equation (2) represents the change in energy of the system when n nodes transmit and (N-n) nodes remain idle. The main function of the program is described next. It ran the simulation of nodes sensors transmitting until no energy remained. It was applied as such:

```
Def Run_Simulation(
Input: E_t, N, sim_counter, tau, exits
Output: Returns the number of successful exits and the
lifetime of a simulated WSN
```
Creates U, a uniform random variable in between 0 and 1.
The function then runs through a for-loop in the range
[0, N], comparing U with Probability(n). If:
U > Probability(N,n-1,tau) and U ≤ Probability(N,n,tau),
then n is the number of node sensors that transmitted at
that given time step. Sim_counter, which represents the
number of timesteps/lifetime is thus incremented by one.
If n=1, then exits is thus incremented by one. Then, the
energy of the system is updated by setting:
E_t = Calc_New_Energy(E_t, n)
If this energy is ≤ 0, then exits and sim_counter is returned, otherwise, the function is recursively called until the base case is completed.

This is the main function used in our WSN models. It successfully simulates an active WSN and returns the number of successful transmissions (in the code referred also as exits, we use this term interchangeably in the rest of the manuscript) and lifetime given a certain τ value. The rest of the functions in the program are used to gather more data on the simulations. There is a function called run_trials which runs the simulation 1000 times and finds the average values returned. Another function called tau_change changes the value of tau for different simulations. The values returned in the end are all plotted through Matplotlib and are displayed in the following sections.

3 Simulating a WSN with a Fixed Tau Value

For these simulation results, we fixed the value of τ on various model WSN's. We graphed the performance in terms of successful packet transmissions, system lifetime, and successful transmissions/lifetime for WSN's with a number of sensor nodes in the range [1, 10]. We tested all the values of τ in the range (0,1] with a step of 0.05. The following graphs represent our findings:

The total amount of successful exits based on simulations of WSN's with fixed values of τ and a set N number of nodes is depicted in Fig. 1. Based on this figure we can see that the number of successful exits increases inversely with N and has a somewhat inverse relationship to τ. The inverse correlation with N is due to the fact that when there are more nodes in the system, there's a greater chance for two or more nodes to transmit during the same timestep, causing a collision and losing data. The correlation with τ shows that a lower transmission probability will lead to the greatest number of successful transmissions in a WSN. The outliers in this plot are the points associated with N = 1. This can be easily explained because if there is only one sensor node in the system, a τ = 1 will make sure the node transmits every timeslot, leading to a higher number of successful exits. Since we need to be able to compare simulations, we will use a WSN model with 10 nodes (N = 10) as our standard of comparison. The performance of different values of τ on this standard model is depicted in Fig. 2. The value of τ that led to the highest number of successful exits was a value of 0.05. The number of successful exits calculated from this was 267. While this value might produce the highest number of successful exits, we still must compare its energy efficiency.

Performance of Transmission Probabilities

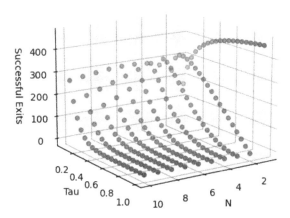

Fig. 1. Relationship between τ, N, and the Exits of simulated WSN's.

The lifetime of our simulations is depicted in Fig. 3. A higher lifetime means that a WSN network can run for longer before completely losing energy. Here we can see that the highest lifetime is a WSN with N = 1 and Tau = 0.05. In general, it seems that a higher Tau value and a higher N correlate to a lower lifetime in our simulated WSNs. However, the lifetime value of a WSN has no practical interest if that WSN cannot successfully transmit data. We decided to analyze the performance of the standard model. From N = 10, the model with the highest lifetime was τ = 0.05. This model ran for 840 time slots. While this may seem like enough evidence to suggest that a Tau value of 0.05 is the most optimal for a WSN, we wanted to further investigate. In order to find the balance between optimizing lifetime and optimizing successful transmissions, we decided to look at the ratio between exits and lifetime.

The ratio between exits and lifetime, Exits/Lifetime, and shows the percentage of successful exits in the WSN throughout the lifetime of the system. A higher Exits/Lifetime means that the WSN has a higher percentage of successfully transmitting data during a timestep. The model with the highest Exits/Lifetime would therefore theoretically be the most efficient WSN. Figure 4 shows the Exits/Lifetime percentages that we calculated for different WSN models. The model N = 1 is once again an outlier since there is only one sensor node in the system. Looking at the standard model, the highest Exits/Lifetime was with τ = 0.1 with a Exits/Lifetime value of 0.3882. This would mean that when τ = 0.1 the system achieves its best performance. However, we observe that this is not the case. Indeed, even though the system achieves an adequate performance with a value

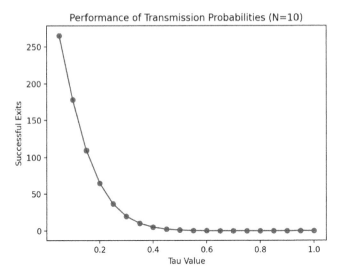

Fig. 2. Successful Exits vs τ on a WSN with 10 sensor nodes.

Performance of Transmission Probabilities

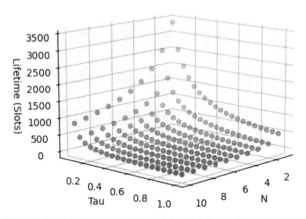

Fig. 3. Relationship between τ, N, and the Lifetime of simulated WSN's.

of τ = 0.1 in terms of the ratio Exits/Lifetime, this relation Exits/Lifetime is unreliable since the lifetime for different settings is not consistent. This is because when τ = 0.1 the network has a relatively smaller lifetime than when τ = 0.05 but a closer successful exits value, then it appears that τ = 0.1 is the best value. This is not the case though, instead τ = 0.1 just ran out of battery quicker. Thus, from our data, for a standard WSN, a fixed τ value of 0.05 is a better choise for successful transmission probability and energy efficiency.

Performance of Transmission Probabilities

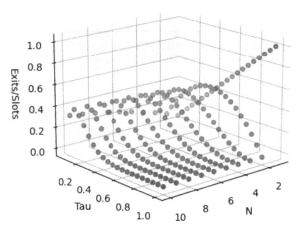

Fig. 4. 3D Relationship between τ, N, and the Exits/Slots percentage for simulated WSN's.

4 WSN with Variable Transmission Probability

After testing the performance of a fixed values of the transmission probability, we propose the use of a variable transmission probability that depends on the residual energy of the system in such a way as to increase the system lifetime by reducing the packet transmissions when the energy left is low, allowing additional time to replace batteries or replenish the nodes in the area of interest. To this end, we propose and analyze the system performance using 16 equations that would produce a tau value based on the current energy of the system. The table containing the equations and their corresponding number of successful transmissions is listed below.

While each of these equations have varying levels of performance, none of them exceed the number of successful exits produced from τ = 0.05 (267). This does not imply that a fixed value of τ produces a better system performance since the other performance parameter is the system lifetime. In this regard, it is expected to have a higher successful packet transmissions with a fixed transmission probability since it is not sensitive to the energy consumption while the proposed variable schemes drastically reduce the packet transmissions as the system evolves and energy is consumed. However, in this work we focus on the total packet transmissions using the variable value of τ and leave for a future work the overall system performance considering the system lifetime as an additional performance parameter. Due to the fact that we propose many schemes for the selection of τ, for illustrative purposes we only show the two best performing equations of τ, that correspond to Eq. 5 and Eq. 3.

Table 1. Shows tau equations with X being the current system energy. Also shows the number of successful exits for each equation on our simulation.

Equations Of Tau		Total Exits (N=10)
|(X-10)cos(10X)|	(/500 to Normalize)	62
(X-10)(X mod 1)	(/500 to Normalize)	68
|(X-10)^2 cos(10X)| / 100	(/2400 to Normalize)	89
exp(-X) sin(X/10)		3
exp(-X/100) |sin(X)|		160
arctan(X-10) cos(5X) / 1.5		10
log(-X+ Total E) (|cos(X)| /3)		12
log(-X+ Total E) (X mod 1 /3)		16
log(-X+ Total E) (|cos(10X)| /3)		11
log-cauchy(mu=1, sigma=1)		17
log-cauchy(mu=1, sigma=1) |cos(5X)|		13
log-cauchy(mu=1, sigma=5)		21
log-cauchy(mu=1, sigma=5) |cos(X)|		15
log-cauchy(mu=0, sigma=5)		18
log-cauchy(mu=0, sigma=5) |cos(X)|		13
log-cauchy(mu=0, sigma=5) (X mod 1)		11

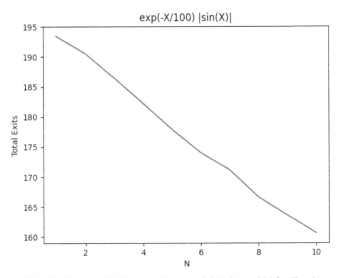

Fig. 5. Relationship between Successful Exits and N for Eq. 4.

Equation 5 entails the highest packet transmissions out of the 16 devised equations of τ. In the standard model it produced the highest number successful exits (Excluding fixed tau findings). Figure 5 shows the performance of Eq. 5 on different WSN models.

We can see that the number of exits decreases linearly as the number of sensor nodes increases in the WSN. This is something that could be looked into as changing this relationship could have the potential to make Eq. 5 a much higher performing equation of τ. Next, we will look at Eq. 3.

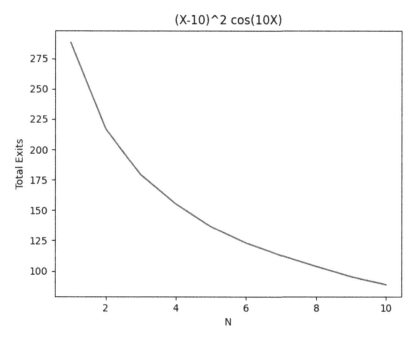

Fig. 6. Relationship between Successful Exits and N for Eq. 5.

Equation 3 had the second highest number of successful exits. Figure 6 displays the graph of the performance of this equation on several models. We see that the number of exits decreases nearly exponentially as the number of sensor nodes increases. This is a downside as the equation is hard to scale for WSN's with a greater number of sensor nodes. Because of this relationship it seems that Eq. 5 has much better chance of being edited and scaled for a larger WSN.

5   Conclusions

This work focuses on the study of Wireless Sensor Networks and selecting an adequate value of τ to increase their energy efficiency and successful data transmission probability. We tested fixed values and several equations of τ with respect to the energy of the system. To analyze the performance of these values, we used metrics such as number of successful exits, lifetime, and exits over slots ratio. From the results derived in this work, we've seen that a fixed tau value of 0.05 achieves the best performance for a WSN in terms of the number of successful packet transmissions. However, we were only able to analyze WSN's with a maximum amount of ten sensor nodes due to computing limits in processing speed. Also, it is expected that a fix value of τ would perform the same number of transmissions irrespective to the residual energy in the system. As such, the use of a variable value of τ is not intended to work for any WSN, since in many cases, the number of transmissions cannot be decreased in benefit of prolonging the system lifetime. For the applications where the network can reduce energy by drastically reducing the packet transmissions, this work may provide a general guide to select the value of τ. Future research could look into optimizing our code in order to analyze the performance of WSN's with a higher number of sensor nodes in the system and study the system lifetime using the proposed mathematical expressions. It would also be interesting to research the performance of equations of tau that have respect to N, the number of sensor nodes in the system as opposed to the current system energy.

Acknowledgements. This work has been partially supported by the MIT International Science and Technology Initiatives (MISTI) and by Instituto Politécnico Nacional.

Conflicts of Interest. The authors declare no conflict of interest.

References

1. Romo Montiel, E., Rivero-Angeles, M.E., Rubino, G., Molina-Lozano, H., Menchaca-Mendez, R., Menchaca-Mendez, R.: Performance analysis of cluster formation in wireless sensor networks Sensors, Special Issue: Smart Communication Protocols and Algorithms for Sensor Networks 17(12:2902), 1–33 (Dic. 2017). ISSN: 1424-8220. https://doi.org/10.3390/s17122902
2. Agarwal, T.: Wireless Sensor Network Architecture : Types, working & its applications. ElProCus (2021, January 25). Retrieved 25 August 2022, from https://www.elprocus.com/architecture-of-wireless-sensor-network-and-applications/#:~:text=The%20wireless%20sensor%20network%20architecture,%2C%20vibration%2C%20sound%2C%20etc
3. Applications of wireless sensor networks. Encyclopedia. (n.d.). Retrieved 25 August 2022, from https://encyclopedia.pub/entry/17294
4. Warneke, B., Last, M., Liebowitz, B., Pister, K.S.: Smart dust: communicating with a cubic-millimeter computer. Computer 34, 44–51 (2001)
5. Olivos-Castillo, I.C., Menchaca-Mendez, R., Menchaca-Mendez, R., Carvalho, M., Rivero-Angeles, M.E.: An Optimal greedy algorithm for the single access contention resolution problem. IEEE Access 7(1), 28452–28463 (Dic. 2019)

6. Phan, C.V., Park, Y., Choi, H.H., Cho, J., Ki, J.G.: An energy-efficient transmission strategy for wireless sensor networr's. In: IEEE Transactions on Consumer Electronics, vol. 56, no. 2, pp. 597–605 (May 2010). https://doi.org/10.1109/TCE.2010.5505976

7. Zhang, W., Zhang, Z., Chao, H.-C., Liu, Y., Zhang, P.: System-level energy balance for maximizing network lifetime in WSNs. IEEE Access **5**, 20046–20057 (2017). https://doi.org/10.1109/ACCESS.2017.2759093

8. Zhang, H., Shen, H., Tan, Y.: Optimal energy balanced data gathering in wireless sensor networks. 2007 IEEE International Parallel and Distributed Processing Symposium, pp. 1–10. Long Beach, CA, USA (2007). https://doi.org/10.1109/IPDPS.2007.370248

9. Azad, A.K.M., Kamruzzaman, J.: Energy-Balanced Transmission Policies for Wireless Sensor Networks. IEEE Trans. Mob. Comput. **10**(7), 927–940 (2011). https://doi.org/10.1109/TMC.2010.238. July

10. Liu, X.: A transmission scheme for wireless sensor networks using ant colony optimization with unconventional characteristics. IEEE Commun. Lett. **18**(7), 1214–1217 (2014). https://doi.org/10.1109/LCOMM.2014.2317789. July

11. Michelusi, N., Zorzi, M.: Optimal random multiaccess in energy harvesting Wireless Sensor Networks. In: 2013 IEEE International Conference on Communications Workshops (ICC), pp. 463–468. Budapest, Hungary (2013). https://doi.org/10.1109/ICCW.2013.6649278

12. Zhao, L., Zhang, H., Zhang, J.: Using incompletely cooperative game theory in wireless sensor networks. In: 2008 IEEE Wireless Communications and Networking Conference, pp. 1483–1488. Las Vegas, NV, USA (2008). https://doi.org/10.1109/WCNC.2008.266

About a Sentiment Analysis Technique on Twitter and Its Application to Regional Tourism in Quintana Roo

Osuna-Galan Ismael[(⊠)], Perez-Pimentel Yolanda, and León-Borges Jose Antonio

División de Ciencias, Ingeniería y Tecnología, Universidad Autónoma del Estado de Quintana Roo, Campus Cancún, Av. Chetumal SM 260, Cancún, México
ismael.osuna@uqroo.edu.mx

Abstract. Sentiment analysis aims to extract general information from texts and understand the opinion, attitude, or emotion of an individual or group of people towards a specific topic. Currently, a source of information used is the messages published on Twitter, which offer possibilities of great interest to evaluate the currents of opinion disseminated through this social network.

However, the enormous volumes of text require tools capable of automatically processing these messages without losing reliability. This article describes a technique to address this problem. This technique uses a variant of a Bi-GRU, a recurrent neural network (RNN) that promises to highlight local and global contextual features of tweets to increase the accuracy of classifying opinions in that social network. Experiments show better performance in tweet analysis, improving accuracy, recall, f-score, and accuracy parameters than traditional techniques. Finally, we identify the advantages and limitations of the system for its application to research on "Pueblos Mágicos" tourism in Quintana Roo.

Keywords: Sentiment analysis · Twitter · Bi-Gru · Temporal CNN · Tourism

1 Introduction

According to data from the Mexican Ministry of Tourism (SECTUR), destinations such as Cancun-Riviera Maya and Mexico City concentrate 58.1% of international tourists in the country, leading to a lack of inclusion in the development of many potential tourist destinations.

In terms of air transportation, the situation is similar. Of the 25 million passengers (about the population of Texas) who arrived on international flights in 2019, 6 destinations concentrated 92.6% of passengers: Mexico City, Cancun, Guadalajara, Monterrey, Tijuana, and Los Cabos. Likewise, it will be necessary to strengthen the sources of information that feed the statistical and geographic systems to promote tourism development. An example of this is the case of Mexican program called "Pueblos Mágicos", where it is necessary to apply essential changes in this matter in the face of the challenges of a more competitive market. At the end of 2018, only 27% of the towns with this denomination have partial statistical information on tourist activity, making it impossible to measure tourism's actual impact in these destinations more than 17 years after its operation.

In this way, the priority objectives of the Tourism Sector Program 2020–2024 (PRO-SECTUR 2020–2024) involve social, ethical, and economic aspects aimed at promoting tourism as a right that includes all sectors of the population, especially the most vulnerable, so that tourism activity permeates all regions, destinations, and communities, as a tool for integration and social reconciliation that generates well-being conditions for society.

One of the strategies seeks to promote the strengthening of statistical and geographic information systems to promote the development of tourism. Moreover, among its specific actions are:

1. Incorporate new applications to improve the operation of the National Statistical Information System of the Tourism Sector of Mexico.
2. Promote the adoption of new technological developments that facilitate the collection, processing, and dissemination of tourist statistical and geographic information.
3. Strengthen the use and generation of tourist statistical information or information related to the sector generated by companies or international organizations for the integral development of tourism.

Efforts must be directed so that the benefits of tourism are equitable throughout the value chain while promoting the conservation of uses customs, territories, biodiversity, identity, culture, language, and legacy of the peoples. In this way, the challenge is to expand the information infrastructure of the "Pueblos Mágicos" under a model focused on the visitor and not on the infrastructure.

In Quintana Roo, the Sustainable Tourism Development Master Plan was developed, which, in addition to promoting tourism, seeks that each action and strategy be carried out based on sustainability, protecting natural, archaeological, and cultural resources. Through a comprehensive vision of management that involves the conception of tourism for development, all the edges must be analyzed to identify areas for improvement and good practices and ensure the generation of information supporting decision-making to formulate better policies from local government to federal cabinets.

Understanding and analyzing human emotions has always been a challenge for many areas of study. However, in the digital age and with the explosion of social media, it has become possible to harness vast amounts of user-generated textual data to extract valuable information about their feelings and attitudes.

Sentiment analysis is a discipline that uses techniques and algorithms to identify, quantify and categorize the emotions expressed in a text. By providing deep insight into people's opinions and perceptions, this discipline offers support for decision-making, product, and service improvement, and understanding social dynamics. In this sense, sentiment analysis has become a fundamental component in today's world, where users' voice is expressed through texts on social networks, reviews, and online comments. Sentiment analysis has various applications in various fields, from market research to online reputation management.

Sentiment analysis was applied to social networks as they began to gain popularity in the early 2000s. Much research explored different ideas for analyzing the emotions and opinions expressed in these digital environments. One of the first significant social media sentiment analysis studies was conducted in 2002 when Pang and Lee [1] introduced a machine learning-based approach to classifying sentiment from movie reviews on the IMDb platform.

In summary, social media sentiment analysis has been applied since the early 2000s, with an increasing focus on Twitter and other popular platforms. Over the years, it has evolved and become more sophisticated, allowing for a deeper understanding of online emotions and opinions.

As social media grew and evolved, interest in sentiment analysis intensified. Twitter became a significant data source due to its text-based nature and many active users. Since 2006, numerous studies ([2–4]) have been carried out, and specific methods have been developed to analyze sentiment in tweets. Twitter sentiment analysis can help identify emerging trends, topics of interest, or shifts in public opinion and can be helpful for strategic planning, product development, and decision-making. With the advancement of technology and the development of more sophisticated algorithms, social media sentiment analysis has become more accurate and effective. Figure 1 shows the main idea of the sentiment analysis.

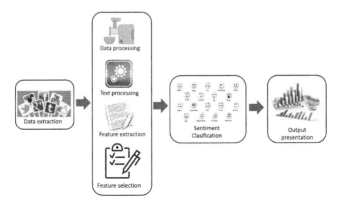

Fig. 1. Steps for the sentiment analysis in social networks.

One of the techniques applied in sentiment analysis is the RNN (Recurrent Neural Network), a type of artificial neural network architecture designed to process and model sequential data or with temporal dependencies. Unlike conventional neural networks, which are designed to process data independently of each other, RNNs can maintain and update internal states as they process each element of a sequence. The GRU (Gated Recurrent Unit) is a LSTM (Long Short-Term Memory) neural network variant. Both were developed to overcome the problem of gradient fading or bursting in standard RNNs. Gradient fading or bursting occurs when gradients (the magnitudes used to adjust the network weights) become small or large as they propagate back through the network layers, hindering learning overall and affecting network performance [5].

The GRU addresses this problem by using gate units to control the flow of information on the network. These gate units help the network decide what information should be retained and what information should be discarded at each step. The GRU has two types of gate units: the update gate and the reset gate. The update gate determines which part of the past information should be kept and which part should be forgotten. The reset gate controls how old information is combined with new incoming information.

Since then, the GRU method has become a widely used tool in natural language processing and has been successfully applied in various tasks, including sentiment analysis, text generation, and other applications related to sequential data processing. Notably, the GRU architecture is an improvement over traditional RNNs, and its introduction in 2014 has been a significant milestone in machine learning and natural language processing. Since then, there have been numerous advances and refinements in GRUs, and a wide range of applications in industry and research use GRU architecture [6].

Temporal Convolutional Networks (TCN) are a variant of Convolutional Neural Networks (CNN) that perform better with sequential data, such as time series or text. TCNs are similar to GRUs and other RNNs in that both are designed to work with sequential data and can capture temporal dependencies in the data. However, there are also some critical differences between them:

Structure: GRUs are RNNs, meaning they process the data stream one step at a time, with the hidden state being updated at each step based on the previous hidden state and the current input. On the other hand, TCNs are CNNs, which means they apply convolutions to the data. In the case of TCNs, these convolutions are applied in a way that respects the temporal order of the data.

Memory: Both GRUs and TCNs can capture temporal dependencies in data. However, GRUs use gating mechanisms to control which information is kept and which is forgotten at each time step, allowing them to capture long-term dependencies more effectively. TCNs, on the other hand, control "memory" through the size of their convolution window (also known as the "receptive field").

Parallelism: One benefit of TCNs over GRUs and other RNNs is that they are inherently parallelizable during training. Because RNNs must process data sequentially, one step at a time, they cannot take full advantage of GPUs and other parallel processing hardware in the same way that CNNs (and thus TCNs) can.

Regarding performance, some studies have found that TCNs can outperform GRUs and other types of RNNs on some tasks, although results may vary depending on the task and the specific implementation of the TCN [7].

Using Python to implement RNN has become much more familiar with the advent of deep learning libraries such as TensorFlow and Keras. TensorFlow is an open-source library for machine learning and neural networks developed by the Google Brain team. Although best known for its deep learning use, TensorFlow supports various traditional machine learning algorithms. (See Fig. 2).

```
import pandas as pd
from tensorflow.keras.preprocessing.text import Tokenizer
from tensorflow.keras.preprocessing.sequence import pad_sequences
from tensorflow.keras.models import Sequential
from tensorflow.keras.layers import Embedding, Bidirectional, GRU, Dense

#Cargar tweets del archivo concentrador
data = pd.read_csv('TWEETS_PM.csv')
#Preprocesamiento de texto
tokenizer = Tokenizer(num_words=5000)
tokenizer.fit_on_texts(data['tweet'])
sequences = tokenizer.texts_to_sequences(data['tweet'])
#Preprocesar los tweets, ajustar a una misma longitud
maxlen = 100
sequences = pad_sequences(sequences, maxlen=maxlen)
#Inicia el modelo
model = Sequential()
model.add(Embedding(5000, 64, input_length=maxlen))
model.add(Bidirectional(GRU(64)))
model.add(Dense(1, activation='sigmoid'))
#Entrenamiento del modelo
model.compile(loss='binary_crossentropy', optimizer='adam', metrics=['accuracy'])
model.fit(sequences, data['sentiment'], batch_size=32, epochs=2, validation_split=0.2)|
```

Fig. 2. Python code for a Bi-GRU technique in tweets.

In 2010, Google began developing DistBelief, its first generation of proprietary systems for machine learning, and by 2015, Google internally used TensorFlow as its second machine learning system, replacing DistBelief. TensorFlow was built to be highly flexible and work with various platforms, from cloud servers to individual devices. TensorFlow 2.0 was released in 2019 as a preview release, and this release includes several significant changes, such as simplifying the programming model by removing redundant sessions and making Eager Execution (an imperative, object-oriented programming interface) the default for most operations. In addition, TensorFlow 2.0 also offers full support for the Keras API, which provides high-level abstractions for building and training deep learning models [8].

2   Related Work

Sentiment analysis has been used in tourism in various areas to understand and assess customer opinion and satisfaction.

Hotel and accommodation reviews: Hotels and accommodation facilities use Sentiment analysis in online comments and reviews. Analyzing the language used in these comments can determine customer satisfaction, identify areas for improvement and obtain valuable information for decision-making in hotel management [9].

Social networks and online opinions: Sentiment analysis helps to monitor and analyze comments and posts on social networks related to tourist destinations, attractions, restaurants, and other tourist services. This analysis helps businesses and destinations understand public perception, spot issues, and respond appropriately [10].

Analysis of survey feedback: Tourism surveys often include open-ended questions where participants can provide comments and opinions. Sentiment analysis is an automatic process for categorizing these comments, which allows for obtaining quantitative information on tourist satisfaction and areas for improvement [11].

Real-time feedback evaluation: Some tourism businesses use real-time sentiment analysis to assess customer feedback and interactions on-site or using services. The customer's suggestions allow them to address issues and improve the customer experience quickly [12].

Analysis of reviews of attractions: Local governments review opinions about restaurants, interests, and other tourist places. It helps users make informed decisions by evaluating the experiences of others and allows properties to identify areas for improvement [13].

2.1 Bi-GRU Architecture

A general model for performing sentiment analysis using LSTM architecture ([14]) is:

1. Data collection and preparation: As in any sentiment analysis, the first step is to collect the appropriate data that contains opinions or sentiments. This data should be labeled or annotated with sentiment labels, such as positive, negative, or neutral. The data must then be prepared using text-cleansing techniques, such as removing punctuation, stopping words, and normalizing text. (See Fig. 3).

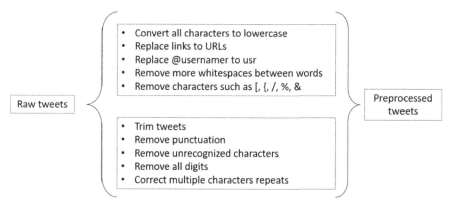

Fig. 3. Preprocessing activities on tweets

2. Splitting data into training and test sets: After collecting and preparing the data, it must be divided into training and test sets. The training set is used to train the LSTM network, while the test set is used to evaluate the performance of the trained model.

3. Representation of the text: The next step is to convert the text into a suitable numerical representation to be processed by the LSTM network. This process uses some techniques such as tokenization, where each word is represented as a token, and the creation of an array of word embeddings that capture the semantic features of the text.

4. Design and training of the LSTM network: In this step, the architecture of the LSTM network is designed. An LSTM is a variant of recurrent neural networks designed

to address the problem of gradient fading and allow long-term dependency learning on data streams. The LSTM network is trained using the training set, fitting the parameters to minimize a loss function, such as cross-entropy, which compares the actual sentiment labels with the model predictions.

5. Model evaluation: The trained LSTM model is tested to validate its performance using the test set. Metrics such as precision, completeness, and F1 score are calculated to assess the model's ability to classify sentiments in the test set correctly.

6. Adjustment and improvement of the model: If the performance of the LSTM model is not satisfactory, adjustments and modifications can be made. These enhancements may include changes to the LSTM network architecture, hyperparameter tuning, regularization techniques such as L1 or L2 regularization, or even exploring more advanced architectures such as Convolutional Neural Networks (CNNs) or Transformers. (See Fig. 4).

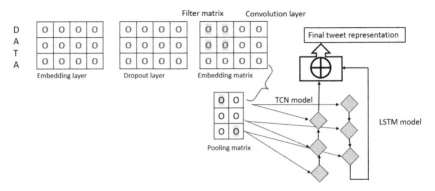

Fig. 4. Sentiment analysis using LSTM: A general scheme.

In [14], the Bidirectional RNNs are shown. Furthermore [15], introduce Bi-GRUs (Bidirectional GRUs), which are GRUs that process the input stream in both forward and backward directions. Bi-GRUs account for the context before and after a given point in the input stream, and this can be useful in many contexts, such as natural language translation, where the meaning of a word can depends on both the context that precedes it and the context that follows it.

The architecture of a Bi-GRU for sentiment analysis could include the following layers and elements:

Embedding Layer: This layer transforms the input words into dense vectors that the network can learn. Embeddings capture more information in fewer dimensions.

Bi-GRU Layer: This layer uses Gate Recurrent Units (GRUs) and operates in both directions. It processes the input sequence from left to right and from right to left and combines the representations at each time step. Bidirectional layers often improve model performance on context-dependent tasks in both directions, such as sentiment analysis.

Dense Layer: A dense (or fully connected) layer that serves as the output layer. This layer can have several units equal to the number of sentiment classes to predict (if it is a multiclass classification), and usually uses a SoftMax activation function. This layer would have a single unit with a sigmoid activation for binary classification (such as positive/negative).

Loss Function: To train the network, we need a loss function. For binary classification, binary cross entropy is commonly used. For multiclass type, categorical cross entropy is often used.

The application of Bidirectional Recurrent Neural Networks with Gate Units (Bi-GRU) in tourism is a relatively new area of research. However, there are several ways in which these models can be helpful.

Sentiment Analysis: The analysis of reviews of hotels, restaurants, tourist attractions, and other tourist facilities provides information on customer satisfaction and helps tourism companies to improve their services.

Demand Prediction: Predicting the demand for travel, hotel rooms, or flight reservations helps tourism companies to manage their resources better.

Machine Translation: Machine translation systems should be developed to facilitate communication between travelers and locals in tourist destinations.

Personalized Recommendations: Local governments should develop recommendation systems that provide customized travel suggestions to users to benefit local businesses.

3   Proposed Model Structure

Studying various deep learning models for sentiment analysis has shown its advantages and disadvantages. Convolution layers in CNN can extract critical features from social media comments, and LSTM can capture contextual information for the words in tweets. Bi-LSTM and Bi-GRU read the vector representation of the input tweet in both directions to analyze in-depth contextual details. Although CNN models can extract essential text features for classification, they ignore the spatial dependencies between the words in tweets that extract features, especially for classifying complex questions. The proposal is to build a set-based learning network using Bi-GRU and TCN. Embedded words are mapped to Bi-GRU, where full contextual information is extracted when the input is read in both directions. Then, the result is sequential contextual information that includes grammatical and semantic knowledge with distant word dependencies present in question. The causal behavior of the convolutional layers in the TCN network can address a long input sequence without facing the problem of the leakage gradient.

Its architecture is designed based on two fundamentals: the causal convolution layer does not allow information to escape from the future to the past, and the framework can take input features of any size mapped to output features of the same size. The dilation in the causal layers demonstrates the advantage of the temporal CNN over the RNN model. The new joint model used by Bi-GRU and TCN is structured to develop a new Bi-GRU-TCN system to analyze sentiments of tourism tweets from "Pueblos Magicos" in Quintana Roo.

3.1   Temporal Convolutional Neural Network

The parallelization of convolutional layers in TCN resembles the time-consuming problem of recurrent networks. The TCN model is built with one 1D convolutional layer and other causal convolution layers; that help pulls out long-term dependencies for sequence modeling.

Sequence modeling aims to find a model that lessens the gap between the predicted and the actual output, as shown in Eq. 1 given below:

$$L[(n_0, n_1, \ldots, n_t), (n'_0, n'_1, \ldots, n'_t)] = L[(n_0, n_1, \ldots, n_t), f(m_0, m_1, \ldots, m_t)] \quad (1)$$

where $(m0, m1, \ldots \ldots, mt)$ is the input sequence, $(n0, n1, \ldots, nt)$ is the output sequence and $(n'0, n'1, \ldots, 't)$ is the predicted output.

The output length of TCN is the same as the input length on using 1D convolutional layers as hidden layers of the same length as the input length. The zero padding is appended in the following layers to maintain the input length.

The prevention of information leakage from the previous to following layers can be achieved using causal convolutional layers, which perform convolution operations between nodes at time t and nodes in the previous layer to get output at time t (Fig. 3). We can see that causal layers do not form recurrent connections; instead, they concentrate on receptive field length, which is faster in training models on long sequences. The receptive field length (Nr) equation is written as

$$N_r = (N_l - 1) * (k - 1) + 1 \quad (2)$$

where Nl is the layer length, and k is the kernel size. On the other hand, such models require many layers to capture adequate historical information in output. This drawback is, dilated convolution layers (Fig. 4(a)) are placed in the model, which skips the input values with steps. A simple solution to this drawback, given by [17], is employing a dilation convolution layer that facilitates the network to perform convolution on a larger area than its length by passing over input values to some steps. The dilation layers stack allows the network to have large receptive fields with few layers without increasing the computation cost. For this network framework, receptive field length Nr is calculated as

$$N_r = \sum_D (k - 1)d \quad (3)$$

where D is the dilation array (d). The exponential increase in dilation factor, $d = O(2i)$, at ith depth of network (Eq. 4) and large filter size (k) together help in maintaining long adequate history size. Equation 4 can be written as

$$N_r = 1 + \sum_{i=1}^{N1-1} (K - 1)2^{i-1} \quad (4)$$

3.2 Gated Recurrent Unit

The step-by-step process of calculating output from one GRU unit:

(a) Reset Gate: This gate chooses which information needs to drop from previous instance. In Eq. 6 Ur and Wr are the weights, $Ht-1$ is the input to previous instance and Br is the bias value.

$$R_t = \sigma(W_r S_t + U_r H_{t-1} + B_r) \quad (5)$$

b) Update Gate: The update gate selects the information which needs to get updated at present instant. In Eq. 7 Uz and Wz are the weights.

$$Z_t = \sigma(W_z S_t + U_z H_{t-1} + B_Z) \tag{6}$$

(c) In the next step, GRU evaluates the candidate memory information of the current instant, as shown in equation where W and U are weights and B is bias value.

$$H'_t = \tanh(WS_t + UR_t H_{t-1} + B) \tag{7}$$

(d) The final out of the GRU cell is calculated as below:

$$H_t = (1 - Z_t)H'_t + Z_t H_{t-1} \tag{8}$$

The tweet representation vector from temporal CNN model and contextual information about tweets from BiGRU model are merged into one representation, which is fed into a fully connected layer. To get the final expression of word at the output layer, we multiply mi and ni:

$$Y_i = m_i \odot n_i \tag{9}$$

The final representation $Y = [y1, y2, \ldots, yn]$ is fed into fully connected layer, followed by SoftMax non-linear layer that forecast the probability distribution over classes. The output calculations are as follow, where Wf is the weight on layer, Bf is the bias value and qi is the label output (Fig. 5):

$$P_k = W_f Y_i + B_f \tag{10}$$

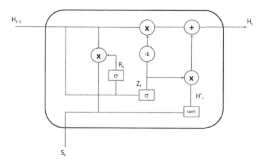

Fig. 5. GRU unit.

The proposed network model is trained on various parameters to minimize the cross-entropy error between actual and predicted output distribution.

$$qi = \exp(Pk)/\sum k \exp(Pk) \tag{11}$$

4 Experiment Results

The training and testing process is performed on a system with Intel Core i7 GPU processor, 8 GB RAM, and Windows 10 operating system in Python 3.10.5 environment using TensorFlow framework. The experiment procedure is discussed as follows:

1. Text-cleaning: Due to the heterogeneity of information, this process is a real challenge for the following reasons: specific tweets share photos or videos and only contain hashtags or emojis in the text; many comments only mention other users, share photos or videos, and do not contain any text; some posts contain prize draws, product promotion or news about the city; most users do not share their location; some tweets use emojis to express opinions in the comments and posts; and some tweets contain questions for other users. We remove user mentions and emoticons to deal with tweets that only contain hashtags or emojis and no text or only mention users. Any tweet that is unrelated to tourism in "Pueblos Mágicos" of Quintana Roo is also discarded by searching for the word tourism in the text of the English tweets and turismo in the Spanish tweets. Additionally, the geo-location was analyzed for those tweets where this was available. Finally, we remove punctuation marks, users, and links, as was the term RT for retweets since when a person retweets, they reiterate the original tweet. Retweets have not been removed because they show acceptance of the original tweet and reinforce what the original tweeter posted.

2. Descriptive analysis: This includes post metrics (hashtag frequency) and finds all the tweets with a location to identify the most visited places. In terms of user metrics, we obtain the frequency of individual posts, retweets, comments, followers, videos, and photos for each user, and this gives us an initial idea of the user's social influence.

3. Tokenization: We first identify the languages in our dataset and then divide each tweet into keywords according to the language. This study uses tweets written in Spanish and English because these languages have the most information.

4. Stop-word removal and stemming: We used the Natural Language Toolkit (NLTK, a platform of Python) to perform this process since it contains both Spanish and English stop-words. The subsequent stemming process also uses NLTK with one stemmer for Spanish and another for English, reducing inflected words to their word stem, base, or root.2. Vector Representation of Question: The union of pre-trained vectors of words present in question gives the vector representation of tweets.

3. Constructing Proposed Ensemble-based Learning Model (Bi-GRU-TCN): The Bi-GRU model is designed with an input layer of pre-trained vector size and hidden layers of 256 dimensions. The TCN model consists of an input layer equal to the length of the pre-trained vector, kernel value 2. Then four residual blocks were replaced sequentially with dilation factors 1,2,4, and 8, respectively. The Bi-GRU and TCN model output is merged into a fully connected layer.

4. Train the proposed framework: With the tweet vector representation, train the Bi-GRU-TCN neural network.

5. Parameters Optimization: The optimized performance of the proposed network is achieved by tuning the model with different parameters. (See Table 1).

6. Framework Evaluation: The accuracy, precision, recall and F-Measure for the proposed model and others is calculated for classifying the sentiments of the tweets. (See Table 2).

Table 1. Network Configuration.

PARAMATER	VALUE
Batch size	10
Epochs	10
Activation function for hidden layer	Relu
Activation function for output layer	Sigmoid
Optimizer	Adam
Learning rate	0.001
Dropout	0.5
Loss function	binary cross-entropy

Table 2. Comparison between different algorithms.

Methods	Accuracy	Precision	Recall	F-Measure
RNN	69	73	72	72
TCN	81	79	78	78
LSTM	80	70	67	66
GRU	82	79	78	78
BiGRU + TCN	88	82	81	81

Once the posts had been collected, they were processed with the following operations: text cleaning, descriptive analysis, tokenization, stop-word removal, and stemming.

1. Text-cleaning: Due to the heterogeneity of information, this process is a real challenge for the following reasons: specific tweets share photos or videos and only contain hashtags or emojis in the text; many comments only mention other users, share photos or videos, and do not contain any text; some posts have prize draws, product promotion or news about the city; most users do not share their location; some tweets use emojis to express opinions in the comments and posts; and some tweets contain questions for other users.

We remove user mentions and emoticons to deal with tweets that only contain hashtags or emojis and no text or only mention users. Any tweet that is unrelated to tourism in "Pueblos Mágicos" of Quintana Roo is also discarded by searching for the word tourism in the text of the English tweets and turismo in the Spanish tweets. Additionally, the geo-location was analyzed for those tweets where this was available. Finally, we remove punctuation marks, users, and links, as was the term RT for retweets since when a person retweets, they reiterate the original tweet. Retweets have not been removed because they show acceptance of the original tweet and reinforce what the original tweeter posted.

2. Descriptive analysis: This includes post metrics (hashtag frequency) and finds all the tweets with a location to identify the most visited places. In terms of user metrics,

we obtain the frequency of individual posts, retweets, comments, followers, videos, and photos for each user, and this gives us an initial idea of the user's social influence.

3. Tokenization: We first identify the languages in our dataset and then divide each tweet into keywords according to the language. This study uses tweets written in Spanish and English because these languages have the most information.

4. Stop-word removal and stemming: We used the Natural Language Toolkit (NLTK, a platform of Python) to perform this process since it contains both Spanish and English stop-words. The subsequent stemming process also uses NLTK with one stemmer for Spanish and another for English, reducing inflected words to their word stem, base, or root.

Content analysis was performed in a seasonal context, and the year was divided into the two periods of spring-summer and autumn-winter. The analysis mainly focuses on structuring the data from texts. It includes the following processes:

1. Word frequency: a separate word frequency analysis for Spanish and English and the word cloud for all the tweets to identify the most commented places. It also enables us to gauge how users perceive these places through words such as beautiful, love, etc.

Table 3. Samples from the test set of each dataset with their sentence, aspect, actual sentiment, and predicted sentiment.

Sentence	Aspect	Actual	Predicted
Te recomiendo pasar por Holbox o Isla Mujeres, ambas buenísimos lugares para pasar el día o más de un día. En Cancún se come mejor en el centro o en el pueblo que en la zona hotelera.;)	Recommendation	Positive	Positive
Punta Mosquito en Holbox el lugar perfecta para pasar un gran día de relax!!	Recommendation	Positive	Positive
Mi hermana siempre que viene, se va a Tulum. No entiendo que le ven de cool a un lugar donde todo está caro, con una zona hotelera dlv que ni pavimentada está, siempre hay balaceras, la playa llena de sargazo y caro alv	Personal Comment	Negative	Negative

2. Sentiment analysis: this entails identifying and classifying each tweet according to feelings. Since this process does not consider the seasonal context because this division did not reveal any relevant results, it was therefore performed globally. Due to the large number of tweets in both Spanish and English, two tools are used. The first tool for classifying Spanish tweets is called Senti-py. The package uses data to train the classifier from Twitter. (See Table 3).

The polarity score is a float within the range [0,1]: values that are less than or equal to 0.3 are negative, values greater than 0.3 and less than 0.6 are neutral, and values greater than 0.6 are positive.

5 Conclusions

This research contributes to the tourism sector by proposing a new deep-learning model for a better classification of comments on Twitter. To this end, a set-based learning model called the Bi-GRU-TCN model is introduced to improve the classification performance. The TCN model is built using four residual blocks sequentially placed after the input layer to extract better long-distance dependent features using dilated convolution layers. At the same time, Bi-GRU captures the contextual information of the words in the dataset. The results of an extensive series of experiments indicate that the proposed model outperforms other deep learning models. The proposed model is fitted with several hyperparameters, and its influence is demonstrated in the experiments.

Finally, although the proposed model achieves good efficiency, we intend to perform various pre-trained word embedding technologies to feed our Bi-GRU model in future work. Also, to get more effective results, we would like to explore alternative variants of RNN models for our problem.

In summary, as future work, it is intended to test different pre-trained word embedding technologies in the proposed Bi-GRU model. In addition, it will seek to explore alternative variants of RNN models to obtain more effective results.

References

1. Pang, B., Lee, L., Vaithyanathan, S.: Thumbs up? Sentiment classification using machine learning techniques. arXiv preprint cs/0205070 (2002)
2. Go, A., Bhayani, R., Huang, L.: Twitter sentiment classification using distant supervision. CS224N project report. Stanford 1(12), 2009 (2009)
3. Kouloumpis, E., Wilson, T., Moore, J.: Twitter sentiment analysis: the good the bad and the OMG!. In: Proceedings of the international AAAI conference on web and social media, Vol. 5, No. 1, pp. 538–541 (2011)
4. Sarlan, A., Nadam, C., Basri, S.: Twitter sentiment analysis. In: Proceedings of the 6th International conference on Information Technology and Multimedia, pp. 212–216. IEEE (2014, November)
5. Cho, K., et al.: Learning phrase representations using RNN encoder-decoder for statistical machine translation (2014). arXiv preprint arXiv:1406.1078
6. Baktha, K., Tripathy, B.K.: Investigation of recurrent neural networks in the field of sentiment analysis. In: 2017 International Conference on Communication and Signal Processing (ICCSP), pp. 2047–2050. IEEE (2017, April)
7. Bai, S., Kolter, J.Z., Koltun, V.: An empirical evaluation of generic convolutional and recurrent networks for sequence modeling (2018). arXiv preprint arXiv:1803.01271
8. Géron, A.: Hands-on machine learning with Scikit-Learn, Keras, and TensorFlow. O'Reilly Media, Inc. (2022)
9. Bian, Y., Ye, R., Zhang, J., Yan, X.: Customer preference identification from hotel online reviews: A neural network based fine-grained sentiment analysis. Comput. Ind. Eng. **172**, 108648 (2022)
10. Alaei, A.R., Becken, S., Stantic, B.: Sentiment analysis in tourism: capitalizing on big data. J. Travel Res. **58**(2), 175–191 (2019)
11. Kelly, C.: Wellness tourism: retreat visitor motivations and experiences. Tour. Recreat. Res. **37**(3), 205–213 (2012)

12. Haddi, E., Liu, X., Shi, Y.: The role of text pre-processing in sentiment analysis. Procedia Computer Science 17, 26–32 (2013)
13. Ali, F., Kwak, D., Khan, P., Islam, S.R., Kim, K.H., Kwak, K.S.: Fuzzy ontology-based sentiment analysis of transportation and city feature reviews for safe traveling. Transportation Research Part C: Emerging Technologies 77, 33–48 (2017)
14. Wang, J., Yu, L.C., Lai, K.R., Zhang, X.: Dimensional sentiment analysis using a regional CNN-LSTM model. In: Proceedings of the 54th annual meeting of the association for computational linguistics (volume 2: Short papers), pp. 225–230 (2016, August)
15. Schuster, M., Paliwal, K.K.: Bidirectional recurrent neural networks. IEEE Trans. Signal Process. 45(11), 2673–2681 (1997)
16. Cho, K., Van Merriënboer, B., Bahdanau, D., Bengio, Y.: On the properties of neural machine translation: Encoder-decoder approaches (2014). arXiv preprint arXiv:1409.1259
17. Mikolov, T., Chen, K., Corrado, G., Dean, J.: Efficient estimation of word representations in vector space (2013). arXiv preprint arXiv:1301.3781

Comparative Study of Pattern Recognition Techniques in the Classification of Vertebral Column Diseases

Alam Gabriel Rojas-López[1]([✉]) [iD], Abril Valeria Uriarte-Arcia[1] [iD],
Alejandro Rodríguez-Molina[2] [iD], and Miguel Gabriel Villarreal-Cervantes[1] [iD]

[1] Mechatronics Section, Postgraduate Department, OMD Laboratory, Instituto
Politécnico Nacional - Centro de Innovación y Desarrollo Tecnológico en Cómputo,
07700 Mexico City, Mexico
arojasl2101@alumno.ipn.mx
[2] Research and Postgraduate Division, Tecnológico Nacional de México/IT
de Tlalnepantla, 54070 Tlalnepantla de Baz, Mexico

Abstract. This work compares popular classifiers based on pattern recognition techniques of supervised learning, including k-Nearest Neighbors, Naïve Bayes, Support Vector Machines, Artificial Neural Networks, and Decision Trees. Such techniques are applied to a dataset related to vertebral column orthopedic diseases. Different parameter values employed by each classifier are tested, resulting in an accuracy of around 80% in almost all approaches, where the k-Nearest Neighbors alternatives were the most accurate. Finally, a brief discussion of particular highlights of how the metrics affect the performances of the classifiers is presented.

Keywords: Vertebral column · disk hernia · spondylolisthesis · kNN ·
Naïve Bayes · SVM · ANN · Decision Tree

1 Introduction

Since the third industrial revolution, one of the main tasks among human efforts has been the automation of processes [27]. The improvement of technological resources has reverberated not only in the automation of the mechanical process, as at the beginning of the industrial revolution, but also in other fields like visual, musical, chemical, and biological, among others. Nowadays, one of the most important is related to the computational field, where mixing maths, logic, and

The first and fourth authors would like to thank the support from Secretaría de Investigación y Posgrado through project No. 20230320.
The third author would like to thank the support from the Dirección de Posgrado, Investigación e Innovación of the Instituto Tecnológico Nacional de México (TecNM) through project No. 16907.23-P.

M. F. Mata-Rivera et al. (Eds.): WITCOM 2023, CCIS 1906, pp. 395–417, 2023.
https://doi.org/10.1007/978-3-031-45316-8_25

electronics has brought more powerful equipment and techniques [5]. In the last decades, some popular techniques are related to pattern recognition, focused on generating new information considering a priori knowledge, whose applications are related to classification, data recovery, regression, and clustering [6,10].

The implementation of the classification techniques based on pattern recognition follows the next steps [31]: i) Generate a dataset of desired information, considering inputs (attributes) and outputs (classes) of a process to be studied [1]. ii) A pre-processing of the information is necessary to check if there are enough instances within the dataset, if the considered attributes are representative, and if the instances' values are correct, among other considerations [16]. iii) Then, a pattern recognition technique is executed/trained to find the best parameters that will be used for the future classification of new instances [20,25]. iv) The previous step requires a validation stage, where the classifier's performance is evaluated on new data (test set) using metrics such as accuracy, recall, or precision [28,33].

The advantage of the classification techniques based on pattern recognition is that they can work with any data from any field rather than just engineering approaches. This makes them useful in works where the information is difficult to represent or is incomprehensible to other areas [8]. An example of this is presented in [30], where an Artificial Neural Network (ANN) classifies, through spatio-temporal data, catchments (and its drivers) through seasonal water quality. Another example is in [14], whose objective was to classify tea according to the season of their harvest according to the FT-IR fingerprinting, accomplishing the task with the Principal Component Analysis (PCA) method. These works consider geographical and climatical values as attributes to improve the engineering/production process, even though the people have no complete background.

Moreover, some works are related to more specialized fields such as health, medicine, and biology, whose attributes are complex to describe/interpret if they are not depured by a specialist. Nevertheless, the classifiers based on pattern recognition still have good outcomes when applied to these cases. An example of this is in [40], whose authors implemented a k-Nearest Neighbors (kNN) classifier to select the control signal based on the surface electromyogram (sEMG) signals. In addition, some works implement more complex/robust variations of an original pattern recognition technique, like in [15]. In that work, the classification is performed with a Convolutional Neural Network (CNN, an ANN variation), which aims to identify and classify hypospadias. A comparison between the CNN and 53 specialists was performed with similar accuracy (90%).

In some cases, the classifiers based on pattern recognition techniques have become so reliable that they are applied to improve medical processes. Like in [24], where a Naïve Bayes (NB) classifier was employed to optimize the treatment of cancer patients after radiotherapy, classifying the patients according to their possible relapse or progression.

Nonetheless, there is no unique pattern recognition technique and even less a technique with a perfect result with any dataset [43]. Considering this, a good/necessary practice (when a classifier is implemented) is to compare multiple pattern recognition techniques, then select the best approach to obtain improvements. It is worth pointing out that even with just one classification technique, the selection of different parameters considerably modifies its performance as presented in [3,12,36,38]. Thus, the better initial approach when a classification is desired, not only multiple classifiers in their simpler version should be tested [2], but also their parameters must be tuned [35].

Considering this works like [45] implement not only the classifiers (ANN and random forest) but also perform comparisons to suggest which classifiers work better with a specific problem based on driver injury patterns in a multiclass perspective problem. Nevertheless, the comparison does not include other classification techniques to compare. Also, a comparison is performed in [42] with different pattern recognition techniques, like kNN, ANN (with radial basis function), and Support Vector Machine (SVM). Those techniques were applied to classify vertebral column disorders. Even if such work performs multiple tests (considering different validation tests and criteria), it does not change the classifier's parameters to check their behavior or try other classifiers.

Furthermore, the use of a preliminary classification comparison gives a more trustworthy selection of classifiers for practical real-life applications and improvement research investigations. In recent years this has been seen in works like [23], where a comparison of machine learning techniques for automatic text classification showed that the kNN classifier got the best results; hence is selected for future research. Also, in works like [13,32,37], multiple classifiers were compared in the medical field for different critical diseases classification (different variants of ANN were the winners by each reference). In such cases, the selection of the most efficient classifier is critical as they are to be applied to problems regarding the patients' medical treatments and quality of life. Even more, in [41], a comparative study of different studies that implement a comparison of pattern recognition techniques for disease classification is performed. The study showed that the most popular classifier among the studies was the SVM, yet the RF classifier got the highest accuracy. This comparison of classifiers' performance can be used to aid researchers in the selection of appropriate pattern recognition techniques for their studies.

Therefore, this work will describe and compare the behavior of different pattern recognition techniques when their parameters are changed/tuned to find the best classifier with the best compromise between precision and simplicity when they are applied to a problem of vertebral column disease classification.

The distribution of this work is as follows: in Sect. 2, a general explanation of the classifiers implemented is given. A description of the dataset to be classified is presented in Sect. 3. Section 4 displays the results of all the variations tested per classifier. A summary of the results and highlights is presented in Section 5. Finally, Sect. 6 describes the conclusions of this work as well as future work.

2 Pattern Recognition Techniques

Since the dataset is already labeled, the proposed approach is related to supervised learning [26]. Therefore, the following methods are implemented.

2.1   K-Nearest Neighbors (kNN)

This approach is based on the proximity of values within a dataset. The method considers the classes of the k nearest instances. The process consists of calculating de distance d_i between the new proposed instance to classify x' and the instances x of the dataset (Table 1 presents popular distance functions [21,39]). Then, after selecting the k nearest instances $\{x_1, \ldots, x_k\}$, the next step is identifying the predominant class of them. The advantage of this method is related to the absence of a training stage, making it a fast classifier. Nevertheless, this method faces three important problems: i) find the correct/representative k value, ii) if the new proposed instance falls in a region where there is no dominant class (where the k-neighbors are equally distributed in two or more instances), and iii) if the attributes are discrete (categorical).

Table 1. Distance functions.

Name	Distance $d(x', x)$
Euclidean	$\sqrt{\sum_{j=1}^{n}(x_j - x'_j)^2}$
Manhattan	$\sum_{j=1}^{n}\lvert x_j - x'_j \rvert$

2.2   Naïve Bayes (NB)

This methodology is based on a probabilistic approach by calculating, given the attributes of an instance, the probability of an event (class) [29]. It considers the prior probability of a k-th class $P(c_k)$ and the verisimilitude probability of a x_i attribute $P(x_i|c_k)$. Thus, when a new instance x' is classified, it calculates the posterior probability using (1). Although this method does not require a training stage, as the previous one, it needs more calculations. This method also has the advantage of being fast to apply, and besides the previous one, it can manage discrete and continuous values. The main drawback is that this method assumes independency between the attributes of the dataset.

$$P(c_k|\{x_1, \ldots, x_n\}) = \frac{P(\{x_1, \ldots, x_n\}|c_k)P(c_k)}{P(\{x_1, \ldots, x_n\})} = P(c_k)\prod_{i=1}^{n}P(x_i|c_k) \quad (1)$$

2.3   Support Vector Machine (SVM)

This method aims to split the instances of a dataset by its classes through a hyperplane (or support vector) [18]. Figure 1 presents an example of how two different classes (represented by red dots and blue dots) are separated by a dotted line (hyperplane). The division aims to minimize the distance of the hyperplane to all the instances of a class. The equation defining the hyperplane is the kernel function $k(x, x')$ [9], Table 2 presents common kernel functions to be implemented in the present work. This method is known to be one of the most accurate because it implements an optimization problem considering all the instances (training stage). However, this characteristic also makes it a slower classifier. The main drawback of this method is presented when it is applied to datasets whose instances have overlapped attribute values. However, this drawback is overcome by calculating more hyperplanes (considering that this makes the method even slower).

Table 2. SVM kernel functions.

Type	k(x,x')
Linear	$\left\langle x^T \dot{x}' \right\rangle$
Polynomial	$\left(\gamma \left\langle x^T \dot{x}' \right\rangle + r\right)^d, \{d \in \mathbb{N} \mid d \geq 2\}$
Radial Basis Function (RBF)	$\exp\left(-\gamma \left\| x - x' \right\|^2\right)$
Sigmoid	$\tanh\left(\gamma \left\langle x^T \dot{x}' \right\rangle + r\right)$

r is a bias value
γ is a weight value

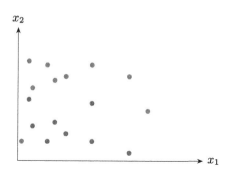

Fig. 1. SVM Linear kernel classifier. (Color figure online)

2.4   Artificial Neural Network (ANN)

This classifier uses a network of neurons, where the neurons within the network are like the one presented in Fig. 2. Each neuron follows two basic steps [22]. First, the neuron solves (2) by adding the product of each i-th input In_i with its corresponding i-th weight ω_i and adding up a bias b of the neuron. Then the result z of the previous step is used in an activation function (Table 3 shows some of the most used activation functions), whose result is used as the input of the following neuron or as the final result in the output layer. Finally, an optimization problem is set to find the neurons' weights and biases that improve the network's performance (training stage). This characteristic makes ANN one of the most accurate and reliable classifiers. Despite this, it is worth mentioning that the training stage is slower than other methods. Also, it is important to point out that other parameters can be modified in the method besides the activation function, such as the solver algorithm (optimization algorithm), the learning rate (step size of the optimization algorithm), and the dimension/structure of the hidden layers.

$$z = \sum_{i=1}^{n} \omega_i In_i + b \qquad (2)$$

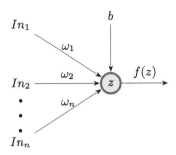

Fig. 2. Neuron diagram.

Table 3. Activation functions of ANN.

Name	Activation function
Linear	$f(z) = z$
Sigmoid	$f(z) = \left\{ \dfrac{e^z}{1+e^z} \right.$
ReLU	$f(z) = \left\{ \begin{array}{l} 0, z < 0 \\ z, z \geq 0 \end{array} \right.$
Hyperbolic	$f(z) = \dfrac{e^z - e^{-z}}{e^z + e^{-z}}$

2.5   Decision Tree (DT)

Unlike the previous methods, this approach is based on logic rather than a mathematical basis. Graphically, it can be similar to the SVM method, but instead of using a hyperplane, DT implements orthogonal division according to attributes [34]. Figure 3 is a basic representation of how the method splits the instances of two classes (red dots and blue dots). The instances have two attributes (x_1 and x_2). The method's behavior is to find a value (within the attribute range) that splits the instances into two groups with elements of only one class. If the new groups do not fit the requirement, the process will be repeated, resulting in a *Tree* of conditional functions. This method depends on many factors like i) the minimum instances quantity to stop the divisions, iii) the number of splits by criteria, iii) and the number of levels of the tree. However, if the classifier is correctly tuned, it becomes one of the most accurate methods because it can classify datasets where the instances have attributes with discontinuous ranges. Nevertheless, this method has drawbacks regarding the different parameters that must be tuned, such as criterion (Gini or entropy to measure impurity), splitter (random or best to select the split point on each node), samples split (minimum number of instances to split a node), and sample leaf (minimum number of instances to convert a node to a leaf/class).

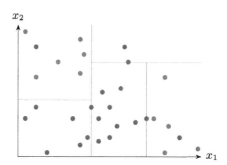

Fig. 3. Decission tree - Two attributes example. (Color figure online)

3   Dataset Description

The dataset is obtained from the Vertebral Column dataset [11] (VCDS). The information was collected and depured by Dr. Henrique da Mota in the Group of Applied Research in Orthopaedics (GARO) of the Centre médico-chirurgical de réadaptation des Massues (Lyon, France). It has 310 instances, each one with the following six biomechanical attributes: i) pelvic incidence (PI), ii) pelvic tilt (PT), iii) lumbar lordosis angle (LLA), iv) sacral slope (SS), v) pelvic radius (PR), and vi) grade of spondylolisthesis (GS). The dataset can be applied to two groups of classification. The first one divides the set into three classes, Normal (100 instances), Disk Hernia (60 instances), and Spondylolisthesis (150 instances). The second classification, a simpler one, only divides between Normal (100 instances) and Abnormal (210 instances). Aiming to prove the classification methods to a more detailed/complete classification, the present work will only focus on the first alternative (three classes).

Before starting with the implementation of the classifiers, it is important to check if the dataset is usable; in this version, the dataset does not omit information in the instances. Nevertheless, the data is imbalanced. This can be confirmed with an Imbalance Ratio IR (3).

$$IR = \frac{\text{Majority class instances}}{\text{Minority class instances}} \tag{3}$$

The theory establishes that the classes in a dataset are imbalanced if $IR \geq 1.5$ [19], so applying this in (5) confirms that the dataset is imbalanced. As a matter of completeness, the relationship between the majority class and the second minority class (Normal class) is also calculated in (4). This is done only to show the wide difference between the classes' instances.

$$IR_2 = \frac{\text{Spondylolisthesis instances}}{\text{Disk Hernia instances}} = 2.5 \tag{4}$$

$$IR_1 = \frac{\text{Spondylolisthesis instances}}{\text{Normal instances}} = 1.5 \tag{5}$$

Such characteristics may reduce the method's capacity because there are not enough instances to perform a representative/fair classification. This problem is faced by an *oversampling* approach [17], specifically the ADASYN technique), creating synthetic instances to produce three classes, each with 150 instances. Also, Fig. 4 presents the heat map of the correlation between the instances' attributes of the datasets, where PR is the less representative attribute. Usually, in this scenario, the attribute can be removed from the dataset to reduce the computational burden. However, considering this is a small dataset with few attributes, there is no difference/improvement. Consequently, all attributes must be considered.

Finally, Fig. 5 and Fig. 6 present the relation between the attributes and the classes. The first refers to a principal component analysis (PCA) that transforms a multivariate dataset into a two-dimension representation. Figure 5 shows that the Normal class (NO) and the Disc Hernia class (SL) share common characteristics (complicating the classification between these classes) and also that there are only a few instances of the Spondylolisthesis class whose characteristics are similar to other classes. In Fig. 6 exists a more detailed representation employing a graphic of parallel coordinates, where each attribute of the instances is plotted. Attributes of the SL class exist within a different value range than the other classes, which is similar to the PCA plot. Nevertheless, Fig. 6 indicates that considering the attributes LLA and SS, there is a slight difference between the instances of the DH and the NO classes. Such information might be useful to understand which attributes are important to consider.

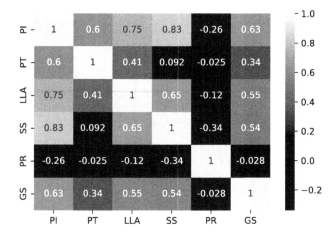

Fig. 4. Heat map of VCDS.

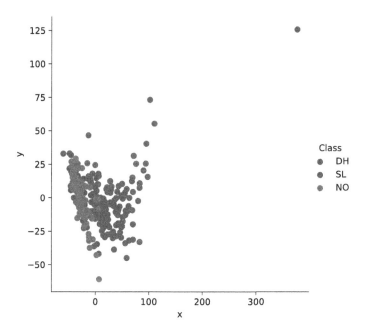

Fig. 5. Principal component analysis of VCDS.

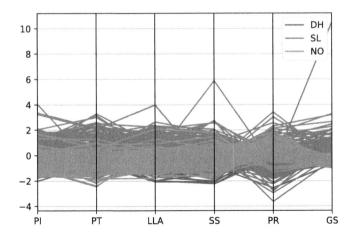

Fig. 6. Parallel coordinates of VCDS.

4   Classification Results

All the classifiers (considering their different parameter configuration) are implemented in Python programming language. The classification methods are implemented from the *scikit-learn* library. All methods use accuracy as scoring, considering that is a popular and reliable metric used in pattern recognition techniques [7,44]; also, the K-Fold Cross-Validation (KFCV) process with $k = 10$ [4] will be used. Specifically, the reported accuracy (acc_{mean}) is the mean value of the accuracy obtained in each of the 10 K-Fold Cross Validation method iterations. The present work implements all the aforementioned variations on each method/classifier, presenting the results by method variance and then a general comparison. Finally, it is worth pointing out that the classifications were carried out on a computer with a CPU Intel® Core™ i7-7700HQ at 2.80 (GHz) with 16 (GB) of RAM.

4.1   kNN Results

Multiple tests were performed, varying the k value from 1 to 20 neighbors and changing the distance metric. Figure 7 presents the results of the Euclidean metric, where the accuracy keeps above 0.8 ($acc_{mean} > 0.8$), where $k = 1$ is the best with an accuracy of $acc_{mean} = 0.95$. Also, for all those k above 6, the accuracy is settled at around 0.82 ($acc_{mean} \approx 0.82$). It is remarkable that the fewer the considered neighbors, the higher the accuracy; however, this might lead to overfitting. Likewise, Fig. 8 presents the results of the Manhattan metric, which are similar to the obtained by the Euclidean distance metric with the difference that for all those k values above 11, the accuracy is reduced below 0.8 ($acc_{mean} < 0.8$).

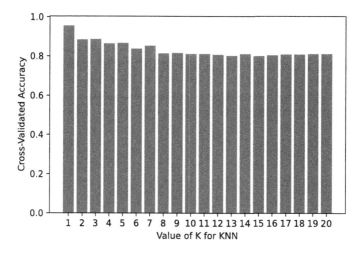

Fig. 7. kNN results - Euclidean distance.

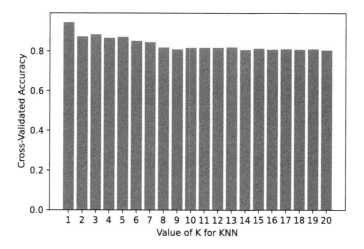

Fig. 8. kNN results - Manhattan distance.

4.2 NB Results

Since the NB method is a simple classifier and only estimates probabilities within the dataset, there are no variations in the parameter values to implement. Thus, only de accuracy scores for $k = 10$ are presented in $acc_{k=10} = \{0.7173, 0.7555, 0.8, 0.7777, 0.7777, 0.7111, 0.6888, 0.7777, 0.6444, 0.7111\}$ with a mean accuracy value of $acc_{mean} = 0.7361$. This method is not as accurate as the previous one but still falls into an acceptable accuracy range.

4.3   SVM Results

Figure 9 compares the kernels. Without considering the sigmoid kernel, they all reach an accuracy above 0.8 ($acc_{mean} > 0.8$), where the linear kernel is the best with a mean accuracy of $acc_{mean} = 0.8339$. On the other hand, Fig. 10 presents the behavior of the polynomial kernel when the degree increase from 2 to 9. Despite the kernel's degree augmentation, the accuracy is not changed, keeping slightly above 0.8 (the 9th degree has the best result with a mean accuracy of $acc_{mean} = 0.8315$).

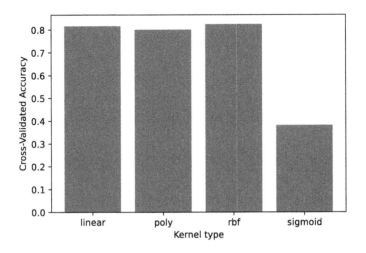

Fig. 9. SVM results - kernel type.

4.4   ANN Results

As this method has multiple parameters to be tuned, each comparison presented may have different characteristics. However, each test changes only one parameter at each time, and at the beginning, the process will implement the default values of the *sklearn* package. Regarding the four first tests, the proposed ANN structure is formed by two hidden layers, each with three neurons. Figure 11 shows the big difference between the Adam solver, with a mean accuracy of $acc_{mean} = 0.6898$, and the other solvers/optimizers. Even though this solver has the best result, it is still below an acceptable range.

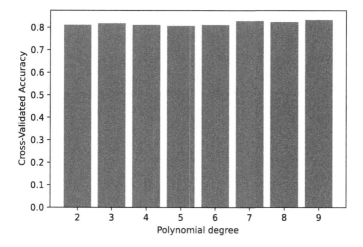

Fig. 10. SVM results - polynomial degree.

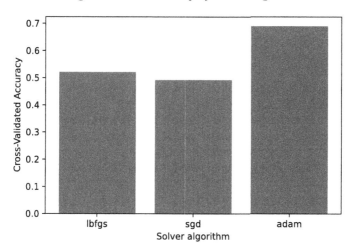

Fig. 11. ANN results - solver algorithm.

Considering the previous information, the subsequent tests will implement the Adam solver. One characteristic of the optimizers is related to their learning rate, where there is a trade-off about its value. The bigger the learning rate, the less accurate the optimizer is. Otherwise, the smaller, the slower the execution of the algorithm, and it might not reach an adequate value. Thus, Fig. 12 presents the behavior of the ANN when the learning rate changes, being 0.001 the best learning rate, with a mean accuracy of $acc_{mean} = 0.6898$.

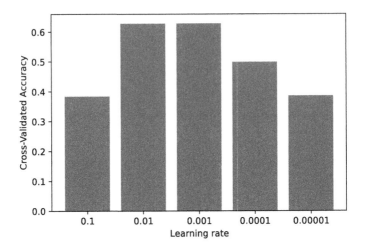

Fig. 12. ANN results - learning rates.

Keeping the same process, the following test will implement the Adam solver with a learning rate of 0.001. Now, Fig. 13 displays the behavior of the different activation functions of the neurons, where the identity and ReLU functions have similar results. The best result is obtained with the identity function with a mean accuracy of $acc_{mean} = 0.7128$.

Finally, the last test keeps the previous parameters (Adam solver, a learning rate of 0.001, and the identity activation function) and proposes different hidden layers structures. Figure 14 presents some proposed structures, where the idea is to show how the accuracy changes when adding layers and increasing neurons per layer. The variances of the test depicted in Fig. 14, represent the structures of the hidden layers applied, where the representation "(#L,#N)" means the "(number of hidden layers, number of neurons per hidden layer)". The first three structures keep the same neurons and add more layers; doing this, the accuracy decreases. The next three structures add one neuron on each layer, which increases the accuracy (even more when the number of layers increases). Finally, the last structure proposes two more neurons to the basic structure (2 hidden layers, 3 neurons). Doing this, the best result is reached with the structure (3L, 5N), which has a mean accuracy of $acc_{mean} = 0.7784$. This is a simple tuning of an ANN based on trial and error. However, it is clear that this classifier's implementation is complex; therefore, many techniques to find the correct hyperparameters have been developed.

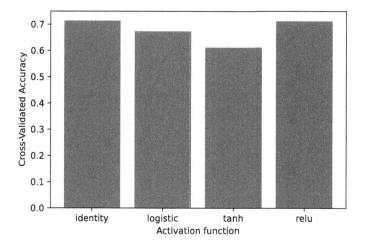

Fig. 13. ANN results - activation functions.

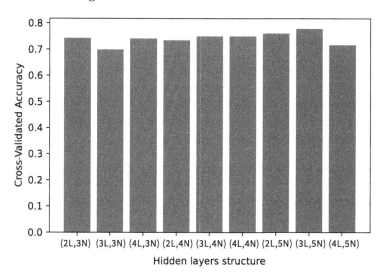

Fig. 14. ANN results - hidden layers.

4.5   DT Results

Sames to the previous method, this approach requires tuning different parameters. Figure 15 shows the response of two popular criteria. Even though there is no significant difference, the entropy criterion has the best result (with a mean accuracy of $acc_{mean} = 0.8449$). As with the previous classifier, the parameter with the best response is used to tune the following parameter. Figure 16 compares two popular splitter techniques, being the best splitter technique the one with the higher accuracy given by a mean accuracy of $acc_{mean} = 0.8449$.

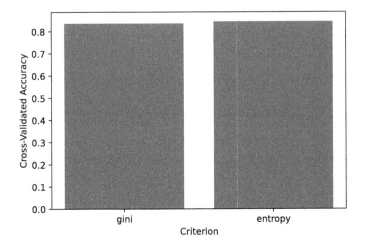

Fig. 15. DT results - criterion.

The following parameter is related to how many levels (depth) the tree will have. Figure 17 shows that the more depth the tree has, the more accurate it becomes in classifying. For example, with a depth of 10 levels, the classifier reaches a mean accuracy of $acc_{mean} = 0.8537$.

The following parameter is about how few instances have to exist in each node to require a new level. Figure 18 shows that this attribute does not affect the performance much. As a matter of completeness, the best value is 3, which gives a mean accuracy of $acc_{mean} = 0.8582$.

The final parameter has a trade-off with the previous one. This parameter establishes how many parameters are required to convert a node to a leaf (last node/class) instead of searching for new levels (split node). Figure 19 presents this characteristic and how even the accuracy is reduced where the best result obtains a mean accuracy of $acc_{mean} = 0.8404$.

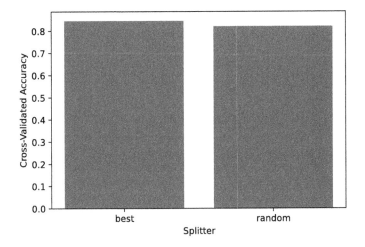

Fig. 16. DT results - splitter.

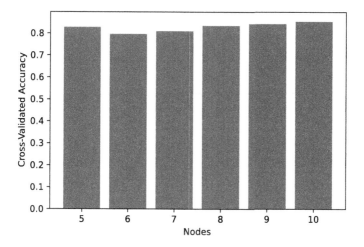

Fig. 17. DT results - nodes.

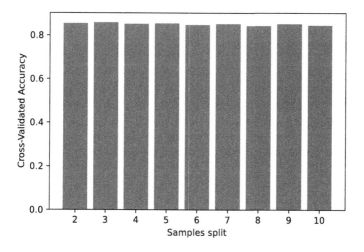

Fig. 18. DT results - sample split.

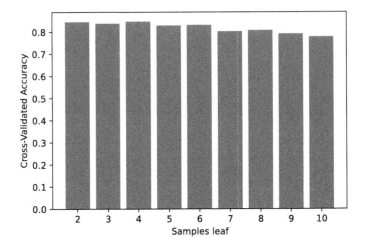

Fig. 19. DT results - sample leaf.

5   Discussion

So far, different pattern recognition techniques based on supervised learning have been implemented. Even though the applied methods consider a similar validation approach, it isn't straightforward to compare them deeper because each implements a different process. However, in this section, a discussion about interesting highlights is presented. Firstly, the kNN classifier has the best outcome (especially when the Euclidean distance is applied), where Manhattan and Euclidean approaches reached a mean accuracy above 0.9 ($acc_{mean} > 0.9$), which can be the consequence of the LLA and SS attributes, whose distribution in Fig. 6 make the distance differences between the classes. On the other hand, the NB classifier has one of the less accurate results with a mean accuracy of $acc_{mean} = 0.7361$, which is attributed to the distribution of the attributes, as observed in Fig. 5 where the elements of the instances of the classes DH and SL are overlapped, even more Fig. 6 shows the overlapped attributes distribution, which reflects no statistical differences and also this is confirmed in Fig. 4 where the correlations between the attributes PI-SS and PI-LLA are elevated (0.83 and 0.75), which affect the NB as it requires independency between the attributes of the dataset.

Furthermore, when classifiers with a more complex operation are implemented, the results might change considerably according to the selected parameters. Such as the SVM classifier, when the sigmoid kernel approach is employed, the classifier has unacceptable results with a mean accuracy below 0.4 ($acc_{mean} < 0.4$). On the other hand, when a linear kernel for an SVM classifier is implemented, the best outcome is reached with a mean accuracy of $acc_{mean} = 0.8339$, whose result wins even when compared to a polynomial kernel of 9th degree. The behavior of these results reflects linearity between the instances of the classes, which makes the sigmoid kernel impractical, hence its unsuitable results.

Even though ANN is a popular classifier, it is very susceptible to tuning, i.e., the selection of different parameters such as the solver, learning rate, and activation function. In this particular problem, modifying the structure/disposition of the hidden layers was the only parameter that represented significant improvements in the classifier's performance. However, the ANN never reaches the mean accuracy of 0.8 ($acc_{mean} < 0.8$)), which makes this method one of the less accurate (as in the NB classifier. Despite the results obtained, it is important to remember that ANN is a popular classifier with a great reported performance, yet its implementation is more complicated than others, and in this particular work (dataset), such effort for tuning is futile as the other techniques have acceptable results.

Considering that the DT classifier is as complex to tune as the ANN classifier (it also has several parameters to adjust), it is interesting that the accuracy in this particular problem is always maintained above 0.8 ($acc_{mean} \geq 0.8$), which makes this classifier as reliable as the kNN classifier and the SVM classifier when a linear kernel is implemented.

Finally, Table 4 is provided to summarize the best results of each classifier, where the second column shows the metrics that produced the outcome, the third column presents the outcome of the respective classifier, and the fourth column displays the solver time required by each classifier. It is evident that kNN is the better approach for this particular dataset, followed by DT and SVM with linear kernel, which makes these particular techniques the best selection for future improvements, not only for this dataset but also for others with similar characteristics as few instances with overlapped attributes. Also, for the sake of completeness, the time consumed by each classifier is presented, even if it might not be a fair comparison, as each method implements different processes. Nonetheless, this information might be useful for future real-life applications where the computational burden is a mandatory requirement, such as in embedded systems. It is interesting that kNN and DT got the best performances with a relatively low computational burden.

Table 4. Classifiers' best results comparison.

Classifier	Metrics	acc_{mean}	Solvertime (s)
kNN	Euclidean distance k=1	**0.95**	0.0374
NB	N.A	0.7361	0.0253
SVM	Linear kernel	0.8339	0.5196
ANN	Adam solver Learning rate = 0.001 Identity activation function Hidden structure = (3 hidden layers, 5 neurons)	0.7784	6.2472
DT	Entropy criterion Best splitter Depth = 10 levels Max samples per level = 3	0.8582	0.0546

6 Conclusions

This work presented the behavior of different classifiers, including the approaches based on common parameter values of each technique. The best performance was obtained by the kNN classifier (with Euclidean distance) when only one neighbor ($k = 1$) is considered, reaching an $acc_{mean} = 0.95$. However, this outcome is attributed to the characteristics of the dataset (overlapped attributes, where only a few of them presented representative differences). Figure 7 and Fig. 8 show that when the number of neighbors k increases in the kNN classifier, the mean accuracy tends around 0.8 ($acc_{mean} \approx 0.8$), which is a similar result obtained by other classifiers.

Also, the best results of SVM and DT are similar (0.8339 and 0.8582); selecting a winner might depend on characteristics such as simplicity of implementation. On the one hand, SVM seems to be only affected by kernel selection, which makes it simpler to tune. On the other hand, there are more metrics to tune with the DT classifier. However, they made only a small improvement in the classifier's performance.

Likewise, the NB and ANN classifiers have similar results (0.7362 and 0.7784). Unlike other classifiers, NB has no parameters (in this work) to be tuned, so the performance hangs completely on the dataset's characteristics (in classes with small probabilistic differences between their instances, the classifier has poor performance). On the contrary, the ANN classifier has considerable parameters to be tuned, and all parameter settings affect the outcome. Even though this work used different parameters, there might be another tuning that improves the results, yet for this particular problem, such effort is in vain as other classifiers reach a better outcome with less struggle.

Finally, as future work, a deeper study about how the classifiers are affected by reducing the dataset's attributes is considered, as well as the use of different scorings besides de accuracy. Furthermore, it is also considered the development/improvement of classifiers based on the best pattern recognition techniques reported here, as well as a comparison with other methods reported in the literature.

References

1. Abraham, A., Falcón, R., Bello, R.: Rough Set Theory: A True Landmark in Data Analysis, vol. 174. Springer, Heidelberg (2009). https://doi.org/10.1007/978-3-540-89921-1
2. Akinsola, J.E.T.: Supervised machine learning algorithms: classification and comparison. Int. J. Comput. Trends Technol. (IJCTT) **48**, 128–138 (2017). https://doi.org/10.14445/22312803/IJCTT-V48P126
3. Alawad, W., Zohdy, M., Debnath, D.: Tuning hyperparameters of decision tree classifiers using computationally efficient schemes. In: 2018 IEEE First International Conference on Artificial Intelligence and Knowledge Engineering (AIKE), pp. 168–169 (2018). https://doi.org/10.1109/AIKE.2018.00038
4. Anguita, D., Ghelardoni, L., Ghio, A., Oneto, L., Ridella, S.: The 'K' in K-fold cross validation. In: ESANN, pp. 441–446 (2012)

5. Bahrin, M.A.K., Othman, M.F., Azli, N.H.N., Talib, M.F.: Industry 4.0: a review on industrial automation and robotic. Jurnal teknologi **78**(6–13), 137–143 (2016)
6. Bishop, C.M., Nasrabadi, N.M.: Pattern Recognition and Machine Learning. Springer, New York (2006)
7. Carvalho, D.V., Pereira, E.M., Cardoso, J.S.: Machine learning interpretability: a survey on methods and metrics. Electronics **8**(8), 832 (2019). https://doi.org/10. 3390/electronics8080832
8. Chiang, L.H., Russell, E.L., Braatz, R.D.: Pattern classification. In: Fault Detection and Diagnosis in Industrial Systems. Advanced Textbooks in Control and Signal Processing, pp. 27–31. Springer, London (2001). https://doi.org/10.1007/978-1-4471-0347-9_3
9. Cristianini, N., Shawe-Taylor, J.: An Introduction to Support Vector Machines and Other Kernel-based Learning Methods. Cambridge University Press, Cambridge (2000). https://doi.org/10.1017/CBO9780511801389
10. De Sa, J.M.: Pattern Recognition: Concepts, Methods, and Applications. Springer, Heidelberg (2001). https://doi.org/10.1007/978-3-642-56651-6
11. Dua, D., Graff, C.: UCI machine learning repository (2017)
12. Duarte, E., Wainer, J.: Empirical comparison of cross-validation and internal metrics for tuning SVM hyperparameters. Pattern Recogn. Lett. **88**, 6–11 (2017). https://doi.org/10.1016/j.patrec.2017.01.007
13. Erdem, E., Bozkurt, F.: A comparison of various supervised machine learning techniques for prostate cancer prediction. Avrupa Bilim ve Teknoloji Dergisi, 610–620 (2021). https://doi.org/10.31590/ejosat.802810
14. Esteki, M., Memarbashi, N., Simal-Gandara, J.: Classification and authentication of tea according to their harvest season based on FT-IR fingerprinting using pattern recognition methods. J. Food Compos. Anal. **115**, 104995 (2023). https://doi.org/ 10.1016/j.jfca.2022.104995
15. Fernandez, N., et al.: Digital pattern recognition for the identification and classification of hypospadias using artificial intelligence vs experienced pediatric urologist. Urology **147**, 264–269 (2021). https://doi.org/10.1016/j.urology.2020.09.019
16. García, S., Luengo, J., Herrera, F.: Data Preprocessing in Data Mining, vol. 72. Springer, Cham (2015). https://doi.org/10.1007/978-3-319-10247-4
17. Gosain, A., Sardana, S.: Handling class imbalance problem using oversampling techniques: a review. In: 2017 International Conference on Advances in Computing, Communications and Informatics (ICACCI), pp. 79–85. IEEE (2017). https://doi. org/10.1109/ICACCI.2017.8125820
18. Géron, A.: Hands-On Machine Learning with Scikit-Learn, Keras, and TensorFlow. O'Reilly Media, Inc., Sebastopol (2022)
19. Haixiang, G., Yijing, L., Shang, J., Mingyun, G., Yuanyue, H., Bing, G.: Learning from class-imbalanced data: review of methods and applications. Expert Syst. Appl. **73**, 220–239 (2017). https://doi.org/10.1016/j.eswa.2016.12.035
20. Hart, P.E., Stork, D.G., Duda, R.O.: Pattern Classification. Wiley, Hoboken (2000)
21. Hidayati, N., Hermawan, A.: K-nearest neighbor (K-NN) algorithm with Euclidean and Manhattan in classification of student graduation. J. Eng. Appl. Technol. **2**(2), 86–91 (2021). https://doi.org/10.21831/jeatech.v2i2.42777
22. Jiang, P., Zhou, Q., Shao, X.: Surrogate Model-Based Engineering Design and Optimization. STME, Springer, Singapore (2020). https://doi.org/10.1007/978-981-15-0731-1
23. Kadhim, A.I.: Survey on supervised machine learning techniques for automatic text classification. Artif. Intell. Rev. **52**(1), 273–292 (2019). https://doi.org/10.1007/ s10462-018-09677-1

24. Kazmierska, J., Malicki, J.: Application of the Naïve Bayesian classifier to optimize treatment decisions. Radiother. Oncol. **86**(2), 211–216 (2008). https://doi.org/10.1016/j.radonc.2007.10.019

25. Kuncheva, L.I.: Combining Pattern Classifiers: Methods and Algorithms. Wiley, Hoboken (2014). https://doi.org/10.1002/0471660264

26. Lehr, J., Philipps, J., Hoang, V., Wrangel, D., Krüger, J.: Supervised learning vs. unsupervised learning: a comparison for optical inspection applications in quality control. IOP Conf. Ser. Materi. Sci. Eng. **1140**, 012049 (2021). https://doi.org/10.1088/1757-899X/1140/1/012049

27. Marengo, L.: Is this time different? A note on automation and labour in the fourth industrial revolution. J. Ind. Bus. Econ. **46**(3), 323–331 (2019). https://doi.org/10.1007/s40812-019-00123-z

28. Mullin, M.D., Sukthankar, R.: Complete cross-validation for nearest neighbor classifiers. In: ICML, pp. 639–646 (2000)

29. Nguyen, T.T.S.: Model-based book recommender systems using Naïve Bayes enhanced with optimal feature selection. In: Proceedings of the 2019 8th International Conference on Software and Computer Applications, pp. 217–222. Association for Computing Machinery, New York, NY, USA (2019). https://doi.org/10.1145/3316615.3316727

30. O'Sullivan, C.M., Ghahramani, A., Deo, R.C., Pembleton, K.G.: Pattern recognition describing spatio-temporal drivers of catchment classification for water quality. Sci. Total Environ. **861**, 160240 (2023). https://doi.org/10.1016/j.scitotenv.2022.160240

31. Pal, S.K., Pal, A.: Pattern Recognition: From Classical to Modern Approaches. World Scientific, Singapore (2001)

32. Panigrahi, K.P., Das, H., Sahoo, A.K., Moharana, S.C.: Maize leaf disease detection and classification using machine learning algorithms. In: Das, H., Pattnaik, P.K., Rautaray, S.S., Li, K.-C. (eds.) Progress in Computing, Analytics and Networking. AISC, vol. 1119, pp. 659–669. Springer, Singapore (2020). https://doi.org/10.1007/978-981-15-2414-1_66

33. Purushotham, S., Tripathy, B.K.: Evaluation of classifier models using stratified tenfold cross validation techniques. In: Krishna, P.V., Babu, M.R., Ariwa, E. (eds.) ObCom 2011. CCIS, vol. 270, pp. 680–690. Springer, Heidelberg (2012). https://doi.org/10.1007/978-3-642-29216-3_74

34. Safavian, S., Landgrebe, D.: A survey of decision tree classifier methodology. IEEE Trans. Syst. Man Cybern. **21**(3), 660–674 (1991). https://doi.org/10.1109/21.97458

35. Sen, P.C., Hajra, M., Ghosh, M.: Supervised classification algorithms in machine learning: a survey and review. In: Mandal, J.K., Bhattacharya, D. (eds.) Emerging Technology in Modelling and Graphics. AISC, vol. 937, pp. 99–111. Springer, Singapore (2020). https://doi.org/10.1007/978-981-13-7403-6_11

36. Shankar, K., Zhang, Y., Liu, Y., Wu, L., Chen, C.H.: Hyperparameter tuning deep learning for diabetic retinopathy fundus image classification. IEEE Access **8**, 118164–118173 (2020). https://doi.org/10.1109/ACCESS.2020.3005152

37. Soni, K.M., Gupta, A., Jain, T.: Supervised machine learning approaches for breast cancer classification and a high performance recurrent neural network. In: 2021 Third International Conference on Inventive Research in Computing Applications (ICIRCA), pp. 1–7 (2021). https://doi.org/10.1109/ICIRCA51532.2021.9544630

38. Sun, J., Zheng, C., Li, X., Zhou, Y.: Analysis of the distance between two classes for tuning SVM hyperparameters. IEEE Trans. Neural Netw. **21**(2), 305–318 (2010). https://doi.org/10.1109/TNN.2009.2036999

39. Suwanda, R., Syahputra, Z., Zamzami, E.M.: Analysis of Euclidean distance and Manhattan distance in the k-means algorithm for variations number of centroid k. J. Phys. Conf. Ser. **1566**(1), 012058 (2020). https://doi.org/10.1088/1742-6596/1566/1/012058

40. Tuncer, T., Dogan, S., Subasi, A.: Surface EMG signal classification using ternary pattern and discrete wavelet transform based feature extraction for hand movement recognition. Biomed. Signal Process. Control **58**, 101872 (2020). https://doi.org/10.1016/j.bspc.2020.101872

41. Uddin, S., Khan, A., Hossain, M.E., Moni, M.A.: Comparing different supervised machine learning algorithms for disease prediction. BMC Med. Inform. Decis. Mak. **19**(1), 1–16 (2019). https://doi.org/10.1186/s12911-019-1004-8

42. Unal, Y., Polat, K., Kocer, H.E.: Classification of vertebral column disorders and lumbar discs disease using attribute weighting algorithm with mean shift clustering. Measurement **77**, 278–291 (2016). https://doi.org/10.1016/j.measurement.2015.09.013

43. Wolpert, D.H.: The supervised learning no-free-lunch theorems. In: Roy, R., Köppen, M., Ovaska, S., Furuhashi, T., Hoffmann, F. (eds) Soft Computing and Industry, pp. 25–42. Springer, London, London (2002). https://doi.org/10.1007/978-1-4471-0123-9_3

44. Zhou, J., Gandomi, A.H., Chen, F., Holzinger, A.: Evaluating the quality of machine learning explanations: a survey on methods and metrics. Electronics **10**(5), 593 (2021). https://doi.org/10.3390/electronics10050593

45. Zhu, M., Li, Y., Wang, Y.: Design and experiment verification of a novel analysis framework for recognition of driver injury patterns: from a multi-class classification perspective. Accid. Anal. Prev. **120**, 152–164 (2018). https://doi.org/10.1016/j.aap.2018.08.011

Security Verification of Instant Messaging Cryptographic Protocols

Gloria O. Olivares Ménez[1,2] (ORCID), Kevin A. Delgado Vargas[1,3] (ORCID),
Felipe Bernstein Mery[4] (ORCID), and Gina Gallegos-García[1,3(✉)] (ORCID)

[1] Instituto Poloitécnico Nacional, Av. Juan de Dios Bátiz S/N,
Nueva Industrial Vallejo, Gustavo A. Madero, 07738 Ciudad de México, Mexico
[2] Escuela Superior de Cómputo, Av. Juan de Dios Bátiz S/N,
Nueva Industrial Vallejo, Gustavo A. Madero, 07738 Ciudad de México, Mexico
[3] Centro de Investigación en Computación, Av. Juan de Dios Bátiz S/N,
Nueva Industrial Vallejo, Gustavo A. Madero, 07738 Ciudad de México, Mexico
ggallegos@cic.ipn.mx
[4] Universidad Mayor, Av. Manuel Montt 367, 7500994 Santiago,
Providencia, Región Metropolitana, Chile

Abstract. There is no doubt that nowadays, the use of smartphones for communication between two or more entities through instant messaging applications has become a trend model in our society. New messaging applications started to emerge and try to replace traditional SMS. In fact, they have become the main communication route, and it is almost impossible to find someone who does not use at least one of these kinds of messaging applications. However, building them with security and privacy in mind of developers was not important in the beginning. In other words, when the popular messaging applications were created, they did not support end-to-end encryption, only standard client-to-server encryption, which gave the service providers access to more private information than necessary. Additionally, information that is exchanged in such instant messaging applications has the characteristic to be sensible that results in the necessity to achieve security services associated with users information, by achieving confidentiality, integrity, and authenticity in sent and received messages. In this article, we present a security verification on the Signal and MTProto 2.0 cryptographic protocols, which are contained in the most commonly used instant messaging applications. The security verification is made by using automatic verification tools and obtained results show that the protocols are flawless in terms of their construction, message delivery logic, and semantics. In other words, they are safe from attacks that automatic protocol verification tools check for.

Keywords: Cryptographic protocol · automatic verification tools · instant messaging · security services

1 Introduction

Nowadays, with the smartphone invention, communicating between entities anytime and anywhere around the globe is not a problem. Actually, according to a

© The Author(s), under exclusive license to Springer Nature Switzerland AG 2023
M. F. Mata-Rivera et al. (Eds.): WITCOM 2023, CCIS 1906, pp. 418–435, 2023.
https://doi.org/10.1007/978-3-031-45316-8_26

study made by the Association of Media Research portal (AIMC, by its acronym in Spanish) [1], the smartphone is the preferred main route for Internet connection. Another study [2] shows that 91.5% of the users on the Internet enter from smartphones and spend approximately 3 h and 39 min surfing on this device. Peer-to-peer communication was not the exception and instant messaging applications emerged, which allow the exchange of texts, files, and images amongst two or more people at the moment. As an interesting fact, 87% of the surveyed in the AIMC study said that they have used an instant messaging service.

Instant messaging applications have a very extensive use, ranging from personal and business use to chat with bots programmed to give answers to predetermined questions. The facilities they grant allow the information that travels on the communication channel to be sensitive or confidential depending on the use, whether personal or business. It makes cybercriminals try to find and exploit vulnerabilities in such applications. For these reasons, instant messaging applications should protect the information that goes through them. In order to achieve that necessity they use cryptographic protocols, which guarantee information security services such as confidentiality, authentication, non-repudiation, and integrity against different attacks [3], such as man-in-the-middle attacks, repetition attacks, parallel execution attacks, messages interception.

This kind of attack takes advantage of vulnerabilities that have not been corrected or considered in the instant messaging applications. As an example, Telegram was made for academic usage, so it does not feature end-to-end encryption activation. Another example could be observed between December 2020 and May 2021, when the highest number of malicious links sent to instant messaging applications was detected [4], reaching a total of 91,242 links, led by WhatsApp with an 89.6% and then Telegram with a 5.6%. The worst part is that the attacks have consequences not only for the users, but for the instant messaging applications, essentially monetary, legally, and in their reputation. Considering the aforementioned, some questions arise: Do the cryptographic protocols ensure the security services they must protect? Can the protocols improve their protection for users? By trying to give answers to these questions, in this paper we present a security verification of the instant messaging applications' protocols, Signal for WhatsApp, and MTProto 2.0 for Telegram, using automatic verification tools, specifically Scyther and Avispa, and the analysis of the vulnerabilities found in such cryptographic protocols.

The remainder of this paper is organized as follows: Section 2 shows some works related to this one. Section 3 describes the two cryptographic protocols we verify, Signal and MTProto 2.0 protocols. Section 4 describes the automatic verification tools we use to verify the cryptographic protocols. Section 5 details how the protocols were verified. Obtained results are presented in Sect. 6. Section 7 highlights our contribution by comparing obtained results with related work. Finally, Sect. 8 closes the document with a synthesis of results and the improvements that could be made in the protocols.

2   Related Work

Today's mobile applications where sensitive user information is stored and transmitted are subjected to malicious attacks, and the instant messaging application is no exception. In fact, messaging applications have changed since their inception, and now they are trying to keep information safe. Talking about instant messaging applications, different cryptographic protocols have been created to try to protect user information and since then such applications and their protocols have been the subject of different analyzes.

In [5] a vulnerability was discovered by Tobyas Boelter, which happens when WhatsApp automatically accepts new public keys of users that already have communication with others, without re-validating them. It provokes that WhatsApp re-sends all the messages in traffic that are identifiable as those that only have a validator, and the receiver has not received or read them.

In [6], the security features of the messaging application Signal is analyzed. The attack model presented considers two possibilities: 1. The session starts, where the attack can only be detected manually by physically checking the QR codes; 2. The session is established and the attacker forces a new communication by receiving the keys from one of the main entities, impersonating the other.

The work in [7] evaluates Telegram's block cipher scheme. They determined, in a theoretical way, that it is not safe under the IND-CCA security, which means that an attacker, with two different ciphertexts and a plaintext, can know with certainty which of the ciphertexts corresponds to the plaintext. In other words, the message confidentiality might be compromised by the attacker.

In [8], a study of the security of cryptographic primitives of the Signal and MTProto 2.0 protocols is presented. In the first one, the constant keys renovation for encrypting and decrypting prevents a possible attacker compromises the keys and accesses to old messages. In MTProto 2.0, they verify theoretically that when an encrypted message is received and when comparing the key message, the verification fails. It is deleted without notifying the sender of any error.

The work presented in [9] shows an analysis of the properties of secure messaging regarding trust establishment, conversation security, and transport security. The analysis compares two applications, WhatsApp and Signal, that use the same Signal protocol to verify how each one satisfies the security properties. It also shows the similarities and differences in how the two applications achieve the desired security of the protocol. However, many of the protocol implementation decisions result in vulnerabilities. The authors state that these vulnerabilities have a low probability of being exploited, since certain conditions must be met for the attack to be successful.

In [10] a comparative analysis between 3 of the most used instant messaging applications is presented, WhatsApp, Telegram, and Signal. The analysis focuses mainly on the protocols used by each one, as well as the security they offer. The paper shows a discussion of the considerations that can influence the impact of application security, such as user base, data collection, and usage policies. Some of the vulnerabilities that each application has had in the last 3 years are presented. Finally, packet sniffing is presented using Wireshark and Fiddler.

In [11] the analysis of the MTProto 2.0 protocol using the ProVerif automatic tool is presented. The different implementations of the protocol are considered, and each protocol is examined in isolation, relying solely on the guarantees provided by the previous ones and on the robustness of the basic cryptographic primitives. In the verifications carried out, the behavior of the users is taken into account, when relevant. The authors found that the rekeying protocol is vulnerable to a theoretical unknown key-share (UKS) attack [12] due to user behavior.

3 Instant Messaging Cryptographic Protocols

According to [3] a cryptographic protocol is a distributed algorithm, which defines a sequence of steps where the actions that are required to be executed between two or more entities are specified, in such a way that a specific security service is achieved.

Most of the time protocols work on an insecure network, where the attacker could read, modify, retain, or delete messages transmitted between entities participating in the protocol. That is the reason why in a cryptographic protocol, the information should travel protected using some cryptographic primitive. In this context, cryptographic protocols are intended to provide confidentiality, entity authentication, information integrity, and non-repudiation.

Cryptographic protocols, which could become exclusives to organizations, are the specific backbone of instant messaging applications. Roughly speaking, the most downloaded instant messaging application around the globe are WhatsApp, Telegram, WeChat, Facebook Messenger, QQ, Snapchat, Line and KakaoTalk. On the one hand, in [13], it is said that Facebook Messenger and WhatsApp were the most used applications in 2021 in the West, while KakaoTalk and Line were the most used in China and Japan. On the other hand, Telegram have increased its users due to the privacy policies published by WhatsApp, reaching 600 million users, however, it is still below WhatsApp with 2 billion users and Facebook Messenger with 1.3 billion [14]. Considering that, the number of users is a determining factor for our choice of cryptographic protocols to be verified, together with the availability of information and the documentation related to the cryptographic protocols used by each of the applications mentioned above. In this sense, WhatsApp and Telegram show the construction of their Signal and MTProto 2.0 cryptographic protocols respectively in a sequential manner. Below, we describe Signal and MTProto 2.0 cryptographic protocols [15,16].

3.1 Signal, WhatsApp Protocol

The Signal protocol, designed by Open Whisper System [15] for the WhatsApp instant messaging application, has end-to-end encryption. According to the official documentation in the WhatsApp page, for the end-to-end connections, the protocol has three main phases: Client Registration, Session Configuration, and Message Exchange.

In the first phase, when a client or a mobile device with the WhatsApp application is registered, it transmits its identity key, a key signed with its signature, and an unspecified number of one-time keys to the server that stores the public keys associated with an identifier corresponding to the user for which they were sent. Then, in the second phase, named session configuration phase, the transmitter establishes an encrypted session between peers, so two users can communicate in a secure and private way. When this session is done, the transmitter and receiver do not need to reestablish it unless, a reinstatement of the application, or a change of device, with the same number, takes place. There is a certain process that needs to be followed for establishing such a encrypted session. They are given as follows:

1. The user (transmitter) who wants to start a conversation asks for the public keys to the server, except the keys of one usage.
2. When the transmitter gets the keys, it saves them in different variables $I_{recipient}$ as the identity key, $S_{recipient}$ as the signed key, and $O_{recipient}$ as the one usage key. It also generates a pair of ephemeral masked keys $E_{initiator}$ with Curve25519 and a bit length of 32 bytes.
3. The transmitter keeps its own identity key ($I_{initiator}$), having a set of four or five keys, depending on the case.
4. The one who wants to initiate the communication, computes, with the obtained keys, a master secret using an ECDH function, which is a secret-sharing scheme where two entities establish a shared secret through an insecure channel.
5. The transmitter uses a function HKDF or HASH for key derivation, in order to obtain the Root and Chain keys of the secret master.

From previous steps it is important to clear up that Curve25519 is a function that allows, through the disposition of a private key, to generate a public key, and, if available, the private key of a user and the public key of another user, to generate a secret shared by both. Until the receiver responds, in all the messages sent by the transmitter, his ephemeral and identity keys are included. If the receiver has the intention of sending messages, he needs to calculate the secret master using his own private and public keys received in the incoming messages and uses, as well as the Hash function for obtaining the corresponding root and chain keys.

Finally, in the third phase, named message exchange, the transmitter and receiver, they both have a message key used in the block cipher AES-256, for encryption, and HMAC-SHA256 for message authentication. This key changes in each sending, and it is derivate from the chain key, which gives security for future keys. Such a chain key alters in two scenarios, message sending and message reception. In the first case, each time a key message is needed, it is computed with HMAC-SHA256. After that, the key Chain is updated with the HMAC-SHA256, so the key messages can not be calculated with this chain key. Finally, when a message is received, new chain and root keys are computed, inducing that the keys are not reused. The description made until now is depicted in Fig. 1.

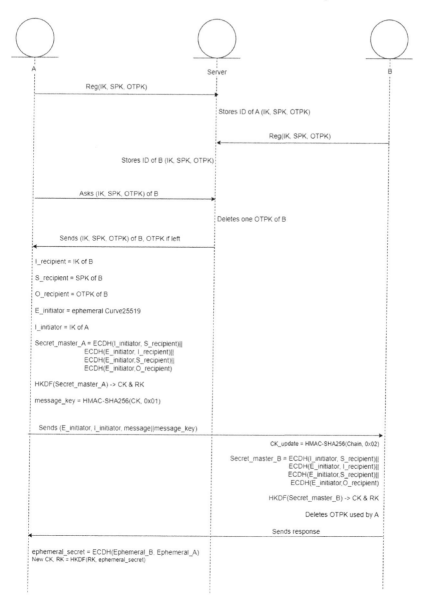

Fig. 1. Signal Sequence Diagram

3.2   MTProto 2.0 Protocol

For the Telegram protocol MTProto 2.0, in the end-to-end connections, there are two main phases: Key Generation and Key Exchange. To define the protocol, it should be considered two users, an initiator, and a receiver. The first action of the initiator, in the Key Generation process, is to get the Diffie-Hellman parameters from an executable method. Then, it tries if the elements are secure and adds an element of aleatory length, if necessary, generated by the server to attach entropy. After checking that, the elements are safe, and the parameter adds the necessary entropy, it ends up calculating a number a of 2048 bits and creates a parameter g_a, with the help of a function, which is included in the request to the receiver when establishing communication.

If the receiver confirms the request, it receives its own Diffie-Hellman parameters, which help with the computation of the number b (similar to a for the initiator) and builds the parameter g_b with the help of a function. Finally, it creates the shared key using g_a and b. The shared key has a footprint parameter that is the same as the last 64 bits of the masked key with the SHA-1 function.

After the receiver's authorization and the creation of g_b, the initiator receives this parameter and produces, on its own, a shared key using g_b and a. Both key's footprints must coincide, so the messages can be sent and processed. If not, the communication ends and the users are notified.

On the other hand, in the message exchange, in order to protect the messages or the plaintext, it commutes itself with a random number of bytes between 12 and 1024, divisible by 16. This result must be added as a part of the shared key. Then, all the previous set is masked with SHA-256 to give rise to the $msg_{keylarge}$ key, part of it is used for the construction of the key message (msg_{key}). Subsequently, the variables SHA-256$_a$ and SHA-256$_b$ are created, which have two addends that are masked with SHA-256, the key message and a shared key extract. They are used for the AES keys (AES $_{key}$ and AES$_{iv}$) production, which are applied in the final cipher of the message. Finally, the message is encrypted with the AES keys, and it is preceded by the message key and the footprint key before being sent. If the receiver wants to read the messages, he must verify that the message key is exactly the same as the 128 intermediate bits that make up the decrypted message masked by SHA-256, added to 32 bytes from the shared key. Details given until now can be found in Fig. 2.

4   Automatic Verification Tools

Cryptographic protocols can be prone to security or semantic failures. Their security verification by using automatic verification tools is defined as a combination of an abstract mathematical model and the requirements regarding its accuracy, together with a formal demonstration that determines if the protocol meets the necessary properties to function optimally. Hence, different tools help in such formal verification. This kind of tools verify their cryptographic properties, including their semantics but only under certain scenarios raised in the tools.

The tools for protocol verification vary depending on how the security verification is performed. They can be divided into two main techniques: the formal model and the cryptographic model. The first one abstracts the cryptographic primitives to functions within a space of symbolic expressions and the security properties to a formal model. In the second one, the primitives are modeled into

Fig. 2. MTProto 2.0 Sequence Diagram

functions of bit strings and the security properties defined in terms of probability and computational complexity of successful attacks [17]. Currently, the formal verification of cryptographic protocols can be done manually or using automatic tools that speed up the process and obtain a more accurate result, since through an automated process a greater number of scenarios can be verified without being prone to errors with respect to the manual verification.

Some of the advantages of using automated verification tools are: Improve accuracy and consistency, increase coverage and depth, find vulnerabilities that are difficult for the human eye to detect, provide exhaustive verification by thoroughly enumerating possible states of the target and verifying all possible paths to the target, without relying on test cases. They also support various formal languages and methods such as assertions, model checking, equivalence checking, and theorem proving. Their disadvantages are: Limited and inflexible dependent on availability and performance of hardware and software, it is necessary large amounts of computational times and verifications may never be completed because they do not have desirability.

In the literature, there are different automatic verification tools such as: CASPER, Tamarin, ProVerif, Verifpal, Scyther and AVISPA, among others. All of them have their own characteristics, protocol description language, advantages and disadvantages. Some of them are described below:

CASPER/FDR [18] uses model checker (FDR) as a compiler to analyze security protocols. It consists of the Casper tool, which translates protocol descriptions into the process algebraic CSP, suitable for checking using FDR. It provides a time-based analysis of using the tool for analyzing a large collection of existing protocols. It can be used either to find attacks upon protocols, or to show that no such attack exists. It is subjected to the assumptions of the Dolev-Yao Model, meaning that the intruder may overhear or intercept messages, decrypt and encrypt messages with keys that he knows, and he even could forge messages, but not perform any cryptologic attacks. It is important to mention that Casper does not cover all the features of security protocols, but it does provide a useful framework for investigating new ideas related to how to model new features within CSP.

Tamarin [19] is a security protocol verification tool written in Haskel, a functional language. It supports both falsification and unbounded verification in the symbolic model. It automates cryptographic protocols with an unbounded number of sessions through two modes: interactive and automated. Although it is considered the most used tool for analyzing and proofing security protocols, it has some limitations. e.g. It only operates in the symbolic model and thus can only capture attacks within that model, and given a certain equational theory. The underlying verification problems are undecidable in general, so Tamarin is not guaranteed to terminate.

ProVerif [20] is an automatic cryptographic protocol verifier developed by B. Blanchet. It is worth mentioning that it can handle many different cryptographic primitives (shared and public-key cryptographic, hash functions, etc.). Also, it analyzes an unbounded number of sessions by using over-approximation and represents protocols by Horn clauses. Some limitations for ProVerif are: It does not support all equations, as a consequence may happen that the pre-treatment of equations by ProVerif does not terminate. For instance, associativity cannot be handled by ProVerif for this reason, which prevents the modeling of primitives such as XOR (exclusive or) or groups.

Verifpal [21] is a software for verifying the security of cryptographic protocols, which uses a symbolic formal verification. It uses a new language named Verifpal language, it is meant to illustrate protocols close to how one may describe them in an informal conversation, while still being precise and expressive enough for formal modeling. Verifpal does not allow users to define their own cryptographic primitives. Instead, it comes with built-in cryptographic functions. The biggest limitation is that Verifpal is still highly experimental software. Using it in a classroom or learning environment is welcome, but it should not yet be relied upon for academic formal verification work.

Scyther and AVISPA automatic verification tools allow a verification of the security of the cryptographic protocols, by validating if a protocol satisfies the security requirements for which it was created [22]. Considering limitations of previous automatic verification tools, we decide to use Scyther and AVISPA as the automatic tools for security verification of the Signal and MTProto 2.0 cryptographic protocols. They can analyze the security of the protocols and the semantics of the security properties that are verified. Additionally, they provide results that can be used to improve the protocol itself, if necessary.

4.1 Scyther

Scyther was developed by Cas Cremers in 2006 [23, 24]. It performs the verification with an unlimited number of protocol executions, provides a graphical interface in which the protocol description and security parameters must be entered. As output, it delivers a report of the resulting analysis and in the event that one or more attacks can be carried out, the tool displays a graph for each one. It can review all possible scenarios. In case one or more attacks are found during the verification, the tool creates and displays a tree, where possible attacks can be observed. It is capable of verifying man-in-the-middle attacks and characterization. In the same way, it can perform a protocol characterization analysis.

Scyther uses the Security Protocol Description Language (SPDL). Such a language allows the verification of claims, manually and automatically, which allows the tool to be requested to validate certain aspects of the protocol (e.g., the secrecy of a value). This provides confidentiality or certain properties necessary for authentication. Finally, the protocol can be analyzed from the point of view of each role, so the tool takes a finite number of possibilities in the execution of the protocol.

4.2 AVISPA

This tool has a graphical interface that allows the user to edit the specifications of a protocol, based on the security service that is expected to be achieved. In the same way, a role-based modular language called HLPSL (High Level Protocol Specification Language) is used. Such a language allows structuring the code in a control flow of complex security properties and different cryptographic primitives. In addition, a language of the tool is presented that allows selecting a simplified HLPSL code. The tool has features, among which is the implementation of analysis techniques, which allows for a step-by-step analysis of the execution of the protocol [25].

Avispa describes five scenarios, each one represented with buttons in its interface: HLPSL2IF, OFMC, ATSE, SATMC and TA4SP. The first one declares a standard scenario, where given the specifications and goals, starting from an initial state, an attack state can be generated due to defects and vulnerabilities. The OFMC button models a malicious entity who is going to make attacks upon weak keys and deficient specifications of algebraic properties of cryptographic operators. It bases its operations in attack restrictions. ATSE allows verifying if identity fraud is possible in the protocol and the actions that the malicious entity can do if it succeeds. SATMC considers the initial state of the protocol and all the scenarios in which security services are not fulfilled. Afterward, it translates those attack scenarios using a model and verifies that those attacks can be executed. Lastly, with TA4SP, tests without limit of sessions can be made. Its logic is based on Genet and Klay's [26] malicious entity knowledge approximation of protocol verification.

5   Security Verification on Cryptographic Protocols

For making the analysis on the cryptographic protocols Signal and MTProto 2.0, it is necessary that we define the scenario for the attacks in each tool. Although AVISPA defines such scenarios within its pre-run configuration, Scyther performs all possible attacks at the same time, in a single run.

5.1   Experimentation

The use of the aforementioned automatic verification tools helps to verify that the designed protocols guarantee security services, such as authentication, confidentiality, integrity and non-repudiation. The equipment used for the installation and subsequent use of verification tools has the following characteristics: Processor: AMD Ryzen 5 - 8 CPUs - 2.1 GHz. Memory: 8 GB RAM. Capacity: 1 TB HDD + 250 GB SSD. Connection speed: 500 Mbps download + 11 Mbps upload. The chosen automatic verification tools have differences in terms of the operating system in which they can be executed. The Scyther tool can be executed on Linux and Windows operating systems, meanwhile Avispa can only be executed on Linux. Therefore, to carry out the execution of the automatic verification tools, it was necessary to install a virtual machine using the Oracle VM Virtual Box software. The Ubuntu 10 system was chosen for both, because the download exists for this Operating System, standardizing executions by a common factor. The tools present a high-level programming environment, in which, based on a protocol code or algorithm, they can check if it is reliable or has vulnerabilities. The configuration of the tools is done for both protocols as follows.

5.2   Methodology

The verification of the protocols is carried out with a methodology that depends on the tool that is being used, so the steps performed with each of them is described below:

Scyther: Step 1. Coding of the protocol in the Security Protocol Description Language. Step 2. Definition of the claims that are sought to verify the security of the protocols. Step 3. Execution of the verification with the following verification and advanced parameters: Maximum number of runs: 2, Matching type: typed matching, Search pruning: Find best attack. Maximum number of patterns: 10. Step 4. Obtaining graphic elements displayed by the verification of the tool to the protocol.

AVISPA: Step 1. Coding of the protocol in the High Level Protocol Specification Language. Step 2. Definition of knowledge among the entities participating in the protocol. Step 3. Selection of the reasoning engines: OFMC (On-the-fly Model Checker), Cl-AtSe (Constraint-Logic-based Attack Searcher), SATMC (SAT-based Model Checker) and TA4SP (Tree Automata based on Automatic Approximations for the Analysis of Security Protocols). Step 4. Obtaining graphic elements displayed by the verification of the tool to the protocol.

5.3 Scyther

For this tool, the entities involved in the process are three: Initiator, Server and Receiver. Subsequently, the variables and functions that will be used in the rest of the code are defined. For both protocols, the use of private and public keys is required. In this sense, the two keys are specified, one public and one secret, and these are inverses of each other. Variable hash functions are specified as well as macros used for long operations indicated in the protocol. Finally, the interactions between the entities and the verifications that are required for the security services are written.

5.4 AVISPA

The first thing to define in this tool are the identifiers that correspond to the users or entities, the types of data, the functions and the keys to use. Then, we proceed with the exchange of messages, where it is indicated which entity is the one that transmits to the other and what is the content of the message sent. Subsequently, the tool requires that it be specified what knowledge each entity has of the variables participating in the protocol. That is, each entity must have knowledge of its private keys as well as the public keys of all other entities. And to start an execution cycle, what nickname is assigned to each one of them. Finally, it is written which service is required to be verified with respect to previously defined variables. Particularly in AVISPA, three goals that are related to those services are evaluated, these are: strong authentication, weak authentication, and confidentiality.

6   Results

Once the process of coding the cryptographic protocols in the automatic verification tools language has been completed, the analysis of the vulnerabilities is identified by different works within the framework of Scyther and Avispa tools. In the following sections, we show the results.

6.1   Security Verification of Signal and MTProto 2.0 with Scyther Tool

When the Scyther tool runs the codification of the Signal and MTProto 2.0 cryptographic protocols in the language that the tool requires to interpret, it showed that with respect to the defined "claim", it does not present any commitment. For each "claim", the result obtained is "Ok". It means, it complies with ensuring the security service and there are no associated attacks. In Fig. 3a and 3b we can see that the execution was carried out with a maximum of two consecutive cycles of the cryptographic protocols. It was made by looking for vulnerabilities and possible attacks. The initial approach was to run the tool without limit of sessions, but when configuring these parameters, the software started an infinite cycle, from which no results were obtained, regardless of the execution time.

Claim			Status	Comments
Wapp	Init	Wapp,i1 Alive	Ok	No attacks within bound
		Wapp,i2 Weakagree	Ok	No attacks within bound
		Wapp,i3 Niagree	Ok	No attacks within bound
		Wapp,i4 Nisynch	Ok	No attacks within bound
		Wapp,i5 Commit Rec,nb	Ok	No attacks within bound
		Wapp,i6 Secret nb	Ok	No attacks within bound
	Server	Wapp,s1 Alive	Ok	No attacks within bound
		Wapp,s2 Weakagree	Ok	No attacks within bound
		Wapp,s3 Niagree	Ok	No attacks within bound
		Wapp,s4 Nisynch	Ok	No attacks within bound
	Rec	Wapp,r1 Alive	Ok	No attacks within bound

				Status	Comments
MTProto	Init	MTProto,i1	Niagree	Ok	No attacks within bound
		MTProto,i2	Nisynch	Ok	No attacks within bound
		MTProto,i3	Alive	Ok	No attacks within bound
		MTProto,i4	Weakagree	Ok	No attacks within bound
		MTProto,i5	Commit Recv,text	Ok	No attacks within bound
		MTProto,i8	Secret text	Ok	No attacks within bound
	Recv	MTProto,r1	Niagree	Ok	No attacks within bound
		MTProto,r2	Nisynch	Ok	No attacks within bound
		MTProto,r3	Alive	Ok	No attacks within bound
		MTProto,r4	Weakagree	Ok	No attacks within bound
		MTProto,r5	Commit Init,text	Ok	No attacks within bound
		MTProto,r8	Secret text	Ok	No attacks within bound

(a)   (b)

Fig. 3. Results obtained from the verification of (a) Signal and (b) MTProto 2.0 with the Scyther tool.

6.2   Security Verification of Signal and MTProto 2.0 with AVISPA Tool

The executions of the Avispa tool for the Signal and MTProto 2.0 cryptographic protocols revealed that they both comply with ensuring the security services that the tool can evaluate. In other words, they are secure. Figures 4a and 4b show obtained results from the analysis that the Avispa tool provides for both of them respectively.

The security verification made by the Avispa tool specifies the compliance of evaluated security services, how many consecutive cycles performed and if it was made bounded or without limit of sessions for a particular scenario.

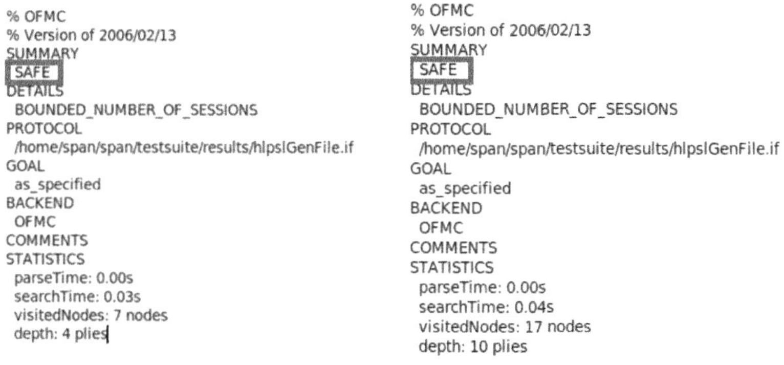

```
% OFMC                                    % OFMC
% Version of 2006/02/13                   % Version of 2006/02/13
SUMMARY                                   SUMMARY
  SAFE                                      SAFE
DETAILS                                   DETAILS
  BOUNDED_NUMBER_OF_SESSIONS                BOUNDED_NUMBER_OF_SESSIONS
PROTOCOL                                  PROTOCOL
  /home/span/span/testsuite/results/hlpslGenFile.if   /home/span/span/testsuite/results/hlpslGenFile.if
GOAL                                      GOAL
  as_specified                              as_specified
BACKEND                                   BACKEND
  OFMC                                      OFMC
COMMENTS                                  COMMENTS
STATISTICS                                STATISTICS
  parseTime: 0.00s                          parseTime: 0.00s
  searchTime: 0.03s                         searchTime: 0.04s
  visitedNodes: 7 nodes                     visitedNodes: 17 nodes
  depth: 4 plies                            depth: 10 plies

        (a)                                       (b)
```

Fig. 4. Results obtained for the (a) Signal and (b) MTProto 2.0 protocols by verifying in the AVISPA tool.

Table 1. Results of AVISPA configurations for Signal and MTProto 2.0 protocols

Setting	Results in Signal	Results in MTPROTO 2.0
HLPSL2IF	Safe	Safe
OFMC	Safe	Safe
ATSE	Safe	Safe
SATMC	Inconclusive	Inconclusive
TA4SP	Not supported	Not supported

Table 1 summarizes obtained results of the security verification on instant messaging cryptographic protocols for each specified scenario. In such a Table we can see that in three scenarios the tool outputs "Safe". It means that ensuring security services is fulfilled, while in two it is not possible to determine it. The reason why it is not possible to determine it is that these two scenarios do not support the modulo or xor operators [27].

7   Discussion

Related work summarized in Table 2 let us see different analyzes that have been carried out on instant messaging cryptographic protocols. These have been carried out with different approaches, ranging from the different functions that the protocols have to in an isolated way, such as sending messages. Another approach have also considered the keys comparison in the execution of specific attacks such as the impersonation attack.

These verifications have been by using manual methods. It means that the way in which the tests can be carried out is by using the application and verifying QR codes in the applications of each user.

The literature review shows that the formal analysis that exists so far focuses on the cryptographic protocols with specific conditions that take into account the behavior of the users. Therefore, the found attack is likely to be unsuccessful.

Unlike the related work, where the analysis is mainly focused on the use of the application, that is, directly on the implementation of the cryptographic protocol, in our security verification the analysis was carried out directly on the construction of the protocol. It was performed with the automatic verification tools, which analyzes the cryptographic primitives and the way the protocol was built with them.

The results we show in Sect. 6 let us know that the protocols are secure within the conditions that the tools verify. However, with the verification of the protocols using AVISPA, two of the results indicate that they are inconclusive or not supported. Therefore, it remains an open problem in the verification of the protocols through the SATMC and TA4SP engines.

In this way, we can say that the protocols are implicitly secure in their construction and semantics. And that, possibly, the vulnerabilities found in the literature do not depend directly on their construction, but on the algorithms used in their implementation, which is out of our scope.

Table 2. Comparison of related work' analysis approaches to messaging applications

Work	Protocol	Analysis approach	Verification method	Tool
[5]	Signal	Message forwarding	Manual	Smartphone
[6]	Signal	Impersonation	Manual	Smartphone
[7]	MTProto	PLE and LBS	Oracle	-
[8]	Signal, MTProto 2.0	Key comparison	Theoretical	-
[9]	Signal	Implementation	Manual	Smartphone
[10]	Signal, MTProto 2.0	Implementation	Packet sniffing	Wireshark and Fiddler
[11]	MTProto 2.0	Unknown key-share	Formal	Proverif
Our	Signal, MTProto 2.0	Protocol Verification	Formal	Scyther and AVISPA

8   Conclusion

In this work, we present a security verification on Signal and MTProto 2.0 instant messaging cryptographic protocols. We focused on the both protocols because they are inside the most used instant messaging applications, called WhatsApp and Telegram. Our security verification was made from a formal protocol verification approach, which allowed verification by including their semantics and security, under only scenarios that the Scyther and Avispa verification automatic tools can evaluate.

After the security verification with the AVISPA and Scyther tools on Signal and MTProto 2.0 instant messaging cryptographic protocols, it is possible to conclude that they do not have vulnerabilities in bounded scenarios, where the limit is the number of consecutive rounds, with each round meaning new information that the attacker is learning from the previous interactions.

As future work, we recommend to pay attention in the way users use the instant messaging applications because there exists certain scenarios that can be defined as the main reasons for vulnerabilities. A first scenario occurs when a change is carried out in the device associated with a particular telephone number, with which the instant messaging applications link the user accounts with the contacts of such a number. Faced with this, the contact should be blocked and request the application to confirm the trust of the contact, also resulting in the interruption of the execution of the cryptographic protocol, which in turn suspends the exchange of messages between the entities. Under this same scenario, in addition to contact blocking, applications must notify the user's contacts when the user changes devices, similar to when the instant messaging application is reinstalled, generating new shared keys. A second scenario, exclusively regarding WhatsApp, occurs with security notifications, since these remain disabled by default and are only activated if the user searches for the option and decides to do so. For any user, these notifications must always exist, regardless of the instant messaging application used. Making the user aware of the events associated with the security of the application leads to taking preventive and corrective measures on time. A third scenario to consider, is related to the MTProto 2.0 protocol, which could be optimized according to the ISO/IEC 19772:2009 standard, in the sense that the encryption process is firstly performed and then the HMAC is applied, ensuring confidentiality, when there may be compromise of the shared key.

References

1. Asociación para la Investigación de Medios de Comunicación | AIMC. https://www.aimc.es/. Accessed 06 June 2023
2. Situación Global Mobile o Móvil 2021. https://yiminshum.com/mobile-movil-mundo-2021/. Accessed 06 June 2023
3. Menezes, A., Vanstone, S.A., van Oorschot, P.C.: Handbook of Applied Cryptography. CRC Press, Boca Raton (1996)
4. Phishing attacks via WhatsApp, Telegram soar in India. https://www.siasat.com/phishing-attacks-via-whatsapp-telegram-soar-in-india-2164308/. Accessed 06 June 2023
5. WhatsApp Retransmission Vulnerability. https://boelter.blog/2016/04/whats-app-retransmission-vulnerability/. Accessed 06 June 2023
6. Schröder, S., Huber, M., Wind, D., Rottermanner, C.: When SIGNAL hits the fan: on the usability and security of state-of-the-art secure mobile messaging. In European Workshop on Usable Security. IEEE, pp. 1–7 (2016) https://doi.org/10.14722/eurousec.2016.23012
7. Jakobsen, J., Orlandi, C.: On the CCA (in) security of MTProto. In Proceedings of the 6th Workshop on Security and Privacy in Smartphones and Mobile Devices, pp. 113–116. (2016). https://doi.org/10.1145/2994459.2994468

8. Andrieş, Ş., Miron, A. D., Cristian, A., Simion, E.: A survey on the security protocols employed by mobile messaging applications, Cryptology ePrint Archive, Paper 2022/088 (2022). https://eprint.iacr.org/2022/088

9. Sajoh, D.I., Atiku, A.U., Naibi, R.S.: Secure messaging: analysis of signal protocol implementation in whatsapp and signal journal of digital innovations & contemp res. In Sc., Eng & Tech. vol. 6, No. 3. pp 63–72, (2018). https://doi.org/10.22624/AIMS/DIGITAL/V6N3P6

10. Bogos, C.E., Mocanu, R., Simion, E.: A security analysis comparison between Signal, WhatsApp and Telegram, Cryptology ePrint Archive, Paper 2023/071 (2023). https://eprint.iacr.org/2023/071

11. Miculan, M., Vitacolonna, N.: Automated symbolic verification of telegram's MTProto 2.0. In Proceedings of the 18th International Conference on Security and Cryptography, SECRYPT 2021, pp. 185–197 (2020) https://doi.org/10.48550/arXiv.2012.03141

12. Blake-Wilson, S., Menezes, A.: Unknown key-share attacks on the station-to-station (STS) protocol. In: Imai, H., Zheng, Y. (eds.) PKC 1999. LNCS, vol. 1560, pp. 154–170. Springer, Heidelberg (1999). https://doi.org/10.1007/3-540-49162-7_12

13. Global Mobile Messaging Forecast 2021. https://store.businessinsider.com/products/global-mobile-messaging-forecast-2021. Accessed 06 June 2023

14. WhatsApp, Messenger, Telegram, Snapchat: quiénes y dónde usan estas aplicaciones. https://cnnespanol.cnn.com/2021/10/06/whatsapp-telegram-snapchat-quien-y-en-donde-se-estan-usando-orix/. Accessed 06 June 2023

15. WhatsApp Encryption Overview Technical white paper. https://www.whatsapp.com/security/WhatsApp-Security-Whitepaper.pdf. Accessed 06 June 2023

16. End-to-End Encryption, Secret Chats. https://core.telegram.org/api/end-to-end. Accessed 06 June 2023

17. Abadi, M., Rogaway, P.: Reconciling two views of cryptography (the computational soundness of formal encryption)*. J. Cryptology 15, 103–127 (2002). https://doi.org/10.1007/s00145-001-0014-7

18. Lowe, G., Broadfoot, P., Dilloway, C.: A compiler for the Analysis of security protocol. Version 1.12, Oxford University Computing Laboratory (2009). http://www.cs.ox.ac.uk/gavin.lowe/Security/Casper/manual.pdf

19. Meier, S., Schmidt, B., Cremers, C., Basin, D.: The TAMARIN prover for the symbolic analysis of security protocols. In: Sharygina, N., Veith, H. (eds.) CAV 2013. LNCS, vol. 8044, pp. 696–701. Springer, Heidelberg (2013). https://doi.org/10.1007/978-3-642-39799-8_48

20. Blanchet, B., Smyth, B., Cheval, V., Sylvestre, M.: ProVerif 2.04: Automatic cryptographic Protocol Verifier, User Manual and Tutorial (2021)

21. Kobeissi, N., Nicolas, G., Tiwari, M.: Verifpal: cryptographic protocol analysis for the real world. In: Bhargavan, K., Oswald, E., Prabhakaran, M. (eds.) INDOCRYPT 2020. LNCS, vol. 12578, pp. 151–202. Springer, Cham (2020). https://doi.org/10.1007/978-3-030-65277-7_8

22. Patel, R., Borisaniya, B., Patel, A., Patel, D., Rajarajan, M., Zisman, A.: Comparative analysis of formal model checking tools for security protocol verification. In: Meghanathan, N., Boumerdassi, S., Chaki, N., Nagamalai, D. (eds.) CNSA 2010. CCIS, vol. 89, pp. 152–163. Springer, Heidelberg (2010). https://doi.org/10.1007/978-3-642-14478-3_16

23. Das, A.K., Odelu, V., Goswami, A.: A secure and robust user authenticated key agreement scheme for hierarchical multi-medical server environment in TMIS. J. Med. Syst. 39(9), 1–24 (2015). https://doi.org/10.1007/s10916-015-0276-5

24. Cremers, C.J.F.: The scyther tool: verification, falsification, and analysis of security protocols. In: Gupta, A., Malik, S. (eds.) CAV 2008. LNCS, vol. 5123, pp. 414–418. Springer, Heidelberg (2008). https://doi.org/10.1007/978-3-540-70545-1_38

25. Armando, A., et al.: The AVISPA tool for the automated validation of internet security protocols and applications. In: Etessami, K., Rajamani, S.K. (eds.) CAV 2005. LNCS, vol. 3576, pp. 281–285. Springer, Heidelberg (2005). https://doi.org/10.1007/11513988_27

26. Genet, T., Klay, F.: Rewriting for cryptographic protocol verification. In: McAllester, D. (ed.) CADE 2000. LNCS (LNAI), vol. 1831, pp. 271–290. Springer, Heidelberg (2000). https://doi.org/10.1007/10721959_21

27. Javed, A.: Formal analysis of CWA 14890-1. In: Prouff, E. (ed.) CARDIS 2011. LNCS, vol. 7079, pp. 314–335. Springer, Heidelberg (2011). https://doi.org/10.1007/978-3-642-27257-8_20

Elaboration of an Information System to Improve Operational Discipline in PEMEX with LAGS Methodology

Vladimir Avalos-Bravo[1](✉) (iD), Meliton Flores Ledesma[2] (iD), and Denisse Guadalupe Melo Lugo[3] (iD)

[1] SARACS Research Group, Instituto Politécnico Nacional, CIITEC, SEPI-ESIQIE, UPIEM, ESIME Zacatenco, Mexico City, Mexico
ravalos@ipn.mx
[2] Instituto Politécnico Nacional, SEPI-ESIQIE, Mexico City, Mexico
meliton.flores@pemex.com
[3] Instituto Politécnico Nacional, ESIQIE, Mexico City, Mexico
dmelol1900@alumno.ipn.mx

Abstract. During the last few years, catastrophic accidents occurred at Petroleos Mexicanos (Pemex), which led to the company working on implementing A Safety, Health, and Environmental Protection Program that contribute to reducing them. To be able to provide the hydrocarbon, oil, and petrochemical pipeline transportation service improvements, the 12 Best International Practices (MPI) of the SSPA System (Safety, Occupational Health, and Environmental Protection) are used to guarantee the safety of the personnel that their works. The present work proposes to develop an information system that allows monitoring one of these 12 MPI called operational discipline, to guarantee rigorous monitoring and compliance of all procedures and operational, administrative, and maintenance instructions of the Work Centers through a methodology that comprises five phases for the development of this information system to Transportation, Maintenance, and Pipeline Services Management operational discipline by collecting the information in a system developed exclusively for this purpose that documents the cases of incidents present in the areas, which records, monitors and controls that documents the operational discipline process shows containing and evaluating the 5 stages of number 6 Best International Practices to standardize the procedures reported by each area.

Keywords: PEMEX · Hydrocarbons · Operational discipline · Information system · LAGS Methodology

1   Introduction

The Board of Directors of Petroleos Mexicanos approved on March 27, 2015, the Agreement for the creation of the Pemex Logistica Subsidiary Productive Company (PLOG) [1], whose purpose is to provide the service of transportation and storage of hydrocarbons, oil, and petrochemicals and other services related to Pemex, Subsidiary Productive Companies (EPS), Subsidiary Companies and third parties, through pipeline transportation strategies and by maritime and land means [1].

In 2017, PLOG declared a network of pipelines (multiple pipelines, oil pipelines, LP gas, and petrochemicals), of 15,233.5 km, to provide the transportation service of hydrocarbons, oil products, and petrochemicals by pipeline and to ensure its availability and reliability, it must have a Comprehensive maintenance plan that allows optimizing human, material, and equipment resources [1].

To provide transportation, maintenance, and operation services through the pipeline, the Pemex Regulatory Control System concentrates and publishes on its website the procedures that govern as regulations and that must be applied and updated by the Transportation Subdirectorate of Pemex Logistics, to avoid the occurrence of accidents and incidents with workers, infrastructure, and the environment, always adhering to the regulatory framework of the SSPA System.

The Management of Transportation, Maintenance, and Pipeline Services to be able to provide transportation services by pipeline for hydrocarbons, oil products, and petrochemicals, uses the 12 Best International Practices (MPI) of the SSPA System and the SAP System to schedule maintenance to its operational infrastructure safely for its workers, facilities, environment, and neighbors to carry out maintenance effectively, with a procedure to improve and mitigate all risks and bad work habits.

Therefore, it uses Element 6 of the 12 MPI of High-Performance Standards (Operative Discipline), to monitor and rigorously and continuously comply with all procedures and work instructions, both operational, administrative, and maintenance of a Work Center. Through the administrative process of having them available with the best quality, effective communication, and compliance to those who apply them and demanding their strict adherence.

1.1   SSPA System

In the years 1995 and 1996 in Petroleos Mexicanos (Pemex) catastrophic accidents occurred that motivated the state-owned Pemex Gas and Basic Petrochemicals to seek an international system that would help reduce incidents, taking advice from the Dupont company with the implementation of the Safety, Health, and Environmental Protection Program [2]. In 1997, Pemex Corporate began with the implementation of SIASPA in Pemex Exploration and Production (PEP), Pemex-Refining, Pemex-Petrochemical, and Corporate, to reduce the number of accidents as shown in Fig. 1.

From 1997 to 2004, the Safety Systems in Petroleos Mexicanos continued and in 2005 the safety systems were relaxed again and the number of accidents and disabling injuries increased in some Pemex facilities, forcing Petroleos Mexicanos to carry out a diagnosis in terms of Safety, Health at Work and Environmental Protection in its infrastructure and critical operations to reduce risks within it, corporate image, and negative impacts on

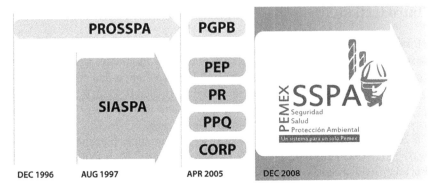

Fig. 1. SSPA, SIASPA implementation at Petroleos Mexicanos [2].

the environment. As a result of this diagnosis, Pemex defines an integrated system called the Petroleos Mexicanos Safety, Health, and Environmental Protection Administration System.

The Pemex-SSPA System is integrated as A set of interrelated and interdependent elements (PROSSPA and SIASPA) and is based on the 12 Best International Practices and organizes the remaining elements into three Subsystems that address Process Safety, Occupational Health, and Environmental Protection, which serve to manage the general aspects of safety, occupational health, and environmental protection, which includes and defines planning activities, responsibilities, practices, procedures [3], analysis root cause, the contractors and the necessary resources to comply with the Policy and the Principles of Petroleos Mexicanos.

1.2 International Best Practices

The 12 MPI are the support on which the ASP Process Safety Administration Subsystems, AST Occupational Health Administration and SAA Environmental Administration are based and through their interaction with Operational Discipline ensure the prevention of incidents and continuous improvement in SSPA as is shown in Fig. 2.

The best international practices are the basis of the PEMEX-SSPA system for safety and are made up of 12 elements that serve to manage the general aspects of safety, health at work, and environmental protection in the company Petroleos Mexicanos and from which the safety policy emanates. SSPA applies to the entire organization. Within its conceptual components are the visible and demonstrated commitment, the SSPA policy, and the responsibility in the line of command. In the structural ones, we have the structured organization, aggressive goals and objectives, high-performance standards, and the role of the SSPA function. The operational elements are effective auditing, incident investigation and analysis, training and coaching, effective communication, and progressive motivation. With this list, the 12 best practices of PEMEX are concluded.

Best international practices are the basis of the **PEMEX-SSPA** system for safety and are made up of 12 elements that serve to manage the general aspects of safety, health at work, and environmental protection in the company Petroleos Mexicanos and from which the safety policy emanates.

SSPA applies to the entire organization. Within its conceptual components are the visible and demonstrated commitment, the SSPA policy, and the responsibility in the line of command.	Structured organization, aggressive goals and objectives, high-performance standards, and the role of the **SSPA** function.	Are effective auditing, incident investigation and analysis, training and coaching, effective communication, and progressive motivation.

Fig. 2. 12 International Best Practices and 3 SSPA Subsystems [4].

1.3   Element 6, High Standards of Performance/operational Discipline

Petroleos Mexicanos and its subsidiary organizations, through the Corporate Directorate of Planning, Coordination and Performance monitor the fulfillment of the Safety, Health and Environmental Protection policy and its principles in their work centers, to establish safe and reliable work environments, with controlled risks in their daily maintenance activities. In recent years, the statistical analysis of the incidents and accidents in Petroleos Mexicanos indicates a clear recurrence of some factors among which are the breach of work procedures which negatively impacts the performance in safety, health, and environmental protection and environmental protection and the various causes that encourage non -compliance in the application stand out:

- Lack of availability of procedures in the areas where they require the use of them.
- Incomplete and/or extensive procedures
- Procedures with a high degree of complexity for consultation
- Lack of clarity
- Lack of update
- Obsolescence (it does not reflect the current conditions or facilities)
- Ignorance, lack of understanding by staff
- Lack of dissemination, and training to staff
- Lack of consistency in its application

The high standards of performance/ operational discipline (OD) are the rigorous and continuous compliance of all work procedures and instructions, both operational, administrative, and maintenance of a work center, through the process of having them available with the best quality and compliance, communicate them effectively to those who apply them and demand their strict attachment [5]. For the above to remain constant and sustainably, it is necessary national and international, including the following: guidelines, technical guides, reference standards, procedures, instructions, rules, and criteria. The transport, maintenance, and duct services management have the availability of infrastructure of duct transport systems, the availability of maintenance programs where the operational technical procedures should be applied, as well as the availability to verify that the Activities out of the program (emergencies) are carried out with security under procedures. It has the Internal Network of Pemex and computer equipment and software for the development of diagnosis and data analysis (SAP, Excel, work orders, procedures, etc.). Table 1 shows the total number of processes concerning the total kilometers per pipeline.

Table 1. Several procedures vs. Pipelines km.

Sector	Number of Procedures	Pipelines kms
Mendoza	171	1,779.230
Guadalajara	133	765.605
NPX-Etano	70	300.000
Tlaxcala	72	720.100
Cardenas	139	2,159.813
Monterrey	217	2,399.808
Topolobampo	100	231.352
Rosarito	138	223.167
Valle Mexico	143	1,024.738
Guaymas	121	250.528
Venta de Carpio	100	696.525
Reynosa	127	761.672
Catalina	96	1,116.809
Victoria	130	1,178.385
Madero	182	1,302.446
Torreon	187	1,657.557
Total:	*2126*	*16,567.735*

1.4 LAGS Methodology

The systems development life cycle is the set of activities that users, analysts, designers, and builders need to carry out to develop and implement a computer-based information system [6]. The LAGS methodology serves as the basis for developing an information system since it considers the life cycle of the development of any computer-based information system.

The proposed methodology is divided into five stages or phases that are described below: Phase 1 Analysis of the operational discipline management system, Phase 2: Design of the operational discipline management system, and Phase 3: Construction of the operational discipline management system. Operational discipline, phase 4:

Implementation of the operational discipline management system, and finally phase 5: Operation of the operational discipline management system.

Each of these phases must include the elements, guides, and suggestions to carry out the process in each phase of the development of this information system for the management of operational discipline in the Sub-Management of Safety and Environmental Protection, dependent on PEMEX Exploration and production.

2 Methodology Application to the Study Case

To carry out the proposed system, it is essential to collect data regarding the number of reports that are handled by area to understand the classification that must be given to the operational discipline according to the type of accident reported.

To facilitate this task, we must start from phase 1 of the methodology called analysis, in this phase, the current situation of the parastatal company will be examined in a general and detailed way through its security area. Will this allow the environment that composes it to be identified and the elements where the problem develops, in addition to considering the available resources and those that are required to establish, what to do? Generating a proposed solution.

Then, phase 2 of the methodology is proposed. It tells us about planning. In this phase, the recommendations and diagnosis proposed in phase 1 are taken, which was the beginning of the change procedure in the analyzed system, in this case, the operational discipline report. This phase, in turn, makes it possible to identify the objectives and plan the activities to be carried out to achieve the objectives set.

Subsequently, phase 3 will be worked on, which is the design and construction of the system to report the operational discipline of the workers. In this stage, we will work with the activities obtained in the previous phase. These actions will be carried out under software that allows feeding the information obtained and modeling it so that it complies with the security standards established by the company, In this way, the representation of the environment to be developed or the work interface will comply with what has been indicated and will be built in this way. This stage follows up on system testing.

Phase 4 will determine the efficiency with which the developed system can count. For this, a pilot test will be carried out, classifying in the menu of the operational discipline reporting system only those that are classified according to Sect. 6 of the 12 PEMEX international best practices. This will allow us to include the risk activities more easily and know how to act when any of these occurs.

Once the previous phase has been completed, the system will be implemented in the work areas of the unit so that the findings can be reported according to the newly assigned classification in Phase 5.

3 Discussion and Results

Once the Analysis and Design phases have been completed according to the LAGS methodology, applying the techniques and tools proposed by these stages, it was possible to obtain the bases for the development of the computer-based Information System, this will be of great importance to simplify the procedures of operational discipline reported.

Performing an analysis of the 2,126 reported procedures, the codes not repeated in 16 sectors of pipelines that shared their total procedure census are reviewed in a dynamic table of Excel, the amount is reduced to 1,939 unique codes of procedures, which are listed below.

Cuenta de Secto:tiquetas de color ▾ Etiquetas de f ▾	Cárdenas	Catalina	Guadalajara	Guaymas	Madero	Mendoza	Monterrey	NPX-Etano	Reynosa	Rosarito	Tlaxcala	Topolobampo	Valle México	Venta de Carpio	Victoria	Total general
PXL-ST-GTMSD	1															1
PXL-ST-GTMSD	1															1
PXL-ST-GTMSD	1															1
PXL-ST-GTMSD-PTO-0007						1										1
955-52190-PO-*	1															1
PXL-ST-GTMSD-J221-IE-300							1									1
PXL-ST-GTMSD-591-51540-PTO-47			1													1
PXL-ST-GTMSD	1															1
PXL-ST-GTMSD-STMDGS-3221-ITO-001						1										1
300-50000-PGA-	1															1
300-50000-PGO	1		1	3	1	1										7
300-50000-PGO-09	1															1
572-51540-PEO-018													1			1
572-51540-PEO-034													1			1
572-51540-PEO-10-STD-MXX-D-10													1			1
572-51540-PEO-12-STD-MXX-D-12													1			1
572-51540-PEO-15													1			1
572-51540-PEO-18-STD-MXX-T-08													1			1
572-51540-PEO-25													1			1
572-51540-PEO-26													1			1
PXL-ST-GTMSO-PO-061													1			1
PXL-ST-GTMSO-PTO-061											1					1
PXL-ST-GTSMD-PE-048													1			1
PXL-ST-GTSMD-PTO-043													1			1
PXL-ST-GTSMD-PTO-044													1			1
PXL-ST-GTSMD-PTO-045													1			1
PXL-ST-GTSMD-PTO-046													1			1
PXL-ST-GTSMD-PTO-047													1			1
PXL-ST-GTSMD-PTO-048													1			1
PXL-ST-GTSMD-PTO-049													1			1
PXL-ST-GTSMD-PTO-050														1		1
ST-GTMSD-LGM-01															1	1
Total general	139	96	133	121	182	171	217	70	127	138	72	100	143	100	130	1939

Fig. 3. Procedures in Dynamic Table organized by code.

Making the classification of the operational discipline only with the 9 Critical Procedures with code GDSSSTPA of the Safety and Hygiene Regulation of Petroleos Mexicanos, these are reduced to 474 procedures registered in the Pipeline Sectors, once the taxonomy has been reviewed to avoid duplication of generated reposts, there are only 63 procedures left according to the following classification:

4 Operational Technical Guide.
9 Critical Procedures.
10 Specific Procedures.
39 Technical Operating Procedure (Fig. 4).

Due to the above, the review of 2,126 operational procedures of the spatiality reported in Fig. 3 was carried out, to correct errors in the taxonomy and avoid duplication of names according to the generated report.

Subdirección de Transporte
Gerecia de Transporte, Mantenimiento y Servicios Ductos

Código	Nombre del Documento Técnico Operativo
PXL-GDSSSTPA-PCS-01	Entrada segura a espacios confinados
PXL-GDSSSTPA-PCS-02	Protección contra incendio
PXL-GDSSSTPA-PCS-03	Equipo de proteccion personal
PXL-GDSSSTPA-PCS-04	Prevención de caídas
PXL-GDSSSTPA-PCS-05	Seguridad electrica
PXL-GDSSSTPA-PCS-06	Bloqueo de Energia y Materiales Peligrosos
PXL-GDSSSTPA-PCS-07	Delimitación áreas de riesgo
PXL-GDSSSTPA-PCS-08	Apertura y cierre de lineas y equipos de proceso
PXL-GDSSSTPA-PCS-09	Izaje de cargas
PXL-GDSSSTPA-PTO-0001	Procedimiento tecnico operativo para la planeacion,programacion, autorizacion, y ejecucion de tr
PXL-GDSSSTPA-PTO-0002	Elaboración y aplicación de análisis de seguridad en el trabajo
PXL-GDSSSTPA-PTO-0003	Auditoria al sistema de permisos de trabajo
PXL-GDSSSTPA-PTO-0004	Auditorias Efectivas
PXL-GDSSSTPA-GTO-001	Guía Técnica Operativa para Elaborar y Actualizar Documentos Técnicos Operativos.
PXL-GDSSSTPA-PTO-0005	Procedimiento Técnico Operativo Tecnología del Proceso
PXL-GDSSSTPA-PTO-0006	ARP Procedimiento Técnico Operativo para Realizar Análisis de Riesgos de Proceso en Instalac
PXL-GDSSSTPA-PTO-0008	Procedimiento Técnico Operativo para Revision de Seguridad Prearranque
PXL-GDSSSTPA-PTO-0032	Procedimiento Técnico Operativo para el Emplazamiento a Paro Seguro de Instalaciones, Equip
PXL-GDSSSTPA-PTO-0034	Procedimiento Técnico Operativo para Realizar Simulacros Operacionales
PXL-GDSSSTPA-PTO-0041	Procedimiento Técnico Operativo para la Administración de Bloqueos/Inhabilitación (bypass) de I

Fig. 4. GDSSSTPA Procedures new classification.

4 Conclusions

The analysis and design proposed in this work are focused on the development of computer-based information systems that allow streamlining and efficient administrative control of operational discipline reports carried out in the. Different areas of SSPA, since it will allow the administrators of these security systems to make decisions related to the data generated given the ease of having the information quickly and easily. This type of technological project is essential to gather the necessary information and implement security measures, as well as improvements that protect personnel from undesired events through diagnoses of poor performance of activities called operational discipline. This makes it possible to reduce investment costs and time, in addition to having benefits for the safety of employees, since systems tailored to the interested parties are obtained, in this case, PEMEX. Likewise, strengthen the areas where these diagnoses are not clear or do not have the correct information.

Among the benefits obtained by implementing the proposed methodology, we find the generation of actions according to the needs to be resolved, the establishment of the cause-and-effect relationship, and the diagnosis of these cases is built starting from the general and reaching the particular. at each stage, it allows rapid detection of training needs, defines functions and activities in a timely manner, adapts to changes, among others.

Currently and in the XXI century, called as the century of knowledge, the use of technology in the management of risks and accidents through computer-based information systems has become a necessity. It is important to mention that there are no guides or directives for the creation of a management system for operational discipline.

PEMEX only has guidelines to follow for the reporting of the operational discipline that satisfies point 6 of the 12 best international practices; however, it does not have a guide for the development of a computer-based information system.

The implemented methodology allowed to change the vision that was had about the operative discipline in the suggestion of sanitation and environmental protection.

As the information obtained was a core part of the development of the system creation process, the results showed a paradigm shift, which allowed a simpler program.

Acknowledgments. This project was funded under the following grants: SIP-IPN: No-20230046 with the support of CIITEC-IPN, and special thanks to Hernan Abraham Perez Flores for the figure's edition.

References

1. IR ASF Homepage (2017). https://www.asf.gob.mx, last accessed 10 May 2023
2. Sandoval, G.: Años acumulados de vida productiva potencial perdidos por accidentes de trabajo en Petroleos Mexicanos. Salud Pública de México, México (1996)
3. Guía Técnica para Procedimiento de Operación y Prácticas Seguras. PEMEX-SSPA, Mexico (2010)
4. Politica y Principios de Operación de SSPA. PEMEX.SSPA, Mexico (2021)
5. Guía Técnica de Disciplina Operativa. PEMEX-SSPA, Mexico (2010)
6. Bauza Guadalupe, Metodología para implementar un sistema de enseñanza aprendizaje virtual presencial en un entorno educativo de nivel superior. México (2006)

ICIS: A Model for Context-Based Classification of Sensitive Personal Information

Sara De Jesus Sanchez(✉) [iD], Eleazar Aguirre Anaya[iD], Hiram Calvo[iD], Jorge Enrique Coyac Torres[iD], and Raul Acosta Bermejo[iD]

Centro de Investigación en Computación CDMX, Instituto Politécnico Nacional, CDMX, Mexico

{sdejesuss2100,jcoyact1900}@alumno.ipn.mx, {eaguirrea,fcalvo, racostab}@ipn.mx

Abstract. Sensitive personal information is at risk of exposure by the institutions it is shared. Institutions are responsible for preserving the privacy of the personal data they hold, even more so, in the case of sensitive data. This paper shows the design of ICIS, a model that considers the context to identify 55 personal data types in unstructured texts of government type documents, regardless the size and type, and then classify each text segment as sensitive personal information, using natural language processing and machine learning techniques. ICIS not only indicates whether a text segment contains sensitive information or not, it also indicates personal data identified in each text segment, their location in the document and whether each text segment is classified as sensitive information. The main contributions of this work are both the identification of personal data and the classification of sensitive information based on the context, and the definition of sensitive personal information, in computational terms.

Keywords: personal data · sensitive information · machine learning · classification · natural language processing · cybersecurity

1 Introduction

The protection of individuals regarding the automated processing of their personal data originates in Convention 108 of the Council of Europe in 1981. One of its main points is to ensure the confidentiality of sensitive personal data by the organizations responsible for it. Organizations must ensure the confidentiality of the personal information for which they are responsible, according to its level of sensitivity, value, and criticality [1, 2].

Personal data, in general, are those concerning an identified or identifiable natural person [3]. Sensitive personal data are a subset of personal data, defined by the European Commission as data that refer to the most intimate sphere of its holder, or whose misuse may give rise to discrimination or entail a serious risk to it, such as racial or ethnic origin, present or future state of health, genetic information, biometrics, religious, moral, philosophical beliefs, political opinions, and sexual preferences. Sensitive personal data are subject to specific processing conditions, as they require robust protection [4, 5].

M. F. Mata-Rivera et al. (Eds.): WITCOM 2023, CCIS 1906, pp. 445–459, 2023.
https://doi.org/10.1007/978-3-031-45316-8_28

Organizations must ensure the security of the personal information for which they are responsible, according to the level of sensitivity, value, and criticality of it. For this reason, classifying it is the basis for reducing security risks. These risks can be enormous for individuals, for organizations and for governments.

In Mexico, there are laws to regulate the processing of personal data carried out by public and private institutions: Ley General de Protección de Datos Personales en Posesión de Sujetos Obligados (Ley General) and Ley Federal de Protección de Datos Personales en Posesión de Particulares (LFPDPPP). These laws establish high penalties, and in the case of sensitive personal data, the penalties can be increased up to twice [6].

The present paper presents the design of ICIS, a model to identify personal data and classify it as sensitive information, in unstructured texts of government documents where the writing style is formal, and the documents vary in types and sizes. ICIS identifies the different types of personal data in each text segment of a document using natural language processing (NLP) and then classifies each text segment as sensitive personal information using machine learning (ML). Both identification and classification consider the context of the data.

2 Related works

Textual classification of sensitive personal information is addressed as a NLP problem, which uses language processing within a document to classify it into a particular category [7].

Graham McDonald et al. used n-grams, grammatical analysis "Part of Speech" (POS) and support vector machines (SVM) with fixed patterns for the classification of sensitivity of texts in English. The use of grammatical analysis for preprocessing is a reference for identifying sensitive text sequences [8].

Yan Liang et al. used incremental learning and similarity comparison (ILSC) for sensitive text classification in Chinese, incremental support vector machine (ISVM), online random forest (ORF), and naive Bayes (nB). These machine learning algorithms were compared [9].

Gousheng Xu et al. employed convolutional neural networks (CNNs) and recurrent neural networks (RNNs) to detect sensitive information in unstructured Chinese texts. They compared these models [10].

Huimin Jiang et al. designed a classifier of sensitive medical data in Chinese with the SVM algorithm, nB and KNN [11].

Ji-Sung Park et al. developed a Data Loss Prevention (DLP) system to classify Korean words into sensitive personal data categories using "Named Entities Recognition" (NER) [12]. The use of NER can be considered to identify entities such as names, places, organizations that could be classified as sensitive information.

NLP techniques have been used for personal data identification, and the methods to classify documents as sensitive information are based on ML.

Personal data is not easy to identify in unstructured text of government documents, because there are different types and sizes, and because it depends not only on whether a text segment contains certain words or formatted identifiers, but on the context. Also, personal data appear only in some text segments of the documents, and we want to know the findings, their locations, and their classifications.

The text preprocessing through segmentation, the personal data categories, stop words elimination, NER and POS, the vectorization with the personal data, in addition to the use of ML algorithms, are taken from the state of the art to identify personal data and classify it as sensitive information.

Sensitive information could be obtained from metadata even in no text documents. There were no sensitive information classification studies that consider metadata. In this study only the file type was read from the metadata, but in the next studies the classification of sensitive information in metadata will be considered.

3 Solution

The objective of the present study was to design a model to identify and classify sensitive personal information in government type documents, using NLP and ML techniques, to prevent its exposure on government organizations sites. This model was named ICIS: Identification and Classification of Sensitive Personal Information.

In ICIS, personal data contained in each unstructured text segment of government documents can be identified considering the context, and then classified as sensitive information, through NLP and ML, regardless of the document's size and type.

Government documents have different formats, ICIS identifies the file type from the metadata, if the document handles text, its content will process.

To locate the findings within the document, it was proposed to classify sensitive information for each text segment with personal data, instead of the whole document.

The ICIS model was designed based on above considerations, such as the different formats, the text segmentation and the context-based identification and classification, as described in 3.1.

Identification and classification of sensitive personal information were proposed to be completely related to the context of the speech. The context analysis is detailed in Sect. 3.2.

3.1 ICIS model

The ICIS model is presented in Fig. 1. The input to ICIS is the file to be analyzed. The output is a json structure with the findings and classification for each text segment in the document.

Fig. 1. The model ICIS.

The model ICIS consisted of six stages in which the text document was analyzed to identify personal data and classify it as sensitive information. The stages are:

A. Metadata and content separation. All files, regardless of their format, have metadata, the format file was read from metadata. Files that handle text (txt, csv, pdf, html, docx, xls, ppt) were analyzed to identify and classify sensitive information in their content. Files in another format were not considered.

B. Text segmentation. The textual content of a document can be segmented into pages, paragraphs, sentences, table paragraphs, or into table sentences: the segmentation is flexible. The segment location indicates the page (p:); or the page and the paragraph (p: pr:), or the page, and the paragraph, and the sentence (p: pr: or:). For contextual analysis this study considered that there was sensitive information in a document if it was related to a person in a text segment, as described in Sect. 3.2.

C. Filtering. Each text segment is cleaned by removing special characters, consecutive white spaces, consecutive tabs, and consecutive line changes.

D. Personal data identification. ICIS identified 55 types of personal data grouped into 10 categories, such as work, academic, clinical, etc. The taxonomy is detailed in Sect. 3.3. Regular expressions, dictionaries, NER, and dependency analysis techniques were used to extract personal data from text segments. Identification was based on context to avoid false positives.

E. Vectorization. Once the identification is done, a vector is formed for each text segment, indicating whether it contained personal data. Initially the 55 features of a text segment vector were set to 0. When personal data are identified, the features values are set to 1. Figure 2 shows a personal data vector for a text segment.

NAME	ADDRESS	BIRTHDATE	RFC	CURP	PHONE	INE	SIGNATURE	EMAIL	PASSWORD	USERNAME	WORKPLACE	JOB POSITION	...	BLOOD TYPE	WEIGHT	HEIGHT
1	0	0	0	1	0	0	0	0	0	0	0	0	...	1	0	0

Fig. 2. Personal data vector for a text segment with 55 binary features.

F. Sensitive personal information classification SPIC. The vectors were classified as sensitive information, using ML. The classification is described in Sect. 3.4.

ICIS output was a json structure with the findings of personal data in the document. An output example is shown in Fig. 3.

The json structure included the analyzed file name, the location of each text segment with findings and within it, the text, the identified data, the four Personal and Sensitive Data Classifications PSDCC and the Sensitive Personal Information Classification SPIC.

In the output example, the file name, segment location, text original segment, findings, and classifications are shown. The text segment is classified as USD because it contains a CURP, as PID because it contains a name and a CURP, as SPD because it contains an allergy, and as *PD* since it contains at least one personal data. Therefore, this text segment is classified as *SI*.

{'Archivo.txt': {
':p:1:pr:8:or:1': {
'TEXTO': René Pérez López tiene una alergia a la penicilina, su curp es PELJ020710MDFRPN04',
'NOMBRES':['René   Pérez   López'],   CURP: ['PELJ020710MDFRPN04'],
'ALERGIA': ['penicilina]],
'CLASIFICADORES': ['USD', 'PID', 'SPD', 'PD', 'SI']}
}}

Fig. 3. ICIS model output example.

3.2 Contextual Analysis

This study considered the context for both identification and classification of the sensitive personal information in a text segment.

For identification, ICIS considered the context of the text segment in which a personal data was found. If the identification was not context-based, false positives would increase, for example 'DEL 2022' would be misidentified as a plate number, although it is a year.

In the identification process, grammar analysis helped to contextualize the personal data, which was identified also by the grammatical structure where it was found. ICIS analyzed the grammar in the text segment where the data was found, not only if it fit a format or matched a word.

For the classification process, ICIS considered the context of the text segment. If a text segment contained sensitive data which was not related to a particular person, it was not classified as sensitive information. To be classified as sensitive information, there must be sensitive data related to a particular person in a text segment.

3.3 Personal Data Type Taxonomy

ICIS is a model to identify and classify sensitive personal information in government documents. The types of personal data to identify in documents could be from different agencies, for example health, academic, social security, energy, and so on. There also could be identity numbers and the personal data listed as sensitive. Figure 4 shows the personal data type taxonomy for ICIS.

The proposed taxonomy contained 55 personal data types grouped in 10 categories. This was the taxonomy ICIS used to identify personal data and sensitive personal data in documents.

It was designed so it is possible to add more data types or to adapt it to any other personal data type taxonomy.

The proposed taxonomy contained 55 personal data types grouped in 10 categories. This was the taxonomy ICIS used to identify personal data and sensitive personal data in documents. It was designed so it is possible to add more data types or to adapt it to any other personal data type taxonomy.

Taxonomía de datos personales									
Identificativos	Electrónicos	Laborales	Tránsito/ Migratorio	Patrimonio	Salud	Académicos	Ideológicos	Intimidad	Características físicas
Nombre	Email	Empresa	Pasaporte	Sueldo	Estado de salud	Escuela	Religión	Preferencia sexual	Iris
Dirección	Contraseña	Puesto	Licencia	Impuestos	Historial clínico	Calificación	Afiliación sindical	Hábito	ADN
Fecha nacimiento	Usuario	Email laboral	Visa	Créditos	Enfermedad	Título	Preferencia política	Relación personal	Color de piel
RFC		Dirección laboral	Placas	Número de tarjeta	Tratamiento	Certificado	Organización civil		Huella dactilar
CURP			NIV	Inversiones	Estudio clínico	Número de cédula			Cicatriz
Teléfono				Afore	Alergia				Tipo de sangre
Firma				Seguros	Condición psicológica				Peso
INE					NSS				Altura

Fig. 4. Personal data type taxonomy

3.4 Sensitive Personal Information Classification

After analyzing the 55 personal data types, we noticed that we could use them in different ways:

- Some could help us to identify a person, like the name or identification numbers.
- Some others are personal data types related to an individual.
- Some, like health data, are sensitive data types related to a person.
- And there are some special personal data types that have a lot of information by themselves.

Because of that, in this study, four personal data classifications are proposed. With their results, the personal information is classified.

Personal Data Classifications. The four Personal Data Classifications PDCC were proposed: Identifier Personal Data IPD, Sensitive Personal Data SPD, Personal Data PD and Unit Sensitive Data USD.

Identifier personal data IPD are types of personal data with which an individual can be directly identified, such as name or official identification numbers.

Personal Data PD, such as academic or labor, related to an individual. There is personal information when personal data is related to a person by an identifier. If PD is found in a text segment without an identifier, there is no personal information.

Sensitive Personal Data SPD is a subset of personal data that by its nature may violate the fundamental freedom or privacy, such as those related to health, ideology, and sexuality of an individual. If sensitive data is found in a text without an identifier, there is no sensitive personal information, because there is no one who can be damaged or discriminated against. There is sensitive information only if sensitive data is related to a person by an identifier in a text segment.

Unit Sensitive Data USD are personal data considered sensitive by themselves because in addition to being identifiers, knowing their formats it is possible to obtain personal information such as age, sex, date, and place of birth. These personal data are sensitive as a unit. In Mexico with data as RFC (Federal Taxpayer Registration) or CURP (Unique Population Registry Id), and certain public tools, sensitive personal information could be obtained.

Personal Information Classification. In this study, the four Personal Data Classifications (IPD, PD, SPD, USD) were used to identify personal data and sensitive personal data in each text segment of a document. We found that there is personal information in a text segment, if it contains personal data related to an individual; and that there is sensitive personal information, if the text segment contains sensitive data related to a person.

With these proposed definitions, the *Sensitive Personal Information Classification* SPIC was proposed. A text segment is classified as sensitive personal information SI when it contains USD, or when it contains SPD and IPD. A text segment is classified as personal information PI when it contains PD and IPD. Otherwise, the text segment is classified as *Not Identified* information NI. The rules for SPIC are proposed and described in Sect. 3.5.

The four PDCC and the SPIC were implemented as ML classifiers. Every classifier was trained to predict if a text segment corresponds to a class. Model training is detailed in Sect. 4.

As described in Sect. 3.1, every text segment in a document is represented by a personal data vector which indicates whether it contained or not, the 55 personal data types. Personal data vectors are the input to the four personal and sensitive data classifiers. Each vector is processed by each classifier.

A new vector is formed with the results of the four PDCC. This vector is the input to the SPIC. Figure 5 shows the ICIS model made up by SPIC and the four PDCC.

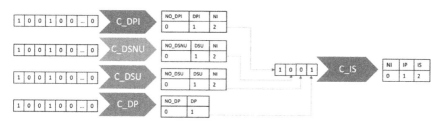

Fig. 5. Personal Information Classification with the four Personal Data Classifications

3.5 Sensitive Information Classification Rules

According to the sensitive personal information definition proposed in Sect. 3.4, in the ICIS model, three rules were proposed to classify information as *Sensitive Personal Information* SPI, as *Personal Information* PI or as *Not Identified* information NI. These classification rules receive as input the outputs of the four Personal Data Classifiers.

A first classification rule was proposed, where a text segment is classified as *Sensitive Personal Information* SPI if it contained USD or if it contained PID and SPD.

$$SPI = USD \lor PID \land SPD \qquad (1)$$

where:

SPI : $Textsegmentcontains Sensitive Personal Information$
PID : $Textsegmentcontains Identifier Personal Data$
SPD : $Textsegmentcontains Sensitive Personal Data$
USD : $Textsegmentcontains Unit Sensitive Data$

A second classification rule was proposed, where a text segment is classified as *Personal Information* PI if it contained PID and PD.

$$PI = PID \wedge PD \tag{2}$$

where:

PI : $Textsegmentcontains Personal Information$
PID : $Textsegmentcontains Identifier Personal Data$
PD : $Textsegmentcontains Dersonal Data$

Otherwise, there is no personal information identified. If the text segment was not classified either as SPI or PI, there was neither personal information nor sensitive information. There is no identified information because there is no person related. The text segment is classified as NI.

$$NI = \neg SPI \wedge \neg PI \tag{3}$$

where:

NI : $Textsegmentcontains No Identified information$
$\neg SPI$: $Textsegmentdoesnotcontain Sensitive Personal Information$
$\neg PI$: $Textsegmentdoesnotcontain Personal Information$

In computational terms, these classification rules defined the *Sensitive Personal Information*, the *Personal* (but not sensitive) *Information*, and the *Not Identified* information. These rules were used to label the vectors in the dataset for the ML classification model.

4   ICIS results

Following the methodology, after adjusting the model design, the experimentation for the classification model was designed, the tests were designed and executed, and their results were analyzed.

Tests were made for the preprocessing modules, for the classification of personal data and for the classification of sensitive information of the ICIS model. In this section the results of the Sensitive Personal Information Classification are presented.

The programming tools and libraries, the datasets used for training and testing to four PSDCC and SPIC are described in Sects. 4.1 and 4.2.

ML algorithms were applied to the four PSDCC (PID, PD, SPD, USD) and to the SPIC. The results of the four PSDCC and the SPIC are shown in 4.3 and 4.4.

4.1   Implementation Tools

The separation, segmentation and filtering preprocessing steps were implemented in python 3.10 with pyCharm, using pyExifTool, doc2txt, beautifulsoup4, python-pptx, xlrd and pdfPlumber tools. Personal data identification, vectorization and the classification were implemented with Spacy, nltk and pandas tools.

4.2   Classification Dataset

In ICIS, the input to the four PSDCC (PID, PD, SPD, USD) is a *Personal Data Vector*. A *Personal Data Vector* is made up by 55 binary features, that is 2^{55} possible combinations. A synthetic unbalanced dataset was generated with 17,000 random binary vectors, labeled according to the classifications described in Sect. 3.4, and to the classification rules proposed in Sect. 3.5. The dataset was partitioned into 70% for training and 30% for testing in all cases.

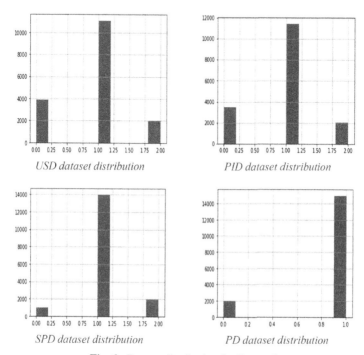

Fig. 6. Dataset distribution for Personal

The dataset distributions for the personal and sensitive data classifications are shown in Fig. 6.

The USD distribution was 24% labeled as NO_USD (0), 64% as USD (1) and 12% as NI (2). The PID distribution was 21% as NO_PID (0), 67% as PID (1) and 12% as NI (2). The SPD distribution was 6% as NO_SPD (0), 82% as SPD (1) and 12% as NI (2). The PD distribution was 11% as NO_PD (0) and 89% as PD (1).

The four PDCC had negative (0) and positive (1) classes, three of them had also a class for unidentified information (2). The positive classes frequencies were higher in all distributions.

The example vectors were randomly generated, so distribution aspects in real environments were not considered. Vectors and distributions are not representative of actual government document texts, where, depending on the institution, most of the personal data might belong to one or two categories in the taxonomy.

4.3 Data Classifications Results

The four Personal Data Classifications were implemented as machine learning classifiers: C_USD, C_PID, C_SPD, C_PD. In each classifier, four ML algorithms were applied and compared to select the best for the ICIS model. A feature selection was made for the creation of the model. The 55 selected features indicate the presence of the personal data in a text segment. The type of learning was supervised, the data was labelled. The size of the vector is not very large. Therefore, the ML classification algorithms applied were: nB, SVM, Logistic Regression (LR) and Decision Tree (DT).

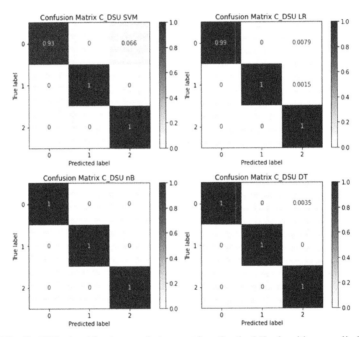

Fig. 7. USD classification confusion matrices for the ML algorithms applied.

USD Classification. Figure 7 shows the confusion matrices for the algorithms applied in the USD classification C_USD. The algorithm with the most true-positives and true-negatives in all classes was nB.

Precision, completeness, accuracy, and f1 metrics are shown in Table 1. The measure of accuracy is not relevant, because the classes are unbalanced. We are interested in recall, because when classifying text segments as unit sensitive data, false negatives are not accepted. The highest recall index is also obtained with the nB algorithm.

The C_PID and C_SPD classifiers have similar metrics, as they also have three classes, and their distributions are very similar to C_USD, as described in 4.1.

DP Classification. The C_DP classifier had a different distribution since it was binary. Figure 8 shows the confusion matrices of the ML algorithms. nB is the one with the most true-positives and true-negatives.

Table 1. USD Classification metrics for the ML algorithms applied.

C_USD	SVM	LR	nB	DT
Precision	0.9795	0.9969	1.0	0.998839
Recall	0.9782	0.9968	1.0	0.998835
Accuracy	0.9782	0.9968	1.0	0.998835
F1	0.9788	0.9969	1.0	0.998837

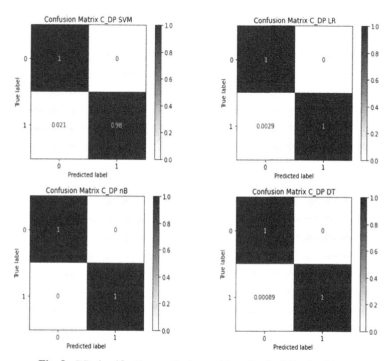

Fig. 8. DP classification confusion matrices for the ML algorithms

Precision, completeness, accuracy, and f1 metrics are shown in Table 2. The measure of accuracy is not so relevant, because the classes are unbalanced. We are interested in recall, because when classifying text segments as personal data, false negatives are not accepted. The highest recall index is also obtained with the nB algorithm.

Therefore, the nB was the selected ML algorithm to implement in the ICIS four personal and sensitive data classifiers (C_DSP).

Table 2. DP classification metrics for the ML algorithms applied.

C_DP	SVM	LR	nB	DT
Precision	0.989858	0.998557	1.0	0.9995552
Recall	0.989648	0.998553	1.0	0.9995548
Accuracy	0.989648	0.998553	1.0	0.9995548
F1	0.989753	0.998555	1.0	0.9995549

4.4 Sensitive Personal Information Classification SPIC result

The SPIC is implemented as a ML classifier C_SPIC and is described in Sect. 3.4. The DT, LR, SVM and nB algorithms were applied and evaluated to select the best for the ICIS model.

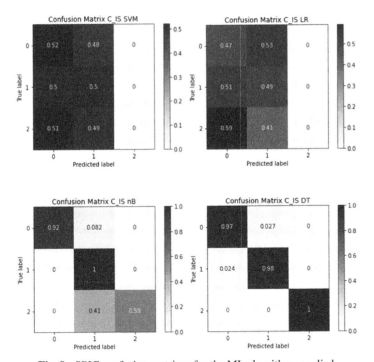

Fig. 9. SPIC confusion matrices for the ML algorithms applied.

Input vectors had 4 selected features, which were the results of the four PSDCC. Due to the small number of features, the dataset was integrated with 100 vectors from the PSDCC, labeled following the sensitive information classification rule defined in 3.5. The SPIC dataset is divided into 70% for training and 30% for testing. The distribution of the SPIC classification is 36% as NI, 33% as PI and 31% as SI.

The best performing algorithm is DT. Figure 9 shows that the confusion matrix with more true-positives and true-negatives, in all its classes is the DT algorithm.

In the C_SPIC, the dataset is balanced, so accuracy is considered reliable. However, again the metric we are interested in is recall because it is not possible to accept false negatives.

Table 3 shows the metrics for the C_SPIC classifier algorithms. The algorithm with the best metrics, including recall, is DT. Therefore, DT was the selected ML algorithm to implement in ICIS sensitive personal information classification model.

Table 3. SPIC classification metrics for the ML algorithms applied.

C_SPIC	SVM	LR	nB	DT
Precision	nan	nan	0.891	0.983
Recall	0.227	0.215	0.741	0.983
Accuracy	0.255	0.240	0.737	0.983
F1	nan	nan	0.809	0.983

5 Conclusions

Personal data could be identified considering the context, using NLP techniques, and classified as sensitive information by ML techniques. This study fulfills the objective of designing a model for the identification and classification of sensitive information in texts, which can help prevent its exposure in public sites documents.

The ICIS model not only indicates whether a text segment contains sensitive information or not, and not only identifies different types of personal data. As described in Fig. 3, in Sect. 3.1, it also indicates the types of personal data that were identified in each text segment, their values, their location in the document and whether the text segment is classified as sensitive information, derived from the classification rules and the four personal and sensitive data classifications proposed.

The main contributions of this work are the identification of personal data based on the context, the classification of sensitive information based on the context and the definition of sensitive personal information, in computational terms.

Unlike state-of-the-art, Personal data was identified and classified, not only by its format, but by its context. Contextual identification and classification were made due to the text segmentation and grammar analysis.

To classify information as sensitive, four personal and sensitive data classifications were defined. For the same purpose, sensitive information classification rules were proposed. These classification rules define, in computational terms, personal information and sensitive personal information.

The four machine learning algorithms performances evaluated for the four personal and sensitive data classifications were excellent, nB was the best, but it could not be compared with the state of the art, since the datasets are different. For the sensitive information classification, the DT algorithm performance was the best, with a small dataset and 4-feature vector. The results of the sensitive information DT classification metrics exceed what is reported in the state of the art, in Sect. 2, but it could not be compared, since the datasets are different.

5.1 Future Work

The implementation of the model in the PICIS platform (Plataforma de Identificación, Clasificación y Monitoreo de Información Personal Sensible) represents a security control oriented to the confidentiality of the personal data, which helps those in charge and responsible in the government institutions to avoid the exposure of sensitive information in public websites. There are agreements with two federal institutions, but it is expected to spread nationwide, initially.

It can be implemented as a security control to avoid exposing sensitive information also from private institutions, since the model is independent of whether the type of writing is legal, commercial or services; it is based on the personal data that is identified in unstructured text, to classify it as sensitive information.

The ICIS model can also be applied as a security control to help prevent the exposure or leakage of holders' personal data, verifying that the documents on their devices are free of sensitive information.

The data identification was according to Mexican regulations, such as license plates, id numbers as Registro Federal de Contribuyentes (RFC), Clave Única de Registro de Población (CURP) or Instituto Nacional Electoral (INE); however, it is possible to adapt the formats of the identification numbers used in other regions or countries.

It is possible to add data types to the taxonomy, adding the identification process, changing the size of the vector, and updating the four personal and sensitive data classifications and datasets.

In addition to analyzing the textual content of documents, it is possible to analyze the metadata of any type of files, not just text, but images, audio, video. In the metadata there may be personal information, such as the author, the place, the equipment with which the document was created, for example. The metadata could also be linked to the textual content of the document.

The classification module used a synthetic dataset; however, it is necessary to test with a real dataset, from documents that are available in public websites of the government institution.

Acknowledgements. This work was supported by Consejo Nacional de Ciencia y Tecnología (CONACyT), Instituto Politécnico Nacional (IPN), Comisión de Operación y Fomento de Actividades Académicas del IPN (COFAA), Programa de Estímulos al Desempeño de los Investigadores del IPN (EDI), Secretaría de Investigación y Posgrado del IPN (SIP), Convenio IPN-OAG-100-2021, Organization of American States (OAS), Cisco and the Citi Foundation, thanks to projects SIP 20222092, SIP 20211758 and the project Plataforma de Identificación, Clasificación y Monitoreo de Información Sensible (PICIS), winner of the Innovation Fund for Cybersecurity Projects in Latin America and the Caribbean 2021, created by OAS, Cisco and Citi Foundation.

References

1. Decree: Decree promulgating the Additional Protocol to the Convention for the Protection of Individuals with regard to the Automated Processing of Personal Data. https://www.dof.gob.mx/nota%5Fdetalle.php?code=5539474 (2018). Accessed Sep 2018
2. Data classification: «Data classification,» OAS. https://www.oas.org/es/sms/cicte/docs/ESP-Clasificacion-de-Datos.pdf (2019)
3. Opinion 42007: Article 291 Working Party Opinion 4, 2007 on the concept of personal data. What is personal data? https://ec.europa.eu/justice/article-29/documentation/opinion-recommendation/files/2007/wp136%5Fes.pdf (2007)
4. European 2021: What personal data are considered sensitive?" https://ec.europa.eu/info/law/law-topic/data-protection/reform/rules-business-and-organisations/legal-grounds-pro cessing-data/sensitive-data/what-personal-data-considered-sensitive%5Fes (2021)
5. EU Regulation 2019: Regulation EU 2019/679 of the European and Council Parlamento of 27 April 2016 on the protection of natural persons with regard to the processing of personal data and on the free movement of such data. https://eur-lex.europa.eu/legal-content/ES/TXT/?uri=CELEX:32016R0679%23d1e1547-1-1 (2016)
6. INAI 2021: Federal Law on Protection of Personal Data Held by Private Parties. https://home.inai.org.mx/?page%5Fid=1870I%26mat=p (2021)
7. Mathkour, H., Touir, A., Al-Sanie, W.: Automatic information classifier using rhetorical structure theory. In: Intelligent Information Processing and Web Mining, Proceedings of the International IIS: IIPWM'05 Conference held in Gdansk, Poland, 13–16 June 2005. Gdansk, Poland (2005)
8. Graham McDonald, C.M.I.O.: Using part-of-speech n-grams for sensitive-text classification. In: Proceedings of the 2015 International Conference on the Theory of Information Retrieval, New York, USA (2015)
9. Liang, Y., Wen, Z., Tao, Y., Li, G., Guo, B.: Automatic security classification based on incremental learning and similarity comparison. In: 2019 IEEE 8th Joint International Information Technology and Artificial Intelligence Conference (ITAIC), Chongqing, China (2019)
10. Xu, G., Qi, C., Yu, H., Xu, S., Zhao, C., Yuan, J.: Detecting sensitive information of unstructured text using convolutional neural network. In: 2019 International Conference on Cyber-Enabled Distributed Computing and Knowledge Discovery (CyberC), Guilin, China (2019)
11. Jiang, H., Chen, C., Wu, S., Guo, Y.: Classification of medical sensitive data based on text classification. In: 2019 IEEE International Conference on Consumer Electronics – Taiwan (ICCE-TW), Yilan, Taiwan (2019)
12. Park, J.-S., Kim, G.-W., Lee, D.-H.: Sensitive data identification in structured data through GenNER model based on text generation and NER. In: Proceedings of the 2020 International Conference on Computing, Networks and Internet of Things. Sanya, China (2020)

Transformational Leadership in Universities During the Pandemic by SARS-CoV-2

Jesus Antonio Alvarez-Cedillo[1] (ID), Ma. Teresa Sarabia-Alonso[2](✉) (ID),
and Teodoro Alvarez-Sanchez[3] (ID)

[1] Instituto Politécnico Nacional, UPIICSA, Ciudad de México, Mexico
[2] Tecnológico Nacional de México, Instituto Tecnologico Superior del Oriente del Estado de Hidalgo, Hidalgo, Mexico
tsarabia@itesa.edu.mx
[3] Instituto Politécnico Nacional, CITEDI, Tijuana, Mexico

Abstract. Currently, education presents important challenges due to the Pandemic we are going through due to SARS-COV-2, which has generated uncertainty in all aspects; hence the importance of incorporating leaders who provide confidence and guidance to their colleagues within organizations has become an indispensable factor. Therefore, this article analyzes leadership styles (positive, ethical, authentic, spiritual, service, and transformational Leadership) as case studies observed in Universities during the Pandemic to identify the leadership style that helps reduce uncertainty in this Pandemic.

Keywords: Universities · Leadership · Transformational Leadership · Institutions of Higher Education First Section

1 Introduction

Currently, companies require competitive advantages to change from a saturated market to a market full of opportunities; however, this is increasingly complicated; Leadership is considered a key resource to achieve organizational goals both with workers and in society (Cruz-Ortiz et al., 2013a, 2013b, 2013c). Human capital is, according to Lev (2001), an intangible resource that is formed throughout its trajectory in the company, which is why they are often primary factors in the construction of business competitiveness.

According to Lupano and Castro (2008), Leadership is essential to guide organizations and human resources towards strategic objectives; It is also vital since it gives the possibility of having the best resources, good planning, control, and supervision, but if you do not have an appropriate leader, it is complex for the organization to survive (Noriega, 2008).

Leadership is a skill that people have to influence their social circle; According to Heifetz, Grashow, and Linsky (2009), a leader is a promoter of change and a generator of a productive imbalance, giving up stability to mobilize the system, motivating people to give their best effort in achieving their goals—expectations, promoting and cultivating a vision that provides meaning to the purposes and objectives of organizations.

M. F. Mata-Rivera et al. (Eds.): WITCOM 2023, CCIS 1906, pp. 460–472, 2023.
https://doi.org/10.1007/978-3-031-45316-8_29

In the present investigation, six types of Leadership are analyzed, which were selected to share both their characteristics and examples of them, this a comparative table is built; In the last part of the article, they are analyzed as a case study of transformational Leadership in Universities during the Pandemic, where it is highlighted that the leader must succeed in enthusing his followers so that they feel identified with the work, that they perform and can perform beyond what could be expected.

2 Literature Review

According to Peiró and Rodríguez (2008), Leadership is crucial in promoting well-being and organizational and occupational health at the individual and collective levels. The above importance has allowed the appearance of different models of positive Leadership, where leaders encourage and try to maintain optimized performance levels through virtuous and eudemonic behaviors (Cameron & Plews, 2012).

Leadership is a skill that people have to influence their social circle; According to Heifetz, Grashow, and Linsky (2009), a leader is a promoter of change and a generator of a productive imbalance, giving up stability to mobilize the system, motivating people to give their best effort to achieve their expectations., promoting and cultivating a vision that provides meaning to the purposes and goals of organizations.

The leader must succeed in enthusing his colleagues so that they feel identified with their work and can perform beyond what might be expected.

According to Noriega (2008), Leadership is intended for followers to achieve common objectives that benefit the organization; he also argues that Leadership can be approached from two lines which are: the personal quality of the leader or as a function within an organization, system, community or society; being the last perspective the one that is studied the most, due to the utilitarian interest that can provide more significant benefit to the company.

According to Lupano and Castro (2008), Leadership is essential to guide organizations and human resources towards strategic objectives; It is also vital since it gives the possibility of having the best resources, good planning, control, and supervision, but if you do not have an appropriate leader, it is complex for the organization to survive (Noriega, 2008).

According to Dinha et al. (2014), two groups of Leadership are categorized, the established and the emerging theories; in terms of the latter, they are oriented towards ethics or positive, which have been the most analyzed, in which are found the of authentic Leadership, servant, spiritual, moral, and transformational Leadership.

The transformational leadership model has become one of the most relevant approaches to understanding the effectiveness of leaders in organizations (Lowe & Gardner, 2001). According to Cruz-Ortiz et al., (2013a, 2013b, 2013c), there is empirical evidence that the behaviors linked to this Leadership have a positive effect on individual and group variables such as employee commitment, motivation, and the efficient execution of tasks, as well as the relationship between variables such as effectiveness and organizational performance. Six types of Leadership, as well as their characteristics, are described below.

2.1 Transformational Leadership

According to the transformational Royal Spanish Academy (RAE), it belongs to or is related to transforming some sentence schemes into others. In the leadership discipline, different theoretical considerations are made about transformational Leadership, this from different epistemic positions of authors such as Bass and Avolio (2006), Velásquez (2006), Lerma (2007), Leithwood, Mascall and Strauss (2009), concluding that this style of Leadership implies a management process in which the modification of the environment represents a fundamental aspect, where the leader must become a motivational factor for organizational change, this being a constant.

Transactional Leadership is based on traditional models; it is based on exchange or transaction; the leader uses power, rewarding or punishing workers based on their performance; it does not go beyond the tasks and is limited to maintaining the normal flow of operations in the organization, with no tendency to strategic development (Contreras & Barbosa, 2013).

There are different postulates which address that traditional Leadership, oriented towards a transactional style (focused on the task), may be insufficient to facilitate organizational change and that, given its characteristics in terms of transformational Leadership, it could favor the adaptation of the organization -as a system-, to the current conditions of the environment, derived from the fact that in this Leadership the role of the leader is focused as an agent of change, which promotes commitment and motivates the team, focused on intangible qualities, seeking to generate relationships, provide values and give meaning to the activities carried out (Almirón V., Tikhomirova A., 2015).

"Transformational leadership seeks to motivate and encourage followers to actively participate in changes in the internal environment, for which it sensitizes each of them so that they empower themselves with the mission and vision; Consequently, they are activated to achieve it, within a healthy work environment, working with enthusiasm, with mystique, responsibility, productivity, a high sense of commitment to the achievement of organizational purposes" (Almirón V., Tikhomirova A., 2015).

According to Velásquez (2006), transformational Leadership is defined as a process of positive change in followers in such a way that there is harmonious collaboration.

3 Methodology

Documentary research collects data and information for research purposes by examining existing documents, such as historical records, government reports, newspaper articles, academic journals, and other written or recorded materials. This research method is used in various disciplines, including sociology, history, anthropology, and political science.

Documentary research aims to gather the information that is already available and analyze it to gain insight into a particular topic or issue. For example, researchers may use this method to investigate social phenomena, historical events, political trends, or economic patterns, among other subjects.

Documentary research typically involves systematically and critically analyzing primary and secondary sources. Primary sources are original documents or materials created when the event or phenomenon is being studied, such as diaries, letters, photographs, or government reports. Secondary sources are written or recorded materials that interpret or analyze primary sources, such as academic articles, books, or documentaries.

The process of documentary research involves identifying relevant sources, analyzing, and interpreting the information, and using the findings to support research conclusions or arguments. Documentary research is a valuable method for conducting research when other data collection forms, such as surveys or experiments, are not feasible or ethical. See Fig. 1.

For this study, published documents from different sources (Scopus & Journal Citation Reports of Clarivate) of information were located, searching for them in January 2020 in virtual libraries, using descriptors such as scientific writing, reviews, and critical reading. The records obtained were between 10 and 50 after the combinations made with keywords such as Leadership, leadership styles, and transformational Leadership; Another type of search was used on the Internet, which was carried out in the search engines "google academic" and "Dialnet" with the exact keywords.

From critical reading, case studies, and different reviews, those documents that contained transformational Leadership with other techniques used, both quantitative and qualitative, were selected in such a way that it will reach an understanding and comparison of each one, following a descriptive review that according to with Day (2005), is one of the most valuable reviews, providing the reader with an update on practical concepts in constantly evolving areas.

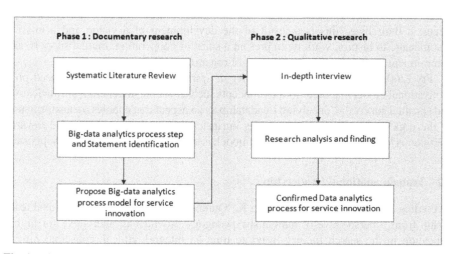

Fig. 1. The process of documentary research. Source Nopsaran Thua Hong Chai et al. Adopt big-data analytics to explore and exploit the new value for service innovation.

4   Leadership styles

According to Fairholm (1997), spirituality reflects the intimate relationship with the inner being as a bearer of moral values. It is important to note that spirituality encompasses more than any organized religion with its principles, dogmas, and doctrines (Zellers & Perrewe, 2003).

This theory of spiritual Leadership emerges within the conventional Leadership framework; more is needed to satisfy the subjects' needs in the organizational environment. Thus, authors such as Fairholm (1997) identified a series of qualities, such as the presence of essential objectives that they have defined, the moral convictions that they have rooted, high intellectual capacity, the social skills they present, and a particular focus on people developing values.

4.1   Spiritual Leadership

In 1996 Fairholm established the first model of spiritual Leadership, which was based on Reave's research where correlations are found between spiritual practices and effective Leadership; He also took ideas from Greenleaf about servant leadership, and thanks to all these contributions, Fairholm managed to cement his model which incorporates the capabilities, needs, and interests of both the leader and the followers, as well as the objectives and goals of the organization.

Spiritual leaders help their followers to be able to articulate their decisions about issues in their lives; this is a result of the development of a vision and a mission that manage to inspire, working to present a spirit of cooperation, mutual support, and commitment to the effective functioning of organizations.

Fry (2003) developed a causal theory of spiritual Leadership that is based on a motivational model that incorporates concepts such as vision, hope, faith, altruistic love, and spiritual survival, Conceiving Leadership as an aspect that enables a transformation of the organization as an entity that is intrinsically motivated and oriented towards continuous learning, as in any emerging model, issues arise that have not been supported.

4.2   Transformational Leadership

According to Rojas O., Vivas A., Mota K., Quiñónez J., (2020), transformational leadership from a perspective of humanistic pedagogy provides an alternative for higher education in the search for new ways to train an integral, ethical, conscious citizen committed to his social reality. Velásquez (2006), transformational Leadership is a style defined as a process of positive change in followers, focusing on transforming others to help each other harmoniously, integrally focusing the organization; which increases the motivation, morale, and performance of its followers; this concept was introduced by Burns (1978).

The most excellent elaboration of the construct corresponds to Bass (1985), who proposed the so-called Multifactorial Theory of Leadership, which conceptualizes Leadership based on defined behaviors articulated based on three factors: transformational Leadership, transactional Leadership, and laissez-faire leadership.

Transformational Leadership has been identified as Leadership that establishes a vision of the future, which is shared with the organization's members, considers individual differences, and acts as a stimulus for achieving organizational objectives and goals.

Transformational leaders are described as capable of motivating their followers to transcend their interests, so they direct their behavior toward achieving collective goals (Bass, 1985).

The transformational leader is considered the opposite of the transactional leader in which he has the characteristic of exchanging behaviors based on rewards (Burns, 1978); on the other hand, transformational Leadership is presented, according to Bass (1999), as the integration of factors such as idealized influence, inspiring motivation, intellectual stimulation, and individualized regard for followers.

The investigations carried out by Bass resulted in the realization of a multifactorial Leadership instrument (Bass, 1985), which has been used to validate the construct and the investigation. As a result, the transformational leadership model has become one of the most critical approaches for understanding the effectiveness of leaders in organizations (Lowe & Gardner, 2001).

With this Leadership, the awareness of the workers is stimulated, who are directed to accept and commit to the scope of the mission stated in the organization. According to Cruz-Ortiz et al., 2013a, 2013b, 2013c), there is empirical evidence that behaviors related to transformational Leadership have a positive effect on individual and group variables such as employee commitment, motivation, and efficient execution of tasks, which Bono, Judge et al. (2006) support where they demonstrate the relationship between the variables of effectiveness and general organizational performance of a company leadership.

4.3 Authentic Leadership

This type of Leadership arises from the attempt to overcome numerous examples of unethical conduct that have recently occurred in the political and business spheres (Luthans & Avolio, 2003); The concept of authenticity has its roots in Greek philosophy, although it was later used by humanistic psychology (Maslow, 1968), it is currently related to areas of positive psychology.

Authentic leaders can be described as those endowed with deep moral convictions, whose behavior is strongly inspired by these ethical principles for the benefit of the collective; they are aware of the actual content of their thoughts, emotions, abilities, value system, and above in which others perceive them, they present qualities such as confidence, optimism, hope, resilience and moral strength (Avolio, Gardner Luthans, May and Walumbwa, 2005). In addition, they avoid behaving in a way that hides their ideas and emotions, even when these could be uncomfortable for followers.

Avolio and Gardner (2005) are the most prominent authors of this orientation; they define, in their model, the components of authentic Leadership linked to the leader: positive psychological capital, moral perspective, self-knowledge, and self-regulation of behavior; in terms of influence processes: personal and social identification, positive modeling of behavior, emotional contagion and social exchange based on reciprocity and congruence; Finally, it also focuses on the followers: self-knowledge, self-regulation, personal development and finally they are oriented to the organizational context.

According to Luthans and Youssef (2004), the interaction of the previous components originates a sustainable competitive organizational advantage that translates into positive returns of a psychological nature; these leaders are perceived as more credible sources of information by their followers and considered generators of goals and well-drawn plans to achieve them.

Avolio et al. (2005) suggest that authentic leaders increase the social identification of followers with organizational principles.

4.4 Servant Leadership

Greenleaf (1977) conceived servant Leadership directly in the organizational context; this derived from the author's significant experience in companies, which is why he builds his reflection, where the servant leader is the one who places the needs, aspirations, and interests of his followers above his own; his deliberate choice is to serve others so that development and success can be achieved in the organization.

The philosophical foundations of servant Leadership are equally rooted in the Christian tradition (Sendjaya & Sarros, 2002). The servant leadership theory emphasizes the concept of service to others and the recognition that the organization's role is to enable the formation of individuals who can contribute to creating a positive organizational environment.

The concept of servant Leadership has presented an alert. However, due to the little support, different systematic investigations have been initiated on it since, in the current context, it is identified as an alert; for example, corporate leaders in the economy have presented unethical conduct.

4.5 Ethical Leadership

Ethical dimensions are present in the models of a transformational, servant, and, especially, authentic Leadership discussed above; Different authors have tried to develop the concept of ethical Leadership as an independent concept; for their part, Brown and Treviño (2006) developed the complete ethical leadership model, which according to their definition, this Leadership is given the task of promoting normatively appropriate behaviors in followers, based on actions they perform as a person, the interpersonal relationships they maintain and the leader, this from a reward system together with transparent communication.

However, there are no conclusive bases to establish it; this is because the behaviors of the leaders are normatively appropriate, leading to being considered subjective. Brown and Treviño (2006) have suggested a set of psychological processes that would explain the relationship between this type of Leadership and behaviors of an ethical nature, such as behaviors that benefit society and antisocial behaviors. These theoretical processes would be related to learning and social exchange. Therefore, ethical leaders can be role models who excel in ethically neutral environments.

4.6 Positive Leadership

Avolio and Gardner (2005) establish that this type of Leadership is conceptually linked to transformational Leadership (Bass, 1985) and authentic Leadership; these two models above are solid empirical support, contrary to positive Leadership, which is still in the affirmation process. According to Cameron (2013), this Leadership is based on the application of positive behavioral principles that arise from disciplines such as positive psychology (Seligman, Steen, Park, & Peterson, 2005) and positive organizational psychology (Cameron, Dutton, & Quinn, 2003).

Positive Leadership has three essential components: the leader focuses on the followers' strengths and abilities that reaffirm their human potential, focuses on results to facilitate above-average individual and organizational performance, and finally focuses on those components that can be analyzed as virtues of the person.

In different studies carried out by Kelloway et al. (2013), it has been found that in work teams led by a positive leader, the members show higher levels of labor well-being and present positive emotions, according to Cameron (2013), it has been managed to demonstrate that positive Leadership increases the performance of followers, as well as their commitment, interpersonal relationships, improving their communication significantly.

Cameron and Plews (2012) argue that the presence of an upbeat leadership style has facilitated the merger of organizations and increased levels of customer satisfaction.

5 Comparison of Leadership Styles

5.1 Results

The observed scenarios belong to the educational sector, in decentralized public Higher Education Institutions (HEIs), so the topic described above is of the utmost importance, considering that this type of leadership is required to transform teachers, increase their motivation and especially its performance, especially in this social crisis caused by COVID-19, where it has brought with it a difficult aspect to manage, this is the result of isolation, the use of technologies such as the Internet of Things (IoT) which allows a connection of all devices to the internet, however this requires prior technical ability, the ability to adapt to this change, eradicating resistance to technology and the internet, but above all due to social limitations, which is why the Transformational leadership is a tool that is required to achieve the goals of the institutions.

Description of Case A

The first scenario studied has an academic director who analyzes the options and trends required by the education sector in his region, due to the fact that during 2019 there is documentary evidence that all teaching staff already implemented technological tools such as Classroom, Edmodo or Moodle. In all the subjects taught at the institution, they also used free applications to carry out activities in synchronous and asynchronous sessions. This is where transformational leadership is identified, where the academic leader became an agent of change, visionary to provide tools, knowledge and skills to its followers, achieving a harmonious coexistence, with this the institution managed to reduce the risk of teachers feeling unprotected or even lost in their academic activities during this pandemic that is going through.

Some strategies implemented as part of the transformational leadership in the HEI, were observed in two aspects, on the one hand, the delivery of talks by experts in the area of psychology who provide recommendations and follow-up to avoid depression or some other mental health disorder among the staff teaching and in the second aspect was the execution of virtual forums where teachers exposed part of the aspects that concerned them that is presented in this online modality, where it is possible to share strategies among peers, generating empathy, motivation and decreasing uncertainty among teachers followers collaboratively.

Description of Case B

Regarding the collection methods used as focus groups and individual interviews carried out in the second institution, it is identified that there was no induction, training or monitoring of the teaching-learning process with technological tools that implement the IoT, in this house of studies the Teachers had to self-train, reviewing video tutorials to use at least one virtual platform that would allow them to communicate with their students, however, more than half continue to use chats such as WhatsApp to assign activities where it is difficult to follow up on activities, all of them These situations encourage the physical and emotional exhaustion of teachers in the face of this pandemic, which is already considered a social crisis, generating frustration and resistance to the implementation of the Internet in the education sector. Opinions of not knowing how to work as a team and not wanting to share are collected the knowledge that has been acquired with their fellow teach.

The analysis of these cases has allowed the understanding of the importance of the existence of a transformational leadership, the educational field is a sector that faces areas of improvement during this pandemic, due to the fact that teachers face the challenge of using the technological tools that are used in the IoT which start from the internet to develop, so it is a skill that is identified with this study that teachers must have, the use of digital resources, which allow the teacher to help them to teach their session, but not only to impart it, but also to provide this accompaniment to the students through these means, as well as to develop the teaching-learning process, but how can they develop it if they do not know them. This is where the importance of people who are visionaries, who seek collaboration and above all that they provide confidence in the decisions that are made, this occurred in case A, where the leader is a true transformational leader, since he identified the world trend on the use of digital tools in education and launched it from before the pandemic is declared, thus reducing academic stress, uncertainty, and bad practices in the academic process.

Transformational Leadership allows turning the leader into an agent of change, which focuses comprehensively on an organization since it analyzes the qualities and abilities of each collaborator, thus increasing motivation and stimulating awareness of the impact of the activities carried out, obtaining, as a result, the commitment to achieve the mission and vision of the company.

The context that was observed is the educational sector in a public Higher Education Institution, which is decentralized, for which the topic described above is of the utmost importance, considering that this type of Leadership is required to transform the teachers, increase their motivation and above all their performance, especially in this social crisis due to SARS-COV-2, so-called by different authors, where it has brought with it an aspect that is difficult to manage, this is the result of isolation, the use of technologies but above all due to social limitation, which is why transformational Leadership is a tool that is required to achieve the goals of the institution.

The universities A studied has an academic director who analyzes the options and trends required by the education sector in the region because, during 2019, all the teaching staff already implemented technological tools such as Classroom, Edmodo, or Moodle in all the subjects taught at the university. Moreover, institution, free applications were also used to carry out activities in synchronous and asynchronous sessions; it is here where transformational Leadership is identified where the academic leader becomes an agent of change and visionary to provide tools, knowledge, and skills to his followers, achieving a harmonious coexistence, with this it was possible to reduce the risk of a teacher feeling unprotected or even lost in this Pandemic that is going through.

Within the strategies implemented as part of the transformational Leadership in the Higher Education Institutions, there are different talks by experts in the area of psychology who provide recommendations and follow-up to avoid depression or some other mental health disorder among the teaching staff, in the same way, they were carried out different virtual forums where teachers exposed part of the aspects that concerned them that is presented in this online modality, where it is possible to share strategies among peers, generating empathy, motivation and reducing uncertainty among followers collaboratively.

Compared to other Universities, where there was no induction, training, or monitoring of the teaching-learning process with technological tools, teachers had to self-train, reviewing video tutorials to use at least one virtual platform that allowed them to communicate with their students. However, many continue to use chats such as WhatsApp to assign activities where it is difficult to follow up on actions; all these situations encourage teachers' physical and emotional exhaustion in the face of this Pandemic, which is already considered a social crisis.

6 Conclusions

The SARS-CoV-2 pandemic has presented unprecedented challenges for universities worldwide, forcing leaders to quickly adapt to new circumstances and make difficult decisions to ensure their students and staff's safety and well-being. In such times of crisis, transformational leadership can play a crucial role in guiding institutions through the challenges posed by the pandemic.

Transformational leadership focuses on inspiring and motivating followers to achieve their full potential through a shared vision and a sense of purpose. This leadership style is particularly effective in times of change and uncertainty, as it encourages creativity, innovation, and adaptability.

During the pandemic, transformational leaders in universities have had to navigate various challenges, including transitioning to remote learning, maintaining academic standards, and ensuring their students and staff's mental and physical well-being. To do this, they must foster a culture of trust, collaboration, and innovation that encourages everyone to work together to find new and creative solutions to these challenges.

Some key traits of transformational leaders in universities during the pandemic include:

1. Vision: Transformational leaders must have a clear and compelling vision for their institution's future, even in times of crisis. They must communicate this vision effectively to all stakeholders and inspire them to work towards it.
2. Empathy: Leaders must be empathetic to the concerns and challenges their students and staff face. It includes understanding the pandemic's impact on mental health and providing appropriate support.
3. Flexibility: Leaders must adapt to changing circumstances quickly and make decisions based on the best available information.
   Innovation: Leaders must encourage innovation and creativity to find new ways of delivering education and support services.
4. Collaboration: Leaders must foster a culture of collaboration and teamwork, bringing together stakeholders from across the institution to work towards common goals.
   In conclusion, in the comparison of the cases analyzed, transformational leadership had a positive impact on the use of digital tools in higher education institutions, influencing the behavior of teachers based on the example of their leader and working as a team to increase competitiveness in the organization, managing to promote teleworking and, above all.

Leadership is a skill that some people have with which they manage to influence their followers. Currently, leaders are born with this skill. However, it is also considered that it can be developed, which is why the importance of this research on the types of Leadership and, above all, the case study that compares the implementation of transformational Leadership that provides the opportunity for its collaborators to have the confidence and certainty that the activities they carry out contribute to the universities in this SARS-COV-2 Pandemic.

There are different types; this is considered an advantage because it allows covering different contexts; without a doubt, it is an essential thing, managing to analyze and identify the type of Leadership that the organization has can be potentiated, allowing increased assertive communication, collaboration, and overall job satisfaction of company members.

From this inquiry, it can be concluded that all the mentioned theories have a significant contribution depending on the conditions to implement since no leadership is better than another; on the contrary, they complement each other, thus allowing organizations to have tools to manage their collaborators, influencing their behavior based on the example of their leader and working as a team to increase business competitiveness.

In conclusion, in the comparison of the cases analyzed, transformational leadership had a positive impact on the use of digital tools in higher education institutions, influencing the behavior of teachers based on the example of their leader and working as a team to increase competitiveness in the organization, managing to promote telework. This research is of great importance because transformational leadership in education is transferred to the different organizations with the students that are being trained, which is why the conclusion reached by Rojas et. al., (2020) is supported, where they reach the conclusion that transformational leadership provides an alternative for higher education in the search for new ways to train a citizen in an integral, conscious and committed way with the social reality that surrounds him.

Acknowledgments.   We are grateful for the facilities granted to carry out this work to the National Council of Science and Technology (CONACYT), Tecnológico Nacional de México and Instituto Politécnico Nacional, the Research and Postgraduate Secretariat with the SIP 20220730, 20231468 projects. Furthermore, to Instituto Tecnologico Superior del Oriente del Estado de Hidalgo and the Interdisciplinary Unit of Engineering and Social and Administrative Sciences and Center for Research and Development of Digital Technology. Likewise, the "Programa de estimulos al desempeño de la investigacion" (EDI), "Programa de estimulos al desempeño docente" (EDD), and "Comision de Operación y promoción de actividades academicas" (COFAA).

References

Lev, B.: Intangibles, Management, Measurement and Reporting, Harrisonburg, Virginia, U.S.A, Ed. Donnelley and Sons, The Brookings Institution (2001)

Lupano, M., Castro, A.: Estudios sobre el liderazgo: Teorías y evaluación. Psicodebate 6: Psicología, Cultura y Sociedad **8**, 107–122 (2008). http://www.palermo.edu/cienciassociales/pub licaciones/pdf/Psico6/6Psico%2008.pdf

Heifetz, R.A., Grashow, A., Linsky, M.: The Practice of Adaptive Leadership: Tools and Tactics for Changing the Organization and the World. Harvard Business Press, Boston, EE.UU (2009)

Noriega, M.: La importancia del liderazgo en las organizaciones. Temas de Ciencia y Tecnología **12**(36), 25–29 (2008). http://www.elfinancierocr.com/gerencia/biblioteca/GuadalupeNoriega-Universidad-Tecnologica-Mixteca_ELFFIL20140425_0008.pdf

Peiró, J.M., Rodríguez, I.: Estrés laboral, liderazgo y salud organizacional. Papeles del Psicólogo **29**(1), 68–82 (2008)

Cameron, K., Plews, E.: Positive leadership in action: applications of POS by Jim Mallozzi, CEO, prudential real estate, and relocation. Organ. Dyn. **41**(2), 99–105 (2012)

Avolio, B.J., Gardner, W.L.: Authentic leadership development: getting to the root of positive forms of Leadership. Leadersh. Q. **16**(3), 315–338 (2005)

Luthans, F., Youssef, C.: Human, social, and now positive psychological capital management: Investing in people for competitive advantage. Organ. Dyn. **33**(2), 143–160 (2004)

Dinha, J.E., Lord, R.G., Gardner, W., Meuser, J.D., Lidend, R.C., Huc, J.: Leadership theory and research in the new millennium: current theoretical trends and changing perspectives. Leadersh. Quart. **25**, 36–62 (2014)

Lowe, K.B., Gardner, W.L.: Ten years of The Leadership Quarterly: contributions and challenges for the future. Leadersh. Quart. **11**, 459–514 (2001)

Cruz-Ortiz, V., Salanova, M., Martínez, I.M.: Liderazgo transformacional y desempeño grupal: Unidos por el engagement grupal. Revista de Psicología Social **28**(2), 183–196 (2013)

Cruz-Ortiz, V., Salanova, M., Martínez, I.M.: Liderazgo transformacional: investigación actual y retos futuros. Revista Universidad & Empresa **15**(25), 13–32 (2013)

Fairholm, G.W.: Capturing the Heart of Leadership: Spirituality and Community in the New American Workplace. Greenwood Publishing Group, Santa Barbara (1997)

Zellers, K.L., Perrewe, P.L.: En: Giacalone, R.A., Jurkiewicz, C.L. (eds.) Handbook of workplace spirituality and organizational performance, pp. 300–313. M.E. Sharpe, Armonk, NY (2003)

Reave, L.: Spiritual values and practices related to leadership effectiveness. Leadersh. Quart. **16**(5), 655–687 (2005)

Fry, L.W.: Toward a theory of spiritual Leadership. Leadersh. Quart. **14**(6), 693–727 (2003)

Burns, J.M.: Leadership. Harper & Row, New York (1978)

Cameron, K.: Practicing Positive Leadership: Tools and Techniques that Create Extraordinary Results. Berrett-Koehler Publishers, San Francisco (2013)

Bass, B.M.: Leadership and Performance Beyond Expectations. Free Press, New York (1985)

Judge, T.A., Woolf, E., Hurst, C., Livingston, B.: Charismatic and transformational Leadership: a review and an agenda for future research. Zeitschriftfür Arbeits-und Organisations Psychologie A&O **50**(4), 203–214 (2006)

Sendjaya, S., Sarros, J.C.: Servant leadership: its origin, development, and application in organizations. J. Leadersh. Organ. Stud. **9**(2), 57–64 (2002). https://doi.org/10.1177/107179190200 900205

Maslow, A.H.: Toward a Psychology of Being, 2nd edn. Van Nostrand, Princeton, NJ (1968)

Brown, M.E., Treviño, L.K.: Ethical dleadership: a review and future directions. Leadersh. Quart. **17**(6), 595–616 (2006). https://doi.org/10.1016/j.leaqua.2006.10.004

Cruz-Ortiz, V.; Salanova, M.; Martínez, I.M.: Liderazgo transformacional: investigación actual y retos futuros. Universidad &Empresa No. 25, pp. 13–32 (2013)

Rojas, O., Vivas, A., Mota, K., Quiñónez, J.: El liderazgo transformacional desde la perspectiva de la pedagogía. Sophia, colección de Filosofía de la Educación **28**(1), 237–262 (2020)

Detection of Mental Health Symptoms in the Written Language of Undergraduate Students Using a Microblogging Platform

Ivan Madera-Torres[1,2], Mauricio Gabriel Orozco-del-Castillo[1](✉), Sara Nelly Moreno-Cimé[1], Carlos Bermejo-Sabbagh[1], and Nora Leticia Cuevas-Cuevas[1]

[1] Departamento de Sistemas y Computación, Tecnológico Nacional de México/IT de Mérida, Mérida, Yucatán, Mexico
{le17081441,mauricio.od,sara.mc,carlos.bs,nora.cc}@merida.tecnm.mx,
mauricio.orozco@itmerida.edu.mx
[2] AAAI Chapter of Mexico (AAAIMX), Mérida, Mexico

Abstract. Adolescents and young adults are increasingly acknowledged as mental health vulnerable populations whose mental health is particularly vulnerable. Conditions such as anxiety and depression are especially prevalent. The detection of these conditions and timely support in educational institutions remains a challenge, as they can have an important impact on the well-being of students and academic performance. In this article we present a new microblogging web platform designed to solve these problems by providing students with a safe, expressive space to freely communicate about topics of interest in their respective communities, providing the chance to do so. This platform encourages users to share their experiences, opinions and concerns. One of the main features of this platform is its seamless integration with various modules that capture valuable metrics of mental health. By linking the results of text analysis with data from commonly used questionnaires for mental health symptom detection, a comprehensive picture of an individual's well-being can be established. In particular, we developed a support vector machine model specifically trained to identify depressive symptoms in the written language shared on the platform. Our findings demonstrate the effectiveness of the microblogging platform in conjunction with the classification model. By leveraging this approach, educational institutions can gain insights into students' mental health by analyzing their written expressions. This integrated system offers a promising strategy for detecting and addressing depressive symptoms among adolescents and young adults, ultimately contributing to improved well-being, academic performance, and targeted support in educational settings.

Keywords: Microblogging · web development · mental health · data analytics

M. F. Mata-Rivera et al. (Eds.): WITCOM 2023, CCIS 1906, pp. 473–486, 2023.
https://doi.org/10.1007/978-3-031-45316-8_30

1   Introduction

Young people, particularly university students, have attracted the attention of various researchers in the field of mental health [13], this is due to the frequency with which university students present difficulties that affect them emotionally, which prevents them from having a correct adaptation community [17]. This phenomenon has led to several mental health problems, particularly anxiety and depression disorders, which have become a serious health and economic problem (accounting over a trillion dollars each year) [19] and tend to interrupt the proper development of the student [17]. Depression, particularly, a precursor to suicide, has a high cure rate if detected and diagnosed early [4]. Therefore, it is very important for institutions to develop collaborative work environments so that the emergence of these issues can be detected and avoided opportunely [10]. Even though institutions nowadays rely on management systems to accelerate student learning, they tend to omit communications technologies such as social networks and microblogging, where students participate in real-time collaborative interactions which more genuinely represent the students' thinking and which shed light into the mental health issues that the student could present [1].

Due to the constant evolution of computer applications, several of them have been used for mental health purposes [7], including social media [26], self-report questionnaires [6], biosignals [8,27], and distributed environments. Distributed environments have gained particular importance in information technologies [3], particularly those that have evolved to become more intuitive and user-friendly, allowing collaborations at very accessible costs [1]. With this in mind, educational institutions have tried to create better learning management systems to reduce the gap which still exists in terms of these types of platforms for students [21]. Even though there have been multiple efforts in this direction, institutions have yet to harmonize three important factors: education, support, and interaction between members of the educational communities [1].

One particular option to strengthen these factors in educational communities is microblogging [5]: a form of communication in which users describe their status in brief posts [22] (usually with a character limit), which can then be shared through social networks, cell phones, Web platforms, etc. Microblogging has been increasingly studied in research as a recent phenomenon in which Twitter® is largely responsible. It is estimated that in 2009 there were more than 32 million people on this platform [9] and that in 2008 11% of the US population had posted on a microblogging site. Some uses of microblogging at the time were particularly intent on sharing information, keeping up with topics of interest, and directly communicating with others [9], and today they are sharing their activities or searching for information [14], including during emergency situations [30].

In recent years, microblogging data has emerged as a valuable resource for detecting mental health symptoms, particularly depression [31]. Numerous studies have explored the detection of depression symptoms using text analysis techniques [18] and machine learning algorithms, such as Support Vector Machines (SVMs) [16] and multi-kernel SVMs [25]. These studies have primarily focused on English and Chinese languages, delving into various aspects of depression

and related tendencies, including rumination [24]. However, one notable gap in
the literature is the scarcity of studies conducted in the Spanish language. This
limitation hinders our understanding of mental health symptoms in Spanish-
speaking populations. To address this gap, there is a need for the development
of an ad-hoc microblogging tool specifically designed for Spanish users. Such a
tool would enable comprehensive research and analysis in the context of Spanish
language and culture, ultimately contributing to a more inclusive and diverse
understanding of mental health.

In this work, we present microblogging as a dual purpose mechanism, first,
as a means of interaction between students, teachers, entrepreneurs, etc., that
allows users to have the freedom to share experiences, opinions, and concerns.
Second, we must detect patterns that denote the student's problems in mental
health through the use of automated natural language processing (NLP) applications and be able to refer him or her to attention if required.

2   Materials and Methods

2.1   Software Development

For the development of the platform, the Scrum methodology was used [12].
Scrum is an agile development methodology which has been reported to be more
productive and effective for these types of purpose than other methodologies [23];
it is based on closing short development cycles known as "Sprints" [23].

The elements of Scrum are described as follows [28]:

- Roles. The specific responsibilities and accountabilities assigned to individuals
  or groups within the development team, product owner, and Scrum master.
  They ensure that the philosophy of the methodology is followed as good as
  possible:
  - Product Owner (owner of the product).
  - Scrum Master (facilitator of collaboration, process adherence, and imped-
    iment removal).
  - Team (development team).
- Events. Events aim to minimize undefined and improvised meetings and to
  establish a series of instances that allow better communication and collab-
  oration in the team [28]. This reduces time spent on lengthy meetings and
  restrictive predictive processes. They also have a "TimeBox" with a fixed
  duration; an event ends when its purpose has been achieved. The events com-
  monly used in Scrum are [28]:
  - Sprint.
  - Sprint Planning.
  - Daily Scrum.
  - Sprint Review.
  - Sprint Retrospective.
- Artifacts. Artifacts provide transparency and the ability to inspect and adapt
  processes so that all team members understand what is being accomplished
  [28]:

- Product Backlog.
- Sprint Backlog.
- Increase.

A schematic diagram of the Scrum methodology is shown in Fig. 1. First, the Product Owner prioritizes the Product Backlog, which is a list of desired features and requirements. Then, the Scrum Team conducts Sprint Planning to determine which items from the Product Backlog will be included in the Sprint and creates the Sprint Backlog. During the Sprint, the Scrum Team works on developing the product increment. At the end of the Sprint, a Sprint Review is held to demonstrate the product increment to stakeholders and gather feedback. The final stage of the cycle is the Sprint Retrospective, where the Scrum Team reflects on the Sprint and identifies areas for improvement. The Sprint ends after the Sprint Retrospective meeting.

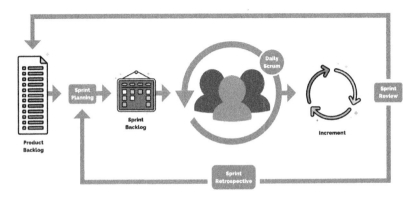

Fig. 1. The Scrum iterative cycle, showing the different elements and operations: Product Backlog, Sprint Planning, Sprint Backlog, Daily Scrum, Increment, Sprint Review, and finally, Sprint Retrospective. Adapted from [22,28]

2.2   Platform Description

The microblogging web platform for support in managing conditions that affect the mood of students allows fostering interaction between students through communities that address the most important topics of interest today or that may be more useful to students with the objective of detecting states of mind that could affect the emotional well-being of students, both in everyday life and at school. In this way, users can communicate through the platform, interact with students of higher and lower semesters to provide support in case of any doubt or concern that may arise, thus promoting teamwork indirectly based on the support given and received by the students that make up the communities; likewise, there are communities dedicated to leisure that allows the students to be free to avoid focusing exclusively on the academic field. The latter provides a tool for the a posteriori analysis of data in order to enhance the early detection of psychological disorders such as anxiety, depression, among other disorders. This detection is proposed through the analysis of text information using NLP techniques that can be collected directly from student publications to detect symptoms in a timely manner and take the appropriate measures to be treated.

The technologies used for the development of the platform were the following:

- Python: Used for backend development and integrated with an Object Relational Mapping (ORM) system.
- Vue.js: Employed for frontend development, enabling the creation of interactive user interfaces.
- PostgreSQL: Utilized as the database management system to handle relational databases.
- Django: Employed for building application programming interfaces (APIs) that facilitate communication between the frontend and backend components of the platform.

2.3   Platform Architecture

The Vue.js framework, as mentioned above, was used for FrontEnd, which together with Buefy (a component library for user interfaces) allowed the platform to be implemented in a responsive, pleasant, and intuitive way for students. Figure 2 presents the architecture of the platform and also shows how the different technologies that were used relate to each other.

The Web platform interacts with the database, which provides the necessary storage for the subsequent analysis of the content of the publications. This is performed through various APIs, which employ the Django framework for the development of the necessary models that adapt to the needs of the platform, the logic of creating, updating, listing, and deleting data, as well as the URLs necessary for consumption of the services. An important point to highlight is where the database is hosted, Heroku, a cloud platform with high accessibility and low cost. Unlike other platforms, Heroku supports a large number of programming languages [11]. Finally, PostgreSQL was used as the database manager. This system uses SQL-relational databases and adapted very well with the Django framework, which provided greater advantages when it came to implementing it and using it in production.

2.4   Platform Functionalities

The main functionality of the platform is the communities module. In order for a student to be able to post and see what other people have already posted, they need to join the community. Figure 3a shows the interface where the student is instructed to perform the said task, in this case, the "Sports" task. Once the student has joined the community, he/she can post publications and can also see the publications that have been made in that community (Fig. 3b).

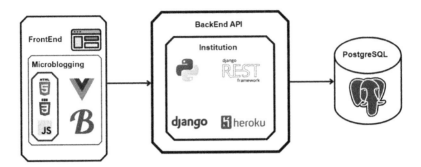

Fig. 2. The services and technologies used in the platform. Those for FrontEnd (left), Backend APIs (center), and database (right).

(a)   (b)

Fig. 3. Interface of the "Sports" community, seen by a student who (a) has not yet joined it, and who (b) has already done so.

In order for a publication to be displayed correctly within a community, the student must first enter the content of the publication in the text input provided by each community to which they are attached and assign it a label that best suits its content.

There are several ways in which an user can interact with a given post, such as rating, reporting and commenting. Rating is done when the student wants to award a prize (in experience points) to a post by another student in the community. For this, the student must select the experience points that he wishes to grant and register them on the platform (Fig. 4a). The experience points will be reflected in the profile of the user who received them. Each student can send a maximum of 5,000 experience points per day (modifiable). Reporting is allowed when a user detects a misplaced post within a community; the platform gives him the option to report it (Fig. 4b). This is important to ensure that the content on the platform is appropriate. Finally, a student can comment on an existing

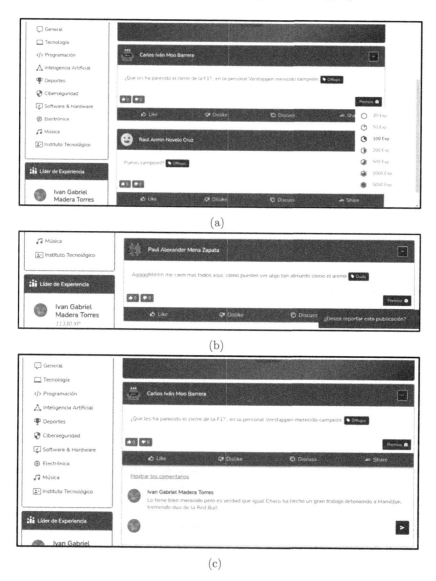

(a)

(b)

(c)

Fig. 4. Possible interactions with a post, such as (a) awarding experience points, (b) reporting a post for removal, or (c) commenting a post.

post by pressing the Discuss button, writing the comment, and submitting it (Fig. 4c).

An administration module for the exclusive use of the administrator of the microblogging platform was also developed. One of the functionalities to which the administrator has access is to see the posts that have been reported as

inappropriate by users and to decide whether they should be removed or remain
on the platform (Fig. 5).

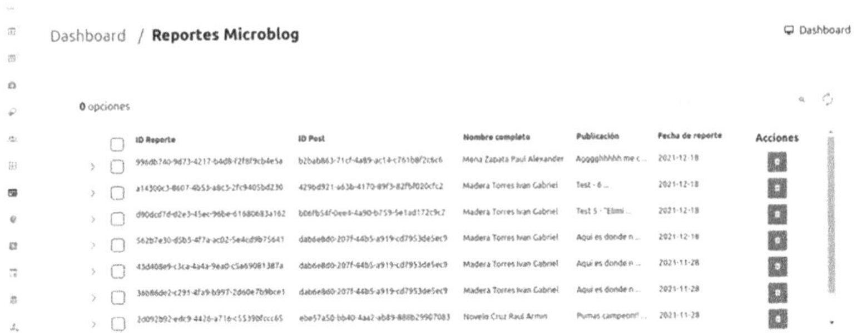

Fig. 5. List of publications that have been reported by students. The list includes IDs
for the report and post, as well as the name of the user, the post itself, the date it was
posted, and the option to remove it.

3   Development and Results

The methodology presented in this document allowed the development and
launch of the microblogging platform for students of the Department of Systems
and Computing of the Technological Institute of Mexico (TecNM)/Technology
Institute of Merida (ITM) during the January-June and August-December 2022
semesters. The platform presented in this work, being part of a comprehensive
system, allows direct association of the results of the text analysis with other
indicators obtained by other modules of the platform to which it belongs, for
example, scores obtained from commonly used questionnaires for the detection
of mental health symptoms, as described in [22]. The original study included
157 undergraduate students. Ethical guidelines and regulations were strictly followed for both the self-report questionnaires and the input of natural language;
all participants provided informed consent. The participant group consisted of
30 females and 127 males, with ages ranging from 17 to 23 years. The results
obtained by this module, CSV files, allow the results from the self-report questionnaires to be directly integrated with artificial intelligence or data science
algorithms.

In particular, our deployment allowed us to capture texts that were subsequently analyzed using a NLP methodology for detecting mental health symptoms. While providing a comprehensive description of the technique is beyond
the scope of this work, we can outline its general design. The data for each user
were linked to their responses to the PHQ-9 questionnaire, a very common questionnaire for assessing symptoms of depression [15]. The scores of all users were

classified ascendingly and separated into four data sets corresponding to quartiles, Q1 (lowest) through Q4 (highest). The words entered into the microblogging platform for all users in the quartiles Q1 and Q4 were pre-processed using common NLP techniques, particularly tokenization, which involved splitting the texts into individual words or tokens, eliminating punctuation signs, prepositions, and other commonly occurring linguistic elements that typically do not carry significant semantic meaning. After preprocessing, we used Word2Vec [20] feature extraction methods to represent each text in a numerical format that ML models could process. Word2Vec is a predictive word embedding model that learns word representations based on their contextual usage. It takes into account the surrounding words of a target word to predict it or vice versa. Next, we used a SVM classifier to train a model using labeled data. Labeled data consisted of user texts that had been manually annotated as "depressed" (Q4) or "non-depressed" (Q1) according to their corresponding PHQ-9 scores. The performance of the SVM model in classifying depressive symptoms in the written language of undergraduate students was evaluated using recall.

In the context of depression screening, recall can be a more effective metric to consider due to the nature of the task. Detecting individuals who may be experiencing depressive symptoms is crucial to ensure that appropriate support and intervention can be provided. By focusing on recall, we aim to minimize false negatives, which are instances where individuals with depressive symptoms are incorrectly classified as nondepressed. To assess the robustness and generalizability of the model, we employed 5-fold cross-validation, and the SVM model was trained and evaluated iteratively using different combinations of training and validation sets. The average recall obtained from cross-validation was 0.7823. While there is room for improvement, these results demonstrate the effectiveness of the NLP-based SVM model in detecting depressive symptoms in the written language of undergraduate students. More research is needed to determine whether more samples will improve the efficacy of the classifier.

For a qualitative analysis, particularly useful for mental health professionals, these datasets were used to generate Word Clouds. Word Clouds, are a commonly-used visual tool to highlight the results of qualitative analyses [2]. They show the words that most often appear in a corpus of words. The size of each word in the Word Cloud corresponds to the frequency of occurrence of it in the corpus, allowing interpreters to analyze differences between distinct corpus and hypothesize possible reasons behind those differences [2]. The Word Clouds corresponding to Q1 and Q4 are shown in Fig. 6. Words such as "creo" ("I believe") occur evidently more often in the Q1 word cloud than in the Q4. These results are consistent with the literature which has identified how the language of the depressed patients is different from those who are not [29].

(a)   (b)

Fig. 6. Word Clouds of users in quartiles (a) Q1 and (b) Q4 according to the PHQ-9 questionnaire results and their inputs to the microblogging module.

4   Discussion and Conclusions

In this article, a microblogging platform was presented as part of a system that allows students to express themselves freely about various topics of interest among communities of students with the same hobbies, preferences, and interests. The development of this tool offers the possibility of allowing students to express themselves, which could be particularly useful when they have emotional difficulties, either in their daily life or at school. This could support the timely detection and prevention of the development of mental health problems, such as psychological disorders, through the textual analysis of the publications made by users. In particular, the platform allowed us to collect the necessary data to apply NLP techniques prior to the application of a SVM, which in turn allowed us to generate Word Clouds for users showing and lacking symptoms of depression, according to the PHQ-9 questionnaire, which is consistent with the reported literature.

The performance of the SVM classifier heavily relies on the availability of accurately labeled data, which, in this particular case, ultimately depends on how the depression symptoms are detected. Obtaining a large and diverse dataset with accurate labels for depressive symptoms may pose challenges. The lack of such database makes it possible for the SVM classifier to struggle to generalize well to unseen data, leading to reduced performance. Also, the choice of features and their representation, such as the Word2Vec embeddings, can influence the performance of the classifier. Inappropriate feature selection or representation may result in the loss of important information or introduce noise. The optimal selection of features for this particular study requires further research.

The classification of depressive symptoms based on written language can be challenging due to the subjective and context-dependent nature of text. Different individuals may express symptoms differently, and the classifier might struggle with capturing nuanced variations in language use. Different approaches to capture text should be considered and the results of the classifier analyzed.

In terms of the platform, to speed up the development process, cutting-edge technologies were used, such as Vue.js, which allows the reuse of code through its components, which helped to have a more readable development and with less repetitive code, in conjunction with Django, which provided a vast amount of functions for the realization of the APIs. These technologies adapted very well with the PostgreSQL database manager system, used to store and manage information from student posts in the various communities.

The development tools were selected due to their scalability, community support and integration capabilities. However, some software development tools might have a steeper learning curve, requiring time and effort for developers to become proficient in their usage. On the other hand, depending on the chosen tools, there may be limitations in terms of customizability or flexibility, which could restrict certain design choices or unique feature implementations. This may suggest considering alternative software development tools, including frameworks or libraries, cloud services and DevOps tools.

Finally, the noninvasive nature of the platform also allows obtaining more reliable data than those obtained by digital tools that ask the user to enter text to answer a particular question, avoiding unnatural information or information that is influenced by the user awareness of being psychologically evaluated. The design of this tool allows the "automatic" generation of data, that is, it frees researchers from tasks that involve submitting the patient to generate texts periodically or as part of extraordinary research protocols and simply allows downloading and analyzing the data.

5 Future Work

The microblogging platform has proved to be useful for research and mental health attention purposes, so it is expected that its operability and functionality will be constantly improved. Among the main improvements that can be added, are the following:

– Enhance representativeness of data: Investigate active engagement of students experiencing psychological distress with the microblogging platform and address any hesitancy to openly share struggles, ensuring a more representative sample.
– Consider alternative methods for visualizing mental health expressions: Recognize limitations of word clouds and explore additional methods or visualizations that capture the context and nuances of students' expressions related to mental health.
– Broaden assessment of mental health dimensions: Expand beyond the PHQ-9 questionnaire to capture a broader range of mental health dimensions and related conditions, ensuring a comprehensive understanding of students' well-being.
– Evaluate alternative machine learning algorithms: Compare the effectiveness of other machine learning algorithms in identifying mental health symptoms in student texts, beyond SVM, to determine the most suitable approach.
– Incorporate user-centered design principles: Involve students in the development process and consider their experiences, concerns, and feedback to improve the platform's effectiveness and user-friendliness.

- Expand socialization spaces and tags: Allow students to create additional socialization spaces and expand the catalog of communities, as well as provide flexibility in adding tags that best fit the content of their publications.
- Enhance post editing and deletion options: Allow users the freedom to edit their posts, add tags if forgotten, and permanently delete posts when desired, while defining editing protocols for NLP and analysis purposes.
- Improve reactions and comments: Expand the diversity of reactions to publications, ensuring they are mutually exclusive, and enable users to respond and react to comments, while incorporating reporting and hiding functionalities for improved security.
- Refine pagination and visibility: Improve the platform's pagination system to exclude hidden publications for a more streamlined user experience.
- Expand publication options: Enable a wider range of publication formats, such as links, images, gifs, and surveys, offering more versatile content creation capabilities.
- Increase training data for SVM classifier and explore alternative ML models: Augment the SVM classifier with more text samples for training and evaluate the performance of different machine learning models in identifying mental health symptoms.

Acknowledgements. This work was supported by projects 13933.22-P and 14601.22-P from Tecnológico Nacional de México/IT de Mérida.

References

1. Al-Maroof, R., Al-Qaysi, N., Salloum, S.A., Al-Emran, M.: Blended learning acceptance: a systematic review of information systems models. Technol. Knowl. Learn. **27**(3), 891–926 (2022). https://doi.org/10.1007/s10758-021-09519-0, https://link.springer.com/10.1007/s10758-021-09519-0
2. Alderson, H., et al.: Sensory profile of kombucha brewed with New Zealand ingredients by focus group and word clouds. Fermentation **7**(3) (2021). https://doi.org/10.3390/fermentation7030100, https://www.mdpi.com/2311-5637/7/3/100
3. Amiri, Z., Heidari, A., Navimipour, N.J., Unal, M.: Resilient and dependability management in distributed environments: a systematic and comprehensive literature review. Clust. Comput. (2022). https://doi.org/10.1007/s10586-022-03738-5, https://link.springer.com/10.1007/s10586-022-03738-5
4. Baek, J.W., Chung, K.: Context deep neural network model for predicting depression risk using multiple regression. IEEE Access **8**, 18171–18181 (2020). https://doi.org/10.1109/access.2020.2968393
5. Bisht, A., Bhadauria, H., Virmani, J., Singh, A., Kriti, N.: Sentiment analysis of micro-blogging sites using supervised learning: a narrative review of recent studies. Int. J. Knowl. Learn. **15**(2), 89 (2022). https://doi.org/10.1504/IJKL.2022.121884, http://www.inderscience.com/link.php?id=121884
6. Orozco-del-Castillo, M.G., Orozco-del-Castillo, E.C., Brito-Borges, E., Bermejo-Sabbagh, C., Cuevas-Cuevas, N.: An artificial neural network for depression screening and questionnaire refinement in undergraduate students. In: Mata-Rivera, M.F., Zagal-Flores, R. (eds.) WITCOM 2021. CCIS, vol. 1430, pp. 1–13. Springer, Cham (2021). https://doi.org/10.1007/978-3-030-89586-0_1

7. Chen, M., Mao, S., Liu, Y.: Big data: a survey. Mob. Netw. Appl. **19**(2), 171–209 (2014). https://doi.org/10.1007/s11036-013-0489-0, http://link.springer.com/10.1007/s11036-013-0489-0

8. Cho, D., et al.: Detection of stress levels from biosignals measured in virtual reality environments using a kernel-based extreme learning machine. Sens. (Switz.) **17**(10) (2017). https://doi.org/10.3390/s17102435

9. Ehrlich, K., Shami, N.S.: Microblogging inside and outside the workplace. In: ICWSM 2010 - Proceedings of the 4th International AAAI Conference on Weblogs and Social Media, pp. 42–49 (2010)

10. Giorgi, G., et al.: COVID-19-related mental health effects in the workplace: a narrative review. Int. J. Environ. Res. Public Health **17**(21), 7857 (2020). https://doi.org/10.3390/ijerph17217857, https://www.mdpi.com/1660-4601/17/21/7857

11. Heroku: Heroku Dev Center (2022). https://devcenter.heroku.com/

12. Hron, M., Obwegeser, N.: Why and how is scrum being adapted in practice: a systematic review. J. Syst. Softw. **183**, 111110 (2022). https://doi.org/10.1016/j.jss.2021.111110, https://www.sciencedirect.com/science/article/pii/S0164121221002077

13. January, J., Madhombiro, M., Chipamaunga, S., Ray, S., Chingono, A., Abas, M.: Prevalence of depression and anxiety among undergraduate university students in low- and middle-income countries: a systematic review protocol. Syst. Rev. **7**(1), 57 (2018). https://doi.org/10.1186/s13643-018-0723-8, https://systematicreviewsjournal.biomedcentral.com/articles/10.1186/s13643-018-0723-8

14. Java, A., Song, X., Finin, T., Tseng, B.: Why we twitter: an analysis of a microblogging community. In: Zhang, H., et al. (eds.) SNAKDD/WebKDD -2007. LNCS (LNAI), vol. 5439, pp. 118–138. Springer, Heidelberg (2009). https://doi.org/10.1007/978-3-642-00528-2_7

15. Kroenke, K., Spitzer, R.L., Williams, J.B.: The PHQ-9: validity of a brief depression severity measure. J. Gener. Internal Med. **16**(9), 606–613 (2001). https://doi.org/10.1046/j.1525-1497.2001.016009606.x

16. Liu, S., Shu, J., Liao, Y.: Depression tendency detection for microblog users based on SVM. In: 2021 IEEE International Conference on Artificial Intelligence and Computer Applications (ICAICA), pp. 802–806. IEEE (2021)

17. Liu, S., Xu, B., Zhang, D., Tian, Y., Wu, X.: Core symptoms and symptom relationships of problematic internet use across early, middle, and late adolescence: a network analysis. Comput. Hum. Behav. **128**, 107090 (2022). https://doi.org/10.1016/j.chb.2021.107090, https://linkinghub.elsevier.com/retrieve/pii/S0747563221004131

18. Lyu, S., Ren, X., Du, Y., Zhao, N.: Detecting depression of Chinese microblog users via text analysis: combining linguistic inquiry word count (LIWC) with culture and suicide related lexicons. Front. Psych. **14**, 1121583 (2023)

19. Martinez, K., Menéndez-Menéndez, M.I., Bustillo, A.: Awareness, prevention, detection, and therapy applications for depression and anxiety in serious games for children and adolescents: systematic review. JMIR Serious Games **9**(4), 1–19 (2021). https://doi.org/10.2196/30482

20. Mikolov, T., Chen, K., Corrado, G., Dean, J.: Efficient estimation of word representations in vector space. arXiv preprint arXiv:1301.3781 (2013)

21. Mohd Kasim, N.N., Khalid, F.: Choosing the right learning management system (LMS) for the higher education institution context: a systematic review. Int. J. Emerg. Technol. Learn. (iJET) **11**(06), 55 (2016). https://doi.org/10.3991/ijet.v11i06.5644, http://online-journals.org/index.php/i-jet/article/view/5644

22. Moo-Barrera, C.I., Orozco-del Castillo, M.G., Moreno-Sabido, M.R., Cuevas-Cuevas, N.L., Bermejo-Sabbagh, C.: Web platform for the analysis of physical and mental health data of students. In: Mata-Rivera, M.F., Zagal-Flores, R. (eds.) WITCOM 2022. CCIS, vol. 1659, pp. 139–156. Springer, Cham (2022). https://doi.org/10.1007/978-3-031-18082-8_9

23. Morandini, M., Coleti, T.A., Oliveira, E., Corrêa, P.L.P.: Considerations about the efficiency and sufficiency of the utilization of the Scrum methodology: a survey for analyzing results for development teams. Comput. Sci. Rev. **39**, 100314 (2021). https://doi.org/10.1016/j.cosrev.2020.100314, https://linkinghub.elsevier.com/retrieve/pii/S1574013720304147

24. Nambisan, P., Luo, Z., Kapoor, A., Patrick, T.B., Cisler, R.A.: Social media, big data, and public health informatics: ruminating behavior of depression revealed through twitter. In: 2015 48th Hawaii International Conference on System Sciences, pp. 2906–2913. IEEE (2015)

25. Peng, Z., Hu, Q., Dang, J.: Multi-kernel SVM based depression recognition using social media data. Int. J. Mach. Learn. Cybern. **10**, 43–57 (2019)

26. Reece, A.G., Danforth, C.M.: Instagram photos reveal predictive markers of depression. EPJ Data Sci. **6**(1) (2017). https://doi.org/10.1140/epjds/s13688-017-0110-z, http://dx.doi.org/10.1140/epjds/s13688-017-0110-z

27. Sánchez-Sánchez, A., Orozco-del Castillo, M.G., Castillo-Atoche, A.: Design and implementation of an interactive photoplethysmography and galvanic skin response based gamepad. In: Mata-Rivera, M.F., Zagal-Flores, R., Barria-Huidobro, C. (eds.) WITCOM 2022. CCIS, vol. 1659, pp. 225–236. Springer, Cham (2022). https://doi.org/10.1007/978-3-031-18082-8_15

28. Scrum.org: The Scrum Framework Poster | Scrum.org (2022). https://www.scrum.org/resources/scrum-framework-poster

29. Seabrook, E.M., Kern, M.L., Fulcher, B.D., Rickard, N.S.: Predicting depression from language-based emotion dynamics: longitudinal analysis of Facebook and Twitter status updates. J. Med. Internet Res. **20**(5), e168 (2018). https://doi.org/10.2196/jmir.9267, http://www.jmir.org/2018/5/e168/

30. Vieweg, S., Hughes, A.L., Starbird, K., Palen, L.: Microblogging during two natural hazards events. In: Proceedings of the 28th International Conference on Human Factors in Computing Systems - CHI 2010, p. 1079. ACM Press, New York (2010). https://doi.org/10.1145/1753326.1753486, http://portal.acm.org/citation.cfm?doid=1753326.1753486

31. Wilson, M.L., Ali, S., Valstar, M.F.: Finding information about mental health in microblogging platforms: a case study of depression. In: Proceedings of the 5th Information Interaction in Context Symposium, pp. 8–17 (2014)

Neural Network-Based Load Identification for Residential Electrical Installations. A Review and an Online Experimental Application

Gerardo Arno Sonck-Martinez[1], Abraham Efrain Rodríguez-Mata[1],
Jesus Alfonso Medrano-Hermosillo[1], Rogelio Baray-Arana[1,2],
Efren Morales-Estrada[1], and Victor Alejandro Gonzalez-Huitron[2(✉)]

[1] Tecnológico Nacional de México, Instituto Tecnológico de Chihuahua, División de
Estudios de Posgrado e Investigación, Chihuahua, México
arno.sm@chihuahua.tecnm.mx
[2] Tecnológico Nacional de México, Instituto Tecnológico de Querétaro,
Santiago de Querétaro, Mexico
alx3416@hotmail.com

Abstract. This study presents the implementation of a feed-forward neural network (FNN) for the classification of household appliances, specifically refrigerators and microwave ovens. The data used in this study was collected using a PZEM-004t sensor, capturing various parameters such as current, power, power factor, frequency, voltage, and energy consumption. The collected data was then preprocessed, including outlier removal, handling missing data, and applying normalization techniques. The FNN model was trained using labeled and sorted data, with current, power, and power factor chosen as input parameters due to their high variation and relevance. The neural network was trained using MATLAB's neural network toolbox, employing a configuration with 12 input nodes, two hidden layers, and an output layer. The model achieved impressive performance during the training stage, with accuracy, fallout, recall, miss, and specificity metrics calculated. In the generalization stage, the model achieved an accuracy of 94% and demonstrated a correct identification rate of approximately 95% with a false positive rate of around 5%. The Area Under the Curve (AUC) value, calculated as 0.9692, further validated the model's robustness and accuracy in appliance identification tasks. The study concludes that the trained neural network has great potential for accurate appliance identification in residential settings, laying the foundation for intelligent energy management practices.

Keywords: load identification · residential energy consumption estimation · neural networks · artificial intelligence · energy management

1 Introduction

Fundamental to energy management systems is the identification of demands in residential electrical installations. It involves identifying the power consumption patterns of individual household appliances and devices. Accurate load identification enables a variety of applications, such as energy monitoring, demand-side management, and the creation of intelligent home automation systems. Traditional burden identification techniques, which rely on manual inspection and measurement, are time-consuming and frequently impractical for large-scale deployments [1,2]. This has prompted researchers to investigate the capability of artificial intelligence techniques, specifically neural networks, to automate and enhance burden identification processes [3–5].

Neural networks are a category of machine learning algorithms that are modeled after the structure and function of the human brain. They are composed of layered, interconnected structures (neurons) that are capable of learning and modeling complex patterns from input data. Due to their capacity to manage non-linear relationships and autonomously extract high-level characteristics, neural networks have attracted considerable interest. Neural networks, when applied to load identification in residential electrical installations, can analyze power consumption data and accurately infer the operation of individual loads [6,7].

Despite the numerous benefits of neural networks in load identification, researchers must address several obstacles. These consist of data acquisition and preprocessing, model selection and optimization, and the interpretability of neural network outputs [8–10]. In addition, the generalization of neural networks across various households, variations in burden behavior, and the potential impact of noise and outliers are areas that require additional research. This section provides a thorough analysis of notable academic studies about load identification in residential electrical installations using neural networks. Different neural network architectures (e.g., feed-forward, recurrent, convolutional), data acquisition techniques (e.g., smart meters, non-intrusive load monitoring), and performance evaluation metrics (e.g., accuracy, precision, recall) are covered in the selected references. Each citation contributes to the advancement of load identification research by providing valuable insights and methodologies [11–13].

The identification of residential electricity consumption is a problem of significant interest to energy distribution companies, consumers, and energy efficiency researchers. Based on the measurement of voltage and current signals at a common access point, the purpose of this task is to determine which types of electrical appliances are connected to an electrical network and how much energy they consume. This information can be used to optimize energy consumption, detect anomalies or faults, implement dynamic pricing systems, or promote energy conservation [14,15].

Identification of electrical charges can be performed either invasive or non-invasive. The intrusive method entails installing individual sensors in every electrical appliance, which is expensive and complicated to operate. The non-intrusive technique, on the other hand, is based on the analysis of voltage and current signals aggregated at a single measurement point, without requiring direct intervention on the devices. This method is more practicable and cost-effective, but also more technically difficult [16–18].

Among the techniques for non-intrusive identification of electrical charges are those based on artificial neural networks (ANNs), which are computational models inspired by the human brain's operations. ANNs can learn intricate patterns from data and apply them to new instances. In the context of electrical charge identification, ANNs can be trained with historical voltage and current data to recognize and correctly classify the distinctive characteristics of each charge type [19].

Future research should focus on addressing the extant obstacles and investigating new avenues in order to improve load identification using neural networks. Integration of additional data sources (e.g., environmental variables, user behavior), transfer learning across households, explainability of neural network decisions, and development of hybrid models combining neural networks with other AI (Artificial Intelligence) techniques are potential research areas. In addition, efforts should be made to evaluate the scalability, robustness, and real-time capabilities of load identification systems based on neural networks [8].

In this paper, an overview of load identification in residential electrical installations using neural networks is provided. We have discussed the advantages and disadvantages of employing neural networks in this domain, with an emphasis on their potential for automating and improving load identification procedures. The exhaustive analysis of academic studies yielded insightful insights into the advancements and future orientations of this research field. By leveraging neural networks, we can improve residential energy management and promote more efficient power consumption.

2 Statement Problem and Model

Optimizing electricity consumption is critical for long-term sustainability and cost-effectiveness because of how integral it is to contemporary life. Knowing the total electric costs of all the building's equipment and gadgets is one technique to cut down on energy use. However, conventional approaches to charge detection are laborious and need human interaction. Research is needed to create and test AI models that can reliably detect electric charges and optimize energy utilization so that this process may be automated using AI [20].

Artificial intelligence has the ability to increase efficiency, decrease energy costs, and hasten the transition to renewable sources of power. By classifying the electric costs of each appliance and fixture in a building, machine learning and deep learning may help maximize efficiency. AI has enabled the development of computationally efficient tools for planning, simulating, controlling, diagnosing, and supplying steady power to residential areas in [21].

The second goal of the technology is to optimize the usage of renewable energy while decreasing the costs associated with producing, transmitting, and distributing power. Fourth, the application of AI to the energy industry is only getting started [22].

On paper as [23], studies are needed to create and evaluate AI models that can correctly recognize electrical charges and reduce energy use. The models should be able to process massive volumes of data and benefit from being trained on labeled data. Ethical and legal concerns in applying AI to the energy industry should also be explored.

Finally, the use of artificial intelligence in the detection of electric charges for the purpose of optimizing energy is a potential field of study. However, further study is needed to design and test AI models that can reliably recognize electric charges and maximize energy efficiency so that this process may be automated. The models should be able to process massive volumes of data and benefit from being trained on labeled data. Ethical and legal concerns in applying AI to the energy industry should also be explored [24].

The methodology employed to address this issue involved utilizing a PZEM-004t sensor to gather current, power, and power factor readings from refrigerators and microwave ovens. This data collection was facilitated through ESP32 development boards and the ARDUINO IoT Cloud, enabling remote monitoring and acquisition. Subsequently, Matlab was utilized for data cleaning, training, and generalization of a feedforward neural network (Fig. 1).

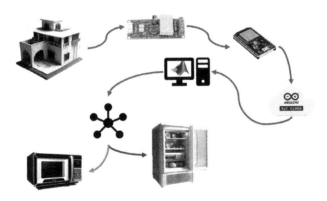

Fig. 1. Problem-solving framework

2.1   Neuronal Networks

Neural networks are information-processing systems inspired by the fundamental cell of the human brain. These networks are composed of artificial neurons that are connected by weighted connections. Neural network learning occurs by adjusting these weighted connections between neurons in different layers. Neural networks are used in many industries, such as medical diagnostics through medical image classification, computer vision, unstructured data understanding, and decision-making. Feed-forward neural networks are the most commonly used, processing data in one direction, from the input node to the output node. There are different types of neural networks, such as the Simple Perceptron, the Hopfield neural network, and convolutional neural networks. Convolutional neural networks are the most widely used today for image processing and pattern recognition. Recently, applications of neural networks and deep learning have been developed also in biomedical fields, such as disease identification and prediction of medical treatment outcomes [25].

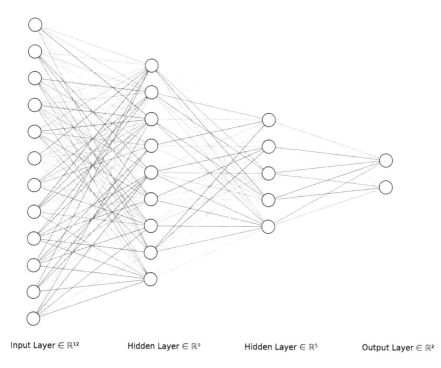

Input Layer $\in \mathbb{R}^{12}$ Hidden Layer $\in \mathbb{R}^9$ Hidden Layer $\in \mathbb{R}^5$ Output Layer $\in \mathbb{R}^2$

Fig. 2. Used neural network in FCNN style

One area of AI that is seeing a surge in interest is convolutional neural networks (CNNs). These networks are examples of deep learning architectures used in fields as diverse as computer vision, computer imaging, and image processing. In order to perform classification and detection, CNNs consume and analyze vast volumes of gridded data before extracting crucial detailed characteristics. The three main kinds of layers in a CNN are the convolutional layer, the clustering layer, and the fully connected layer. The photos' features are extracted and classified using these layers [26]

There are several current uses for convolutional neural networks. Object recognition in video and still pictures, voice recognition, medical image classification, spotting financial fraud, predicting consumer behavior, illness detection, and identifying traffic patterns are just a few of the many applications. Today, convolutional neural networks (CNNs) are among the most potent techniques for computer vision and image processing [27].

Picture processing, object identification, picture classification, computer vision, and many more current applications all make use of convolutional neural networks, which are a kind of artificial intelligence. Image feature extraction and classification are performed by these networks, which are deep learning architectures. Today, convolutional neural networks (CNNs) are among the most potent technologies for image processing and computer vision [28].

On the other hand, feed-forward neural networks have demonstrated their effectiveness and versatility in various domains. In one study [29], a real-time hand gesture recognition model utilizing surface electromyography (sEMG) signals showcased accurate and swift gesture recognition, even before their completion. Another study [30] focused on power quality disturbances in the power grid, combining a visual attention mechanism with a feed-forward neural network to accurately classify single and combined disturbances, surpassing existing methods. Additionally, the potential of feed-forward neural networks in dynamic environments was highlighted in [31], where an algorithm optimized these networks for dynamic data-driven applications. Furthermore, ResMLP [32], an architecture based on multi-layer perceptrons, achieved remarkable accuracy/complexity trade-offs on ImageNet for image classification tasks. These findings emphasize the efficacy of feed-forward neural networks in handling complex classification tasks and improving the quality of power supply while showcasing their adaptability to different domains beyond traditional image classification.

3   Data Collection and Preprocessing

The data utilized in this study was gathered using a PZEM-004t sensor, enabling the measurement of current, power, power factor, frequency, voltage, and energy consumption of the household appliances. These data were collected at regular intervals of 1 s and transmitted to the Arduino cloud using an ESP32 device.

Subsequently, the data was downloaded in CSV format and subjected to an in-depth analysis. The objective of this analysis was to identify parameters exhibiting significant variance. Through this analysis, the most relevant attributes were selected for the subsequent training of the feed-forward neural network.

Following the identification of pertinent parameters, the data underwent an extensive preprocessing phase. Potential outliers were removed, missing data was handled, and normalization techniques were applied to ensure consistency and comparability across the entire training dataset.

Before employing the data for neural network training, each data sample was labeled and sorted according to its corresponding appliance. Furthermore, the dataset was divided into two subsets: one for training the neural network and another for model validation.

This preprocessing and data preparation stage ensured that the feed-forward neural network model was trained and evaluated using clean, labeled, and appropriately separated data. This step is crucial for achieving accurate and reliable results in appliance identification and energy consumption estimation.

3.1 Data Analysis

Data analysis revealed that the parameters exhibiting the highest variation in the collected dataset were current, power, and power factor. Although energy consumption also showed significant variance, it was omitted from the present analysis due to multiple readings within the same histogram interval caused by its accumulation over time (see Fig. 3).

In the case of alternating current (AC), there is a phase difference between current and voltage due to inductive and capacitive loads. The current and power readings obtained from the sensors are referred to as apparent current and apparent power, respectively. The real current and power are phase-shifted with respect to the voltage and are related through the power factor, which corresponds to the cosine of the phase angle.

Hence, it was decided to utilize current, power, and power factor as the input parameters for training the neural network. This choice allows capturing the essential characteristics of the electrical signals, considering the phase relationship between current and voltage and the influence of the power factor.

By incorporating current, power, and power factor as input features, the neural network can effectively learn the complex relationships and patterns in the data, enabling accurate identification of household appliances and estimation of energy consumption.

4   Neural Network Training

For training the neural network, we utilized the neural network toolbox in MAT-LAB. The objective was to develop a feed-forward neural network with exclusive output capable of distinguishing between two appliances: microwave ovens and refrigerators. Various configurations were tested, and an appropriate configuration was identified, consisting of 12 input nodes, two hidden layers with 9 and 5 neurons respectively, and an output layer with two neurons (see Fig. 2).

The activation function employed in the network was the sigmoid function, which allows for non-linear transformations of the input data. The cross-entropy function was chosen as the performance function, as it provides an effective measure of the network's accuracy in classification tasks. The Levenberg-Marquardt backpropagation algorithm was employed as the training function, which offers efficient convergence and robustness for training the network.

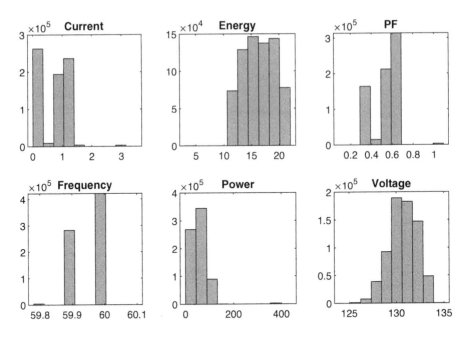

Fig. 3. Histograms

5   Performance Evaluation

The feed-forward neural network demonstrated remarkable performance during the training phase. As depicted in Fig. 4, the Mean Squared Error quickly converged to below 0.02 within a mere 218 epochs.

In addition to this, the following performance metrics were computed to assess the network's accuracy in distinguishing between microwave ovens and refrigerators:

1. Training Stage Performance:

– Accuracy: 98.7%
– Fallout: 0.5% - Represents the proportion of microwave ovens incorrectly identified as refrigerators.
– Recall: 97.9% - Indicates the proportion of refrigerators correctly identified by the network.
– Miss: 0.5% - Corresponds to the proportion of refrigerators erroneously classified as microwave ovens.
– Specificity: 99.5% - Reflects the proportions of the network in correctly identifying microwave ovens.

2. Generalization Stage Performance:

– Accuracy: 94%

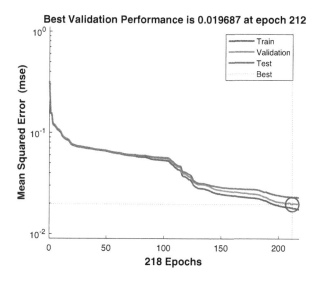

Fig. 4. Receiver operating characteristic curve (ROC) in generalization phase

- Fallout: 8% - Represents the proportion of microwave ovens incorrectly identified as refrigerators.
- Recall: 96.2% - Indicates the proportion of refrigerators correctly identified by the network.
- Miss: 8.4% -Corresponds to the proportion of refrigerators erroneously classified as microwave ovens.
- Specificity: 92% - Reflects the proportions of the network in correctly identifying microwave ovens.

In this analysis, a true positive indicates the correct identification of a refrigerator, whereas a true negative represents the accurate identification of a microwave oven. The visualization of all the preceding results can be observed in Fig. 5.

The Receiver Operating Characteristic (ROC) curve provides valuable insights into the performance of our model. It illustrates that we achieve a correct identification rate of approximately 95% with a false positive rate of around 5% when evaluated on the generalization dataset. This indicates that our model is effective in distinguishing between microwave ovens and refrigerators. Furthermore, the Area Under the Curve (AUC) value, which measures the overall performance of the ROC curve, is calculated to be 0.9692. This high AUC value further confirms the robustness and accuracy of our model in appliance identification tasks (Fig. 6).

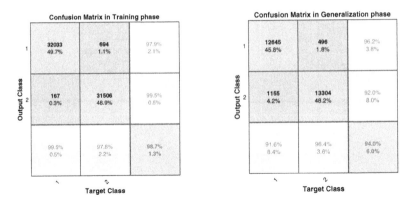

Fig. 5. Confusion matrices

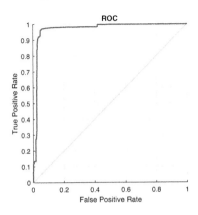

Fig. 6. Receiver operating characteristic curve (ROC) in generalization phase

6   Conclusions

This study presents a successful implementation of a feed-forward neural network for the classification of refrigerators and microwave ovens, achieving remarkable accuracy. The findings highlight the potential of the trained neural Network in appliance identification within a household, thereby facilitating more efficient energy management. The key conclusions drawn from this research are as follows:

The trained neural Network exhibited an impressive overall accuracy of 94%, indicating its robustness in classifying the target appliances. The fallout rate, which measures the proportion of misclassified microwave ovens as refrigerators, was recorded at a low value of 8%. Conversely, the recall rate, representing the network's ability to accurately identify refrigerators, achieved a rate of 96.2%. The miss rate, indicating the proportion of refrigerators falsely classified as microwave ovens, stood at 8.4%. Furthermore, the specificity of the network, signifying its precision in recognizing microwave ovens, reached a commendable level of 92%.

The Area Under the Curve (AUC) value, calculated to be 0.9692, underscores the superior performance of the model in appliance identification tasks. This metric substantiates the efficacy of the trained neural Network in effectively discriminating between refrigerators and microwave ovens.

Overall, the outcomes of this study emphasize the potential of the trained neural Network as a powerful tool for accurate appliance identification in a residential setting. The model's exceptional accuracy, as validated by the AUC value, lays the foundation for advancing intelligent energy management practices within households.

It is important to acknowledge that this study focused on a specific set of appliances, and further investigation is necessary to assess the generalizability of the model to a wider array of devices.

In conclusion, this work demonstrates the substantial benefits of the trained neural Network for appliance identification in residential environments. The findings contribute to the advancement of energy-efficient practices and provide valuable insights for researchers and practitioners working in the field of smart home technologies.

References

1. Kundu, A., Juvekar, G.P., Davis, K.: Deep neural network based non-intrusive load status recognition. In: 2018 Clemson University Power Systems Conference (PSC), pp. 1–6. IEEE (2018)
2. Alam, S.M., Ali, M.H.: A new subtractive clustering based ANFIS system for residential load forecasting. In: 2020 IEEE Power & Energy Society Innovative Smart Grid Technologies Conference (ISGT), pp. 1–5. IEEE (2020)
3. Paul, S., Upadhyay, N., Padhy, N.P.: Residential appliance identification using 1-D convolutional neural network based on multiscale sinusoidal initializers. IEEE Trans. Industr. Inform. 18(11), 7444–7453 (2022)
4. Grover, H., Panwar, L., Verma, A., Panigrahi, B.K., Bhatti, T.S.: A multi-head convolutional neural network based non-intrusive load monitoring algorithm under dynamic grid voltage conditions. Sustain. Energy Grids Netw. 32, 100938 (2022)
5. Moradzadeh, A., Mohammadi-Ivatloo, B., Abapour, M., Anvari-Moghaddam, A., Gholami Farkoush, S., Rhee, S.-B.: A practical solution based on convolutional neural network for non-intrusive load monitoring. J. Ambient. Intell. Humaniz. Comput. 12(10), 9775–9789 (2021). https://doi.org/10.1007/s12652-020-02720-6
6. Vanting, N.B., Ma, Z., Jørgensen, B.N.: Evaluation of neural networks for residential load forecasting and the impact of systematic feature identification. Energy Inform. 5(4), 1–23 (2022)
7. Wu, X., Han, X., Liang, K.X.: Event-based non-intrusive load identification algorithm for residential loads combined with underdetermined decomposition and characteristic filtering. IET Gener. Transm. Distrib. 13(1), 99–107 (2019)
8. Yang, H., Jiang, J., Chen, G., Zhao, J.: Dynamic load identification based on deep convolution neural network. Mech. Syst. Signal Process. 185, 109757 (2023)
9. Huang, L., Chen, S., Ling, Z., Cui, Y., Wang, Q.: Non-invasive load identification based on LSTM-BP neural network. Energy Rep. 7, 485–492 (2021)

10. Hu, X., Zeng, Y., Qin, C., Meng, D.: Bagging-based neural network ensemble for load identification with parameter sensitivity considered. Energy Rep. **8**, 199–205 (2022)
11. Buchhop, S.J., Ranganathan, P.: Residential load identification based on load profile using artificial neural network (ANN). In: 2019 North American Power Symposium (NAPS), pp. 1–6. IEEE (2019)
12. Freire, V.A., de Arruda, L.V.R.: Identification of residential load patterns based on neural networks and PCA. In: 2016 12th IEEE International Conference on Industry Applications (INDUSCON), pp. 1–6. IEEE (2016)
13. Ali, M., Djalal, M.R., Arfaah, S., Fakhrurozi, M., Hidayat, R.: Monitoring and identification electricity load using artificial neural network. In: 2021 7th International Conference on Electrical, Electronics and Information Engineering (ICEEIE), pp. 1–6. IEEE (2021)
14. Yang, T., Ren, M., Zhou, K.: Identifying household electricity consumption patterns: a case study of Kunshan, China. Renew. Sustain. Energy Rev. **91**, 861–868 (2018)
15. Hamdi, M., Messaoud, H., Bouguila, N.: A new approach of electrical appliance identification in residential buildings. Electr. Power Syst. Res. **178**, 106037 (2020). https://doi.org/10.1016/j.epsr.2019.106037
16. Klemenjak, C., Reinhardt, A., Pereira, L.: Non-intrusive load monitoring: a review. IEEE Trans. Smart Grid **14**(1), 769–784 (2023). https://doi.org/10.1109/TSG.2022.3189598
17. Liang, J., Liu, J.: On enabling collaborative non-intrusive load monitoring for sustainable smart cities. Sci. Rep. **11**(1), 1–13 (2023). https://doi.org/10.1038/s41598-023-33131-0
18. Kocaman, S., Akkaya, K.: Non-intrusive load monitoring using multi-label classification methods with feature selection. Electr. Eng. **102**(4), 2245–2259 (2020). https://doi.org/10.1007/s00202-020-01078-4
19. Santoso, A., Prasetyo, A.: Monitoring and identification electricity load using artificial neural network. In: 2021 7th International Conference on Electrical, Electronics and Information Engineering (ICEEIE), pp. 1–6. IEEE (2021)
20. Makala, B., Bakovic, T.: Artificial intelligence in the power sector (2020)
21. Ahmad, T., et al.: Artificial intelligence in sustainable energy industry: status quo, challenges and opportunities. J. Clean. Prod. **289**, 125834 (2021)
22. Ahmad, T., et al.: Energetics systems and artificial intelligence: applications of industry 4.0. Energy Rep. **8**, 334–361 (2022)
23. Forootan, M.M., Larki, I., Zahedi, R., Ahmadi, A.: Machine learning and deep learning in energy systems: a review. Sustainability **14**(8), 4832 (2022)
24. Farzaneh, H., Malehmirchegini, L., Bejan, A., Afolabi, T., Mulumba, A., Daka, P.P.: Artificial intelligence evolution in smart buildings for energy efficiency. Appl. Sci. **11**(2), 763 (2021)
25. Liu, W., Wang, Z., Liu, X., Zeng, N., Liu, Y., Alsaadi, F.E.: A survey of deep neural network architectures and their applications. Neurocomputing **234**, 11–26 (2017)
26. Gulzar, Y., Hamid, Y., Soomro, A.B., Alwan, A.A., Journaux, L.: A convolution neural network-based seed classification system. Symmetry **12**(12), 2018 (2020)
27. Sabuhi, M., Zhou, M., Bezemer, C.P., Musilek, P.: Applications of generative adversarial networks in anomaly detection: a systematic literature review. IEEE Access **9**, 161003–161029 (2021)

28. Hussain, N., et al.: A deep neural network and classical features based scheme for objects recognition: an application for machine inspection. Multimed. Tools Appl. 1–23 (2020)

29. Zhang, Z., Yang, K., Qian, J., Zhang, L.: Real-time surface EMG pattern recognition for hand gestures based on an artificial neural network. Sensors **19**(14), 3170 (2019)

30. Zhang, Y., Zhang, Y., Zhou, X.: Classification of power quality disturbances using visual attention mechanism and feed-forward neural network. Measurement **188**, 110390 (2022)

31. Gölcük, İ, Ozsoydan, F.B., Durmaz, E.D.: An improved arithmetic optimization algorithm for training feedforward neural networks under dynamic environments. Knowl.-Based Syst. **263**, 110274 (2023)

32. Touvron, H., et al.: ResMLP: feedforward networks for image classification with data-efficient training. IEEE Trans. Pattern Anal. Mach. Intell. **45**, 5314–5321 (2022)

Interactions in the Digital Learning Ecosystem in Teacher Learning Outcomes

Diana C. Burbano G[(⊠)] and Jaime A. Álvarez

University of Santiago de Cali, Cali -Valle, Colombia
1diana.burbano02@usc.edu.com, jaimejoyero@msn.edu.co

Abstract. Learning environments and interactions in educational contexts generate transformations in student learning outcomes, in which conceptual, methodological, and investigative trends are identified; from those assumed by learning environments and their mediations, conceptions, origins, and characteristics that emphasize those who learn, knowledge, and the educational community. Based on this research work, an app with augmented reality about autopsies is proposed, used by professionals in health sciences (semester 11) when considered for learning. This look proposes a space constituted by two design experiments and they were correlated with the conceptual design of an interactive digital learning ecosystem, in this way the learning environments as an object of the study propose a domain articulation space as a theoretical and practical perspective about the complexity of educational technological phenomena; operationalized in different phases: planning, learning outcome mediated by (personal learning environmental (AVA virtual learning environment – didactic sequence), and reflection on the teaching pedagogical praxis. At the same time, digital technologies are in the process of expansion and generalization in educational systems, allowing communication between students and teachers. Therefore, it is necessary to think about new pedagogical practices that promote knowledge processes, dynamic practices thought from the encounter in otherness and interactions with a multi-situated thought or group cognition, to the bidirectional relationships between systems, virtual and human educational environments.

Keywords: learning environments · learning interactions · digital learning ecosystem · significant experiences · legal medicine app

1 Introduction

Information and communication technologies (ICT), increasingly pose new challenges and possibilities in the educational field. However, the focus cannot be solely on the use of these technologies since teachers with new skills and a continuous training process are needed in the knowledge society. Disruptive trends in technologies [1] reveal cognitive configurations that, in some cases, focus on "learning", privileging interactivity, under the assumption that in this way meaning is conferred on experiences and applicability of the content. Learned to real-life situations. Another interest focuses on socialized learning, observing an experiential introspective trend, which aims to strengthen inter-active structures in relation to the community and the culture, this is seen as a way of manifesting comprehensive training from mediations pedagogical In addition, it is necessary to consider the implications that these mediations have for specific didactics, given that nowadays, teaching and learning communicable knowledge in the context of higher education is not the same as in the last century. This contrasted with today had these tools in terms of the production of multiple mental representations of knowledge objects. Therefore, its study, understanding, and analysis lead to research in educational contexts. Following the reflections of Erazo [2], the concept of "technological media-tion" supposes such a complexity that it intervenes in the multiple processes of cultural transformation that we are witnessing, in the midst of which the teaching and student subjectivities of the last decades are constituted. To speak of mediation is to go beyond the simplistic position that assumes that the media-recipient relationship is of cause and effect. Authors such as Martín-Barbero [3] and Serrano [4], introduced the term in our context and placed the media-audience relationship in a network of interactions.

Consequently, learning is taking on other dimensions and the role of the teacher is also changing. Today, learning is ubiquitous, and this is how m-Learning must include the ability to learn from anywhere, at any time, and without a physical connection to the network. So, the teacher, based on what exists on the Internet, can use technology as an artifact, tool, or instrument, in the sense of putting it at the service of teaching and learning.

Cognitive ecologies do not consider technology as an independent factor of people but rather understand it as a dimension that produces meaning. Seen from this perspec-tive, technology is understood as a human dimension. Beyond the devices, the tech-nological universe configures societies, understood as individual and social *collective devices of subjectivation* [5]. Technological *ecosystems* or *cognitive ecologies* are the aforementioned societal configurations. Understanding the phenomenon of technolog-ical mediations in education implies the recognition of an emerging system that arises from the tension between the instrumental paradigm (media and pedagogy) centered on educational institutions, with the ecosystemic paradigm, open and tending to techno-scientific development. Cultural transformation, an issue that occurs outside the school context, whose dynamics come from *digital media*.

In this article, learning environments are discussed, they are the best of the academic community for new forms of relationship with learning. They arise, mainly, from a genuine concern of the pedagogical praxis for the need to generate significant learning in the subject of necropsies with augmented reality. This bet was fed by deep reflections of teachers in their professional practice; by the way, learning spaces are configured. In this sense, learning environments as interaction scenarios in which other possible ways of generating symbiosis in teaching and learning processes are proposed.

2   State of Art

Information and communication technologies (ICT), increasingly pose new challenges and possibilities in the educational field. However, the focus cannot be only on the use of these technologies given that teachers with new skills and a continuous training process are needed in the knowledge society. Disruptive trends in technologies [6] reveal cognitive configurations that, in some cases, focus on "learning", privileging interactivity, under the assumption that in this way meaning is conferred on experiences and applicability of the content. Learned real-life situations. Another interest focuses on socialized learning, observing an experiential introspective trend, which aims to strengthen interactive structures in relation to the community and the cultural, this is seen as a way of manifesting comprehensive training from mediations pedagogical In addition, it is necessary to consider the implications that these mediations have for specific didactics, given that nowadays, teaching and learning communicable knowledge in the context of higher education is not the same as in the last century. This contrasted with today had these tools in terms of the production of multiple mental representations of knowledge objects. Therefore, its study, understanding, and analysis lead to research in educational contexts.

2.1 Collaborative Learning of the Teacher in the App-Mediated Learning Ecosystem (Augmented Reality): Key in the Online Educational Ecosystem

Personal Learning Environments (PLE), starting in the 21st century, began to develop and implement new technologies; defined by Castell "Knowledge Society" (SC), directed by the automation and easy access to Collaborative Learning courses (AC), determining that the organizations that make up the PLE, are in its entirety characteristics and processes of access to the information such as search ports, digital skills of teachers (Ministry of Sciences, 2020 plan); with other app application plans (augmented reality), from the integration of existing updated personal learning environments, for which it is desired to make the implementation of this system more effective in innovative processes, directed towards the creation and innovation in terms of functional products for the information society [7], in which the criteria for the diagnosis of educational practice (EP) are identified, mediated by technological devices, from which the following learning models emerge: PLE and PLN [8].

2.2 Intersubjectivity and Mediation

Intersubjectivity occurs when there is a core of shared meanings. With this condition, it is possible to initiate a dialogical and negotiation process of meanings in the search for coincidences [9] here the intervention of the teacher becomes important to sustain the states of Intersubjectivation with their students and to broaden the base of coincidences about the study [10]. In this process, the student and the teacher interactively modify their perspectives; the teacher tries to appropriate the meanings of the student and the student seeks to signify the contributions of his teacher. As a negotiation of meanings progresses, different levels of intersubjectivity are produced, in which the teacher interprets better the meanings of the student, and the student perfects the conceptual meanings of its cognitive structure [11].

2.3 Computational Thinking (CT) from a Socio-constructivist Perspective

The concept of Computational Thinking (CT), a high-level skill, related to a specific conceptualization model of human beings, develops ideas and links with abstract-mathematical and pragmatic thinking. The PC is not synonymous with the ability to program a computer, it requires thinking at levels of abstraction and is independent of devices. It has the characteristic of combining abstraction and pragmatism, it is based on mathematics, a world of ideas, and it is developed through engineering projects that interact with the real world; computational concepts, communicating with other people, and managing aspects of our daily lives [12].

2.4 Computational Thinking and Augmented Reality

Computational thinking seeks to solve problems by fulfilling a certain sequence of steps in the process through a methodology that uses technological elements; In this sense, some characteristics of computational thinking that support its greater adoption in learning strategies are a. formulating problems allow the use and knowledge of RIC as an aid in the proposed solution, b. Organize information sequentially for understanding, c. Obtain a structure of information through models and simulations. d. advance solutions through the structure of Algorithmic Thinking (AP), e. Identify, analyze, and implement solutions to achieve an effective and efficient mix of steps and resources.f. systematize and translate the structure of problem-solving. g. when using the PC, it is evident that the skills to obtain maximum performance in the sense of skills are necessary in the computational world, with specific features (for example, with data and results gateways), but equally for the rest of the activities that lead to some type of learning or development, the analysis has at least three dimensions, where each one is constituted without being exclusive or separated from the rest, a domain of study and research such as 1. Dimension of the situation of collaboration (group size, time period, affordances, communication, technological devices), 2. Type of Strategies and 3. Characteristics of "learning" and forms of collaboration [13, 13] (Table 1).

Table 1. Lists the cognitive components in relation to the variable intuition and reasoning in computational thinking.

Dual Cognitive Processing		
Autor	Intuition	Reasoning
Schneider & Schiffin (1977)	Automatic	Checked
Chaiken (1980)	Heuristic	Systematic
Fodor (1983)	modular input	High Cognition
Evans	Heuristic	Analytical
Reber (1993)	Implicit	Explicit

(continued)

Table 1. (*continued*)

Dual Cognitive Processing

Autor	Intuition	*Reasoning*
Epstein (1994)	experiential	Rational
Hammond (1996)	Intuitive	Analytical
Stanovich (1999)	System 1	system 2
Smith & DeCoster (2000)	associative	Based on Rules
Nisbett et.al	holistic	analytical
Wilson (2002)	Subconscious	Aware
Strack & Deutsch (2004)	Impulsive	Thoughtful
Toates (2006)	Limited to stimulus	high order
Stanovich & Stanovich	Algorithmic Mind	reflective mind

Author: Own source

The challenges of education in the 21st century, "contemporary education" arises, must be approached from a holistic perspective in the current learning society, given that social and cultural changes demand us to change the worldview of education in the century. XVI. The academic community then speaks of a comprehensive educational action to encompass the totality of being and apply the concept of holism in the teaching-learning process, in the role of the student, the role of the teacher, and the contents of the personal learning environment Finally, the importance of the commitment that we must acquire as educators to respond to the demands that our society demands in relation to education is highlighted.

2.5 The Role of the Teacher in Learning Analytics

In the trend of learning analytics or also called "Intelligent learning" mediated by "mobile learning" it is widely used in student media (whether university or college), as well as marketing and business, because it is a platform agile, seen from a technological point of view, because it allows easy access to information, carrying out a strict staggering of the things that are to be provided to the user, as well as access to the information sought by static means such as a database; therefore, all information related to ubiquitous media is more effective due to access and also "interaction with the medium and search", related to platforms that are commonly used from Web 2.0 to Web 4.0; (16) which integrate the information contained, in platforms that are connected through a network, allowing interaction with the external environment, which is located in classrooms or places where the software is available, showing that these platforms are robust.

3 Methodology

The methodological design of this research is oriented towards training in learning outcomes in eleven-semester medical school students in an educational institution through the development of the APP technological resource with augmented reality in practice scenarios; based on technological mediations in relation to mobile applications focused on M-Learning, which is associated with a learning theory conceived from five dimensions: individual productivity, interaction with other individuals, objects of study, educational work and cultural heritage, scientific method and technological, which allow pedagogical transformation by promoting the development of a learning route within the course, guided by ICT [15], in this way the inclusion of mobile technology in different models has generated the development of technological applications in education with a socio-technical perspective, which shows the interactions between "mobile technologies and the educational field", and how they are revolutionizing the new educational processes, in the field of mediations applied to Education. The research phases are Phase I: it was developed within the research project (augmented reality neuropathy published in the book clinical autopsy from the ethnographic context) [16] and financed by the authors of this research.

Following scientific rigor, the following instruments were implemented: A questionnaire composed of Likert scale questions was designed that sought to know the level of knowledge of students about augmented reality after their training experience.

Phase II: Qualitative analysis (focus group sample 22 students lay medicine students), augmented reality (learning result in usability test pedagogy).
Phase III: Analysis **of** descriptive inferential and correlation validate the hypothesis.
Phase IV: Data validity Conbrach's alpha.

3.1 Research Design

In the present investigation, the study methodology is based on "interactions in learning ecosystems", carried out in the year 2020–2022, in higher education institutions (IES); The research aimed to analyze the implementation of learning environments from the conceptual and methodological component while contributing to the process of curricular integration and technological innovation. In this way, the importance of addressing aspects related to the characteristics of the learning ecosystem, activities, student-teacher-patient-colleague interactions, and practice scenarios is recognized. The design (DBR) was implemented that helps to understand the complex nature of real-life design learning problems [17, 18]. This methodology is frequently used to improve learning and teaching in mobile applications about legal medicine in medical students; Characterized by iterative cycles of theory-based reflection, analysis, and refinement, DBR aims to create individual tools or services and their respective learning practices to address specific challenges in learning outcomes.

The development of the research involved working with an experimental group, with a number of medical students twenty-three (23) of semester eleven, in which the participation of men and women was presented, in addition, it is important to highlight that the group had students from different parts of the department as well as from very similar socioeconomic strata among the participants.

Taking into account the characteristics of the investigation, a logical sequence was carried out that allowed the components to be developed in relation to a. Qualitative techniques, b. quantitative techniques, c. Analysis and decision making as referred to in Fig. 1, Logical sequence for the research design Fig. 1. (Own source).

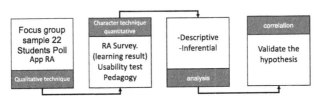

Fig. 1. Research phases

The objective of carrying out this research is oriented to compare the development in the learning results, through the application of the pre and post-test, making use of a didactic strategy that led to the development of skills through the APP-realidad mobile application augmented.

The legal medicine subject has a temporary duration of sixteen weeks (16), where the third week of class development was used to carry out the pre-test and from the fourth week, the mobile tool was introduced, in the eleventh week it was carried out the evaluation of the post-test and in the fourteenth week a usability test was carried out with the students that allowed knowing the inclusion of the use of Learning and Communication Technologies (TAC) in the classroom, within the subject. Additionally, a follow-up was carried out through the application of the work carried out by the students in the different spaces proposed through the processes of interaction and collaboration, the monitoring of the activities allowed the teacher to motivate the participation of the students, as well as to encourage those who do not participate, facilitating feedback processes in real-time.

In relation to the design, implementation, and validation of the technological resource, the creation of a specific design was generated in the subject of legal medicine through an app with augmented reality DTAPP with the intention of a teacher-student interaction configured in two levels of abstraction Fig. 2. However, the process focuses on conceptual and technological integration in a learning ecosystem. A first version of a DBAPP conceptual design was configured, which is validated through experimental design through the presentation of three cases derived from a conceptual analysis.

Phase 1. A problem in the learning outcomes (didactic sequence) is identified and analyzed in medical students prior to the experimental phase of the app on the subject of pathology (2020 years of registration), in the present investigation we propose a DBAPP framework with augmented reality that generated an approach to the formulation of practical needs based on scientific evidence, such variables as learning outcomes, practice scenarios with augmented reality in legal medicine subject, design practices, by integrating with mockus prototype design Fig. 3.

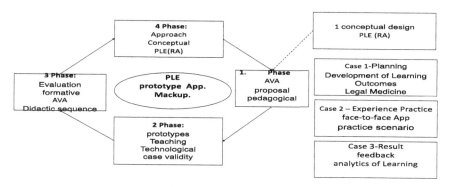

Fig. 2. Research design

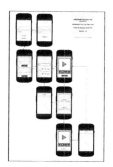

Fig. 3. Wireframe mockup

Phase 2. Initially, in 2020, the first app was registered with the virtual learning environment without augmented reality, which presents significant learning results when validating it. However, we continue the research line, we carry out our second experimental phase in the theme of the app with augmented reality in the subject of legal medicine, for which a certification of teachers in digital content and content curation (institutional certification of the IES) and interinstitutional repositories.

Phase 3. Some pre-designs were made through the app's thread diagram, user manual, AVA (virtual learning environment), learning outcomes (faculty curriculum plan), new sketches of the prototypes with the teachers in charge (credentials of doctors in educational sciences), experimentation with external peers and attached to the faculty in relation to design, implementation, and validation of prototypes.

Phase 4. An approximation to the DBAPP conceptual design of the teacher was made, in the last phase of the investigation a prototype of the DBAPP made in the experimental phase derived from the teacher-student interaction making the proposal is made.

3.2   Design Experiment (Cases)

During the experimental phase, the technological prototype was designed and validated in relation to interdisciplinary work and validated by external peers with the aim of collecting information on the DBAPP design. The purpose of the experimental phase was to test the DBAPP components, in order to improve the design and examine their appropriation in practice scenarios in relation to interactions, which involved a higher education institution. The main objective is to analyze the teaching interaction when interacting with technologies and how this knowledge is integrated into the DBAPP design.

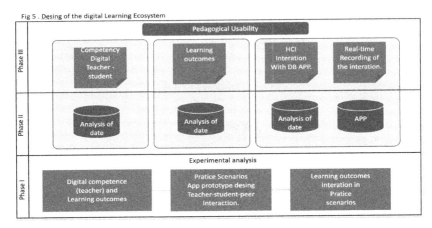

Fig. 4. Design of the digital learning ecosystem

3.3   Case 1: Assessment of Digital Competence, Mockup

Learning Outcomes
Case 1: Digital competence and learning outcome.

Objective: Criteria for evaluating ICT skills (Min Science) and learning outcomes: Teaching rubric.

Validation process in the DBAPP planning phase.

Sample: 23 students (SIGA).

Teachers: 3 teaching staff of the IES, the sample was taken in relation to the payroll of the institution, at the time it is a small sample.

Procedure:
Teachers received training in digital teaching skills within the framework of Min Sciences and in content curation in instructional design. Under the ADDI questionnaire, teachers reflect on their experiences in a questionnaire.

In the present study, the levels of digital skills and experience in digital learning ecosystems were analyzed.

Prototype: Self-assessment tool for assessing competence.

Evaluation: Content analysis in digital skills.

3.4 Case 2: Design, Implementation, and Validation of App Application (Augmented Reality). Expert Evaluation

Sample: Teachers work collaboratively to build learning ecosystems. The experimental phase of software design and interdisciplinary work of instructional design, piloting, and wireframes tests. 3 plant teachers participated, participated in the present study which participated in the pilot test, which had eligibility criteria.

Procedure: Enlistment: Phase I: Teacher training in instructional design and software, DRAPP conceptual approach, design, and app application implementation.

Prototype: Development of thread diagram for the app, conceptualization of DRAPP, entry to the platform, and socialization in practical scenarios by teachers.

Evaluation: In the present study, the pedagogical usability test was carried out (results).

Includes interactions with DLR (collective–individual).

3.5 Case 3: pedagogical usability

Goal: Interaction of teachers in DB APP.

Sample: Three teachers attached to the program with academic credentials at the PhD training level: contribute to the design and implementation of DB APP.

Procedure: In 1 year, in collaborative work, the teachers created the DB and tested the designs (72), and tested in the different practice scenarios. The evaluation instrument is pedagogical usability.

Prototype: The evaluation tool is an online questionnaire for pedagogical usability and Monkey.

Evaluation: It was carried out with the Google formats, monkey formats in the app, and online format with the pedagogical usability criteria.

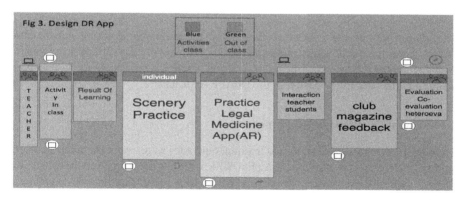

Fig. 5. Desing DB APP necropat

3.6 Consent to Participate in the Study

In line with internationally accepted standards to ensure the ethical treatment of people involved in scientific research, an informed consent form was developed. The document will explain to the research participants in the focus groups the nature of the study, its objectives, as well as the right not to participate or to suspend their participation at any time, and the confidentiality of the information provided to the participants.

3.7 Data Analysis Plan

The proposed methodology is complementary (quantitative and qualitative), the analysis of the data obtained according to their nature will be performed. For the processing and analysis of quantitative data, the statistical software SPSS version 4.0 for Windows, was used. First, the descriptive statistics will be kept, including frequencies, calculation of measures of central tendency (mean, median, and mode), and dissension (variance and standard deviation). The analysis is performed between differences of groups (T students test for independent samples and analysis of variance of a factor) and the degree of association or relationship between the variables (Pearson's correlation coefficient and chi-square tests).

The qualitative information collected will be analyzed with the MaxQda software, version 2018. The interviews are made recorded in audio format and subsequently transcribed and incorporated into the software for the organization and classification of data, summarizing and tabulating them (data reduction). It will be done following the inductive method, based on the information obtained, the analysis categories will arise. Therefore, following the suggested methodology, qualitative data will pass to an analytical description to extract relevant information.

4 Results

This section presents the results that emerge from the experimental design in these three phases: learning results, design, and implementation of new practices in app development with augmented reality, experimental phase, and practice scenarios. In the last section, we present the conceptual design of the DbAPP for teachers.

4.1 Evaluation of Design Experiments

Through the design, digital skills and learning outcomes were evaluated in teachers and students through neuropathy app mediation. 90% of the teachers perceived the evaluation as necessary in the process improvement plans. 10% report that the self-assessment makes them reflect on their pedagogical practice.

Main outcomes:

The three teachers who participated in this study determined that digital skills were necessary and that design and implement a learning ecosystem through a necropat app due to the prevailing need for practice scenarios in health sciences.

Upon entering the digital ecosystem, we monitor the activities and practices in the subject of legal medicine offering the student feedback activities and interdisciplinary management. We consider constant planning and evaluation in the development of integrated learning outcomes in the three phases.

Continuous training is carried out in the planning of DRAPP, and digital skills described by the Ministry of Sciences.

Design and enactment of practices.

In cases 1 and 2, h5p activities are carried out, they are trained and a conceptual approximation of the DBAPP design is carried out. The following practice scenarios are proposed:

Inverted classroom. Students collaboratively apply knowledge in legal medicine to problem resolution.

Problem-based learning: Problem-based learning. Student work teams are created, with each team member having a clear role. Students define the clinical case of interdisciplinary study, indicating the expected results and a timeline. To achieve the goal of the project, individuals continually engage in collaborative interactions with DBAPP.

Learning in practice scenarios: clinicopathological correlation.

Task-based learning. An example of an LD designed as a flipped classroom activity is described in Fig. 3 using the LePlanner web application.

Activities are carried out individually and collaboratively (Fig. 6).

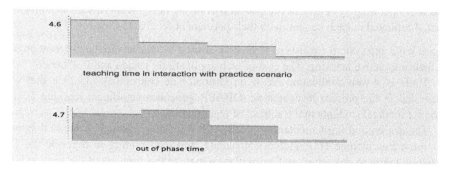

Fig. 6. App Interaction necropat

The teachers who participated in the present study (n = 3) mentioned that the use of DB APP provides automatic feedback for the students based on their interactions,

Evaluate the digital ecosystem in class.

The teacher who participated in this study monitors the activities of the didactic sequence in real-time with continuous feedback activities. Figure 4. The analysis of the answers of the professors showed in relation to the constant feedback when implementing the design in the learning of the students happen as expected. Research has shown that teachers primarily struggle to choose pedagogical actions in response to data.

Impact on the interactions and learning of the necropat application (augmented reality).

The students through the necropat application allowed to imagine interactive virtual elements of general pathology using mobile devices; necessary learning in the diagnosis of the future doctor.

Disruptive trends in augmented reality offer improvements in the design maintenance and delivery of digital content in real environments such as generating learning outcomes. Generate motivation in the student to direct any technological advance that is obtained with augmented reality to academic training determining that it serves as support in educational processes.

In the present study, the traditional pedagogical transformation towards collaborative learning mediated by the necropat app and significant experiences was evidenced, which motivated training processes of diagnosis and clinical treatment plan.

4.2   Conceptual Design of a Digital Learning Ecosystem

In this section, a conceptual design of DLE for teachers' situated learning will be proposed. Design experiments carried out as studies to understand the pedagogical, technological, and methodological aspects integrated into the design of the integrated DRAPP have not been validated in design experiments.

Dimensions of the proposed DBAPP

The technological dimension of our DBA APP is an app application (necropat), mediated in the learning of teachers and students. These are online web applications (android and IOS operating systems), developed as part of the design experiments described in Sect. 4 reflected in each session with their permanent feedback. (See Fig. 5).

Phase I: the app system consists of web services used by teachers in the different phases of their interactive learning. The cost of web applications Tinada and LePlanner.

Tinda is a web application based on Drupal. The conceptual approach that was generated in the present investigation, DBAPP, generates significant learning in real time for medical students in the subject of legal medicine.

The design and implementation of DB APP were done through a thread diagram, the interfaces include H5P, includes metadata, and data mining to describe the DB based on learning outcomes, and curricular themes. In the contents of the session with their respective themes, they generate interactions and provide feedback in real-time, generating a habit in the students.

Phase II: The phase analyzes the information in databases and stores the records of learning outcomes in relation to each topic. Interactions are automatically annotated with a specific category (domain concept used in taxonomies and domain models), linking students to learning outcomes.

Teachers base digital skills on their pedagogical praxis; by generating innovative proposals mediated by disruptive trends.

5   Conclusions

Most of the evaluation proposals in university contexts of medical students in relation to learning outcomes correlating Computational thinking focused on the computing or programming skills that the students possessed.

The augmented reality necropat app has advantages over traditional teaching methods. Realism, interactivity, motivation, and interest in learning are the most important factors to highlight, evidenced in students from their use of this tool.

The design and implementation of an app with augmented reality as a didactic in teaching and learning inspire them in computational thinking PC computational thinking of university students. Assessments are part of a broader project to bring computational thinking to practice scenarios in university educational contexts with an interdisciplinary collaborative group.

There is a wide base of instructional design models, and the one chosen in the present investigation is the AVA; notwithstanding the theoretical development considered as frameworks for the development of training modules or classes (theoretical and practical), doing so in accordance with its guidelines and precepts, the possibility of learning, of encouraging the participation of students so that they learn faster and obtain learning results in the students.

Currently Learning Analytics help us solve some problems in which we find ourselves immersed; for example, it is an excellent aid for diagnostic and formative evaluation in the adaptability of learning resources, to improve personalized planning within the PLE (personal learning environment), and for real-time tutoring. Likewise, it can also help us to establish models associated with competencies and learning outcomes (in addition to validating their effectiveness).

From the results of the study on "interactions in the digital Learning ecosystem in teacher Learning outcomes", some conclusions grouped from the dimensions that were proposed in the study are presented, to give way to recommendations that are considered in the learning design of real-life through DBR (design-based research) in collaborative environments.

Learning environments are academic bets for new ways of relating to learning. They arise, mainly, from a concern of the teaching group for the learning needs of the students. These bets feed on deep reflections of teachers for their professional practice; by the way in which learning environments are configured as interaction scenarios in which other possible ways of organizing teaching-learning processes are proposed.

The environments also bet on the creation of an educational community, where students, teachers, and interdisciplinary clinical management; participate in the learning process. This finding widens the view on the actors and on the forms of participation that mediate learning.

This study showed that some topics of digital ecosystems and learning environments are more visible than others. Topics such as the recognition of the characteristics of the students, clinical management of the study of legal medicine combined with augmented reality, the approach of disciplinary knowledge, the establishment of conditions in meaningful learning in real-time, the teacher-student relationship, communication, or evidence of pedagogical intent, are more frequent (greater than 70%); followed by the work from an interdisciplinary perspective, student-student interaction, student teacher, external peer students or evidence-based interdisciplinary clinical management (30%).

The integrated DBAPP was validated in phases II and III in future research. Comprehensive validation requires a study that encompasses in a single intervention all the important phases, pedagogical, social, and pedagogical approaches. A large-scale and longer-term study of the digital learning ecosystem is needed.

5.1 Discussion

The report 2020 [19] "Visions transforming education and training through advanced technologies" was published, it includes a series of articles that propose feasible scenarios for the year referring to the uses of ICT in educational institutions. They propose the transformation of the daily life of students in schools, innovation in teaching methods, educational materials, and evaluation, as well as the radical change of what we now conceive as the physical space of the classroom and therefore, of course, the emergence of new demands on the training and functions of the teaching staff.

The author Barriga [20] points out that "if we assess the way in which technological developments have been introduced in the field of education, we see that it has had a significant impact on education, in the sense that a change is being promoted, deep in the educational paradigms.

The work in [21] presents AR as one of the prevailing usage trends that have a significant presence in aspects related to training. The objective of this research work is to pretend that the reader finds motivation to direct any technological advance that is obtained with augmented reality to academic training determining that it serves as a support for the educational process.

The learning objects in AR are presented as useful educational materials for the learning of medical students, an aspect in which we agree with the work of [22, 22];

[24] Augmented reality (AR) has revolutionized the field of medicine by offering innovative and promising tools. By combining virtual elements with the physical world, AR has been used to improve diagnosis guide surgical procedures, train medical professionals, and improve the patient experience.

Students show a high level of motivation when incorporating these tools into educational practice, and they perceive them to be truly useful. In this sense, we can point out that we agree with the contributions made by different authors [25, 25]. In medical diagnosis, augmented reality allows more detailed and precise visualization of images in the anato – a pathological study in legal medicine. His ability to blend the virtual with the physical opens up a world of possibilities and promises a bright future in advancing modern medicine.

Students and residents can practice virtual procedures in simulated environments, where they can interact with organs and anatomical structures in a precise and realistic way. This provides hands – on learning opportunities without endangering patients and speeds up the process of acquiring medical skills.

This research has been funded by Direccion General de Investigaciones of Universidad Santiago de Cali under call No. 02-2023

Bibliography

1. Christensen, C.M., Baumann, H., Ruggles, R., Sadtler, T.M.: Disruptive innovation for social change. Harward Bus. Rev. **84**(12), 58–65 (2006)

2. Erazo, E.S.P.: The impact of the digital expression media on the processes of formation of architects and architecture. Latin Am. J. Soc. Sci. Childhood Youth **11**(2), 769–781 (2013). https://doi.org/10.11600/1692715x.11221170912
3. Martin-Barbero, J.: From media to mediations: communication, culture, and hegemony. Andres Bello Agreement (1998)
4. Serrano, M.: Social Mediation, Akal edn. Buenos Aires (2008)
5. Joao, O.: Sociedad de la informacion. Investigaciones, analisis y opiniones (ejercicios doctorado). San Salvador (2003)
6. Wing, J.: Computational thinking and thinking about computing (2008)
7. Christensen, C.M., Baumann, H., Ruggles, R., Sadtler, T.M.: Disruptive innovation for social change. Harward Bus. Rev. **84**(12), 58–65 (2006)
8. Castañeda, L., Adell, J.: Entornos personales de aprendizaje: claves para el ecosistema educativo en red. Marfil, Alcoy (2013)
9. Muñoz, H.A.: Mediaciones tecnologicas: nuevos escenarios de la parctica pedagogica. Prax. Saber **7**(13), 199–216 (2016)
10. Battro, A.M., Denham, P.J.: La educacion digital. (version digital). Editorial Emece (1997)
11. Fainholc, B.: cLa tecnologia educativa apropiada: una revisita a su campo a comienzos del siglo. Revista Rueda. Universidad Nacional de Lujan (2001)
12. E. &. G. -. M. D. Bording: Principios del pensmiento computacional. En Aparici 6 Garcia Marin. Comunicar y educar en el mundo que viene, pp. 177–191 (2018)
13. Tellez Ramirez, M.: Pensamiento computacional: una competencia del siglo XXI. Edu. Sup. Rev. Cient. Cepies. **6**(1), 23–32 (2019)
14. Zapata-Ross, M.: Pensamiento Computacional: Una nueva alfabetizacion digital. RED. Revista de Educacion a Distancia (46) (2015)
15. Chen, Y.-L., Cheng, L.-C., Chuang, C.-N.: A group recommendation system with consideration of interactions among group members. Expert Syst. Appl. **34**(3), 2082–2090 (2008)
16. Soler, J.A.A.: Autopsia clinica desde el contexto etnografico. Editorial Universidad del Cauca, Popayan (2023)
17. Herrington, J., Reeves, T.C., Oliver, R.: A guide to Authentic e-Learning. Routledge (2009)
18. Liu, G.-Z., Hwang, G.-J.: A key step to understanding paradigm shifts in e-learning: towards context-aware ubiquitous learning. Br. J. Educ. Technol. **41**(2), E1–E9 (2010). https://doi.org/10.1111/j.1467-8535.2009.00976.x
19. Montecé-Mosquera, F., Verdesoto-Arguello, A., Montecé-Mosquera, C., Caicedo-Camposano, C.: Impacto De La Realidad Aumentada En La Educación Del Siglo XXI. Eur. Sci. J. **13**(25), 129 (2017)
20. Barriga, F.: Educacion y nuevas tecnologias de la informacion: ¿hacia un nuevo paradigma educativo innovador? Universidad Nacional Autonoma de Mexico, Mexico (2007)
21. Cabero, J., Barroso, J.: Posibilidades educativas de la Realidad Aumentada. Revista de Nuevos Enfoques en Investigacion Educativa **5**(1), 46–52 (2016)
22. Yeo, C.T., Ungi, T., Uthainual, P., Lasso, A., McGraw, R.C., Fichtinger, G.T.: The effect of augmented reality trainig on percutaneous needle palcement in spinal facet joint injections. IEEE Trans. BioMed. Eng. **58**, 2031–2037 (2011)
23. Wu, H.-K., Lee, S.W.-Y., Chang, H.-Y., Liang, J.-C.: Current status, opportunities and challenges of augmented reality in education. Comput. Educ. **62**, 41–49 (2013). https://doi.org/10.1016/j.compedu.2012.10.024
24. Bower, M., Howe, C., McCredie, N., Robinson, A., Grover, D.: Augmented Reality in education – cases, places and potentials. Educ. Media Int. **51**(1), 1–15 (2014)
25. B. P.: REalidad Aumentada en la escuela: tecnologia, experiencias e ideas. Educon TIC (2013)

26. Han, J., Jo, M., Hyun, E., So, H.-J.: Examining young children's perception toward augmented reality-infused dramatic play. Educ. Technol. Res. Dev. **63**(3), 455–474 (2015). https://doi.org/10.1007/s11423-015-9374-9
27. Li, Z., Bouazizi, I.: Light Weight Content Fingerprinting for Video Playback Verification in MPEG DASH. Samsung Research America (2013)
28. Muller, C., et al.: Open source column: dynamic adaptive streaming over HTTP toolset. In: ACM SIGMM Records (2013)
29. Timmerer, C., Griwodz, C.: Dynamic adaptive streaming over HTTP: from content creation to consumption. In: MM'12 (2012)

CRAG: A Guideline to Perform a Cybersecurity Risk Audits

Isaac D. Sánchez-García[(⊠)] (iD), Tomás San Feliu Gilabert (iD),
and Jose A. Calvo-Manzano (iD)

Universidad Politécnica de Madrid (UPM), Escuela Técnica Superior de Ingenieros
Informáticos, Madrid, Spain
isaacdaniel.sanchez@alumnos.upm.es, {tomas.sanfeliu,
joseantonio.calvomanzano}@upm.es

Abstract. The cybersecurity risk audit is a relatively new field. The objective of cybersecurity risk audits is to identify deficiencies or deviations in cybersecurity countermeasures. Currently, cybersecurity risk audit guidelines do not include an internal control approach that aligns with cybersecurity standards such as ISO 27001 or the NIST CSF. Internal control is essential for addressing cybersecurity risk audits. This article proposes a cybersecurity risk audit guideline called CRAG (Cybersecurity Risk Audit Guideline), created using the SADT (Structured Analysis and Design Technique) model. CRAG aims to be comprehensive in the various applications that a cybersecurity risk audit guideline can have. The CRAG guideline consists of seven steps and 28 activities, as well as the content that the resulting audit report should include. Additionally, this article provides guidelines for its proper implementation, as well as examples of its potential applications.

Keywords: Cybersecurity · Risk · Audit · Guideline · Information security · Internal control

1 Introduction

Cybersecurity has emerged as a significant issue for most organizations worldwide, with potential consequences for the accuracy and dependability of financial reports as well as audit quality. In 2016, the Center for Audit Quality (CAQ) of the American Institute of Certified Public Accountants (AICPA) published a document outlining the role of external auditors in relation to cybersecurity risks faced by companies (Center for Audit Quality, 2019). According to the CAQ, the external auditors' responsibilities encompass two key areas: the examination of financial statements and internal control over financial reporting (ICFR), as well as disclosures. Previous studies examining the auditors' role in relation to companies' cybersecurity risks have focused on the impact of actual cyber breaches, highlighting the increased risks of material misstatement and weaknesses in internal controls [1–5].

Internal control influences the perception of the importance of risk management reports. The internal control system is fundamental in the risk management of multinational companies. By better understanding the contributions of an internal control system, we can improve communication between the parent company and the company's

M. F. Mata-Rivera et al. (Eds.): WITCOM 2023, CCIS 1906, pp. 517–532, 2023.
https://doi.org/10.1007/978-3-031-45316-8_33

subsidiaries, as well as encourage greater participation of the subsidiaries in corporate policies related to risk management [6].

Internal control is essential for addressing cybersecurity risk audits. Autores como Chalmers K. et al. [7] mencionan la relevancia que tiene el control interno en la mejora de los procesos organizacionales relacionados a tecnologías de la información. Así mismo Haislip J. et al. [8] realizaron pruebas sobre el efecto de la experiencia del auditor en tecnología de la información (TI) en la calidad del control interno y documentaron una asociación positiva entre ambas variables, ya que la probabilidad de que las empresas informen debilidades en el control interno de TI está asociada negativamente con la presencia de un auditor con experiencia en TI.

Most models such as ISO 27004 [9], NIST CSF [10], COBIT [11], lack the guidelines provided by internal control guidelines as COSO ERM [12], IAASB [13], or the Sarbanes-Oxley Act [14].

The cybersecurity risk audit completes the cycle of continuous improvement in cybersecurity risk management [15]. The cybersecurity risk audit, as part of the monitoring and review of a cybersecurity risk management system, refers to the countermeasures established during the risk treatment stage [5].

One of the main objectives of cybersecurity risk audits is to ensure the operational effectiveness of countermeasures within a specified time period. Cybersecurity risk audits rely on control objectives established in catalogs or taxonomies of countermeasures as a reference for forming an opinion [16].

The cybersecurity risk audit is considered a relatively new field when it comes to internal control. Some of the current problems are: 1) The absence of standardized frameworks results in a lack of universally acknowledged and consistent guidelines for conducting cybersecurity audits. This lack of standardization can lead to variations in audit methodologies and challenges in comparing and benchmarking audit outcomes across diverse organizations [17]. 2) The swift progress of technology presents fresh obstacles for cybersecurity audits. Auditors must stay up to date with emerging technologies and the risks they entail in order to conduct comprehensive evaluations effectively [17]. 3) Auditors may not possess the essential knowledge and expertise in cybersecurity required to adequately assess and evaluate an organization's security controls and practices. This deficiency in expertise can hinder their ability to effectively analyze and assess the effectiveness of an organization's security measures [2].

Previous work was carried out to identify taxonomies of countermeasures and related risk management models [18, 19]. In these systematic mapping reviews (SMR) it was identified that the current cybersecurity risk management models and their countermeasures do not integrate the vision of internal control for their evaluation. The identification of the need for an audit guide focused on cybersecurity, which incorporates internal control guidelines, was made possible thanks to the previously mentioned SMRs.

The present research work aims to create a proposal for a cybersecurity risk audit guideline. This proposal for a cybersecurity risk guideline takes into account current guidelines on cybersecurity risks, internal control, and auditing. The objective is to standardize how to conduct a risk audit in the field of cybersecurity, making it adaptable and serving as a support for auditors when conducting specific cybersecurity risk audits.

This research work is organized as follows: Sect. 2 (method) presents the method and its justification for the creation of the guideline for cybersecurity risk; Sect. 3 (CRAG guideline) presents the details of the proposed cybersecurity risk guideline; Sect. 4 (Application & use) presents the application and use of the guideline, and Sect. 5 presents the conclusions and future work.

2 Method

For the development of the Cybersecurity Risk Audit Guideline (CRAG), the Structured Analysis and Design Technique model by Congram & Epelman (SADT) was selected [20], The requirements analysis and definition model identify and defines the key requirements that the standard must meet. This involves understanding the needs and expectations of users and stakeholders, as well as considering relevant technical, operational, security, and quality aspects.

The SADT model was chosen because it provides a robust structured method for modeling hierarchical systems, and for this research, it offers the opportunity to define and analyze the properties and attributes of the guidelines and actors involved in conducting cybersecurity risk audits. The SADT model has been selected because its main function is to identify graphical relationships and evaluate their efficiency in a structured manner, as mentioned by authors such as Islamova et al. [21] They have applied it in the management and improvement of processes. In addition, Olbiort J et al. [22] The SADT model has been used to represent information flows in cybersecurity-related investigations, highlighting its usefulness for concept mapping and information flow representation.

Additionally, studies have been identified related to cybersecurity or risks that utilize the SADT model for the creation of models, frameworks, or tools. For example, the studies by [23], and [24] use the SADT model to relate concepts and objectives of risks or threats.

2.1 SADT model

The SADT model consists of four main stages: Analysis, Design, Development, and Transition, which are described below:

Analysis: In this stage, the different components and functions of a system are identified and analyzed. It is used to understand the structure and operation of the system by breaking it down into smaller parts. Techniques such as flowcharts, context diagrams, and structure diagrams can be used to graphically represent the system and its interactions.
Design: In this stage, solutions are defined, and relationships between system components are established. More detailed diagrams, such as hierarchical structure diagrams and process diagrams, are created to describe how the components of the system are organized and operated. Interfaces and technical specifications can also be defined in this stage.
Development: In this stage, the physical or logical implementation of the system takes place. The system components are built according to the specifications and designs defined in the previous stages. This may include software development, hardware configuration, and component integration.

Transition: In this stage, testing is carried out, the system's functionality is verified, and it is implemented in its production environment. Acceptance tests are conducted, and final adjustments are made to ensure that the system meets the established requirements and expectations. Training and support can also be provided during the system transition.

The specific organization and industry involved play a role in determining the context of a cybersecurity risk audit, which can vary. Nonetheless, in broad terms, such an audit is carried out to evaluate the efficiency of an organization's cybersecurity protocols and pinpoint potential vulnerabilities or deficiencies that may result in security breaches or data breaches. The objective of the audit is to assess the organization's adherence to applicable standards, regulations, and industry best practices within the realm of cybersecurity.

2.2 Cybersecurity Risk Audit

The objectives of the cybersecurity risk audit serve the following purposes: Assess the effectiveness of the organization's cybersecurity controls, policies, and procedures in mitigating risks and protecting sensitive data.

Evaluate compliance with applicable laws, regulations, and industry standards, such as ISO/IEC 27001[25], NIST Cybersecurity Framework [10], PCI DSS [26], CIS8 [27], and any specific sector-specific regulations.

Identify potential vulnerabilities or weaknesses in the organization's information systems, network infrastructure, applications, and data storage that could be exploited by malicious actors.

Review incident response and disaster recovery plans to ensure they are comprehensive, up-to-date, and aligned with industry best practices.

Evaluate the effectiveness of employee training and awareness programs regarding cybersecurity to ensure employees are well-informed and vigilant about potential risks.

Consider applicable standards and regulations.

After analyzing the ISO/IEC 27001[25], NIST Cybersecurity Framework [10], PCI DSS [26], and CIS8 standards [27], minimum domains were identified that should be considered in an initial integrated phase of cybersecurity risk audit.

The scope of the cybersecurity risk audit may include at least the following: Network infrastructure, including firewalls, routers, switches, and wireless networks. System and application security, including operating systems, databases, web applications, and mobile applications. Access controls and user management, including user authentication, authorization, and privileged access management. Data protection and encryption, including data classification, encryption methods, and key management. Security incident management, including monitoring, detection, response, and recovery processes. Physical security controls, such as access controls to data centers and server rooms. Third-party vendor management and assessment of their cybersecurity practices, if applicable. Compliance with applicable regulations, standards, and contractual obligations.

3   CRAG Guideline

The CRAG guideline was developed considering international standards for both cybersecurity and internal control. The purpose of the CRAG guideline is to address cybersecurity risk audits, taking into account aspects beyond technical and traditional ones.

The creation of the CRAG guideline used the SADT model as a starting point, incorporating the phases of internal control audit defined in COSO ERM and complementing them with the stages of security risk management proposed by ISO 27001, as shown in Fig. 1.

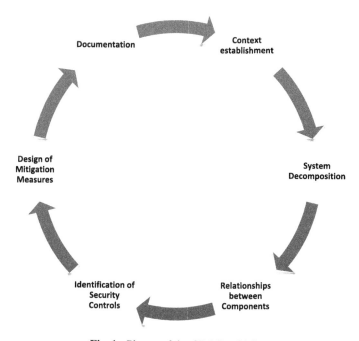

Fig. 1. Phases of the CRAG guideline

3.1   SADT Model Applied to Create CARG Guideline

For the creation of the CARG guideline, the following phases were considered, considering and adapted the SADT model:

Context establishment: Identify the context of cybersecurity risk audit, considering applicable standards and regulations. Establish the objectives and scope of the audit (See Fig. 1).

System Decomposition: Break down the cybersecurity system into its main components, such as technological infrastructure, information assets, business processes, and security policies. Identify key areas that need to be evaluated during the audit. These areas will be defined based on general classifications of standards such as ISO 27001, NIST CSF (See Fig. 1).

Relationships between components: Determine the interactions and relationships among the components of the cybersecurity system. For example, how information assets are protected by physical security controls defined in policies and procedures (layered security model) [28] (See Fig .1).

Identification of Security Controls: Establish how different controls relate to the system components and contribute to mitigating cybersecurity risks.

Risk Assessment: Evaluate cybersecurity risks associated with each system component, considering the identified security controls and requirements of applicable standards. Determine the impact and likelihood of occurrence of identified risks (See Fig. 1.).

Design of Mitigation Measures: Establish corrective and preventive actions to reduce risks to an acceptable level (See Fig. 2).

Documentation: Document the results of the cybersecurity risk audit. This may include creating diagrams showing the structure of the cybersecurity system, identified risks, recommended security controls, and proposed mitigation measures (See Fig. 1).

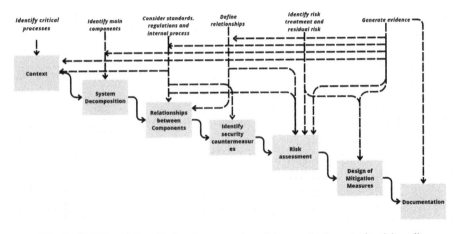

Fig. 2. SADT model applied to the concepts and stages of cybersecurity risk audit.

3.2 Definition of CRAG Guideline Activities

Within each of the phases of the CRAG guideline, a series of activities were established as shown below:

Context Establishment and System Decomposition
Within the establishment of the CRAG guideline, the following activities were defined (see Fig. 3) for the establishment of the context and the decomposition of the system:

Establish audit scope: Defines the boundaries and extent of the audit. Which systems, assets, and processes will be evaluated? Will it focus on a specific area of the organization

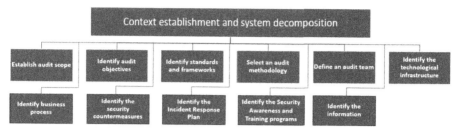

Fig. 3. Activities of the context and the decomposition of the system

or the entire company? The scope should be clear and specific to ensure that all relevant aspects are covered.

Identify audit objectives: Establishes the purposes and goals of the audit. What is expected to be achieved with the cybersecurity risk audit? These may include identifying vulnerabilities, evaluating existing controls, reviewing compliance with policies and regulations, among others.

Identify standards and frameworks: Identifies the standards and frameworks that will be used as a basis for evaluating cybersecurity controls. This could include internationally recognized standards such as ISO 27001[25], NIST Cybersecurity Framework [10], COBIT [11], among others. These frameworks provide a solid structure for assessing the organization's cybersecurity posture.

Select an audit methodology: Defines the approach and methods that will be used during the audit. This may include personnel interviews, documentation review, penetration testing, risk analysis, among others. The methodology should be consistent and rigorous to ensure the objectivity and thoroughness of the audit.

Define an audit team: Establishes who will be the members of the audit team. This may include internal and external auditors, cybersecurity experts, and other professionals with technical knowledge. It is important for the audit team to have the necessary experience and skills to adequately assess cybersecurity risks.

Identify the technological infrastructure: This component refers to the hardware, software, and network infrastructure that supports an organization's information systems. It includes servers, workstations, routers, firewalls, intrusion detection systems, encryption mechanisms, and other security technologies. Protecting the technological infrastructure is crucial for maintaining the confidentiality, integrity, and availability of information assets.

Identify the information assets: Information assets encompass the data and information that an organization collects, processes, stores, and transmits. This includes sensitive customer data, financial records, intellectual property, trade secrets, employee information, and other valuable or sensitive information. Proper protection of information assets is vital to prevent unauthorized access, data breaches, and other security incidents.

Identify the business processes: Business processes represent the workflows, procedures, and activities that an organization undertakes to achieve its objectives. These processes can involve various departments and functions, such as finance, human resources, operations, and marketing. Integrating cybersecurity measures into business processes helps ensure that security requirements are considered throughout the organization's operations.

Identify the security policies: Security policies establish the rules, guidelines, and best practices that govern an organization's approach to cybersecurity. These policies cover areas such as password management, data classification, access controls, acceptable use of assets, incident response procedures, and employee awareness training. Well-defined and communicated security policies provide a framework for consistent and effective security practices.

Identify the security countermeasures: Security controls are the technical and procedural measures implemented to protect the organization's systems and data. These controls can include network firewalls, intrusion detection systems, antivirus software, encryption mechanisms, access controls, authentication mechanisms, and security awareness training programs. Security controls are designed to prevent, detect, and respond to cyber threats.

Identify the incident response plan: An incident response plan outlines the steps to be taken in the event of a cybersecurity incident. It defines the roles and responsibilities of the incident response team, the procedures for detecting and reporting incidents, the containment and recovery processes, and communication protocols. An effective incident response plan helps minimize the impact of security incidents and enables a timely and coordinated response.

Identify the security awareness and training programs: The human element is a critical component of a cybersecurity system. Security awareness and training programs educate employees about cybersecurity best practices, policies, and procedures. These programs help employees understand their roles and responsibilities in protecting information assets and recognizing and reporting potential security threats.

Relationships Between Components
Within the establishment of the CRAG guideline, the following activities were defined (see Fig. 4.) for the Relationships between Components:

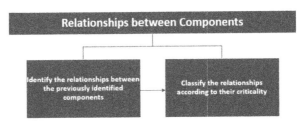

Fig. 4. Activities of the context and the Relationships between components Phase.

Identify the relationships between the previously identified components: Relationships are established when there are dependencies between more than one component that needs to be secured.

Classify the relationships according to their criticality: Establish a criticality rating considering the potential impacts if the critical process supported by the components being evaluated ceases to operate or experiences a security failure.

Identification of Security Countermeasures

Within the establishment of the CRAG guideline, the following activities were defined (see Fig. 5.) for the Identification of Security Countermeasures:

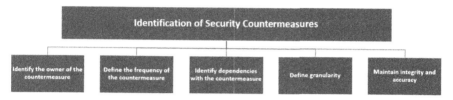

Fig. 5. Activities of the Identification of Security Countermeasures phase

Identify the owner of the countermeasure: Define the person responsible for the management and execution of the control.

Define the Frequency of the Countermeasure: Establish how many times the control is executed within a certain period of time.

Identify Dependencies with the Countermeasure: Identify if the control has any dependencies with the execution of a process or control.

Define Granularity: Clarify if the control operates uniformly across the organization or if there are variations in its execution.

Maintain Integrity and Accuracy: In the case of information used for the execution of the control (reports and records), the integrity and accuracy of the reports must be considered.

Risk Assessment

Within the establishment of the CRAG guideline, the following activities were defined (see Fig. 6.) for the Risk Assessment:

Fig. 6. Activities of the Identification of Risk Assessment phase

Collect samples: Samples are used to evaluate and obtain evidence about a larger population or dataset. The selection of samples allows the auditor to examine a representative sample of items instead of reviewing all the elements of a complete population, which would be impractical in most cases.

Evaluate operational effectiveness: The operational effectiveness of a countermeasure refers to its ability to fulfill its purpose and achieve desired results in the realm of security. A countermeasure is a measure taken to prevent, mitigate, or counteract a specific threat or risk within a specific timeframe.

Identify deviations: The process of detecting discrepancies or irregularities between the examined information and applicable standards, policies, laws, or regulations. These deviations may indicate deficiencies in internal controls, non-compliance with standards, or potential risks for the organization.

Identify observations: Control observations are findings or results identified during an audit that indicate deficiencies in an organization's internal controls. These observations reveal areas where controls are not functioning effectively or do not meet established standards, policies, or requirements.

Assess the probability of countermeasure failure: The probability of countermeasure failure refers to the likelihood that a countermeasure will not perform as expected or be effective in mitigating or countering a specific threat or risk. It is important to assess and understand the probability of countermeasure failure to make informed decisions about implementing additional measures or adopting alternative approaches.

Assess the impact of risk materialization: The assessment of the impact of risk aims to evaluate the potential negative consequences or effects that could occur if a risk materializes. The assessment of risk impact is essential for understanding and prioritizing the risks faced by an organization and making informed decisions about risk management.

Design of Mitigation Measures

Within the establishment of the CRAG guideline, the following activities were defined (see Fig. 7.) for the Design of Mitigation Measures:

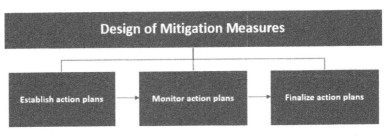

Fig. 7. Activities of the Identification of Design of Mitigation Measures phase

Establish action plans: The main objective of the action plan is to address the identified deficiencies, implement corrective measures, and enhance the organization's processes and internal controls.

Monitor action plans: Monitoring the audit action plans is crucial to ensure that corrective actions are effectively implemented, and the identified deficiencies are resolved.

Finalize action plans: The closure of the audit action plan is performed once all the corrective actions have been implemented and the identified deficiencies from the audit have been addressed.

Documentation

An audit report is a formal document that summarizes the findings, conclusions, and recommendations resulting from an audit conducted in an organization, process, system, or project. This report is prepared by the auditor or audit team and is presented to the organization's management or other relevant stakeholders. It consists of the following elements:

Header: The report should start with a header indicating the report title, audit identification, issuance date, and the intended recipients.

Executive Summary: This is a brief section that provides an overview of the key findings and conclusions of the audit. The executive summary should be clear and concise, giving a general idea of the audit results.

Audit Scope: The audit scope is described, including the objectives, areas, or processes that were examined during the audit. This helps establish the context and limitations of the audit.

Audit Methodology: The methodology used during the audit is detailed, including the techniques and tools employed, the audit criteria used, sources of information, and any other relevant information about how the audit was conducted.

Audit Findings: The specific audit findings are presented, i.e., the deviations, non-compliance, or areas for improvement identified during the audit process. These findings should be clear, specific, and supported by documented evidence.

Audit Conclusions: The general conclusions based on the audit findings are presented. The conclusions should be objective and supported by facts and evidence collected during the audit.

Recommendations: Recommendations are provided to address the identified deviations and improve the audited processes or systems. These recommendations should be practical, achievable, and focused on continuous improvement.

Annexes: Annexes may be attached to the audit report, such as supporting documents, evidence records, or any other relevant information that substantiates the findings and conclusions.

4   CRAG Applications, Comparison and Use

In this section, the fields of application of the CRAG cybersecurity risk audit guideline (Sect. 4.1) are first presented, then a brief comparison between CRAG, ISO 27004 [9], NIST CSF [10], COBIT [11], and SOX-COSO [12] is presented (Sect. 4.2), followed by the necessary considerations for the application of CRAG (Sect. 4.3).

4.1   CRAG Application

The CRAG cybersecurity risk audit guideline focuses on assessing the effectiveness of security controls and the protection of information assets within an organization. Some common areas of application for a cybersecurity audit include:

Security posture evaluation: Cybersecurity audits are used to evaluate an organization's current security posture. They help identify the strengths and weaknesses of implemented security controls, risk management practices, and protection of information assets.

Regulatory compliance: Cybersecurity audits are conducted to ensure compliance with specific regulations and standards related to information security. These regulations may include legal requirements, industry standards, and privacy and data protection compliance norms.

Third-party assessment: Cybersecurity audits are conducted on third-party providers or vendors to assess their security practices and ensure that they meet the required standards and contractual obligations.

Identification of risks and vulnerabilities: Cybersecurity audits allow for the identification of risks and vulnerabilities in an organization's systems, networks, and applications. This helps prioritize risk mitigation actions and strengthen security defenses to protect information and critical assets.

Penetration testing: Cybersecurity audits may include penetration testing or ethical hacking tests, where simulated cyber-attacks are conducted to assess the resilience of an organization's systems and networks. This helps identify vulnerabilities and provides recommendations for improving security.

Evaluation of incident management: Cybersecurity audits evaluate an organization's readiness and capability to detect, respond to, and recover from security incidents. Incident response plans, monitoring practices, and recovery capabilities are reviewed to ensure effective incident response.

Continuous improvement: Cybersecurity audits provide a foundation for continuous improvement of controls and security practices. Audit findings and recommendations help the organization identify areas for improvement and implement corrective and preventive measures to strengthen security over time.

4.2   CRAG Comparison

Comparing in general the proposed CARG guidelines, the participation of the entities mentioned by ISACA in the BMIS model was validated. [29]: 1) Process, 2) People, 3) Organization, and 4) Technology. These four entities must be considered, guaranteeing security at all levels (strategic, operational, and technical). The comparison between CRAG, ISO 27004, NIST CSF, SOX-COSO and COBIT is presented in Table 1.

Upon conducting the comparison, it becomes evident that CRAG takes into account various attributes. These include the strategic-level design factors of countermeasures established by SOX-COSO, as well as technical and operational attributes from NIST CSF and ISO 27004. Moreover, CRAG also incorporates a cross-request feature. To effectively assess the Entities and sources of light within the CRAG model, it is deemed necessary to apply a case study within any organization.

4.3   CRAG Use

For the proper application of CRAG, it is necessary to take into consideration a series of recommendations as shown below:

Table 1. CRAG guideline comparison.

Guideline	Entities	Focus Level
ISO 27004	Process, People, Technology	Operational, Technical
NIST CSF	Process, Organization, Technology	Operational, Technical
SOX-COSO	Process, People, Organization	Operational, Strategic
COBIT	Process, Organization, Technology	Operational, Strategic
CRAG	Process, People, Organization, Technology	Operational, Technical, Strategic

Countermeasure Taxonomies: In the identification of technological elements, it is important to consider international classifications, such as existing cybersecurity countermeasure taxonomies. An example would be the categorization conducted by Sanchez-Garcia et al., [18] which provides a classification of countermeasure taxonomies applied to cybersecurity.

Models for conducting risk assessments: Currently, there are a large number of risk assessment models available. The assessment can consider both quantitative and qualitative variables. Therefore, it is recommended to consider these models in the implementation of CRAG. An example is the study by Sánchez-García et al. [19] which identifies applicable risk assessment models for cybersecurity risks.

Considerations of internal control: For the proper implementation of CRAG, it is important to consider that internal control auditing is closely related to cybersecurity risk auditing. Therefore, it is suggested to consider the evaluation of design factors mentioned by the COSO [30] internal control framework and the Sarbanes-Oxley Act [14].

5   Conclusions and Limitations

During the cybersecurity risk audit phase of the risk management process, there is often confusion or misunderstanding regarding the concepts and goals involved. If the cybersecurity risk audit is not conducted properly, it can create challenges in achieving the established objectives within a management system.

5.1   Limitations of This Research Work

One of the limitations of this research work is the need to test the efficiency of the CRAG guideline in real-world case studies of cybersecurity risk audits. A pilot test is planned to be conducted in an organization where the accuracy of reports and observations identified using the CRAG guideline can be measured.

Another limitation or potential bias is the difficulty in comparing and obtaining common benchmarks for guidelines that have such different approaches, such as internal control guidelines, information security guidelines, and cybersecurity guidelines.

The CRAG guideline is recommended for evaluating specific cybersecurity counter-measures, as applying it to countermeasures created for another possible field may not take into account specific needs of that field.

5.2 Research Findings, Knowledge Gaps

In this research work, best practices and audit requirements focused on cybersecurity were collected from international standards such as ISO 27001, the NIST Cybersecurity Framework, CIS Controls 8, and COBIT, complemented by internal control models such as COSO and the SOX Act. These practices were aligned and grouped together to create the Cybersecurity Risk Audit Guideline (CRAG).

Auditors, as defined by Aditya [31], identify three stages in every audit: 1) establishing the context, 2) conducting the audit, and 3) preparing the audit report.

Using the SADT model, relationships and common steps were identified among the standards, models, and guidelines, which were then adapted for application in cybersecurity risk audits. The CRAG guideline consists of seven steps and 28 activities.

5.3 Future Research Directions

Within the lines of future research, it is deemed necessary to identify specific concepts and objectives of cybersecurity risk audits and incorporate them into the CRAG guideline. Additionally, evaluating the guideline in a company to validate its efficiency in assessing cybersecurity countermeasures is considered a future research direction.

Finally, it is believed that after evaluating and further maturing the CRAG guideline, it is possible to incorporate quantitative parameters that aid in conducting an objective cybersecurity risk audit.

Based on the needs identified in this research work, it is considered necessary to adapt the CRAG guideline into a cybersecurity risk management model to complement the complete cycle of risk monitoring and review.

References

1. Li, H., No, W.G., Boritz, J.E.: Are external auditors concerned about cyber incidents? evidence from audit fees. Auditing: A J. Pract. Theory **39**(1), 151–171 (2020). https://doi.org/10.2308/ajpt-52593
2. Rosati, P., Gogolin, F., Lynn, T.: Audit firm assessments of cyber-security risk: evidence from audit fees and sec comment letters. Int. J. Account. **54**(03), 1950013 (2019). https://doi.org/10.1142/S1094406019500136
3. Tom Smith, T.J., Higgs, J.L., Pinsker, R.E.: Do auditors price breach risk in their audit fees? J. Inform. Syst. **33**(2), 177–204 (2019). https://doi.org/10.2308/isys-52241
4. Li, H., No, W.G., Wang, T.: SEC's cybersecurity disclosure guidance and disclosed cybersecurity risk factors. Int. J. Account. Inf. Syst. **30**, 40–55 (2018). https://doi.org/10.1016/j.accinf.2018.06.003
5. Calderon, T.G., Gao, L.: Cybersecurity risks disclosure and implied audit risks: evidence from audit fees. Int. J. Audit. **25**(1), 24–39 (2021). https://doi.org/10.1111/ijau.12209

6. Beuren, I.M., Machado, V.N., Dall Agnol, A.J.: Relevance of internal controls for risk management: empirical evidence from the perception of its executors and reviewers in a multinational company. Corporate Governance: Int. J. Bus. Soc. **23**(6), 1233–1250 (2023). https://doi.org/10.1108/CG-05-2022-0200

7. Chalmers, K., Hay, D., Khlif, H.: Internal control in accounting research: a review. J. Account. Lit. **42**(1), 80–103 (2019). https://doi.org/10.1016/j.acclit.2018.03.002

8. Haislip, J.Z., Masli, A., Richardson, V.J., Sanchez, J.M.: Repairing organizational legitimacy following information technology (IT) material weaknesses: executive turnover, IT expertise, and IT system upgrades. J. Inf. Syst. **30**(1), 41–70 (2016). https://doi.org/10.2308/isys-51294

9. International Organization for Standardization: "ISO/IEC 27004:2016," Information technology — Security techniques — Information security, 2016. https://www.iso.org/standard/64120.html. Accessed 24 Oct 2022

10. National Institute of Standards and Technology: NIST Cybersecurity framework. In: Proceedings of the Annual ISA Analysis Division Symposium, vol. 535, pp. 9–25 (2018)

11. Information Systems Audit and Control Associatio: COBIT 2019. www.isaca.org/COBIT (2018). Accessed: 08 May 2022

12. Galligan, M.E., Rau, K.: COSO in the cyber age (2015)

13. IAASB: International Auditing and Assurance Standards Board. https://www.iaasb.org/ (2023). Accessed 22 May 2023

14. Public Company Accounting Oversight Board. Sarbanes Oxley Act. (2002)

15. Al-Matari, O.M.M., Helal, I.M.A., Mazen, S.A., Elhennawy, S.: Integrated framework for cybersecurity auditing. Inform. Secur. J. **30**(4), 189–204 (2021). https://doi.org/10.1080/19393555.2020.1834649

16. European Confederation of Institutes of Internal Auditors: 'Risk in focus 2021. Hot topics for internal auditors. https://www.eciia.eu/wp-content/uploads/2020/09/100242-RISK-IN-FOCUS-2021-52PP-ECIIA-Online-V2.pdf (2020)

17. Duncan, B., Whittington, M.: Compliance with standards, assurance and audit: Does this equal security? In: ACM International Conference Proceeding Series, Association for Computing Machinery, pp. 77–84 (2014). doi: https://doi.org/10.1145/2659651.2659711

18. Sánchez-García, I.D., Feliu Gilabert, T.S., Calvo-Manzano, J.A.: Countermeasures and their taxonomies for risk treatment in cybersecurity: a systematic mapping review. Comput. Secur. **128**, 103170 (2023). https://doi.org/10.1016/j.cose.2023.103170

19. Sánchez-García, I.D., Mejía, J., Feliu Gilabert, T.S.: Cybersecurity risk assessment: a systematic mapping review, proposal, and validation. Appl. Sci. **13**(1), 395 (2022). https://doi.org/10.3390/app13010395

20. Congram, C., Epelman, M.: How to describe your service. Int. J. Serv. Ind. Manag. **6**(2), 6–23 (1995). https://doi.org/10.1108/09564239510084914

21. Islamova, O.V., Zhilyaev, A.A., Bozieva, A.M.: SADT technology as a tool to improve efficiency in the use of process approach in management of engineering enterprise. In: 2016 IEEE Conference on Quality Management, Transport and Information Security, Information Technologies (IT&MQ&IS), IEEE, pp. 65–68 (2016). https://doi.org/10.1109/ITMQIS.2016.7751903

22. Olbort, J., Röhm, B., Kutscher, V., Anderl, R.: Integration of communication using OPC UA in MBSE for the development of cyber-physical systems. Procedia CIRP **109**, 227–232 (2022). https://doi.org/10.1016/j.procir.2022.05.241

23. Bygdas, E., Jaatun, L.A., Antonsen, S.B., Ringen, A., Eiring, E.: Evaluating threat modeling tools: microsoft TMT versus OWASP threat dragon. In: 2021 International Conference on Cyber Situational Awareness, Data Analytics and Assessment (CyberSA), IEEE, pp. 1–7 (2021). https://doi.org/10.1109/CyberSA52016.2021.9478215

24. Derradji, R., Hamzi, R.: Multi-criterion analysis based on integrated process-risk optimization. J. Eng. Des. Technol. **18**(5), 1015–1035 (2020). https://doi.org/10.1108/JEDT-08-2019-0201
25. Microsoft Global: ISO/IEC 27001:2013 Information Security Management Standards (2021). https://docs.microsoft.com/en-us/compliance/regulatory/offering-iso-27001. Accessed 01 Sep 2021
26. Security Standards Council: PCI DSS Quick Reference Guide. www.pcisecuritystandards.org (2018)
27. Center for Internet Security: CIS Critical Security Controls® CIS Critical Security Controls. www.cisecurity.org/controls/ (2021)
28. Yildiz, M., Abawajy, J., Ercan, T., Bernoth, A.: A layered security approach for cloud computing infrastructure. In: 2009 10th International Symposium on Pervasive Systems, Algorithms, and Networks, , pp. 763–767. IEEE (2009). https://doi.org/10.1109/I-SPAN.2009.157
29. ISACA: An Introduction to the Business Model for Information Security. www.isaca.org (2009)
30. Mancero Arias, M.G., Arroba Salto, I.M., Pazmiño Enríquez, J.E.: Modelo de control interno para pymes en base al informe COSO – ERM. Universidad Ciencia y Tecnología **24**(105), 4–11 (2020). https://doi.org/10.47460/uct.v24i105.375
31. Aditya, B.R., Ferdiana, R., Santosa, P.I.: Toward modern IT audit- current issues and literature review. In: 2018 4th International Conference on Science and Technology (ICST), pp. 1–6. IEEE (2018). https://doi.org/10.1109/ICSTC.2018.8528627

Adversarial Attack Versus a Bio-Inspired Defensive Method for Image Classification

Oscar Garcia-Porras[1](✉)(ID), Sebastián Salazar-Colores[2](ID),
E. Ulises Moya-Sánchez[3](ID), and Abraham Sánchez-Pérez[3]

[1] Universidad Autónoma de Querétaro, Santiago de Querétaro, Querétaro, Mexico
ogarcia41@alumnos.uaq.mx
[2] Centro de Investigaciones en Óptica, León, Guanajuato, Mexico
sebastian.salazar@cio.mx
[3] Dirección de Inteligencia Artificial del Gobierno de Jalisco, Guadalajara, Jalisco, Mexico
{eduardo.moya,abraham.sanchez}@jalisco.gob.mx

Abstract. Adversarial attacks are designed to disrupt the information supplied to Artificial Intelligence (AI) models causing a failure in their intended purpose. Despite late state-of-art performance on computer vision tasks like image classification, AI models can be vulnerable to adversarial attacks. Hence, to mitigate this risk the AI models require additional steps. This research presents the implementation of a novel bio-inspired defense method against adversarial attacks. The defense is based on the use of a deterministic monogenic layer at the top of a ResNet-50 convolutional neural network model used for image classification with the CIFAR-10 data set. The results show the ConvNet with the bio-inspired defense approach outpacing the regular convolutional architectures, this can be translated into increased resistance to adversarial attacks and greater reliability of artificial intelligence models. The Structural Similarity Index Measure (SSIM) and the Peak Signal-to-Noise Ratio (PSNR) metrics were measured on the bio-inspired layer activations to obtain a quantitative explanation of the improvement. The results obtained from this research expose the potential performance of the monogenic layer in confronting adversarial attacks and encourage further expansion of the knowledge in the field of the monogenic signal for AI purposes.

Keywords: Adversarial attacks · Deep neural networks · Image classification · Monogenic signal

1 Introduction

Computer vision intends to similarly accomplish the ability to see and understand visual information as humans, this task for computer vision requires the

Supported by the Mexican governmental institute Consejo Nacional de Humanidades Ciencias y Tecnologías (CONAHCyT).

use of methods and techniques to analyze, understand, and extract relevant information from the visualized data. Deep neural networks (DNN) and specifically convolutional neural networks (ConvNets) are commonly used in computer vision tasks, due to their capacity to extract higher-level features from the input data to process the information and be capable of accomplishing the required computer vision tasks [1]. State-of-art neural networks are achieving outstanding performance on these tasks, demonstrated by several studies, where most of them are related to image classification [2–4]. Image classification can be required for basic real-life tasks and many researcher's work has been focused on building data sets to train neural networks for several purposes, some data sets a related to numbers, animals, plagues, or even tasks used for medical purposes where the best outcome performance of the ConvNet is critical [5–8]. Current state-of-art performance from the ConvNets models can be affected by feeding images processed by an adversarial attack (adversarial examples) to the pre-trained ConvNet models, leading to miss classification and further malfunction in the ConvNet intended purpose [9]. The impact on ConvNet performance caused by adversarial attacks is a challenge that needs to be addressed. To date, several investigations have been exploring alternatives to confront affectations generated by adversarial examples improving the performance of the ConvNets, nevertheless, there is not an effective general solution to address adversarial examples, which leaves room for further investigation [10–18].

The experimental setup was based on adversarial examples computed by using the Foolbox library [19] and the CIFAR-10 data set [20]. The outcomes of the evaluation demonstrate the improvement in robustness and performance of ConvNets with the bio-inspired layer.

2   Monogenic Signal and Adversarial Attacks

2.1   Monogenic Signal

The most accepted 2D generalization of the 1D analytic signal is known as the monogenic signal. The basis of the monogenic signal is the analytic signal, which is the complex representation of a one-dimension signal. The analytic signal can be seen as an identity split in image processing and recognition, in its polar representation two characteristics from the complex signal are obtained: the local amplitude (local quantitative measure of the information) as the modulus and the local phase (local qualitative measure of the information) as the argument [21].

Equations that define the 1D analytical signal (f_A) from an original function (f) [22]:

$$f_A = f - i f_{Hi} \tag{1}$$

where f_{Hi} is the Hilbert transform:

$$f_{Hi}(x) = \frac{1}{\pi} \int_{-\infty}^{\infty} \frac{f(x)}{\tau - x} d\tau \tag{2}$$

Obtaining the amplitude (A) and phase (ϕ) from f_A:

$$A = |f_A(x)| = \sqrt{[f(x)]^2 + [f_{Hi}(x)]^2} \tag{3}$$

$$\phi(x) = \arctan\left(\frac{f_H(x)}{f(x)}\right) \tag{4}$$

However, in real life, there are various types of signals especially those that work at different scales, hence it is required to use a filter to focus on a specific part. Commonly to overcome this problem the use of a band-pass filter centered on the required spot of the frequencies may be the solution. Gabor, log-Gabor, Poisson, Cauchy, and Gaussian derivative are some of the filters that can work for the solution [23].

The analytic signal generates a single imaginary value, but in the case of a two dimensions signal two imaginaries values will be required to represent each dimension. To obtain these two imaginary values the quaternionic algebra and the riesz transform (a generalization of the Hilbert transform) will be required. In its general basic form, the monogenic signal can be expressed as [21]:

$$f_M = f + if_{R1} + jf_{R2} \tag{5}$$

where f_R are the riesz transforms. This research gets the approximation by a filter quadrature, $f' = g * f$ where $*$ is the convolution operator and $g = g(x, y)$ is a Gabor function. Rewriting the original function:

$$J_M = \mathcal{F}^{-1}\left(J + J_1 + J_2\right) \tag{6}$$

where, $J = \mathcal{F}(f)\mathcal{F}(g)$, $J_1 = \mathcal{F}(f)\mathcal{F}(g)f_{R_1}$ and $J_2 = \mathcal{F}(f)\mathcal{F}(g)f_{R_2}$.
The riesz transforms are defined by:

$$f_{R_1}(u) = \frac{u_1}{||u||} \tag{7}$$

$$f_{R_2}(u) = \frac{u_2}{||u||} \tag{8}$$

where, $||u|| = \sqrt{u_1^2 + u_2^2}$, u_1 and u_2 are the frequency components.
Returning to the main three representations of each pixel, the local amplitude of the monogenic signal can be defined by:

$$A_M = \sqrt{J^2 + J_1^2 + J_2^2} \tag{9}$$

Local phase (J_ϕ) and local orientation (J_θ) associated to J are defined by:

$$J_\phi = \arctan 2\left(\frac{J}{|J_R|}\right) \tag{10}$$

$$J_\theta = \arctan\left(\frac{-J_2}{J_1}\right) \tag{11}$$

where $J_R = J_1 + J_2$.

The final result from applying the equations will provide both of the required characteristics: the local phase (ϕ) and the local orientation (θ), both are visually represented in Fig. 1.

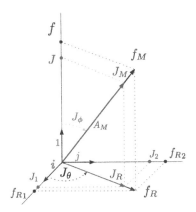

Fig. 1. Geometric representation of the monogenic signal for one pixel.

The outcomes obtained from the monogenic signal provide the tools required to explore its application and associated techniques in the context of adversarial attacks, this may allow the development of robust defense mechanisms against adversarial attacks in image classification tasks.

2.2 Adversarial Attacks and Defensive Methods

Nowadays, deep neural networks (DNNs) have an extendable and more common use in day-to-day activities where computer vision tasks are required, nevertheless, DNNs are vulnerable to adversarial examples, which can result in incorrect outcomes and failure of the model's intended purpose [24]. There are two main types of adversarial attacks: black-box attacks and white-box attacks, which were classified according to the level of information they use from the target model structure to generate the adversarial examples [11]:

- Black-box attack: It only requires access to the input data to generate the affectation. This type of attack lacks knowledge of the target model structure.
- White-box attack: This type of attack know the target model structure (i.e. activation functions, training data, gradient information, among others). Its attack can be more complex and it can generate adversarial examples to deviate outcome classification to a specific class of the data set (i.e. Projected Gradient Descent (PGD) [25]).

This research is focused on the white box attack: Projected Gradient Descent(PGD) [25], example exposed in Fig. 2.

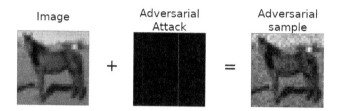

Fig. 2. Adversarial example generated by using the Foolbox library into an image from CIFAR-10, with a $L_{inf}PGD$ adversarial attack (epsilon = 0.5 and steps = 20).

Adversarial attacks are a real issue to be considered as a risk for the security of the artificial network models [10]. Hence, it is required to work on defensive methods to mitigate adversarial attacks. Many defensive methods with variable countermeasure techniques have been implemented where three main types of defensive methods can be categorized into model optimization, data optimization, and additional network [11].

Model optimization has different techniques where the robustness of the model will be implemented directly on the main structure of the deep neural network trying to complicate the appropriation of the model structure parameters to the adversarial attack. Some of the known approaches to mitigate the affectation of the adversarial examples use the idea of transferring knowledge between networks, which will reduce the capability of the adversarial attack to acquire information from the DNN structure, this is known as defensive distillation [12], some use a coder and decoder in the model to get gradient masking, which will reduce the adversarial attack capability of getting knowledge from the DNN by hiding gradients to the attacker [13] and some of them use a U-Net network as an image denoising network, which intention is to eliminate noise and restore the image to its true values [14].

On the other hand, data optimization tries to tackle the problem by processing the adversarial examples before the classification network, or in some cases it directly handles the process on the adversarial examples during training. Adversarial training is oriented toward training the neural network with a mix of adversarial examples and clean samples, so it can learn from both cases and differentiate the adversarial example from the clean image [15]. Some investigations try to pre-process the adversarial example, feature compression is one of this type, it uses a method to compress from 24-bit pixel to 12-bit pixel and uses a second process to reconstruct the affected image [16]. Another technique is the input reconstruction, where some investigations use image transformations (image clipping and re-scaling, depth reduction, JPEG compression, total variance minimization, and image quilting), trying to get variable and effective image information [17], in the same way, an adversarial example defense methodology based on GANs, which work removing the noise by generating an image with random noise that at the end of the process should approximate its distribution to the distribution of the clean samples [18].

Several methods have shown relative effectiveness by using different techniques, but there is no universally effective solution, leaving room for further exploration and improvement of defensive methods against adversarial attacks.

3   Monogenic Front Layer for Deep Neural Networks

The inspiration behind the concept of the monogenic layer was based on the knowledge of the mammalian visual system properties from the primary cortex V1, which special characteristics denote invariance to contrast and illumination changes [26]. The special characteristics of the monogenic layer contribute to confronting adversarial examples by its benefit of handling variations in image contrast and illumination [27].

Previous studies about the monogenic layer support the outstanding performance of the monogenic layer in addressing variations in image contrast and illumination [27,28]. The objective of the current research is to further expand knowledge about the monogenic layer by conducting experiments specifically on the PGD white-box attack to understand the effectiveness of the monogenic layer as a defense mechanism against adversarial attacks.

3.1   Structure of the Model

To mitigate the affectations of the adversarial attack, the monogenic layer is positioned at the beginning of the processing pipeline, before the DNN. The process of the monogenic layer is to extract the local phase and local orientation from each image. The local phase and local orientation are computed as separate images at the end of the monogenic layer processing, then the images will continue the process of feature extraction through the layers of the convolutional neural network so the DNN can learn from them, and at the end of the processing pipeline, the probability for the classification task is provided by the output of the network's dense part (Fig. 3).

4   Methods and Materials

4.1   Hardware and Software

The code was built using Python 3.10.6. The deep neural network model development and the handle were performed by using the libraries of Pytorch 1.12 and Pytorch-lightning 1.9.5. A computer with 64 GB Ram, 12 GB memory size GPU NVIDIA GeForce RTX3080Ti, and Ryzen 7 eight-core process was used to perform the experiments shown in this research.

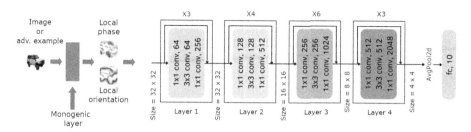

Fig. 3. Visual illustration of position and processing of the monogenic layer.

4.2 Data Set

Cifar-10 consists of 60,000 color images with a size of 32×32 in 10 classes, with 6,000 images per class. Normally 50,000 images are for training and 10,000 images are for testing. The classes are conformed by: airplane, automobile, bird, cat, deer, dog, frog, horse, ship, and truck.

4.3 Image Quality Metrics

The functionality of the monogenic layer can be measured by comparing the structural modification of the local phase and local orientation obtained from the images before the adversarial attack and after the adversarial attack. The quantitative results of the comparison may be obtained by calculating their similarity by using image quality metrics.

Some of the most common metrics utilized to measure image fidelity are Structural Similarity Index Measure (SSIM) and Peak Signal-to-Noise Ratio (PSNR).

Structural Similarity Index Measure. The SSIM metric takes into consideration image structure and dependencies, its functionality process is based on image signals and their strong neighbor dependencies. SSIM is defined by [29]:

$$SSIM(x, y) = \frac{(2\mu_x\mu_y + C_1)(2\sigma_{xy} + C_2)}{({\mu_x}^2 + {\mu_y}^2 + C_1)({\sigma_x}^2 + {\sigma_y}^2 + C_2)} \quad (12)$$

where x and y are two arrays of size N $\times$ N, μ_x, μ_y, σ_x^2 and σ_y^2 are the mean values and variances respectively, σ_{xy} is the covariance of x and y, while C_1 and C_2 are small positive constants that stabilize each term.

Peak Signal-to-Noise Ratio. The PSNR is another metric used for signal fidelity measurement, however, this metric tends to have low performance due to its limitations in measuring structural distortions [30].

$$PSNR = 10 \log_{10} \frac{L^2}{MSE} \qquad (13)$$

where L is the range of the pixel intensities from the analyzed image.

Both of these metrics (SSIM and PSNR) were implemented computationally using the methods from the Scikit-image library [31].

5   Experimental Setup

5.1   Monogenic Signal

The monogenic layer was implemented based on Eqs. (1–11) with a Gabor filter.

5.2   Data Set

The CIFAR-10 data set was obtained from the torchvision library and handled by torch DataLoader with several transformations: random crop = 32 and padding = 4, random horizontal flip, and normalized (mean = 0.4914, 0.4822, 0.4465 and standard deviation = 0.2023, 0.1994, 0.2010) for the training data set. In the case of the test data set the transformation only took the normalization with the same values previously mentioned.

5.3   Adversarial Attack

The Fool box library [19] was used to compute the L_{inf} PGD adversarial attack. The setting used for the attack were: step = 20, random start, range of bounds = [−2.42906, 2.75373], and ϵ values: 0.1, 0.2, 0.3, 0.4, 0.5, 0.6, 0.7, 0.8, 0.9, 1.0, by using the Fool box library. The value of 20 steps and random start were selected as common values used on several investigations [32–34], the range of bound was selected according to the minimum and maximum value of the images data set after the initial transformation and the epsilon values where selected to cover a wide range of values (Fig. 4).

5.4   Deep Neural Network for Image Classification

ResNet-50 [35] without pre-trained weights was the neural network chosen for this research. Some modifications were made to the original model to accept the input of the local phase and local orientation obtained from the monogenic layer. The principal characteristics of the resulting deep neural network are summarized in Table 1 and graphical representation may be visualized in Fig. 3.

Cross-entropy and Stochastic Gradient Descent were implemented on this neural network as the loss function and the optimizer function, both computed using the Torch library [36]. The resulting total trainable parameters of the deep neural network were 23.5 million.

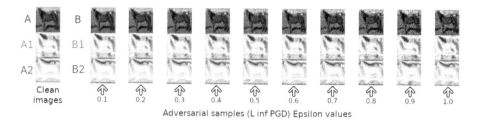

Fig. 4. Example of one image processed by several epsilon values. A is the clean image, A1 is the local phase (ϕ) of A, A2 is the local orientation (θ) of A, B is the adversarial example produced by its corresponding epsilon, B1 is the local phase (ϕ) of B and B2 is the local orientation (θ) of B as corresponding to their epsilon values.

Table 1. Summary of the modified model ResNet-50.

Layer name	Output size	Content	
Layer 1	32 × 32	Conv 1 × 1, 64 Conv 3 × 3, 64 Conv 1 × 1, 256	×3
Layer 2	16 × 16	Conv 1 × 1, 128 Conv 3 × 3, 128 Conv 1 × 1, 512	×4
Layer 3	8 × 8	Conv 1 × 1, 256 Conv 3 × 3, 256 Conv 1 × 1, 1024	×6
Layer 4	4 × 4	Conv 1 × 1, 512 Conv 3 × 3, 512 Conv 1 × 1, 2048	×3
	1 × 1	AvgPool2d, 10-d fc, softmax	

The performance of the monogenic layer in image classification was obtained by comparing the classification rate from two models: one without the monogenic layer and one with the monogenic layer. In both of the experiments, the same images were attacked by the same adversarial attack by the same epsilon values with the same number of steps.

Both of the models were trained with the 50,000 train images and tested with the 10,000 test images previously split by the CIFAR-10 author [20].

6   Results and Analysis

The performance of the monogenic layer was measured by obtaining the image signal fidelity using PSNR and SSIM metrics calculated accordingly to each pair of images for each epsilon value (B-A, B1-A1 and B2-A2, may reference in Fig. 4).

The PSNR and SSIM values obtained for each pair of images had better metrics for the local phase and local orientation than the clean images. An

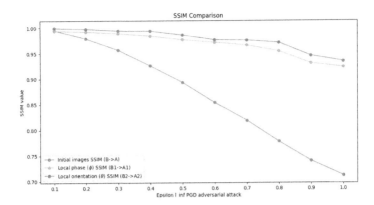

Fig. 5. SSIM calculated at diverse epsilon values for one image (horse showed in Fig. 4).

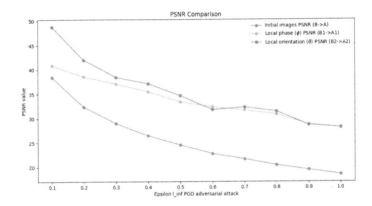

Fig. 6. PSNR calculated at diverse epsilon values for one image (horse showed in Fig. 4).

example of the results obtained by processing the image of the horse shown in Fig. 4 can be seen in Fig. 5 and Fig. 6.

The results shown in Fig. 5 and Fig. 6 predict a good direction on the performance of the monogenic layer. Nevertheless, the need for a more reliable result by analyzing a sample containing more images is needed for a more reliable result. 3,000 images from the 10,000 test images were randomly selected and the same previous process to obtain an image quality metric was performed. The results are exposed in Fig. 7 and Fig. 8.

Figure 7 shows the box plots of the SSIM measured for the 3,000 images at each of the epsilon values. The box plots from the SSIM for the local phase and the local orientation show a more compact distribution, higher mean values, and fewer outliers than the box plot from the SSIM for the clean images.

Figure 8 shows the box plots of the PSNR measured for the same 3,000 images sample at each of the epsilon values. The box plots exhibited a more scattered distribution but indicated that the local phase and the local orientation values

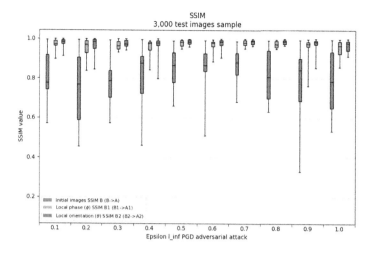

Fig. 7. SSIM box plot from 3,000 random images at diverse epsilon values.

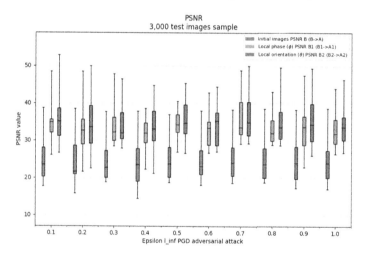

Fig. 8. PSNR box plot from 3,000 random images at diverse epsilon values.

had a more centered distribution and higher mean values than the clean images at all epsilon values.

The results of the classification task showed a more stable top-1 accuracy for the model with the monogenic layer compared to the model without the monogenic layer. The best accuracy achieved for each model: 0.8674 for the model without the monogenic layer and 0.7641 for the model with the monogenic. The top-1 accuracy of the model with the monogenic layer could be improved by modifications to the DNN, but the results were suitable for comparing the performance of both models.

The results show a more stable performance on the model with the monogenic layer, as evidenced by the stable accuracy through the increment of epsilon values (Fig. 9).

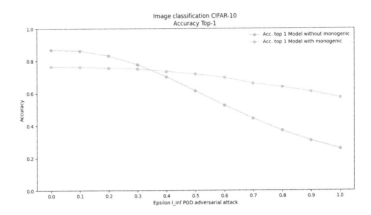

Fig. 9. Image classification accuracy top-1 metric.

Comparing the decrement rate based on its maximum classification accuracy from each of the model's testing processes may provide a different perspective on the comparison of both models. Figure 10 also shows a more stable classification accuracy through the increment of epsilon value for the monogenic model, but in this case, it is more notable the difference of performance. In the case of the highest epsilon evaluated (1.0) where the image is highly perturbed the model without the monogenic layer was reduced to 30% of its max classification top-1 accuracy and in the case of the model with the monogenic layer it was only reduced to 75% of its max classification top-1 rate accuracy.

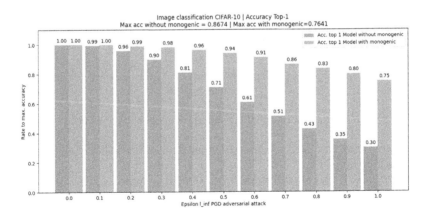

Fig. 10. Decrement rate based on maximum testing accuracy from both models tested.

7 Discussion

Deep neural networks are vulnerable to adversarial attacks [9], leading to false predictions [24] and the need for defenses to maintain reliable security in real-life computer vision tasks.

This research focused on exposing the vulnerability of a neural network, specifically ResNet-50, against a white-box attack ($L_{inf}PGD$) using the CIFAR-10 data set for image classification.

The monogenic layer as a defense method to confront adversarial examples was implemented in this research. The results obtained from this research expose the potential performance of the monogenic layer in confronting adversarial examples. Although there is no fully efficient defense method against adversarial attacks this research demonstrates the potential usage of the monogenic signal for defense purposes.

The favorable results obtained in this research, along with previous research on the monogenic signal [27,28], are evidence that encourages further investigation to expand the knowledge in the field of the monogenic signal for Artificial Intelligence purposes.

Suggestions for further investigation would include increasing test accuracy for the model with the monogenic layer, conducting experiments with trainable parameters with the monogenic layer [28], and evaluating its performance against diverse adversarial attacks and data sets.

Acknowledgments. This academic research was supported by the Mexican governmental institute Consejo Nacional de Humanidades Ciencias y Tecnologías (CONAH-CyT), in the engineering postgraduate faculty of the Universidad Autónoma de Querétaro (UAQ) specifically on the financial support on the author (CVU: 1176674) M. Sc. studies.

References

1. Bengio, Y.: Learning Deep Architectures for AI, 1st edn. Now Publishers Inc., Dept. IRO, Université de Montréal, Canada (2009)
2. Tan, M., Le, Q.: EfficientNetV2: smaller models and faster training. In: Meila, M., Zhang, T. (eds.) International Conference on Machine Learning, vol. 139, pp. 10096–10106. PMLR (2021)
3. Kolesnikov, A., et al.: Big transfer (BiT): general visual representation learning. In: Vedaldi, A., Bischof, H., Brox, T., Frahm, J.-M. (eds.) ECCV 2020. LNCS, vol. 12350, pp. 491–507. Springer, Cham (2020). https://doi.org/10.1007/978-3-030-58558-7_29
4. Ridnik, T., et al.: TResNet high performance GPU-dedicated architecture. In: IEEE Winter Conference on Applications of Computer Vision (WACV), pp. 1399–1408. IEEE (2021)
5. Deng, L.: The MNIST database of handwritten digit images for machine learning research [best of the web]. IEEE Signal Process. Mag. **29**, 141–142 (2012)
6. Song, H., Kim, M., Lee, JG.: SELFIE: refurbishing unclean samples for robust deep learning. In: Chaudhuri, K., Salakhutdinov, R. (eds.) International Conference on Machine Learning, vol. 97, pp. 5907–5915. PMLR (2019)

7. Amarathunga, D., Ratnayake, MN., Grundy, J., Dorin, A.: Image data set of two morphologically close thrip species: western flower thrips and plague thrips. Monash University (2022)
8. Lee, R.S., et al.: A curated mammography data set for use in computer-aided detection and diagnosis research. Sci. Data **4**(170177), 1–9 (2017)
9. Madry, A., et al.: Towards deep learning models resistant to adversarial attacks. In: 6th International Conference on Learning Representations, ICLR 2018 - Conference Track Proceedings (2018)
10. Jagielski, M., et al.: Manipulating machine learning: poisoning attacks and countermeasures for regression learning. In: IEEE Symposium on Security and Privacy (SP), pp. 19–35. IEEE (2018)
11. Liang, H., et al.: Adversarial attack and defense a survey. Electronics **11**(8), 1283 (2022)
12. Papernot, N., et al.: Distillation as a defense to adversarial perturbations against deep neural networks. In: IEEE Symposium on Security and Privacy (SP), pp. 582–597. IEEE (2016)
13. Folz, J., et al.: Adversarial defense based on structure-to-signal autoencoders. In: IEEE Winter Conference on Applications of Computer Vision (WACV), pp. 3568–3577. IEEE (2020)
14. Liao, F., et al.: Defense against adversarial attacks using high-level representation guided denoiser. In: IEEE/CVF Conference on Computer Vision and Pattern Recognition, pp. 1778–1787. IEEE (2018)
15. Kannan, H., Kurakin, A., Goodfellow, I.: Adversarial logit pairing. Cornell University (2018)
16. Jia, X., et al.: ComDefend: an efficient image compression model to defend adversarial examples. In: IEEE/CVF Conference on Computer Vision and Pattern Recognition (CVPR), pp. 6077–6085. IEEE (2019)
17. Guo C., et al.: Countering adversarial images using input transformations. Cornell University (2017)
18. Pouya S., Maya K., Rama C.: Defense-GAN: protecting classifiers against adversarial attacks using generative models. Cornell University (2018)
19. Rauber, J., et al.: Foolbox native: fast adversarial attacks to benchmark the robustness of machine learning models in PyTorch, TensorFlow, and JAX. Journal of Open Source Software **5**(53), 2607 (2020)
20. Krizhevsky, A.: Learning multiple layers of features from tiny images. University of Toronto (2009)
21. Felsberg, M., Sommer, G.: The monogenic signal. IEEE Trans. Signal Process. **49**, 3136–3144 (2001)
22. Granlund, G.H., Knutsson, H.: Signal Processing for Computer Vision, 1st edn. Springer, New York (2013)
23. Bridge, CP.: Introduction to the monogenic signal. Cornell University (2017)
24. Chakraborty, A., et al.: A survey on adversarial attacks and defences. CAAI Trans. Intell. Technol. **6**(1), 25–45 (2021)
25. Carlini, N., Wagner, D.: Towards evaluating the robustness of neural networks. In: IEEE Symposium on Security and Privacy (SP), pp. 39–57. IEEE (2017)
26. Hubel, D.H., Wiesel, T.N.: Receptive fields, binocular interaction and functional architecture in the cat's visual cortex. J. Physiol. **160**(1), 106–154 (1962)
27. Moya-Sanchez, E.U., et al.: A bio-inspired quaternion local phase CNN layer with contrast invariance and linear sensitivity to rotation angles. Pattern Recogn. Lett. **131**, 56–62 (2020)

28. Moya-Sanchez, E.U., et al.: A trainable monogenic ConvNet layer robust in front of large contrast changes in image classification. IEEE Access **9**, 163735–163746 (2021)
29. Wang, Z., et al.: Image quality assessment: from error visibility to structural similarity. IEEE Trans. Image Process. **13**, 600–612 (2004)
30. Wang, Z., Bovik, A.C.: Mean squared error: love it or leave it? A new look at signal fidelity measures. IEEE Signal Process. Mag. **26**, 98–117 (2009)
31. Van-der-Walt, S., et al.: Scikit-image: image processing in Python. PeerJ **2**, e453 (2014)
32. Jin, G., et al.: Enhancing adversarial training with second-order statistics of weights. In: IEEE/CVF Conference on Computer Vision and Pattern Recognition (CVPR), pp. 15252–15262. IEEE (2022)
33. Addepalli, S., et al.: Towards achieving adversarial robustness by enforcing feature consistency across bit planes. In: IEEE/CVF Conference on Computer Vision and Pattern Recognition (CVPR), pp. 1017–1026. IEEE (2020)
34. Robustness (Python Library). https://github.com/MadryLab/robustness. Accessed 18 July 2023
35. He, K., et al.: Deep residual learning for image recognition. In: IEEE Conference on Computer Vision and Pattern Recognition (CVPR), pp. 770–778. IEEE (2016)
36. Collobert, R., Kavukcuoglu, K., Farabet, C.: Torch7: a matlab-like environment for machine learning. In: BigLearn, NIPS workshop. LIDIAP (2011)

Technological Tools for Inventory Control in Fac Stores

Clara Burbano Gonzalez, Lorieth Bocanegra Jurado(✉), Valentina Rodriguez Caviedes, Emavi, Victor Rodriguez Yáñez, and Marco Fidel Súarez

Military Aviation School, Cali Valle de Cauca, Colombia
{lbocanegraj,vrodriguezc}@emavi.edu.co

Abstract. Inventory control is an element of great importance for the development of large, medium and small companies, for this reason the main objective of this study is to create an app implementing QR code for inventory control in Air Force warehouses. Colombiana, which will allow carrying out the inventory management method in the warehouses of the Colombian Air Force, making use of technological tools in the globalized world to facilitate control in this type of areas and functions. This will allow for a more rigorous control of inventory administration and management of administrative processes for the warehouses of the aeronautical logistics center, miscellaneous, aerial weapons and ground weapons, thereby generating doctrine in the logistics process, standardizing activities and controls for the inventory management and warehouse control. This leads to obtaining as a result a correct decision making facilitating the execution of the activities of the warehouses that will allow having an essential strategic stock to guarantee the operations of the Colombian Air Force, in the same way it reflects the opportunity to improve the operation of this area of great importance for the daily operation of the institution's activities. This being essential for the correct development of the institutional mission, ensuring that we always have the products regardless of the conditions that may arise, such as a possible war.

Keywords: Inventory management · Strategic stock · Inventory classification

1 Introduction

In any organization, the entry and exit of goods or services is of vital importance; hence the importance of inventory management, companies such as: government agencies, educational institutions and private companies; More and more different organizations are striving to achieve an inventory control information system for the supply chain. Therefore, to achieve effective inventory control, there must be adequate coordination and cooperation between the elements of the system, this project focuses on the state of the distribution warehouses of the different elements in each part of the institution (López & Lopez, 2011).

Therefore, in this article called "Technological tools for inventory control in warehouses" the results of a research process are presented where the purpose is to develop

M. F. Mata-Rivera et al. (Eds.): WITCOM 2023, CCIS 1906, pp. 548–566, 2023.
https://doi.org/10.1007/978-3-031-45316-8_35

and implement an app through the QR code for inventory control in warehouses. The warehouses of the Colombian Air Force.

The theme of this article corresponds to a series of concerns that have arisen in the training process, evidencing shortcomings and opportunities for improvement within inventory control in the warehouses of the Colombian Air Force, because it is evident in theory and in practice. The need to delve into the administration of inventories and management of administrative processes for the warehouses of the aeronautical logistics center, miscellaneous, air weapons and ground weapons, thereby generating doctrine in the logistics process, standardizing activities and controls for inventory management and the warehouse control.

The theoretical foundation of the research is supported by the theory of Inventory Management defined as the inventory management process, so that its amount can be reduced to the maximum, without affecting customer service, through adequate planning and control (Cespón Castro, 2012), despite appearing to be a technical process, brings relevant theoretical, conceptual and practical advances through the use and appropriation of technology, they manage to solve problems in warehouse control.

Some SMEs that sell and offer their products in large quantities, it is important to be able to verify in detail the activities that are carried out and to be able to exclusively analyze the white line of the inventory (washing machines and refrigerators), which occupy the majority of the percentage of the space used, Nowadays, in the main warehouse, it is the one that is almost at the top, since 80% of its limited space is being occupied.

Currently within the warehouse area there are regularly certain excesses in inventory, identifying another problem is the large number of days that inventory rotates; this naturally generates high costs for storage, risks and deterioration of the product, as well as loss amounts due to accidents. The common problem is the excess of inventory turns out to be the heel of quiles of some companies that keep stock for sale, being the hoarding of the stock that is naturally known as overstock (Sifuentes, 2020, p.8).

In this order of ideas, the Ibero-American Foundation for Higher Studies (FIAEP) points out that the misuse of inventories in warehouses and supplies, as well as the purchase of products in inadequate quantities and times, generally increase costs, production is varied and exceeds the volume of the limit in the warehouse, because of this, the cash must be reduced to the rent, insurance and utilities to be paid or the like, sometimes it forms groups of workers so that there can be a low profit. In addition, it indicates that the loss of materials is part of another factor that increases the cost of goods sold on a large scale, an acceptable loss would be 2% to 30% of the inventory value (Sifuentes, 2020).

Because currently a company cannot be considered innovative without the support of information and communication technologies (ICT) to manage business processes. By implementing new technologies, large companies have revolutionized their productivity, however, their adoption is also possible in small and medium-sized companies, which can see the growth opportunities they face, without spending millions (Hernández, et al., 2021).

One of the alternatives used in this problem is based on QR codes; QR codes are a tool that today has positioned itself as an app for businesses around the world. By innovating internally in a company's processes, its image benefits from others in an exponentially competitive field.

Innovation regarding the implementation of QR codes in different areas of the company is focused on the development of inventory control systems through QR codes, this, in order to demonstrate that this tool helps small companies to reduce time and costs compared to barcodes. In the same way, it reduces the difference in the inventory record (Hernández, et al., 2021).

The most relevant issue in this project focuses on the importance of establishing control of elements or tools found in different warehouses of each group of the force, for this, implementing a QR code is viable for precise control of the tools with the help of an app in order to easily use and access this technological tool for officials of the Colombian Air Force; The problem is located in the lack of control of tools or elements in warehouses that provide supply such as: spare parts, maintenance tools, implements for electronic work, there is no control regarding the time and the person who uses this tool, which It is part of the different warehouses found in each Force Group.

In the same way, different causes can be generated for the situation, such as the time exceeded in the use of the objects and the ignorance of the personnel that makes use of the object. One of the possible consequences that may arise corresponds to not having a guarantee for loss or damage of the tools designed for officials who therefore require the expenses or budget to cover the gap left by a lost or damaged object in a warehouse. They can be increased, disproportionate budgetary values destined to administrative obligations of the Group that has this type of novelty, all for not having an adequate control with technological tools, which have greater precision and speed than a process or manual control.

Consequently, a description and a forecast is generated regarding the use and knowledge of technological tools, such as the QR code, through an easy-to-use app for people who require daily use of the different elements found in warehouses., promoting control and information regarding the users who make use of the objects, however, to contribute to the success of the purpose that is to be achieved with the app. It is important that the officials who use the elements carry out the due diligence in the app, in order to have a record of each object and promote the objective, which is to have control over the elements of the warehouse.

In order to achieve the objective, it is intended to create an app to implement a QR code that will allow inventory control of the different warehouses of the Colombian Air Force, and that will be of great help to corroborate the catalog or have information regarding the users who require the tools that are supplied in the warehouse.

This article intends to present the results of an information system that allows to control the activities that are carried out in the warehouse, in this way it is expected that by implementing the information system it will allow the creation of important and significant results that will be reflected in the management. Inventory, in order to save time, effort and paperwork after information for users.

2 Referential Framework

2.1 Background

In the Bibliotic University of Harvard Institutional digital repository in the article by Castillo (2015) he mentions that: "Qr codes are virtual supports where information is stored and can be shared, users display the information through the mobile phone that can provide with data of interest or simply share news". It is a digital resource that allows information to be systematized, allows processes to be simplified, information to be compressed and shared immediately.

QR codes are two-dimensional barcodes for the coded programming of information, currently it is widely used and we find it not only in food products, in magazines, books, posters, flyers, promotions, etc. In the search for information on degree work that involves Qr codes, it is found in the digital repository of the Complutense University of Madrid in the work of Naranjo (2015) in which he states that: "Qr codes are digital media that at the same time Being allies in the educational field facilitates the acquisition of materials or resources that serve as a complement to the teaching-learning process".

Salazar (2019) points out that "the barcode is a standardized language useful for uniquely identifying commercial and logistic units. This tool is useful for the application of automatic information capture systems".

The Global Trade Item Number barcode (GTIN, governed by GS1, hereinafter GTIN), consists of two main parts: 11.

Code: The alphanumeric or numerical representation that identifies the unit of marketing, logistics, etc., as shown in Fig. 1.

Fig. 1. Barcode. Reference: Salazar (2019).

Symbol: The graphical representation of the code that allows the capture of its information automatically through reading, as shown in Fig. 2

"A system of bars is 'the two out of five'. Each digit is represented by five bars. Two of which are wider than the other three. A thin bar is a binary 0 and a thick one is a 1. The thick bar is three times as wide as the thin one. Two wide bars should always appear as a protective measure to avoid errors. The position of the broad lines determines the digit." (Arranz, 2002).

The barcode technology used in the logistics sector proposes its use and application for a better control of the product in a company, thus obtaining a series of advantages and an interesting use of resources.

Fig. 2. Barcode symbol. Reference: Salazar (2019)

In Mexico, for example, a project was developed under the objective of designing, developing and implementing an information system that would allow the registration of articles, control their import and export, as well as all the necessary operations in the warehouse of the Technological Institute of Saltill; in which an application has been developed with the intention of keeping it installed on one or more computers, this application would be permanently available to potential users responsible for the Department of Resources and Materials, only for the warehouse area, with the measures of mandatory security so that it is accessible to the people responsible for the warehouse area, to be able to access the information related to the items in stock, in this way, within the conclusions they express that although it was not possible for them to make the publication once created given Because it was in that process, the level of information that would be processed in this space gives way to more investigations to make changes, for example, warehouse users requesting needs that arise in inventory management, then the system it can be managed through the facility's network, in addition, the information generated by the system would facilitate the work of other departments (López & López, 2011).

In the United States, in 2018, Pradeep Pai, in his thesis: "Adaptable inventory management system for a hospital supply chain", established difficult inventory management as a problem because demand, prices and policies of the products offered by the hospital are always changing. The objective was to develop a monitoring system to determine the range of hospital products in order to maintain the effectiveness of the proposed system. The search type has been applied, the results show the cost savings of the supply chain, as well as the optimization of the request time, on the other hand, it shows that the level of service has increased thanks to the performance of the system. In this context, the service level is considered a reference, since it can help to verify the status of the inventory (Hidalgo Santos, 2019).

In 2018, Finland Zelioli Luca in his thesis: "Automated Inventory Application", a company where his research was carried out whose name is LappiHuaina, dedicated to the sale of honey in Germany, described how his problem pointed to human error when updating the inventory, also reported that the process to carry out the inventory was always slow because they needed communication from the commercial agents to inform the amount of honey that was sold and, in turn, by text message it was required to place the order for the delivery of new jars of honey. Honey. The objective was to create an app that will have an automated inventory to reduce work hours and minimize errors in the inventory process of a small business. Therefore, it has been widely accepted by the workers of the company as it is a very useful and necessary upgrade to change the old process. In this context, the communication process of a product is considered as a reference, because through it is verified if a product has been specified for manufacturing (Hidalgo Santos, 2019).

In Peru during the year 2019, a study with the objective of determining the impact of a mobile application integrated with QR codes in the control of inventories in the company of Inversiones Muchari SAC "MD CENTROPLAC", taking into account that its main problem was based on relying on response times to get their product feedback, causing inventory backlogs, as well as not knowing for sure which products should be included in a project, causing a delay in delivering the customer's project from The company, thus, found within the results, an increase of 9.3% in the accuracy of supply per order, coupled with the increase of 34.52% for the level of service, therefore, it was concluded that the mobile application integrated with code QR improved the inventory control process in the company (Hidalgo Santos, 2019).

To determine the influence of mobile applications on inventory control in the company ALTOKEE E.I.R.L.S, located in Peru, a study was carried out where they stated that mobile applications improved inventory control in it, since it allows to improve inventory accuracy. And expedite inventory rotation, helping to achieve the objectives of this survey and corroborate the hypotheses. Similarly, this survey makes recommendations to implement new technologies to work more efficiently and quickly, such as QR and barcode readers. As well as mobile printers for product labeling (Sifuentes, 2020).

In Colombia, in 2017 an investigation was carried out, whose objective was focused on developing an inventory system based on QR code that helps to plan and evaluate the movement of merchandise and sales, where the products are registered in an organized, fast, simple and accessible to all users adapted to the needs of the store, in which they concluded that The use of the QR code as a merchandise coding system is perfectly adapted to the needs of the store because it is two-dimensional, allows quick reading in all directions, creating an advantage over other codes (barcodes) since its readability would be applied to the surface of the shoe (Vargas & León, 2017).

2.2 Conceptual Framework

Microsoft 365
We must be clear that Office 365 is a Microsoft suite that allows us to work with Office tools that we all know and the most current collaboration applications, such as Microsoft Teams, SharePoint, Forms, OneDrive, as well as other applications such as Power Automate, PowerApps and Power Virtual Agents. All this from any device and anywhere, with an internet connection.

Power Apps
On many occasions, either because we are carrying out a technical review or carrying out a commercial action with a client, if we had an application from which we could carry out certain procedures, this would greatly speed up our work. In this way, we would not have to wait to get to the office to fill out the work reports or simply to consult some

customer data. Power Apps is part of the Microsoft 365 suite, so if we already work with it within our company, we can enjoy this tool without having to make an additional payment. In addition, Power Apps is capable of directly accessing the 42 data that is 28 stored within Microsoft 365, so it would not be necessary to carry out any additional development to obtain the data of our company. However, another of its main advantages is that we can connect our applications with more than 260 connectors. These connectors will allow us to obtain the data of our business that is stored in external applications and work with them without the need to develop a connection layer for each one. Asana, Salesforce, Jira, Trello, Slack, SQL Server, Azure, are just a few examples that we can find.

Software is called a logical system of computer assemblies that make it possible to perform specific problems or tasks in a computer system. There are many types of software that we can use to carry out this project, such as system, programming and/or application.

To begin with, the meaning of each one is defined: 1) System Software: Runs all the applications for a system to operate correctly, includes drivers and components; 2) Programming software: They allow the development of new software, they are usually used by programmers; includes compilers, interpreters, and text editors; and 3) Application software: It facilitates tasks for computer media (computers, tablets and/or cell phones), it is used in assisted design programs such as video games, it uses telecommunications and productivity applications.

When defining a database, it is given as a set of information ordered for transmission, analysis and recovery. They are generated as a product of the human need to generate and store information in a systematic way, allowing orderly storage and easy information retrieval. We currently have a large number of types of databases, they are characterized according to what is required by the user, for example: 1) Static: Business intelligence, they are read-only, information can be extracted, but the existing one can never be modified; 2) Dynamics: They handle processes of constant updating, reorganization, addition and deletion of content.

They are also classified according to their content in: 1) Bibliographic: Reading content, ordered from key information such as data, areas, titles, among others; 2) Full text: It is handled with texts or documentaries, considered as primary source; 3) Directories: Totally personalized data lists such as emails, numbers, names, etc.; and 4) Specialized: Contains technical information, created by the needs of the public that uses the information.

2.3 Theorical Framework

By scanning a QR code using your smartphone, you get immediate access to its content. The QR code reader can then perform an action, such as opening the web browser to a specific URL. Other actions may be triggered, such as storing a business card in your smartphone's contact list or connecting to a wireless network. Today, QR codes can be seen on brochures, posters, magazines, etc. You can easily spot these two-dimensional barcodes around you. QR codes allow you to interact with the world through your smartphone.

Today the barcode has become one of the most important international standards in the world, used mainly in the unique identification of commercial and logistic units.

The bar code is a coding system, according to Roger C. Palmer, it is an automatic identification technology by means of the orderly coding of the graphically summarized information through series of lines and parallel spaces of different thicknesses. The barcode is a form of data entry using a parallel arrangement of vertical bars and spaces that contains encoded information. This information can be read by optical devices (optical readers), which send the read information to a computer (or terminal) just as if it had been typed manually.

Specifically, a QR Code extends the data available to any physical object and creates a digital measure for marketing operations. This technology enables and accelerates the use of mobile web services: it is a very creative digital tool. QR codes are easily identifiable by their square shape and by the three boxes located in the upper and lower left corners.

A barcode reader or scanner can record data 5 to 7 times faster than an experienced typist. A system that uses barcode technology to obtain information in real time, a procedure that is difficult to perform by other manual means, such accurate and real-time information helps to track and control the products (or the data from which is automating) that in the long run will help to improve decision-making by having accurate and timely information.

In the communication of key strategies, indicators and even projects of organizations, SharePoint lists are very important as tools to present the status of these elements of corporate measurement.

There are more complex definitions that include some other aspects. There are some points that it is necessary to review when creating a SharePoint list, to be sure that this tool will work and fulfill its purposes.

One of the most important features of a good database list is its display. In data analysis, and to know clearly how we are doing, it is important that what is shown in the lists of our programs is supported by graphics, information, data and organization that are understandable for the work team. From them, it will be possible to start taking action. Its main objective is to carry out the follow-up of the processes or business units of the organization, and in this way present and make decisions on time. Ideally it should contain information.

Databases are essential for the development of systems in all organizations. A database is an organized collection of information, structured so that it can be easily accessed and managed. The data is managed through a database management system; The most specialized databases, having a great capacity to handle millions of records or data, make it easier for us to use them on a large scale and in different circumstances according to our needs. A datum allows us to describe an object. We can call such an object an entity, for example, a house in which people live. The house is the entity and the number of people living in the house is a piece of data, which in this case is numeric.

There are different types of data that can be held in a database: character, numeric, image, date, currency, text, bit, decimal, and varchar. There are more or less adequate databases depending on the type of data, and there is a process to convert data into information, since a single piece of data by itself does not represent anything if we do not see it in contrast to others. This is how behaviors are identified.

2.4   Historical Framework

This research article is framed in the context of inventory control in the Colombian Air Force through a mobile application. To understand the importance and relevance of this approach, it is necessary to briefly review the historical context of inventory control in this institution.

The Colombian Air Force (FAC) is one of the branches of the Colombian Military Forces in charge of the defense and air security of the country. Throughout its history, the FAC has experienced various technological advances and changes in its logistics processes, including inventory management and control in its aeronautical warehouses.

In the past, inventory control in the FAC was carried out manually and in physical format, which implied multiple challenges. Paper records and spreadsheets were prone to errors, loss of information, and difficulties in updating and tracking inventories. These traditional methods were neither efficient nor effective for proper management of available resources and tools.

With the advancement of information and communication technologies, new opportunities arose to improve inventory control in the FAC. The appearance of mobile devices and the development of mobile applications have opened up new possibilities to optimize logistics processes and guarantee a more accurate and up-to-date control of inventories.

In this context, the need to develop a specific mobile application for inventory control in the FAC aeronautical warehouses has been identified. This application will allow the safe and efficient registration of tools and users, the monitoring of the locations of the tools and the generation of reports and statistics for better decision making.

The use of mobile applications for inventory control is not new in the business and logistics field. Various organizations have successfully implemented this type of technological solutions, obtaining significant improvements in the efficiency and precision of inventory control processes.

QR (Quick Response) codes are barcodes widely used in marketing and business applications to include links to web pages, among other things. Currently, a large number of electronic devices such as smartphones or tablets have applications capable of capturing such information, allowing its user to store it and share it with other users. There are some examples of its application in education, although no examples have been found in the area of Chemical Engineering. In this context, the work presented is the implementation and evaluation of QR codes in Chemical Engineering teaching laboratories with access to multimedia teaching content.

Barcodes are optical-electronic devices that interpret linear shapes contained in an image that are processed as relevant data for a certain organization. These devices emit a beam of laser light (they can use other technologies as well) that interprets the information by passing the laser through the encoded image (barcode). This device is considered a data entry device, and the data it scans is sent to a computer connected either by cable or wirelessly (InformaticaModerna.com, 2016).

QR codes are made up of numerous small squares, which are the ones that contain the information. Within a QR code we can distinguish different parts, as can be seen in

Fig. 1. The application that we have on our Smartphone/Tablet collects all the information that the QR provides, taking into account the position and alignment and returns the information to us. Content, in the form of an image, text, URL, email, telephone, message, contact, location, among others, in conclusion, the possibilities it offers us are enormous.

The barcode consists of a coding system created through a series of lines and parallel spaces of different thicknesses. It is generally used as a control system since it facilitates the commercial activity of the manufacturer and the distributor, therefore it does not offer information to the consumer, but operations data applied to identify products, keep track of inventories, loading and unloading of merchandise, reduce sales service times. One of the main advantages is that the data stored in a barcode can be read accurately and quickly.

3 Methodology

3.1 Research Method

3.1.1 Inductive

This article is based on an inductive method since we will follow a series of patterns to get to the implementation of a mobile application, in which you will have control of the different tools through information tables, PowerApps applications, SharePoint lists and the use of QR and bar codes, to register each item and information of the users of the tools.

Analysis of the current situation: An exhaustive analysis of existing inventory control procedures and systems in the Colombian Air Force will be carried out. Data will be collected on currently used inventory recording, tracking and management methods.

Mobile application development: A customized mobile application will be developed using mobile application development tools. The application will contain functionalities such as the registration of inventory inputs and outputs, stock consultation, report generation and critical level alerts.

Implementation and testing: The mobile application will be implemented in a representative sample of Colombian Air Force units. Functional tests will be carried out to evaluate the usability, precision and effectiveness of the application in inventory control.

Data Collection: During the implementation and testing period, data will be collected on the use of the mobile application, such as the time of inventory registration, the accuracy of the data entered and the efficiency of inventory management.

Descriptive analysis: A descriptive analysis of the data collected will be carried out to evaluate the effectiveness of the mobile application in inventory control. Metrics such as inventory recording accuracy, error reduction, improved visibility, and time saved in inventory management processes will be examined.

Expected Results:
This study is expected to provide a detailed description of inventory control in the Colombian Air Force through the use of a mobile application. The results will allow us to understand the effectiveness and benefits of the implementation of the application in terms of data accuracy, improvement in operational efficiency and reduction of errors.

In addition, possible limitations and challenges in the implementation and use of the mobile application will be identified, which will provide valuable information for future improvements and optimization of inventory control in the Colombian Air Force.

3.2 Type of Research Approach

3.2.1 Descriptive

Because the data collected from the warehouses is measured by statistics and we answer for each order request. We will carry out a study of which material or spare part is most required by the warehouses and thus have more accurate data on future requirement forecasts.

The objective of this study is to carry out a descriptive investigative approach about inventory control in the Colombian Air Force through the implementation of a mobile application. The current situation of inventory control will be examined, the characteristics and functionalities of the proposed mobile application will be described, and the benefits and limitations of its implementation will be analyzed.

Methodology:
Analysis of the current situation: An exhaustive analysis of existing inventory control procedures and systems in the Colombian Air Force will be carried out. Data will be collected on currently used inventory recording, tracking and management methods.

Mobile application development: A customized mobile application will be developed using mobile application development tools. The application will contain functionalities such as the registration of inventory inputs and outputs, stock consultation, report generation and critical level alerts.

Implementation and testing: The mobile application will be implemented in a representative sample of Colombian Air Force units. Functional tests will be carried out to evaluate the usability, precision and effectiveness of the application in inventory control.

Data Collection: During the implementation and testing period, data will be collected on the use of the mobile application, such as the time of inventory registration, the accuracy of the data entered and the efficiency of inventory management.

Descriptive analysis: A descriptive analysis of the data collected will be carried out to evaluate the effectiveness of the mobile application in inventory control. Metrics such as inventory recording accuracy, error reduction, improved visibility, and time saved in inventory management processes will be examined.

3.2.2 Quantitative

We are based on the collection of data and numerical collection of the articles or objects that are kept in a warehouse or in the place where the (pilot plan) is studied, which, in this case, will take as an example the elements that are borrowed, of the different GRUAC laboratories, to generate control over the elements through the application.

The collection of information through surveys of experts on the subject of inventory management in aeronautical warehouses also allows us to quantify which of the characteristics most chosen by these personnel, we can add to our application.

Forecast Models: Forecasting techniques, such as moving average or exponential smoothing, will be applied to predict future demand for products and assist in inventory planning.

Inventory analysis: Key inventory metrics, such as service level, replenishment time, and inventory turns, will be calculated to assess the efficiency of current inventory control.

Variability analysis: Statistical techniques will be used to analyze the variability of inventories and determine the amount of safety inventory necessary to avoid shortages.

Inventory optimization: Inventory optimization techniques will be applied, such as the periodic review model or the reorder point, to determine the optimal quantities of replenishment and adequate inventory levels, taking into account that the application allows us to obtain data which They make optimization much easier.

3.3 Information Sources

In the project, we used the primary type of information source, since we were in direct contact with the people who experienced the problem (teachers, laboratory workers and program directors) of lack of control of the elements of the laboratories or aeronautical warehouses.

3.4 Techniques for Collecting Information

In the project we can show that the two techniques they need to collect information were used, such as non-participatory observation, since we are foreign to the place where we are conducting the investigation, we have the alternative of the witnesses or the group which has the daily routine of being in the place where the problem was found, therefore it should be added that the interview is also used, to find out what kind of experiences and problems the group of people who work and know the system that is in place in the GRUTE lives and above all in the aeronautical warehouses of EMAVI where the problem to be investigated arises.

3.5 Data Analysis and Processing Plan

Questions were asked and all kinds of information was requested for the different groups of the CACOM 7 unit (GRUAC, GRUCA, GRUTE, GRUSE) focusing on the way in which objects are controlled in places where elements that are constantly stored use for officials or personnel who are part of each group. There is a big problem with the time in which they return an object or the loss of it, since there is no record of the people who have it and the established time of the same.

Our main basis for creating the mobile application is based on the data from the warehouses, the material supplied, that the availability of the tools in the warehouse is compatible with each possible delivery and/or loan time. With all this data collected, they begin to be organized and compiled in tables and thus generate the different connections in Microsoft 360 required for the creation of an app, after that we must take into account that not all personnel would have access to it, only personal authorized since it would generate conflicts, possible losses or even change of information by unreliable personnel, in the administrative part of the application (backend).

4 Results

For the validation project of the mobile application for inventory control in the aeronautical warehouses of the Colombian Air Force, the following types of usability can be used:

Learning usability: Evaluate the ease with which users can learn to use the mobile application, especially in relation to the use of QR and barcodes. You can measure the learning curve, the intuitiveness of the interface and the clarity of the instructions related to reading and recording information through these codes.

Accessibility usability: Evaluate the accessibility of the mobile application, ensuring that users can access information and functionalities effectively and safely. This includes compatibility with different mobile devices, adaptability to different screen sizes, support for assistive technologies, and the ease of reading and scanning QR and barcodes.

Error Recovery Usability: Evaluate the ability of the mobile application to help users recover from errors or problems during the registration and inventory control process. This includes the presence of clear error messages, the ability to undo actions, and the ease of correcting incorrect or incomplete information.

User satisfaction usability: Evaluate the general experience of users when using the mobile application, including their satisfaction with the interface, ease of use and effectiveness in inventory control. User comments and feedback can be collected to measure their level of satisfaction and make improvements based on their needs and preferences.

By using these types of usability, the effectiveness of the mobile application can be evaluated and validated in terms of its accessibility, efficiency and user satisfaction, ensuring that it meets the specific objectives of the project regarding the safe, efficient and organized registration of inventories in the aeronautical warehouses of the Colombian Air Force.

Figure 3 is shown below in representation of the cyclical form of the usability of the application.

4.1 Graphic Functionality of the Application

The selection of the button for the user screen (see Fig. 4) allows us to register (in case of having an ADMI role or visualizing which users are registered in case of having a USER role).

Fig. 3. Barcode. Reference: Salazar (2019).

Fig. 4 allows us to see the main screen and the options it gives us to be able to register users and/or products. In the case of the users button, the other part of image 4 appears, where users can be seen. Registered, their role and different options to add, filter, reload, delete, edit and observe data (arrow).

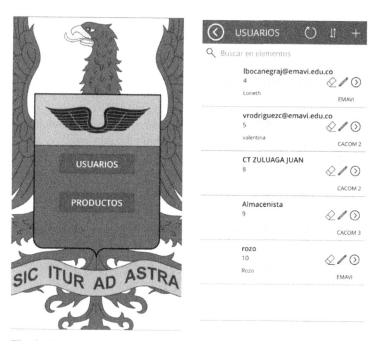

Fig. 4. Main screen, with button selection for user screen. Reference: Own.

Figure 5 shows that, when selecting the plus icon, this allows (in the event that the role of the person using the application is an ADMI) to show the bars where the mail is registered, Role and unit in which the new user is registered.

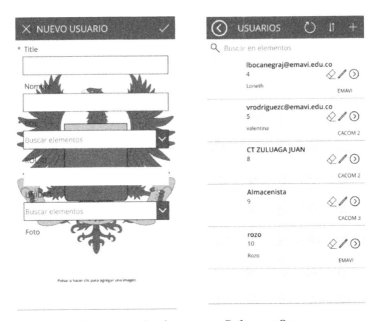

Fig. 5. Selection for new user. Reference: Own.

The drop-down lists, presented in Fig. 6, contain different items depending on their reference, options to select whether a User or an Administrator is going to be registered, also in the Unit where the person to be registered is located.

The following tools in Fig. 7 allow, in the case of being an Administrator, to edit user information and delete it, for users it only allows the preview.

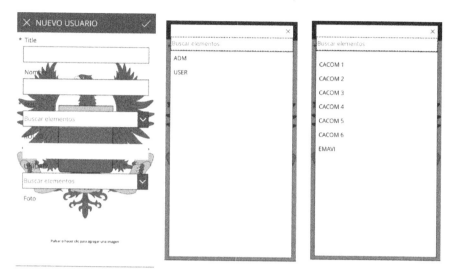

Fig. 6. Drop-down lists. Reference: Own.

Fig. 7. Editing, deletion and preview tools. Reference: Own.

5   Discussion

At this point of the article, a discussion is presented on the use of an application based on Power Apps for inventory control in the Colombian Air Force. The current challenges in inventory management are examined and a technological solution is proposed that offers efficiency and significant improvements in the control of logistics resources. The benefits of the application, its main features are discussed, and possible limitations and practical considerations for its successful implementation are explored.

Inventory control plays a fundamental role in the operation of any organization, and the Colombian Air Force is no exception. The efficient management of logistics resources, such as spare parts, tools and equipment, is essential to maintain the operational readiness and response capacity of the institution. However, traditional inventory control methods can present challenges, such as data entry errors, lack of real-time visibility, and difficulties in communication between different units and departments.

In response to these challenges, the implementation of a Power Apps application is proposed as an efficient technological solution for inventory control in the Colombian Air Force. Power Apps is a low-code application development platform that allows you to create custom, intuitive, and scalable solutions without the need for in-depth programming knowledge. This application can be used on mobile devices, which facilitates access and recording of data in real time, anywhere and at any time.

The Power Apps application offers several significant features and benefits to improve inventory control in the Colombian Air Force. First of all, it enables the digitization of inventory registration and tracking processes, eliminating the need for paper records and reducing manual errors. In addition, it offers an intuitive and easy-to-use interface, which facilitates adoption by staff and reduces the learning curve.

Another important advantage of the Power Apps application is its ability to integrate with other existing systems and databases in the Colombian Air Force. This allows greater visibility and traceability of inventories, as well as better coordination and communication between different units and departments. In addition, the application can generate reports and analyzes in real time, which provides valuable information for decision making and the optimization of inventory levels.

However, it's important to keep in mind some practical considerations and potential limitations in your Power Apps app deployment. Availability of suitable mobile devices and reliable connectivity must be ensured for use in the field. In addition, security and access control protocols must be established to protect the integrity of the data stored in the application.

6   Conclusions

A mobile application with integrated technology was developed for reading QR and bar codes that, through the scanner, identifies information from the data registered by a user on a tool.

It responds to the need to integrate options that perform a new registration of objects in a quick and organized way.

The impact of the application is evaluated and approval of the application is generated by the end user.

Appendix I

To complement the monitoring of the processes followed in the development of the application, we have the following requirements:

1. Identification of administrators and users: An identification system is implemented through an ID and a role assigned to each user. Administrators have additional privileges to access specific functionality.
2. Registration of tools and users: A button is incorporated for administrators to select whether they want to register a new tool or a new user. By clicking on the corresponding button, a form will open where the relevant data is entered, such as name, description, category and other relevant details.
3. QR and Barcode Search: To make finding tools easier, a QR and Barcode Scan button is included. By using the camera of the mobile device, the user can scan the code of the tool and get the corresponding information automatically.
4. Search via search bar: In addition to code scanning, a search bar is provided where users can enter keywords, names or descriptions to search for specific tools. As you enter your search term, a database query is performed to find matches and display relevant results.
5. Recording and storage in SharePoint: All data entered, whether it is user or tool records, is recorded and stored in SharePoint tables. This allows to have a centralized and accessible database to perform queries and generate reports later.

It is important to mention that the development of the application has been carried out following the best user interface design practices, ensuring an intuitive and easy-to-use experience. Usability aspects, such as the logical layout of the elements, the use of clear labels and visual feedbacTo complement the monitoring of the processes followed in the development of the application, we have the following requirements:

1. Identification of administrators and users: An identification system is implemented through an ID and a role assigned to each user. Administrators have additional privileges to access specific functionality.
2. Registration of tools and users: A button is incorporated for administrators to select whether they want to register a new tool or a new user. By clicking on the corresponding button, a form will open where the relevant data is entered, such as name, description, category and other relevant details.
3. QR and Barcode Search: To make finding tools easier, a QR and Barcode Scan button is included. By using the camera of the mobile device, the user can scan the code of the tool and get the corresponding information automatically.
4. Search via search bar: In addition to code scanning, a search bar is provided where users can enter keywords, names or descriptions to search for specific tools. As you enter your search term, a database query is performed to find matches and display relevant results.
5. Recording and storage in SharePoint: All data entered, whether it is user or tool records, is recorded and stored in SharePoint tables. This allows to have a centralized and accessible database to perform queries and generate reports later.

It is important to mention that the development of the application has been carried out following the best user interface design practices, ensuring an intuitive and easy-to-use experience. Usability aspects, such as the logical layout of the elements, the use of clear labels and visual feedback, have been considered to provide a friendly and efficient interface have been considered to provide a friendly and efficient interface.

The validation of the application will be carried out through the participation of experts in the field, who will evaluate the functionality, usability and the relationship between the inventory records and the control panels. Your comments and suggestions will be collected and considered to make further improvements and optimizations in the application, ensuring its effectiveness and compliance with the objectives established in the research document.

References

Álvarez-Hornos, F.J., Sanchis, M.I., Ortega, A.C.: Implantación y evaluación de códigos QR en laboratorios docentes de ingeniería química. @ tic. revista d'innovació educativa (13), 88–96 (2014)

Arroba Salto, J.E., Angulo Rosales, Y.A., Naula Valla, S.M.: Control de inventarios y su incidencia en los estados financieros. Observatorio de la Economía Latinoamericana. https://www.eumed.net/rev/oel/2018/11/inventarios-estados-financieros.html (2018)

Cabrera Solarte, J.M.: INAP–Herramienta para la administración de un inventario de aplicaciones en uso por la empresa XM (2021)

Castillo Valbuena, D.A. Desarrollo y soporte a los casos de uso para mejorar la productividad de los colaboradores del Banco de Bogotá (2021)

Cordero Ortiz, L.E., Hoyos Vega, N.C.: Códigos QR en árboles y plantas ornamentales como estrategia pedagógica para el fortalecimiento del PRAE y el cuidado de la flora de la Institución Educativa La Unión (2020)

Fernández, O.L.D.: Sistema de registro e impresión de datos de ganados en código QR (Doctoral dissertation, Universidad Nacional) (2015)

Hernández-Castillo, C.-U., Gutiérrez-Zozaya, S.-J., Zapata-Rebolloso, A.: Sistema de control de inventarios aplicando códigos QR Inventory control system applying QR Codes. 1, 11 (2021)

Hidalgo Santos, C.F.: Aplicación móvil integrada con código QR para el control de inventario en la empresa "MD CENTROPLAC" Santa Anita – 2019. Repositorio Institucional – UCV. https://repositorio.ucv.edu.pe/handle/20.500.12692/44481 (2019)

López, M. M. S., & López, L. M. V.: Sistema de Información para el Control de Inventarios del Almacén del ITS 41, 7 (2011)

Mamani Anave, N.I.: Sistema web de gestión de inventarios basado en código QR. Caso: empresa" ITSEVEN" (Doctoral dissertation) (2016)

Nogales Pérez, C.M.: LOS CÓDIGOS QR EN EL PROCESO ENSEÑANZA APRENDIZAJE (Master's thesis, Ambato: Universidad Tecnológica Indoamérica) (2019)

Rafael, M.: ¿Para qué sirve un código QR además de para ver cartas de restaurantes? (Revista Digital INESEM) (2022)

Sifuentes Farfán, V.A.: Aplicación móvil basada en plataforma Android para el proceso de control de inventario integrado con código QR en la empresa Altokee E.I.R.L. Repositorio Institucional – UCV. https://repositorio.ucv.edu.pe/handle/20.500.12692/51503 (2020)

Vargas Guzmán, K.A., León Castañeda, D.M.: Implementación de Código QR como Método de Codificación, para Sistema de Inventario a Través de Un Aplicativo Móvil y Servicios Web. http://repository.udistrital.edu.co/handle/11349/5967 (2017)

Author Index

M. F. Mata-Rivera et al. (Eds.): WITCOM 2023, CCIS 1906, pp. 567–568, 2023.
https://doi.org/10.1007/978-3-031-45316-8

Printed in the United States
by Baker & Taylor Publisher Services